ECONOMIC PREHISTORY

ECONOMIC PREHISTORY

PAPERS ON ARCHAEOLOGY BY
GRAHAME CLARK

Emeritus Disney Professor of Archaeology
University of Cambridge

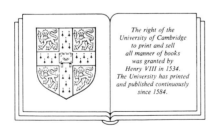

The right of the
University of Cambridge
to print and sell
all manner of books
was granted by
Henry VIII in 1534.
The University has printed
and published continuously
since 1584.

CAMBRIDGE UNIVERSITY PRESS

CAMBRIDGE

NEW YORK   PORT CHESTER

MELBOURNE   SYDNEY

Published by the Press Syndicate of the University of Cambridge
The Pitt Building, Trumpington Street, Cambridge CB2 1RP
40 West 20th Street, New York, NY 10011, USA
10 Stamford Road, Oakleigh, Melbourne 3166, Australia

First published 1989

Printed in Great Britain at the University Press, Cambridge

British Library cataloguing in publication data

Clark, Grahame
Economic prehistory: papers on archaeology.
1. Archaeology 2. Man, Prehistoric
I. Title
930.1   GN740

Library of Congress cataloguing in publication data

Clark, Grahame. 1907–
Economic prehistory: papers on archaeology/Grahame Clark.
    p.   cm.
Includes index.
ISBN 0-521-34481-6
1. Economics, Prehistoric. 2. Man, Prehistoric. 3. Economics.
Prehistoric–Europe. 4. Europe–Antiquities. I. Title.
GN799.E4C53 1988
936–dc19   87–35093

ISBN 0 521 34481 6

ACKNOWLEDGEMENTS

Cambridge University Press is grateful to the following for permission to reprint material first published by them: Addison-Wesley Publishing Company (item 28); *Antiquity* (1, 2, 3, 5, 7, 23, 24, 27); Archaeological Survey of India (31); Aris and Phillips (11); Duckworth and Company Ltd (20); *Economic History Review* (6, 10); Editions de l'Ecole des Hautes Etudes en Sciences Sociales, Paris (15); Instituto de Arqueología y Prehistoria, Universidad de Barcelona (17); Oxford University Press (21); Peabody Museum of Archaeology and Ethnology, Harvard University / University of New Mexico Press (13); the Prehistoric Society (4, 32); the Royal Danish Academy of Science and Letters (22); The Royal Society, London (19); Ulster Archaeological Society (16).

CONTENTS

PREFACE

In undertaking to make these contributions to the study of economic prehistory available in convenient form, the Cambridge University Press has flattered but at the same time embarrassed their author. Economic prehistory has long since been incorporated in the practice and teaching of prehistory, not least in the hands of his own pupils. As might be expected, the subject has been carried to a more sophisticated level in recent decades, and no one is more keenly aware of this than the author of the papers included in the present volume. Since these were first published in a number of periodicals and collective volumes, addressed in some cases to overseas readers, a certain amount of repetition is to be expected, however careful the selection. Again, since publication has been spread over a number of years, it follows that in a developing field they reflect changes in perspective and on occasion even outright contradictions. No attempt has been made to take account of these. If thought worth reprinting as early essays in a field now generally accepted as needing further research, it seems important that they should appear in their original form, warts and all.

The author may be permitted to make a further observation. Although he remains convinced of the importance of learning more about how prehistoric communities obtained and utilized food and other resources he also remains convinced that they did more than survive and perpetuate themselves by exploiting the resources of their respective ecosystems. Men, even prehistoric men, did not live by bread alone. Indeed, it has always been the author's conviction that prehistoric economies themselves can be fully understood only if it is accepted that in pursuing them men have from remote times always been influenced by a variety of interacting factors, social, technological and even ideological. Economies are worth intensive study because it is only by practising them successfully that men are capable of realizing their full potential as human beings. If man has indeed made himself, he has only been able to do so by means of his economies. Yet however important economic prehistory may be, it is only one approach, however essential, to our understanding of the emergence of specifically human societies. If economies need to be studied in their correct ecological contexts, it is no less important to remember that the communities involved were distinguished and informed by their own distinctive cultures. Economic prehistory is not so much the key as a useful approach to the study of early man.

THE PUBLISHED WORKS OF GRAHAME CLARK

An asterisk indicates a paper reprinted in the present volume.

1928   'Discoidal polished flint knives: their typology and distribution', *Proceedings of the Prehistoric Society of East Anglia*, 6, 40–54.

1931   'The dual character of the Beaker invasion', *Antiquity*, 5, 415–26.

   'A note on North European arrowheads', *Man*, 31, no. 23, 23–5.

   'Notes on the Beaker pottery of the Ipswich Museum', *Proceedings of the Prehistoric Society of East Anglia*, 6, 356–61.

   With Binnall, R. 'Note on two flints from Hastings', *Man*, 31, no. 247, 250.

1932   'The curved flint sickle blades of Britain', *Proceedings of the Prehistoric Society of East Anglia*, 7, 67–81.

   'The date of the plano-convex flint-knife in England and Wales', *The Antiquaries Journal*, 12, 158–62.

   'Fresh evidence for the dating of gold Lunulae', *Man*, 32, no. 46, 40–1.

   The Mesolithic Age in Britain, xxiii, 223p., 60 figs. Cambridge: Cambridge University Press.

   'A microlithic flaking site at West Heath, W. Harting', *Sussex Archaeological Collections*, 73, 145–55.

   'Note on some flint daggers of Scandinavian type from the British Isles', *Man*, 32, no. 223, 186–90.

   'A Stone Age site on Swaffham Prior Farm', *Proceedings of the Cambridge Antiquarian Society*, 32, 17–23.

1933   'The classification of a microlithic culture: the Tardenoisian of Horsham', *The Archaeological Journal*, 90, 52–77.

   'Early settlement at Runcton Holme, Norfolk. Part 1. The first occupation: Neolithic and Beaker remains', *Proceedings of the Prehistoric Society of East Anglia*, 7, 199–202.

   'Mesolithic sites on the Burtle Beds, near Bridgewater, Somerset', *Man*, 33, no. 65, 63–5.

'Palaeolithic implements from S. W. Transjordan', *Man*, 33, no. 152, 147–9.

With Piggott, S. 'The age of the British flint mines', *Antiquity*, 7, 166–83.

In collaboration with Godwin, H. and M. E. and Macfadyen, W. A. 'Report on an early Bronze Age site in the South-Eastern fens', *The Antiquaries Journal*, 13, 266–96.

1934   *'Archaeology and the State', *Antiquity*, 8, 414–28.

'Derivative forms of the *petit tranchet* in Britain', *The Archaeological Journal*, 91, 32–58.

'A late Mesolithic settlement site at Selmeston, Sussex', *The Antiquaries Journal*, 14, 134–58.

'Recent researches on the post-glacial deposits of the English fenland', *The Irish Naturalists' Journal*, 5, 144–52.

'Some unrecorded finds of microliths from England', *Proceedings of the Prehistoric Society of East Anglia*, 7, 421–3.

With Godwin, H. and M. E. and Clifford, M. H. 'A Bronze Age spearhead found in Methwold Fen, Norfolk', *Proceedings of the Prehistoric Society of East Anglia*, 7, 395–8.

With Hazzledine Warren, S., Godwin, H. and M. E. and Macfadyen, W. A. 'An early Mesolithic site at Broxbourne sealed under boreal peat', *Journal of the Royal Anthropological Institute of Great Britain and Ireland*, 64, 101–28.

1935   'The prehistory of the Isle of Man', *Proceedings of the Prehistoric Society*, 1, 70–92.

With Godwin, H. and M. E. and Clifford, M. H. 'Report on recent excavations at Peacock's Farm, Shippea Hill, Cambridgeshire', *The Antiquaries Journal*, 15, 284–319.

1936   *The Mesolithic settlement of Northern Europe: a study of the food-gathering peoples of Northern Europe during the early post-glacial period*, xvi, 283p., 74 figs., 8 pls. Cambridge: Cambridge University Press.

'Report on a late Bronze Age site in Mildenhall Fen, West Suffolk', *The Antiquaries Journal*, 16, 29–50.

'The timber monument at Arminghall and its affinities', *Proceedings of the Prehistoric Society*, 2, 1–51.

With Hazzledine Warren, S., Piggott, S., Burkitt, M. C. and Godwin, H. and M. E. 'Archaeology of the submerged land surface of the Essex coast', *Proceedings of the Prehistoric Society*, 2, 178–210.

1937 'Scandinavian rock-engravings', *Antiquity,* 11, 56–69.

1938 'Early man', *Victoria History of the County of Cambridgeshire and the Isle of Ely,* edited by L. F. Salzman, Vol. 1, 247–303. London: Oxford University Press.

'Microlithic industries from tufa deposits at Prestatyn, Flintshire, and Blashenwell, Dorset', *Proceedings of the Prehistoric Society,* 4, 330–4.

'The reindeer hunting tribes of Northern Europe', *Antiquity,* 12, 154–71.

1939 *Archaeology and society,* xv, 220p., 31 figs., 24 pls. London: Methuen.

'Further note on the tufa deposit at Prestatyn, Flintshire', *Proceedings of the Prehistoric Society,* 5, 201–2.

With Rankine, W. F. 'Excavations at Farnham, Surrey (1937–8): the Horsham culture and the question of Mesolithic dwellings', *Proceedings of the Prehistoric Society,* 5, 61–118.

1940 'New World origins', *Antiquity,* 14, 117–37.

Prehistoric England, viii, 120p., 110 pls. London: Batsford.

With Godwin, H. 'A late bronze Age find near Stuntney, Isle of Ely', *The Antiquaries Journal,* 20, 52–71.

1942 *'Bees in antiquity', *Antiquity,* 16, 208–15.

1943 *'Education and the study of man', *Antiquity,* 17, 113–21.

1944 *'Water in antiquity', *Antiquity,* 18, 1–15.

1945 'Ancient sites', *The National Trust: a record of fifty years' achievement,* edited by J. Lees-Milne, 29–41. London: Batsford.

*'Farmers and forests in Neolithic Europe', *Antiquity,* 19, 57–71.

'Man and nature in prehistory, with special reference to Neolithic settlement in Northern Europe', *Conference on the problems and prospects of European archaeology held at the University of London Institute of Archaeology September 16–17, 1944,* 20–8. London: University of London Institute of Archaeology.

1946 *From savagery to civilisation,* ix, 112p., 24 figs., 4 pls. London: Cobbett Press. Translated into German and Hungarian.

*'Seal-hunting in the Stone Age of north-western Europe: a study in economic prehistory', *Proceedings of the Prehistoric Society,* 12, 12–48.

1947 *Archaeology and society,* 2nd ed. xv, 222p., 29 ills, 24 pls. London: Methuen.

*'Forest clearance and prehistoric farming', *Economic History Review*, 17, 45–51.

'Sheep and swine in the husbandry of prehistoric Europe', *Antiquity*, 21, 122–36.

*'Whales as an economic factor in prehistoric Europe', *Antiquity*, 21, 84–104.

1948 'The development of fishing in prehistoric Europe', *The Antiquaries Journal*, 28, 45–85.

*'Fowling in prehistoric Europe', *Antiquity*, 22, 116–30.

'Objects of South Scandinavian flint in the northernmost provinces of Norway, Sweden and Finland', *Proceedings of the Prehistoric Society*, 14, 219–32.

Prehistoric England, 4th ed. viii, 120p., 110 ills. London: Batsford.

1949 'A preliminary report on excavations at Star Carr, Seamer, Scarborough, Yorkshire, 1949', *Proceedings of the Prehistoric Society*, 15, 52–65.

'Report on excavations on the Cambridgeshire Car Dyke, 1947', *The Antiquaries Journal*, 29, 145–63.

1950 'The earliest settlement of the West Baltic area in the light of recent research', *Proceedings of the Prehistoric Society*, 16, 87–100.

'Preliminary report on excavations at Star Carr, Seamer, Scarborough, Yorkshire, 1949', *Proceedings of the Prehistoric Society*, 15, 52–65.

1951 *'Folk-culture and the study of European prehistory', *Aspects of archaeology in Britain and beyond: essays presented to O.G.S. Crawford*, edited by W.F. Grimes, 49–65, London: H. W. Edwards.

1952 'The Mesolithic hunters of Star Carr', *Transactions of the Lancashire and Cheshire Antiquarian Society*, 63, 183–90.

'Die mittlere Steinzeit', *Historia Mundi*, 1, 318–45.

'*Prehistoric Europe: the economic basis*', xix, 349p., 180 figs., 16 pls. London: Methuen. Translated into French, Italian, Polish and Russian.

1953 'Archaeological theories and interpretation: Old World', *Anthropology today: an encyclopedic inventory*, prepared under the chairmanship of A. L. Kroeber, 343–60. Chicago: Chicago University Press.

*'The economic approach to prehistory: Albert Reckitt Archaeological Lecture, 1953', *Proceedings of the British Academy*, 39 215–38.

'The groove and splinter technique of working reindeer and red deer antler in Upper Palaeolithic and Mesolithic Europe', *Archivo de Prehistoria Levantina*, 4, 57–65.

With Fell, C. I. with an appendix by Burkitt, M. C. 'The early Iron Age site at Micklemoor Hill West Harling, Norfolk, and its pottery', *Proceedings of the Prehistoric Society*, 19, 1–39.

With Thompson, M. W. 'The groove and splinter technique of working antler in Upper Palaeolithic and Mesolithic Europe', *Proceedings of the Prehistoric Society*, 19, 148–60.

1954   *The study of prehistory: an inaugural lecture*, 35p. Cambridge: Cambridge University Press.

With chapters by Walker, D. and Godwin, H., and Fraser, F. C. and King, J. E. and with an appendix by Moore, J. W. *Excavations at Star Carr: an early Mesolithic site at Seamer, near Scarborough, Yorkshire*, xxiii, 200p., 80 figs., 24 pls. Cambridge: Cambridge University Press.

1955   'A microlithic industry from the Cambridgeshire fenland and other industries of Sauveterrian affinities from Britain', *Proceedings of the Prehistoric Society*, 21, 3–20.

'Notes on the Obanian with special reference to antler- and bone-work', *Proceedings of the Society of Antiquaries of Scotland*, 89, 91–106.

1956   'Star Carr: a Mesolithic site in Yorkshire', *Recent archaeological excavations in Britain: selected excavations 1939–1955 with a chapter on recent air-reconnaissance*, edited by R. L. S. Bruce-Mitford, 1–20. London: Routledge and Kegan Paul.

With Godwin, H. 'A Maglemosian site at Brandesburton, Holderness, Yorkshire', *Proceedings of the Prehistoric Society*, 22, 6–22.

1957   *Archaeology and society: reconstructing the prehistoric past*, 3rd ed. 272p., 52 ills, 24 pls. London: Methuen. Translated into Dutch, Italian and Spanish.

1958   'Blade and trapeze industries of the European Stone Age', *Proceedings of the Prehistoric Society*, 24, 24–42.

'O. G. S. Crawford 1886–1957', *Proceedings of the British Academy*, 44, 281–96.

1959   'Perspectives in prehistory: presidential address', *Proceedings of the Prehistoric Society*, 25, 1–14.

1960   With contributions by Higgs, E. S. and Longworth, I. H.
        'Excavations at the Neolithic site Hurst Fen, Mildenhall, Suffolk
        (1954, 1957 and 1958)', *Proceedings of the Prehistoric Society*, 26,
        202–45.

1961   'The first half-million years: the hunters and gatherers of the
        Stone Age', *The dawn of civilization: the first world survey of
        human cultures in early times,* edited by S. Piggott, 19–40.
        London: Readers Union.
            World prehistory: an outline, xiii, 283p., 12 pls, 7 maps.
        Cambridge: Cambridge University Press. Translated into
        Dutch, French, German and Italian.

1962   *Prehistoric England,* Revised paperback ed. 200p. London:
        Batsford.
            'A survey of the Mesolithic phase in the prehistory of Europe
        and South-West Asia', *Atti del VI Congresso Internazionale
        delle Scienze Preistoriche e Protohistoriche,* Vol. 1, 97–111.
        Rome: Congresso Internazionale delle Scienze Preistoriche e
        Protohistoriche.
            With Godwin, H. 'The Neolithic in the Cambridgeshire fens',
        Antiquity, 36, 10–23.

1963   'Neolithic bows from Somerset, England, and the prehistory of
        archery in North-Western Europe', *Proceedings of the
        Prehistoric Society,* 29, 50–98.

1965   'Radiocarbon dating and the expansion of farming culture from
        the Near East over Europe', *Proceedings of the Prehistoric
        Society,* 31, 58–73.
            'Radiocarbon dating and the spread of farming economy',
        Antiquity, 39, 45–8.
            *'Traffic in stone axe and adze blades', *Economic History
        Review,* 2nd series, 18, 1–28.
            With Piggott, S. *Prehistoric societies,* 356p., 95 figs., 8 pls, 4
        maps. London: Hutchinson. Translated into French.

1966   *'The invasion hypothesis in British archaeology', *Antiquity,* 40,
        172–89.
            *'Prehistory and human behaviour', *Proceedings of the
        American Philosophical Society,* 110, 91–9.

1967   'Foreword', *The Haua Fteah (Cyrenaica) and the Stone Age of
        the South-East Mediterranean,* by C. B. M. McBurney, xii-xiv.
        Cambridge: Cambridge University Press.
            The Stone Age hunters. 143p., 137 ills. London: Thames and
        Hudson. Translated into Japanese and Portuguese.

1968   *'Australian Stone Age', *Liber Josepho Kostrzewski octogenario a veneratoribus dicatus*, edited by Konrad Jazdzewski, 17–28. Warsaw: Zaklad Norodowy im Ozzolinskich.

'The economic impact of the change from late-glacial to post-glacial conditions in Northern Europe', *Proceedings VIIIth International Congress of Anthropological and Ethnological Sciences 1968 Tokyo and Kyoto.* Vol. 3, 241–4. Tokyo: Science Council of Japan.

1969   *World prehistory: a new outline, being the second edition of World Prehistory*, xvi, 331p., 16 pls., 10 maps. Cambridge: Cambridge University Press. Translated into Hungarian, Portuguese, Serbo-Croat, Spanish and Swedish.

1970   *Aspects of prehistory*, xiii, 161p., 23 figs., 4 pls. Berkeley: University of California Press.

'Primitive man in Egypt, Western Asia and Europe in Mesolithic times', *Cambridge Ancient History*, 3rd ed., edited by I. E. S. Edwards, the late C. J. Gadd and N. G. L. Hammond. Vol. 1 pt. 1, 90–121. Cambridge: Cambridge University Press.

With Piggott, S. *Prehistoric societies*, Revised ed. 352p., 95 ills., 8 pls., 4 maps. Harmondsworth: Penguin. Translated into Greek and Polish.

1971   *'The expansion of man with special reference to Australia and the New World', *Mélanges de préhistoire, d'archaeocivilisation et d'ethnologie offerts à André Varagnac*, 157–66. Paris: Sevpen.

'A shaped and utilized beaver jaw from Ulrome, Holderness, Yorkshire (E. R.)', *The Antiquaries Journal*, 51, 305–7.

1972   *'The archaeology of Stone Age settlement: Oliver Davies lecture for 1972', *Ulster Journal of Archaeology*, 35, 3–16.

'Foreword', *Papers in economic prehistory: studies by members and associates of the British Academy major research project in the early history of agriculture*, edited by E. S. Higgs, vii–x. Cambridge: Cambridge University Press.

Star Carr: a case study in bioarchaeology, 42p. Reading, Mass.: Addison-Wesley.

1973   'Bioarchaeology: some extracts on the theme', *Current Anthropology*, 14, 464–70.

'The cultural landscape', *Nature in the round: a guide to environmental science*, edited by N. Calder, 68–78. London: Weidenfeld and Nicholson.

*'Seasonality and the interpretation of lithic assemblages',

Estudios dedicados al Prof. Dr. Luis Pericot, edited by J. Maluquer de Motes, 1–13. Barcelona: Universidad de Barcelona. Instituto de Arqueologia y Prehistoria.

1974 *'Prehistoric Europe: the economic basis', *Archaeological researches in retrospect*, edited by G. R. Willey, 31–57. Cambridge, Mass.: Winthrop Publishers Inc.

1975 *The earlier Stone Age settlement of Scandinavia*, xxv, 282p., 63 figs., 19 tables, 16 maps. Cambridge: Cambridge University Press.

1976 *'A Baltic cave sequence: a further study in bioarchaeology', *Festschrift für Richard Pittioni zum siebzigsten Geburtstag*, edited by H. Mitscha-Marheim, H. Friesinger and H. Kerchler, *Archaeologia Austriaca*, Beiheft 13, 113–23.

   *'Domestication and social evolution', *Philosophical Transactions of the Royal Society*, series B, 275, 5–11. (Republished in *The early history of agriculture: a joint symposium of the Royal Society and the British Academy*, organized by J. Hutchinson, J. G. D. Clark, E. M. Jope and R. Riley, 5–11, Oxford: Oxford University Press for the British Academy.)

   'New perspectives in Canadian archaeology: a summation', *New perspectives in Canadian archaeology: proceedings of a symposium sponsored by the Royal Society of Canada, 22–23 October 1976*, edited by A. G. McKay, 237–48. Ottawa: Royal Society of Canada.

   *'Prehistory since Childe' (the first Gordon Childe memorial lecture), *Bulletin of the Institute of Archaeology*, 13, 1–21.

1977 *'The economic context of dolmens and passage-graves in Sweden', *Ancient Europe and the Mediterranean: studies presented in honour of Hugh Hencken*, edited by V. Markotic, 35–49. Warminster: Aris and Phillips.

   World prehistory in new perspective, 3rd ed. xx, 554p., ills. Cambridge: Cambridge University Press. Translated into Italian and Spanish.

1978 *'Neothermal orientations', *The early postglacial settlement of Northern Europe: an ecological perspective*, edited by P. Mellars, 1–10. London: Duckworth.

1979 *'Archaeology and human diversity', *Annual Review of Anthropology*, 8, 1–20.

   'Geoffrey Hext Sutherland Bushnell 1903–1978', *Proceedings of the British Academy*, 65, 587–93.

*'Primitive man as hunter, fisher, forager and farmer', *The origins of civilization: Wolfson College lectures 1978,* edited by P.R.S. Moorey, 1–21. Oxford: Clarendon Press.

Sir Mortimer and Indian archaeology (Wheeler memorial lectures, first series 1978), 83p., 21 ills. New Delhi: Archaeological Survey of India.

'Discussion of section 3 [The interaction of ethnic groups]', *Space, hierarchy and society: interdisciplinary studies in social area analysis,* edited by B. C. Burnham and J. Kingsbury, 241–44. (British Archaeological Reports International Series, 59.) Oxford: British Archaeological Reports.

1980 'Foreword', *The Cambridge encyclopedia of archaeology,* edited by A. Sherratt, 8. Cambridge: Cambridge University Press.

Mesolithic prelude: the Palaeolithic-Neolithic transition in Old World prehistory, viii, 122p., 32 figs. Edinburgh: Edinburgh University Press. Translated into Japanese.

*'World prehistory and natural science', J.C. Jacobsen memorial lecture, *Historisk-filosofiske Meddelelser,* 50, 1–40.

1981 *'Some remarks about the inter-relations between archaeology and natural sciences', *Proceedings of the third international symposium on flint 24–27 May 1979, Maastricht,* edited by E. F. G. Engelen. *Staringia,* 6, 8–10.

1983 *'Coastal settlement in European prehistory with special reference to Fennoscandia', *Prehistoric settlement patterns: essays in honour of Gordon R. Willey,* edited by E. von Z. Vogt and R. M. Leventhal, 295–317. Albuquerque, N. M.: University of New Mexico and Harvard: Peabody Museum of Archaeology and Ethnology.

The identity of man as seen by an archaeologist, xvi, 184p., 56 ills. London: Methuen. Translated into Italian, Portuguese and Spanish.

1985 'Ellis Hovell Minns, 1874–1953', *Proceedings of the British Academy,* 71, 597–602.

'Gertrude Caton Thompson, 1888–1985', *Proceedings of the British Academy,* 71, 523–31.

*'The Prehistoric Society: from East Anglia to the world', *Proceedings of the Prehistoric Society,* 51, 1–13.

1986 'Foreword', *Stone Age prehistory: studies in memory of Charles McBurney,* edited by G. N. Bailey and P. Callow, xiii–xiv. Cambridge: Cambridge University Press.

'John Mulvaney', *Papers presented to John Mulvaney*, edited by C. C. Macknight and J. P. White, *Archaeology in Oceania*, 21, 1.

Symbols of excellence: precious materials as expressions of status, ix, 126p., 43 figs., 10 pls. Cambridge: Cambridge University Press.

1989   *Prehistory at Cambridge and beyond*, x, 176p., 61 figs., Cambridge: Cambridge University Press.

Festschriften to Grahame Clark

1971   'Contributions to prehistory offered to G. Clark', edited by J. Coles, *Proceedings of the Prehistoric Society*, 37, ii.

1976   *Problems in economic and social archaeology: a tribute to Grahame Clark*, edited by G. de G. Sieveking, I. H. Longworth and K. E. Wilson, xxvi, 626p., ills. London: Duckworth.

PART I

ECONOMIC PREHISTORY

CHAPTER I

_____

BEES IN ANTIQUITY

As purveyors of honey and wax, substances rated high by early man, bees would seem to deserve more attention from archaeologists than they have in fact received. In this respect they serve to point a moral. The tendency has all too frequently been to concentrate on those aspects of ancient cultures which lend themselves most easily to classification, to the neglect of those which promise the closest insight into the working of the societies under review, thus inverting the true outlook of the archaeologist and turning him away from the activities of human beings towards a world of abstractions. The thesis one would like to urge is that the prime concern of archaeology is the study of how men have lived in society, of how within the social framework they have striven to satisfy and multiply their wants. From such a standpoint the means adopted to gratify the taste for sweet things, a taste shared by man and beast and physiological in its basis, merits at least as much attention as current fashions in safety-pins and other topics beloved of 'museologists'.

Honey is by far the most ancient source of sugar. For all practical purposes beet-sugar is little more than a century old. The process of extraction was, of course, based on Marggraff's original discovery of 1747, but it was not until some years later that it was put on a commercial basis: the first factory was opened in 1801 and from the decade 1830–40 the success of the new industry may be said to have been assured. The exact origin of cane-sugar remains obscure, though it is known to be of high antiquity. It was certainly to cane-sugar that Strabo referred when, quoting Nearchus, the famous admiral of Alexander the Great, he wrote of reeds being found in India which 'produce honey, although there are no bees'.[1] After a long, but as yet unmeasured history in India and southeastern Asia, sugar-cane cultivation spread with almost startling rapidity in two separate movements, first with the Moors to Egypt, Sicily and South Spain, where it is mentioned in the 10th century, and where in Granada and Andalusia it had become a common crop by the 12th century,[2] and secondly, to Madeira and the Canaries and so to Brazil and the West Indies in the wake of New World discovery. Cane-sugar may be said to have flooded into Europe as both the plantations and the facilities for trans-Atlantic travel developed.

The combined result of sugar-cane cultivation and the extraction of sugar from beet has been to make sugar far more abundant in modern times than

3

1.1 Raiding the wild bees' nest. A scene from rock-paintings at Las Cuevas de la Araña, Valencia, Spain. (After Hernandez-Pacheco)

ever before.[3] The comparative scarcity of sugar in the past only served to enhance the importance of honey, the only source of supply available. But honey is something far more than a pleasant sweet; its dietetic value is high, it is a potent ingredient of intoxicating drinks and it has an attractive smell, which the ancient Egyptians recognized by using it in the manufacture of perfumes.

The many virtues of honey have made it a substance eagerly sought after from the earliest times. At first no doubt it was by seeking out the nests of wild bees that honey was obtained and we may imagine that wild honey played an important part in the diet of palaeolithic man, wherever conditions were favourable. A sidelight on the quest for honey is thrown by a painting from the rock-shelter art of eastern Spain at Las Cuevas de la Arana, whereon the artist depicts a man actually raiding a nest.[4] Wild honey certainly plays an important role in the dietary of modern primitive peoples at a food-gathering level of culture. Indeed, Donald Thomson, describing a group of natives of Cape York Peninsula, Queensland, goes so far as to claim that wild honey or 'sugar bag' is 'probably the most valuable single article of diet' available to them.[5] The equipment used by the Cape York people in the collection of the honey comprises a long cane or rod of pliant wood, with a frayed brush at the end to mop it out of hollows in trees and receptacles of bark to contain it, both adequate for the purpose but neither of them likely to leave any archaeological trace.

The collection of wild honey must have been a laborious business involving movement over wide areas, so it is not surprising to find that bees were domesticated at an early date. In ancient Egypt, where the evidence is best preserved, honey featured among offerings from the earliest times;[6] bee-keepers were an officially recognized profession and honey formed part of the divine revenues. Honey was eaten freely, particularly on certain feast days. It was commonly used in the preparation of pastries and as a medium for the preservation of dates. The ancient Eygptians also appreciated the intoxicating qualities of honey and sometimes mixed it with their wine. The use of honey in the preparation of strong drink certainly goes back to the Early Bronze Age in Europe, for analysis of the sediment in the birch-bark pail from the Guldhøj oak-coffin burial in Denmark showed that honey and myrtle had been added to cranberry wine. Mead, the drink of our Anglo-Saxon forefathers, was essentially a liqueur obtained by boiling drained honey combs. A similar beverage ('metheglin') was popular in Ireland in days gone by.[7] Mead (*pur'e*) is still consumed among some of the Finno-Ougrian peoples. As a mild laxative honey was utilized by the physicians of ancient Egypt, and we may assume that its properties in this direction were well appreciated in the peasant communities of prehistoric and medieval Europe.[8]

Bees-wax has played a part hardly less important than honey, although in rather different fields. Its chief merits are that it can be modelled with facility, that when molten it takes the minutest impressions of a mould and that, once hardened, it retains its shape in any temperature normally experienced. The artistic possibilities of wax as a medium have been appreciated from the earliest times. Wax was used by the ancient Egyptians, not only to seal the nose, eyes and mouth of mummies, but also to model the mask.[9] It is possible that the ancestral wax masks cherished by patrician Roman families[10] derive ultimately from this Egyptian source. In the same line stood the royal models at Westminster and the wax figures of Madame Tussaud's. The realism possible to the modeller in wax was appreciated by the magicians of ancient Egypt, who in the practice of their calling made frequent use of bees-wax.[11] In this connexion it is interesting to recall Breasted's reference to the celebrated lawsuit in which certain individuals were prosecuted for endeavouring to bring harm to Ramses III by practising on a wax image.[12] From later times one may cite the medallion art of the Renaissance and Flaxman's originals for Wedgwood pottery designs as examples of the possibilities of bees-wax. For the lowlier craftsman, also, bees-wax had many uses. Lucas notes, for instance, that it was used by the ancient Egyptians to provide a transparent surface covering for painted surfaces and to lute on vase covers.[13]

The wealth of evidence from ancient Egypt makes it clear that bees-wax as well as honey must have been produced in considerable quantities, facts which point to intensive apiculture in the Nile valley during ancient times. Of the methods employed the tomb-paintings give us only partial information. In a scene on the tomb of Rekhmara (18th dynasty) we see bees being smoked out and their honey extracted: one man is depicted holding the torch, while a second removes the honey by hand and a third stores it in large jars.[14] Other scenes show jars of honey being sealed. Some indication as to the nature of the hives used in ancient Egypt is given in the tomb-paintings, which illustrate both pots and thick rolls of papyrus employed for this purpose.

Direct evidence of the use of bees-wax in prehistoric Europe is hardly to be expected, but its employment on the widest scale would seem to be indicated by the prevalence of the *cire perdue* method of casting. It has recently been argued that the open stone moulds characteristic of the Early Bronze Age, previously interpreted as designed to cast the metal itself, were in fact meant to prepare the wax models, later to have been cased in clay, melted out and replaced by molten metal.[15] In any case it is certain that the method was extensively employed during the later stages of the Bronze Age and it is a fair inference that bees-wax was the medium.

It may be assumed that both honey and bees-wax were consumed on a large scale in prehistoric Europe. What is not established is the extent to which these substances were gathered from the nests of wild bees or were the product of apiculture. That the distinction is likely to be elusive in a primitive society is well brought out by considering the methods of obtaining honey still employed by peoples dwelling on the margins of settled economy in the great forests of Northern Europe, under conditions not dissimilar from those which obtained much earlier in more favoured parts of the continent. Among the Finno-Ougrian peoples of the Volga-Kama region described by Manninen,[16] the quest for wild honey grades almost imperceptibly into the production of garden honey. Even in the most primitive stage we find some element of proprietorship: thus a man, finding a swarm of wild bees in a tree while ranging far away from human settlement, will mark the trunk with his house sign, so establishing a lien over any honey that might eventuate. A Wotjak peasant of the late 19th century might 'own' in this way upwards of a hundred honey trees distributed over a wide area of forest. Similar conditions obtained in parts of medieval Europe as we know from 'the numerous legal provisions about the disputes over swarms and the hunting of wild bees' mentioned by Bolin,[17] as well as from the importance of 'bee-forests' as sources of taxation.[18] In wooded country the wild bee commonly nests in holes made in trees by wood-peckers and other natural agents, so that in the normal way it would be necessary to remove some of the trunk to get at the honey. The Finno-Ougrians improved on nature to the extent that they enlarged such holes in trees frequented by wild bees, closing them by a pair of boards, one perforated to allow the passage of bees; then when autumn came one of the boards could be removed allowing honey to be extracted with ease.[19] Another indication of the somewhat sophisticated stage of wild honey collection among the Finno-Ougrians is to be seen in the elaborate climbing stirrups with sharp metal hooks, by means of which the hunter could haul himself up trunks giving scanty foot-hold. A definite step towards control had been taken in areas where wild bees were habitually lured to trees previously prepared by the cutting of artificial holes, duly covered over with boards: bees enticed by honey to take up residence in trees thus dealt with were well on the way to domestication. Finally, among some communities, regular 'bee gardens' were formed by concentrating a number of timber 'hives', each formed by a section of tree trunk treated in the same way and commonly provided with a small roof. By forming such 'bee gardens' close to human settlement long journeys were avoided and the bees themselves brought under increasingly close control.[20]

On the general question of the origin and diffusion of apiculture, the antiquity of the art can be proved for Egypt, and is rendered likely for Mesopotamia by the fact that the wild honey bees are known to have flourished in neighbouring regions during antiquity.[21] It would seem a fair assumption that apiculture spread from the early centres along with other elements of settled civilization. On the other hand we may assume that the collection of wild honey had long been practised over the regions into which the arts of higher civilization were diffused and it is at least arguable that 'intermediate' stages, like those met with among the Finno-Ougrians, were due to contact between the two in areas on the fringe of settled civilization. The importance attached to bee-keeping in Classical times and its prevalence in peasant economies from the Dark Ages onwards both suggest that apiculture was deep-rooted in European economy. Moreover it seems unlikely that the quantities of bees-wax needed for *cire perdue* casting on a generous scale could easily have been secured from wild bees. On the whole it looks as though bee-keeping goes back at least to the Bronze Age in Europe.

In conclusion it is perhaps worth reflecting that the nature of early settlement and land-utilization in prehistoric Europe was pre-eminently such as to favour the production of honey. There is an old saying that where there is good wool there also will be found sweet honey. In view of the prodigious number of flowers necessary to produce any quantity of honey it is evident that a landscape given over very largely to pastoral activities will tend to favour bees as opposed to one heavily cultivated.[22] Viewed in this light the biblical description of Palestine as a land 'flowing with milk and honey'[23] falls into line with Strabo's assertions that among the products of Brundisium the 'honey and wool are among those that are strongly commended',[24] that 'wax, cheese and honey' were among the main products exchanged by the people of the Alps for the necessaries of which they were short,[25] and that Attic honey, more particularly that from the slopes of Mount Hymettus, is rated 'the best in the world'.[26] The fact that comparatively little ground was given over to the plough and that wide pasturages and extensive woodlands made up the bulk of the countryside resulted in ideal conditions for bee-keeping of an elementary order. In this way, through the activities of bees, the pastoral background of Bronze Age Europe helped materially to fashion the most characteristic products of the period. Which tell us more, the bees or the bronzes? A question-begging question. In the study of any society, past or present, no aspect can safely be omitted, for all are interdependent.

Notes

1 *Geography*, xv, i, 20.
2 *Cambridge Economic History of Europe*, i, 355.
3 This is illustrated for instance by the following figures for estimated sugar consumption in Great Britain: in 1700, 10,000 tons, in 1800, 150,000 tons, and in 1885, 1,110,000 tons.
4 Reproduced from Francisco Hernandez-Pacheco, 'Escena Pictoria con Representaciones de Insectos de Époco Paléolitica', *Real Soc. Española de Hist. Nat.*, T.d. 50 Ann., pp. 62–7, Madrid, 1921. An analogous scene is probably represented in the Cueva de la Vieja, Alpera.
  I have to thank Mr M. C. Burkitt for his great kindness in looking out and reproducing this illustration and for providing the full reference. Absence from libraries has, in general, prevented me from doing more than indicate in broad outline the scope of what I believe to be a subject of importance for the student of early man.
5 *Procs. Prehist. Soc.*, 1939, v, 220.
6 F. Hartmann, *L'Agriculture dans l'ancienne Egypte*, Paris, 1923, pp. 205–6.
7 E. E. Evans, *Irish Heritage*, Dundalk, 1942, p. 78.
8 Possibly the honey buried in a glass bottle in a Romano-British grave at Bartlow Hills was therapeutic in intention. See L. C. West, *Roman Britain: the objects of trade*, Oxford, 1931, p. 24. Pliny, *Nat. Hist.*, xxii, 50, is eloquent on the medical virtues of honey.
9 A. Lucas, *Ancient Egyptian Materials*, p. 132; Hartmann, *op.cit.*, 208.
10 E.g. Pliny, *Nat. Hist.*, xxxv, 2 and xxi, 49. Pliny makes the point that wax can easily be made to take colours.
11 Lucas, *op. cit.*, 133, found that, though friable, bees-wax from Egyptian tombs appeared to have undergone no drastic change. From eleven instances he established a range of melting from 64° to 70°c, which compares with 63°c for modern commercial bees-wax.
12 *Ancient Records*, iv, 220, para 454.
13 *Op. cit.*, 132 and 133.
14 Hartmann, *op. cit.*, 204–6.
15 *Procs. Soc. Ant. Scot.*, lxix, 424–30.
16 I. Manninen, *Die Finnisch-Ugrischen Völker*, Leipzig, 1932, 215–17, and 243–4.
17 *Cambridge Economic History of Europe*, i, 483. An example of such a dispute is that in which the people of the city of Riga were involved with the Livs in 1349 over the ownership of honey trees.
18 E.g. in 15th-century Lithuania. See Rutkowski, *ibid.*, 409
19 Sufficient would be left for the winter. Any that remained would be collected in the spring.
20 Strabo must have been referring to hives like those in use among the Finno-Ougrians when he wrote that 'In Hyrcania . . . bees have their hives in the trees, and honey drips from their leaves.' Similar hives were said to have been in use in Media and Armenia: *Geography*, ii, i, 14.

21 See note 20. Strabo also refers to the bitter honey of Colchis: *Geography*, xi, ii, 17.
22 It should be remembered that fodder-crops like clover played a very minor role in prehistoric times.
23 Equally significant is Isaiah's reference (vii, 15, 22) to a diet of curdled milk and honey, symbolizing invasion and the conversion of agricultural into pastoral districts.
24 *Geography*, vi, iii, 6.
25 *Ibid.*, iv, vi, 9.
26 *Ibid.*, ix, i, 23.

CHAPTER 2

WATER IN ANTIQUITY

The basic importance of food in the daily lives both of individuals and of communities, and the all-pervading influence upon outlook and social structure exercised by the methods adopted to ensure its adequate supply have become more and more widely recognized among students of ancient society during recent years.[1] Rather less attention has yet been paid to water,[2] that other necessity of life, bound up so intimately with the distribution and density of human settlement, and linked at the same time with man's exploitation of his physical environment. Yet water-supply merits the closest attention, not only of those who approach prehistory from a functionalist point of view, but of all those whose studies are in the last resort based on archaeological material. In the first place, the connexion between human settlement and sources of water offers a cardinal clue to the location of ancient sites; in the second, the dampness of wells and springs has made for conditions favourable to the preservation of objects, organic as well as inorganic, which in the course of time have found their way into their recesses; and in the third, the veneration in which sources have been held has fostered from time immemorial the deposition in their waters of offerings as welcome to the archaeologist as to the spirits themselves.

The relations between water-supply and human settlement through the ages have not by any means been simple; on the contrary, they have been essentially reciprocal, subject to perpetual readjustment in the course of time. If on the one hand settlement may be restricted by shortage, on the other human requirements may lead to an increase in the supply of water made available. Nature imposes certain limits, but within these there is scope for a wide range of adjustment. It must be obvious that in any local study consideration should first be given to the natural possibilities of the region, to the climate, the distribution and character of its natural sources and to the occurrence or otherwise of subsoil water. For present purposes I shall confine myself to a general consideration of the manner in which men have sought to adjust the supply of water to their social needs under varying cultural conditions and within the limitations imposed by nature.

A primary factor in the evolution of artificial methods of water-supply has been a growth in the density of settlement, in itself a concomitant of cultural progress. Obviously men living under nomadic or semi-nomadic conditions

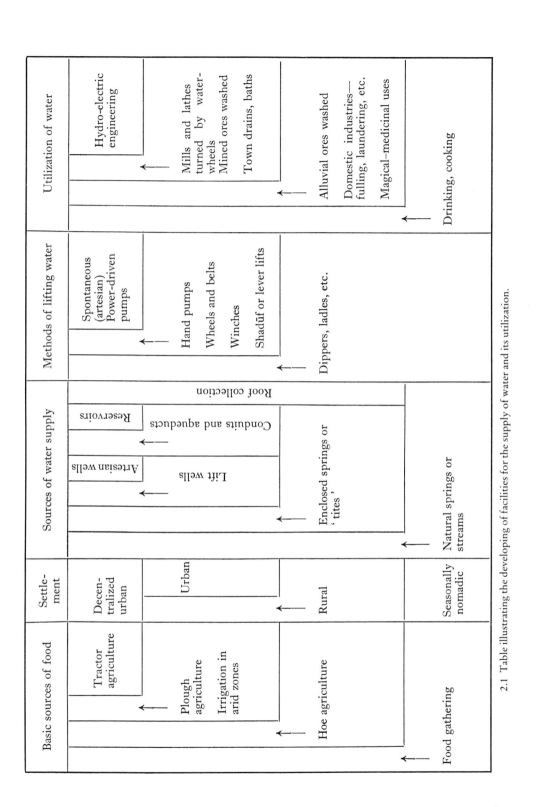

2.1 Table illustrating the developing of facilities for the supply of water and its utilization.

would be free to wander from one natural source of water to another. Like the beasts and their water-holes, they would find these sources adequate to their needs without artificial improvement. Under such conditions live some of the simpler peoples of our own day; under such, we may be certain, lived our forebears of Palaeolithic and mesolithic antiquity.

In temperate Europe, subjected to the complex and disturbing events of the Quaternary Ice Age, it is unlikely that we shall ever obtain much direct evidence about the actual settlements of Lower Palaeolithic man. In areas such as North Africa and contiguous parts of Asia, on the other hand, it is possible to study his habitat substantially unaltered, save for the effects of desiccation, whereby verdant parklands have been transformed into more or less arid wastes, lakes have dried up or contracted and springs failed. Here the quest for Palaeolithic man should centre first and foremost on the now extinct, but once vital, sources of his water supply. Most significant in this respect are the excavations carried out in the Kharga Oasis by Miss G. Caton-Thompson; by detecting and dissecting the fossil springs upon which the Acheulian men of the region depended, and extracting shapely 'hand-axes' from tufa bearing the imprints of the oak-leaf, she has in effect opened up a vast and fascinating field of research. As she herself wrote of her discovery: –

' . . . in the "fossil" spring deposits of Kharga Oasis we have a magnificent chance of resolving the stratigraphical succession of the Stone Age industries, which are represented both in the depression itself, and so prolifically upon the bounding scarp; and it seems not unlikely that the deposits themselves, with marked evidences of alternations of quiescence and great activity of water discharge, may provide us with an unexpected instrument of great value in palaeo-climatic enquiry'.[3]

Not until Upper Palaeolithic and Mesolithic times does one meet in Europe with adequate evidence bearing on the siting of open dwelling-places. A fact which leaps first to the eye is that, whether one looks to the caves of the Dordogne or the Vézère or to the earth-houses of the Don or the Desna, we find Upper Palaeolithic man camping by river courses, in caves or shelters in the gorges through which their waters run, or in houses on their banks.[4] The attraction of rivers is even more clearly seen when one considers Mesolithic Europe,[5] although it must be remembered that rivers were sought for their fish as much as for their water. More decisive is the evidence of such springs as the Schüssenquelle, south of the Federsee in Württemburg, from the peats and tufas of which were excavated flints, bones and antlers worked by Upper Palaeolithic hunters,[6] or the spring at Farnham, Surrey,[7] round the head of which Mesolithic food-gatherers scooped out the floors of their winter dwellings, and to which repaired men of successive periods up to Roman times.

Throughout the ages, indeed, springs have remained foci of human settlement and as such sign-posts to the discerning archaeologist. More than that, they are capable of yielding invaluable evidence of natural conditions prevailing at different periods. Calcareous tufa such as is deposited in spring water is always worth attention, since it may not only disclose the former presence of a spring and consequently of human settlement, but may also yield impressions or actual remains of contemporary vegetation and animal life. As Hulth and Sernander were the first to show in Scandinavia,[8] the mere fact of excessive tufa formation may, even in temperate countries, betoken periods of heavier rainfall and more active springs. Before valid conclusions can be drawn for a given area, however, it is necessary to assemble a substantial body of evidence in the form of archaeological finds in true stratigraphic relation to calcareous deposits, on the lines followed in the Swabian Alps and the Black Forest by Reith.[9] Work on the recent calcareous deposits of this country remains in its infancy, but has already confirmed the heavier rainfall of Atlantic times for which other evidence is available.[10]

In proportion as man began to assume a greater measure of control over his physical environment, basing his subsistence to an ever-growing extent on food won by his productive labour, and bending to his own purposes the physical properties of an ever-widening range of material substances, so his outlook in relation to his water-supply shifted from acquiescence to purposeful mastery. The history of man's control over his supply of water is thus only one aspect of that of his general control over nature, although one with a special relevance to the problems of human settlement. Man has sought to control water primarily for domestic and agricultural needs, but increasingly also for mining and industrial purposes. The essence of this control has been to make water available at the time and place and of the quality and in the volume required. This has been achieved, broadly speaking, by lifting, conducting and storing water, or more often by a combination of two or all of these.

A common device for securing a ready supply of water from a natural spring breaking the surface of the ground was to reinforce the sides, either with stones or wood; by such means a sufficient depth of water was accumulated to make it easy to collect in buckets, dippers or other receptacles. The reinforcement of the sides of the spring also had the effect of keeping the water clean and preventing the silting up of the springhead. To denote such artificially improved springs C. E. N. Bromehead[11] has recently revived the old Cotswold term 'tite'. Enclosed springs or tites may be considered the first improvement on the natural spring and, as such, are of remote antiquity. Yet for the needs of small communities such economical adaptations must long have sufficed. Among the prehistoric peasant peoples of Europe tites were in general use for domestic purposes, nor have they passed out of memory even in the rural England of today. The Jutish farms of the pre-Roman Iron Age excavated by Hatt were furnished with stone-lined tites, comprising funnel or saucer-shaped holes at the bottom of shallow, oval or circular depressions, from which water was drawn directly, sometimes with the aid of a recumbent boulder stepping-stone or in the case of deeper ones by a stone step projecting from the sides.[12]

An alternative method of reinforcing the sides of a natural spring by means of a short section of hollow tree-trunk was resorted to during the Bronze Age of northern and central Europe and can be observed in use down to the present day in backward parts of peasant Europe.[13] In a simple form it is exemplified by the spring at Budsene on the Danish island of Moen, enclosed in a hollow alder trunk. The fact that this yielded women's ornaments of bronze, girdle-cases and armlets, in addition to a miscellaneous collection of animal bones, suggests that we have to do here with women's votive offerings to the spring's godhead.[14] Springs, indeed, have seldom been regarded merely as sources of water. Bubbling from the ground, ever renewed and ever pure, it is hardly surprising that springs should have impressed early man by their magical potency. That well-worship, or at least the association of divinities with wells, flourished in prehistoric Europe we can feel sure from the attitude of the early Church, which beginning by interdicts ended by adoption;[15] the saints' 'wells' of Cornwall – actually all of them are enclosed springs, not wells[16] – are but the Christianized versions of pagan godheads.[17] As more positive evidence one might cite the gold signet-ring from Mycenae, whereon was depicted the 'adoration of a sacred spring descending from a height within a walled temenos, and its source sheltered by three trees within a little enclosure',[18] or Homer's reference to the Achaians offering hecatombs to the immortals 'round about a spring . . . beneath a fair plane-tree whence flowed bright water',[19] in each of which there is associated an element of tree-worship, an association illustrated in our own folk-lore by the custom of pinning rags to trees and bushes close to springs. In his study of the holy 'wells' (sic) of England R. C. Hope has shown that divination of the future from the behaviour of bubbles rising from the casting of pins or coins, physical healing, especially for eye diseases, skin troubles, and the infirmities of old age, and the promotion of fruitfulness among women have all played their part, alongside with worship, in recent folk-lore. More elaborate, but of the same general class, is the famous spring of St Moritz.[20] Here, post-dating an earlier phase, represented by a much decayed shaft, were found two larchwood shafts (one 1.83 m. high and 1.12 m. in diameter, the other 2.35 m. high and 0.78 to 1.07 m. in diameter) enclosed within a double rectangular enclosure of the same wood, the inner of plank, the outer of block-house construction. From the base of the shallower of the two shafts were recovered a series of bronzes, dated to the transition between Reinecke's c and d phases of the Bronze Age and comprising two bronze hilted swords, both sticking vertically into the bottom, a pin, a dagger with broken tang and the upper part of a sword blade, bronzes which can only be interpreted in

such a context as votive offerings. In this particular case one may safely guess
that the offerings were made in the hope of healing; situated some 1775 m.
above sea-level in an Alpine valley, scanty in traces of early settlement, St
Moritz would appear already at this early date to have been a place of
pilgrimage made famous by the healing virtues of its chalybeate springs.[21]
Thus already in the Bronze Age there is evidence that the peoples of
prehistoric Europe made substantial offerings to springs as sources of fertility
and healing, offerings later commuted to coins and pins.

An obvious advance on the enclosed spring or tite was the well in the sense
defined by C. E. N. Bromehead as a 'means of obtaining water from the earth
vertically beneath the spot at which it is required, where it is not obviously
present at the surface'.[22] In the well, tapping subterranean supplies, we have a
radically new departure, even if superficially, and from a formal standpoint it
may not always be easy to draw a hard and fast distinction between a shallow
well and a deep tite. Whereas a spring either breaks surface or at least betrays
itself by such visible signs as the vapours, frogs, toads or damp-loving plants
specified by Pliny and Vitruvius as propitious to the seeker after water, the
sinking of a well involved a definite break with everyday experience, an
incursion into the unknown and, until comparatively recently, the unpre-
dictable.[23] The sinking of wells was not only a new departure psychologically; it also involved heavy economic burdens. The well shaft itself had to
be dug, boring, at first by hand augers and only since 1832[24] by machine,
being a relatively modern process. Then the shaft had to be lined or steined to
retain the sides and exclude impurities. The greater depth of wells made it the
more necessary to enclose their heads, if only to prevent children falling
down the shafts. Moreover, once constructed, wells had to be maintained, for
which purpose various forms of steps or foot-rests were commonly provided
in the shaft. More burdensome still was the day to day operation of wells,
involving, in place of the facile scooping of water from the natural spring or
homely tite, the labour of hauling the water up the shaft, a task which
nevertheless was lightened by a variety of lifting appliances.

Sufficient has been said to make it evident that wells can hardly be regarded
as a necessary or inevitable link in a chain of development from the flowing
spring. On the contrary they represent a revolutionary innovation which can
only have come about through the play of powerful social forces. The
necessity for artificial sources of water supply was brought about by pressure
of population, at once a cause, an index, and a consequence of man's
increased control over nature. This growth of population resulted in an
increased density of areas of primary settlement and in an expansion into
poorer regions previously neglected because deficient in natural supplies of
water. With the rise of urban centres the natural sources of water locally
available ceased to be adequate, on the one hand because deficient in volume
and on the other because contaminated through long-maintained and over-

dense settlement. Moreover city life meant not only that more people required water, but that more people required more water; the dirt and congestion of urban life meant that artificial facilities for bathing and washing and the provision of adequate sanitation became necessities of public health rather than luxuries. Small wonder is it that the provision of a pure and abundant supply of water has been a prime aim of city fathers since men first dwelt in cities. Thirst and pestilence between them were powerful stimuli.

Wells, tapping subterranean sources, were one of the obvious solutions to the problems of urban water supply, and occur throughout the ancient world in the zone of urban life. Within the wide range of geographical endowment and cultural differentiation prevailing there was ample scope for variety, both in construction and in the devices used for raising water. To turn first to construction, the simplest type of well was, obviously, that cut in rock sufficiently firm to require no artificial steining. Where the rock was suitable one might expect to find such 'primitive' wells at any period among peoples acquainted with the idea of well-sinking. Examples familiar to British archaeologists are those Roman wells sunk through the chalk of Cranborne Chase investigated by General Pitt-Rivers.[25] Yet, in the ancient East and in the Mediterranean basin, where urban civilization first spread on the European mainland, we find, side by side with such simple wells, a wide range of others which appear, as it were, fully differentiated and sophisticated in construction, in the earliest contexts.

Thus, the wells of Mohenjo-Daro, among the very oldest in the world, had their circular shafts, ranging in diameter from two to seven feet, lined throughout with specially contrived wedge-shaped bricks. Low brick copings, surrounded by brick pavements worn with hollows where the water-jars once stood, finished off the well-head and served to keep it clean. Water-logging in the lowest levels prevented the excavators from ascertaining the total depth of the wells, many of which are known however to date from an early stage in the history of the city. Indications of additions to the brick linings given by clearly marked joints show that as the level of the city rose on its own rubble, so the steining of the wells had to be built up to keep their heads above ground. In such a manner did the pressure of social life, in the form of long continued settlement on the same site, increase the labours of the water-drawers. Today as the well-shafts stand clear of the excavated portions of the city mound, they resemble nothing more than grotesque factory chimneys.[26]

An entirely distinct use of fired clay for lining well-shafts is that met with in the Eastern Mediterranean. Thus the well in the courtyard of the Mycenaean megaron palace of Phylakopi was lined by a succession of tubular sections of fired clay, each some 2 ft. 1½ ins. to 2 ft. 3 ins. in diameter and 2 ft 10½ ins. in length and having one end flared for retaining the next in sequence. The shaft was excavated to a depth of 9 metres when the work was halted by water. Oval holes in the earthenware sections gave foot-hold and hand-grip to anyone ascending or descending the shaft.[27] Not dissimilar was the well excavated by Sir Arthur Evans in the town area northwest of the Palace of Knossos, although in this case each section was built up of three parts. This Cretan well (10.4 m. deep and 69 cms. in diameter) was in use during the Roman period, but may be more ancient in origin.[28]

Stone is another obvious material for steining wells and its use can be shown from early times. Particularly skilful was the work of the Etruscan well-builders, who contrived shafts of splayed or bell-shaped profile with constricted mouths.[29] Easier to construct must have been the stone-lined wells of the Romans, built with an even batter from constricted base to open mouth. A detail of interest revealed during the excavation of such wells at the Saalburg were the timber footings designed to keep the well bases from being choked by silt.[30]

In central and western Europe the Romans commonly used timber for steining wells. Generally this took the form of a square sectioned framework filled in by wooden planking. In the case of deep shafts, such as some of those on the Saalburg which reached up to 24 metres, the excavation seems to have been carried out in stages, the sides of the shaft being steined down to a safe depth, before resuming work at a lower level. As each successive stage was dug on a more restricted area, the profiles of such well-shafts were characteristically stepped at the lower levels.[31] The upper portion of the well-shaft was commonly left unsteined, the sides being battered to give a funnel-shaped section. Where, as in Roman Silchester, the shafts were comparatively shallow, it commonly happened that the timber frame extended less than half way up.[32] Occasionally, as at London[33] and Silchester,[34] the base of the well-shaft was lined by a wooden tub from which the top and bottom had been removed. At Silchester, also, wattlework, held in place by a ring of stakes, was used to stein the lower portion of an 18 ft. well-shaft.[35] The Romans were evidently practised well-sinkers, and judging from the numbers found on some of their stations, were prodigal of new shafts. Thus at the Saalburg no less than 98 wells were found, of which no more than 3 appear to have been in use at any one time, implying the frequent sinking of new ones. Their wells were hand-dug, the well-sinker descending by a ladder[36] and presumably having his spoil lifted by the type of winch normally used to raise water.

In northwestern and central Europe true wells appear either as direct Roman innovations, or, in regions outside the limits of the empire, as the probable result of Roman influence. At least in such regions wells cannot be shown to have occurred before the spread of Roman domination over contiguous areas. Those that are known from the opening centuries of our era in barbarian Europe belong to one of two main types, one lined with planks set into a framework of vertical corner-posts, the other of morticed plank construction. A good example of the frame type is the wooden well at Stickenbüttel, near Cuxhaven, explored by Karl Waller.[37] The shaft, which has a funnel-shaped upper portion, was sunk into a low ridge above marsh-level through sand and loam to fresh-water-bearing sand. Originally the well had been a rather shallower 'tite', a funnel-shaped hollow lined by turf sods, enclosed by a stone setting and approached by a sloping path with three oak sleepers acting as steps. The wooden shaft, which superseded this primitive tite, comprised four square uprights pointed at the base and grooved for the reception of the side planks, the edges of which were bevelled so as to allow a neater fit. The lowermost course of planking was mortised to the uprights and reinforced by vertical timbers retained on the inside by another course of horizontal planking. The top of the shaft was 2.3 m. below ground level and the base 5.8 m. According to the pottery the Stickenbüttel well, the earliest in north Germany, dates from the period between the 2nd century B.C. and the 1st century A.D. An example of a wooden well-lining composed entirely of mortised side planks is that at Domslau, nr. Breslau, described by J. Richter[38] and dated by Jacob Friesen to the 3rd–4th centuries A.D.[39] Sunk down to water-bearing sands, the shaft was 1.4 m. deep and set at the base of a funnel-shaped opening extending 1.65 m. below ground-level. Both the funnel itself and the timber shaft were coated and packed with blue-grey clay.

Having considered well-shafts, attention must next be directed to the lifting apparatus made necessary by their depth. In ancient times there were two types in general use, a lever apparatus adapted to relatively shallow wells and various forms of winding and drawing apparatus for deeper ones. The former consisted of a long beam oscillating at the apex of a forked upright on the see-saw principle, the receptacle for the water being attached by a rope or long pole to one end of the beam, the other end of which was weighted to secure a counterpoise and so ease the task of drawing water. Such a device, the *shaduf* of modern Egypt, is of remote antiquity. It made its appearance, along with a simple type of plough, in the Egyptian Old Kingdom;[40] it was known in ancient Babylonia;[41] in China it came in during the Han period,[42] and at the present day it is still used extensively in Egypt and North Africa,[43] Asia Minor, India,[44] Italy, Iberia, the Balkans,[45] Germany, Sweden, Finland,[46] Hungary,[47] Poland, the East Baltic States and White Russia. In North Africa today the *shaduf* is used to some extent in connexion with irrigation and there is reason to think that this may indeed have been its primary use. A possible link between the ladle or scoop and the balanced lever apparatus may be seen in the pivoted ladle observed by Wakarelski in Bulgaria in present day use for scooping water from irrigation channels.[48]

An alternative method of lifting water from wells, and one that, before more modern developments, was necessitated for deeper wells, was to raise it in a receptacle attached to a rope or chain, by a process of hauling, either directly by the hands or indirectly on some form of winch or spindle. Use of the simpler method of hand-haulage may be betrayed, as it was at Mohenjo-Daro, by grooving of the lips of wells or their copings. Positive evidence for the use of winding devices is not often forthcoming from ancient sites, which makes all the more interesting such finds as those made by Jacobi at the Saalburg. For shallow wells the Roman occupants of this frontier stronghold used iron hooks on poles,[49] but from deeper ones they wound up their water buckets on hempen ropes, either on grooved wheels revolving on metal pins,[50] the diameter of the wheel depending on the depth of the well, or on spindle-shaped rollers like that found at Herculaneum.[51] As Wakarelski has pointed out,[52] the length of time required to raise water from a deep well, even where some form of winch was available, would be such as to render desirable some form of protection from the weather. This accounts for the often elaborate roofs found over wells in many parts of Europe at the present day; no doubt excavation in the immediate neighbourhood of ancient well-heads would often reveal traces of similar structures.[53] With the harnessing of animals to winches much of the drudgery of raising water from draw-wells was eliminated, although, as Wakarelski states, this appears to have been almost confined to the Mediterranean zone. The pump, by means of which water was pushed or sucked to the surface, was a device familiar to the Romans,[54] and, mechanically operated, still plays a role superseded only in part by the spontaneous uprush of water from modern artesian wells.

An obvious alternative to tapping subterranean sources was to conduct supplies from a distance to the spot required. To a limited extent this could be effected by the actual carriage of water in skins or jars, but such was normally limited to the local distribution of water from spring or well-head. Travellers crossing arid zones might carry water between water-holes, and men defending a waterless eyrie might make hazardous descents and carry water back to the garrison,[55] but in so doing they would be reacting to exceptional circumstances; under the conditions of normal and rational existence men have availed themselves, when they wished to convey water, of its fluidity and its capacity, given a sufficient overall drop, to surmount obstacles between source and place of use. For example, the ancient Minoans conducted water from the limestone spring of Mavrokolybo to the Palace of Knossos by means of a descending and ascending conduit,[56] implying a practical knowledge of the fact that water finds its own level. It is of course on this principle that the modern use of water-towers for the distribution of water is based. As Bromehead has pointed out, much experience in the conducting of water must have been gained in the course of irrigation.[57] The idea of extending the area of fertility by cutting irrigation channels, when applied to the problem of increasing domestic water supply, took the form of constructing artificial conduits or canals. In the forested regions of north-western, northern and central Europe such are still made of wood, open channels cut from solid split timbers or built up from boards, or whole trunks hollowed to the shape of tubular pipes. Timber pipes, often with iron hoops at their joints, were used for distributing water in the cities of northwestern Europe until recent times, while open canals of wood boards can still be seen from the roadside or the train window in use for canalizing drainage down steep slopes in areas of heavy rainfall and poor land-drainage. Similar open channels made of terracotta were used by the Mycenaeans for drainage purposes, having been found at Tiryns and at Phylakopi.[58] Closed water pipes of terracotta were also in early use in the Mediterranean area. From Minoan Crete we find a refinement in the tapered pipes, designed to impart a shooting motion to the flow of water and so prevent an accumulation of silt, excavated by Sir Arthur Evans.[59] The Romans, master plumbers of antiquity, conducted water in pipes and open canals of terracotta, stone, wood and lead.[60] Such forms of artificial channel were used not only to collect and distribute domestic water supplies, but also for irrigating gardens, for drainage and for many other purposes. In their monumental aqueducts, designed to carry fresh water to the inhabitants of great urban centres, the Romans carried the supply of water for domestic use to a level only surpassed in recent times.

The modern method of supplying great centres of population from a distance involves the use of reservoirs to make the flow of water independent of seasonal change. The storage of water in tanks and cisterns has of course played a part in the history of water supply from early days. Water accumulated in this way might issue from springs, like that from the Perseia spring near Mycenae carried by the Mycenaeans in stone conduits and stored in long narrow stone cisterns.[61] More often it was rainwater collected from the roof, or even, as at Knossos, from flights of steps.[62] In areas of low rainfall rainwater collected in this way formed an important source of supply. In modern Melos, for example, rainwater, collected on flat roofs sloping slightly to one corner and conducted by pipes to tanks below ground level, is made to last some households the whole year round.[63] As will be shown later, the peculiar properties of rainwater made it of special value for industrial purposes, even where other sources were available for domestic requirements. Thus it may be that the Mycenaeans, who stored spring water in stone cisterns, used the large lead containers found on their sites for storing rainwater.[64]

In northern and central Europe a number of wood-lined shafts have been discovered, which may, as Jacob Friesen has argued,[65] have served in most instances as water cisterns rather than as wells; where, indeed, the shafts are sunk into impermeable clay their interpretation as wells is one that will not bear examination. Jacob Friesen regards them specifically as rainwater cisterns, although in no case, it must be confessed, have traces of dwellings been found in proximity, a fact quite probably due to lack of adequate examination. Structurally these well-like wooden cisterns resemble closely the wooden shaft at Stickenbüttel. Thus the cistern found during the construction of the Mittelland canal near Algermissen, near Hildesheim,[66] and dated to the beginning of our era had squared oak uprights mortised at the base to a rectangular framework and grooved to retain the side planking. The shaft was sunk into a blue clay, deficient in ground water, but admirably adapted for holding it. The cistern itself was some 3½ m. deep and the head of the timber lining was approximately 4 m. below ground level. Rectangular sockets for steps were found in some of the side planks. Closely similar was the so-called 'well' at Gamla Uppsala described by Olsson,[67] distinguished only by its slightly ruder construction, the corner uprights, ladder rungs and side-planks being left untrimmed and the uprights, pointed at the base, being rammed directly into the subsoil. The Romans frequently built wood-lined cisterns in their frontier posts along the *limes*, which, since they were adequately provided with well-water for drinking, were almost certainly for storing rainwater for industrial purposes. As Jacobi has pointed out,[68] the ancients esteemed rainwater for certain purposes owing to its softness and its freedom from the salts commonly dissolved out of the rock through which well water passes. Rainwater would be especially useful for dyeing, fulling, the washing of linen[69] and the preparation of flax.[70] There is evidence that rainwater was collected, presumably for home industries, as early as Hallstatt times in Germany.[71]

As has been shown, elaborate methods of assuring supplies of drinking water and facilities for washing and for the disposal of sewage and drainage appear as functions of city life. Like wells and aqueducts, drains appear at a high stage of development among the earliest urban communities. Thus the people of the Indus Valley, to whose wells I have already alluded, devised the most complete, as it is among the most ancient, system of drainage yet discovered. House drains of brick cemented with mud or gypsum mortar, or clay pipes, were connected with brick-lined street drains by which refuse was carried out of the city. Both house and street drains were provided with sumps from which solid matter could be collected. As the city grew on its accumulated rubble the drainage channels had frequently to be deepened and eventually replaced. Moreover, to cope with the Indus floods great corbelled culverts had to be built on the outskirts.[72] The first people on the European mainland to sink wells, the Mycenaeans, were also the earliest to devise elaborate systems of drainage. Thus at Tiryns Schliemann found that the courtyards of the megara were so tilted that rainwater drained naturally into the mouths of shafts by which it was conducted to horizontal drainage channels below ground-level.[73] At Phylakopi drains built of stone flags and rough stone blocks were found immediately below the surface of many of the streets, the main line of drainage being such as to give a sufficient fall.[74] The Mycenaean inhabitants of Phylakopi built stone sinks in the walls of their houses,[75] the outlets of which issued into the street drains. The ordinary type of domestic bath used in Greece and the Aegean during the Mycenaean period was a splayed open pottery bowl about 40 inches in diameter having paintings of spirals and other designs on the inside. A complete pottery bath of this kind found during the excavation of the Mycenaean city at Phylakopi was bedded on a slab of ironstone placed in the corner of a room.[76] Many years earlier the great Schliemann had found a fragment of such a bath at Tiryns.[77] Doubtless, also, it was to such that Homer referred when he spoke of men being washed by female attendants in 'polished baths';[78] on a terracotta of early, but unknown, date from Cyprus we can see a bather squatting on his heels with water being poured over him by a woman.[79] For bathing of a formal or ritual character the Mycenaeans had stone floored bathrooms with outfalls into the street drains and small plaster-receptacles set into the wall which may once have held oil or unguents. Such a bathroom was explored by Schliemann close by the larger of the two megara at Tiryns.[80] From time immemorial women have sought water to wash their laundry, but only in the most advanced societies has this need been met by elaborate artificial means. As a rule textiles would be carried to the riverside and washed on the spot, though where the source of supply was spring-water it might be necessary to provide troughs, like the 'fair troughs of stone, where wives and daughters of the men of Troy were wont to wash bright raiment' in the waters of the twin fountains which fed 'deep-eddying Skamandros'.[81]

There seems little doubt that the origins of artificial supplies of water for domestic purposes are closely bound up with irrigation. The idea of intensifying and at the same time extending human settlement by supplementing the supplies of water naturally available is not only analogous with that of extending the area of cultivation and increasing the yield of the land, but is to a large extent its logical outcome. Historically it was precisely in those great river valleys of the Old World where irrigation was first practised that urban civilization first developed, and as we have seen it was pressure of urban conditions which stimulated the development of artificial means of water-supply. While, as I have stressed, deep wells were born of the necessities of city life, methods of conducting water from distant sources and of lifting it from shallow wells on the lever principle seem to have been derived from experience gained in the manipulation and control of water during irrigation. It was in connexion with irrigation also that the water-wheel first came into use, as a lifting device. The spread of rotary devices for lifting water in the Balkans during recent centuries, wheels with scoops attached to their circumference or drums revolving belts with scoops, has recently been discussed by Wakarelski, to whom the reader is referred for illustrations. The origin of such is to be found in the ancient centres of civilization where irrigation was practised; endless chains of pots were used to water the hanging gardens of Babylon[82] and similar devices were referred to in Egyptian papyri of the 2nd century B.C.[83] To this day water is lifted from the deeper wells of Algeria by an endless chain of buckets revolving on geared wheels.

The rotary method of lifting water was early applied to the problem of draining mine-workings. In particular the screw-pump or water-screw, originally devised by Archimedes of Syracuse (287–212 B.C.) for raising Nile water for irrigation works, was widely used in the Roman mines of Spain and south France. Consisting of a wooden cylinder with a helical copper vane or screw on a wood core, the Archimedean screw rotated by men working a treadmill was capable of lifting water approximately five feet. Arranged in a series at successive levels, it was possible to raise water a considerable height, though at ever-increasing cost in man-power.[84] Many well-preserved examples have been recovered from Roman mines and their mode of operation is illustrated by models and wall-paintings.[85]

The use of the water-wheel for lifting water must have suggested a ready means of utilizing its inherent power, a development pregnant with possibilities for lightening the burden of human labour. The power of flowing water was early applied to the recovery of two of the most precious metals of antiquity, gold and tin. Alluvial gold dust, first seen sparkling in the water of a stream, was most easily separated in a wood trough or dish, shaken in flowing water which carried off the lighter sand. Mined gold could be separated from worthless dust by spreading the pulverized ore on an inclined board and pouring on water in the manner described by Diodorus Siculus.[86] A further step was to conduct water where it was required to utilize its scour; thus, Strabo wrote of the Iberian gold-washers that 'they flood the waterless districts by conducting water thither, and thus they make the gold dust glitter'.[87] Here we seem to have a further application of methods of conducting water originally gained through irrigation. Indeed, the activities of gold-seekers seem on occasion to have brought them directly into competition with cultivators; when the Salassi, who dwelt among the foothills between the Po and the Alps, deviated the waters of the Durias river to wash mined gold they came into conflict with 'the people who farmed the plains below them, because their country was deprived of irrigation'.[88] Again, in early times and throughout most of the Middle Ages the tinners of Cornwall used to recover the heavier ore by shovelling some of the tin 'bed' into an inclining wooden waterway or 'tye' and then by vigorous stirring help the flowing water eliminate the lighter waste.

But it was through the utilization of the force of flowing water by means of the wheel that water-power was to make its greatest, albeit retarded, contribution. In early times the most important application of the power generated by wheels turned by flowing water was to milling corn. The water-mill not only superseded the tedium of hand-querns, but transformed milling from a domestic occupation to a trade. The earliest references to rotary mills driven by water-power date from the 1st century B.C., but the invention seems to have made slow headway in the Classical World owing no doubt to the cheapness of slave labour. Not until the 4th century A.D. do references, among them the well-known one of Vitruvius, become common. A mill resembling that described by Vitruvius, with the difference that it was overshot instead of undershot,[89] was excavated by the Americans in the Agora at Athens, being dated to the time of Leo I (A.D. 457–474).[90] From earlier in the same century, also, we have what according to G. Brett[91] is the only representation of a water-wheel in Roman art on the recently uncovered mosaic in the Great Palace of Byzantium. It seems likely that Brett is correct in his view that the overshot mill may be a development of the Late Empire. On the feudal estates which followed the break-up of the Empire water-mills underwent a rapid development, a consequence in part no doubt of the disintegration of slavery, and the miller emerged as one of the leading figures of medieval society. Already by Domesday there were more than 5000 mills in England.[92] There is evidence, also, in the pot-stone industry of the Alps that as early as the 1st century A.D. the Romans had harnessed mountain torrents to turn lathes.[93]

It is only in our own day that the possibilities of water-power have been fully realized. Up to the present the prodigious power unloosed by hydro-electric engineers has been largely wasted in warfare, and the plants and dams, when not geared to the production of weapons of war, have themselves been destroyed by air attack or demolished in the wake of retreating armies. Directed into constructive channels the electrical energy generated by water-power is capable not only of ameliorating conditions of work, by banishing smoke and fumes, but of positively transforming society. By increasing leisure and doing away with the necessity of concentrating industry and population in the immediate neighbourhood of the sources of power, hydro-electrical engineering may yet go far to redress some of the worst evils of the Industrial Revolution, restoring the balance between town and country. Moreover the very scale of the projects involved in the harnessing of water-power to the production of electrical energy inevitably favours collective as opposed to individual enterprise. So, from the Stone Age to the 20th century has water reflected the image of society; first the food-gathering tribes camping round their springs; then the lowly peasants with their village tites; next the town-dweller and his aqueducts and wells with their diverse appliances and his water-driven mills and lathes; and finally the men of the future, breaking loose from the city bounds, banishing smoke and fumes and winning leisure for themselves and the control of energy for society at large.

Notes

1 The basic importance of food supply has been stressed by the present author in his *Archaeology and Society*, pp. 152–8, where references will be found to some of the most outstanding work in the archaeological reconstruction of ancient food supply. In the field of anthropology Audrey I. Richards' *Hunger and Work in a Savage Tribe* (1932) and her later monograph *Land, Labour and Diet in Northern Rhodesia* (1939) may be cited as illustrating the new trend.

2 Reference should, however, be made to C. E. N. Bromehead's excellent paper, 'The Early History of Water-Supply', *Geog. J.*, xcix, 1942, 142–51, 183–96.

3 *Man*, 1931, no. 91.

4 *Proc. Prehist. Soc.*, v, 1939, 100–3.

5 J. G. D. Clark, *The Mesolithic Settlement of Northern Europe*, 1936, pp. 23–4, and *Proc. Prehist. Soc.*, iii, 1937, 472–5.

6 R. R. Schmidt, *Die Diluviale Vorzeit Deutschlands*, 1912, fig. 12.

7 J. G. D. Clark and W. F. Rankine, 'Excavations at Farnham, Surrey', *Proc. Prehist. Soc.*, v, 1939, 61–118.

8 J. M. Hulth, 'Über einige Kalktuffe aus Westgötland', *Bull. Geol. Inst. Univ.*, Uppsala, iv, 1898.

9 A. Reith, 'Vorgeschichtliche Funde aus dem Kalktuff der Schwäbischen Alb und des württembergischen Muschelkalkgebiets', *Mannus Z*, 1938, pp. 562–84.

10 E.g. flint and chert implements of Late Mesolithic appearance have been obtained from tufa deposits at Prestatyn, Flint, and at Blashenwell, Dorset, the mollusc assemblages from which have been diagnosed by Dr Wilfred Jackson and Mr A. S. Kennard, respectively, as indicative of a rainfall higher than that prevailing today. See J. G. D. Clark, *Proc. Prehist. Soc.*, iv, 1938, 330–4; v, 1939, 201–2.

11 *Op. cit.* 142.

12 E.g. G. Hatt, *Aarbøger*, 1938, 161–5 and figs. 29–32; also 199–201 and figs. 73–5.

13 For example, one closely resembling that from Budsene is illustrated from modern Bulgaria by C. Wakarelski in his 'Brunnen und wasserleitungen in Bulgaria', *Folk-Live*, 1939, taf. 2c.

14 C. A. Nordman, *Aarbøger*, 1920, pp. 63ff.; J. Brønsted, *Danmarks Oldtid*, ii, p. 202, fig. 187.

15 Well worship was interdicted by the Council of Tours A.D. 567, and proscribed by the laws and canons of kings Egbert, Edgar and Cnut, but the 26th canon of St Anselm, 1102, merely enjoined that 'no one attribute reverence or sanctity to a dead body or a fountain, without the Bishop's authority'. R. C. Hope, *The Legendary Lore of the Holy Wells of England*, 1903, p. xx.

16 Although sometimes enclosed by elaborate masonry, or even, as in the case of St Madern's 'well', Madron, by a complete chapel, they remain rites from which water could be scooped directly.

17 R. C. Hope, *op. cit.*, pp. 112–15, suggests that the votive tablet inscribed to the goddess Coventina, which, together with 24 altars and a number of vases, rings, beads, brooches and coins, was recovered from a well at Carrawburgh on the Wall, were deposited by the guardians or priests of the well fleeing the Theodosian persecution.

18 Sir A. Evans, *Palace of Minos*, iii, 137–8.

19 *Iliad*, ii, 305–7.

20 As evidence of the persistence of the custom of depositing coins, one may quote the instance of the children's spring at Tolgs skn., Norrviding hd., Småland, from which were recovered no less than 540 silver and 5394 copper coins, ranging in date from Magnus Eriksson, 1319–64, to Oscar ii. *Vitt. Akad. Månadsblad*, 1903–5, pp. 3–8.

21 J. Heierli, 'Die bronzezeitliche Quellfassung von St Moritz', *Anz. für Schweizerische Altertumskunde*, N. F. Bd. ix, 1907, 4 Hft, pp. 265–78; M. M. Lienau, 'Die bronzezeitliche Quellfassung von St Moritz', *Mannus Z.*, x, 1908, 25–30.

22 *Op. cit.*, 142.

23 The first well sited on strictly scientific principles to reach water in agreement with anticipation appears to have been sunk in Derbyshire in 1795. Bromehead, *op. cit.*, 149.

24 *Ibid.*, 151.

25 General Pitt-Rivers excavated two wells in the Romano-British settlement at Woodcuts, Rushmore. Although the recovery of the metal handle and bands of a wooden bucket from the bottom of one of these (188 ft deep) shows it once to have been in use, the well proved on excavation to be quite dry and remained so until refilled. In such a manner wells may sometimes give indication of a lowering of the local water table. *Excavations in Cranborne Chase*, 1887, i, 27–8, and pl. v.

26 E. Mackay, *The Indus Civilization*, 1935, pp. 49–52, 57–8.

27 C.C. Edgar, *Excavations at Phylakopi in Melos*, 1904, fig. 51.

28 Sir A. Evans, *The Palace of Minos*, iii, pp. 255–9 and figs. 175, 176.

29 O. Montelius, *La civilisation primitive en Italie*, 1895, pp. 495 ff. and pl. 108, nos. 1 and 2.

30 H. Jacobi, 'Be- und entwässerung unserer limes Kastelle', *William Dorpfeld Festschrift*, Berlin, 1933, pp. 49–70.

31 *Ibid*, abb. 6, no. 4.

32 Thus two wells at Silchester, 27 ft. and 21 ft. deep, were steined for 13 ft. and 7 ft. respectively. *Archaeologia*, lvii, 93–4.

33 *Arch. J.*, xiii, 274.

34 *Arch.*, lviii, 415.

35 *Arch.*, lvii, 94.

36 The remains of a ladder with fir uprights and oak rungs were found at the bottom of what appeared to be an unfinished well at Silchester. *Arch.*, lvii, 244.

37 Karl Waller, 'Der Stickenbüttler Brunnen', *P.Z.*, xx, 1929, 250–65.

38 J. Richter, 'Zur vorgeschichtlichen brunnenkunde', *M.A.G.W.*, liii, 1923, 49–68.

39 *Op. cit.*, 35.

40 For a representation in a tomb painting, see P. Leser, *Entstehung und verbreitung des Pfluges*, 1931, abb. 342. Wooden *shaduf* hooks were recovered by Petrie from graves 249 and 558 at Tarkhan, dating from the IInd and IIIrd dynasties; see *Tarkhan I and Memphis*, 1913, p. 25 and pl. x, no. 6.

41 H. Prinz, *Weltwirtschaftliches Archiv*, 1916, bd. 8, p. 11.

42 Leser, *op. cit.*, abb. 343.

43 *Ibid.*, p. 541.

44 *Ibid.*, abb. 345.

45 For an illustration of a modern Bulgarian example, see Wakarelski, *op. cit.*, fig. 6.

46 Leser, *op. cit.*, abb. 344.

47 *Antiquity*, 1938, pl. iv, opp. p. 361.

48 Wakarelski, *op. cit.*

49 H. Jacobi, *op. cit.*, abb. 6, no. 15.

50 *Ibid.*

51 *Ibid.*, abb. 7, no. 3.

52 Simple draw wells in northeast Bulgaria and the Dobrudja observed by C. Wakarelski were sometimes as much as 100 m. deep.

53 *Lothr. Jahrb*, 1910, xxii, p. 509, pl. 41.

54 O Paret, *Die Römer in Württemburg*, iii, s. 101 and abb. 65, illustrates a reconstruction of a Roman well-house.

55 The question of the supply of water in the hill-forts of southern England has frequently been discussed. In war men are willing to act – may be compelled to act – in a manner that

normally would appear irrational. Under the conditions of primitive tribal warfare, a hill-top garrison would find little difficulty in fetching sufficient water from the valley, although dependence on an external source of water-supply must have placed barbarians at a fatal disadvantage when opposed by a civilized foe.

56 *Palace of Minos*, II, pp. 462–3.

57 *Op. cit.* 183.

58 *Tiryns*, fig. 118; *Phylakopi*, fig. 57.

59 *Palace of Minos*, III, fig. 173.

60 Jacobi, *op. cit.*, abb. 8.

61 H. Schliemann, *Mycenae and Tiryns*, 1878, p. 141.

62 Sir Arthur Evans has described (*Palace of Minos*, III, 236–51 and fig. 169 c) the ingenious methods employed to carry the rainwater round the angles formed by successive flights of steps and the devices for catching sediment.

63 A picturesque detail mentioned by C. C. Edgar, *op. cit.*, 49 is that it is usual to let the first rainfall of the season escape, since the roof is general fairly dirty from the family having slept there during the summer months.

64 Thus six circular lead containers with bronze edgings were found in the Shaft Graves at Mycenae (G. Karo, *Die Schachtgräber von Mykenai*, Munich, 1930, pp. 160 and 231), while Wace found a mass of molten lead in burnt houses at Mycenae.

65 K. H. Jacob-Friesen, 'Die Ausgrabung einer urgeschichtlichen Zisterne bei Algermissen, Kr. Hildesheim', *Nachrblt. für Niedersachsens Vorgeschichte*, 1925, N. F., No. 2, 35.

66 *Ibid.*, 29–36.

67 M. Olsson, ' En forntida brunn vid Gamla Uppsala', *Upplands Forminnesförenings Tidskr.* XXVIII.

68 *Op. cit.*, p. 60. On the Saalburg the larger cisterns were shallow, oblong structures, 8 by 9 metres in plan and 1 metre deep.

69 Sir A. Evans, *Palace of Minos*, III, p. 243.

70 E.g. flax is retted by steeping in soft water.

71 Thus a clay cistern, presumably for storing rainwater, was found immediately outside the outer wall of the living-room of one of the rectangular wooden houses of the Hallstatt stronghold of Neuhäusel, Westerwald: F. Behn, *Kulturgesch. Wegweiser Röm.-Germ. Central Mus. Nr. 2 Das Haus in Vorrömischer Zeit*, p. 23.

72 For a concise description, see Mackay, *op. cit.*, pp. 42–9.

73 Schliemann, *op. cit.*, pp. 204, 238 and 245.

74 Edgar, *op. cit.*, p. 50 and fig. 36.

75 C. C. Edgar, *op. cit.*, fig. 44.

76 Edgar, *op. cit.*, pp. 13, 14 and 139 ff.

77 Schliemann, *op. cit.*, pl. XXIV, d, e.

78 *Odyssey*, IV, 49–50.

79 *Bull. de corresp. Hell.* 1900, p. 515.

80 *Op. cit.*, fig. 117.

81 *Iliad*, XXII, 154–7.

82 *Ecclesiastes*, chap. XII.

83 According to V. G. Childe, *What Happened in History*, 1942, p. 224.

84 See T. A. Rickard, *Man and Metals*, pp. 421–4 and fig. 49.

85 See a terracotta from Alexandria of Ptolemaic date (B.M. no. 37563); also a wall painting at Pompeii (*Illustrated London News*, 17 December 1927).

86 See Rickard, *op. cit.*, pp. 209–12. Diodorus was quoting from Agatharchides of Ciredus who visited the Egyptian gold mines in 170 B.C.

87 Strabo, Loeb transl. 3. 2. 8.

88 Strabo, Loeb transl. 4. 6. 7.

89 In an overshot mill the water is canalized and its force increased. According to G. Brett, 'Byzantine Water-Mills', *Antiquity*, 1939, pp. 354–6, the overshot mill may be a development of the Late Empire.
90 A. W. Parsons, 'A Roman water-mill in the Athenian Agora', *Hesperia,* v. 70 ff.
91 Illustrated by Brett, *op. cit.*
92 See *Antiquity*, 1939, xiii, 266.
93 For details of the industry, which survived in remote valleys up to the present day, reference should be made to Rütimeyer's *Ur-ethnologie der Schweiz*, pp. 94 ff. In the modern survivals the water was canalized in open wooden leads with a sudden drop close to the wheel, the axle of which was used to turn the pot. The industry was mentioned by Pliny in his *Nat. Hist.*, xxxvi, cap. 22.

CHAPTER 3

FARMERS AND FORESTS IN
NEOLITHIC EUROPE

The role of Neolithic man as a breeder of domesticated animals and plants has long been recognized as one of high significance in the evolution of culture, and the spread of farming has been commonly accepted as marking one of the most significant phases in European prehistory. Much less attention has been paid to the manner in which the earliest farmers pioneered the European wastes and, in creating the conditions needful for their way of life, laid the foundations for later prehistoric settlement. One reason for this is the widely held theory that Neolithic man was only capable of colonizing 'open' country, having perforce to avoid forest areas. It will be my aim in this article to show that this theory rests on false premises, and that, far from being hostile, forests paid a vital part in the spread of farming from the genial centres of the ancient world over the savage spaces of northen Europe.

If the idea that Neolithic man shunned the forest has exercised something of a hypnotic influence on the study of early settlement, this may be due in part to the characteristically circular form of argument in which some of its chief protagonists have indulged. Broadly speaking it has been argued that, since Neolithic man was unable to clear the forest for himself, he can only have settled areas naturally 'open' or free from forest trees, and, conversely, that areas known to have been settled by Neolithic man cannot have been forested at the time of his settlement. Particularly subtle has been the way in which the theory, in reality so unscientific, managed to secure at least the appearance of sanction from the natural sciences; hypotheses founded on botanical and geological data were systematically seized upon to justify the thesis of an 'open' countryside at the time of the Neolithic colonization, and the framers of these very hypotheses were encouraged to draw comfort from the supposed 'fact', in reality only a prejudice, that early man was incapable of settling forest country. Here we see in truth the baleful results which accrue from false cooperation, in reality mere collusion, between the human and natural sciences, when, instead of each testing the hypotheses of the other in terms of data established by its own discipline, each uses the hypothesis of the other as the foundation of proof for its own theory.

One example of this is given by the loess, that famous 'corridor' through the forests of central Europe, along which the Danubian farmers are

29

supposed to have advanced unhindered by any necessity of clearing the land of forest trees. The legend appears to have originated in a gratuitous pronouncement by the celebrated geologist A. Penck in 1887.[1] Remarking on the proclivity of the Neolithic settlers of central Europe for the loess, Penck volunteered the astonishing statement that, since it was unlikely that the colonizers would have recognized 'instinctively' that certain parts of the forest were more suitable than others for cultivation, it was quite probable that the loess was as free from forest as the prairies of North America.[2] While agreeing that the early farmers could hardly have been guided 'instinctively' to the most likely cultivable soils, one must protest that natural vegetation, which could well have been forest, might have afforded an outstanding clue. According to Carl Schott,[3] the English pioneers in Ontario of the late 18th–early 19th centuries selected ground for cultivation precisely on the criterion of observed forest growth.[4] Equally unfortunate is Penck's reference to the prairies. One of Schott's most interesting points is that before the European colonization the North American prairies were in fact given over to hunting peoples, cultivation being carried on in plots cleared from the forest by the Indians. It is true that Penck did no more than suggest the forest-free character of the loess in Neolithic times, but his hypothesis was eagerly appropriated as a ready 'explanation' of the Danubian colonization, and there is no doubt that his reputation as a geologist gave it an impetus in no way merited by his argument. One may even suspect that its transformation into an article of faith was assisted by a certain confusion in the minds of some of those concerned between the conditions which gave rise to the loess and those which obtained at the time of its colonization by Neolithic man. When in 1905 J. Hoops[5] published his classic book on the trees and cultivated plants of German antiquity, he accepted as a fact that the earliest farmers of southern Germany settled the loess because it was free from forest rather than for its fertility or ease of working.

More far-reaching in its effects on the study of early settlement in Europe was the *Steppenheidetheorie* put forward by R. Gradmann[6] and distorted by a tribe of followers in the field of *Siedlungsgeschichte*. It was of the essence of Gradmann's thesis that prehistoric settlement was virtually confined to open country of a steppe-like character, among which the loess was of course included. He relied to a great extent on the coincidence in central and southern Germany of what he regarded as relics of a *Steppenheide* flora, a mixed association of shrubs, grasses and bushes with an occasional stunted tree, with the settlement areas of early man; both man and plants spread, according to his view, during a warm, dry climatic phase hostile to forest growth. Of almost equal importance to his thesis was the dogma that human communities at a low stage of culture were incapable of clearing the forest: it was the decline of forests under the influence of dry, warm conditions, which alone made it possible for Neolithic man to settle in Europe. In order to account for the continued occupation of the cultivated zones during a period when the forests recovered to attain the flourishing state reflected in the writings of classical authors, it was conceded that the pre-Roman inhabitants of Europe were capable of resisting encroachments by the forest, even if incapable of initiating clearance.

Gradmann's thesis appeared to find some support from researches on the gross stratigraphy of Scandinavian and German raised bogs (*Hochmoore*). On the basis of his own work on the bogs of south Sweden and on the researches of A. Blytt on the post-glacial deposits of Norway, R. Sernander advanced his celebrated hypothesis of a twice-repeated cycle of continental (Boreal and Sub-boreal) and oceanic (Atlantic and Sub-atlantic) climatic phases since the Ice Age in Scandinavia.[7] When in 1923 Gams and Nord-hagen[8] extended this sequence to southern Germany, they were in effect claiming that it was valid for regions remote from the Baltic, and independent of the well-known geographical changes which marked the post-glacial period in that part of the world. Meanwhile, C. A. Weber[9] had stressed the importance of the *Grenzhorizonte*, dividing the older from the newer *Sphagnum* peat in the north German raised bogs; this he claimed to mark the close of a period of at least a thousand years, during which peat had ceased to form. Students of *Siedlungsgeschichte*[10] were not slow to equate this period with Sernander's Sub-boreal phase, accepting it as further proof that climate was substantially drier during Neolithic times than today. Evidently, it was the return of continental conditions during the Sub-boreal period, which brought about the replacement of forests by an open vegetation of *Steppen-heide* character, and so, in Reinerth's graphic – but, as so often, wildly inaccurate – phrase, opened the door to the Neolithic settlers![11]

Weber's interpretation of the *Grenzhorizonte* was by no means unchallenged by his fellow-workers, but since the phenomenon only dates in general terms from the close of the Bronze Age, and is one which in any case should be handled by a professional botanist, it will not be further discussed here. What concerns us more closely is the duration of the Sub-boreal phase, which the *Grenzhorizonte* is supposed to have brought to an end. Apart from the question, whether in fact a Sub-boreal phase in the sense used by Sernander ever existed, which is doubted by an increasing number of authorities, it may be noted that Danish and Swedish workers have generally equated the transition from Atlantic to Sub-boreal with that from the Dolmen to Passage-grave stage of the northern Neolithic. This equation, if valid, would of course leave the main Neolithic colonization of Europe comfortably within the moist, equable, Atlantic phase. As is well known, this is confirmed for our British branch of the Neolithic 'Western' culture by the evidence of snail shells from the causewayed camps and the long barrows.

The real test of the relevance of the Blytt-Sernander hypothesis came with the growth of comprehensive and exact knowledge of the development of vegetation during post-glacial times, first made possible by pollen-analysis, a technique not fully demonstrated until 1916. When the palaeo-botanists at length, after tedious research, succeeded in working out the sequence of forest development in different parts of Europe, they found no evidence of any pronounced fluctuation during Neolithic and Bronze Age times. On the contrary, the work of pollen-analysts has dealt a mortal blow to the *Steppenheide* theory. Here I may cite the work carried out by Karl Bertsch[12] in Swabia, that very region which provided Gradmann with his botanical 'evidence'. The crucial fact established by pollen-analysis is that during the time, when according to the Blytt-Sernander theory a continental type of climate should have prevailed, both the silver fir and the beech achieved their widest spread. Yet each of these trees was damp-loving, and the beech, in particular, was in that region intolerant of a continental type of climate; indeed, the palaeobotanists tell us that one reason for the lateness of their spread was precisely the remoteness of the areas to which they had withdrawn to escape the severely continental conditions of the last Ice Age. As P. Keller[13] pointed out, about the same time, in discussing the forest history of Switzerland, the mere fact that the beech achieved its widest distribution during the Neolithic and Bronze Age periods shows that there cannot have been any contemporary climatic fluctuation sufficient to cause the thinning or disappearance of existing forests. Indeed, according to H. Nietsch[14] there is evidence that the beech spread into regions which today have a rainfall below the minimum needed for this tree to flourish, suggesting that at the time of its maximum spread conditions must have been more and not less favourable to forest-growth than to-day.

The researches of botanists have fully confirmed the former existence of a steppe flora in the existing temperate zone of Europe,[15] but this vegetation, which flourished only until overtaken by the forests advancing into the zone vacated by the ice-sheets already in the Pre-boreal period, had nothing to do with the Neolithic settlers. On the contrary, the earliest farming communities did not penetrate Europe until the re-colonization by forest trees was far advanced, although, as we have seen, still in full swing. From the time of the Neolithic settlement, there is, it is true, evidence for a recrudescence of grasses and for the appearance of a number of plants other than forest trees, but all the indications point to farming as itself the cause for this. One may begin by referring to the pioneer researches of the Danish botanist, J. Iversen,[16] who found evidence of an abrupt decline in the pollen of forest trees and a corresponding rise in that of other vegetation at levels in bogs contemporary with the Neolithic settlement. In the bog of Ordrup this same level was marked by an extensive charcoal layer, suggesting that the decline in forest trees was the direct result of burning. That this burning was brought about by deliberate action on the part of the Neolithic farmers is indicated by the appearance around the same level of the pollen of plants introduced by man or which followed in his footsteps, notably cultivated cereals and meadow weeds such as the plantain, the 'white man's trail' of the North American Indians. A similar marked change at the Neolithic level has recently been demonstrated by Dr H. Godwin[17] for Hockham Mere in the northern Breckland. In this Godwin sees the beginning of the process whereby the region changed from a closed mixed oak forest to the open heath we know today. Although unable, as yet, to advance direct evidence of the mechanism of this change, Godwin favours Iversen's suggestion that it was wrought by forest clearance on the part of Neolithic man. Thus, so far from the Neolithic settlement being made possible by a decline in the vigour of forests due to climatic causes, it was this settlement itself which initiated the process of forest destruction at the hands of man.

As to the all-pervading character of the woodlands at the peak of the forest period, the eminent British ecologist A. G. Tansley expressed himself in no uncertain terms in 1911:[18]

There is no doubt that by far the greater part of the British Isles were originally covered by forest: in England the whole of the east, south and midlands, except perhaps some of the chalk downs and some of the poorer sands, and of the north and west probably everything but the summits of the higher hills; in Wales the alluvial plains of the larger rivers and the valley sides up to similar altitudes; in Scotland the great central lowland plain, the flat shores of the northern firths on the east coast, and the sides of the valleys running into the heart of the Highlands; in Ireland presumably the central plain and the hill country up to a considerable altitude.

Tansley's inferences, which were derived in the main from his studies of existing plant associations in relation to soil-types, have been comprehensively confirmed by later intensive work on the history of vegetation by means of pollen-analysis and other methods. There is now a broad measure of agreement that forests once covered nearly the whole of western Europe below the tree-line, apart from the sea-shore, excessively poor sandy areas, beaver-meadows, salt-springs and the like. If some would still maintain reserve on the antiquity and origin of certain open pasturages, it is notable that in his magnificent new book Tansley wrote:[19]

It is hard to believe that the chalk and oolite uplands were not covered with forest in the warm damp climate of Atlantic times, since this was essentially a forest climate in which deciduous forest attained its maximum extension in this country and in western Europe generally. Oak will not, it is true, form good trees on the shallow chalk and limestone soils, but yew, ash and beech will and do.

As we have seen in the case of the Breckland, pollen-analysis of mere sediments has shewn that even this unpromising region supported dense oak forest at the time of Neolithic man's appearance. Broadly speaking we may conclude that regions capable of yielding crops were forested when the first farmers appeared upon the scene.

The implications of this will become clearer as we consider examples of Neolithic settlement. One may begin with the Danubian peasants, who, as is well known, settled almost exclusively on the loess, spreading from one patch to another as they extended their area of colonization. Now, we have it on the authority of the botanist Tüxen[20] that the loess of the Middle Rhenish area, settled by the Danubians with special intensity, carried an oak-mixed forest with hazel undergrowth. Moreover, it has been pointed out by Nietsch,[21] that the only soils in this area too poor to support forest, namely the sands of the Rhine-Main triangle, were either ignored or at best very sparsely settled by the several groups of Neolithic colonizers penetrating this part of Germany. The inference is unavoidable that the Neolithic farmers were more concerned with the ease of working and fertility of the soil than with its forest cover. A point to be noted is that, although a fertile soil might support a dense vegetation, this would be offset to some extent by the comparatively small area which it would be necessary to clear, but the crucial fact is that the Danubians colonized soil which competent authority pronounces to have been forested. The only conclusion to be drawn is that the Danubians were not only fully capable of clearing, but did in fact clear the ground of forest.

Even more instructive is the Neolithic settlement of Denmark and North Germany, since here we can observe two separate cultures in close proximity, each apparently adapted to distinctive soil-types with different forest coverings. The primary zone of the northern megalithic colonization lies within the limits of the last major glaciation (Weichsel-Würm) and predominantly within the Baltic end-moraine, whether in east Jutland, Schleswig-Holstein, northern Brandenburg, Mecklenburg or Pomerania. The secondary spread of the culture, on the other hand, over northwest Germany and north Holland, extended onto the ground moraines of the older (Elster-Saale) glaciation, soils subject to more prolonged weathering.[22] Evidently it was the fertile soils of the ground moraines which were chiefly sought by the northern megalithic folk, preference being given in the first instance to the younger and less weathered soils. Yet it is important to note that fertility was not the only criterion which determined the choice of ground. As Prof. G. Schwantes[23] has emphasized in the case of Schleswig-Holstein, the megalithic sites are found on the poorer, sandier, rather than on the richer, loamier soils of the glacial drift: in other words, as Fox[24] has shown so clearly for southern England, the early farmers sacrificed fertility in some measure to ease of working; it was of no use to clear the heavy clay lands, however rich the potential yield, if the equipment for cultivating them was lacking. As for the forest covering of the ground moraines cultivated by the northern megalithic folk, Schwantes cites the botanist W. Christiansen for the view that this was most probably dry oak-mixed-forest, as opposed to the damp oak-hornbeam association of the heavier soils. Yet this should not make us overlook the fact that over the whole area of their distribution from the North Sea to the margin of the Russian steppes the northern megalithic peoples chose for settlement territories, which at the time were covered by the oak-mixed-forest. Of these people Nietsch wrote in lyrical mood.[25]

Where the oak trees grow best, there find they the best fields, there their cattle prosper, and they themselves bide as energetic and doughty peasants of the woodland . . .

By contrast, the single-grave or battle-axe people of central Jutland and Schleswig-Holstein occupied poor glacial outwash sands, carrying an oak-birch association of a type which under the influence of burning and of grazing animals would rapidly degenerate into heath. An interesting point made by Schwantes[26] in this connexion is, that whereas the oak-mixed forest provided the best sustenance for cattle and swine, the oak-birch association was more suited to sheep. Perhaps it was in consequence of a more pronouncedly pastoral mode of life that, in contrast with the megalithic people, whose houses and settlements have been found quite commonly, the settlements of the single-grave people have proved elusive.

As to Britain, although doubts remain in some quarters as to the vegetation natural to parts of the chalk, the distribution of Neolithic sites as a whole makes it certain that here also forest clearance must have been carried out at that time. It must be admitted that in lowland Britain many of the sites relating to Neolithic people of 'western' origin have so far been found on stretches of chalk, which, it may still be argued, may in parts have been free of forest trees at the time of the Neolithic colonization. There is, however, by no manner of means an exclusive correlation between the 'western' people and the chalk: even in southern England this is very far from true, as witness, among many others, the finds of Neolithic 'A' pottery from the Fens, [27] from the submerged land-surface of the Essex coast,[28] from the site of the Abingdon 'camp' on the Thames gravel[29] and from Great Ponton, Lincs.[30] As to the settlement areas of the Neolithic communities, who from their homes in the forests of northern Europe reached us from across the North Sea, these comprised first and foremost soils favoured by the dry oak mixed forest; only secondarily did these Neolithic 'B' people spill over into chalk areas settled by the 'westerners', with whom in some regions they inter-mingled.

Much can be learned from the placing of our megalithic tombs and long barrows. A point, on which Fox[31] once commented as a 'curious fact', is that

many of the chambered cairns and long barrows of the Neolithic Age are inconspicuously placed in hollows, or on slopes, instead of in the position we regard as more normal – on ridges and shoulders of the hills. If the hills were originally forest-clad, this inconsistency is what might have been expected since in forest one cannot judge where the dominant positions are . . .

By contrast, the round barrows of the Bronze Age and later periods are commonly sited with accuracy so as to break the sky-line, having presumably been erected at a time when the cleared area was already extensive.[32] Again, many megaliths and long barrows are visibly placed on soils well suited to the growth of trees. It is a striking fact that about one in six of the long barrows visited by Crawford, when collecting material for his book, were situated in spinneys, plantations or woods, most commonly of beech trees.[33] Excavation of some of the Cotswold cairns has shown them to be overlying a seam of red clay, which according to geological opinion is the product of natural weathering of the limestone and which can with confidence be assumed to have carried forest. At Nympsfield a beechwood with ash and larch grows on the same clay only a short distance from the cairn, the mollusca from which have significantly been interpreted by Kennard as indicating 'a rather damp scrub woodland, for typical grassland forms are absent'.[34]

Very suggestive evidence comes from Wales. As Grimes recognized from his field surveys, many of the Welsh monuments were erected on sites which according to all the rules one would expect to have been forested in early times. In 1936 he drew attention to the placing of megalithic tombs on valley flanks or spurs, or even on valley bottoms in Carmarthenshire.[35] Again, in 1939, he emphasized that those of the Black Mountains of Brecknockshire were normally situated on the lower slopes below the existing tree-line.[36] Although Grimes had no occasion to refer to it at the time, Hemp had in fact already published evidence pointing strongly in the same direction. Of the situation of the tomb of Bryn yr Hen Bobl, Hemp wrote in 1935[37] that:

the wide view of the Caernarvonshire mountains, which it once commanded, is now partly hidden by the trees which cover the steep fall of the terrace down to the water . . . There is no sign that any of the ground in the immediate neighbourhood has ever been under cultivation, and it still carries many ancient trees; two of them, oaks whose age must be measured by centuries, grow on the summit of the cairn itself.

Whether in his allusion to the 'wide view' Hemp was referring to a hypothetical 'open' countryside in Neolithic times, or whether to the clearings made in the primeval forest, is not clear from the context, but the analysis of charcoals obtained from the site and identified by Mr Hyde makes it probable that the surroundings of the cairn would under natural conditions have been of the 'damp' oakwood type. Hyde commented:[38]

If it be assumed that the specimens constituted a fair sample of the tree flora of the period in the immediate neighbourhood of the site, then it may be concluded that the predominant vegetation was oakwood. In view of the fact that the predominant subsoil is boulder clay, it seems probable that the woods were of the 'damp' oakwood type, with Common Oak (*Quercus Robur L. sens. str.*) dominant: the high proportion of hazel is consistent with this supposition. The high percentage of hawthorn probably indicates abundant scrub growth . . .

The significance of Bryn yr Hen Bobl is all the greater that the terrace on which it is found, only 3½ miles long and 1½ miles broad, bordering the shores of the Menai Straits 100 ft. above high water, originally carried at least 17 megalithic tombs.

That some at least of our megaliths were erected on ground which naturally bore forest – and 'damp' oak forest at that – would seem to be pretty firmly established. Whether, as Grimes suggests,[39] the cairns were built on land cleared for farming, is more doubtful. The possibility should be considered that the tombs were set up in clearings made for the purpose in the virgin forest. In view of the sanctity of forests among many ancient peoples, this cannot lightly be brushed aside. Nearly a century ago, M. Maury, à propos of this very point, cited the case of a 'dolmen' known as the 'Calvaire de la Motte', situated in the ancient forest of Duault, and added that 'en Allemagne, c'est souvent dans la profondeur des forêts, à l'ombre des bocages, sous de hautes futaies que l'on découvre ces antiques tombeaux connus sous le nom de Hunengraeber . . .'.[40] Whether certain of the megalithic tombs of Cotswold and Wales were built on fresh clearings or on older established ones is, yet, subsidiary to the main point that their construction presupposes that Neolithic man was able to clear forest, in some instances of the 'damp' oakwood type.

The distribution of archaeological sites and finds in relation to soils regarded by ecologists as naturally forest-bearing shows, if we reject, as we have done, the thesis of a catastrophic natural declension of the post-glacial forests, that Neolithic man must have been fully capable of clearing the forest for himself. This brings us into direct conflict with the second main prop of Gradmann's theory, the idea that the primeval forest was unbelievably hostile to human settlement. At its crudest, the conception of the *Siedlungsfeindlichkeit* of the forest was expressed by Hoops in the succinct phrase '*Der Urwald ist der Feind und nicht der Freund des Menschen*'.[41] In point of fact, as recent German authorities have themselves admitted,[42] such a negative point of view has contributed in no small fashion to obscure our understanding of the interrelations of men and forests. So far from forests being actively antagonistic to man, the boot was if anything on the other foot: in Maury's words 'l'humanité ne se développe qu'au détriment de la végétation arborescente . . .'.[43] In the face of an advance in culture so striking as that implied in the adoption of farming, we are surely entitled to expect a marked inroad on forests. In order to practise the new economy in Europe, Neolithic man had no choice but to encroach upon the forest, not only directly to cultivate the soil, but even more pervasively through his domestic stock. In addition it should be remembered that the rapid growth in the density of population made possible by the new economy greatly increased the call made upon forests as sources of raw materials needed for a wide range of activities.

Man had, indeed, already established harmonious relations with the forest in Mesolithic times. It is only natural that Hoops[44] should have rejected the view justified by modern research that the primeval forest gave shelter to communities of food-gatherers and hunters. The supposed 'hiatus' in the human settlement of Europe between the end of the Ice Age and the spread of farming was seized upon as convincing evidence of the incorrigible hostility of the forests, which, spreading into Europe, expelled the hunting tribes adapted to tundra and steppe and maintained an impenetrable front until thinned by natural processes during the Sub-boreal phase of aridity. As a matter of fact, when Hoops wrote, discoveries at Mullerup, Mas d'Azil, and Fère-en-Tardenois had already shown that the 'hiatus' was itself an illusion. Today we know that, although certain Mesolithic groups shunned the forest, keeping to such areas as the poorest sands, uplands above the tree-line and the sea-shore, others on the plain of northern Europe had already adapted themselves to forest conditions.[45] The Maglemosians not only used a wide range of forest products, but worked wood on a substantial scale. For felling and working timber they had axes and adzes of flint and stone, the latter even ground on occasion and rubbed smooth,[46] prototypes of the ubiquitous Neolithic celt. Yet, although he may have opened up small areas round his dwelling and obtained trunks for his dug-out boats,[47] Mesolithic man had no motive for clearing the forest on any extensive scale. Thus, before the introduction of farming, early man made no serious inroad on the forest. On the other hand, he was far from shunning it completely. Certain Mesolithic groups made themselves at home in the woods, got to know their riches and initiated that exploitation by gathering, based on intimate knowledge of natural yields, which was to play a part of no mean importance to the successive peasant communities of Europe down to medieval and even later times. The suggestion that forest clearance may have begun on a restricted scale prior to the spread of farming is confirmed by the evidence of the Finnish dwelling-places, inhabited by communities basically Mesolithic in their mode of life, although contemporary with the megalithic and battle-axe cultures of the southern Baltic. Many of the old sites were overgrown by forest subsequent to their abandonment in the Stone Age and revealed only by modern clearance.[48]

Since, as we have seen, the most desirable soils supported forest at the time, it was necessary for the earliest farmers to clear the ground before they could begin to cultivate it. If this has proved a hard doctrine for some prehistorians, it is because they envisage clearance of a far more drastic and definite character than in fact took place. M. Grenier's challenging claim[49]

la véritable histoire de l'âge neolithique, c'est, avec la domestication des animaux et l'invention de l'agriculture, la conquête de la terre sur la forêt

is valuable for drawing attention to a neglected aspect of Neolithic activity, but gives a false impression of thoroughness and permanence. What in reality we have to envisage, is the temporary clearance of restricted areas carried out in successive stretches of forest, many of which re-established themselves as the farmers and their stock moved elsewhere. The Neolithic farmers were small in numbers, and since they practised an extensive mode of agriculture, seldom tilling any given patch of soil for more than a few years and frequently breaking up new ground, they must have occupied at any particular moment a much smaller area than the total distribution of relevant archaeological finds might suggest. Again, it is likely, although we need more precision on this point, that tillage played a smaller part than stock-raising in the economy of the Neolithic communities of Europe. Indeed, could we but have flown over Neolithic Europe, it is possible that we might have failed to observe that patches of the endless forest were in fact being utilized by small, scattered communities of farmers.

An essential element in the system of extensive, temporary cultivation, such as obtained in Neolithic Europe, was the clearance of forest by fire. The potash contained in the ash, which resulted from the burning of timber and shrubs, greatly increased the return from the cleared area. We have it on the authority of Manninen[50] that among the Finno-Ougrian peoples ground cultivated according to the principles of *Brandwirtschaft* yielded from fifty- to ninety-fold of rye, as compared with a bare fifteen- to twenty-fold from ordinary ploughland in the same area. This rich potash dressing was only one of the bounties which accrued to those who cultivated clearings in the forest. Carl Schott[51] tells us that the early colonists of southern Ontario had only to scratch the newly cleared ground with rake or harrow in readiness for the seed and that not until five or six years did they as a rule need to use the plough. Similarly, according to Manninen,[52] it was usual among the Finno-Ougrians merely to harrow in the seed among the ashes of the burnt forest. By contrast the task of breaking up the mythical 'open' grassland, the treeless corridor of *Steppenheide* imagined by Gradmann, might well appear beyond the capacity of the Neolithic farmer, who, be it remembered,[53] had to make do without a plough!

It has sometimes been doubted whether the foliaceous trees, with which Neolithic man was mainly confronted in Europe, would have been as amenable to burning as the coniferous forests with their carpets of inflammable needles and pine-cones, such as are met with in Finland, where the practice of forest burning survives. While it is possible that more intensive preparation may on occasion have been called for, there is no doubt that foliaceous trees were burnt during the colonizing days in southern Ontario, during historical times in France,[54] and, what is more to the point, in Neolithic Europe. The only instance from prehistory certainly established is that from the Ordrup bog in Denmark described by Iversen and already mentioned (p. 32), but it is worth recalling what may have been indications of similar intentional burning from the area north of the Swiss lake-settlement of Robenhausen, which at the time were interpreted as debris blown from the settlement when burning in a strong south wind.[55]

Important though burning must have been as a method of forest clearance, it was by no means the only one available. As in Ontario and modern Finland, the axe must have played an essential part in clearing the forests of Neolithic Europe. There is ample archaeological evidence of Neolithic man's capability with the axe. He used timber lavishly in building his houses[56] and tombs[57] and for his dug-out canoes,[58] inherited, as we have seen, from forest-dwelling groups of the Mesolithic age. Nor should the numerous experiments made to test the efficacy of Neolithic flint and stone axes be left out of account. Sir John Evans quoted the case of a Mr Sehested's wooden hut, the trees for which 'were cut down and trimmed with stone hatchets ground at the edge',[59] and recalled experiments by the Vicomte Lepic showing how 'with a polished Danish flint hatchet 8 inches in diameter, hafted in part of the root of an oak, an oak-tree 8 inches in diameter was cut down without injury to the blade'.[60] More recently Prof. Jacob-Friesen has demonstrated that a fir-tree 17 cm. in diameter can be felled in seven minutes using an axehead of chipped flint, and in five with one of polished stone.[61] This last experiment is particularly interesting, indicating, as it appears to do, that a polished is empirically superior to a chipped axe for felling trees: such a difference, if not induced by other factors, such as the shape or weight of the axes or differences in their materials, would be sufficient to account for the added labour involved in polishing chipped ones. The circumstances under which polished axes are found is sometimes suggestive. Thus, four stone axes, two of them showing signs of heavy use, together with a stone axe hone, were found on the site of Bryn yr Hen Bobl; in no case were they associated with any of the burials and the only reasonable explanation for them is that they were used in the original clearance. Again, there is such a case as that cited by M. Grenier,[62] in which numerous broken polished axes were found in the course of modern deforestation within a radius of two kilometres of the spring of Bonnefontaine near the right bank of the Saar in Lorraine, evidently indicating an ancient clearance over which the forest had successfully re-established itself. It may be accepted that the axe of flint or stone was fully capable of felling trees and that in fact it played a vital part in deforestation. Indeed, it is only in the light of this that we can explain the abundance and ubiquity of the implement and the high regard paid to it by Neolithic man, as witness the elaborate flint-mines and the intricate trade by which he sought to ensure a supply of the best material available. No doubt the flint-mines at Grimes Graves were worked primarily to provide the axes needed in clearing the mixed oak forests of the Breckland!

It has sometimes been implied[63] that an obligation to remove the stumps of felled trees was among those which deterred prehistoric man from colonizing forest country, but in fact our Neolithic farmers need never have shifted a single one, at least until they were far in decay. We have not to go back very far in time to find that in some forest regions tree stumps were suffered to rot in the ground, even where the plough was habitually employed. F. Mager[64] has shown from his researches on the economic history of the Duchy of Schleswig and again on that of old Prussia that the usual practice of the peasants in these regions during the 17th, 18th and early 19th centuries was to cultivate the soil between the stumps until they finally disappeared, growth in the meantime being kept in check by browsing animals. Rather similar practices have been described by Manninen for the Wotjaks of the Volga-Kama region, whose agriculture was based on the burning and felling of successive areas of forest.[65] The Finns, likewise, cultivated between the pine-stumps of their clearings,[66] as we are reminded by a passage in the Kalevala epic, wherein the voice of the aged Väinämöinen is likened to 'the hoe among the pine-roots'.[67] There is further confirmation from the European settlement of southern Ontario during the period after 1783, described by Schott,[68] according to whom the colonists simply left the stumps in the ground until they could be dragged out without trouble; it is interesting to note that whereas the stumps of foliaceous trees rotted sufficiently to be easily removed after eight or ten years, those of conifers were far more tenacious and often showed no signs of decay after fifty years. A striking fact recorded by Schott is that in the year 1880 some 46 per cent of the fields of York County, first colonized by white men in 1790, showed tree stumps, even though by this time Ontario had become one of the main granaries of Europe.

There remains one agent of deforestation, of which the predominating importance has been admitted by ecologists and economic historians alike, namely the domesticated animals of the early farmers. Until the various fodder crops, such as sown grasses, clover and the various members of the genus *Brassica* – e.g. swedes, turnips, cabbages and kale – were established as field crops, not as a rule before the 18th century, the feeding of stock during the winter months remained a leading problem of European husbandry.[69] Full use was made of hay from natural grassland, straw from grain crops and stubble, but to a great extent it was upon the forests that farmers had to depend to bring even a minimum of livestock through the winter. As Parain[70] wrote of French medieval economy, the forests

were the peasants' providence. They fed his horses . . ., his cattle, his sheep, his goats, with their leaves – eaten green in summer and gathered dry in winter – and the grass of their open glades. His pigs ate the acorns and beech-mast . . . the forest provided a part, but often a great part, of the feed of every kind of domestic animal.

Pig-sties were often built in the woods and there, according to Lord Ernle,[71] 'during most months of the year' the swine ranged in quest of 'roots, wild pears, wild plums, crab apples, sloes, haws, beech-mast and acorns'. The familiar fact that woods were commonly assessed in Anglo-Saxon charters and in the Domesday Survey as providing 'pannage' for so many swine is only one indication of their economic significance.[72] Forests were equally vital for sustaining cattle and sheep, which grazed on leaves, herbage and shoots and during the winter months were fed with almost everything but the solid wood of the trunks. Characteristic is Fitzherbert's (1523) advice to farmers to lop and top their trees in winter 'that thy beasts maye eate the brouse, and the mosse of the bowes, and also the yues (ivies)'.[73] The lopping of trees for fodder is even now met with among some of the more backward European peasant communities.

If such conditions obtained in medieval times, when bread had already become established as the staff of life, they must have applied with even more force to times when stock-raising played a proportionately greater part. The forest must have been even more integral to prehistoric than to medieval farming: it was as vital to the pastoral as to the agricultural side of husbandry. In reality it is impossible to isolate the effects on the forest of the two leading aspects of mixed farming: browsing beasts, by thinning under-growth and scrubs, around the tilled areas, must have helped prepare the way for clearance when it became necessary to shift cultivation to fresh zones of forest; and it was on his stock also that the Neolithic farmer must have relied to keep down unwanted growth on his very imperfectly cleared plots. The same factor must be taken into account when considering the fate of areas which reverted to waste in the normal course of extensive agriculture. At first, no doubt, the forest succeeded in re-establishing itself on all but the poorest soils, as, according to Iversen, occurred in the Ordrup bog. Yet, as settlement grew more dense and the effects of grazing became more concentrated, there is little doubt that by eating off the seedlings in the way described by Tansley,[74] domestic animals must have prevented the rejuvenation of wood-lands and on an ever wider scale brought about their extinction. It is obvious that in the course of prehistoric times grazing animals must have come to exercise an immense effect on the nature of the countryside.

In conclusion, a word must be said about the limitations on prehistoric settlement imposed by the heavier and less pervious clays, the effect of which has been to canalize early settlement within fairly narrow limits and impose a certain uniformity of pattern on successive stages in the colonization of many regions.[75] This was not lost upon upholders of the *Steppenheidetheorie*. Gradmann himself regarded the 'lack of any geographical progress in land-settlement from the Neolithic period through the Bronze Hallstatt and La Tène periods to the threshold of the Roman period'[76] as one of the outstanding facts of prehistory. Hoops[77] argued that, had the prehistoric colonization been due to forest clearance, it would surely have been extended as technical means improved, bronze replacing stone and flint, and iron bronze, and conversely that since this did not occur, at least on a commensurate scale, settlement must have been confined to naturally 'open' ground. In reality of course there was a marked development in the prehistoric colonization, only this took the form in the main of a more intensive settlement of the area already occupied.[78] The barrier to expansion was not imposed to any serious extent by vegetation: the 'damp' oak-mixed forest might have been more difficult to burn than the 'dry', but an oak-tree remains an oak whether durmast or sessile, and in any case we know that Neolithic man cleared 'damp' oakwoods to build his megalithic tombs. The point is that until, at the very close of the prehistoric era, the farmer possessed a heavy wheeled plough, he was unable to tackle the heavier, less easily drained, soils. The contrast between the areas settled by prehistoric man and those shunned by him was not as between forested and 'open' lands, or even as between 'densely' and 'lightly' forested, so much as between those which he could and those which he could not cultivate.

Notes

1 A. Penck, 'Das Deutsche Reich' in A. Kirchhoff's *Länderkunde des Erdteils Europa*, I, 1887, s. 441. I have been unable to check the reference and have had to rely upon the excerpt quoted by J. Hoops, *Waldbäume und Kulturpflanzen im germanischen Altertum*, Strasbourg, 1905, s. 98–9.

2 Penck is quoted as having written of the early farmers that ... 'wenn nicht gerade abgenommen werden soll, das dieselbe instinktiv innerhalb grosser Waldflächen den besten Feldboden rodete, so ist wohl wahrsheinlich, das sie die Lössdistrikte in waldfreien Zustande als Wiesengebiete vorfand, ahnlich den Prärien des nordamerikanischen Westens', *op. cit.*, s. 441.

3 C. Schott, 'Urlandschaft und rodung. Vergleichende betrachtungen aus Europa und Kanada', *Z. d. Ges. f. Erdkunde zu Berlin*, 1935, s. 81–102; See s. 100.

4 Dr H. Godwin, F.R.S., to whom I am deeply indebted for reading this article in typescript and offering valuable criticism, tells me that the great American ecologist F. E. Clements based his work on 'Plant Indicators' on this very possibility. In modern American and Continental forestry practice it is usual to estimate the condition and potentialities of the soil from the nature of the ground flora. We may be sure that early man accumulated sufficient lore on this subject to enable him to decide where to make his clearances.

5 Hoops, *op. cit.*, s. 99: 'Es ist also nich sowohl der fruchtbare Lössboden als solcher, sondern der waldfreie Charakter seiner Oberfläche, mit andern Worten, es sind die einstigen Tundra- und Steppenflächen, die den ackerbauenden Neolithiker genau so, wie früher den paläolithischen Menschen, in erster Linie anzogen.'

6 R. Gradmann, *Das Pflanzenleben der schwabischen Alb*, 1st edn, 1898; 2nd edn, 1900; 3rd edn, 1936; 'Das mitteleuropäische landschaftsbild nach seiner geschichtlichen Entwicklung', *Geogr. Z.* 7 (1901), 361–77 and 435–47; 'Beziehung zwischen Pflanzengeographie und Siedlungsgeschichte', *Geogr. Z.* 12 (1906), 305–25, etc.

7 R. Sernander, *Die schwedischen Torfmorre als Zeugen postglazialer Klimaschwankungen*, Geologkongr. Stockholm, 1910.

8 H. Gams and R. Nordhagen, 'Postglaziale Klimaänderungen und Erdkrustenbewegungen in Mitteleuropa, *Mitt. Geogr. Ges.*, Munich, 1923.

9 C. A. Weber, 'Was lehrt der Aufbau der Moore Norddeutschlands über den Wechsel des Klimas in postglazialer Zeit', *Z. d. Deutsch, Geol. Ges., bd.* 62, s. 143–62.

10 E.g. E. Wahle, *Ostdeutschland in jungneolithischer Zeit, ein prähistorisch-geographischer Versuch.*, Mannus Bibl. no. 15, Wurzburg, 1918, s. 98.

11 H. Reinerth, *Die Jüngere Steinzeit der Schweiz*, Augsburg, 1926, s. 16–29.

12 K. Bertsch, 'Klima, Pflanzendecke und Besiedlung Mitteleuropas in vor und fruhgeschichtlicher Zeit nach den Ergebnissen der pollenanalytischen Forschung', *Rom. Germ. Komm.*, 18 Ber., 1928, Frankfurt a.M.

13 P Keller, 'Pollenanalytische Untersuchungen am Schweizer Mooren und ihre floren-geschichtliche Deutung', *Veroff. des Geobot. Int. Rubel in Zurish*, 1928.

14 H. Nietsch, *Wald und Siedlung im Vorgeschichtliche Mitteleuropa*, Mannus Bibl. no. 64, 1939, see s. 48–51.

15 E.g. R. Schütrumpf, 'Die paläobotanisch-pollenanalytische Untersuchung', in A. Rust, *Das Altsteinzeitliche Rentierjägerlager Meiendorf*, Neumünster, 1937, s. 11–47.

16 J. Iversen, 'Land occupation in Denmark's Stone Age', *Dan. Geol. Unders.* 11 R. Nr. 66, Copenhagen, 1941. Note, also, comments by Dr. H. Godwin in *Nature*, vol. 153, p. 511. Some implications of Iversen's work were suggested by the present writer in a lecture at the London Univ. Inst. of Archaeology's Conference in the summer of 1944.

17 H. Godwin, 'Age and origin of the "Breckland" heaths of East Anglia', *Nature*, vol. 154, p. 6.

18 *Types of British Vegetation*, ed. by A. G. Tansley, Cambridge, 1911, pp. 65–6.

19 A. G. Tansley, *The British Isles and their vegetation*, Cambridge, 1939, p. 164.

20 R. Tüxen, 'Die Grundlagen der Urlandschaftsforschung. Ein Beitrag zur Erforschung der Geschichte, der anthropogenen Beeinflussung der Vegetation Mitteleuropas', *Nachr. aus Niedersachsens Urgeschichte*, 1931, s. 59–105. See s. 77 and s. 88–9.

21 Nietsch, *op. cit.*, s. 180–1.

22 Nietsch, *op. cit.* s 155–67.

23 G. Schwantes, *Geschichte Schleswig-Holsteins*, Bd. I, Vorgeschichte, Lief., 1–7, Neumünster, 1939, s. 462 ff.

24 Sir Cyril Fox, *The Personality of Britain*, 1st edn, p. 79.

25 Freely translated from the original (Nietsch, *op. cit.*, s. 167): 'Wo die Eichen am besten wachsen, finden sie den besten Acker, gedeiht ihnen das Vieh, und sie selber bleiben tatkräftige wehrhafte Waldbauern . . .'

26 Schwantes, *op. cit.*, s. 461.

27 E.g. *Ant J.*, xv, pp. 302–3.

28 *Proc. Prehist. Soc.*, 1936, p. 188.

29 *Ant. J.*, vii, 1927, pp. 438–64; viii, 1928, pp. 461–77.

30 *Ant. J.*, xv, 1935, pp. 347–8.

31 *Op. cit.*, 1st ed., pp. 48–9 Absent from the current (4th) ed.

32 Mr H. A. Hyde, Keeper of Botany at the National Museum of Wales, has recently published evidence on this point from the Middle Bronze Age Pond Cairn, Glam. (*Archaeologia* 87, pp. 175–6). He states that, while it would be unsafe to reconstruct a picture of local vegetation from the samples examined, yet 'the use as fire-wood of so much gorse, bracken, hawthorn and hazel, in comparison with oak and ash, probably indicates that locally at least the forest had already been destroyed and replaced by grassland and scrub; indeed on the botanical side no such direct evidence for early deforestation seems previously to have been published'.

33 O. G. S. Crawford, *The Long Barrows of the Cotswolds*, Gloucester, 1925, *passim*, e.g. nos. 2, 3, 13, 19, 23, 27, 41, 42, 44, 52, 57, 61, 66, 68. In addition one may note that the Giant's Cave, Luckington, bush-grown when visited by Crawford, was covered by 'some oakes and other trees and boscage' in Aubrey's day; also what appears to have been a chambered tomb, described by George Clinch as deep in a thick wood at St Margaret's, in the Black Mountains of Herefordshire, *ibid.*, nos. 78 and 61 respectively, was not to be found at the time of Crawford's visit.

If the reader refers to the photographs of Danish and north German chambered tombs reproduced by Brøndsted (*Danmarks Oldtid*, 1, figs. 112, 113, 144, 146, 148), Sprockhoff (*Die nordische Megalithkultur*, Berlin, 1938, Taf. 1, 3, 4, 5, 6, 7, etc.) and Schwantes (*op. cit.*, taf. 14, abb. 209, 210), he will find ample evidence for the occurrence of such monuments under trees.

34 *Proc. Prehist. Soc.*, 1938, p. 212

35 *Proc. Prehist. Soc.*, 1936, p. 114.

36 *Proc. Prehist. Soc.*, 1939, pp. 120–1.

37 *Archaeologia*, LXXXV, 1935, p. 253.

38 *Ibid*, p. 281.

39 *Proc. Prehist Soc.*, 1936, p. 114.

40 L. F. A. Maury, *Histoire des grandes fôrets de la Gaule et de l'ancienne France*, Paris 1850, pp. 163–4.

41 Hoops, *op. cit.*, p.9.

42 E.g. Schwantes, *op. cit.*, s. 458; Nietsch, *op. cit.*, s. 159.

43 Maury, *op. cit.*, p. 320.

44 Hoops, *op. cit.*, s. 91 ff.

45 V. G. Childe, 'The Forest Cultures of Northern Europe: a Study in Evolution and Diffusion', *J. R. A. L.* LXI, 1931, pp. 325–48; also J. G. D. Clark, *The Mesolithic Settlement of Northern Europe*, Cambridge, 1936.

46 Clark, *op. cit.*, p. 105.

47 For Mesolithic dug-out canoes and paddle-rudders, *ibid.*, pp. 107–9.

48 J. Ailio, *Die steinzeitlichen Wohnplatzfunde in Finland*, Helsingfors, 1909, bd. I, s. 2; bd. II, s. 150.

49 A. Grenier, 'Aux origines de l'économie rurale', *Annales d'historie économique et sociale*, t. 2e, 1330, p. 28.

50 I. Manninen, *Die Finnisch-Ugrischen Völker*, Leipzig, 1932, s. 274–5.

51 Schott, *op. cit.*, s. 98–99.

52 Manninen, *op.cit.*, s. 30.

53 We reject alike the antiquity of the notorious Walle plough and validity of the Bodman 'reconstruction'.

54 Marc Bloch, *Les Caractères originaux de l'histoire rurale française*, Oslo, 1931, pp. 27–9.

55 F. Keller, *The Lake Dwellings of Switzerland*, trs. London, 1866, p. 47.

56 E.g. R. R. Schmidt, *Jungsteinzeit-Siedlungen im Federseemoor*, I. Lief, Augsburg, 1930, s. 64, 66, 67, etc.

57 E.g. Giants' Hills, Lincs. C. W. Phillips, *Arch.*, LXXXV, pp. 47–8, 49, 59.

58 It is possible that the flint and stone axes found respectively in the Erith and Clyde dug-out canoes may have been used to hollow them out or possibly to fell the parent tree. See *Ant. J.*, VI, p.127.

59 Sir John Evans, *The Ancient Stone Implements . . . of Great Britain*, 2nd ed. London, 1897, p. 69.

60 *Ibid.*, p. 162.

61 Quoted from Nietsch, *op. cit.*, s. 70.

62 Grenier, *op. cit.*, p. 29.

63 E.g. by Fox, *op. cit.*, 1st ed, p. 71; 4th edn, p. 79.

64 F. Mager, *Entwicklungsgeschichte des Kulturlandschaft des Herzogtums Schleswig in historischer Zeit*, Breslau, 1930; also 'Die Rodungsfrage in Altpreussen', *Jhrber. d. Universitätsbundes*, Konigsberg, 1934, quoted by Schwantes, *op. cit.*, s 462–3 and Schott, *op. cit.*, s. 86 f.

65 Manninen, *op. cit.*, s. 245.

66 G. Retzius, *Finnland. Schilderungen aus seiner Natur, seiner alten Kultur und seinem heutigen Volksleben*, Berlin, 1885, s. 42–5.

67 Runo XXI, 350, Everyman edn, vol. I, p. 248.

68 Schott, *op. cit.*, 96–9.

69 C. S. Orwin, *The Open Fields*, Oxford, 1938, pp. 52–6.

70 C. Parain, 'The evolution of agricultural technique', *The Cambridge Economic History of Europe*, I, Cambridge, 1941, pp. 118–68, p. 162.

71 Lord Ernle, *English Farming Past and Present*, 5th edn (ed. Sir A. D. Hall), London 1936, pp. 16–7.

72 E.g. H. C. Darby, 'Domesday woodland in East Anglia', *Antiquity*, 1934, pp. 211–15, and F. W. Morgan, 'Domesday woodland in Southwest England', *Antiquity*, 1936, pp. 306–24.

73 Quoted from Orwin, *op. cit.*
74 Tansley, *op. cit.*, p. 66. Tansley quotes A. C. Forbes (*The Development of British Forestry*, London, 1910, p. 7) for the view that one cause of the British Isles and the seaboard of western Europe being among the most poorly wooded parts of Europe may be that the mild winters of Atlantic regions allow grazing all the year round.
75 This was one of the chief lessons from Fox's epoch-making study, *The Archaeology of the Cambridge Region*, Cambridge, 1923.
76 Gradmann, *op. cit.*, 1901, s. 374.
77 Hoops, *op. cit.*, s. 100.
78 Intensive study of different areas has shown that, in fact, extensions of the area of settlement during prehistoric times did sometimes occur, e.g. in central and southern Germany. See Nietsch, *op. cit.*, s. 209–10.

CHAPTER 4

SEAL-HUNTING IN THE STONE AGE OF NORTH-WESTERN EUROPE: A STUDY IN ECONOMIC PREHISTORY

Although it has been widely recognised that the bones of seals occur on Stone Age sites in various parts of north-western Europe, no comprehensive attempt to clarify the history and estimate the role of seal-hunting in the economy of Stone Age Europe has yet been made.[1] The research, on which the present paper is based, is part of a programme to further knowledge of prehistoric times by the study of social activities. Seal-hunting is here considered, not because it gave rise to objects which need classifying and dating, but simply because it was an activity of vital interest to certain coast-dwelling communities in north-western Europe during the Stone Age. If the physiological approach is stressed, this is not to depreciate the morphological: in point of fact the more we discover about any human activity the more fitted we become to interpret correctly the material objects or structures associated with it.

Archaeology is rarely sufficient to recover the way of life of early man. The problem of seal-hunting in antiquity, which is after all basically biological, is one of those which can only be resolved by several convergent disciplines. The foundations of the present study have been laid by zoologists, men who, like Winge, Holmquist, Pira, Degerbøl and others, have given us precise information about the seals hunted by early man, through patient identification of bones and teeth from archaeological deposits, or who, by their observation of the life habits and distribution of the various species in the field, have, like Collett, Nordqvist, Nansen and Fraser Darling, enabled us to visualise the opportunities open to the old hunters. Very important contributions have also been made by quaternary geologists, such as Munthe and Sauramo, both in dating stray finds and still more in establishing the situation of the sea-coasts at different stages of the Stone Age, so helping us to assess the limits within which the evidence for coastal settlement at this time has survived. Again, we are more likely to interpret the archaeological traces of seal-hunting correctly, if guided by the light of ethnology rather than that of nature: the value of Eskimo parallels has been illustrated by Mathiassen's study of the blubber lamps of the Ertebølle people, referred to later. Even more telling, because of historical continuity, are analogies drawn from the folk culture of northern Europe, whether still or recently extant, or whether recorded by earlier observers. The value of this source has recently been emphasised by Brøgger (1940, 166) in a passage which deserves to be quoted:

To be able to approach any understanding at all of the culture of antiquity, it is absolutely necessary to begin with what we know to-day – to know the elements in the peasant culture still found in Norway and Sweden some 50 to 100 years ago; to know something of life along the coast and at sea, in the forests and amid the mountains, on the land, the fields, the pastures, the hinterland and the mountain farms. Without knowing something of this, one will never attain to the heart of anything comprised within the ancient culture.

As regards seal-hunting especially valuable information has been collected by Ekman, Lithberg, Sirelius, Berg and Svensson. Use has also been made of historical sources, such as early annals or sagas, and later works, like the great map and book of Olaus Magnus (1539 and 1555), L. J. Debes' description of the Faroes (1676) or Martin Martin's (1703) of the Western Isles of Scotland.

ZOOLOGICAL BACKGROUND

It is known that the following species of seal were hunted by the Stone Age inhabitants of north-western Europe, viz:

Phoca hispida Schreber, Fabr. (syn P. *foetida* Fabr.).

Commonly known as the 'ringed seal' from the irregular oval rings of light grey with darker centres on its sides; also, 'hair seal' (*hispidus*=hairy) and, having reference to its habits, 'floe-rat.'

P. groenlandica Erxl.

The shape of the dark markings, more pronounced in the case of males, which contrast with a greyish white ground colour, has caused this species to be known as the 'harp-seal' or 'saddle-back.'

Halichoerus grypus Fabr.

Generally known as the 'grey seal.'

Phoca vitulina L.

Generally known as the 'spotted seal,' owing to the prominent irregular bluish-black spots on a lemon yellow ground, but often referred to as 'common' due to its relative abundance round the shores of Britain.

In the interests of brevity and consistency, I shall refer to the species in this paper respectively, as ringed, harp, grey and spotted seals.

No remains of either the hooded seal (*Cystophora cristata* Erxl.) or the bearded seal (*Erignathus barbatus* Erxl.) have yet been recorded from sites of the European Stone Age. At the present day both are found off the coasts of the extreme north of Norway, but they only spread further south rarely and sporadically (Collett, 1911, 435 and 414).

Generally speaking the four species hunted in the Stone Age are found to-day in the circumpolar regions of the northern hemisphere, and in contiguous areas, but certain differences ought to be noted. The ringed seal is that most commonly met with in the far north, where it is found off the coasts of Greenland and Labrador, and from Coronation Gulf in northern

Canada across the Behring Straits and along the arctic coasts of northern Eurasia to the Kara and Barents Seas. This species does not move far afield and individuals seldom range into more southerly waters: during the last hundred years only a few specimens have been recorded from the east coast of England;[2] off the Norwegian coast it is rarely met with, except in the extreme north on the margins of the Barents Sea; it is uncommon in Danish waters; and it appears to be unknown on the western coast of Sweden. The rarity of ringed seals on the shores of the North Sea and in the Skagerrak and Cattegat emphasises the isolation of those found so commonly in the northern parts of the Baltic.[3] Zoologists consider that the ringed seals of the Gulfs of Bothnia and Finland and of the northern parts of the Baltic, as also those of the lakes of Saima, Ladoga and Onega, the Caspian Sea and the great lakes Baikal, Aral and Kuku-noor, are relicts from times when all these waters were connected with the Arctic Seas.[4]

The harp seal, to quote Fridtjof Nansen's excellent description (1925, 56–7), 'is distributed over the entire Polar Sea north of the Atlantic Ocean, from St Lawrence Bay, Newfoundland, Hudson Bay and the western part of the Canadian Arctic Islands (from about 95°W. Long.) to the west, over Davis' Straits, the northern Norwegian Sea, and Berents Sea to Kara Sea in the east.' Since, unlike the ringed seal, which is able to make breathing holes through ice, the harp seal 'usually keeps to the drift ice near the edge of the pack . . . and disappears from the ice as soon as it closes up,' its northerly range is more restricted. On the other hand, the harp seal is more mobile and during the summer months it ranges great distances in herds, seeking food often far beyond the drift ice. In normal years the harp seal visits the coasts of northern Norway, but abnormal ice-conditions in the Barents Sea may, as happened in the cold winter of 1902–3, cause it to spread further south;[5] in the spring of 1903 there were many records of its appearance on the east coast of Scotland[6] and at least one found its way as far as the river Teign.[7] A point to note is that, unlike the ringed seal, the harp seal is conspicuously absent, except as a rare visitor, from the Baltic (Ekman, 1933, 30).

The distribution of the grey seal is more restricted than that of either the ringed or the harp seal, but it is found much more generally in European waters. It occurs around Spitzbergen, Iceland and Greenland, and off the east coast of North America down to Nova Scotia. In European waters it is met on the coast of Norway as far north as Tromsø; in the Baltic, where it extends into the territory of the ringed seal as far as the Gulf of Bothnia; and off the northern and western fringes of the British Isles, where it is mainly concentrated round the Orkneys, Shetlands and Hebrides and the coast of Donegal, although still occurring in Cornwall, at certain points on the Welsh coast and occasionally even off the Norfolk shore.[8] Like the harp seal, the grey seal is gregarious and spends the summer fishing at sea, returning to traditional grounds for breeding.

The spotted seal is found to-day on either shore of the N. Atlantic and Pacific oceans and is common along the coasts of Greenland and Spitzbergen. Even more than the grey seal, however, its range extends into seas more southerly than those frequented by the ringed and harp seals. On the western shore of the Atlantic it reaches as far south as New Jersey and on the eastern down to the Straits of Gibraltar. Up till the early 19th century it was still very abundant round the coasts of Britain, but persecution has so reduced its numbers and restricted its range that to-day it 'is probably never seen . . . on the English coast except off Cornwall, Northern Yorkshire, Northumberland and Cumberland,' though 'still common all round the coasts of Ireland and of West and North Wales, and North-east and West Scotland, the Orkneys, Shetlands, Hebrides, and the great islands off the coast of North Britain' (Sir H. Johnston, 1903, 197–200). Across the North Sea the spotted seal is to-day the commonest species,[9] and it abounds in the south-western Baltic, being hunted as far north as Sandön Island (Ekman, 1933, 29) and Esthonia (Leinbock, 1932, 10). Like all the species considered, other than the ringed seal, the spotted seal is gregarious. It resembles the ringed seal in that it is relatively stationary throughout the year. It prefers shallow water and frequents sandy or pebbly shores, sand-banks, river estuaries and similar localities,[10] although in pursuit of salmon it will penetrate rivers up to 20 or 30 kilometres (Hentschel, 1937, 44).

THE EVIDENCE FOR SEAL-HUNTING IN THE STONE AGE[11]

Positive evidence for seal-hunting during the Stone Age (fig. 4.1) consists primarily of the remains of seals from the middens of ancient settlement sites, supplemented in a few instances by chance discoveries of seal bones associated with harpoon heads and incorporated in the bed of the Litorina Sea, where this has been left high and dry by a relative lowering of the sea-level in recent times. It is important before embarking on further discussion to appreciate the limitations of this evidence and to realise how unequally it has survived.

So far as coastal settlements are concerned, it should be remembered that, thanks to geographical changes since the close of the Ice Age, only limited stretches of the Stone-Age coasts are available for study above modern sea-level. Alone in the areas most depressed by the weight of the Pleistocene ice-sheets – regions in which we should hardly expect to find abundant traces of human colonisation until a comparatively late stage – are coast-lines dating from most phases of post-glacial time available, since it is only there that the land gained almost progressively on the sea as the ice-sheets contracted. No coastal sites dating from the Stone Age – and consequently few traces of seal-hunting – on the other hand, can be expected from areas so remote from

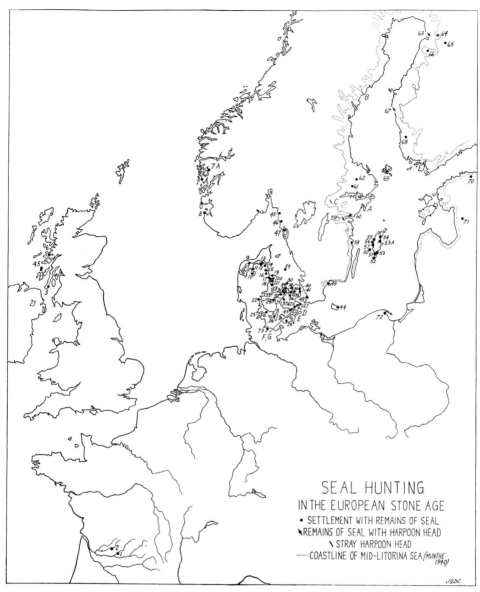

4.1 Map showing seal-hunting stations (1–73) and stray harpoons (A–H)

centres of isostatic displacement as to have been affected solely or predominantly by eustatic movements of sea-level, since here the old coasts are submerged, often at considerable distances from the modern shore. Between the two extremes are zones of special importance to our problem, in which the two processes were more evenly balanced, sometimes one and sometimes the other gaining the mastery, and from which, in consequence, we have ancient strand-lines dating in the main from the Atlantic and 'Sub-boreal' stages of post-glacial time. Allowance must also be made for great variations in the degree to which organic remains have survived, even where the sites of coastal settlements are available; bones of many species are available in quantities on some sites and from others are quite absent.

One can point to no coastal settlements dating from Late Glacial times in north-western Europe in territories known to have been settled by Upper Palaeolithic man, for the excellent reason that, even if they existed, which has yet to be proved, they would be below modern sea-levels. Certain well-marked strand-lines dating from Mesolithic I are available in Norway and in the Finnmarkian there is a well-defined coastal culture, but unfortunately no trace of organic material has survived (Bøe and Nummedal, 1936, 133). The position is little better from Mesolithic II, since in the best populated regions few traces of coastal settlement have survived above modern sea-level. Not until the stage of the Litorina Sea (Mesolithic III and Neolithic) is it possible to judge the extent of coastal settlement and even for this period the evidence is restricted geographically to the northern parts of the British Isles (Movius, 1942, Fig. 11), Scandinavia and parts of the Baltic area; elsewhere, including southern Britain, France, and Low Countries, north-western Germany and the southern shores of the Litorina Sea from Kolding Fjord to Memel, the contemporary coasts are submerged below modern sea-level. Yet, there are good reasons for believing that the areas from which evidence of coastal settlement have survived are in fact among those where seal-hunting was most intensively developed; in particular, it is precisely from these areas that we have most evidence for seal-hunting in Europe during modern times.

The earliest evidence available for seal-hunting comprises seal-bones from deposits of Upper Palaeolithic age in the Dordogne,[12] namely the left and right mandibles of the same individual from an Aurignacian level under the rock-shelter of Castanet in the valley of the Vézère and a single mandible from a late Magdalenian level in the cave of Raymonden on the Isle, another tributary of the Dordogne river, which itself flows into the Gironde. It is unnecessary to suppose with Lartet and Duparc[13] that the seals were caught on the distant sea-coast, possibly during a seasonal migration, and carried inland to the caves; the simpler explanation is that the seals were slaughtered in the immediate neighbourhood of the sites yielding the bones. As was pointed out by M. Harlé, the distinguished palaeontologist (1913), there is no reason why this should not have been the case, even though the finds were made some 200 and 190 kilometres from the existing coast and, by presumption, even further from the contemporary sea. Harlé quotes modern records of seals observed in such rivers as the Oder, Rhine and Loire, up which they will often ascend distances of 400 kilometres from the sea in pursuit of salmon. Representations of seals engraved on objects from the cave deposits (fig.4.2), like the bear's tooth from the Magdalenian burials at Duruthy, Sordes, and the pieces from the rock-shelter of Mège at Tejat, from Montgaudier, Brassempouy and Gourdan (Capitan, Breuil, Bourrinet and Peyrony, 1906, 210–211), suggest they were seen at least occasionally by the cave artists. Indeed, it is difficult not to think that the Tejat and Montgaudier engravings were studies from the life, or at least that the artists were working from quite recent impressions. These works of art bear sure witness to the interest attracted by the occasional seal, which found its way into the interior of the country by way of rivers and so intruded into the environment familiar to the reindeer-hunters.

There is no evidence for seal-hunting in the Late Glacial or Pre-boreal stages in the north and very little from the Boreal (Mesolithic II) time. A single tooth was found in the raised beach at Campbeltown, Kintyre, with an Early Larnian flint industry, but, since the latter was 'apparently derived from (an) old ground surface and washed inland' and no other traces of fauna were found (Movius, 1942, 177–8), it may well be that the association is more apparent than real. The forepart of a lower jaw-bone from the Maglemose site of Svaerdborg, Zealand, which at the time of the Ancylus Lake was more distant from the coast than it is to-day, is regarded by Degerböl as an amulet (1933, 376). If this interpretation is correct, it argues not only for contact with the coast, but also for the existence of coast-dwellers. Lastly, one may quote the bones from Kunda as an indication that seals were hunted in the Ancylus Lake.

It is not until a period contemporary with the Litorina phase of the Baltic that coastal settlements from the Stone Age are normally accessible for study, and from this time we meet with plenty of evidence for seal-hunting within the geographical limits already indicated. There are conclusive indications that the Obanian people of Argyllshire pursued seals, since bones of two species have been identified from two of their middens on the island of Oronsay (Caisteal-nan-Gillean and Cnoc Sligeach) and from a third on the tiny islet of Risga in Loch Sunnart. The presence of layers of blown sand in the Oronsay middens and the small size of Risga show that we have to deal with intermittent settlement, which in the case of Risga at least must have been of a seasonal character and may even have been connected directly with seal-catching. On the other hand it may be emphasised that the evidence for seal hunting during the Stone Age in Scotland is comparatively meagre,[14]

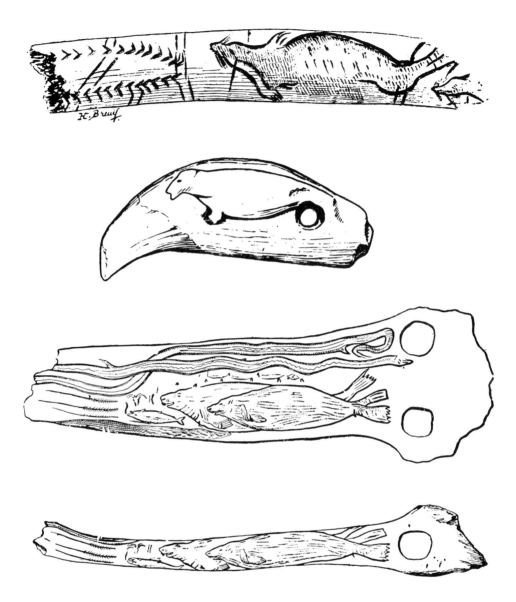

4.2 Representations of seals on objects of Upper Palaeolithic age from the Dordogne: top, Mège, Tejat (c. 3/2); middle, Duruthy, Sordes (1/1); bottom, Montgaudier (c. ½) (After Breuil, Lartet and Cartailhac)

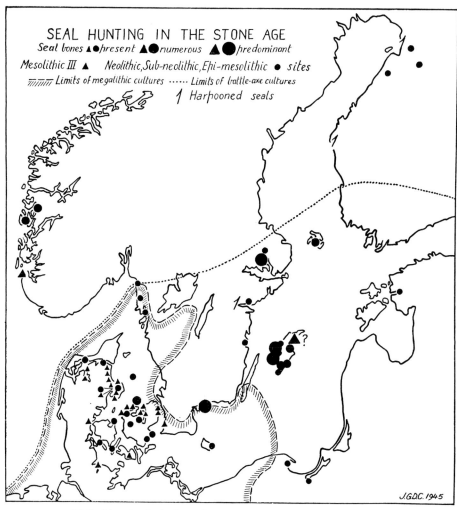

4.3 Seal-hunting in the Stone Age

even in the area where the old coastal sites are still above water, and there is no suggestion that the activity was developed to anything like the same extent as in the Baltic.

Approximately half the Stone Age sites in north-western Europe known to have yielded remains of seal are concentrated on the old Litorina shores of northern and eastern Jutland and of the Danish islands (fig. 4.3). Yet it ought not to be inferred from this that Denmark was the most important focus of seal-hunting during the Litorina time. The concentration of dots on the distribution map is due to the fact that coastal sites from this time happen to be available around much of Denmark and that conditions for the preservation of bone are particularly favourable there; evidence of seal-hunting

during the Stone Age has merely survived to a greater extent than in some
other parts of Scandinavia, where it was in all probability much richer. As a
matter of fact the mammalian fauna from the Ertebölle (Mesolithic III) sites
of Denmark is predominantly made up of forest species, principally red deer,
roe deer and wild pig, with the aurochs in substantial strength: seal remains in
no case account for more than a comparatively small proportion of the
whole. On the other hand the fact that seal bones have come from some
twenty of their dwelling-places and middens suggests that seal hunting
played a definite, if restricted, role in the economy of the Ertebölle people.

In estimating the place of seal-hunting in the following Neolithic period,
the varying cultural status of the different groups inhabiting Denmark at this
time must be taken into account. As might be expected of an area having a
vigorous native stock of Mesolithic tradition, among whom Neolithic culture
was introduced from outside, one meets with a wide range of response to
culture contact, from total rejection through varying stages of acceptance of
the new ideas. A few groups of coast-dwelling Ertebölle people, such as those
at Sölager and Klintesö, maintained their way of life virtually unimpaired by
the Neolithic colonization, and can best be described as Epi-mesolithic.
Others, like those represented by the settlement at Strandegaard, although
basically Mesolithic in tradition, yet appear to have absorbed elements from
the groups of Neolithic colonizers, whose dead are found sometimes in flat
earth-graves and commonly in megalithic 'dolmens'; such groups may be
termed Sub-neolithic or, more specifically, Sub-megalithic. Finally there are
settlements, such as Havnelev and Lindö, the artifacts from which conform
substantially to those found in the 'dolmens' and 'passage graves' of the
northern megalithic group.

Until more is known it would be unprofitable to try and estimate any
differences that may have existed in the part played by seal-hunting among
the various communities of Neolithic age in Denmark. Even in comparing
the data from Atlantic and 'Sub-boreal' times in Denmark, it has to be
remembered that many settlements were occupied either continuously or
intermittently during both periods and that only in certain cases have bones
from the different levels been segregated; in at least one instance where this
was done, namely at Langö on Fünen, it was found that traces of seal-hunting
were confined to the Neolithic levels. It follows that some of the occurrences
of seal-bones in Denmark listed as Mesolithic III ought more properly to be
classified as of Neolithic age. Evidence of seal-hunting has been found on at
least sixteen sites of Neolithic age in Denmark and it is from this period that
we have the first indication of intensive activity, notably on the island of
Hesselö in the Cattegat, which has yielded over four hundred corner teeth,
among other remains, of the grey seal. The small size of the island – it is less
than a mile long – and the fact that the seals were predominantly young
individuals suggest that the site of Hesselö was a sealing station, to which

Archaeological periods in Denmark	Cultural and economic status			Climatic phases	Forest zones (Jessen)	Baltic stages
Neolithic	Neolithic (farming) e.g. Havnelev (Megalithic)	Sub-neolithic (predominantly food-gathering) e.g. Strande- gaard	Epi-mesolithic (food-gathering) e.g. Sølager (Ertebølle IV)	'Sub- boreal'	VIII	Litorina Sea
Mesolithic III	Ertebølle (I-III) (food-gathering)			Atlantic	VII	
Mesolithic II	? (Coasts submerged)			Boreal	V-VI	Ancylus Lake
Mesolithic I	? (Coasts submerged)			Pre- boreal	IV	Yoldia Sea

4.4 Table illustrating the development of coastal culture in Denmark during post-glacial times

recourse was made possibly over a period of years at the breeding season of the grey seal. The comparative isolation of the island – still more marked in the case of Anholt, where also grey seal bones occurred in a Neolithic context – implies a certain facility in navigation at this time, for which other evidence will be cited.

Round the ancient shores of Norway conditions for the survival of animal bones have in general been bad, with the saving exception of certain rock-shelters, occupied in some cases already from the Stone Age. From three such, Viste, near Stavanger, Ruskenesset near Bergen and Skipshelleren, near Stamnes, seal bones have been obtained in some quantity. At Viste remains of grey seal were common and the harp seal was also represented. An interesting point is that cod bones (*Gadus morrhua*) predominated among the fish and in fact formed a notable feature of the deposit, a fact which, as Brögger pointed out at the time (1908, 23), implies that the Viste people were capable of fishing from boats. Whether the site in fact dates from the Mesolithic III time of the Danish area, as is usually stated, or whether it represents a survival in a part of Scandinavia which remained outside the megalithic colonization, does not seem to be conclusively settled. Ruskenesset, on the other hand, must date on the evidence of flint daggers and hollow-based arrow-heads, not to mention some fragments of bronze, from the period of the Stone Cists at the close of the Stone Age. To judge from the presence of bones of domesticated animals and from the impressions of barley grains on sherds, the seal-hunters of Ruskenesset were farmers, who, as was common in Norway up till recent times, supplemented their food-supply by seasonal hunting and fishing. Just as at Viste the pig was the commonest mammal represented among the food waste, so at Ruskenesset it was another forest creature, the red deer, which predominated; yet seal bones were again second in abundance, in this case the spotted seal, and remains of cod were likewise conspicuous among the fish. Although a report on the fauna from Skipshelleren has yet to appear, Dr Böe has kindly informed me that seal bones occurred there freely in the Stone Age levels and that among them bones of the spotted seal were conspicuous, including many quite young ones. Further north, seals are represented on rock-engravings attributed to the Arctic dwelling-place people at Rödöy (Gjessing, 1936, pl. viib) and Finnhågen, Valle (Gjessing, 1932, pl. xxviii), both in the province of Nordland. At the former the seal is accompanied by a porpoise, an elk, and, significantly, a boat (fig. 4.6).

Evidence relating to seal-hunting during the Stone Age in Sweden has survived very unequally. As a rule bones have disappeared from the old dwelling-places, leaving traces behind them in the form of phosphate, it is true, but bequeathing no evidence by which they could be identified. Only in Gotland have we an appreciable number of finds, a consequence no doubt of the limestone element in the island's build. Thus the surviving evidence from ancient sites gives no reliable indication of the relative importance of seal-hunting in different parts of the country. While no doubt conditions differed during the Stone Age, it is suggestive that, if we take into account the number of seals qualifying for government premiums during the period 1902–6 from different parts of the Swedish coast, we find that the provinces north of Uppland, which earned the most premiums, have yielded no finds, while the return for Gotland which has produced nearly half the Stone Age sites was among the lowest for any provinces in Sweden.[15]

The great majority of the Swedish finds date from a time contemporary with the Neolithic civilization in the south-west Baltic. Only from two sites, Limhamn and Gislause, have we any evidence of seal-hunting of Mesolithic III age, and in neither instance is this impressive: from the former, the evidence consists of only one bone from a disturbed part of the cultural deposit, while the archaeological material from the latter is of indeterminate character and the site is dated only in its relation to old strand-lines. The Stone Age seal-hunters of Sweden appear in general to have dwelt on the fringe of the contemporary Neolithic world, at a period contemporary with that of the passage-graves in the south. Culturally speaking, the dwelling-place people can best be described as Subneolithic: basically Mesolithic in tradition and way of life, they were yet influenced by the farming economy of more advanced cultures to the south and east. The degree of Neolithic influence varied from group to group. At such sites as Siretorp, Stora Förvar, Visby and Västerbjers the bones included a perceptible element of domesticated forms, additional to the ubiquitous dog, and the last two mentioned yielded thick-butted flint axes, which could well have come from passage graves (Nihlén, 1927, Fig. 101 and Stenberger, 1939, 80). The economy revealed by the fauna from other sites, like the middens of Anneröd, Rörvik

and Rotekarrslid in Bohuslän, Åloppe and Sotmyra in Uppland and most of
the Gotland dwelling-places appears to have been based on hunting and
fishing, and traces of specifically domesticated forms, other than the dog, are
absent. In any case hunting was very important to these people, whether or
not they managed to supplement their food by exchange or by a low form of
farming culture.

Owing to defects in the evidence, it is often difficult to assess the relative
importance of seal-hunting in the chase, but the impression is that this was
considerable. In no case was the assemblage of bones from any one of the
Bohuslän middens sufficient to justify a reliable estimate, although if we
aggregate the material we find that seals formed quite an important element in
the fauna. At Siretorp, despite a number of bones of domestic species, seals
accounted for some 84 per cent of the fauna (E. Dahr, in Bagge and
Kjellmark, 1939, 242–5). Further north, at Vivastemåla in Småland, evidence
that quantities of animal refuse had been discarded by the dwelling-place
people was revealed in the high phosphate-content of the soil (Bagge, 1941,
23), yet only four pieces of bone survived; of these, the three identifiable
fragments belonged to seals. Thanks to more favourable conditions our
information about the animals hunted by the dwelling-place people of
Gotland is much fuller and we receive a livelier impression of the importance
of seals: thus, seal bones predominated in the lower levels of Stora Förvar, at
Visborgs Kungsladugård and Gislause, while at Hemmor, Gullrum and
Visby, at which latter they amounted to over a third of the total bones, they
formed a substantial element; at Alvena and Hoburgen the evidence is
insufficient to allow us to do more than assume the fact of seal-hunting. In
Uppland the fauna from Sotmyra is too meagre to tell us much, but from the
well-known station of Åloppe more than 10,000 identifiable bones were
obtained in the excavations of 1902, three-fifths of which belonged to fish
and a number of which belonged to birds. Of the mammals, the ringed seal,
represented by over a hundred individuals, was the predominant species, pig
being second and elk third in importance. Taken as a whole, we are justified
in interpreting the Swedish finds as proof that the Subneolithic dwelling-
place people of that country, and particularly of the Baltic coasts and of
Gotland, were keen seal-hunters and that the seal played a role of substantial
importance in their economy.

Judging by what we know of later history, this was almost surely true of
the dwelling-place people of Finland, but in this case very little evidence
survives. The same causes, which have deprived us of all but a handful of their
antler and bone artifacts, have also destroyed the evidence, which their
discarded meat bones might have provided. As it is, there are only a few
flakes of burnt bone from which to deduce the kinds of animal hunted by the
Sub-neolithic Finns (Ailio 1909, p. 6). From such evidence as we possess, it
appears that, apart from fish, the commonest species represented were elk,

4.5 Sub-Neolithic harpoon-heads from Sweden: 1 Norrköping, Östergotland (Statens
Hist. Mus. 13476); 2 Djursnas, Ösmo skn, Södermanland (Statens Hist. Mus. 3940);
3 Örnsköldvik, Ångermanland (Statens Hist. Mus. 1303); 4 Hemmor, Gotland
(Statens Hist. Mus.); 5 Örebro district (?), Närke (Statens Hist. Mus.)

4.6 Rock-engraving at Rödöy, Nordland, Norway.

beaver and ringed seal, the latter being identified from four sites on the mainland, Honkala, Nimisjärvi, Pitkäsaari and Uotimäki; in addition, the site of Jettböle in the Aaland Islands has yielded numerous bones of the harp seal.

Owing to the submergence of the Litorina coast, finds of seal-bones on archaeological sites are rare from the south shores of the Baltic. However, in an area where the Litorina coasts are still above sea-level, there is a record of seal-bones from the dwelling-place of Rinnekalns at the northern end of Lake Burtneck in Latvia, among an assemblage which included domestic species, as well as many wild animals of the forest. Further west, on the Putziger Wiek, seal bones were numerous on a coastal settlement of the Polish Corded Ware or Battle-axe people at Rzucewo; at this Neolithic site the bones of domesticated animals predominated, but the seal bones formed a substantial proportion of those of wild animals. Finally, it may be noted that seal-bones have been dredged from the Ertebølle (Mesolithic III) site in Kiel Fjord, off Ellerbek, one of that great preponderance of Stone Age sealing stations at present submerged by the sea.

There remain three finds of seal skeletons, found by chance in clays deposited in the Litorina Sea on either side of the present Gulf of Bothnia, which from the circumstance of their each being accompanied by barbed points can be interpreted as victims of Stone Age man. The first discovery of this kind was made in 1907 during excavations for the foundations of the new city hall of Norrköping. The bones of a fairly young ringed seal, accompanied by a bone harpoon head (fig. 4.5, no. 1; fig. 4.7, no. 2), were found in the clay bed at approximately the level of the Baltic Sea at the present day; since the Litorina Sea level is estimated to have been approximately 60 metres higher when the clay was deposited, the seal must have sunk in deep water and come to rest on the sea-floor. A second find was made while draining a fen at Närpes in 1935, when a complete harpoon head of elk bone (fig. 4.7, no. 3) was recovered from the ribs of a skeleton of a harp seal lying curled up in a deposit formed on the floor of the Litorina Sea, through the waters of which it had evidently sunk, mortally stricken. Thirdly, there is the discovery in a brick-works near Oulu during the winter of 1936–7 of a barbed point of elk bone, unfortunately incomplete at the lower end (fig. 4.7, no. 1), amidst a heap of ringed seal bones, dated to a fairly advanced stage of the Litorina Sea, a find which might well relate to the comb-ware site at Muhos, a few miles away, where a few flakes of ringed seal bone have been recovered. It is further worth noting that, in addition to many finds from unrecorded deposits, three harpoon-heads have been found by chance in deposits formerly part of the bed of the Litorina Sea: two of these from Södermanland and Närke respectively (fig. 4.5, nos. 2 and 5), are perforated at the base, the former doubly; the third, from Ångermanland (fig. 4.5, no. 3), is formally distinct, being barbed on both edges and having a spade-shaped base, and may not have been connected with seal-hunting.

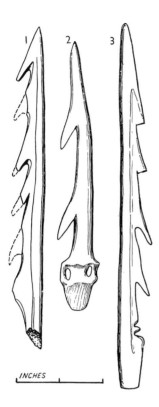

4.7 Harpoon-heads from the bed of the Litorina Sea: 1 Oulu, Österbotten, Finland (elk bone); 2 Norrköping, Östergotland, Sweden; 3 Närpes, Österbotten, Finland (elk bone)

ANALYSIS OF THE SEALS HUNTED IN THE STONE AGE

Analysis of the proportions in which the different species were hunted throws light upon the nature of the hunting and upon the former distribution of the seals. The finds from the Dordogne show that during Late Pleistocene times ringed and harp seals reached at least as far south as the Gironde estuary, up which individuals presumably passed to the river Dordogne and its tributaries. Although traces of both have been found in deposits laid in the waters bordering the Scandinavian ice-sheet, there is no evidence that these or any other seals were hunted in northern Europe, either in Upper Palaeolithic or in Mesolithic I times. There are signs that during Mesolithic II times in this area the ringed seal was being hunted in the northern part of the Ancylus Lake (Kunda), while the grey seal was slaughtered at its south-western end (Svaerdborg) and had certainly spread as far north as Skattmansö in Uppland

(Munthe, 1895). But it is only from the period of the Litorina Sea that there is sufficient evidence to reach any firm conclusions about the proportions in which the different species of seal were hunted and then only for the Baltic and contiguous areas. From the Obanian stations of Scotland such evidence as we have is consistent in showing that the grey seal and spotted seal were each hunted, both species being present in the area to-day.

The distribution of finds of the various species of seal from Stone Age sites in the Baltic and its approaches is shown on fig. 4.8, in which the area is divided into the following zones:–

I. Approaches to the Baltic: W. Norway, W. Sweden and Denmark outside the Belts.
II. The south-western Baltic: Denmark within the Belts and coasts of Germany and S. Sweden as far east as Rügen.
III. The middle Baltic: from Rügen to Fårö (north of Gotland).
IV. The northern Baltic and Gulfs of Finland and Bothnia: north of Fårö.

Table showing the number of finds with archaeological associations of the various species of seal in each zone: percentages (in brackets) refer to the occurrence of each species zone by zone

			Zone I	Zone II	Zone III	Zone IV	Totals
Ringed seal	..	..	3 (7%)	1 (7%)	5 (23%)	8 (67%)	17
Harp seal	..	..	12 (29%)	5 (37%)	10 (45%)	3 (25%)	30
Grey seal	..	..	22 (52%)	6 (43%)	6 (27%)	1 (8%)	35
Spotted seal	..	..	5 (12%)	2 (14%)	1 (5%)	nil	8
Total	..	..	42	14	22	12	90

In interpreting this evidence, it has to be remembered that two factors must have operated, namely the distribution of the various seals at the time of the Litorina Sea and the capacity of the hunters of the period, which, in view of limited technical means, may well have varied according to species. So far as the ringed seal is concerned, the evidence is consistent with the relict character of the species in the north Baltic and the gulfs: the fact that it accounts for two-thirds of the finds in Zone IV is balanced by its rarity in Zones I and II. The relative abundance of the harp seal, especially in Zones II and III, where it accounts for over two-fifths of the occurrences of seals, has attracted a good deal of attention, since climatic conditions are generally supposed to have been more equable, with a mean annual temperature rather higher than those prevailing to-day, when it is virtually absent from the Baltic. Noting that at least 10 individuals of this arctic species were found in 80 square metres of the Visby dwelling-place, Holmquist (1912, 72–3) maintained that the harp seal must have been established for breeding in the Gotland area. Harp seals were hunted as far north as the Aaland Islands

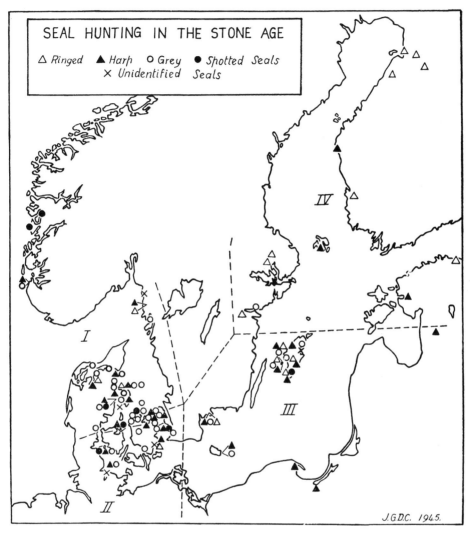

4.8 Map showing types of seal-hunting in different parts of Scandinavia during the Stone Age. (For definitions of zones I–IV, see p. 64).

(Jettböle) and the Gulf of Bothnia, where, in addition to the specimen from Närpes, two were recovered from Litorina clay at Sundsvall on the Swedish side (Adlerz, 1906) of the Gulf. Ekman (1933, 31 and 1935, 199–200) has suggested that the harp seals of the Litorina Sea ought to be explained as relics from the Sub-arctic Yoldia Sea; the absence of finds from the stage of the Ancylus Lake, when the Baltic basin was shut off from the outer sea, he accounts for by pointing out that potential sources of evidence are submerged. On the other hand, Pira (1926, 131–3) has shown that at Stora Förvar on Stora Karlsö, the harp seal was absent in the lower levels, appearing in the middle and disappearing again in the upper, as though penetrating the Litorina Sea from outside, establishing itself for a period and leaving. What is certainly established, is the presence of this arctic species in the Litorina Sea at the height of the Stone Age seal-hunting. Ekman (1933, 32–3) has suggested that conditions may have been more favourable for the formation of drift ice than to-day, thanks to the greater salinity of the Litorina Sea and the consequent formation of a superficial layer of fresh water.

The commonest species of seal on the Stone Age sites in Zones I and II is the grey seal, which, as well as being found on the largest number of sites, often occurs in abundance. The spotted seal, at present much the commonest species in these zones, is meagrely represented in the Stone Age material, a fact interpreted by Pira (1926, 134) as indicating that it reached the Baltic basin comparatively late. The possibility ought not to be excluded that the rarity of the spotted seal is more apparent than real, and that, in fact, this species was not slaughtered in numbers proportionate to its occurrence in nature. Some support can be found for this in the fact that, unlike the grey seal, the spotted seal does not establish itself on rocks during the breeding season, and that its young takes to the water within a few hours of birth; the spotted seal is thus free from the seasonal clubbing which is still the scourge of the grey seal (Prichard, 1936, 191). Yet, it will not have been forgotten that the inhabitants of Ruskenesset and Skipshelleren on the west coast of Norway appear to have hunted this species with marked success. Its rarity in the Baltic can, therefore, hardly be ascribed to any special difficulty in its hunting. One can only assume that the spotted seal was in fact much rarer in the western Baltic than it is to-day and it may well be that the conditions which favoured the harp seal were uncongenial to the spotted seal.

THE METHODS USED IN HUNTING

Before fire-arms came into general use for seal-hunting, methods had to be adapted closely to the distinctive habits of the various species, and more particularly in early times, when technical means were limited, hunters must have taken full advantage of fleeting or periodic opportunities. Seals are especially vulnerable at their breeding seasons, particularly the ringed harp and grey seals which spend the first few weeks of their lives on the ice or the rocks, as the case may be, where their elders will often try to defend them, only too often to share their fate: although well able to elude human enemies when in open water, seals are relatively helpless on land, even though at an earlier stage of their evolution this was their proper element. It also happens that young seals are particularly valuable at the stages immediately before taking to the water, after spending the opening weeks of their lives accumulating resources against the day when they have to fend for them-selves. According to observations made off the Frø Islands, near Trondheim, the grey seal cub has fattened to such effect by the age of three weeks that it will yield, in addition to 12/18 kg. of meat, some 20/30 kg. – in rare instances up to 60 kg. – of blubber, much of which it loses in the following months of struggle (Collett, 1881, 383–4). There is thus a double motive for pursuing seals at the breeding season; the young and their elders are accessible on dry land and the former have reached a temporary peak of well-being.

Although it is to be regretted that zoologists have not invariably reported on the age-grouping of the seals represented on ancient sites, a practice which ought surely to be standard and is equally important for domesticated animals, there is a good deal of evidence to suggest that the Stone Age hunters took full advantage of the opportunities given by the breeding seasons of the various species of seal. At Åloppe it was noted that the majority of the bones of the ringed seal, which predominated among the mammalian remains from the site, belonged to very young individuals. The abundant remains of grey seals from Hesselø, and also from the lower levels of Stora Förvar, were likewise predominantly those of young individuals; at the latter site Pira observed 'a great number of mandibles and other skeletal remains of very young and new-born grey seals' (Pira, 1926, 130). Even the spotted seal, the young of which take to the water a few hours after birth, seems to have been hunted during the breeding season off the west coast of Norway, to judge from the finds of Ruskenesset and Skipshelleren: at the former the bones represented individuals ranging from adults to newly born seals, while at the latter the bones were mostly those of quite young seals. It is likely that several, if not all, of these sites were located with direct reference to the breeding-places of the seals and were in fact occupied during the breeding season for the express purpose of securing young seals and their parents. From his very careful study of the fauna from Ruskenesset, which, as we have seen, dates from the time of the Stone Cists, Brinkmann concluded that the site was certainly inhabited during the summer and may well have been settled exclusively at this season. Remains of ox and sheep and a few impressions of barley-grains on potsherds show that the Ruskenesset people were farmers and it may be supposed that they repaired to the encampment under the rock-shelter during an interval in the farming year, which coincided with or at least included the breeding-season of the spotted seal (May-June at present). In this way they filled the period between seed-time and harvest, which before the development in Scandinavia during the Iron Age of intensive farming, involving summer hay-making, must have been comparatively slack, by engaging in hunting and fishing activities. By such means reserves of food could be built up for the winter months.

Owing to the great importance of seals in the economy of the people of the circumpolar regions, there is plenty of evidence relating to their hunting methods (*e.g.* Birket-Smith, 1936 and Mathiassen, 1928). Even more valuable is information about seal-hunting on the Atlantic sea-board of Europe and in the Baltic basin available from early descriptions and from surviving or recently extant folk usage. Not only do geographical conditions at the present day resemble those in the same area during the Stone Age more closely than those of Greenland or northern Eurasia, but it is possible, at least for parts of the Norwegian coast and the Baltic area, to demonstrate continuity of tradition from prehistoric to recent times.

We owe the survival of seal-hunting in the very areas where it was carried on in the Stone Age in part to the fact that, like fishing and other forms of hunting, it was incorporated as a seasonal activity in the farming economy of communities, which, since Neolithic times, have been on the margin of cereal cultivation and stock-raising. It may well be that it is as a result of this that up till modern times the rights of seal-hunting, at least for the most favoured spots, have commonly been vested in the hands of farmers and landowners. In his description of the yearly 'fishing of seals' in the Western Isles, which was held at the end of October, the breeding-season of the grey seal, Martin Martin (1703: 1934 edn, 133) tells us that the right of sealing on the favoured rock of Eousmil belonged to the farmers of adjacent lands, and the monks of Iona are said to have enjoyed rights over a seals' breeding-place on a rocky islet near Mull (Joyce, 1903, 11, 129). The old law and custom of Norway recognised the exclusive rights of land-owners to breeding places of the grey seal (Hjort and Knipowitsch, 1907, 40–1). Similar conditions prevailed in Gotland, where, up till 1865, sealing off the locality of Näsboudden was vested in the owners of five neighbouring estates: the activity was of sufficient consequence for the owners to form a gild, members of which styled themselves 'seal comrades' (*kutbussar*) and bound themselves to man seven boats – six two-man boats and a yawl – and to share the catch (Lithberg, 1914, 118–22). The old style of hunting was only changed by the fall in the price of seal-blubber and the more extensive use of fire-arms during the 19th century.

Seal-hunting no longer plays an integral part in the farming economy of the Scandinavian coasts, but survives mainly as a form of pest-extermination, encouraged by state subsidies; the damage done by seals to the valuable salmon fisheries, among others, necessitated active measures, so soon as the hunting declined as part of the normal economy of coastwise farming. The introduction of fire-arms has brought less drastic changes than might have been imagined. Although first applied to seal-hunting in the middle of the 16th century (Sirelius, 1934, 94) it was not until three hundred years later that their use became general for this purpose. Even to-day firearms have their limitations. Shooting is wasteful, because adult seals sink more or less rapidly (although their buoyancy varies according to species and condition), and the very range at which they can be shot means that many are lost. Thus, it may often happen that practices of remote antiquity survive because they conform to biological realities.

The principal methods, other than shooting, used in modern times for hunting seals on the Atlantic coasts of Europe and in the Baltic basin were clubbing, netting, spearing or piking and harpooning, practised alone or in combination. The choice of method varied according to the species of seal, as well as to the prevailing geographical and climatic conditions and to the season.

The practice of stunning seals by clubbing them is as a rule confined to gregarious species and among these is peculiarly well adapted to the grey seal, which unlike the harp or spotted variety establishes itself for breeding in caves or on rocks well above sea-level. A graphic description of the hunting of grey seals in their caves at the breeding season in the Faroes is given by Debes (1676, 170–1), who tells how first the adults and then the fat young ones were clubbed and their throats cut by the light of great candles, fifty seals often being taken in this way in a single cave. We have many descriptions of the slaughter of the grey seal in the Western Isles of Scotland. Martin Martin (*op. cit.*, 133–4) tells how the sealers would 'embark with a contrary wind' to avoid giving scent to the seals and ensure against being driven out to the Atlantic and how when 'quietly landed, they surround the passes, and the signal for the general attack is given from the boat, and so they beat them down with big staves. The seals at this onset make towards the sea with all speed, and often force their passage over the necks of the stoutest assailants, who aim always at the forehead of the seals, giving many blows before they be killed . . .' At any rate before the Grey Seals Protection Act of 1914 was passed, the clubbing of the seals was an annual event at the breeding season, when the mother seals nursed their helpless pups on the rocks and some of the big bulls lay with their families. Hesketh Prichard's account (1936, 15–17) of the clubbing on Haskeir, a rocky island off Uist, to which grey seals repair year after year for breeding, is reminiscent of Martin's: 'The crew of the boat quietly land, the passes to the sea are blocked, and a savage slaughter with clubs and staves becomes the order of the day, or rather of the night . . . The seals are hit at the root of the nose, and the first, or at any rate, the second blow, should kill . . .' Similar practices obtained at favoured points on the coast of Norway. Collett (1881, 385) has described how in the Frö Islands off Trondheim the clubbing was planned to catch the young grey seals at their plumpest, immediately before leaving for the open sea; the cubs were killed by a blow on the snout from a two-foot wooden club. In Møre, seals were chased ashore within living memory by throwing stones from boats and there clubbed to death (Shetelig and Falk, 1937, 88). There is also evidence for seal-clubbing in the Baltic: grey seals are surprised as they lie basking on skerries off the coasts of Östergotland and Gotland, beaten senseless by iron-shod clubs and despatched by knives (Berg and Svensson, 1934, 54); and clubbing is still used especially for young seals by the seal-hunters of the Esthonian islands of Kihnu and Ruhnu in the Gulf of Riga

(Leinbock, 1932, 10). Nordqvist (1899, 26) has described how the method is used in conjunction with ice-hunting for ringed seals. The hunters stop up the breathing holes, by means of which this species maintains itself under the fast ice of coastal inlets, by plugging them over a limited area with wooden stakes, so forcing the seals to come to a central hole for breathing: when the seals appear they are clubbed senseless and dragged out of the water.

The use of nets for hunting seals may well have been suggested by catching individuals accidentally in fishing-nets, for seals are great robbers; they are commonly caught in salmon nets at the present day.[16] The practice was certainly wide-spread in modern times and is considered by Sirelius (1934, 91–2) to be of great antiquity. According to Martin Martin (1703: 1934 edn, 133–4) one of the ways of catching seals in the Western Isles was to stretch nets of horsehair 'contracted at one end like a purse' across narrow channels. Nets were used extensively in Finland: in the autumn they would be set close by favourite rocks so as to catch the seals as they jumped into the sea and later in the season they would be stretched across the inlets through which the seals passed on their way to the ice (Sirelius, 1934, 91–2). Linnaeus (1745, 156, 184 and 270), on his journey of 1741, noted that nets were used to catch seals on rocks off the shores of Öland and Gotland, and there are more recent records of this method of catching seals in conjunction with clubbing, both on the shores of Fårö in the north and on the Flisen rocks of Näsboudden in the south of Gotland (Lithberg, 1914, 118–20).

Thanks to their appetite for fish, seals can be caught fairly easily by means of traps. Among those in recent use in the Baltic area were fall-traps with trap-doors and scissor-traps with barbed jaws which snap to when the bait is taken (Ekman, 1910, 252–4). The affection of female seals for their young is also turned to advantage by the hunters. When, during an assault on a herd of seals at the breeding season, some of the adults escape, the young are sometimes used as lures, mounted as live-bait on one point of a three-pointed hook at the end of a line; mother seals responding to the calls of their offspring are then caught by their fore-flippers on the remaining points of the hook (Sirelius, 1934, 92 and abb. 152).

Iron-headed seal-spears or pikes with single barb were in common use in the Baltic area during modern times, both for slaughtering grey seal cubs and also in conjunction with other weapons for securing dead or wounded seals, which might otherwise have sunk or escaped (Ekman, 1910, 232–3). It must be remembered that, whereas in the Western Isles or on the coast of Norway the cubs of the grey seal are born in the autumn, as a rule at traditional breeding-places on rocky skerries, in the northern parts of the Baltic the breeding takes place in February and March. For this purpose the seals, after spending most of the year further south, move north into the Gulf of Bothnia, the waters of which freeze for some distance from the shore and which at the height of the season become completely cut off from the Baltic

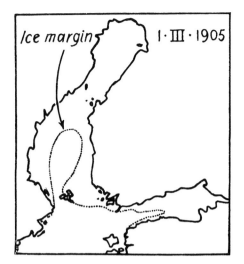 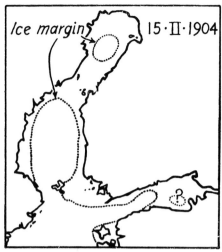

4.9 Map showing maximum extent of ice in the northern Baltic during the winters of 1904–5 (After *Atlas de Finlande*)

by an ice-barrier (fig. 4.9). The seals give birth to their young on ice-floes on the margin of fast ice surrounding the water, which remains open in the centre of the northern part of the Gulf. In the portion of Olaus Magnus' *Carta marina* of 1539 here reproduced (fig. 4.10) the open water of the Gulf of Bothnia at this season is shown, together with the northern edge of the ice barrier. It will be noted that one of the seals visible on the ice-floes is suckling a cub. The hunters, clad in dark clothing to confuse the seals, are shown kneeling on ice-floes with their boats, from each of which the heads of victims may be seen protruding, prudently secured by lines to their waists. Such hunting could be hazardous, as is illustrated by the story of the seal-hunters of Fårö, who in the spring of 1603 were carried on ice-floes to the skerries of the Stockholm area owing to a sudden change of wind. In modern times the Gotlanders usually worked in parties of five or six, one of which would be stationed on shore to watch for changes in the wind. The pikes wielded by the Bothnian hunters depicted by Olaus Magnus resemble those still in use in Finland and employed in Gotland in modern times (fig. 4.11, 1), having a strong barb and apparently being secured to their shafts by sockets. Lithberg (1914, 120–1) tells how hunters used to stalk grey seals on the skerries of Fårö to within 10 or 20 paces, and then rushing upon their victims, drive home their pikes, sometimes one in either hand.

It remains to consider the harpoon with movable head set in a shaft and secured to a line, a weapon which plays a role of immense importance among the Eskimo, whether used from kayaks in open water or in the various forms of ice-hunting (Birket-Smith, 1936, 80–6). In the northern Baltic and the Gulf of Bothnia the harpoon survives especially for hunting the ringed seal in winter through the ice. The idea is to harpoon the seal at the moment it comes to breathe at one of its several holes: the harpoon head is driven into the seal, but the hunter retains the handle and line, the latter of which he pays out until the victim tires and can be drawn up through the hole enlarged for the purpose.

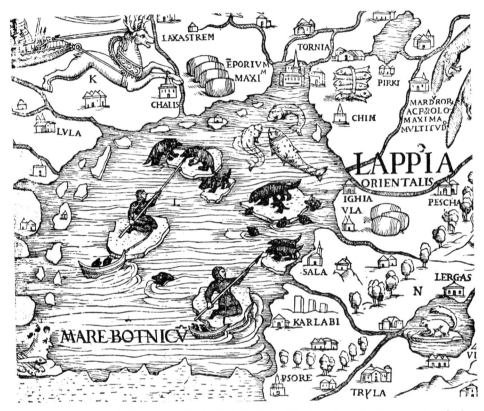

4.10 Seal-hunting at the head of the Gulf of Bothnia, from the *Carta marina* of Olaus Magnus (1539) (By courtesy of the British Museum)

Among the Eskimo we know that the hunter adapts his methods to ice-conditions: when severe frost has given rise to smooth ice in some protected fjord, he will shoe himself in sandals made from the skin of some hairy animal so as to move noiselessly, and, listening for the snorting of seals at their holes, make for each in turn; with snow on the ice each step would betray the hunter by the crunch, so there is no choice but to sit and wait at a selected hole until the seal appears. The *Máupoq* method, as it is termed by the Eskimo, is also found among the Samoyeds, the Finns (Sirelius, 1934, 91) and the Swedes (Ekman, 1910, 232–3). Off the coast of north Sweden hunters are said to lure seals to the breathing-holes, clad in white clothing (Berg and

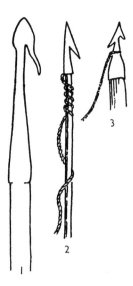

4.11 Modern gear for catching seals in the Baltic: 1 Swedish pike; 2 harpoon in use c. AD 1700, Roslagen, Sweden; 3 iron harpoon-head of the type used today in Finland and Esthonia (After Ekman)

Svensson, 1934, 54–5). The harpoons at present used in the north Baltic are of iron; they are socketed and have one or two barbs (fig. 4.11, nos. 2, 3). Seals appear also to have been harpooned in ancient Ireland. To judge from the story related in the Book of Lismore of the servant of Brigit, who struck a seal, after securing the line to one hand, and was dragged by it across the sea to Britain (Stokes, 1890, p. 196), the Irish harpoons must have been most effectively contrived!

When we ask, which of these methods were practised in the Stone Age, we find ourselves faced with problems, many of which are inherent in the nature of the evidence. Archaeologically there is no proof that seals were clubbed in the Stone Age, since no clubs have survived; even if under exceptional conditions wooden clubs were preserved, it would be difficult to connect such primitive objects specifically with seal-hunting. On the other hand, since we know that the Stone Age hunters slew seal-cubs in large numbers on their breeding grounds, the probability is great that they used wooden clubs. This is rendered all the more likely by the fact that the pike does not appear to have been used for seal-hunting until iron had become common in the north. No traces have so far come to light of coarse-meshed sealing-nets although the fact that portions of fishing-nets have survived from the Stone Age encourages one to hope that, if such in fact were used at this period, the evidence may one day be found. Some of the most effective forms of traps used for seal-hunting are of iron or steel, but others, such as the fall-trap, could have been constructed in the Stone Age.

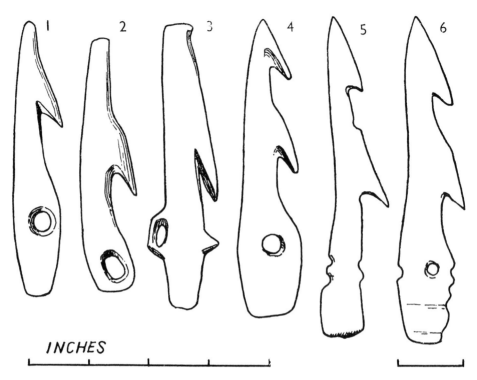

4.12 Sub-Neolithic harpoon-heads from Gotland: 1-3 Stora Förvar (after Schittger and Rydh); 4–6 Västerbjers (after Stenberger)

The only weapon, to which we can point with certainty as having been used by Stone Age man for hunting seals, is the harpoon. First and foremost we must look to the harpoon-heads already mentioned as having been found with the skeletons of seals in deposits formed on the floor of the Litorina Sea. Each of the Finnish specimens was made from a split elk bone and has long tapering barbs, some of which are broken short, on one edge. That from Närpes (fig. 4.7, no. 3) has two notches at the base for securing the line, but the lower end of the Oulu specimen (fig. 4.7, no. 1) is missing. The harpoon head from Nörrkoping on the Swedish side of the Litorina Sea resembles those from Finland in the form and position of the barbs, but the number of these is smaller and the method of attaching the line is also different, the base having two perforations arranged side by side.

Thanks to such finds as these, it is permissible to interpret as sealing-harpoons a number of analogous objects recovered from ancient settlement sites which have yielded seal-bones, and even, though with less certainty, a series of stray finds made from time to time in Denmark, Sweden and Finland. Much evidence has undoubtedly been lost through the decay of bone and antler artifacts: there is only a handful of bone artifacts, none of them certainly parts of harpoons, from the dwelling-sites of the Finnish dwelling-place people (Ailio, 1909, 43), although we know from the Närpes and Oulu finds, as well as from a stray find of a single-barbed harpoon head with a perforation at the base from Muolaa, that these people used to hunt seals by means of these weapons. Elsewhere in the Baltic region, however, there are many sites rich in seal bones and in bone artifacts and from these we may recognize many harpoon heads perforated at the base. The dwelling-places on Gotland and Stora Karlsö are especially rich. One may begin by citing the antler harpoon head from Hemmor (Nihlén, 1927, fig. 64), which resembles that from Nörrkoping in having two barbs and differs only in having a single perforation instead of a pair and in being provided with a contiguous groove for stabilizing the loop attaching it to the line (fig. 4.5, no. 4). The commonest type of harpoon is that with a single barb and a single perforation through the swollen base of the stem: at least a dozen have been illustrated from the site of Stora Förvar, which sheltered groups of Sub-neolithic seal-hunters (Schnittger and Rydh, 1940, pl. I, 7–17 and pl. II 1 and 9) (fig. 4.12, nos. 1–3), and another from the sealing station of Visby (Nihlén, 1927, fig. 104, 1). Since the only other mammal at all well represented on these sites is the pig, which so far as is known is not hunted by this method, it seems fair to assume that the harpoon-heads were used to catch the seals whose bones either predominate or are strongly represented. The type of harpoon favoured by the Sub-neolithic community of farmers and hunters of Late Passage Grave Age at Västerbjers, whose settlement and cemetery have recently been investigated (Stenberger, 1939; 1943), had two barbs both on the same edge, but showed a variety of devices for securing the line; as a rule the lower part of the harpoon head was perforated (fig. 4.12, no. 4), but sometimes it was thought sufficient to cut notches on either side (fig. 4.12, no. 5) and occasionally these devices were combined to make doubly sure (fig. 4.12, no. 6). The harpoon heads from the graves were buried with male skeletons, which only confirms that seal-hunting was, as might have been expected, a masculine occupation (fig. 4.13). Although we can point to no unambiguous harpoon heads of the type known to have been used for seal-hunting from the Ertebølle middens of the Danish Litorina coasts, Mathiassen (1938) has published a number of stray examples, barbed on one edge and perforated at the base, which he attributes to this culture and considers to have been employed for harpooning seals. These harpoons, all of which were found on or close to the coast or marine deposits, include two from Møen, two from the Praestø area in South Zealand and one from a natural shell deposit at Svinninge Vejle in the northern part of the island. A few harpoon-heads with single barb and basal perforation are known from rock-shelters on the Norwegian coast, as at Skipshelleren (Böe, 1934, pl. 1, 3) and Skjåvik, Finnmark (Gjessing, 1938, fig. 5); in the former instance seal bones were present in some quantities, but no information is yet available about the fauna from the latter site. Antler harpoons were used by the Obanian people of western Scotland, but there is no good evidence that such were applied to seal-hunting in this area during the Stone Age.

Until more has been established about the ice-conditions prevailing in the Litorina Sea, it is impossible to estimate the part played by ice-hunting at this time. As already stated, some authorities consider it likely that ice was more and not less prevalent in the Litorina Sea than in the Baltic (fig. 4.9), and in connection with this there is the fact, generally accepted, that colonies of harp seals were established in the Gotland area, a species which is generally closely linked with drift ice. At least we may take it that the Gulf of Bothnia was extensively frozen during the winter and it is probable that, as at the present day, ringed seals were harpooned at their breathing-holes; traces of such ice-hunting could be seen in the stray harpoons and particularly in the skeletons of ringed seals accompanied by harpoons from deposits formed on the floor of the Gulf at the time of the Litorina Sea. On the other hand, the harpoon associated with the skeleton of a harp seal at Närpes must indicate harpooning or spearing from a boat or from the ice-margin, since this species does not make breathing-holes through the ice.

A point of some interest in connection with ice-hunting is the role played by dogs, which incidentally form the only domesticated species represented on the dwelling-place sites of Finland, other than those showing traces of influence from the battle-axe cultures: in modern Finland dogs were used to scent out the breathing-holes of seals (Sirelius, 1934, 89);[17] among the Chukche dogs were used to drag home dead seals (Nordenskiöld, 1881, 1, 97); and it may even be that in the Stone Age of northern Scandinavia they were used to drag sledges for seal-hunting. Certainly we know from the discovery of wooden runners in the bogs that sledges had come into use in Scandinavia as early as Atlantic times (Clark 1939, 127–8). The importance of the sledge in modern ice-hunting for seals in the Gulf of Bothnia has been stressed by Ekman (1910, fig. 95) and Sirelius (1934, 92). In Finland it is usual at the time of the spring thaw to carry small boats on the hunting sledges.

For most of the year even in the northern Baltic and all the year round on the coasts of Norway and Scotland seal-hunting was necessarily carried on predominantly on or from the open sea. The occurrence of sealing stations on islets, like Hesselö, Stora Karlsö, Risga and others, some of which appear to have been visited only during the breeding seasons, reflects a lively activity in navigation. The importance of boats for seal-hunting is obvious when we remember that grey seals normally congregate on rocky skerries and that the harp seal breeds on drift-ice. Further, as has already been noted, the provision of boats was one of the main functions of the old seal-hunting guilds.

A further indication that boats were used extensively at this time is to be found in the evidence for deep-sea fishing: both at Viste and at Ruskenesset

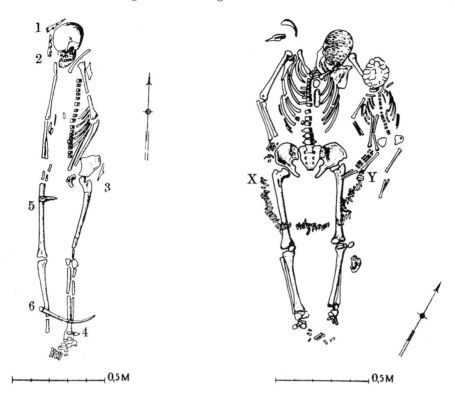

4.13 Burials from the Sub-Neolithic cemetery of Västerbjers, Gotland: left, man accompanied by seal harpoon-heads (1–4), leister-prong (5) and perforated antler tine (6); right, woman, accompanied by an infant and with a cloak fringe of perforated seals' teeth (X–Y) across the thighs. (After Stenberger)

quantities of cod-bones were found, as well as those of ling and haddock.

As to the type of craft used for work at sea we may feel confident that it can hardly have been the dug-out canoe, however useful this may have been for fishing inland waters. Some lighter and more easily handled craft was needed by the seal-hunters.

As there is no evidence that light craft of plank construction were available in this area during the Stone Age, it is likely that skin-covered craft of the same general character as those used for the purpose by the Eskimo were employed. Some indication of the hunting-craft used by the 'Arctic' dwelling-place people of Scandinavia is given by the Norwegian rock-engravings attributed to these people. As Gjessing (1936, 197) has shown, various features of the boats depicted in the engravings at Forselv and Rödöy in Nordland and at Evenhus near Trondheim, recall the construction of skin-boats (fig. 4.6). Gjessing aptly compares them with the Eskimo *umiak*, the profiles of which recall strongly those of the Norwegian engravings: the straightness of the keels and gunwales, the steepness of the bows and sterns and in particular the projections at either end of the gunwale, corresponding with the top of the frame, all support the analogy. Nearer home the paddle-curragh of Donegal displays a similar profile and it is relevant that in the old days seal-skins were used to cover these craft (Evans, 1942, fig. 97 and p. 150).

THE ECONOMIC ROLE OF
SEAL-HUNTING IN THE STONE AGE

To communities dependent on the chase, or in whose economy hunting still played a role of importance, the seal was valuable for its blubber, its skin, its flesh, its blood and its bones. The blubber, which insulates the seal and adheres to the skin when this is removed from the carcase, is especially important as a source of oil, whether for human consumption, for medicinal purposes, for use as fuel or as an illuminant, or for industrial purposes, and it is notable that the decline of the old-style seal-hunting in the Baltic area during the 19th century is attributed to a fall in the price of this commodity (Nordqvist, 1899, 31; Ekholm, 1910, 261). Linnaeus (1745, 215) noted that the fat was eaten fresh instead of butter, as well as being used for cooking omelets, while it is said that pan-cakes baked in the oil were considered as delicacies in Gotland up till recent times (Lithberg, 1914, 122). As a remedy for various ills, seal oil has been used internally and externally both in the Celtic fringe of Britain (Prichard, 1936, 192) and in Finland. Its use for heating and lighting has for obvious reasons been especially prominent in the circumpolar zone with its long winter nights, yet we are also told (Ekholm, 1910, 260) that oil from seal blubber was used for lighting in the Baltic area up till modern times, which gives added point to Mathiassen's comparison (1935) between the oval pottery lamps from the kitchen-middens of the Ertebølle (Mesolithic III) culture of Denmark and those stone lamps used by the Eskimos. In his suggestive paper Mathiassen showed that many of the Ertebølle sites with clay lamps had also produced seal-bones and, further, that chemical analysis of scrapings from the inner surface of one of the Mesolithic lamps had revealed the presence of small quantities of fat. While the archaeological evidence offers no clue to other subsidiary uses, it is perhaps worth noting that according to Olaus Magnus (book 20, chap. 6), writing in the mid-sixteenth century, blubber was employed in Scandinavia for greasing ships' planks and working leather.

Although of less importance than blubber in the Baltic area during historic times, seal skins have nevertheless been put to a variety of uses, and it is reasonable to suppose that in earlier times, when alternatives were more restricted, their role was at least as great. Among Eskimo communities seal-skins are used extensively for tents, clothing, dog-harness and boats (Mathiassen, 1928, 78–9, 88, 94–5, 132–3 and 170–2). The dwelling-place people of Finland and Sweden, who certainly hunted seals, can in some instances be shown to have lived in tent-like structures (Ailio, 1909, 11, 136–7) and it is possible, although not of course established, that they used the skins of seals, as well as of land mammals, for this purpose. Movius (1942, 183) had this in mind when he surmised of certain stone rubbers from the Obanian midden of Caisteal-nan-Gillean that they were used 'for the preparation of seal skins for shelter or clothing.' While no traces of actual clothing have been found among any of the Stone Age communities which engaged in seal-hunting in north-western Europe, significant evidence on this point is forthcoming from the Sub-neolithic cemetery at Västerbjers in Gotland, dating from the late passage grave period (M. Stenberger, 1939, 70–1; 1943, 96). In several instances, all of them women, individuals appear to have been buried in cloaks reaching down to the thigh, the lower fringes formed of perforated animal teeth (fig. 4.13). We have no evidence that these people wove textiles and analogies argue that the garments were of leather. While the source of this leather is open to conjecture, it is significant that the great majority of the teeth belong to seals. Similar finds of perforated seal teeth were noted in two of the Visby burials (O. V. Wennersten, 1909, 202).

Another function of seal-skins, appreciated alike by the Eskimo and by the fishermen of Donegal, was to cover frame boats, for which they were peculiarly well adapted owing to their toughness. Seals were, indeed, hunted off the Donegal coast primarily for their skins (Joyce, 1903, 11, 129), which were also used for clothing. According to historical sources, seal-skin thongs were used both for maritime transport and for land-haulage. In describing to his lord, King Alfred, what conditions were like in his native Halgoland, Ohthere is reported to have said that ship-ropes were made from whale hide and seal hide and that two ropes, one of each material, sixty ells long, were among the tribute customarily rendered by the Finns (Bosworth, 1855, 44–5). Writing of the Western Isles of Scotland some seven or eight centuries later, Martin Martin (1934 edn, 136) noted that seal-skin was 'by the natives cut in long pieces, and then made use of instead of ropes to fix the plough to their horses, when they till the ground.' According to Debes (1676, 171) the Faroe Islanders used the skins for shoes. In our own day Finnish peasants have been accustomed to use seal-skin for a variety of domestic requirements, including bags and boots (Sirelius, 1934, 94).

Seal-meat appears to have been eaten in parts of Europe down to comparatively recent times, especially among the poorer sections of the population, one reason for its survival being that it was regarded as fish[18] and was therefore eaten on fast days. We know that 'seal-meat was eaten more than any other kind of flesh, at any rate in the late Middle Ages' among the Viking settlers of Greenland (Nörlund, 1936, 64). If seal-meat was eaten in agricultural communities in modern times, one many feel reasonably sure that in similar areas it was consumed on a more substantial scale both before the introduction of farming and during its early days. The occurrence of discarded seal-bones on so many dwelling-places suggests that this was the case during the Stone Age. The common European practice in historical times appears to have been to eat the meat salted or smoked, a useful stand-by in time of need. Martin Martin described how in the Western Isles 'the natives salt the seals with the ashes of burnt sea-ware, and say they are good food,' slyly adding that 'the seal, though esteemed fit only for the vulgar, is also eaten by persons of distinction, though under a different name, to wit, ham . . .' (1934 edn, 135–6). According to Collett (1881, 385), the fishermen of the Trondheim area ate the flesh and blubber of young seals salted and found them 'to taste tolerably well, as the young ones only subsist on the milk of the mother.' Seal flesh used to be salted for human consumption in Gotland, where it may also be noted, front flippers were esteemed an especial delicacy (Lithberg, 1914, 122). A liking for seal flippers, hung like game, has been reported from many areas, including Labrador (Prichard, 1936, 112) and the territories of the Iglulik Eskimo (Mathiassen, 1928, 206). The practice of saving seal blood by plugging and sewing up wounds is well known among Eskimos (*ibid.*, 41) and it is worth noting that up till modern times it was customary for the seal-hunters of Västerbotten to fortify themselves with bags of meal or groats mixed with seal blood (Ekman, 1910, 260).

After stripping the seal of its skin with the inner layer of blubber, removing the meat and storing the blood, the hunter was left with the bones and teeth. The former he used as raw material for implements and weapons. Proof of this has commonly been forthcoming where the bones used by prehistoric seal hunters have been determined by zoologists. Thus, it was found that the majority of the bone harpoon heads from Stora Förvar on Stora Karlsö were made from seal-bones, a point of added interest when it is remembered that, so far as one can tell from analogy, these objects were used for hunting seals. More than 60 out of a total of 375 bone awls from the same site were determined as made from seal fibulae (Schnittger and Rydh, 1941, 64); it may be suggested that many of these were used to perforate seal-skins for sewing. As already indicated, the teeth were perforated and sewn along the lower margins of cloaks to serve as fringes among the Sub-neolithic folk of Gotland.

CONCLUSIONS

As to the origins and earliest development of seal-hunting in Europe comparatively little is known, owing to the submergence of the sea-coasts dating from Late Glacial and Early Post-glacial times in the west and to the disappearance of bone from the earliest coastal dwelling-places of the north. Evidence from the Dordogne allows us to suppose that, in Upper Paleolithic times, at least those seals which found their way up rivers, presumably in pursuit of fish, were slaughtered as opportunity offered.

Although we have certain hints that seals were hunted on the shores of the Ancylus Lake, it is only from coastal sites of the Litorina Sea and from contemporary shore settlements in North Britain that we have definite evidence for well-developed coastal activities, in which seal-hunting played a part. Yet, although the Ertebølle people of Denmark, and to a less degree the Obanians of western Scotland, certainly hunted seals, the evidence shows that during Atlantic times this activity was still of minor importance. It was only in Scandinavia during 'Sub-boreal' times (Jessen's Zone VIII) that seal-hunting developed into an occupation of major importance, more especially among the Sub-neolithic dwelling-place people of Finland, Gotland, Sweden and south-western Norway.

The fact that a big development of seal-hunting in Scandinavia coincided with the establishment of Neolithic farming cultures in contiguous areas is surely no coincidence. The marked intensification of activity among food-gathering groups on the margin of farming in the Late Stone Age – and seal-hunting is, as a matter of fact, only one of several fields of activity to reveal a stimulus at this time – was a direct result of proximity to Neolithic communities and reflects in the most interesting manner the influence exerted by a higher upon a lower form of economy. Above all the more populous communities, made possible by the practice of farming, provided a market for wild products, which imposed far greater demands on the hunting and catching economy than were involved in the mere providing of subsistence for the small and sparsely settled groups of food-gatherers themselves: over and above what was needed for subsistence according to the old style of Atlantic times, it was now necessary to secure materials for export. There is no evidence that the contacts between the two economies were one-sided. On the contrary, the demands from either side were reciprocal and were satisfied by exchanges: a real market existed for wild products on the one hand and for the products and accompaniments of farming culture on the other.

To this very day the islanders of Kihnu and Ruhnu in the Gulf of Riga, among whom seal-hunting survives as a specialised calling, trade seal oil and skins against corn, salt, iron and other goods from the Esthonian mainland (Leinbock, 1932, 10–12). A similar relationship between hunter-fisher groups and farmers must have existed along a much more extended front in remote antiquity, a front overlapping on either side of the contemporary limit of farming culture. Apart from the domestic and industrial utility of the various seal products, the meat, whether dried, smoked or salted, and the fat must have been especially valuable as a stand-by for the winter months. No less impelling was the desire of the hunter-fishers to raise their standard of living by barter with more advanced neighbours. Economic convenience and a certain social emulation thus combined to promote exchanges, for which archaeological evidence already exists. Thus it was found that, whereas the inland Neolithic farming community at Havnelev in south-east Zealand imported a certain quantity of seal-meat, the contemporary hunter-fisher group at Strandegaard, some 18 km. to the south-west and situated on the old coast, obtained beef and a few polished flint celts; while it can hardly be proved that exchanges took place between individual communities, such evidence does indicate an interchange of commodities, accompanied by a certain diffusion of industrial forms, as between inland farming and coastal hunter-fisher groups in Zealand during Neolithic times.

Equally, the evidence from Gotland, and notably from Västerbjers, suggests that seal-hunting played an important part in the economy of some communities on the margin of, and in the process of adopting, farming. Again, in certain areas it persisted as a seasonal activity among populations of peasants. The continuity of seal-hunting from the Stone Age up to the present day is demonstrated by numerous finds from the Bronze and Iron Ages, both in Scandinavia and in North Britain. It was indeed mainly as a part-time occupation of peasants that seal-hunting survived in Scandinavia and to a lesser degree in North Britain up till modern times. Even where it continued in certain especially favoured localities to exist as a specialised calling, seal-hunting had long ceased to provide the basis of subsistence, serving, on the contrary, as a medium for exchange against farm-produce.

Notes

1 The neglect of seal-hunting in archaeological text-books is almost complete. Even so compendious a work as Menghin's *Weltgeschichte der Steinzeit* (648 pp.) is silent. For mentions, see V. G. Childe, *Dawn of European Civilization*, 2nd edn, 11 and 194.

2 E.g. one was caught on the Norfolk coast in 1841 (W. H. Flower, 1871, 506), and another on the coast of Lincolnshire in 1871 (Sir H. Johnston, 1903, 202).

3 The rarity of the ringed seal in Danish waters to-day is illustrated by the fact that only one specimen was included among the 819 seals qualifying for the government premium for the period Oct.15, 1889 to Aug. 15, 1890, as against 574 spotted and 244 grey seals (Nordqvist, 1899, 26–7). On the Baltic coast of Germany the ringed seal is rarely found west of the island of Rügen.

4 Nordqvist (1899), who made a special study of the divergences resulting from this isolation, found that the seals of the Baltic and of the Karelian lakes diverged least from those of the Arctic and concluded that they were probably separated later than those of the Caspian and of the Asiatic lakes.

5 During the season 1902–3 harp seals appeared on the Norwegian coast as far south as Vesteraalen and Helgeland (Nansen, 1925, 58–60).

6 *Annals of Scottish Natural History*, 1903, 184.

7 *The Zoologist*, 1903, 312.

8 According to Sir H. Johnston (1903, 206), several were caught in the Severn early in the 19th century and one was killed on the coast of the Isle of Wight as late as 1857.

9 According to Hentschel (1937, 42), the spotted seal accounted for 93 per cent of seals killed off the coasts of Denmark between 1919 and 1926.

10 As noted by Miller and Skertchly (1878, 361) the locality known as Seals' Sand between the outfalls of the Nene and the Ouse is a favourite for spotted seals in the Wash, where they are 'frequently seen in large numbers . . ., basking on the sand banks.'

11 For details and references, see Appendix [omitted from this volume].

12 It may, however, be noted that the monk seal, a species at home in the Mediterranean and adjacent parts of the Atlantic and generally referred to as a separate sub-family (Monachi-

nae), has been recorded from the Grotte de Grimaldi. See V. Gotte, *La Provence Pléistocène*, fascic, 1, p. 43. The monk seal was hunted in the eastern Mediterranean during Homeric times.

13 See *Matériaux*, 1874, 144.

14 Mr A. D. Lacaille has kindly referred me to the record of grey seal bones from a midden at Inchkeith in the Firth of Forth (see *Catalogue of the National Museum of Antiquities of Scotland*, 1892 edn, p. 250, nos, 63–4). The age of this midden is, however, uncertain: the archaeological evidence is inconclusive and the fauna, which included, in addition to the seal bones, ox, pig, sheep, horse and rabbit, seems to indicate, either admixture or a late date.

The absence of seal bones from the recent excavations at Skara Brae, Orkney, is all the more noteworthy, in that seals are still to be seen around the Bay of Skail on which the site is situated (Childe, 1931, 96–7). Miss Margery I. Platt of the Royal Scottish Museum, Edinburgh, has been kind enough to confirm the lack of seal remains from Scottish Neolithic sites. Until a larger number of coastal settlements from this time have been investigated, however, dogmatism on this point would be unwise.

15 According to the table given by S. Ekman (1910, 262), 230 seals were killed for each 10 kilometres of coast in Norbotten and 283 in Vasterbotten: the comparable figure for Gotland was only 22.

16 Many of the records of harp seals off the east coast of Scotland in 1903 were made by salmon fishermen, who found them entangled in their nets. *Ann. Scot. Nat. Hist.* 1903, 184.

17 A more active use of dogs for hunting seals is that reported from the Faroes in the 17th century by Debes (1676, 166–7). The islanders trained dogs to sneak upon sleeping seals from the leeward and hold them fast by the throat until the arrival of their owners.

18 Cf. Olaus Magnus, bk 20, chap. 7 and Martin Martin, 1934, 136.

References

ADLERZ, G. 'Phoca groenlandica i Litorina-aflagring', *Geol. För. Förh.*, Stockholm, bd. 28, 1906, 189–93.

AILIO, J. *Die steinzeitlichen Wohnplatzfunde in Finland*, Helsingfors, 1909.

ALIN, J. and HENRICI, P. 'En bohuslansk Kokkenmodding pa Rotekarrslid, Dragsmark', Gothenburg, *Goteborgs och Bohuslans fornminnesforenings Tidskrift*, 1935, 1–42.

ALMGREN, O. 'Upplandska stenaldersboplatser,' *Fornvannen*, Stockholm, 1906, 1–19 and 101–18.

ANDERSON, J. 'Notes on the contents of a small cave or rock-shelter at Druimvargie, Oban; and of three shell-mounds in Oronsay', *Proc. Soc. Ant. Scot.*, XXXII, 298–313.

BAGGE, A. *Stenaldersboplatsen vid Vivastemala, Vastrums Socken, Smaland*, Kgl. Vitt. Hist. och Ant. Akad. Handl. Del. 37:7, Stockholm, 1941.

BAGGE, A. and KJELLMARK, K. *Stenaldersboplatserna vid Siretorp i Blekinge*, Kgl. Vitt. Hist. och Ant. Akad., Stockholm, 1939.

BECKER, C. J. 'En Stenalderboplads paa Ordrup Naes in Nordvestsjaelland', *Aarboger*, Copenhagen, 1939, 199–280.

BERG, G. and SVENSSON, S. *Svensk Bondekultur*, Stockholm, 1934.

BIRKET-SMITH, K. *The Eskimos* (trans.), London, 1936.

BISHOP, A. HENDERSON, 'An Oronsay Shell-mound – a Scottish Pre-Neolithic site,' *Proc. Soc. Ant. Scot.*, XLVIII, 52–108.

BØE, J. *Boplassen i Skipshelleren pa Straume i Nordhordland*, Bergens Museums Skrifter, nr. 17, 1934.

BØE, J. and NUMMEDAL, A. *Le Finnmarkien. Les origines de la civilisation dans l'extrême-nord de l'Europe*, Inst. f. Sammenlignende Kulturforskning, Oslo, 1936.

BOSWORTH, THE REV. J. *A literal English translation of King Alfred's Anglo-Saxon Version of the Compendious History of the World*, London, 1855.

BRINKMANN, A. and SHETELIG, H., *Ruskenesset. En stenalders jagtplass*, Norske Oldfund, III, Christiana, 1920.

BRØGGER, A. W. *Vistefundet. En aeldre stenalders Kjokkenmodding fra Jaederen*, Stavanger, 1908. *Den arktiske stenalder i Norge*, Videnskabsselskabets Skrifter II, Hist.–Filos. Kl. 1909, nr. I. Christiania.
'From the Stone Age to the Motor Age', *Antiquity*, 1940, 163–81.

BROHOLM, H. C. 'Langofundet. En Boplads fra den aeldre Stenalder paa Fyn,' *Aarboger*, Copenhagen, 1928, 129–190.

BROHOLM, H. C. and RASMUSSEN, J. P. 'Ein steinzeitlicher Hausgrund bei Strandegaard, Ostseeland,' *Acta Archaeologica*, II, 1931, 265–78.

BRØNDSTED, J. *Danmarks Oldtid*, 3 vols., Copenhagen, 1938.

CAPITAN, BREUIL, BOURRINET and PEYRONY. 'L'Abri Mège. Une station magdalénienne à Teyjat (Dordogne)', *Rev. de l'école d'anthropologie de Paris*, VI (1906), 196–212.

CHILDE, V. G. *Skara Brae: a Pictish Village in Orkney*, London, 1931.

CLARK, J. G. D. *The Mesolithic Settlement of Northern Europe*, Cambridge, 1936.   *Archaeology and Society*, London, 1939.

COLLETT, R. 'On *Halichoerus grypus* and its breeding on the Fro Islands off Throndhjemsfjord in Norway,' *Proc. Zool. Soc. London*, 1881, 380–87.

DARLING, F. FRASER. *A Naturalist on Rona*, Oxford, 1939.
Island Farm. London, 1943.

DEBES, L. J. *Faerœ et Foeroa reserata: That is a Description of the Islands and Inhabitants of Foerœ*, (trans. from the Danish), London, 1676.

DEGERBØL, M. 'Danmarks Pattedyr i Fortiden i Sammenligning med recente Former,' *Vidensk. Medd. fra Dansk naturh. Foren.*, bd. 95, 1933, 357–641.
'Subfossile Fisk fra Kvartærtiden i Danmark,' *Vidensk, Medd. fra Dansk naturh. Foren.*, bd. 108, 1945, 103–60.

EBERT's *Reallexikon der Vorgeschichte*, Berlin, 1924–32.

EHRLICH, B. 'Succase. Eine Siedlung der jungsteinzeitlichen Schnurkeramiker im Kreise Elbing', *Elbinger Jahrbuch*, 12–13.

EKHOLM, G. 'Tva nyupptackta upplandska stenaldersboplatser', *Upplands Fornminnesforenings Tidskrift*, XXXIII, 1918, 1–22.

EKMAN, S. *Norrlands jakt och fiske*, Uppsala, 1910.
Djurvarldens utbredningshistoria, Stockholm, 1922.
'Die biologische Geschichte der Nord- und Ostsee,' *Die Tierwelt der Nord- und Ostsee*. (Edt. G. Grimpe), Lief. XXIII, teil Ib, 1–40, Leipzig, 1933.
Tiergeographie des Meeres, Leipzig, 1935.

EVANS, E. ESTYN. *Irish Heritage*, 2nd edn, Dundalk, 1942.

FLOWER, W. H. 'On the Occurrence of the Ringed or Marbled Seal (*Phoca hispida*) on the coast of Norfolk, with remarks on the Synonymy of the Species', *Proc. Zool. Soc. London*, 1871, 506–12.

FRODIN, O. 'En svenska kjokkenmodding,' *Ymer*, 1906, 17–35. Stockholm.

GJESSING, G. *Artiske Helleristninger i Nord-Norge*, Oslo, 1932.
Nordenfjelske Ristninger og Malinger av den arktiske Gruppe, Oslo, 1936.
'Der Kustenwohnplatz in Skjavika. Ein neuer fund aus der jungeren Steinzeit der Provinz Finmarken,' *Acta Archaeologica*, IX, 1938, 177–204.

HARLÉ, E. 'Lagomys de la grotte de la Madeleine et Phoque de l'abri Castanet (Dordogne),' *Bull. Soc. Géol. de France*, 4th ser. XIII, 1913, 342–51. Paris.

HENTSCHEL, B. *Naturgeschichte der nordatlandischen Wale und Robben*, Handbuch der Seefischerei Nordeuropas, bd. III, hft: I, Stuttgart, 1937.

HJORT, J. and KNIPOWITSCH, N. *Bericht über die Lebensverhaltnisse und den Fang der nordischen Seehunde*, Conseil permanent international pour l'exploration de la Mer, Rapports et Procès-Verbaux, vol. VIII, Copenhagen, 1907.

HOLMQUIST, O. 'Tierknochen aus den steinzeitlichen Wohnplatzen in Visby und bei Hemmor sowie aus einem Olandischen Ganggrabe', *Kgl. Vetenskapsakademiens Handl.*, N.F., bd. 49, 71–5, Stockholm, 1912.

INDREKO, R. 'Vorlaufige Bemerkungen uber die Kunda-Funde', *Sitzungsber. d. gelehrten Estinischen Ges.*, Tartu, 1934, 225–98.

JANSON, S. and HENRICI, P. 'En boplats fran yngre stenaldern vid Rorvik i Kville socken,' *Goteborgs och Bohuslans fornminnesforenings Tidskrift*, 1936, 57–91.

JOHNSTON, SIR H. *British Mammals*, Woburn Library, London, 1903.

JOYCE, P.W. *A Social History of Ancient Ireland*, London, 1903, 2 vols.

KJELLMARK, K. 'En stenaldersboplats i Jaravallen vid Limhamn', *Antiqv. Tidskr. f. Sverige*, del. 17, nr. 3, 1904, 1–142.

KOSTRZEWSKI, J. 'Uber die jungsteinzeitliche Besiedlung der polnischen Ostseeküste', *Acta Congr. Sec. Arch. Balticorum Rigae*, 1930, 55–64, Riga, 1931.

LEINBOCK, F. *Die materielle Kultur der Esten*, Zur Estnischen Kulturgeschichte, Tartu, 1932.

LEPPAAHO, J. ET AL. 'Narpion ja Oulujoen Kivikauden hyljeloydot', *Suomen Museo*, XLIII (1936), 1–37.

LINDQVIST, S. 'Nordens Benalder och en Teori em dess Stenaldersraser', *Rig*, 1918, 65–84.

LINNAEUS, C. V. *Olandska och Gothlandska Resa*, Stockholm, 1745.

LITHBERG, N. *Gotlands Stenalder*, Stockholm, 1914.

LONNBERG, E. 'Om nagra fynd i Litorina-lera i Norrkoping 1907' *Arkiv. f. Zoologi*, bd. 4, no. 22, 1–27, Stockholm, 1908.

MADSEN, A. P.; MULLER, S.; NEERGAARD, C.; PETERSEN, C. G. J.; ROSTRUP, E.; STEENSTRUP, K. J. V.; and WINGE, H. *Affaldsdynger fra Stenalderen i Danmark*, Copenhagen, 1900.

MARTIN, MARTIN. *A description of the Western Islands of Scotland*, Orig. publ. London, 1703; quotations from Stirling, 1934. edn.

MATHIASSEN, T. *Material culture of the Iglulik Eskimos*, Rep. 5th Thule Expedition 1921–4, vol. VI, no.1, Copenhagen, 1928.

'Blubber lamps in the Ertebølle culture?' *Acta Archaeologica*, VI, 1935, 139–152.

'Some unusual Danish harpoons', *Acta Archaeologica*, IX, 1938, 224–8.

'Havnelev-Strandegaarde', *Aarboger*, 1940, 1–55.

(with DEGERBØL, M. and TROELS-SMITH, J.) *Dyrholmen. En Stenalderboplads paa Djursland*, Kgl. Danske Videnskab. Selsk. Ark.-Kunsthist. Skr., Bd. 1, Nr. 1, Copenhagen, 1942.

Stenalderbopladser i Aamosen, Nordiske Fortidsminder, III, 3, Copenhagen, 1943.

MILLER, S. H. and SKERTCHLY, S. B. J. *The Fenland Past and Present*, London 1878.

MOVIUS, H. J. *The Irish Stone Age*, Cambridge, 1942.

MUNTHE, H. 'Om fyndet av grasal i Ancylusleran vid Skattmanso i Uppland', *Geol. Foren. Forhandl.* bd. 17, 1895, 583–9.

MUNTHE, H. and HANSSON, H. 'En ny boplats fran aldre stenaldern pa Gotland,' *Fornvannen*, 1930, 257–85.

MUNTHE, H. 'Om Nordens, framst Baltikums, senkvartara Utveckling och Stenaldersbebyggelse', *Kungl. Sv. Vet. Akad. Handl.*, bd. 19, no.1, Stockholm, 1940.

NANSEN. F. *Hunting and Adventure in the Arctic*, London 1925.

NIHLEN, J. *Gotlands Stenaldersboplatser*, Stockholm, 1927.

NORDENSKIOLD, A. E. *The Voyage of the Vega round Asia and Europe*, London, 1881.

NORDMANN, V. 'Danmarks Pattedyr i Fortiden', *Danmarks geol. Unders* III R., nr. 5. Copenhagen, 1905.

NORDQVIST, O. 'Beitrag zur Kenntniss der isolirten Formen der Ringelrobbe (*Phoca foetida* Fabr.)', *Acta Soc. pro Fauna et Flora Fennica*, XV, no.7, 1–43. 1899.

NORLUND, P. *Viking Settlers in Greenland*, London and Copenhagen, 1936.

OLAUS MAGNUS. *Carta Marina et descriptio septentrionalium terrarum*, Rome, 1539. *Historia de gentibus septentrionalibus*. Rome, 1555.

PIRA, A. 'On bone deposits in the cave "Stora Forvar" on the Isle of Stora Karlso, Sweden', *Acta Zoologica*, bd. 7, 123–217. Stockholm, 1926.

PRICHARD, H. H. *Sport in Wildest Britain*. London 1936.

SAURAMO, M. 'Ein harpunierter Seehund aus dem Litorina-ton Nordfinnlands,' *Quartar*, 1 (1938), 26–35. Berlin.

SCHNITTGER, B. and RYDH, H. *Grottan Stora Forvar pa Stora Karlso*, Kungl. Vitt. Hist. och Ant. Akademien, Stockholm, 1940.

SCHWANTES, G. *Geschichte Schleswig-Holsteins Bd. I. Vorgeschichte*, Lief. 1–7, Neumünster, 1939.

SHETELIG, H. and FALK H. *Scandinavian Archaeology* (transl.), Oxford, 1937.

SIRELIUS, U.T. *Die Volkskultur Finnlands. I. Jagd und Fischerei* (transl.) Berlin, 1934.

SIVERTSEN, E. *On the Biology of the Harp Seal*, Hvalradets Skrifter, nr. 26, oslo, 1941.

STENBERGER, M. 'Das Vasterbjersfeld. Ein Grabfeld der Gangraberzeit auf Gotland', *Acta Archaeologica*, x, 1939, 60–105.

    Das Grabfeld von Vasterbjers auf Gotland, Kungl. Vitt. Hist. och Ant. Akademien, Stockholm, 1943.

STOKES, W. *Lives of the Saints from the Book of Lismore* (edited and translated). Oxford, 1890.

WENNERSTEN, O. V. 'Boplats fran Stenaldern i Visby', *Fornvannen*, 1909, 198–212.

WESTERBY, E. *Stenalderbopladser ved Klampenborg*, Copenhagen, 1927.

WINGE, H. 'Om jordfundne Pattedyr fra Danmark', *Vidensk. Medd. fra Dansk nat. Foren.*, 1904, 193–304.

WINTHER, J. *Lindø: en boplads fra Danmarks yngre Stenalder*, 2 vols., Copenhagen, 1926 and 1928.

CHAPTER 5

WHALES AS AN ECONOMIC
FACTOR IN PREHISTORIC EUROPE

Archaeologists have long been aware that whales were extensively utilized by dwellers on the Atlantic sea-board of prehistoric Europe.[1] The frequent discovery of cetacean bones in ancient middens and, in regions such as the extreme north of Scotland and the Orkneys, of implements and other objects fabricated from them prompts one to inquire into the source of the whales. Were some of them hunted, or did prehistoric man confine himself to stranded specimens? Again, it is interesting to speculate on the various ways in which whales, whether hunted or stranded, contributed to the economy of early man.

Most authorities have assumed that stranded whales provided at any rate the main source of supply and some have doubted whether whale-hunting entered the picture at all in early times. Professor V. G. Childe (1931, 97) remarked of the Neolithic settlement at Skara Brae in Orkney that whale-bones 'turned up in considerable quantities, but the amount found hardly presupposes an organized whaling industry. One or two stranded whales would provide all the material actually unearthed', and in a later work the same author (1935, 248) leaves it to be inferred that the whale bones used by the broch-builders of northern Scotland were derived from the skeletons of stranded whales. Again, referring to cetacean bones from Danish kitchen-midden sites of the Ertebølle culture, Dr V. Nordmann (1936, 127–8) expressed doubts whether the boats available at the close of Mesolithic times were adequate for hunting whales and preferred to attribute the finds to stranded specimens. On the other hand, Dr Therkel Mathiassen, whose experience of Eskimo whale-hunting gives his opinion in this matter peculiar weight, had in the previous year (1935, 150) suggested that whales were hunted by the Ertebølle people. No one can doubt that stranded whales were an important source of supply in prehistoric, as in much later historical times, and conclusive evidence for this will be cited at a later stage in this article. The question at issue is how far, if at all, whales were hunted in prehistoric Europe.

Before the discussion can usefully proceed, it needs to be emphasized that many different species of the Order *Cetacea* are found in European waters and that these vary greatly in size, habits, distribution and ease of capture. It is essential, if any valid conclusions are to be reached, that the characteristics

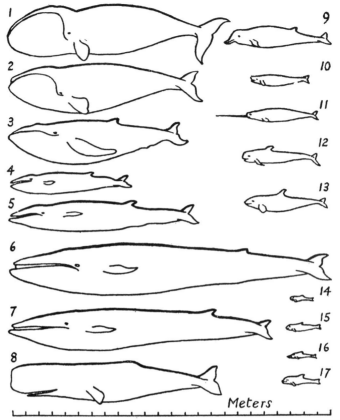

5.1 Whales commonly found in European waters. (After Hentschel, 1937.) For key, see fig. 5.8

of the species illustrated by fig. 5.1. should be distinguished,[2] especially in so far as these influence their mode of capture. At the same time it will be convenient to review some of the main facts about the development of the several whale fisheries of historical times, since in this way it is possible to limit the number of species which could have been pursued under prehistoric conditions.

One may begin with the Baleen Whales, distinguished from the Toothed Whales by the horny plates of whalebone or baleen, which hang from their upper jaws and serve to retain the small organisms upon which they feed. Of the two families of Baleen Whales in our area, the first to be considered will be the Right Whales, from which the Rorquals are marked off by the furrows on the lower jaw and throat and by the fin on the rear part of the back. Of the two Right Whales, the Greenland species can be eliminated as the object of hunting in prehistoric Europe, since the fishery did not begin until whalers began to penetrate effectively the region of pack-ice in which it is at home, early in the 17th century. According to Norman and Fraser (1937, 209–11), the fishery began in the Spitzbergen, Jan Mayen and East Greenland area in 1611, spread to Baffin's Bay in 1719 as the original waters became depleted, and ended up, from 1843 until about 1900, in the Behring Strait and the Okhotsk Sea. The Greenland Whale, which formed the back-bone of the industry during the 17th and 18th centuries, is now one of the rarest in the seas.

The Biscay or Atlantic Right Whale, on the other hand, was certainly hunted as far back as the Dark Ages. The fishery was strongly developed by the Basques, who attacked the females as they penetrated the bays of Gascony to bring forth their young during the winter. According to Fischer (1881), to whose monograph the reader is referred for details, the fishery was at its height during the 12th and 13th centuries, on the decline in the 17th and almost extinct in the 18th. When it began remains obscure, although it would appear from Fischer's account to have been active already by the 10th century.[3] Traces of the look-out towers used by the Basques to spot whales and of the furnaces, in which, after harpooning and dismembering ashore, their fat was melted, can still be seen at several points on the coast (Fischer, 1881, 24). When the inshore whale-fishery declined, the Basques went further afield and, according to Schreiner (1927, 303), had already established fisheries off Ireland, Iceland and Norway by the 15th and 16th centuries.

There is, however, some evidence that the Biscay or Atlantic Whale was hunted on the Norwegian coast long previous to this. In the course of his report to King Alfred on the resources of his native Helgeland, Ohthere described how with five companions he had in the course of two days slain 60 whales, each 48 ells long, the largest 50 (Ross, 1940, 21). What these lengths signify in our measurements is uncertain: Schreiner (1927, 302) is inclined to equate an ell with a foot, but Ohthere speaks of walruses, the males of which reach some 14 feet in length, as being not longer than 7 ells. In any case the whales hunted off the coast of Helgeland were certainly large enough to make Ohthere's bag on the tall side. For reasons which will become apparent, there is no question of Ohthere's whales being identified with the larger Rorquals. Equally, as Schreiner noted, the Greenland Whale must be ruled out as a species habitually hunted on the Norwegian coast, since it keeps close to the ice-margin. It seems that Ohthere can hardly have been referring to any other than Biscay Right Whales. Archaeological support for this comes from a stone slab grave at Hundholm, Tysford, in Helgeland, which yielded, in addition to iron weapons dating from the 8th and 9th centuries, an unworked hyoid bone of a large whale, interpreted by Schreiner as a hunter's trophy and identified tentatively as belonging to a Biscay Right Whale.

Arguing back from historical times, the question whether the Biscay Right Whale was hunted in prehistoric times must remain open. It should be remembered also, that although large, the Right Whales are comparatively docile and can be taken with quite simple tackle. Murdoch (1892, 275) has described how the Eskimo of Point Barrow used to hunt the Greenland Whale from *umiaks*, skin-covered boats of a type current in Europe certainly as early as the Late Stone Age (Clark, 1946, 37). The Eskimo would paddle up to the whale and strike it with a heavy harpoon-head mounted on a detachable shaft and secured to floats. Every time the whale came up to breathe it would be struck again, a fresh harpoon head having in the meantime been mounted in the original shaft and many other *umiaks* and their crews having joined in the fray. Finally when sufficiently wearied, it would be despatched by a heavy lance mounted with a flint head (Murdoch, 1892, 240–1).

As a family the Rorquals or Finwhales were mostly neglected by early whalers on account of their speed and lack of buoyancy, combined with their large size (Norman and Fraser, 1937, 236). Scoresby's observation that a harpooned Rorqual ran out 480 fathoms, or more than half a mile of line, in approximately a minute, gives some idea of their power. Serious pursuit of most species had to wait until the perfection of the harpoon gun in 1865 by Herr Svend Foyn, whose station at Vadsö in Finnmark was the first base for the new fishery. The only exceptions were the Humpback Whale, which when inshore could be hunted by common hand harpoons and lances, but which had the grave disadvantage of sinking, necessitating a wait until decomposition had generated enough gas to float the corpse to the surface, and the Lesser Finwhale, which was only a third the size of the Blue Whale and even so could only be taken under very special local conditions, such as obtained in two bays in the immediate area of Bergen. According to Eschricht's account (1849, 16–17) of the hunting during the 18th and early 19th centuries, a watch was kept at the season when the whales were accustomed to penetrate these bays and wide-meshed nets made from bast were kept in readiness to cut off their retreat. Any disposition to charge the net, which was of course incapable of holding a whale and was intended rather to terrify, was checked by beating the water with wooden mallets and so by setting up a commotion heading the creature back into the inlet. Once securely within, the whale was met with a hail of arrows fired from cross-bows, each marked with the owner's name to secure a share of the quarry. Only when the whale, after many attacks, was seen to be near its end, did the boats approach close enough for the harpoons to be hurled in – and even then it was left to tire awhile before being towed to shore by a fleet of small boats. From first to last the struggle sometimes lasted as many as nine days and nights, which only goes to emphasize the toughness even of the smaller Rorquals: as a family and under normal circumstances these must be considered to have been beyond the range of the prehistoric hunter.

Of the three families of toothed whales commonly found in European waters, only the true Dolphins were the object of well established fisheries during early historical times. The hunting of the Sperm Whale, a dangerous customer, up to 20 metres in length, but capable of jumping clear and of destroying boats, is said to have begun off New England about 1712. The other member of the family *Physeteridae*, the Bottle-nosed Whale or Dogling, was comparatively easy to catch, but the 'Dogling-field', where they concentrate between mid-April and the end of June, is remotely situated north of the Faroes and Shetlands and south of Jan-Mayen; moreover, as Debes commented in 1676 (181), with reference to individuals caught in the Faroes, 'the flesh and fat of these Doglings are not good to eat'.

Neither species of the *Delphinapteridae* family can have played a significant part in prehistoric hunting. The White Whale, like the Greenland Right Whale, is an arctic species, which, though formerly much hunted in the Spitzbergen area by Norwegians and Russians, and though still taken by nets in the White Sea, only rarely occurs further south; for instance schools of White Whales appeared in Christiania Fjord in the spring of 1903, following a very severe winter, during which they were hunted in the Bergen area. The Narwhal, the long tooth of which so fascinated medieval people, is equally arctic in habit, only rarely penetrating temperate waters.

By contrast with many of the whales so far discussed, several of the eight species included under the family *Delphinidae* are known to have been hunted in Europe during historical times and none can be deemed to have been beyond the powers of prehistoric man. The Pilot or Caa'ing Whale, which centres on the Faroes, where it is still taken (Annandale, 1905, 44), used once to be hunted also in the Orkney and Shetland Islands (Harmer, 1927, 36–7) and in the Hebrides (Martin, 1934 edn, 88). From the many surviving accounts, ranging from Debes (1676) up till modern times, it is evident that an extremely primitive method was used: the whales were headed off from the open sea by boats, herded into a chosen inlet and actually driven ashore, a proceeding made possible by the way this species instinctively follows its leader in a blind rush. In this way hundreds of Pilot Whales might be killed in a single day and it has been recorded that no fewer than 16,299 were so taken in the Faroes between 1835–44 (Eschricht, 1849, 16–17).

The Dolphin most abundant in European waters is the Common Porpoise, which habitually moves in small shoals near the coast and penetrates fjords and river estuaries, sometimes venturing considerable distances upstream.[4] As might be expected, records of the catching of Porpoises during the historical period are very numerous. For the most part these relate to the accidental entanglement of Porpoises in fishermen's nets, but there are nevertheless indications that specialized Porpoise fisheries existed in some parts of Europe. Although no regular fishery existed on the Atlantic seaboard of France, there is evidence that one was carried on on the coast of Normandy between the estuaries of the Couesnon and the Bresle and that this was already active by the 10th century and remained so into the 14th (Fischer, 1881, 175). Two fisheries were carried on in Danish waters. One of these was devoted to the Porpoises, which appear in the Isefjord, Zealand, often in shoals of over a hundred, towards the end of March at the time of the Spring Herring and remain until the trees turn green; centred mainly on Jaegerspriis, and carried on by means of nets, this fishery used to yield up to between 300 and 400 Porpoises a year. A more prolific fishery was carried on from Middlefart, Fyen. This was aimed at the Porpoises which assemble in great shoals to pass through the Little Belt on their way out of the Baltic, a movement beginning in November and substantially complete by Christmas. Up till about 1880 the fishery was controlled between St Martin's Day (Nov. 11th) and Candlemas (Feb. 2nd) by a guild of Porpoise hunters, which still mustered ten boats of three as late as 1849 and in 1593 had numbered thirty-six members. The hunt was conducted by beating the water so as to head the shoals into bays across which nets had been stretched in preparation; over a thousand Porpoises were often dragged ashore in this way in the course of a year (Eschricht, 1849, 15–16; Japha, 1909, 119).

There is less information about the pursuit of other species of Dolphin in European waters, but mention should be made of the hunting well into the 19th century of the great shoals of White-sided Dolphins and Killer Whales, which used occasionally to penetrate certain bays in the immediate area of Bergen. One of the largest catches, that made on Dec. 31st, 1834, accounted for some 700 (Eschricht, 1849, 16–17).

A review of what is known about the hunting of the main species of whale in European waters during historical times has shown that several can be ruled out as possible quarries of prehistoric man; in this category must be numbered most of the large kinds, including the Greenland Right Whale, the various members of the Rorqual family and the Sperm Whales. Others, again, such as the Narwhal, the Bottle-nosed Whale and the White Whale, can have played only a very restricted and minor part during Post-glacial times in Europe. On the other hand, it has been shown that Biscay Right Whales, Porpoises, Pilot Whales and other Dolphins have been hunted during historical times by quite primitive methods.

Before turning to interpret the evidence from prehistoric times a word must be said about an alternative source of supply, namely whales stranded in the ordinary course of nature without human intervention, which might on *a priori* grounds be considered the more primitive. Owing to the importance attached by modern zoologists to exact records of strandings, there is plenty of evidence available for recent times. Records have been maintained for the British Isles as a whole since 1913, when the scheme for reporting stranded whales to the British Museum became effective. Within certain limits such records form a useful guide to the numbers of stranded whales available to early man. A number of the specimens noted in the reports have been

STRANDED RORQUALS
1913–1926

5.2 Map showing distribution of rorquals stranded on the shores of Britain between 1913 and 1926

wounded or disabled by modern whaling or fishing activities and might be held to inflate the totals, but against this must be off-set the fact that the records are very unlikely to be complete, especially for the smaller species and for unfrequented stretches of coast. Analysis of the 407 strandings[5] recorded on the coasts of Britain between 1913–26 (Harmer, 1927) shows that, although as many as 178 relate to the Common Porpoise, no less than 14 out of the 19 species listed by Hentschel are represented as well as three rarer species.[6] Of special relevance is the fact that over the same period an average of exactly four Rorquals were stranded yearly; although well distributed, it is worth noting (fig. 5.2) a local concentration in the extreme north in Caithness and Orkney. On the much shorter coast of Holland, it may be noted that a dozen Rorquals were recorded between 1903 and 1916 (van Deinse, 1918, 192–3). In a striking study of occurrences of whales in the Baltic during historical times, it has been shown by Japha (1909) that since 1800 no less than 15 of Hentschel's 19 species were represented out of a total of 55 strandings (other than of Porpoises); among these were no less than 17 Rorquals.

That strandings of whales should so often have been recorded in past centuries only reflects their economic value and it is significant that such records are mainly concerned with ownership. Rights were often meticulously defined: in a charter dated 18 April 1148, granted by Pope Eugenius III to Hilary, Bishop of Chichester, confirming the property of the church, it was made clear that the bishop was entitled to 'any whale found on the land of the church of Chichester, except the tongue, which is the King's', but that in the case of one found elsewhere in the diocese his rights extended to 'the right flipper only' (Peckham, 1946). When, as must often have happened, the vulgar fell upon the carcase of a lord's whale, the machinery of the law was invoked to secure redress and this gave rise to more documentary evidence. Thus, on 15 January 1281 there was issued a Commission of oyer and terminer touching persons who cut off and carried away part of a whale cast ashore at Thornham and Titchwell, being the wreck of Isabella de Albini, Countess of Arundel (le Strange, 1916, 191). It is worth noting that in the first half of the 14th century stranded whales were commonly assessed at £100, as was the case with two washed ashore on the Lincolnshire manors of Friskeney and Sutton, belonging to Alice, Countess of Lincoln, and carried away by certain men, pertaining to whom Commissions were appointed in February, 1340 (*ibid.*, 284). Commenting on the magnitude of this customary fine, le Strange remarked that it was 'difficult to believe that any whale could have been worth a sum equivalent to £1000 to £1200 of our money today' (*op. cit.*, 280). While doubtless designed to act as a deterrent, such a sum may not have been wholly fantastic in the circumstances of the day, when whales were comprehensively utilized and farming was still at a low stage of productivity. In his great *Historia de gentibus septentrionalibus*, published at Rome in 1555, Olaus Magnus maintained that the proceeds of a single whale might fill between 250 and 300 waggons and yield meat for salting, blubber for lighting and heating, small bones for fuel, large ones for house-building and hide sufficient to clothe 40 men (Book 21, cap. 20 and 24).

Before property rights were so well defined, the stranding of a whale, representing as it did in its carcase not merely wealth, but a period of well-being for an entire community, must have been a frequent cause of conflict between rival claimants. In the Icelandic Saga of Grettir the Strong[7] the story is told of how the news of the stranding of a large Rorqual at Rifsker spread afield and of how 'all the famous who could get away went to the whale'. 'The first to arrive were Flosi and the men of Vik, who at once began to cut up the whale, carrying on shore the flesh as it was cut. Then there came the men of Kaldbak with four ships.' On their leader, Thorgrim, laying claim to the whale, Flosi straightway challenged him and Thorgrim saw he was outnumbered. But 'then there came a ship across the fjords, the men rowing with all their might. They came up; it was Svan of Hol from Bjarnafjord with his men, and he at once told Thorgrim not to let himself be robbed.' Then the struggle began and the men of Vik fared ill, until help came with the appearance of Olaf with ships from Drangar, whose arrival turned the tables and enabled Flosi to win the day. A verse was composed on these doings:

> Hard were the blows which were dealt at Rifsker;
> no weapons they had but steaks of the whale.
> They belaboured each other with rotten blubber,
> Unseemly methinks is such warfare for men.

The records from historical times are sufficiently numerous and wide-spread to suggest that strandings must have occurred in substantial numbers on the Atlantic coasts of Europe during prehistoric times. There is plenty of evidence that this was indeed so. In the days when the Wash extended further into the Fenland than it does today numerous whales were stranded and their skeletons incorporated in the Post-glacial silts; among the species identified from skeletal remains may be included the Greenland Right Whale, the Killer Whale, the Bottle-nosed Dolphin and the Porpoise (Skertchly, 1877, 120; Miller and Skertchly, 1878, 342). Further north, the Firth of Forth must have been a veritable deathtrap to whales at the time of the deposition of the carse clays, when it extended some twelve miles west of Stirling. Even in modern times whales are stranded in the Firth, as witnessed by the three recorded by Sir Robert Sibbald between 1689–92 and by the Blue Whale stranded at Longniddry in 1869 (Turner, 1912, 11 and 40): when able to swim many miles further up the estuary, as they could during the period of the Litorina submergence, whales ran a commensurately greater risk of being caught by the falling tide. Evidence that many whales suffered this fate is given by the number of their skeletons found during the last 130 years around the former shores of the Firth (fig. 5.3), information about which was assiduously collected by Sir William Turner (1889 and 1912) and others. Although only a few of the whales have been accurately identified as to species, it has been shown that the Rorquals, including the great Blue Whale, were strongly represented, creatures which, since they can hardly have been hunted by early man, must be regarded as having been stranded. It is of outstanding interest that despite the casual conditions under which many of the early discoveries were made, traces of the implements used for removing the blubber and flesh were found in no less than four instances, viz.:

Airthrey: the skeleton of a whale, estimated at 72 ft in length and identified by Sir Wm. Turner as that of a Blue Whale, was found in 1819 close to the east gate of approach to Airthrey Castle.
'Two pieces of stag's horn . . ., through one of which a hole of about an inch in diameter appears to have been bored' were recovered from close by the skeleton (Turner, 1889, 790; 1912, 5–6).
Burnbank, Blair-Drummond: the skeleton of a large whale, brought to light under

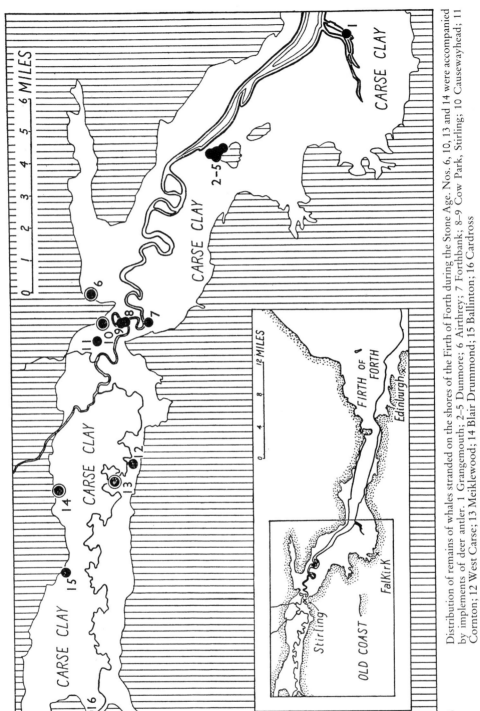

5.3   Distribution of remains of whales stranded on the shores of the Firth of Forth during the Stone Age. Nos. 6, 10, 13 and 14 were accompanied by implements of deer antler. 1 Grangemouth; 2–5 Dunmore; 6 Airthrey; 7 Forthbank; 8–9 Cow Park, Stirling; 10 Causewayhead; 11 Cornton; 12 West Carse; 13 Meiklewood; 14 Blair Drummond; 15 Ballinton; 16 Cardross

four feet of coarse clay when digging a ditch in 1824, was accompanied by a piece of perforated deer's antler with traces of a wooden handle (Turner, 1889, 790).

Meiklewood: during draining operations in 1877 on Woodyett farm on the Meiklewood estate, the skeleton of a Rorqual came to light: 'resting upon the front of the skull and lying vertically in the blue silt, was an implement made of the horn of a red-deer . . . A piece of wood, 1¾ inches long, occupied the hole in the antler . . .' (Turner, 1889, 790–1).

Causewayhead: several portions of the skeleton of a whale were revealed during the cutting of a drain from the village towards the river Forth in 1897. One end of a rib of the whale is said to have shown traces of human work and 'a short distance from the ribs a part of the beam, with one of the tines, of the antler of a red deer was found' (Munro, 1898, 291–2; Turner, 1912, 110).

Discussing the earlier notion that the antler objects found with the whales were 'harpoons', Turner interpreted them quite rightly as implements designed to despoil 'the carcase of its load of flesh and blubber' (1889, 791). The head of the axe (fig. 5.4) found with part of its wooden handle against the skull of the Meiklewood Rorqual might have well served this purpose. A comparable discovery may be cited from the peninsula of Helgenaes, East Jutland, where in an old beach deposit of the Litorina Sea, revealed in the drained Vaengesö, the skull of a Common Rorqual was found in 1920; in the course of its removal by an assistant of the Danish Geological Survey there came to light eight flake axes, two stump-butted stone axes and three flint flakes, the equipment used by Stone Age man to despoil the carcase (V. Nordmann, 1936, 127–8). Here, indeed, from the Stone Age shores of the Firth of Forth and of Eastern Jutland we are confronted by the prehistoric equivalent of the iron tools depicted by Olaus Magnus at work on a 90-foot Rorqual stranded near Tynemouth in August, 1532 (fig. 5.5).

Turning now to the whale-bones from the prehistoric dwelling-places mapped on fig. 5.6, we must face a difficulty which pervades all attempts at interpreting the evidence furnished by prehistoric archaeology, namely the unequal standards of research prevailing in different parts of Europe. As previously emphasized, it is vital to the present discussion to take full account of the several varieties of whale represented; yet, outside the Scandinavian countries and Holland, only a few of the cetacean bones from archaeological sites have been classified as to species. Thus, as regards the material from the Mesolithic midden at Téviec off the coast of Morbihan we are merely appraised of the presence of remains of a large variety of whale and of a small species of toothed whale. Again, very few of the cetacean bones from archaeological (as distinct from geological) sites in the British Isles have been identified:[8] we know that Porpoises were represented at Kent's Cavern and Kintradwell, Sperm Whale at Hoxay and Killer Whale at Keiss and Kintradwell, but it is tantalizing, for instance, to read of the rich material from Skara Brae featuring such items as the jaw-bones of a 'large whale' or the head of a

5.4 Axe head of antler

5.5 Despoiling the carcase of a stranded whale, 1532 (Olaus Magnus)

'small whale'. One can only say that except in so far as they represent Right Whales, remains of large ones like the 'fragments of limb bones and vertebrae of a very large whale' from a midden near Gullane or the Rorqual bones from Caisteal-nan-Gillean, are likely to derive from stranded specimens of species beyond the reach of prehistoric hunters. On the other hand, it would be interesting to know, for example, whether the bones of the Pilot Whale are represented on prehistoric sites in regions where a primitive form of hunting survived until modern times; concentrations of finds in such an area might suggest a prehistoric origin. Again, one would like to know to what extent the smaller Dolphins were represented on the Scottish sites. Meanwhile, it can safely be said that stranded whales must have been an important element in the economy of Orkney, Caithness, parts of the east coast and the Hebrides throughout prehistoric times, and it is worth pointing out that since the larger stranded whales were despoiled as they lay on the shore, being too heavy to move, their bones would as a rule only occur on sites if brought there for use;[9] whale-meat and blubber may, for instance, have played a much greater part in the diet of the Skara Brae people than even the fairly numerous bones imply.

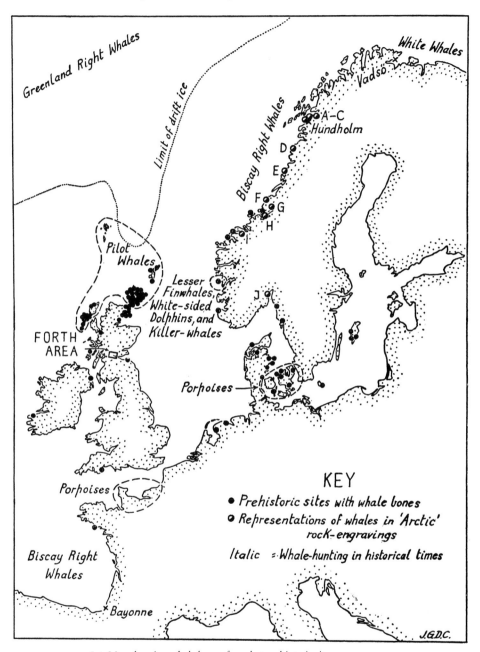

5.6 Map showing whale bones found at prehistoric sites

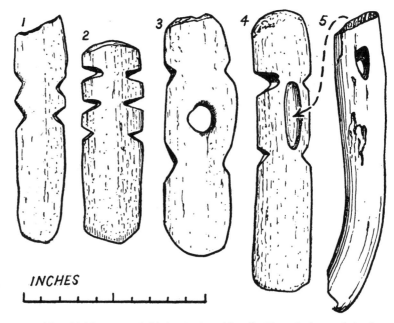

INCHES

5.7 Eskimo blubber mattock blades (1–4) and handle (5) made from whale ribs and
wood. 1–2 from Baffin Land and Hudson Bay area (Boas, 1907, fig. 214); 3–5 from
the Naujan find, Repulse Bay, N. Canada (Mathiassen, 1927, pl. XXI)

In this last connexion one may refer to the adzes (and a couple of axes)
made from the distal ends of ox metapodials, which have been described
(Childe, 1931, 124) as 'quite the most distinctive tool manufactured' at Skara
Brae, some 25 examples having been found there during the excavations of
1927–30. Puzzled to account for these, Professor Childe asked 'what was
there to hack with an adze on a treeless island'? One can only suggest that
they were used for detaching slabs of blubber from stranded whales. The
same explanation may be advanced for the large heart-shaped blades of slate
or schistose stone, perforated for the insertion of a wooden handle, of which
over a hundred were found in the Late Bronze Age level at Jarlshof (Curle,
1933, 100–1). Again, in his report on objects from the wheel-house site at
Foshigarry, N. Uist, the late Graham Callander described (1931, 351–2) a
series of slabs of cetacean bone, having several pairs of triangular indentations
in the sides (fig. 5.9), a type which he recognized as occurring, sometimes
with a perforation, in brochs and wheel-houses in the Orkneys, but for
which no very convincing explanation was offered. Yet, precise analogies
exist (fig. 5.7) in the mattock blades of whale rib excavated from the ruins of
Eskimo houses in the territory from north-west of Hudson Bay to W.
Greenland, where in the frozen soil the wooden handles to which the blades
were lashed at right-angles may still survive (no. 5). As regards their function,
Dr T. T. Paterson informs me that he has observed similar mattocks used for

NOTE The various species are numbered with reference to fig. 5.1		Danish sites	Swedish sites*	Norwegian sites	Totals from sites	Representations on rock-engravings
Balaenidae (Right Whales)	1. Greenland	1	—	—	1	—
	2. Biscay	—	—	—	—	—
Balaenopteridae (Rorquals)	3. Humpback	—	—	—	—	—
	4. Lesser Finwhale	—	—	—	—	—
	5. Sei-whale	—	—	—	—	—
	6. Blue Whale	1	—	—	1	—
	7. Common Rorqual	—	—	—	—	—
Total Baleen Whales		2	—	—	2	—
Physeteridae	8. Sperm Whale	1	—	—	1	—
	9. Bottle-nosed Whale	—	—	—	—	1?
Delphinapteridae	10. White Whale	1	—	—	1	—
	11. Narwhale	—	—	—	—	—
Delphinidae (True Dolphins)	12. Pilot Whale	—	—	1	1	1
	13. Killer Whale	3	1	2	6	3
	14. Common Porpoise	10	3	3	16	20
	Risso's Dolphin	—	—	—	—	—
	15. White-sided Dolphin	—	—	1	1	—
	White-beaked Dolphin	1	2	—	3	—
	16. Common Dolphin	1	1	—	2	—
	17. Bottle-nosed Dolphin	1	—	—	1	—
	Dolphin *sp.* ?	1	—	—	1	4
Total Toothed Whales		19	7	7	33	29
TOTAL WHALES		21	7	7	35	29

* In addition, *Mesoplodon bidens* occurred at a West Swedish site.

5.8 Table showing the incidence of different species of whale among remains from prehistoric sites and among representations on Stone Age rock-engravings of Scandinavia

removing blubber from a large whale driven ashore in the Disco Bay area of W. Greenland as recently as 1937. It is reasonable to suppose that the wheel-house and broch people of northern Scotland and the islands used their heavy whale rib mattocks for a similar purpose.

It is possible to speak with far more assurance about the remains of whales on early sites in Denmark, Norway and Sweden, since in these countries they have almost invariably been identified closely, making possible tabulation of their occurrence[10] species by species for each of the areas (fig. 5.8). From this it appears that the types of whale, which we have agreed were beyond the reach of prehistoric hunters, are barely represented: only one of the five species of Rorqual is present, namely the Blue Whale already described as having been stranded on the Litorina shore in East Jutland; and the Sperm

5.9 Mattock blades made from whale ribs and probably used for detaching blubber, from a wheel-house at Foshigarry, N. Uist. (By courtesy of the National Museum of Antiquities of Scotland)

Whale is indicated only by a single tooth, doubtless from a stranded specimen. Apart from the Greenland Right Whale, represented by a single tail vertebra, all the rest of the cetacean remains are those of Toothed Whales, 31 out of 33 of which belong to the true Dolphin family, half being Common Porpoises. Too much emphasis should not be laid on the absence of the bones of large whales from dwelling-sites, especially in an area in which small use was made of cetacean bone as a raw material. All the same, the overwhelming predominance of the species of whale known to have been hunted by primitive methods during historical times in Europe is sufficiently striking, and the possibility that they were hunted already during prehistoric times cannot be dismissed. On the other hand, the faunal evidence alone certainly does not prove the case.

There is, however, another source of evidence capable of giving us an insight into the very mentality of the prehistoric hunters, namely the rock-engravings of the Arctic Art Group, reviewed in a previous volume of *Antiquity* (1937, 56–69). In this art we see delineated, together with enigmatic signs, boats and human figures, outlines of the beasts on which the hunter depended for his life, among which, in addition to elk, reindeer, bear, water birds, halibut and seals, are no less than 29 representations of whales: of these there is not one example of the species which we have seen to be beyond the reach of primitive hunters; apart from a possible Bottle-nosed Whale, all are true Dolphins, at least two-thirds being Porpoises, but Killer Whales and a Pilot Whale (fig. 5.10) were also included. As if this is not enough, there is a close association between representations of whales and of boats or of quarry, such as seals and halibut, the capture of which likewise implies the use of boats: whales are shown at each of the three sites where skin-covered

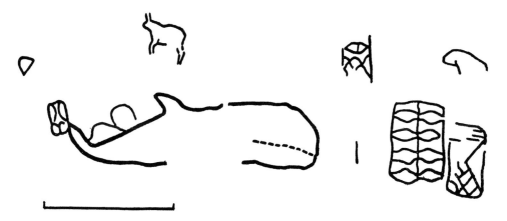

5.10 Rock-engraving at Strand, S. Trondelag, Norway, showing a pilot-whale. Scale of 1 metre. (After Gjessing)

5.11 Rock-engraving at Rødøy, Nordland, Norway, showing a man in a skin-boat, a seal and porpoise (After Gjessing)

boats are represented (Rødøy (fig. 5.11), Forselv and Evenhus), at both those at which seals are depicted (Rødøy and Valle) and at two (Valle and Skogerveien) where halibut are featured. From all this it seems legitimate to conclude that Porpoises, Killer Whales and Pilot Whales were hunted on the Norwegian coast already during the Stone Age. The fact that the proportions in which the different species are represented in the rock-art agree strikingly with those in which their skeletal remains occur on the Scandinavian sites, further suggests that similar hunting was practised on the coasts of Denmark and West Sweden and Gotland.

The conclusion at which we have arrived, then, is that, while stranded whales certainly played an important part in prehistoric, as in medieval times, particularly in North Scotland and the islands, there is evidence that Porpoises, Pilot Whales, Killer Whales and possibly other species of Dolphin were hunted already during the Stone Age, at any rate in Scandinavia. Yet it needs to be emphasized that, if we may judge from the relatively small numbers of bones from early sites, these were not pursued on a scale comparable with seals, which during their breeding seasons must have been considerably easier to secure (Clark, 1946, 27ff.).

One may end by considering in more detail the economic benefits which accrued to prehistoric man from whales, whether hunted or stranded. The flesh and blubber of many kinds of whale were important sources of food, light and warmth. Even at the time of Annandale's description (1905, 37–45) the Pilot Whale provided the people of the Faroes with a useful quota of oil, while the meat, salted in casks or dried in strips, was boiled down as winter-feed for cattle, especially after a poor hay harvest. In the 17th century the flesh was still used as human food: Debes tells how the islanders 'partly melt the fat of the whale to make Train Oil, salting the rest with black salt, to make use of it as of Bacon' and how they 'dry and eat the flesh when it is fresh, the same looking and smelling as Beef; and what they cannot straight consume they cut into long segments and hang it up to dry in the wind, consuming it afterwards in time, as other smoked flesh' (1676, 176–7). Porpoise meat, again, although classified by one mid-17th century writer as

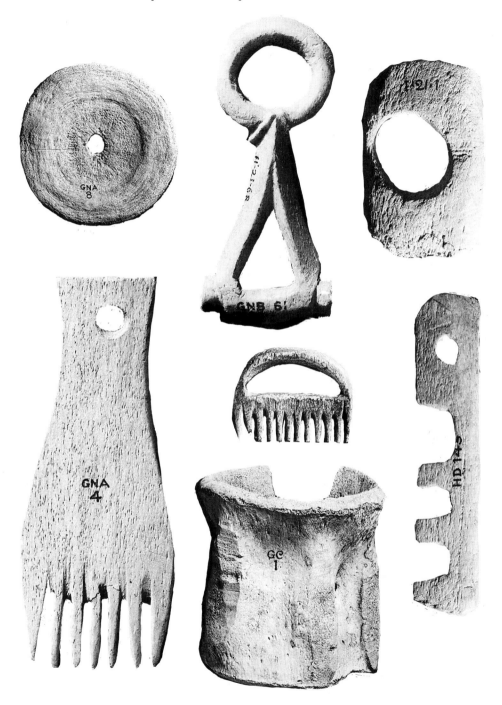

5.12 Objects of cetacean bone from Scottish Iron Age sites: 1, 3, 5 Foshigarry, N. Uist; 2 Bac Mhic Connain, N. Uist; 4 Bowermadden, Caithness; 6 Burray, Orkney; 7 Stenabreck, N. Ronaldsay, Scales: 6, 9/20; 1, 11/20; 3, 2/3; 5, 9/10; 2, 4, 7, 1/1. (By courtesy of the National Museum of Antiquities of Scotland)

'of very hard digestion, noysome to the stomack, and of a very grosse, excrementall and naughty juyce' (Venner, 1650, 106), was esteemed sufficiently highly in earlier times for the great to exert themselves to ensure supplies. As late as the reign of King James V of Scotland, Porpoise meat was bought for the royal kitchens (*Bannatyne Club*, 1836, p. XI). In Saxon times Porpoises were evidently valued: we find six Porpoises detailed as a payment under a lease entered into between the Abbot and community of Bath and Archbishop Stigand between 1061–5 (Robertson, 1939, doc. CXVII); according to a manorial survey dating from the 11th century Porpoises were reserved to the lord of the manor of Tidenham, Gloucester (*ibid.*, doc. CIX); and in 979 Ethelred II is said to have encouraged the export of Porpoises from the Seine fishery to London, by exempting ships carrying them from Rouen from the *tonlieu* (Fischer, 1881, 175, no. 3). The flesh even of some of the larger whales was eaten during historical times in Europe. At the height of the Basque fishery the meat of the Biscay Right Whale was regularly sold in the markets of Bayonne, Biarritz and other towns in the area, and it is worth noting that the tongue was specifically reserved to the Church (*ibid.*, 24–6), as in the Chichester Charter it had been to the King (see p. 94). The presumption that whale-meat was eaten in prehistoric times is all the stronger in that the bones of the smaller species are commonly found with other meat-bones in midden-deposits. Only when the problem of bringing cattle satisfactorily through the winter had been solved by the introduction of fodder crops in the 17th and following centuries did whale-meat fade from the normal dietary of European peoples.

In certain instances the skins of whales are used for leather. Boots and shoe-laces can be made from the skin of the White Whale (Norman and Fraser, 1937, 288), and Ohthere numbered ship-ropes made from whale-hide and seal-skin among the tribute customarily paid by the Finns to his people in Helgeland (Bosworth, 1855, 44–5).

Whale bones served many purposes. Baleen itself, which among the Eskimo is employed for a multitude of purposes, was used in ancient Ireland for making saddletrees, sieve-bottoms and, when suitable wood was lacking, hoops for small vessels (Joyce, 1903, 11, 288). Particularly in such areas as the extreme north of Scotland and the Islands, whale bones afforded a useful raw material for implements. At Skara Brae the caudal vertebrae of small whales were hollowed out to contain pigments and more capacious basins were made from the vertebrae of large ones (Childe, 1931, 136). Similar vessels were used by the wheel-house and broch builders of Orkney, Shetland, Caithness and the Hebrides, as well as by Late Bronze or Early Iron Age people at Kingston Bucis, Sussex. As we have already shown, portions of rib were shaped to form the blades of blubber mattocks. In addition, cetacean bone was used in Northern Scotland and the islands during the Iron Age for fabricating a variety of objects, commonly made further south of the bones of domesticated animals or of metal, as for instance weaving-combs, perforated mallet-heads, knife-handles and copies of metal hair-combs, keys, harness-pieces and the like (fig. 5.12). Elsewhere in prehistoric Europe whale bones were used much more rarely, but a harpoon head made from this material was found at the Ertebölle site of Gudsø Vig, Jutland.

Locally, also, whale bone played an important part in house-construction, as it did in the old Thule culture (Mathiassen, 1927, 132–55), and as, according to Olaus Magnus (see p. 94), it still did in northern Europe up to the 16th century. The archaeological evidence, indeed, extends as far back as Neolithic times. At Skara Brae, Childe (1931, 48) found traces of cetacean bone in an aperture, possibly a joist-hole, in the wall of a passage and earlier excavations at the same site revealed the jaw-bones of a large whale lying across the hearth of a hut, as though fallen from above, suggesting that they had formed roof supports (*PSAS*, VII, 208 and 432).

Another use for the bones, particularly the small ones, if we again follow Olaus Magnus, was as fuel, a usage which likewise finds parallels among the mammoth hunters of Upper Palaeolithic times. Fresh cetacean bones were still used as an alternative to peat in the Faroes, certainly up till the beginning of the present century (Annandale, 1905, 38), which makes all the more significant Childe's observation (1931, 52) that an ash heap, overlying and in front of the fire-place of a Skara Brae hut, 'consisted principally of a mass of charred whale-bones mixed with burnt shells and bones'. Use of the large bones of whales for roofing and of small ones for fuel must be taken into account when estimating the relative importance of whales in the economy of a people from the contents of their middens. Even more important is it to remember that, except in areas where cetacean bone was used as a raw material for tools, stranded whales, a single one of which might enlarge the prospects of a primitive community for a whole season, would normally leave no trace at all in the rubbish heaps of an ancient dwelling-site.[*]

Notes

1 Several species of whale penetrate the Mediterranean and some are at home there, but there is no indication that whales were economically important in ancient any more than in modern times. Dolphins are particularly numerous and were commonly depicted by the Minoans, as in the well-known fresco in the 'Queen's Megaron' at Knossos; although the barbarians of the Black Sea used their fat for oil and ate their flesh salted, the Greeks and Romans regarded dolphins auspiciously as guardians of mariners and refrained from slaying them, except for medicinal purposes (Keller, 1909, 408–10).

2 On the advice of Dr F. C. Fraser of British Museum (Nat. Hist.), to whom I am greatly indebted for reading this paper in typescript and for help in other ways, I have followed Hentschel's system of 1937. Latin names, with the English equivalents used in the text, are shown in fig. 5.8.

3 T. Southwell (1881, 50) maintained that the fishery was established 'as far back as the 8th or 10th century'.

4 Porpoises were observed in the Thames at Teddington in the winter of 1917–18 and one was actually stranded at Venlo, on the Maas, more than 200 miles from the sea (Harmer, 1927, 20–1). According to Fischer (1881, 171), they penetrate 40 km up the Charente and pass up the estuary of the Garonne as far as Bordeaux.

5 Strandings of more than one individual of the same species are counted as one, if occurring on the same day at the same locality.

6 *viz. Mesoplodon bidens, m. mirus and Ziphius cavirostris.*

7 Grettir was born in 996 and died in approximately 1031. The Saga was written down in the 13th century, but its surviving version dates only from the 15th. Quotations are made from the Everyman Edition.

8 In the case of Scottish finds, it must be remembered that many of the surviving whale-bones, especially in the far North, have been artificially shaped, which would often preclude accurate zoological determinations.

9 The geographical distribution of objects made from cetacean bone in Scotland suggests that the material was not at this time widely traded; for instance all the finds are within some four miles of the coast.

10 i.e. the number of different sites at which the species is represented, regardless of the number of individuals involved.

* The article when originally published included an appendix (pp. 100–2), omitted here.

References

Anderson, J. *Scotland in Pagan Times: The Iron Age*, Edinburgh, 1883.

Annandale, N. *The Faroes and Iceland*, Oxford, 1905.

Bannatyne Club, The. *Excerpta e libris domicilii domini Jacobi Quinti regis Scotorum.* MDXXV–MDXXXIII, Edinburgh, 1836.

Beveridge, E. *North Uist: Its Archaeology and Topography*, Edinburgh, 1911.

Beveridge, E. and Callander, J. G. 'Excavation of an Earth-house at Foshigarry, and a Fort, Dun Thomaidh, in North Uist', *PSAS*, LXV (1931), 299–357.

Boas, F. 'Second Report on the Eskimo of Baffin Land and Hudson Bay', *Bull. Am. Mus. Nat. Hist.*, XV (1907), 371–570.

Bosworth, Rev. J. *A literal translation of King Alfred's Anglo-Saxon version of the Compendious History of the World by Orosius*, London, 1855.

Brinkmann, A. and Shetelig, H. *Ruskenesset. En Stenalders jagtplass,* Norske Oldfund, III, Christiania, 1920.

Brøgger, A. W. *Vistefundet. En aeldre stenalders kjokkenmodding fra Jaederen,* Stavanger, 1908. or *Kulturgeschichte des Norwegischen Altertums*, Oslo, 1926.

Catalogue of the National Museum of Antiquities of Scotland, new edition, Edinburgh, 1892.

Childe, V. G. *Skara Brae, a Pictish Village in Orkney*, London, 1931.

    The Prehistory of Scotland, Edinburgh, 1935.

Clark, J. G. D. 'Seal-hunting in the Stone Age of North-western Europe: A Study in Economic Prehistory', *Proc. Prehist. Soc.*, XII (1946), 12–48.

Curle, A. O., 'Account of further excavation in 1932 of the prehistoric township of Jarlshof, Shetland', *PSAS*, LXVII, 82–136.

Debes, J. *Faeroæ et Faeroa reserata: That is a Description of the Islands and Inhabitants of Faeroe* (transl.) London, 1676.

Degerbøl, M. 'Danmarks Pattedyr i Fortiden i sammenligning med recente Former' *Vidensk. Medd. Nat. For.*, bd. 95, 357–641, Copenhagen, 1933.

Deinse, A. B. van. 'Over de Vinvisschen om de Landen in de Noordzee gestrand tusschen de Jaren, 1306–1918', *Zool. Meded. Mus. Nat. Hist. Leiden*, Deel IV, Afl. 1, 179–245.

Engelstad, E. S. *Ostnorske Ristninger og Malinger av den Arktiske Gruppe*, Oslo, 1934.

Eschricht, D. F. *Untersuchungen uber die nordischen Wallthiere*, Leipzig, 1849.

Fischer, P. 'Cétacés du Sud-Ouest de la France', *Actes Soc. Linn. Bordeaux*, XXXV (4th ser., V), 1881, pp. 5–219.

Giffen, A. E. van. 'Die Fauna der Wurten', *Tijdschrift der Nederlandsche Dierkundige Vereeniging*, 2e ser. d. 13, 1914, 1–166, Leiden.

Gjessing, G. *Arktiske Helleristninger i Nord-Norge*, Oslo, 1932.

Nordenfjelske Ristninger og Malinger av den arktiske gruppe, Oslo, 1936.

Grettir the Strong, Saga of. Transl. from the Icelandic by G. A. Hight. Everyman Edition.

Grieve, S. *The Great Auk, or Garefowl*, London, 1885.

Harmer, Sir S. F. *Report on Cetacea stranded on the British Coasts from 1913 to 1926*, British Museum (Nat. Hist.), London, 1927.

Henrici, P. 'Benfynd fran boplatsen vid Rorvik', *Goteborgs och Bohuslans fornminnesforenings Tidskr.*, 1936, 82–91.

Hentschel, E. *Naturgeschichte der nordatlantischen Wale und Robben.* Handbuch der Seefischerei Nordeuropas, bd. III, hft. 1, Stuttgart, 1937.

Japha, A. 'Zusammenstellung der in der Ostsee bisher beobachteten Wale', *Schr. Phys.-okonom. Ges. Konigsberg*, XLIX Jhg. (1909), 119–89.

Joyce, P. W. *A Social History of Ancient Ireland*, London, 1903.

Keller, O. *Die antike Tierwelt*, 2 bd, Leipzig, 1909 and 1913.

Le Strange, H. *Le Strange Records*, London, 1916.

Martin, M. *A Description of the Western Isles of Scotland* (orig. publ., London, 1703), Stirling, 1934.

Mathiassen, T. *Archaeology of the Central Eskimos*, II, *The Thule Culture and its position within the Eskimo culture*, Copenhagen, 1927.

'Blubber lamps in the Ertebolle culture?' *Acta Archaeologica*, VI, 1935, 139–52.

Mathiassen, T., Degerbol, M. and Troels-Smith, J. *Dyrholmen. En Stenalderboplads paa Djursland*, Kgl. Danske Vid. Selsk. Ark.-Kunsthist. Skr., bd. 1, nr. 1, Copenhagen 1942.

Miller, S. H. and Skertchly, S. B. J. *The Fenland Past and Present*, Wisbech, 1878.

Morris, D. B. 'The Whale remains of the Carse of Stirling', *The Scottish Naturalist*, 1924, 137–40; also, *Stirling Nat. Hist. and Arch. Soc. Trans.*, 1923–4, 142–6.

Movius, H. J. *The Irish Stone Age*, Cambridge, 1942.

Munro, R. 'The Relation between Archaeology, Chronology and Land Oscillations in postglacial times', *Arch. J.*, LV (1898), 59–85.

Murdoch, J. *Ethnological results of the Point Barrow Expedition*, 1881–3, IXth Ann. Rep. Smithsonian Inst., Washington, 1892.

Nihlén, J. *Gotlands Stenaldersboplatser*, Stockholm, 1927.

Nordmann, V. *Menneskets Indvandring til Norden*, Dan. Geol. Unders. III R. Nr. 27, Copenhagen, 1936.

Norman, J. R. and Fraser, F. C. *Giant Fishes, Whales and Dolphins*, London, 1937.

Olaus Magnus. *Historia de gentibus septentrionalibus*, Rome, 1555.

Peckham, W. D. *The Chartulary of the High Church of Chichester*, Lewes, 1946.

Péquart, M. and S.-J. *Téviec. Station-nécropole mésolithique du Morbihan.* Arch. Inst. Pal. Hum. Mem. 18, Paris, 1937.

Robertson, A. J. *Anglo-Saxon Charters*, Cambridge, 1939.

Ross, Alan S. C. *The Terfinnas and Beormas of Ohthere*, Leeds, 1940.

Schriener, K. E., in *Osebergfundet*, bd. v, 301–4, Oslo, 1927.

Skertchly, S. B. J. *The Geology of the Fenland*, London, 1877.

Southwell, T. *The Seals and Whales of the British Seas*, London, 1881.

Turner, Sir W. 'On some implements of Stag's Horn associated with whales' skeletons found in the Carse of Stirling', *Rep. of the 59th Meeting Brit. Assoc.*, 1889, 789–91.

The Marine Mammals in the Anatomical Museum of the University of Edinburgh, London, 1912.

Venner, T. *Via recta ad vitam longam*, London, 1650.

Winge, H. 'Om jordfundne Pattedyr fra Danmark', *Vidensk. Medd. Nat. For.*, 1904, 193–304. Copenhagen.

Winther, J. *Lindø: en boplads fra Danmarks yngre Stenalder*, vol. 2, Rudkjobing, 1928.

CHAPTER 6

FOREST CLEARANCE AND
PREHISTORIC FARMING

The subject of forest clearance in prehistoric Europe has suffered a neglect for which it is easy to account, but which is none the less deplorable: easy to account for, because prehistorians have believed that the early farmers avoided forests; deplorable because this belief, now demonstrably out of accord with facts disclosed by science, has obscured a proper understanding of the earliest phases of agrarian history. In this brief article examination will be made of some of the main implications of the knowledge now available about the natural vegetation which confronted the pioneers of agriculture as they penetrated the European wastes, particularly as these bear on the problem of clearance and on the character of prehistoric farming.

As I have shown elsewhere,[1] the theory that early man was incapable of clearing forest and therefore shunned it, cultivating areas naturally devoid of trees or at most only lightly forested, was formulated by R. Gradmann at the close of the 19th century and sedulously fostered over a period of some forty years.[2] As time passed thesis hardened into doctrine, drawing virtue from discoveries which appeared to be favourable, but sufficiently powerful to override doubts. Although not founded on a basis of solid proof, such as only palaeobotanical research could provide, the theory had the practical merit of offering an explanation which tallied with the more obvious facts. When archaeologists plotted their finds on maps showing the drift geology, they found that the symbols concentrated on the lighter, pervious soils and were absent from the heavier, impervious ones. Now, until the Forestry Commission began to change the face of our countryside, it was a matter of observation that the lighter soils were normally free from extensive tree-growth and that such forested areas as remained were as a rule situated on the heavier soils. The suggestion that the lighter soils were settled in prehistoric times because they were free from forest seemed therefore very plausible, and was more readily accepted, since it conformed to the determinist trend of geographical teaching, now happily outmoded. The alternative, that the regions first settled by farming communities are barest of trees because most completely cleared, was overlooked.

At this point it should be made clear that no attack is intended on the method of distributional study pioneered in this country by O. G. S. Crawford and Cyril Fox, whose maps yield information of permanent value.

In his *Archaeology of the Cambridge Region*,[3] Fox showed beyond cavil how, by plotting the finding-places of archaeological material relating to successive periods on a series of maps, a clear impression could be gained of the progress of human settlement in the area studied. As a direct outcome of this procedure he was able to distinguish clearly between primary and secondary areas of settlement, the former comprising the lighter, pervious soils, such as gravel, sand and chalk, the latter heavier, impervious clay soils.[4] Recognition of an intermediate group of loams has modified but not impaired the value of this generalization, the validity of which has been tested and verified in many parts of Britain. It is not the soils, but their 'natural' vegetation, which I am out to discuss here.

Gradmann and his supporters did, indeed, advance botanical arguments to support their case: not content with reiterating that the helplessness of prehistoric man compelled him to settle territories free from forest, they sought to show that the areas he settled were in fact open. Briefly, it was observed that certain species of plants, regarded as characteristic of steppes and heaths, occurred on soils frequented by early man and notably on the loess, that famous corridor of migration into Central Europe. These plants, it was next supposed, were relics of a steppe-and-heath (*Steppenheide*) flora, which in prehistoric times extended over the soils settled by the early farmers, providing them with that treeless landscape then considered to have been so well adapted to their mode of life and to their technical equipment. It is important to note that no proof could have been offered at the time the *Steppenheidetheorie* was formulated, because the techniques needed to provide exact information about the nature of the vegetation existing at specific stages of prehistoric time were not yet available. On the other hand, it is remarkable that Gradmann and his followers closed their eyes to the possibility that the steppe and heath elements found to-day in the flora of areas settled ever since Neolithic times might have resulted from prehistoric forest clearance. But the theory was too well founded: was it not laid down that clearance was beyond the capacity of the earliest farmers?

To return to British archaeology, both Fox and Crawford, the latter in his capacity as Archaeology Officer to the Ordnance Survey, attempted to effect a correlation between types of soil (which they seem to have accepted as constant since prehistoric times) and vegetation, as a basis for restoring 'natural woodlands' on the maps used for plotting their archaeological distributions. It is important to appreciate that both approached their task in a conservative and scholarly spirit: they were determined to show nothing which could not be justified and, starting from the modern map almost empty of forest, they confined themselves more or less strictly to restoring woodland to those heavy, impervious soils, which could be shown to have supported forest extensively in earlier historical times. As a result it is not surprising that their estimates of the former extent of forests were conservative[5] in relation to the views previously expressed by ecologists, such as A. G. Tansley,[6] who had stated emphatically in 1911 that

There is no doubt that by far the greater part of the British Isles was originally covered with forest: in England the whole of the east, south and midlands, except perhaps some of the chalk downs and some of the poorer sands, and of the north and west probably everything but the summits of the higher hills . . .

Crawford was careful to state on the margin of the *Ordnance Survey Map of Neolithic Wessex* (1932) that with certain specified exceptions (exceeding by far what Tansley was prepared to allow) it was 'not claimed that all the open areas on the map were free from trees'. Yet, it can hardly be denied that so conservative a restoration of forest encouraged the notion that naturally 'open' country was more extensive than professional ecologists, even at that time, were prepared to admit.[7] Too many of those who followed ignored the safeguards and reservations of the pioneers and boldly equated the light, pervious soils on which prehistoric settlement was concentrated with open or, at best, lightly wooded country. In point of fact, investigators in this country were influenced, if not directly or indirectly by the teachings of Gradmann, at least by a common nexus of ideas.

The more exact knowledge we have to-day of the vegetation existing in Neolithic times rests on analysis of the fossil pollen released by the species of which it was composed.[8] The technique of pollen analysis was perfected in Sweden in 1916, spread over central Europe during the nineteen-twenties and began to be extensively applied in Britain in the following decade. It allows us to determine with astonishing precision the character of the vegetation of an area at any particular time and to trace developments over a period. Thus, it is possible to discover how important forest trees were in relation to heath plants or grasses, what trees were dominant in the forests and even, within limits, how far cereals were cultivated in the area. The old method of 'restoring' former vegetation by estimation can therefore be discarded in favour of the precise records of observed fact offered by the palaeobotanists.

The result of thirty years of work by means of the new methods has been to show that forests were the dominant feature of the European landscape at the time of the first spread of farming. Stretching like a mantle over the land up to their northern limits of growth, they varied in composition according to soil and other factors, but were broken only by mountains sufficiently high to protrude above the tree-line and by occasional gaps caused by soils too poor to support tree-growth or for that matter even the most miserable agriculture. The soils favoured by the early farmers, notably the loess of Central Europe, supported vigorous forests. Since Dr Alice Garnett[9] has so recently discussed the character of the vegetation covering the loess regions in prehistoric times, I will only allude to Tüxen's intensive study[10] of the north-west German area, from which he concluded that the loess supported a

mixed oak forest (oak, elm and lime), together with some hazel, and that
many of the elements of Gradmann's *Steppenheide* flora, at present found in
the area, were typical components of the former forest surviving from its
clearance. More recently, Dr H. Godwin, F.R.S., has obtained analogous
results from his study of the development of fossil vegetation incorporated in
the muds of Hockham Mere, near the northern edge of the Breckland.[11] At
the time of Neolithic man's arrival in the area the vegetation of the
surrounding Breckland was that of closed mixed oak forest, but thereafter
there ensued a progressive decline in forest trees and a corresponding rise in
the importance of grasses, heath plants and rib-wort plantain. It is significant
of a fundamental change of attitude that Godwin, like Tüxen, should have
sought a likely explanation of the origin of heathlands in clearance by
Neolithic man.

What then becomes of that other prop of the *Steppenheidetheorie*, the
supposed inability of Neolithic man to cope with forest? If we accept the
findings of modern palaeobotanists, it follows that clearance must have been
carried on in the zone of primary settlement effectively enough to allow
farming operations and in the course of time to bring about widespread
changes in plant ecology and ultimately in the character of the soil itself. Even
if for the moment we leave aside the new conception that the primary zone of
settlement was to a large extent forested under natural conditions, there
remain instances where Neolithic man penetrated the secondary zone of
heavy, impervious clays, which on any showing must be allowed to have
carried forest. Let me quote as an example the experiences of Mr W. F.
Grimes in the course of field investigations undertaken for the Ordnance
Survey. Of the Neolithic people in south Wales Grimes wrote

Most of their monuments certainly occur in parts which we may suspect at that time
to have been open or comparatively open country; on the other hand, it is difficult to
resist the conclusion that some at least of the tombs could only have been erected
after a certain amount of clearing had been done,

and of a particular monument that it was

so thoroughly overgrown that its site was lost to people living near it, and was only
rediscovered after prolonged searching.

Such observations[12] ought in themselves to dispose of the notion that
Neolithic man was unable to clear forest if he wished.

Nor is there lacking evidence to show how this clearance was accomplished. It is a commonplace, but one which has been widely ignored, that the
beginning of farming in the Old World is everywhere accompanied by
polished axes of flint or stone. Now it may be granted that such tools could
have been and indeed were used for carpentry, but this craft was by no means
introduced by Neolithic man, and we can hardly find in it a sufficient
explanation for the ubiquity of the axes. Rather must we suppose that the axe

played a part in preparing the way for the new economy introduced at this stage; in Neolithic times, as ever afterwards, the axe was pre-eminently the symbol of the pioneer. It is significant, further, that the polishing of flint should have been developed at this particular juncture, for it has been shown by experiment that polished axes are notably more effective than chipped ones for felling timber. The extra labour bestowed on polishing flint axes was linked with the development of one of Neolithic man's basic modes of subsistence, and it is worth remembering also that polished celts mounted adze-wise with the edge at right-angles to the handle must often have served as the blades of hoes. No doubt it was these overriding needs that caused the early farmers to go to such lengths to secure the best material for their axes, trading stone from afar and burrowing deep into the chalk to tap veins of flawless flint. We may suppose that the flint-mines at Grimes Graves, near Brandon, were sunk primarily to supply axes for clearing the mixed oak forests of the Breckland area: forests which sheltered the droves of red deer, whose antlers provided tools for mining, and the rare forest-haunting Bechstein's Bat, whose bones were found in the mines.[13] Many axes must have been broken in the course of clearance and discarded, a fact which becomes apparent to anyone who walks the fields in an area settled by Neolithic man. It was indeed the discovery of such, in an area assarted during recent historical times and which must therefore have reverted to forest since its original clearance, that led Albert Grenier to exclaim 'la véritable histoire de l'age néolithique, c'est, avec la domestication des animaux et l'invention de l'agriculture, la conquête de la terre sur la forêt'.[14]

Another agent of clearance, doubtless used in conjunction with the axe, was fire. Important evidence of this has recently come to light in Denmark, where layers of charcoal occur at Neolithic levels in the bogs. Study of the fossil pollen from samples, taken from vertical sequences passing through such levels, has shown that the usual oak forest, to which the megalithic people of northern Europe were peculiarly attached, flourished up to the time of the burning. The decline of tree pollen and the rise in the proportions of that of herbs and grasses confirms the fact of clearance, while the appearance of the pollen of cultivated cereals and of a number of weeds, including plantain, points to farming.[15] A feature of the sections is that quite soon they show clear evidence of reversion to forest. The Neolithic clearance was, in fact, temporary, partial and very local. The burnt layers reflect the passing of small farming communities, which for a few years sowed the clearings and then moved on to clear other stretches of the rolling forests. There is little doubt that we are in the presence, already in Neolithic times, of the regime of *Brandwirtschaft*, the farming economy based on the burning of vegetation, which still survives on the northern fringe of farming in Sweden, Finland and Carelia, as well as in the Carpathians, and which was known sporadically even in France up till quite recent times.[16]

The practice of burning felled trees and scrub to clear the land must have played a role of great importance in the earliest European agriculture. It was not merely that the burning cleared the soil, but the resultant ash left so rich a dressing of potash that among the Finno-Ougrians of modern times the yield might be three or four times that of normal cultivated fields.[17] Again, the clearings in the forest needed only the minimum of cultivation to produce crops: for the first few years, according to Carl Schott,[18] the colonists of southern Ontario had only to rake or harrow the ashes among the tree-stumps to receive the seed, a fact which explains why ploughs need not have played a part of great importance in the opening phases of European agrarian history.[19]

Continuous cropping of the cleared area without rotation of fallow rapidly exhausted the potash and stored fertility and involved a frequent shifting of the cultivated area. Assuming that only a sector at a time was cleared, the area of forest within a workable radius of a settlement might have lasted perhaps a generation before a move became imperative: the substantial rectangular farm-buildings, commonly between 20 and 35 metres in length, found on Neolithic sites in central, northern and north-western Europe,[20] denote hardly less and seem to belie the characterization 'more or less nomadic' bestowed by Curwen[21] on British farmers of this stage. Yet even the most elaborate of their settlements were periodically abandoned – occupation of the famous 'Danubian' village of Köln-Lindenthal on the loess south-west of Cologne, one of the few of its period to be completely excavated, was interrupted on three separate occasions during a period of between three and four centuries, while the community shifted to another part of the forest to begin a new cycle of clearance and cultivation. This abandonment of cleared areas not only tallies with the results of Danish bog research, to which reference has been made, but also explains the rapidity with which the Danubian peasants spread over the loess belts from Moravia to the Rhine in the course of a few centuries.

In summarizing the development of British agriculture, Curwen termed the initial phase, ushered in with the spread of Neolithic cultures, the Pastoral Stage. So far as Europe as a whole is concerned, it may be thought that, since the relative importance of stock-raising and cereal-cultivation may have varied greatly as between the various Neolithic groups and since our knowledge is still very rudimentary on this point, we should do better to speak rather of a stage of 'shifting agriculture', a term which has the added merit of contrasting more exactly with Curwen's following stage of 'settled agriculture'. In the case of Britain it is possible, according to existing ideas, to assign the introduction of settled agriculture, with fixed fields and villages, to the Late Bronze Age, but it is too early yet to date the transition in the various parts of the Continent. Indeed, although the distinction is worth preserving as a concept, it would be wrong to regard it as marking a clear-cut division, except where, as in the case of Britain, settled agriculture was introduced from overseas. What we have to envisage in Europe generally is rather a development from one stage to the other, a development which must have varied in *tempo* according to local geographical and social conditions. In this process forest clearance played an important part.

So long as sufficient virgin forest remained within the area of light, easily worked soils, which constituted the zone of primary settlement, the primitive regime of shifting agriculture, associated with tree-felling and *Brandwirtschaft*, could maintain itself intact. In this connexion it is worth recalling that we have actual evidence from Denmark that the forest, at least on certain soils, was capable of regenerating itself after clearance, thus allowing a repetition of the cycle, which at Köln-Lindenthal would appear to have been repeated four times. Yet, after a few centuries, the system must have begun to break down as forest regeneration ceased to meet the need, a process which was presumably more rapid in some areas than in others. The effect of grazing animals in preventing the regeneration of forest was doubtless one of the main agents operating to make permanent the temporary clearances of shifting agriculturalists, but this would naturally have produced a more immediate effect in areas, such as central Jutland, where a poor sandy soil relapsed easily into heath, than in others with rich morainic soils. It is becoming evident that, so far as the poorer soils are concerned, extensive heathlands had already been created as a result of clearance by the end of Neolithic times; thus, the economy of the 'Single-Grave people' of central Jutland was more pastoral in character than that of the Megalithic folk in the eastern zone, and it is significant that their barrows have been shown in some instances to overlie heathland soils.[22] As for the richer soils, it is easy to see that even here, once regeneration had failed in any area to keep pace with clearance, the equilibrium of the old system would soon be upset. The point at which this was reached in any area can only be fixed by palaeobotanical research. Effective clearance of the area of primary settlement need not of itself have given rise to settled agriculture. If, as is widely held, stock-raising predominated over cereal cultivation even on richer soils during the earlier stages of farming, it is conceivable that shifting agriculture may have persisted for centuries in association with pastoral activities. But if permanent forest clearance was not necessarily the immediate cause of the change from shifting to settled agriculture, it was certainly a necessary preliminary.

During the opening phases of settled farming, when colonization was still restricted almost entirely to Fox's zone of primary settlement the pervious soils of which could be worked by means of light ploughs, there may well have been a lull in forest clearance, except in marginal areas, during which the land previously won was cultivated in short broad fields. When the time came to expand into the secondary zone of less pervious but potentially richer soils, a stage marked in central and north-western Europe by the appearance of the heavy four-sided plough and the long narrow strip field, there was initiated a fresh and quite distinct campaign of forest clearance. The main difference between the two is that, whereas the earlier was integral in its first vigour to a regime of shifting agriculture and was for some time only temporary in character, the later was necessitated by the extension of settled agriculture and consequently involved from the very beginning the permanent assarting of woodland, a process which has long engaged the attention of economic historians.

Notes

1 'Farmers and forests in Neolithic Europe', *Antiquity* (1945), pp. 57–71; 'Man and Nature in Prehistory, with special reference to Neolithic settlement in Northern Europe', *Occasional Paper* no. 6, pp. 20–8, Univ. of London Inst. of Archaeology (1945).

2 *Das Pflanzenleben der schwäbischen Alb* (1st edn 1898; 3rd edn 1936).

3 (Cambridge, 1923.)

4 Most clearly formulated for the eastern area in his Presidential Address to the Prehistoric Society of East Anglia for 1933, *P.P.S.E.A.* (1933), VII, 149. For its application to the country as a whole, see his *The Personality of Britain* (1943), 4th edn, pp. 54ff. and 88f.

5 *Archaeology of the Cambridge Region*, XXII.

6 *Types of British Vegetation*, pp. 65–6.

7 A painstaking estimate of former vegetation 'before the process of clearing the woodlands began, and after the establishment of physical and climatic conditions approximating to those of the present day' was given by H. A. Wilcox in *The Woodlands and Marshlands of England*, published by the University of Liverpool in 1933, but completed six years previously. Her estimate of prehistoric woodland (map A) was more liberal than archaeologists allowed and she even went so far as to doubt the status of the East Anglian heaths (pp. 14, 31) and of the Chalk Downs (p. 26).

8 H. Godwin, 'Pollen analysis. An outline of the problems and potentialities of the method', *New Phytol.* (1934), XXXIII, nos. 4 and 5.

9 'The loess regions of Central Europe in prehistoric times', *The Geographical Journal* (1945), CVI, 132–43.

10 R. Tüxen, 'Die Grundlagen der Urlandschaftsforschung. Ein Beitrag zur Erforschung der Geschichte, der anthropogenen Beeinflussung der Vegetation Mitteleuropas', *Nachr. aus Niedersachsens Urgeschichte* (1931), pp. 59–105.

11 'Age and origin of the "Breckland" heaths of East Anglia', *Nature* (1944), CLIV, 6.

12 P. 6 of the Explanation accompanying the *Map of South Wales showing the distribution of Long Barrows and Megaliths* issued by the Ordnance Survey, Southampton, 1936.

13 *Report on the Excavations at Grimes Graves, Weeting, Norfolk, March-May, 1914*, p. 218.

14 'Aux origines de l'économie rurale', *Annales de l'histoire économique et sociale* (1930), p. 28.

15 J. Iversen, 'Land occupation in Denmark's Stone Age', *Danmarks Geologiske Undersögelse* (Copenhagen, 1941), II R., nr. 66.

16 M. Bloch, *Les caractères originaux de l'histoire rurale francaise* (Oslo, 1931), p. 27.

17 I. Manninen, *Die Finnisch-Ugrischen Völker* (Leipzig, 1932), pp. 274–5.

18 Carl Schott, 'Urlandschaft und Rodung. Vergleichende Betrachtungen aus Europa und Kanada', *Z. d. Ges. f. Erdkunde zu Berlin* (1935), pp. 98–9.

19 The antiquity of the plough in Europe has been befogged by the extravagant claims of 'Nordic' propaganda, especially in relation to inadequately dated bog-finds. Recent evidence points to ploughs having come into use during the stage of shifting agriculture, but little is known about their importance in relation to hoes or even more primitive

implements. P. V. Glob, *Acta Archaeologica* (1939), has elaborated V. G. Childe's original suggestion (*The Danube in Prehistory*, p. 45) that obliquely perforated 'shoe-last hoes', of the type commonly found in central Europe, were mounted as plough-shares. It has also been noticed that criss-cross plough-furrows, of the type associated with the light plough and found under Iron Age houses in Jutland by Professor G. Hatt (*Aarbøger for nordisk Oldkyndighed og Hist.* (1941), pp. 155ff.), occur under round barrows in Holland, one of which near Gasteren, Anloo, Drenthe, can be dated to the Early Bronze Age (A. E. van Giffen, 'Grafheuvels te Zwaagdijk, Gem. Werversshoof (N.H.)', *West-Friesland's Oud en Nieuw* (1944), xvii, 121-243, esp. 131 ff.).

20 Such have been found in the Danubian (e.g. Köln-Lindenthal: W. Buttler and W. Haberey, *Die Bandkeramische Ansiedlung bei Köln-Lindenthal*, Berlin, 1936), North Megalithic (e.g. Troldebjerg: J. Winther, *Troldebjerg. En bymaessig Bebyggelse fra Danmarks Yngre Stenalder*, Rudköbing, 1935 and 1938), and Western Neolithic (e.g. Lough Gur, Co. Limerick: *Proc. Prehist. Soc.* (1939), p. 249 and (1946), pp. 147–9; and Ronaldsway, Isle of Man, unpubl.) culture groups.

21 E. C. Curwen, 'The Early Development of Agriculture in Britain', *Proc. Prehist. Soc.* (1938), 27–51, table.

22 For a useful summary with references, see Professor G. Schwantes, *Die Vorgeschichte Schleswig-Holsteins (Stein- und Bronzezeit)* (Neumünster, 1939), pp. 456–7.

CHAPTER 7

FOWLING IN PREHISTORIC EUROPE

Fowling has seldom played a part in the food-quest at all comparable with that of hunting or fishing: the situation of St Kilda, where during the 17th century the 180 inhabitants are held by Martin[1] to have consumed annually some 22,600 Solan Geese (Gannets) and of which the Rev. Macaulay exclaimed in 1758 ' . . . deprive us of the Fulmar, and St Kilda is no more',[2] is an exception which only proves the general rule. Yet, we know that birds helped to vary the diet of most of the communities of prehistoric Europe and that catching them was an activity of economic importance, especially at certain seasons of the year. The only scientific way of estimating the part played by fowling in the economy of any prehistoric group is through an accurate knowledge of the total fauna represented in the food debris, with special regard to the relative proportions of the different species. While this is too seldom available, there is in the aggregate sufficient data to show how far prehistoric man depended on fowling to supply himself with food. As to the methods used, direct evidence of this is all the harder to come by, since these were mainly of a kind to leave little or no tangible trace behind them. Throughout prehistoric times fowling remained at a primitive stage of development, but fortunately the methods used still survived in Europe down to modern times and most are still practised to-day, whether among peasant peoples in the remoter parts of the continent or among poachers nearer home.

One of the first points to emphasize is that the early fowlers relied only to a very limited extent upon taking birds on the wing. This is not to say that the bow and arrow were never used for birds: among the bones from the Hamburgian reindeer-hunters' camp at Meiendorf in Schleswig-Holstein were the pelvis of an Arctic Grouse, apparently perforated by an arrow discharged from below, and the breast-bone of a Crane with no less than four arrow wounds,[3] wooden arrowheads or bolts of the broad-headed type used among modern circumpolar peoples for shooting certain birds, as well as small fur-bearing mammals, have recently been found on Maglemosian sites in Danish bogs (fig. 7.1);[4] and there is literary evidence that eagles were shot by bow and arrow in Classical Greece, as they are among some primitive peoples to-day. But, until firearms became generally available, shooting

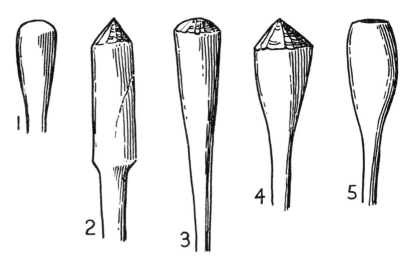

7.1 Blunt-ended wooden arrowheads (1/2): 1, 2 Mesolithic (Danish Maglemosian); 3–5 Modern (Burjat, Wogul and Eskimo)

played only a restricted part in fowling. Slings were probably concentrated, as in later times, on small birds travelling in large flocks, like the field-fares killed in such vast numbers on their way from north Russia to winter in the German woods.[5] Throwing-sticks were a favourite weapon of sportsmen in ancient Egypt[6] for taking wild-fowl as they rose from the reeds and it is possible that the wooden throwing-sticks from the Danish Stone Age site of Brabrand Sø[7] were used for a similar purpose.

A further point which needs emphasizing is that many of the devices used in medieval times for catching birds are thought to have emanated from the classical world and can hardly have been available to prehistoric man save perhaps in certain parts of the Mediterranean zone. According to Lindner[8] these included the use of bird-lime and of nets: the former was employed for taking small birds on the branches of trees and also for catching hawks which were decoyed by a bird tethered between an arched stick coated with the concoction;[9] the latter was of special value for taking coveys of partridges and other ground-birds. Although the use of tame falcons was developed as a sport at an early date in the Near East, the method did not reach Scandinavia until the Migration period and is not generally considered to have spread to Britain until the 9th century A.D.[10] In fact, prehistoric man must in the main have relied upon the various types of snare and trap which occur over extensive tracts of Eurasia and North America and which still survive in parts of Europe, and in the case of birds unable to escape by flight upon the even more primitive methods of clubbing or simple seizure.

An obvious victim of direct attack was the Great Auk (*Alca impennis*),[11] which although agile enough on the sea was quite incapable of flight and was easily taken during the short breeding season on land. As its flesh was quite good to eat, despite a fishy flavour, and kept well when salted, and since the fat, the gullet and the stomach also had their uses, there is no wonder that coast-dwellers went for it from early times. Even the brutish Neanderthalers found its capture within their compass, as bones from La Cotte de St Brelade and from Devil's Tower, Gibraltar, testify. Little is known about the coastal settlements of Upper Palaeolithic man, but bones of the Great Auk have been recovered from Grimaldian deposits in the Grotta Romanelli in Apulia on the heel of Italy, and what may well be a representation of it has been recognized at El Pendo near Santander[12] on the north coast of Spain (fig. 7.2). In post-glacial times the Great Auk no longer reached the Mediterranean, but its bones have been recovered from prehistoric middens from Morbihan to the coast of Norway almost to the Arctic Circle (fig. 7.3). The fact that substantial numbers of individuals were represented at Whitechurch, White-park Bay and Klintesø and the presence at Sejrö and Aakvik of remains of young ones confirm that the birds were slaughtered on or near the breeding-places. The find-spots are hardly numerous enough to show whether prehistoric man caused any reduction in the breeding-area of the Great Auk, which certainly bred as far afield as Caithness, Bohuslän and Western Norway as late as the Early Iron Age. The harrying and final extinction of the species was an affair of modern history.[13]

Many kinds of water-bird, including geese, ducks and swans, are comparatively clumsy during the moulting season and it is then that fowlers would concentrate their attack. It is true of the circumpolar people generally, among

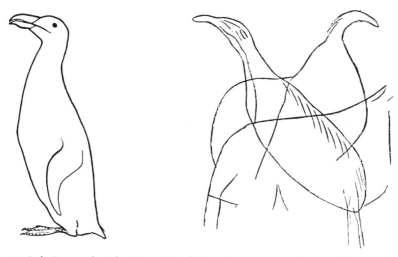

7.2 Left, Great Auk; right, Upper Palaeolithic rock-engraving at El Pendo (After Breuil)

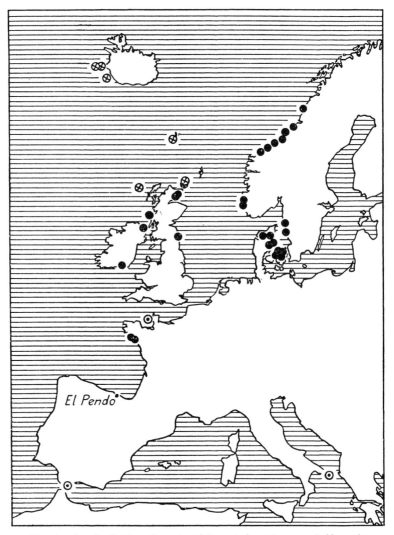

7.3 Map showing distribution of remains of Great Auk on sites occupied by early man

whom fowling is comparatively important, that, as Boas[14] said of the Central Eskimo, 'by far the greater number of birds are caught during the mo[u]lting season'. It was while the geese were in moult that the Lapps of Finnmark ran them down with the help of dogs,[15] just as the natives of Kamtschatka were doing when Krasheninnikov described them two hundred years earlier,[16] and it is at this season that the Eskimo chiefly employ their characteristic bird-dart with side members mounted low down the shaft.[17] Our own English fenmen incurred the wrath of Henry VIII for attacking wildfowl 'in the summer season, at such time as (they) be moulted, and not replenished with feathers to fly . . . in such wise that the brood of wild-fowl is almost thereby wasted and consumed'.[18] Birds can also be taken at a disadvantage when sitting or before they have left the parental nest as fledglings. The inhabitants of the Westman Islands in the Faroes club young gannets and fulmar petrels to death on the nest just before they are ready to leave and take Guillemots and Razorbills, when sitting, by passing nooses round their necks from above.[19] Aleuts and Greenlanders grab cormorants from their nests by night.[20] But it would be superfluous to multiply examples, since the practice of attacking wild-fowl while in moult or on the nest corresponds to basic physiological facts and can reasonably be expected among any people unprovided with fire-arms.

Snares, consisting of nooses of sinew, hair or vegetable fibres secured to wooden stakes, although largely displaced during historical times in Europe by nets, are still very widely distributed and rank as one of the most primitive of fowling devices. They are especially suited to ground birds like Ptarmigan and Arctic Grouse, which prefer running alongside and seeking an opening through an obstacle to clearing it, and are easily taken by nooses attached to forked sticks placed in gaps in a low hedge of birch twigs set in the snow. The Arctic Grouse is still snared in huge numbers in the mountain valleys of northern Norway and on the fells of Lapland and it is particularly to be noted that the trapping is carried on during the season of snow.[21] Similar snares are also widely used to catch water birds, though in this case it is usual to employ lines with a number of nooses (fig. 7.4). Martin noticed horse-hair gins in use on St Kilda[22] and the great Linnaeus observed lines of snares set on the shores of the Baltic island of Färo to catch sea-birds.[23] In Finland, lines are stretched across swimming routes leading to favourite pasturages of wild fowl or close to the shore just in front of a nesting-place, and ducks, divers, swans, geese and even cranes are secured.[24] The Tungus of the Lena Delta set snares across spits of land frequented by wild geese and use a boy or a woman to drive the birds into them.[25] In Siberia, snares are set under water to take swans by the neck when grubbing up the roots of water grasses.[26] Although actual traces of such devices can hardly be expected to survive from early times, unless by the rare chance which preserved one from the Bronze Age in north Sweden,[27] it is safe to assume that they were used during prehistoric times in a wide variety of ways to catch many kinds of ground-bird and water-fowl.

It is worth emphasizing that the evidence of bird remains from archaeolo-

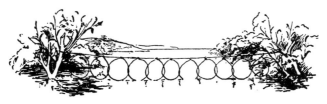

7.4 Siberian duck-snares (after Macpherson)

gical sites may be expected to throw light on much more than the extent and character of the fowling activities carried on by different communities. At all times fowling is regulated to a greater or less degree by the habits and seasons of the various kinds of bird inhabiting or visiting the territory in question. Under primitive conditions, when only the simplest methods were available, the dependence on such biological factors as breeding and moulting, must have been, as we have shown, all the closer. Bird bones should therefore be able to tell us much about the times and seasons during which prehistoric sites were occupied. Indications furnished by the occurrence of migrants or by signs of fowling activities limited to a particular time of the year should throw important light on problems of human settlement and incidentally illustrate the value of an ecological approach to prehistory.

In turning first to the material from the Upper Palaeolithic caves, it should be noted that by no means all the species represented can be related to human activities. Many occupied the caves on their own account, often during intervals in their tenancy by man, and remains of others were introduced by beasts of prey like the Arctic fox. To be quite sure which species were introduced into cave deposits as the result of fowling activities on the part of man, we need far more detailed information about the occurrence and condition of the bird remains than is normally available. One of our best sources of information about the birds represented in the fauna of the Dordogne caves is still the chapter contributed by the ornithologist Milne-Edwards to Lartet and Christy's *Reliquiae Diluvianae*.[28] The fact which stands out from his survey is the abundance and widespread occurrence of the Arctic (Willow) Grouse (*Lagopus albus*). Indeed, the Arctic Grouse, together with the less strongly represented Ptarmigan (*L. mutus*) is the only bird which we can state positively to have been the object of organized fowling by the Upper Palaeolithic cave-dwellers. The condition of the bones, which exhibit clear-cut marks from flint knives, but lack signs of gnawing by beasts of prey, satisfied Milne-Edwards that they really were left-overs from human meals. Both Arctic Grouse and Ptarmigan were again strongly represented in the Magdalenian deposits of the south German caves, including Schweizersbild, Sirgenstein and Wildscheuer,[29] and Arctic Grouse accounted for some 90 per cent of the large quantity of bird remains obtained from Magdalenian deposits in the more recently excavated Petersfels in the same region.[30] Magdalenian man's interest in the Arctic Grouse is reflected in a little-noticed engraving on a reindeer antler stave from Isturitz (fig. 7.5).[31] The occurrence of the Arctic Grouse in such large numbers among his food debris reflects an open landscape with clumps of birches and, to judge from surviving practice, implies the use of snares during the season of snow cover, an interesting confirmation that the rock-shelters and caves were occupied during the winter months.[32]

By contrast, remains of the Arctic Grouse are much less numerous from

7.5 Engraving of a bird, probably an Arctic Grouse, on a piece of reindeer antler from Isturitz, Basses-Pyrénées (After Passemard)

the summer camps of the related Hamburgians of North Germany, and it is significant that, as already noted, at least one individual from Meiendorf showed evidence of having been shot by bow and arrow while in flight. The most numerous birds represented on the Hamburgian sites were wild geese and swans, which must have nested around the lakes and ponds of the tunnel-valleys frequented by the reindeer-hunters during the summer months and were doubtless taken while still on the nest or in moult. The occurrence of at least one crane, and of remains of young birds (swan, sea-gull and, probably, goose) at Meiendorf[33] confirms that the sites were occupied during the summer. Combining the results from the caves and the summer camps, we may conclude that during Upper Palaeolithic times, or at least among the Magdalenians, Arctic Grouse and Ptarmigan were snared during the winter and occasionally shot during the summer and that geese and swans were taken at their most defenceless periods, while on the nest or in moult.

Much the largest and best studied assemblages from Mesolithic sites are those from Denmark. They fall into two distinct groups, one from inland bogs, associated with the Maglemosian culture and of Boreal age, the other from coastal middens of the Ertebølle culture dating from Atlantic times. The bird remains from the chief Maglemosian sites on Zealand,[34] namely Müllerup, Svaerdborg, Holmegaard and Øgaarde, agree closely in general composition, differing mainly in the case of species represented only by single individuals. The birds reflect pretty accurately an inland bog habitat which was not however very far distant from the sea, and which was hemmed in by forest. The only ground-birds represented are a few Capercailzies, doubtless from the pine woods which covered much of the drier ground.

Fresh-water species are by far the commonest and these included the two most abundantly represented, namely Wild Duck and Mute Swan (*Cygnus olor*), as well as Grebe, Coot and Heron. In addition, several species of predominantly sea-birds were taken by the Maglemosian fowlers, including cormorants and gulls and divers of various species, though none of these are represented by more than one or two individuals.

Marine birds are naturally much more strongly represented in the Ertebölle middens.[35] Capercailzie are again the only ground-birds, a reminder that even in Atlantic times pines were not entirely displaced by trees tolerant of warmer conditions. Freshwater species include Wild Duck and Great Crested Grebe, but sea-birds predominate, including many types of duck, auks (predominant among which was the Great Auk already discussed), Cormorants, Gannets and gulls, chiefly Herring and Great Black-backed, and divers. Whooper (*Cygnus Cygnus*) and Bewick's (*C. bewicki*) Swans occur on almost every site, the former often in substantial numbers.

The two assemblages differ markedly in respect of season. The birds from the Maglemosian sites confirm the generally accepted view that these were occupied only during the summer months.[36] The presence of Cranes and of numerous Mute Swans, as well as of young Cormorants and Sea Eagles, indicates occupation during the summer, while the absence of winter migrants argues for their abandonment during the colder months. The story is very different for the coastal middens, from which Herluf Winge cited no less than thirteen winter guests, including, in addition to the two species of swan, several kinds of divers and ducks. Indeed, it was winter migrants which provided the chief victims for the coastal fowlers – at Sølager no less than 29 humeri of Whooper Swan were identified, 57 of Eider, 14 of Common Scoter, 82 of Velvet Scoter and at least 92 of Goldeneye. Arguing from the bird bones alone, it might be tempting to interpret the middens as exclusively winter sites, since the summer migrants common on the bog-sites, such as Mute Swans and Cranes, are conspicuously absent and the sole summer migrants, Honey Buzzard from Aamølle and Pelican from Havnö, are represented only by single bones. Yet we know from Winge's study of the mammalian fauna that the midden sites were in fact occupied throughout the year.[37] The correct interpretation of the bird bones would seem to be that the Ertebølle people carried on their fowling activities principally during the winter months, when numerous migrants frequented the coasts, to be taken in the main no doubt by such rows of snares as Linnaeus noted on the strand of Färo.

Sea-birds contributed to the food-supply of hunter-fishers on the coasts of many other parts of Europe. In western Norway the rock-shelter of Viste, near Stavanger,[38] yielded traces of twenty-seven species, of which no less than twenty-three are attributed to fowling activities by early man. Once again, the only ground-bird is the Capercailzie of the pine forests. Great Auk and Guillemot are the species represented by the largest number of individuals, but remains of Wild Duck, swan, a number of sea-ducks, among them Eider and Scoter, three species of grebe and several gulls and divers also occur. The importance of swimming birds on the coasts of Norway is reflected in the art of the Arctic hunter-fishers: a duck-like bird is represented in a flat bone carving from the cave of Solsem on Leka (fig. 7.6) and swans, geese and ducks are depicted on rock-engravings at Leiknes, Bardal and Hammer,[39] the latter (fig. 7.7) showing what appears to be a brood of young accompanied by adults, all looking in one direction and mostly swimming hard with necks outstretched. Sea-birds were also pursued by the Obanians of western Scotland, the Cnoc Sligeach midden on Oronsay[40] yielding 'great quantities of the bones of marine species', among them Great Auk, Razorbill, Gannet, Cormorant and various gulls. The Tardenoisians of Téviec, a small island off the coast of Morbihan, also took the Great Auk, as well as a large number of different kinds of bird, mainly water-fowl, amongst which Wild Duck and Widgeon were most numerous.[41]

Fowling continued to supply an element in the food-supply of farming communities, particularly those on the sea-coast or in the immediate neighbourhood of lakes or marshes. The inhabitants of the Swiss lake-villages[42] took large numbers of Wild Duck and it is possible that they caught some of these by baiting double-pointed gorges,[43] bone versions of which have turned up on many of their sites. The method, which is widely used for catching fish, is also employed on the north-west coast of North America, in Alaska and in northern Asia[44] for taking duck and actually survives for this purpose on the Swiss Untersee.[45] It is likely that this method was also employed by the prehistoric fowlers of the Norwegian coast. Herons were also killed in quite large numbers by the lake-dwellers and it is worth noting that these were formerly caught in Britain on hooks baited with roach or dace and secured to a stone weight.[46] The discovery of several bones of the Whooper Swan at Robenhausen is interesting, since this bird only reaches Switzerland during the most severe winters and its presence shows that the pile-villages were occupied even when the lakes were frozen. Wild Duck was also the chief quarry of the Glastonbury lake-villagers,[47] but the most

7.6 Bone outline carving of a duck-like bird from the cave of Solsem, Leka, north-west Norway (Trondheim Museum 10815)

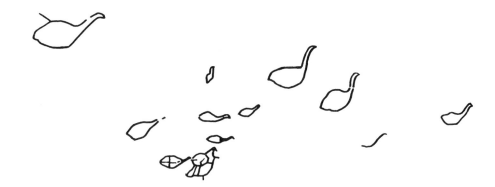

7.7 Arctic rock-engraving at Hammer, north-west Norway, showing a brood of swimming birds (After Gjessing)

interesting finds from the settlement were the remains of the Crested Pelican, including several young individuals, a sure sign, if one were needed, of occupation during the summer months. In the far north of the British Isles, finds from burial chambers and settlements in Orkney and Shetland[48] show that the prehistoric farmers of these parts caught much the same birds as the Obanian hunter-fishers, and for that matter as the St Kildans of modern times.

For the most part fowling was carried on in early times to provide meat, although in certain cases there were valuable adjuncts.[49] The feathers of some birds were particularly sought after. Down was probably collected from nests, as it is to-day among some primitive peoples,[50] but its production in bulk under conditions of quasi or complete domestication only arose under the stimulus of demand from the towns. According to Gustav Klemm,[51] the breeding of tame geese among the ancient Germans developed to meet the demand for feathers from Classical Italy. Incidentally, as has been surmised in the pages of *Antiquity*,[52] the taming of geese could easily have arisen from the practice of raiding the birds while the young were still in the nest; indeed, Macpherson[53] had noted long previously that the Lapps of Finnmark habitually hunted the White-fronted Goose while in moult and took the goslings home for fattening. Among the uses to which the bones of birds left over from meals were put was to stamp pottery, the articular ends being impressed on the clay while it was still soft to produce a variety of decorative patterns. As was first shown in *Antiquity*,[54] this method of decorating pottery was practised by the Peterborough or Neolithic 'B' people of Britain. It is tantalizing that, although the name-site of the culture yielded bird-bones,[55] none of these were identified. Certain sea-birds produced valuable oil; the inhabitants of St Kilda used the oil of Fulmar Petrels for their lamps[56] and the Westman islanders used it also as a spread, like butter;[57] according to Annandale[58] it took only ten Fulmars to yield a litre of oil. Again, the gullet and stomach of the Great Auk were used by Icelandic fisherman for making floats.[59]

In the case of birds of prey, it seems unlikely that these were killed for meat, when so many other birds easier to catch and more generally regarded as palatable were available. It is true that some peoples eat the flesh of eagles – an 18th century observer[60] noted that this was regarded as a delicacy in the Ukraine and among the natives of Kamtschatka – but some other explanation is needed to account for the presence of so many remains of these birds on prehistoric sites. It is reasonable to suppose that birds of prey were killed among prehistoric farmers as vermin: eagles, in particular, whose depredations include the carrying off of young lambs, have been harried by sheep farmers during historical times and their rapid decline in the Scottish Highlands is closely linked with the spread of sheep runs.[61] The Swiss lake-villages, it is worth noting, have yielded remains of Kites, Goshawkes, White-tailed Eagles, Golden Eagles and Sparrow-hawks[62] and birds of prey are known from the Glastonbury lake-village,[63] several prehistoric sites in Orkney and Shetland[64] and many other habitations of farming communities.

The notion that birds of prey were killed as vermin can hardly be applied to account for their presence, often in considerable numbers, on the settlements of hunter-fishers, nor is it the only possible explanation for their presence on those of prehistoric peasants. The suggestion made by the Danish zoologist, M. Degerbøl[65] to account for the numerous remains of White-tailed Eagle at the Maglemosian site of Øgaard, that they were killed for their feathers, needed for fletching arrows, is worth some fuller consideration. The occurrence at Øgaard is no isolated one:[66] remains of the same kind of eagle were found at each of the three other classic Maglemosian sites on Zealand, as well as in most of the Ertebølle middens, and on Mesolithic sites as widely separated as Viste and Téviec. It has long been recognized that the Maglemosians were skilled archers and excavations in the peat-bogs during the war have brought to light a couple of single-piece wooden bows with constricted hand-grips and a number of wooden arrow-shafts.[67] The recovery of arrows with feathers intact can hardly be expected from the bogs, since, although feathers will survive when desiccated – Tut-ank-amen's tomb yielded a large number of fletched arrows[68] – they perish under conditions of water-logging which preserve wood and many other organic materials: if proof were needed one might point to the arrow-shafts from the famous Iron Age bog-finds of Vimose[69] and Thorsbjerg,[70] which tantalizingly show impressions of the threads used to bind on the feathers. From representations[71] on calcareous pebbles from La Colombière it is certain that the feathering of projectiles goes back to Upper Palaeolithic times, and there is every reason for thinking that a device so calculated to steady the flight of an arrow was used by the Mesolithic inheritors of the old hunting tradition.

What reason is there to suppose that they used eagle feathers for this particular purpose? One must admit that concrete evidence is unlikely, for the reason stated, ever to be forthcoming. Yet, it is highly probable. The use of eagle feathers for fletching, particularly the pinion, but also the tail feathers, is extremely widely distributed in northern Eurasia and in parts of North America, and, indeed it survived until comparatively recently in Finland and in Scandinavia. According to Macpherson,[72] the province of Manchuria was still rendering yearly tribute to Pekin towards the end of the 19th century in the form of three hundred skins of the Large Spotted Eagle (*Aquila clanga*), the tail feathers being used to make fans for mandarins and the pinion ones for fletching the famed Manchu arrows. The Japanese also required eagle feathers for their arrows. So great was the demand that feathers were imported from primitive peoples living to the north. It is related by C. H. Hawes[73] of his travels in Sakhalin at the beginning of the present century that the Gilyaks pressed him to shoot White-tailed Eagles for their tail-feathers, 'for which they declared the Chinese gave them three dollars', and, again, that the same people removed young eagles from the nest and reared them in the hopes of selling the tails to the Japanese. A similar practice was reported by an 18th century traveller[74] in the Kuriles, where there was hardly a yurt without its eagle, fed constantly to provide the feathers needed for fletching arrows or for trade to distant islanders, presumably Japanese.

Eagle feathers were also used for fletching arrows among the Beothuc Indians of Labrador,[75] the Eskimo of Greenland[76] and the Golds of the Amur.[77] At the other end of the circumpolar zone the feathers of the White-tailed Eagle were used for the same purpose in Finland up to the 18th[78] and in Scandinavia during the 16th century.[79] To judge from the passage in Olaus Magnus[80] referring to the reaction of eagle feathers when brought up against those of the humbler bird in the same quiver, the eagle must have been supplemented by the goose as a source of feathers for fletching by the middle of the 16th century in the north, a process which had long before been carried to its logical conclusion in the more intensely farmed areas of Europe where goose feathers reigned supreme during medieval times.[81] As to the antiquity in Europe of this use of the eagle's feathers, one need only cite Hesiod's description[82] of the arrows of Hercules 'at the back end covered with the feathers of a dusky eagle'. This, combined with the fact that eagles were commonly shot by bow and arrow accounts for Aesop's fable, 'The Eagle and the Arrow', in which the victim is made to regret ''tis an added grief that with my own feathers I am slain', a conceit of which later poets made ample use, among them Byron:

So the struck eagle, stretched upon the plain,
No more through rolling clouds to soar again,
View'd his own feather on the fatal dart,
And wing'd the shaft that quiver'd in his heart.
English Bards and Scotch Reviewers

Considered as so much raw material the pinion and tail feathers of the eagle are eminently suited for fletching arrows, but not notably more so than those of the goose. Certainly it was not for their physical properties alone that eagle feathers were preferred so long among so many different peoples. Their efficacy was not merely mechanical; it was also magical. The archer wished to direct the aim and increase the force of his arrow by appropriating something of the eagle's power and keenness of vision. Among modern primitive peoples the potency of the eagle is identified not only with the pinions on which it soars in the heaven, but also with the beak and claws by which it secures its prey. The association of bird beaks with hunting luck is quite common – raven beaks for instance are used as amulets by Aleut hunters[83] and the natives of Kamtschatka and the Kuriles[84] wear puffin bills round their necks as talismans. Eagle claws were used even in 19th century Europe to cure various ills: Landt recorded in 1810 that they were applied in the Faroes as remedies for jaundice;[85] and in Finland they were used together with bear claws for scratching the painful place.[86]

A regard for the beaks and claws of eagles and other members of the family *Falconidae* can be traced far back in European prehistory. At least three cases can be cited from the Early Bronze Age of England of falcon beaks associated with burials, two of them of archers. Mortimer records 'the upper part of a hawk's head and beak' from barrow c.38 at Driffield, East Yorkshire.[87] It lay on the pavement of a stone cist in front of a bowman accompanied by his beaker and accoutred with bronze dagger and archer's wrist-guard of bone. Thomas Bateman had previously noted two analogous finds: 'the beak of a bird of the falcon species' discovered among the animal bones in Slip Lowe, a small barrow near Wetton, Staffs., under which was buried a young archer accompanied by two flint arrowheads;[88] and the lower mandible of a hawk from a barrow near Stakor Hill, Buxton, found with two flint implements between two inhumation burials secondary to a burial accompanied by a beaker and a piece of bronze.[89] Although Thurnam refers to 'the claw of an eagle or vulture in the collection at Stourhead',[90] there appears to be no trace of this in Colt Hoare's book or in his collection, now in Devizes Museum.[91] From the Stone Cist period of south Sweden one can cite four eagle claws, perforated for suspension, found together with a bone pin in grave 2 of barrow 1 at Abekås, Skivarps sn., Scania.[92] Lastly, it is worth noting that the Danish mesolithic site Hallebygaarde yielded the claw joint of a White-tailed Eagle showing distinct cut-marks.[93] These beaks and claws are concrete evidence for the regard in which the eagle and its relations were held in prehistoric Europe. If ever a prehistoric arrow is found with its feathers intact, the odds are long that these will prove to come from the pinions or tail of an eagle.

Notes

1 M. Martin, *A Late Voyage to St Kilda*, p. 457 (orig. publ. 1698), Stirling, 1934.

2 Quoted from James Ritchie, *The influence of man on animal life in Scotland*, Cambridge 1920, p. 147. Fowling has also been developed to an exceptional degree in the Faroes. For an excellent description, see Kenneth Williamson's *The Atlantic Islands* (London). ch. 6, which appeared while this article was in press.

3 A. Rust, *Das altsteinzeitliche Rentierjägerlager Meiendorf,* Neumunster, 1937, s. 108, taf. 53.

4 C. J. Becker, 'En 8000-aarig stenalderboplads i Holmegaards Mose', *Fra Nationalmuseets Arbejdsmark*, 1945, pp. 66–7.

5 G. Klemm reckoned that some 1,200,000 field-fares were taken in this way every year in E. Prussia alone. *Allgemeine Culturwissenschaft. Die materiellen Grundlagen menschlicher Kultur*, Leipzig, 1855, s. 117.

6 J. G. Wilkinson, *Manners and Customs of the Ancient Egyptians,* London, 1837, vol. III, p. 38.

7 L. Franz, 'Alteuropäische Wurfhölzer', *P. W. Schmidt Festschrift* (ed. W. Koppers), Vienna, 1928, s. 800–8.

8 K. Lindner, *Die Jagd im frühen Mittelalter*, Berlin, 1940, s. 339–40, 409.

9 According to Lindner, this consisted of mistletoe berries, dried, pounded, soaked in water for twelve days and again pulverized.

10 H. Shetelig and H. Falk, *Scandinavian Archaeology*, Oxford, 1937, p. 306; *Encyclopaedia Britannica*, 11th edn, vol. x, p. 141.

11 For a general account, see Symington Grieve, *The Great Auk, or Garefowl. Its history, archaeology and remains*, London, 1885. A more comprehensive account is given by W. Blasius in Naumann's *Naturgeschichte der Vögel Mitteleuropas*, bd. XII, 169–208. Many of the finds of Great Auk remains from archaeological sites have been made since. For the Broch of Eyre reference and for information about the bones from Elsay, I am indebted to Miss D. M. A. Bate.

12 H. Breuil *et al., Les Cavernes de la région Cantabriques*, Monaco, 1911, pp. 38–9.

13 The last pair was killed in June, 1844, on the islet of Eldey, south-west of Iceland.

14 Franz Boas, 'The Central Eskimo', *6th Ann. Rep. Bureau of Ethnology*, Washington, 1888, pp. 401–669; see p. 512.

15 H. A. Macpherson, *A History of Fowling*, Edinburgh, 1897, p. 122.

16 S. Krasheninnikov, *History of Kamtschatka and the Kurilski Islands, with countries adjacent* (J. Grieve's transl.), Gloucester, 1764, pp. 158–9.

17 J. Murdoch, *Ethnological Results of the Point Barrow Expedition, 1881–83*, Washington, 1893, pp. 210–11; K. Birket-Smith, *Ethnography of the Egesminde District*, Copenhagen, 1924, p. 352.

18 An acte agenst Destruccyon of Wyldfowle. 25 Henry VIII, cap. II. Quoted from H. C. Darby, *The Draining of the Fens*, Cambridge, 1940, p. 9.

19 N. Annandale, *The Faroes and Iceland*, Oxford, 1905, p. 123. See also Williamson, *op. cit.*

20 W. Jochelson, *History, Ethnology and Anthropology of the Aleut*, Carnegie Inst. Pub. 432, Washington, 1933, pp. 53–4.

21 U. T. Sirelius, *Die Volkskultur Finnlands, I. Jagd und Fischerei*, Berlin, 1934, s. 65–6. J. Böe, *Le Finnmarkien*, Oslo, 1936, p. 254.

22 *Op.cit.*, p. 316.

23 C. von Linné, *Ölandska och Gothländska Resa*, Stockholm, 1745, p. 204.

24 Sirelius, *op. cit.*, p. 66.

25 Macpherson, *op. cit.*, pp. 222–3.

26 *Ibid.*, p. 231.

27 E. Granlund, *Sver. Geolog. Unders. ser. Ca. Avhandl. och Uppsatser,* no. 26, p. 143. I have to thank Dr Gosta Berg of Stockholm for this reference.

28 London, 1865–75, pp. 226–47.

29 R. R. Schmidt, *Die diluviale Vorzeit Deutschlands*, Stuttgart, 1912, s. 169, 191, 207.

30 E. Peters and V. Toepfer,'Der Abschluss der Grabungen am Petersfels bei Engen im badischen Hegau', *Prähist. Zeit.,* XXIII (1932), s. 155–99, esp.s. 166.

31 E. Passemard, 'La caverne d'Isturitz', *Rev. arch.,* XV (1922), pp. 1–45, esp. p. 40, fig. 38.

32 R. de St.-Périer, 'Les migrations des tribus magdaléniennes des Pyrénées, *Rev. anthrop.* May-June 1920. Cf. *Proc. Prehist. Soc.* V (1939), p. 268.

33 A. Rust, *op. cit.* s. 55–7.

34 H. Winge, *Aarbøger*, 1903, pp. 194–5; 1919, p. 128–9; 1924, pp. 28–9; and M. Degerböl in T. Mathiassen *et al., Stenalderbopladsen i Aamosen,* Copenhagen, 1943, pp. 190–1.

35 H. Winge, 'Om jordfundne Fügle fra Danmark', *Vidensk. Medd. fra den naturhist. For. i. Kjöbenhavn* (1903), pp. 61–109.

36 J. G. D. Clark, *The Mesolithic Settlement of Northern Europe,* Cambridge, 1936, p. 90.

37 *Affaldsdynger,* Copenhagen, 1900, p. 195; V. Nordmann, *Menneskets Indvandring til Norden,* Copenhagen, 1936, p. 128. Clark, *op. cit.,* p. 51.

38 A. W. Brøgger, *Vistefundet. En aeldre stenalders kjokkenmodding fra Jaederen,* Stavanger, 1908, pp. 9–11.

39 *Leiknes:* G. Gjessing, *Arktiske Helleristninger i Nord-Norge,* Oslo, 1932, pl. IX; G. Hallström, *Monumental Art of Northern Europe from the Stone Age,* Stockholm, 1938, p. 107. *Bardal;* G. Gjessing, *Nordenfjelske Ristninger og Malinger av den arktiske gruppe,* Oslo, 1936, pp. 47–50, pl. LVII; Hallström, *op. cit.,* pp. 300–2, pl. XXIV. *Hammer:* Gjessing, 1936, *op. cit.,* pp. 25–9, pl. LIV.

40 *Proc. Soc. Ant. Scot.,* XLVIII, p. 105.

41 M. and S. -J. Péquart, *Téviec. Station-nécropole mésolithique du Morbihan,* Paris, 1937, pp. 101–2.

42 L. Rütimeyer, *Die Fauna der Pfahlbauten der Schweiz,* Zürich, 1862, s. 113–15; H. Reinerth, *Die Jüngere Steinzeit der Schweiz,* Augsburg, 1926, table in App. II; also, *Das Federseemoor,* Leipzig, 1936, s. 70.

43 F. Keller, *The Lake Dwellings of Switzerland and other parts of Europe,* London, 1866, pl. XIV, 23, 24.

44 E. Krause, 'Vorgeschichtliche Fischereigeräte und neuere Vergleichsstucke', *Z.f. Fischerei,* bd. XI, Berlin, 1904, s. 133–300, esp. s. 228–9.

45 Keller, *op. cit.,* p. 67.

46 Macpherson, *op. cit.,* p. 213.

47 A. Bulleid and H. St. G. Gray, *The Glastonbury Lake Village,* Glastonbury, 1911, pp. 631–7.

48 One of the best studied collections of bird remains from a Scottish archaeological site is that from Jarlshof, Shetland, dealt with by Miss M. Platt, and ranging in age from Late Bronze Age to Norse (*Proc. Soc. Ant. Scot.* LXVII, p. 135; LXVIII, p. 318). For sea birds from a Neolithic deposit in a chambered cairn nr. Midhowe, Rousay, Orkney, see *Proc. Soc. Ant. Scot.* LXVIII, p. 349. It is interesting to note that the Iron Age level in a chamber of a stalled cairn on Eday, Orkney yielded remains of at least 28 Cormorants, as well as lesser numbers
Soc. Ant. Scot. LXXI, pp. 152–3).

49 For a description of the uses to which bird-products were put in the Faroes, see Kenneth Williamson's 'The Economic Importance of Sea-Fowl in the Faeroe Islands', *Ibis,* LXXXVII (1945), pp. 249–69.

50 E.g. by the Aleuts. Jochelson, *op. cit.,* p. 53.

51 *Handbuch der Germanischen alterthumskund,* Dresden, 1836, s. 135.

52 W. H. Riddell, 'The Domestic Goose', *Antiquity*, 1943, p. 150.
53 *Op. cit.*, p. 222
54 Miss D. M. Liddell, 'New Light on an Old Problem', *Antiquity*, 1929, pp. 283–91.
55 *Archaeologia*, LXII, p. 335.
56 Ritchie, *op. cit.*, p. 147.
57 Annandale, *op. cit.*, p. 115.
58 *Ibid.*
59 Grieve, *op. cit*, pp. 119–20.
60 G. W. Steller, *Beschreibung von dem Lande Kamtschatka*, Frankfurt, 1774, s. 194.
61 E.g. Ritchie, *op. cit.*, p. 130.
62 Rütimeyer, *op. cit.*
63 Bulleid and Gray, *op. cit.*
64 E.g. Jarlshof (*Proc. Soc. Ant. Scot.* LXVIII, p. 318); chambered cairn near Midhowe, Rousay (*ibid.*, p. 349); Iron Age level, stalled cairn, Calf of Eday (*Proc. Soc. Ant. Scot.* LXXI, pp. 152–3).
65 M. Degerbøl in Mathiassen *et al.*, *op. cit.*, p. 191. The Øgaarde Maglemosian site yielded 13 humeri, as well as other bones, of the White-tailed Eagle.
66 E. Dahr had previously drawn attention to the large number of bones of the same species from the seal-hunting station at Siretorp, Scania, in A. Bagge and K. Kjellmark, *Stenåldersboplatserna vid Siretorp i Blekinge*, Stockholm, 1939, pp. 242–5.
67 Becker, *op. cit.*, figs. 3, 4.
68 Howard Carter, *The Tomb of Tut-ankh-amen*, vol. III, London, 1933, p. 139 and pl. XLVI
69 C. Englehardt, *Vimose Fundet*, Copenhagen 1929, p. 23 and pl. 14, no. 23.
70 C. Englehardt, *Denmark in the Early Iron Age*, London, 1866, p. 58, pl. 12, no. II.
71 L. Mayet and J. Pissot, *Abri-sous-roche préhistorique de la Colombière*, Lyon, 1915, figs. 47, 56 and pl. XXI, no. I and XXII, no. I. I am indebted to Professor Dorothy Garrod for help on this point.
72 *Op. cit.*, p. 181
73 *In the Uttermost East*, London, 1903, pp. 176, 231.
74 Steller, *op. cit.*, s. 194.
75 *J. R. Anthrop. I*, IV (1875), p. 29.
76 B. Adler, *Der Nordasiatische Pfeil*, Suppl. Bd. XIV, Inst. Arch. f. Ethnog, Leiden, 1901, s.13.
77 *Ibid.*
78 Dr Itkonen kindly showed me arrows fletched with eagle feathers in his department of the National Museum at Helsingfors. He informs us that eagle feathers were preferred up till the end of the 18th century in Finland. Cf. Sirelius, *op. cit.*, s. 33.
79 Olaus Magnus, *Historia de gentibus septentrionalibus*, Rome, 1555, bk. 19, cap 6.
80 *Ibid.*, bk. 19, cap. 7.
81 Riddell, *op.cit.*
82 *The Shield of Hercules*, v, 135. Quoted from Bohn edn, 1856, p. 57.
83 Jochelson, *op. cit.*, p. 77.
84 S. Krasheninnikov, *op. cit.*, p. 153.
85 G. Landt, *A Description of the Feroe Islands*, London, 1810, p. 219.
86 Information from Dr Itkonen.
87 Mortimer, *Forty Years' Researches*, pp. 274–5 and fig. 740; also Grahame Clark, *Prehistoric England*, p. 99.
88 Bateman, *Vestiges*, p. 97.
89 *Ten Years' Diggings*, p. 80. The Director of the City Museum, Sheffield, Mr J. W. Baggaley, kindly informs me that this is still preserved in the Bateman Collection (J.93.549) and that it agrees in size with the mandible of a Peregrine Falcon. In the Appendix to his *Ten Years' Diggings* (p. 299), Bateman refers to two species of *Falconidae* from his excavations 'unrecognizable from the remains, but one rather large'.
90 *Archaeologia*, XLIII, p. 541.
91 I have to thank Mrs M. E. Cunnington for kindly verifying this.

92 J.-E. Forssander, 'Från hällkisttid och äldre bronsålder i Skåne', *Medd. Lunds univ. hist. mus.* (1931–2), pp. 8–24, see p. 15 and fig. 3, no. 5.

93 M. Degerbøl in Mathiassen *et al., op. cit.*, p. 200. A claw joint of a White-tailed Eagle, artificially perforated, was found in an Iron Age urn in a barrow at Holme, south of Aarhus (Winge, 1903, *op. cit.*, p. 101).

CHAPTER 8

FOLK-CULTURE AND THE STUDY OF
EUROPEAN PREHISTORY

When the history of British Archaeology comes to be written, it is safe to say that the name of O. G. S. Crawford will bulk more largely than the record of his own substantial achievements in research. He is likely to be remembered both as an innovator and even more for the stimulus he gave to others.

Above all, Crawford has emphasized the unity of human history and the proper subservience of archaeology to that unity. In defining the scope of his new periodical *Antiquity*, he wrote:

Our field is the Earth, our range in time a million years or so, our subject the human race . . . The past often lives on in the present. We cannot see the men who built and defended the hill-top settlements of Wessex; but we can learn much from living people who inhabit similar sites today in Algeria. From such, and from traditional accounts of Maori forts we learn, by comparison, to understand the dumb language of prehistoric earthworks. Thus to see the past in the light of the present is to give it light and substance; this is the old anthropological method of Tylor and Pitt-Rivers and it has too long been neglected by archaeologists. Some familiarity with the habits and outlook of primitive communities is essential . . . [1]

While the majority of his professional colleagues have necessarily been engaged upon the discovery, preservation and classification of the dry-bones of prehistory, Crawford has always hankered to restore the flesh and blood and to make the past a reality to the living generation. By so doing he has notably succeeded, more perhaps than is always realized, in attracting a wider audience for his colleagues, and on occasion he has even penetrated the reserve of experts hardened in the art of evading reality. He has dared to hint that archaeological evidence can only yield history when it has been interpreted, and to suggest that it can only be interpreted adequately by taking account among other things of survivals from the past. It is the purpose of the present essay to discuss how the study of Folk-Culture may be used to advance knowledge of the prehistoric past.

Archaeology, the science of reconstructing the past from its surviving material traces, depends upon essentially vestigial evidence. In this respect it has much in common with those natural sciences which have to do with the more or less remote past. All are compelled to interpret evidence about the past to some degree in terms of what may be observed in the present. Just as the student of the Pleistocene Ice Age turns to areas where glacial conditions still obtain, or the palaeontologist considers fossil bones in relation to living animals, so must the archaeologist strive to reconstruct the vanished world of antiquity by reference to existing societies. This point of view was well expressed more than a hundred years ago by a professional zoologist, Sven Nilsson of Lund, whose interests centred first on the victims of early man and only later shifted to the hunters themselves. Approaching prehistoric archaeology by way of natural science, he felt positive that:

If natural philosophy has been able to seek out in the earth and to discover the fragments of an animal kingdom, which perished long before man's appearance in the world, and, by comparing the same with existing organisms, to place them before us almost in a living state, then also ought this science to be able, by availing itself of the same comparative method, to collect the remains of human races long since passed away, and of the works which they left behind, to draw a parallel between them and similar ones, which still exist on earth, and thus a way to the knowledge of circumstances which *have been*, by comparing them with those which still exist.[2]

Sir John Lubbock emphasized the same point when he claimed that:

If we wish clearly to understand the antiquities of Europe, we must compare them with the rude implements and weapons still, or until lately, used by savage races in other parts of the world. In fact the Van Diemaner and South American are to the antiquary, what the opossum and the sloth are to the geologist.[3]

Before considering more closely some of the implications of applying the evolutionary ideas of natural science to the study of the works of early man, it seems important to recall that analogies are seldom exact, more particularly when drawn from different fields of knowledge. As Professor Dorothy Garrod has recently stressed,[4] the archaeologist is necessarily concerned with factors distinct from and altogether more complex than those which control the organisms and processes of external nature: whereas the natural sciences deal with phenomena which conform to natural laws, archaeology is concerned with the results of human activities and with a multitude of unique events conditioned by cultural and even personal factors – in a word, with the phenomena of history. The task of reconstructing the life of prehistoric communities is therefore likely to be far more difficult and hazardous than deducing the behaviour of Pleistocene glaciers from observation of existing glaciers obedient to verifiable laws. It was doubtless an awareness of this inherent difficulty – an awareness not always shared by prehistorians – that prompted G. M. Trevelyan to exclaim in a recent lecture[5] that he knew 'of no greater triumph of the modern intellect than the truthful reconstruction of past states of society . . . by the patient work of archaeologists, antiquarians and historians'.

When one passes beyond the range of recorded history the difficulty of understanding past ages is magnified, since one finds oneself deprived of that direct access to the thought of earlier generations which only the written word allows. On the other hand, the very magnitude of human progress gives the hope, if one studies mankind as a whole, of discerning, as it were, a sequence of economico-social states, and of identifying these as they outcrop on the surface of present time.

Long ago, Edward B. Tylor taught that, since civilization has been attained by way of earlier stages of savagery and barbarism, the study of 'primitive' cultures surviving in areas remote from civilization, and of survivals from earlier stages incapsulated in civilized societies, offered a most promising source of knowledge about remote antiquity. General Pitt-Rivers went so far as to wrote[6] that:

The existing races, in their respective stages of progression, may be taken as the *bona fide* representatives of the races of antiquity . . . They thus afford us living illustrations of the social customs, forms of government, laws, and warlike practices, which belong to the ancient races from which they remotely sprang, whose implements, resembling, with but little difference, their own, are now found low down in the soil . . .

Stated dogmatically this doctrine is open to the objection that there are in fact no really primitive peoples living today. Modern savages have a history precisely as long as that of the most highly civilized peoples, only it does not happen to have been written down. It is inconceivable that even savage communities would have retained their culture substantially unmodified over the immense periods of time which have elapsed since the Old Stone Age. Not only must they have been subject to changes in their natural environment, but, even more important, they must have been influenced directly or indirectly by the emergence and expansion of groups at progressively higher stages of cultural evolution. Again, while on the one hand they must often have acquired elements of higher culture, on the other they must frequently have been driven into less desirable habitats and sustained cultural impoverishment or even loss. So far as the acquisition of culture is concerned, this must have applied, as we shall see, with even more force to those barbarous communities, which actually provided the foundations of civilization itself. Primitive man in the strict sense lived in the remote past and so can only be studied directly by prehistoric archaeology. The greatest caution is needed in using existing savages as sources for reconstructing primeval savagery. There is a real danger of setting up a vicious circle and of assuming what one is trying to discover.

Yet, as the earlier anthropologists led by Tylor insisted, much can still be learnt by the comparative method. The more weight is attached to the operation of historical factors in the building of individual cultures, the more significant become the broad fields of agreement between distinct social groups at analogous stages of development. When, for example, such widely separated groups as the Bushmen, Vedda, Andamanese and recently extinct Tasmanians are compared, they are all found to be limited by what Thurnwald termed a common 'cultural horizon'.[7] Fundamentally, such limitations relate to the degree of control attained by social groups over external nature and to the scope of choice implicit in such control; they mark significant stages in the evolution of culture.

It follows that we ought to be very careful to interpret the material traces of extinct societies by reference to recent ones at the appropriate stage of development. To assess Upper Palaeolithic art in terms of Bond Street, or even of the values current among the barbarian societies responsible for Stonehenge or Maiden Castle, would be anachronistic. Mr H. G. Wells may have exaggerated, but he was certainly pointing a useful moral, when he wrote[8] of some popular writers on prehistory that:

They made out the early savage to be a sort of city clerk camping out; they presented the men of Ur and early Egypt as if they had been the population of Pittsburgh or Paris in fancy dress. They minimized or ignored the fact that these people were not only living under widely differing stimuli, but reacting to them in ways almost as much beyond our immediate understanding as the mental reactions of a cat or a bird.

Granted that the cultures of the past ought to be considered in terms of existing ones at a comparable stage of development, it is inevitable that in studying the men of the Old Stone Age recourse should be made to those remote areas, where alone savage communities have survived until recent times. Already in 1865 Tylor had compared the stone implements of the Tasmanians with those of Palaeolithic man,[9] and it was under his influence that W. J. Sollas delivered his famous course of lectures on 'Ancient Hunters and their modern representatives' before the Royal Institution in 1906,[10] in which he compared successive stages of the Old Stone Age respectively with the Tasmanians, Australians and Bushmen. In the last edition of his book published under the same title,[11] he compared the Mousterians with the Tasmanians, the Aurignacians with the Bushmen and the Magdalenians with the Eskimo. After what has been said about the danger of accepting living groups as genuinely primitive, it is interesting to note how Sollas character-ized the stone industries of the Australians as comprising 'a heterogeneous collection to which almost all the Palaeolithic and even some of the Neolithic industries have made their several contributions'.[12]

If few have chosen to follow in the footsteps of Sollas, this may in part be a symptom of the divergence between archaeological and ethnological studies, which grew more pronounced as each began to specialize, the one on the classification and dating of the relics of extinct cultures, the other on the functioning of living communities. But Sollas' approach was not only unfashionable; it was also overdaring. Not content with pointing analogies, he tried to establish genetic relationships between fossil and living cultures at the level of savagery. He maintained the hypothesis that successive groups of Palaeolithic hunters have

one by one been expelled (from Europe) and driven to the uttermost parts of the earth: the Mousterians have vanished altogether and are represented by their industries alone at the Antipodes; the Aurignacians are represented in part by the Bushmen of the southern extremity of Africa; the Magdalenians, also in part, by the Eskimo on the frozen margin of the North American continent . . .[13]

As to the latter, he claimed:

The evidence could scarcely be more definite; the osteological characters of the Eskimo, which are of a very special kind, are repeated by the Chancelade skeleton so completely as to leave no reasonable doubt that it represents the remains of a veritable Eskimo, who lived in southern France during the Magdalenian age.[14]

Claims which go so far beyond the available evidence often daunt rather than stimulate, but at least they make one conscious of the stupendous gaps in knowledge even of the bare bones of prehistory. Again, Sollas was surely right to imply that remains of extinct cultures can only be interpreted with any certainty through modern analogues, if a continuous historical sequence can be demonstrated between them. So far as possible, also, it is desirable that the cultures under comparison should share a common environment, or at least that they should be adjusted to similar physical conditions.

For both these reasons, it may be suggested, prehistoric archaeologists – and more especially those concerned with barbarous communities based on farming and consequently rooted to the soil of a particular homeland – might well pay more attention to the Folk-Culture of the area in which they happen to be working. This is not to say that analogies drawn between the prehistoric farming cultures of Europe and existing cultures in more distant areas are without value. One remembers how instructive to students of Iron Age hill-forts were the articles on Maori and Algerian hill-forts in the first volume of *Antiquity*,[15] or again how valuable was the light thrown on our Neolithic camps by those of the pastoral Beni Mguild of Morocco, to which attention was drawn by Crawford in one of his stimulating notes.[16] Yet analogies between phenomena torn from their historical contexts may be very deceptive. In the case of Palaeolithic archaeology it is inevitable that comparisons should normally be made with remote areas, to which the old hunters in some cases migrated and where alone the old mode of life survives. Since Neolithic and to some extent since Mesolithic times, however, it is possible to trace continuity of settlement down to our own day. The peasant basis, prehistoric in origin and incorporating even elements from the old hunter-fisher way of life, persists in the Folk-Culture of the highly civilized parts of Europe.

Folk-Culture is the term generally applied to the way of life of the rural element in civilized communities, 'those who are mainly outside the currents of urban culture and systematic education'.[17] Such a limitation is regarded by some as a temporary expedient – Iorwerth Peate claims, for instance, that 'Folk-Culture must ultimately include the study of every class and element in the human community'[18] – but the term will be used here in its normal connotation. At the same time no consideration of the rural elements of a modern civilized community can be worth much which fails to take urban culture into account. It is the rural substratum which preserves continuity with the prehistoric past, but it would be quite wrong to imagine that this has not itself been affected, often profoundly, by the urban superstructure. Just as culture is diffused from more to less highly civilized regions, so within a society is it devolved from a higher to a lower stratum, using the term 'higher' in the sense, not of 'superior,' but of 'historically more advanced'. That men look upwards for their fashions, however much it may offend the egalitarian, has been true of past ages, as it remains more than ever true in this Century of the Common Man.

To the student of Folk-Culture this is often sufficiently evident, as in the case of the Barvas pottery of Lewis, which, in addition to pots of prehistoric character, comprises 'crude imitations of tea-pots, tea-cups, sugar-basins, etc., in the local unglazed fabric'.[19] Another familiar instance is provided by the Welsh turnery products which include such genteel forms as candle-sticks and egg-cups,[20] as well as bowls and dippers of Neolithic ancestry. Before assuming that any particular element of Folk-Culture is in fact a survival from ancient times, therefore, it is essential to be sure that continuity has in fact been established between the features under comparison. By means of a critical historical method, it should be possible to strip away the civilized accretions and reveal the essential barbarian core.

Wherever civilization has developed, there are liable to be survivals from earlier times in the culture of the countryside, from which the prehistorian can profit. The felaheen of Egypt continue to go about many of their daily tasks as their forefathers did in the days of the Pharaohs, largely unaffected by the cosmopolitan life of Alexandria or Cairo. Again, as Leonard Woolley and other excavators in Mesopotamia have been quick to recognize and turn to profit, the Iraqi peasant continues to build with mud and reeds in much the same fashion as in the days of Al'Ubaid. In Europe, the evidence has survived best in areas least affected by the Industrial Revolution, such as the Celtic fringe of Britain, the Scandinavian countries, the Alps, the Balkans and the Mediterranean basin. Although it has been studied most systematically in Scandinavia,[21] we have vigorous schools of Folk Culture today in these islands,[22] where indeed the tradition goes back to Martin Martin (1655/60–1719), an observer of the first rank, whose book, *A Description of the Western Isles of Scotland*, attracted Boswell and Johnson to the Hebrides and still remains of value to the student.[23] The subject has also been intensively studied by German scholars, to whom we owe many valuable works on special fields. In the south of Europe, on the other hand, archaeologists have for the most part been obliged to study the local Folk-Culture for themselves.

The most obvious way in which a study of Folk-Culture can help prehistorians is by interpreting objects otherwise enigmatic. One may first quote an example from the Aegean, where, as Stanley Casson once wrote in *Antiquity*:[24]

The economic condition of peasant and small-town life . . . particularly among the islands, hardly differs in simplicity or complexity from what it was either in the Bronze Age or in Classical Greek times. The average islander and coast-dweller still lives on the same food, and in similar houses to those of his ancestors.

When the excavators of the Minoan sites of Gournia, Phaistos, Hagia Triada, Tylissos and Knossos in Crete, came across discs of clay and rarely of marble, they classified them summarily as 'tables either sacred or otherwise, or else as the lids of pithoi';[25] only when Stéphanos Xanthoudídes came to enter them in the inventory of the Candia Museum did he recognize them for what they were – the upper discs of potter's-wheels, made intentionally heavy to give momentum, like those still used on the island for the manufacture of pithoi. This example of the wheel-disc shows how comparisons with modern Folk-Culture will often yield information about the activities as well as the mere forms of the past. The correct identification of circular discs of clay or marble is certainly not to be despised, if only for improving the accuracy of museum labels: more valuable still is the insight it gives into the manufacture of the great storage jars which played so important a part in Minoan economy.

Another notable instance of the value of drawing on Folk-Culture is the way in which the mat impressions found on the bases of early hand-made pottery from Palestine, Greece and the Aegean Islands were explained. At first it was thought that the impressions were received while the pots stood drying on mats before being fired in the kiln,[26] but J. L. Myres maintained that the impressions were made through vessels being built up and rotated on mats, an explanation which was also favoured by Wace and Thompson[27] and which recent work in connection with the Jericho pottery has strongly confirmed. G. M. Crowfoot was able to show that, where coiled mats were involved, the centres of the mats normally coincided with the centres of the pot-bases, suggesting that the pots were in fact set firmly on mats and rotated on them. Even more decisive, to my mind, was her observation of the actions of a woman potter in the Palestinian village of Yabed near Jenin, of whom she wrote:[28]

The mat was moved round when the potter wished to give attention to another aspect of the pot. In this movement of the mat, short and discontinuous as it is, one may see, fossilized, one of the early steps in the evolution of the wheel.

In this last connection it may be significant that mat impressions seem to occur on pot bases at just those points in the archaeological record immediately before the potter's wheel is introduced.

Archaeologists have found settlement sites, with their traces of house-forms, granaries and storage-pits, more informative about the economic and social life of antiquity than even the tangible products of handicrafts. Under such exceptional conditions as those in the Swiss Lakes or round the margin of the shrunken Federsee in Württemburg, the wooden floors of structures survive relatively intact and these will often provide a pattern, by means of which the form of buildings in less favoured areas can be reconstructed from wall-slots or post-holes. Even so, the significance of many features, especially the various pits and ancillary structures on prehistoric sites, will often escape the archaeologist who tries to interpret them in terms of his own limited experience, and only too often resorts to guess-work or adopts some conventional and arbitrary 'explanation'. Of recent years there has been a strong move, particularly evident among German prehistorians, to tap the resources of European Folk-Culture in this field. Franz Oelmann led the way in his reconstruction of the Gallo-Roman farmstead at Mayen[29] and in the evidence he brought forward to support the view that the so-called house-urns were in fact models of granaries.[30] Following his example, Werner Buttler spent two months exploring peasant settlements in Hungary, Rumania and Yugoslavia, to equip himself for writing the report on the Köln-Lindenthal excavations.[31] The danger of such an approach is of course that prehistorians are liable to select evidence from Folk-Culture which suits their own interpretations of the archaeological evidence, and having once found such confirmation to desist from further criticism of what is observed in excavations. The fact that Buttler was able to find Balkan gypsies living in huts with floors scooped out of the ground, for instance, confirmed him in the belief that the irregular hollows at Köln-Lindenthal and other sites were really dwellings. On the other hand, when Paret exposed the falsity of this and showed that the hollows were nothing more than quarries for the wall materials of long houses, he relied purely and simply on a critical evaluation of the archaeological evidence.[32]

Yet there is no kind of doubt about the value of interpreting marks in the sub-soil in the light of what is known of the buildings and habits of communities available for study at first hand. It was by regarding the hollows in the chalk revealed by the excavations of the Prehistoric Society at Little Woodbury,[33] near Salisbury, in this way that Gerhard Bersu was able to interpret pairs of post-holes as traces of the frames still used in the wetter parts of the Continent for drying hay and corn, and deep hollows, the 'pit-dwellings' of some British archaeologists, as storage-pits, used for a few years and hurriedly filled in with tips of rubbish and spoil. One effect of reducing dwellings to the status of temporary cellars has been to alter our ideas radically as to the role of hill-forts in the life of Iron Age Britain.[34]

More fundamental even than settlement sites to an understanding of economic and social realities is the mode of subsistence of prehistoric communities. Observations of existing societies of similar status is of the first importance in making possible a correct interpretation of the archaeological and biological evidence revealed by excavation. But we ought not to rely upon mere analogy: economic and social life, despite ethnic movements and technological 'revolutions,' in fact underwent a continuous development down to modern times, and it is important when collating the data of prehistoric archaeology with that of modern Folk-Culture to remember that Economic History forms a true connecting link.

First and foremost the study of European peasant life should assist in interpreting the evidence relating to farming in antiquity. But it is also the case, especially in areas marginal to the main farming zones, that activities originating from an earlier stratum of economic life have also survived in the peasant culture. In areas such as Scandinavia and the Baltic States the peasants have been obliged for the last 3,000–4,000 years or so to supplement the inadequate returns from farming by practising various forms of hunting and catching: here the same rhythm of ploughing, sowing and harvesting, interspersed with hunting and catching the same land and sea mammals, the same fowls and fishes, has persisted since prehistoric times.[35] Locally, even, as with the islanders of Kihnu and Ruhnu in the Gulf of Riga, who specialize in seal-hunting and exchange fats and skins for the grain, iron and salt of the Esthonian mainland,[36] there are still exhibited conditions like those on the margins of farming culture during Neolithic times, when hunting and fishing activities were stimulated among survivors of the northern Mesolithic groups by the development of a market among the encroaching peasants. Study of such activities not only throws light on the balance of economic life in earlier times, but may also yield important information on methods. As I have shown in detail elsewhere,[37] usages still surviving in northern Europe, or which have been described by observers during recent centuries,[38] have given us a deep insight into the methods used by the men of the Stone Age for catching seals. Similarly in studying methods of fishing or fowling practised in antiquity much can be learnt from recent practice in the area concerned.

As for farming itself, practices still survive in our own continent, which illustrate the processes involved in domesticating plants. The role of women is exemplified by the fact, noted by Maurizio,[39] that the collection and preparation of the wild cereal *Glyceria fluitans*, which flourishes in marshy areas and until recently was widely used for groats in eastern Europe, was, at least in East Prussia, entirely in their hands. Brockmann-Jerosch[40] has further shown how in the case of certain plants, such as the alpine sorrel (*Rumex alpinus*), which until recently was used as human food, often in the form of a kind of *sauerkraut*, in Scandinavia and the Alps, it is possible to observe different stages between the gathering of the wild form and its domestication. Since, like several other plants, including the nettle, the fibres of which were used as early as the Late Bronze Age for textiles,[41] the alpine sorrel flourishes on the manure and offal which naturally collects around farmsteads, it could easily be gathered wild: the first step taken towards ensuring a plentiful supply came with fencing off the natural crop to prevent its being trodden and soiled by cattle, as is done today by Swiss farmers who use it for fodder. In areas where the soil discourages growth and where in consequence sorrel does not colonise farmsteads, Alpine farmers will often take spontaneously the trouble to plant it and so ensure a supply of what is now in some senses a domesticated plant. The symbiosis between men and plants, based on the qualities of the excrement and midden material associated with human settlement, may well explain how domestication developed by easy transition from collecting: it has for instance been observed that the Chukchi will not only utilize the vegetation which flourishes on the organic matter in their refuse, but that they will also save the seeds of favoured plants and sow them around their habitations,[42] a practice which could easily arise by insensible gradations from discarding the débris of food-plants. The lack of any clear demarcation between the gathering and cultivation of plants and the hunting and herding of animals, which appears when real life is studied, should not only make us critical of dogmatic writing on the subject of 'economic revolutions' in the remote past, but will also help us to interpret correctly the organic remains from such sites as the Swiss lake-villages. Again as has been shown elsewhere,[43] it is still possible to observe among the Finno-Ougrian peoples studied by Manninen[44] and others, every stage in the transition from the hunting of wild-bee honey to a developed apiculture.

Many of the actual processes of early farming and most of the associated forms of material culture still survive in parts of Europe to edify the prehistorian. Thus the system of burning successive areas of forest (*Brand-wirtschaft*), which has recently been traced back to the Stone Age in Denmark[45] and in many parts of Europe is attested by history, still survives among the Finno-Ougrians.[46] The implements of tillage, and especially the plough, which have in their development affected so profoundly the history of agriculture and the organization of rural society, have as a rule survived from antiquity only in representations, frequently difficult to decipher, or in fragmentary form. As Paul Leser and many others have shown,[47] it is only when considered in relation to the wooden ploughs still in use in parts of Europe and to illustrations and descriptions from historic times that one can interpret satisfactorily the indications which have come down to us from prehistory. The same applies in varying degrees to devices for harvesting, threshing, storing and grinding grain, as well as for securing fodder for livestock. Means of transport, both on land and water, are another aspect of material equipment represented very unevenly in the archaeological record, but commonly surviving in primitive form in modern peasant cultures. In their work on the development of skis and sledges in Finland and Sweden from the Stone Age to the present day, Sirelius and Berg[48] have given outstanding demonstrations of the value of collating archaeological finds with more recent material in the same area.

So far it has been shown how it is frequently possible, by taking account of the Folk-Culture of a region, whether still existing or described by earlier observers, to throw light upon the material culture forms of antiquity, or upon the economic activities which gave rise to them, even when the archaeological evidence is incomplete or obscure. What also needs to be emphasized is that only by comparison with existing peasant cultures can one easily appreciate just how vestigial the archaeological record normally is. It is true that exceptionally well preserved finds give us an occasional insight into this, but it is only by contemplating the equipment of a living peasant group at a more or less comparable level that one understands it fully. The importance of wood-work and of even less durable substances, such as basketry, wicker-work and bark can hardly be overrated, and yet all of them are sparsely or capriciously represented in the archaeological record of prehistory. Conversely, it is seldom realized how provisional must be conclusions, even about the material culture of a community, when drawn from such a narrowly limited range of evidence as that upon which archaeology has normally to rely. The very concentration on the material evidence, which distinguishes modern archaeology, the careful scrutiny, the accurate description and illustration, the circumstantial method of publication, all tend to make us feel that the conclusions reached are more valid and more firmly based than they often can be.

Even more far-reaching is the reflection that even if a complete range of the material equipment of a prehistoric group could be recovered – and the focussing of research on sites capable of yielding organic materials, together with advances in archaeological technique, encourages the hope that great advances may be made along this road – the problem of interpreting this correctly would still remain more complex than is always allowed. When one reflects upon the part played even by such a characteristic 'fossil' as pottery in a living culture, one realizes how false some of the conventional assumptions made by prehistoric archaeologists are liable to be, unless checked by a knowledge of other aspects of life. One has only to imagine how the great expansion in the distribution of the black hand-made ware of Jutland[49] during the XVIIIth and early XIXth centuries, when it found its way by pack-horse and water as far afield as Holland in the west, Livonia in the east and Vienna in the south, might have been misinterpreted, had it occurred a couple of thousand years earlier! So far from reflecting a period of prosperity in Jutland, this actually co-incided with a time of acute depression, during which farmers had to lean heavily on the products of domestic industry: with the return of prosperity after 1864 the hand-made pottery of Jutland declined so rapidly that it was necessary to save it from extinction. This shows how essential it is to study material culture in relation to general economy, the evidence for which in the case of prehistoric communities must come largely from biological studies of the remains of animal and plant life. Beyond this, of course, it is necessary in studying any community, to consider the prevailing ideas and concepts which in the long run determine its behaviour. Observation of living communities stresses not only the complexity of economic life, but also its limitations as a source of information about prehistoric times.

Notes

1 *Antiquity*, 1927, 1 and 3.
2 Quoted from the Introduction (p. lx) to the 3rd edn (1868) of *The Primitive Inhabitants of the Scandinavian North*, originally published at Lund in 1843.
3 *Prehistoric Times, as illustrated by Ancient Remains, and the Manners and Customs of Modern Savages.* London 1865, 336.
4 *Environment, Tools and Man*, Cambridge. 1946. 8ff.
5 *History and the Reader.* The third annual lecture of the National Book League (Cambridge, 1946), p. 17.
6 J. L. Myres (ed.), *The Evolution of Culture and other Essays*, Oxford, 1906, 53.
7 R. Thurnwald, *Economics in Primitive Communities*, Oxford, 1932, 36–7.
8 *The Work, Wealth and Happiness of Mankind*, London, 1934, 31.
9 *The Early History of Mankind*, London, 1865, 195.
10 *Science Progress*, 1909 (iii, 326–53; 500–33; 667–86).
11 *Ancient Hunters*, 3rd edn, 1924, Oxford, *passim*.
12 *Ibid.*, 258.
13 *Ibid.*, 599.
14 *Ibid.*, 591.
15 *Antiquity*, 1927, 66–78 and 389–401.
16 *Ibid.*, 1933, 344–5.
17 *Encyclopaedia Britannica*, 14th edn, Vol. 9, 444.
18 *Antiquity*, 1938, 321.
19 E. C. Curwen, *Antiquity*, 1938, 282.
20 *Guide to the Collection of Welsh Bygones*, National Museum of Wales, 1929, pl. xxxiv (top, middle) shows a candlestick.
21 The study of Scandinavian Folk-Culture, of which Olaus Magnus (*Historia de gentibus septentrionalibus*, Rome, 1555) was the pioneer, is now based on a broad popular following, thanks to the well-known folk-museums – Skansen, Bygdöy, Lyngby, etc. – and to such museums as the splendid Nordiska Museet at Stockholm. It is also taught at the universities and is the subject of intensive research. The most telling symbol of Scandinavian leadership in this field is the periodical *Folk-Liv*, founded in 1937, and edited by Dr Sigurd Erixon, Professor at the *Institutet för Folk-livsforskning* in Stockholm, on behalf of the Gustavus Adolphus Academy for Ethnological and Folklore Research at Uppsala.
22 Notably in Wales, where the policy first pursued by T. H. Thomas, John Ward and others has been developed under the leadership of Sir Cyril Fox, Director of the National Museum at Cardiff, and of Iorwerth C. Peate, Keeper of the Department of Folk-Culture in the same museum (*Guide to the Collections of Welsh Bygones*, Cardiff, 1929; *The Welsh House*, London, 1940), and in Ireland, where after an abortive start (A. C. Haddon and C. R. Browne, *P.R.I.A.*, Vol. 2, ser. 3 (1893, 768–830)), the task has recently been resumed

under Scandinavian stimulus and notable work done, especially by E. Estyn Evans (*Antiquity*, 1939, 207–22; *Irish Heritage*, Dundalk, 1942). The Western Isles have attracted attention since the XVIIth century, in recent generations from F. W. L. Thomas (*P.S.A.S.* III, 127–44), Dr Arthur Mitchell, whose *The Past in the Present* (Edinburgh, 1880) evidently influenced the future editor of *Antiquity*, and, among others in our own day, Dr E.C. Curwen (*Antiquity*, 1938, 261–89). Important studies based mainly on material from England and Wales, but related to a wider background, have been made by R. U. Sayce.

23 Martin was born in Skye, graduated at Edinburgh, and as a young man acted as governor to the heirs of leading families on the island. He travelled extensively collecting information, which he communicated to the Royal Society in 1697. His book first appeared in 1704. It has recently been reprinted with other items by Mackay of Stirling (1934).

24 1938. 466. cf. F. S. Xanthoudides, 'Some Minoan potter's-wheel discs', *Essays in Aegean Archaeology*, Oxford, 1927, especially pp. 119–20.

25 Xanthoudides, *op.cit.*, 111.

26 C. C. Edgar in *Excavations at Phylakopi in Melos*, 1904, 94–6.

27 A. J. B. Wace and M. S. Thompson, *Prehistoric Thessaly*, Cambridge, 1912, figs. 136 and 187.

28 *Liverpool Annals, of Archaeology and Anthropology*, xxv (1938), 3–11.

29 'Ein gallorömischer Bauernhof bei Mayen', *Bonner Jahrbücher*, hft. 133 (1938), 51–140.

30 'Hausurner oder Speicherurnen?' *ibid.*, hft. 134 (1929), 1–39.

31 'Gruben und Grubenwohnungen in Südosteuropa', *ibid.*, hft. 139 (1934), 134–44; also in *Antiquity*, 1936, 25–36 (transl.).

32 O. Paret, 'Vorgeschichtliche Wohngruber?' *Germania*, Vol. 26 (1942), 84–103.

33 'Excavations at Little Woodbury, Wiltshire, Part 1', *Proc. Prehist. Soc.*, 1940, 30–111.

34 Grahame Clark, *Prehistoric England*. London, 1940, 88.

35 This has been well brought out by Prof. A. W. Brøgger in *Antiquity*, 1940, 163–81.

36 F. Leinbock, *Die materielle kultur der Esten*, Tartu, 1932.

37 'Seal-hunting in the Stone Age of north-eastern Europe; a study in Economic Prehistory', *Proc. Prehist. Soc.*, 1946, 12–48.

38 E.g. by Olaus Magnus in his *Historia de gentibus spetentrionalibus*, Rome, 1555, Book 20, cap. 5; L. J. Debes, *Faeroe et Foeroa reserata*, London, 1676, 166–71; Martin Martin, *op. cit.* (1934 edn), 133–4.

39 A. Maurizio, *Die Geschichte unserer pflanzennahrung von den Urzeiten bis zur Gegwart*, Berlin, 1927, 44–8.

40 H. Brockmann-Jerosch, 'Die altesten Nutz- und Kulturpflanzen', *Vierteljahrsschrift d. Naturforsch. Ges. in Zürich*, 62 (1917), 80–102.

41 A good description of the use of nettles by European peasants in recent times has been given by M. Hald, 'The Nettle as a Culture Plant', *Folk-Liv*, 1942, t. VI 28–49. Cf. Manninen, *Die Finnisch-Ugrischen Volker*, Leipzig, 1932, 185 and 352–3, for a useful account of the methods used by the Mordwins and Ob-Ougrians. For the occurrence of textiles made from nettle fibres in the Late Bronze Age of Denmark, see *Aarbøger*, 1943 99–102.

42 Maurizio, *op. cit.*, 17–18.

43 'Bees in Antiquity', *Antiquity*, 1942, 208–15.

44 Manninen, *op. cit.*, 215–17, 243–4.

45 J. Iversen, 'Land Occupation in Denmark's Stone Age', *Danmarks Geologiske Undersogelse*, II R., nr. 65, Copenhagen, 1941. See also *Antiquity*, 1945, 61 and 67–8.

46 Manninen, *op. cit.*, 30.

47 P. Leser, *Entstehung und Verbreitung des Pfluges*, Münster, 1931.

48 For many references, see G. Berg, *Sledges and Wheeled Vehicles*, Nordiska Museets Handlingar, 4, Stockholm, 1935.

49 Axel Steensburg, 'Hand-made Pottery in Jutland', *Antiquity*, 1940, 148–53.

CHAPTER 9

THE ECONOMIC APPROACH TO PREHISTORY

For more than one reason it was appropriate that in opening this biennial series of Reckitt Archaeological Lectures Professor Stuart Piggott should have chosen to speak on William Camden and the *Britannia*.[1] Those who were present on that occasion will agree that the lecturer covered his field with singular felicity and no one is more keenly aware than he who is now called upon to follow of the high standard of wit and learning set by the first Reckitt Lecturer. By thus celebrating the quarter-centenary of the birth of William Camden the Academy acknowledged in a manner the place of antiquarianism in the genesis of archaeology: it was surely right to emphasize that the studies, which Camden did so much to further, gave birth to and nurtured the early childhood of those methods of distilling history from material remains that we recognize as specifically archaeological.

Yet, if Camden's role in the prologue to archaeology is acknowledged, it is only right to recall that in Professor Piggott's words the prime object of the *Britannia* was 'to establish Britain as a member of the fellowship of nations who drew their strength from roots struck deep in the Roman Empire'.[2] Camden was concerned with history in the restricted sense of that term and it is only natural that he should have relied first and foremost on literary sources: when he had recourse to archaeological evidence he confined himself almost entirely to coins or to monuments mentioned by ancient authors – such notice as he took of what we should now term prehistoric antiquities was perfunctory even when he was impelled to wonder by their very grandeur. Of Stonehenge he grieved mightily 'that the founders of this noble monument cannot be trac'd out'[3] and in his Preface he made no secret of his doubts about the chances of discovering the truth about the first inhabitants of Britain, who 'had other cares and thoughts to trouble their heads withal, than that of transmitting their originals to posterity' and who, even had they so desired, could not 'have effectually done it'.[4] The fact is that Camden lived at a time before scholars conceived it to be possible to learn anything worth knowing about peoples who had left no written records.

The achievements of prehistoric archaeology during the last century and a half and more particularly during the last fifty years have shown, on the contrary, how much it is possible to recover of the unwritten history of mankind through diligent study of material remains. It would indeed be tedious to expatiate on the merits of archaeological research in the rooms of an Academy which has done so much to advance its cause. The suggestion one would make rather is that archaeological data has exerted if anything too exclusive a fascination over students of prehistoric times. A certain professional myopia is a common penalty of success and this is especially true of a subject like archaeology: it is not merely that the evidence on which it depends perpetually increases with the progress of exploration and the refinement of technique, but – thanks to the growth of museums and despite the bombs – it survives and accumulates in the form of tangible objects, objects moreover which are often aesthetically and sometimes even financially attractive in themselves. It is small wonder that archaeologists should often have succumbed to their own material and squandered on empty analyses of form energies which might more profitably have been devoted to the understanding of prehistory.[5] It was inevitable that the earlier generations of prehistorians should have been engrossed in the collection and classification of data and it is certain that for a long while to come such activities will continue to absorb a large part of the time of those engaged in prehistoric research. Yet, already for some quarter of a century a sound beginning has been made with the writing of prehistory, at least in those few territories for which the preliminary and essential work of chronological and cultural definition has been brought to the requisite degree of precision.[6]

It is widely accepted today that prehistory ought to be classified as a historical discipline: in the sense that it is concerned with development and change in the sphere of human affairs this is hardly to be questioned. Yet it seems essential to recognize that prehistory differs radically from the kind of history based even in some measure on written sources, not merely in its methods and procedures, but also in what it is capable of telling us. Since it is anonymous, prehistory can take no cognizance of the moral and psychological problems confronting individuals: it is concerned and can only be concerned with social problems; its subject-matter is culture, whether in the abstract or in relation to a specific community, region, or period. In this lecture I shall be concerned in effect with the study of the economic aspects of prehistoric cultures.

At this point it is well to reflect on what we mean by culture in the present context. If current archaeological usage is vague – the term is loosely applied to denote congruencies among such traits as happen to be at hand as a result mainly of accident or of haphazard excavation – this is due partly to the inherently vestigial nature of the archaeological record, but partly also to lack of awareness of the achievements of the social sciences and of their implications for archaeology. As an expedient the archaeological usage can be defended, but it can hardly be accepted as more than a temporary necessity: indeed, one might measure the validity of archaeological studies by the degree to which they approximate in their reconstruction of ancient cultures to the functioning entities investigated by modern anthropologists. For their part the anthropologists have defined culture in numerous ways – in their recently published *Culture. A Critical Review of Concepts and Definitions,*[7] Professors Kroeber and Kluckhohn marshal no less than 166 significant definitions in 7 categories, not to mention 100 statements under 6 heads – revealing a diversity of definition which transcends temperamental differences and the varying levels of abstraction sought or attained by individual authors and emphasizes both the many-sidedness of culture and the multiplicity of ways in which it can usefully be approached.

One of the few things on which all authorities agree is the artificiality of culture: culture is not something that sprouts from rocks or trees – it is made by man and is man's distinctive contribution to the totality of nature or being. Further, there is a significant measure of agreement among the authors cited by Kroeber and Kluckhohn[8] in recognizing different dimensions of culture, which, though variously labelled, may conveniently be termed material, social, and spiritual. The first of these, categorized by Franz Boas[9] as including

the multitude of relations between man and nature; the procuring and preservation of food; the securing of shelter; the ways in which the objects of nature are used as implements or utensils; and all the various ways in which man utilizes or controls, or is controlled by, his natural environment: animals, plants, the inorganic world, the seasons, and wind and weather,

in effect defines pretty closely the aspect of culture which comes directly within the purview of economic prehistorians and at the same time emphasizes the theme I have particularly in mind, namely, the interplay between culture, habitat, and biome, as illustrated by the food and raw materials consumed by prehistoric communities.[10]

The artificiality of culture is in itself a sufficient argument against studying prehistory as though it was a natural science. Yet it is surely an equal error to suppose that culture is something outside nature: man after all is a natural organism and his culture is in essence a traditional medium for harmonizing social needs and aspirations with the realities of the physical world, that is with the soil and climate of the habitat and with all the forms of life, including man himself, that together constitute the biome. One reason for the inadequate treatment of prehistory has been that prehistorians have too often failed to remember that archaeology is only one of a number of disciplines needful for advancing their subject. It is largely because the economic activities of man, in the course of which he utilizes natural resources to support the way of life patterned by his social inheritance, illustrate so vividly the interrelations of culture and physical environment that their study is so rewarding.

Students of modern primitive societies are in the happy position of being able to study in detail, not only the overt activities of economic life, but also, through language, the way in which different preliterate peoples classify and organize their knowledge of their physical environment. Donald Thomson, for instance, was able to observe directly how the Wik Monkan of northern Queensland 'classified the types of country as accurately and as scientifically as any ecologist, giving to each a name and associating it with specific resources, with its animal and vegetable foods and its technological products',[11] or, again, how they divided the year into 'a cycle of four, or more accurately, of five, seasons, each with its distinctive and characteristic climatic and other conditions, and each related to a food-supply, and hence to a definite kind of occupation'.[12] Alternatively one might quote from a recent report by Paul A. Vestal on the Ramah Navaho, an agricultural and stock-raising group of the American south-west:

Of the 465 uncultivated plant species collected in the area, there were only three of which no Navaho name was given when shown to two or more informants, and for one of these a use was known ... the people are observant of their plant-surroundings, and can readily distinguish between plants of major, secondary, or minor importance in their lives. ... Plants enter into all their activities from birth until death. The uses of plants are multiple, and from the Navaho standpoint they fit into that harmony of related parts which is the Navaho view of the universe, and with which the people must make harmonious connections for an abundant life.[13]

This detailed knowledge of ecological conditions was as much a part of the Wik Monkan or Navaho way of life as the tools they made from natural products. The same must have been true of prehistoric man, but in his case we can only infer this from a study of biological traces.

Modes of subsistence confront us with the most vital aspect of economic life or indeed of life itself, since, not merely does survival itself depend on food, but the methods by which food is acquired affect more or less closely all other departments of cultural life. From a theoretical viewpoint subsistence represents no more in essence than the appropriation of animal and plant substances for the nourishment of human beings at standards and in manners conditioned by the societies to which they belong. As such it reflects both the economic level and the individual characteristics of different cultures. Above all, it illustrates how, in the case of man, the preliminaries to even such an overtly biological activity as eating conform to patterns of social behaviour. A knowledge of the methods by which early man maintained life is essential to an understanding both of individual cultures and of the process of change unfolded in prehistory.

Under the economic and social conditions prevailing in Upper Palaeolithic and Mesolithic times – the earliest for which we yet have adequate documentation – it must be conceded that the field of choice open to individuals or communities was limited by the varieties of animal and plant occupying the habitat. One may emphasize, though, that, if freedom of choice was limited by biological and ultimately by physical factors, this by no means disposes of it. Freedom of choice is after all very relative and no living organism or association of such can exist unless by coming to terms with the extraneous factors which condition to a greater or less degree all forms of life. Other animals, indeed, conform instinctively to these, but it is after all the hall-mark of man that he behaves at least ideally with reference to an artificial pattern evolved and transmitted by society. The evolution of culture, indeed, has been a story of ever-widening range of choice. Already among primitive hunter-fishers there was scope for the exercise of preference – at the most elementary level, for instance, there was the choice from among those available of which animals to hunt and which plants to gather and in what proportions.

It is not difficult to measure accurately the proclivities of prehistoric hunters in regard to meat, since bone commonly survives and the practice of extracting the marrow makes it obvious which animals have served for food. For instance, the fauna from the Magdalenian cave of Petersfels (fig. 9.1) in south-east Baden[14] reflects, in the rarity of forest and the abundance of

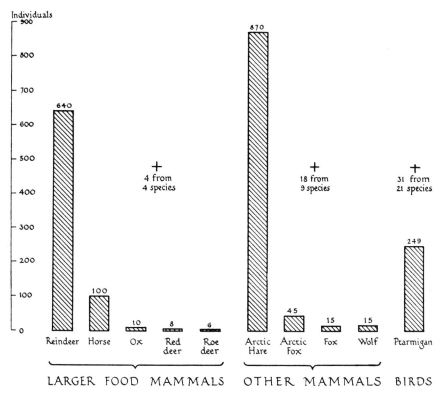

9.1 Faunal remains from the Magdalenian cave of Petersfels

tundra-steppe species, the ecological conditions prevailing there at a particular phase of Late Glacial times. Yet, if it would be folly to interpret such a table solely in economic terms, it would be wrong to do so in purely zoological ones. The skeletal material from Petersfels, apart perhaps from a few rodents, is, like that from any other archaeological site, the product of human selection: it represents social choice operating within the limits set by definable biological and physical factors. By and large the Magdalenians of Petersfels relied for their meat (as well as for many of their most important raw materials) on reindeer and to a lesser degree on wild horses, but during the season of snow cover they evidently trapped Ptarmigan, Arctic Fox, and Arctic Hare. On the other hand the Late Glacial stations of Meiendorf and Stellmoor[15] (fig. 9.2) show an unrelieved predominance of reindeer. Analysis of the faunal remains makes it clear that the sites were inhabited only during the summer. During this time of the year the hunters attached themselves to

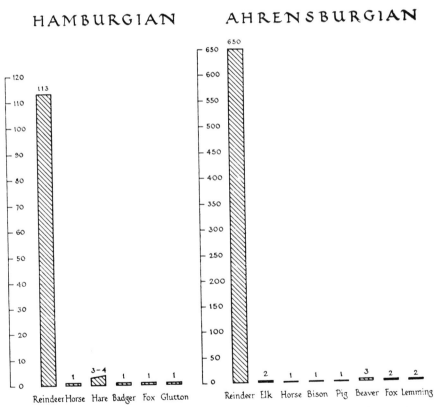

9.2 Faunal remains from Meiendorf and Stellmoor. The Hamburgian figures relate to fauna from Meiendorf and from the lower level at Stellmoor combined, the Ahrensburgian ones to the upper level at Stellmoor

reindeer herds during their migrations to the north, depending on them almost entirely for meat, clothing, and shelter, as well as drawing on their antlers and bones for tools and weapons, so that almost every item in the archaeological inventory of both cultures finds an explanation in terms of the hunting or utilization of this one animal. By contrast, the animals hunted by the inhabitants of east Yorkshire during the initial Pre-boreal phase of the Post-glacial period, as illustrated by the fauna from Star Carr (fig. 9.3), belonged, almost without exception, to forest-dwelling species.[16] Further, in this case we appear to be confronted with the food and industrial debris of the winter months, and it has to be admitted that none of the animals available to the Mesolithic hunters encouraged specialized hunting to the extent that the gregarious and migratory reindeer undoubtedly did. Even so, the Star Carr people showed a marked preference for Red Deer, though they took Aurochs, Elk, and Roe Deer in considerable numbers. Examples could

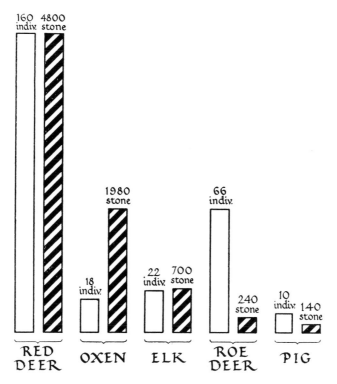

9.3 Faunal remains from Star Carr. The numbers of individuals represented among the material actually recovered from Star Carr were half those shown, but allowance has to be made for areas unexcavated and for the fact that antler and horn had decayed on the northern part of the site.

be multiplied, but my point will have been made if I have shown that an element of social choice existed, even if the range within which this could be exercised was limited by the facts of climate and animal and plant ecology. What above all else limited the possibilities of life for the hunters of Petersfels, Meiendorf, or Star Carr was the nature of their economy.

The great turning-point in prehistory, the point at which men first escaped from the closed cycle of savagery and became free to advance towards literate civilization – often termed the Neolithic revolution, though it should be remembered that the great discovery of domestication must in fact have been made by Mesolithic hunters and gatherers[17] – may be conceived of as in essence the outcome of a change of attitude on the part of human societies towards the animals and plants with which they were associated. This change was fundamentally from a predatory to a productive régime, away from mere seizure and appropriation to protection, nurture, and selective breeding, so that from among wild species men were able to elicit others endowed with qualities which they regarded as desirable. The species domesticated by human societies over the course of generations were moulded in conformity with the ideas and requirements of these societies and so acquired characteristics determined at least in some measure by the cultural patterns of the societies into which they were in a sense incorporated by domestication. Viewed from a slightly different angle the change was one from a relatively passive to an active, dynamic attitude towards nature: men ceased to be satisfied not merely with the character of the animals and plants they found around them but also with their distribution. The need to expand the area within which crops could be grown and herds grazed sprang logically from the control of breeding by domestication. The increased density of population which this made possible, together with the advances in technology which flowed from and at the same time encouraged these, created demands which could most easily be met by expanding the territories over which farming could be carried on. It was, of course, the spread of the new economy from western Asia and north Africa which marked for successive zones of Europe the transition from Mesolithic to Neolithic culture. The magnitude of this change, which transcended the purely economic sphere and affected the entire social structure and spiritual outlook of the peoples concerned, can only be fully appreciated in biological terms. The introduction of farming to temperate Europe was nothing less than majestic, not only in its historical consequences, but also as an achievement in creative evolution. It implied not merely the introduction of domesticated animals and plants into an environment quite different from that in which they were originally bred, but also the modification of the incoming economy to suit these different conditions and conversely the initiation of processes by which the physical environment was itself ultimately transformed to accord with developing social needs.

From the point of view of prehistoric research it is these biological and specifically ecological changes which provide the fullest and most reliable index of the progress and extent of the economic transformation wrought during Neolithic times. Neither of the archaeological traits identified by the earlier prehistorians with the introduction of Neolithic culture were in themselves of great significance: the polishing of flint axe and adze blades is still, it is true, of local value as an indicator, even though the technique was taken over from the working of antler, bone, and stone practised by upper Palaeolithic and Mesolithic hunters;[18] and it now appears that farming antedated the appearance of pot-making in the Old as well as in the New World,[19] quite apart from the fact that the manufacture and use of pottery by no means implies the practice of husbandry.[20] As farming techniques developed, the material equipment needed for tilling the soil, harvesting crops, and the like forms an increasingly valuable source of evidence, but in the earliest stage this was hardly the case: primitive stock-raising could be carried on without leaving any trace in the archaeological record; and crops could be grown without elaborate tillage and harvested by reaping-knives indistinguishable from those employed for gathering wild grains.[21] The most decisive criteria for determining the origin, spread, and progress of farming are biological, notably indications of domestication exhibited by remains of animals and plants, and evidence of ecological disturbance resulting from the practice of farming and from the ever-increasing transformation of the habitat which this entailed.

The practice of agriculture inevitably involves occupation of the soil in a manner more intimate and more intensive than does hunting and gathering: conversely the increasing intensity with which the habitat was settled reflects the dynamism of the new economy with its accompanying growth of population and technological advance. It is hardly too much to claim that we owe our present understanding of the agricultural prehistory of temperate Europe in the first instance to biologists working within the general framework of Quaternary Research.[22] From the very beginning agriculture had to be carried on at the expense of, although also in partnership with, the existing vegetation. The Neolithic settlers were really only the forerunners of deforestation, since, as Iversen and his botanical colleagues over much of north-western Europe have shown,[23] the first clearances were strictly temporary in character. Iversen's hypothesis that the Neolithic pioneers practised the slash and burn system, clearing small patches, burning the undergrowth and felled timber (in so doing enriching the soil with potash), taking two or three crops and passing on to fresh tracts of forest, is supported by economic history and comparative ethnology as well as being confirmed experimentally: there is after all plenty of evidence for the practice in medieval Europe[24] and during the colonization of eastern North America;[25] it survived until yesterday in the forests of Finland and Carelia,[26] and it still operates among primitive agriculturists in many parts of the world today, notably in Malaya where its progress has been so admirably recorded from the air.[27] The whole process of clearing, burning, and raising cereal crops has recently been reproduced in Jutland by the authorities of the National Museum of Denmark, using only such equipment as was available to Neolithic man; and it is significant that cereals were only able to compete with weeds on soil mixed with ash from the burning.[28]

It is in the light of this hypothesis that we are enabled for the first time to view the earliest agriculturists of temperate Europe as functioning in a convincing setting. The disconnected distribution of the Danubian peasants, the apparent speed with which they spread over their extensive loess-lands,[29] the frequency with which even their most important settlements were abandoned and reoccupied,[30] all these and many other details fit easily into the context of *Brandwirtschaft*. It is for instance amusing to note the effect of the new concept on our evaluation of so familiar and so solid an archaeological fossil as the shoe-last celt. So long as we thought of the loess as an open corridor it seemed most reasonable to interpret the *Schuhleistenkeil* as an implement of tillage – plain ones as hoe-blades[31] and perforated ones as plough-shares.[32] Once the forest cover and the régime of slash and burn is accepted, there is no need for hoes, let alone ploughs, since the seed had only to be raked among the ashes,[33] and there is every occasion for felling trees and for working wood: so it was really no surprise when re-examination[34] of the shoe-last celt revealed a slightly hollow working-edge, a feature meaningless in relation to a hoe-blade, but very much in keeping with the D-shaped section and pointing beyond doubt to use as an adze. Thus, not even the most established types are impervious to ideas, a main function of which in archaeology should be to lead us back to reinterpret the material data. Any regrets for that discarded landmark of prehistory, the shoe-last hoe, will be more than compensated for by the reflection, brought home with increasing force by the continued revelation of traces of massive timber-framed houses, that the Danubian peasants had every need for their adzes as well as every opportunity to use them.

The ecological approach has further provided a convincing clue to the changes in land-utilization which underlie so much of the later prehistory of our region. The initial phase of shifting agriculture could endure only so long as forest regeneration approximated to the rate of clearance. It was inevitable that the growth of population made possible by farming, not to mention the depredations of livestock maintained under a very imperfect system of domestication,[35] should have slowed down and in due course brought to an end the whole cycle. The crisis of subsistence, reflected for instance in the widespread movements of warrior herdsmen at the close of Neolithic times, was to some extent deferred by the annexation of marginal lands and by the intensification of herding and hunting: in the long run, though, it could be resolved only by adopting a more settled and at the same time a more intensive form of agriculture.

Precisely when the new régime, based on permanent as distinct from temporary clearance of forest and involving the cultivation of definite fields by means of the *ard*,[36] the light oxdrawn implement of tillage evolved in the dry farming zone of the Near and Middle East, spread into successive parts of temperate Europe is still subject to research. The system seems to have worked well enough on the light, relatively well-drained soils of the area first taken up for tillage in temperate Europe,[37] but inevitably the time came once again when the needs of a growing population outstripped the available sources of food and towards the end of the prehistoric period it became necessary to incorporate intermediate loams and ultimately to make a start on the heavier clay soils. With the colonization of the secondary area of settlement new problems arose,[38] which the onset of wetter conditions only served to emphasize, and it was in response to these that the régime familiar from medieval times was originally developed. The topic of land-utilization during prehistoric times is indeed one of inexhaustible interest, but we must not lose sight of the object of all this activity, namely, the supply of animal and plant protein, more even in flow and more substantial in volume than was possible under a régime of hunting, fishing, and gathering.

The importance of research on the nature of domesticated animals and plants as a source of information about the economy of prehistoric farmers need hardly be emphasized, having in fact been widely recognized ever since the revelation of the Swiss lake-villages a hundred years ago.[39] On the other hand the purely historical questions which occupied the older prehistorians – the sources of different domesticated species and the routes by which they were diffused – have now been replaced or at least supplemented by others more functional in character. Among such one may note the relative importance of domesticated and wild forms (by which the respective roles of hunting and stock-raising can be measured); the character and degree of domestication; the proportions in which different species were maintained, considered in relation to the total environment;[40] and the precise manner in which different species contributed to the subsistence of the societies which maintained them. Many of these questions – like the more elementary ones already treated when speaking of hunting groups – are capable of scientifically precise answers, in the sense that they are susceptible of exact statistical treatment. Further, when material from successive periods, is analysed, any significant trends or developments are likely to be made manifest. This is well seen in the results of Hans Helbaek's work on cereals imprinted on hand-made pottery and other clay-fictiles.[41] The beauty of his method is that it rests on a random selection – on imprints of whatever material happens to have lain about while potting was actually in progress – and that the cultural and temporal relevance of the data is automatically fixed by the pottery on which imprints occur. Even when restricted to Denmark, the country where it was first worked out,[42] the method disclosed changes in the composition of crops, for instance the swing during the Bronze Age from wheat to barley and the appearance towards the end of prehistoric times of such crops as oats and rye. Now that it is being applied to a much more extensive territory, including the British Isles, and that the imprints are being interpreted in conjunction with other sources of information, it is beginning to throw light on such topics as the origin and spread of domesticated species and in some instances even on the sources of folk-movements indicated by archaeology. Thus, just as the functionalist school of anthropology, though avowedly anti-historical in bias, has in practice made it possible for the first time to appreciate what is involved in social evolution, so in the case of prehistoric crops the ecological approach is making possible a renewed and more profound understanding of genetical-historical problems.

It rarely happens that we can supplement inferences drawn from discarded meat-bones or impressions of plants with more direct evidence about the food of prehistoric man. The autopsy recently carried out in the National Museum of Denmark by the chief pathologist of a Copenhagen hospital, assisted by a specialist in forensic medicine, on the body of an Early Iron Age man recovered from a bog at Tollund, near Silkeborg, Jutland, is one of the rare instances to the contrary.[43] When the digestive tract was washed out, it was found to contain the residue of a kind of gruel, recalling that described by Pliny as the common diet of peasants in Greece and Italy. The chief ingredients were barley, linseed, Cameline seed, and the fruits of *Polygonum lapathifolium*, a common weed of cultivation, but remains of fifteen other plants including oats and a number of weeds were also identified. Traces of most of these plants have been found on contemporary settlements in Denmark and there seems no doubt that the peasants of this period were fond of certain oil-bearing seeds and, further, that they took the trouble to gather the seeds of a number of weeds. The investigation of residues in various kinds of container is a not uncommon source of information about food and drink: thus, the evidence from Tollund is reinforced by the discovery of a quantity of linseed and Cameline seed, evidently from a perishable container, in an Iron Age house at Østerbølle, Jutland[44] and as regards drink one recalls the long-published evidence from Danish burials – cranberry wine mixed with myrtle and honey from the Bronze Age and a brew of barley, cranberry, and bog myrtle from the Roman Iron Age.[45] Although occasional clues to methods of cooking are given by finds of ovens, baking platters, and the like, it has to be admitted that we know far less about the ways in which food was prepared than we do about the selection and provision of the actual raw materials, despite the profound significance of cuisine as an expression of culture.

If prehistoric man lived by eating animals and plants, he depended equally on natural substances, whether organic or otherwise, for the fabric of his material culture, seeking out what he needed and shaping it to meet the requirements of his social life. The artifacts, whether structures, objects of utility, ornaments, or works of art, on which archaeology mainly depends may be thought of as embodiments of ideas, which, however, could only be realized through techniques applied to materials present in or elicited from the natural environment. Thus we are faced in the sphere of technology with the same kind of dynamic relationship between culture and ecosystem that we encountered in the case of subsistence. Whereas in the animal world raw materials were utilized to satisfy merely instinctive needs, among men their very selection has from the beginning been determined by cultural considerations (fig. 9.4). If prehistory is the study of man's growing control over forces external to himself down to the time when through his invention of writing he first emerged on the stage of history, it is significant that this progress has for over a hundred years been epitomized for archaeologists by the dominant

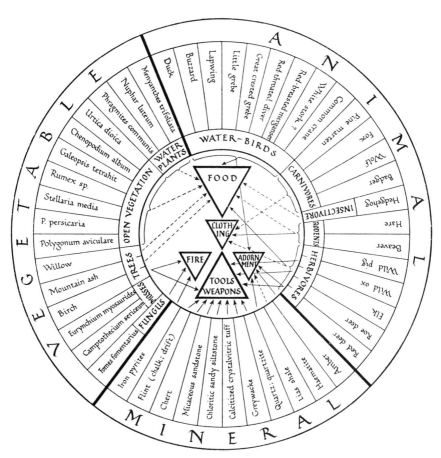

9.4 Selected raw materials and their use by early man at the mesolithic site of Star Carr

raw materials used for implements and weapons.[46] By and large prehistoric man used the materials available to him which most adequately fulfilled his requirements within the limits of his capacity to shape them: his selection of raw materials thus provides important information about the extent of territory from which he obtained supplies, whether by seasonal migration or trade, and about the pattern of his social needs, as well as about the general level of his technology.

	Antler or horn	Cranium	Mandible	Teeth	Vertebral column	Ribs	Scapula	Humerus	Radius	Metacarpal	Phalange	Ilium	Femur	Tibia	Metatarsal
RED DEER	▨			▨											
OX	?									▨			▨		▨
ELK	▨									▨					
ROE DEER															
PIG															

9.5 The use of animal bones at Star Carr

One of the most striking characteristics of the technology of modern primitive peoples is the use made of materials derived from wild animals and plants – skins, sinew, bone, antler, wood, bark, resin, stems, leaves, and so on – and no doubt such materials played a much more prominent role among prehistoric peoples subject to the limitations of a stone-age technology than the archaeological record suggests: even so antler and bone often survive in sufficient quantities to provide adequate material for study. When one considers the items selected by any group of stone-age man from among the skeletal remains of the animals take for food, it soon becomes evident that we are confronted with the results of discrimination; that this discrimination is the outcome of cultural inheritance and of the actual mode of life pursued; and that in consequence this choice is as germane to prehistoric studies as the material equipment fabricated from the raw materials in question.

One may illustrate this by reference to the hunters of Star Carr[47] (fig. 9.5). Of their principal food-animals they ignored the roe deer and wild pig; of aurochs they used only the metapodials and femurs and these exclusively for making a particular kind of leather-working tool; of elk they utilized the lower portions of the antlers and the attached frontal bone for mattock-heads, the small lateral metapodials for bodkins and, in rare instances, splinters from the metapodials for barbed points; but, most instructive of all, in the case of their principal quarry, red deer, they entirely neglected the limb bones and ribs, concentrating on the antlers, almost every one of which they turned to account as sources of material for their favourite barbed spearheads. The blanks from which these objects were made were won by cutting parallel grooves up and down the beam and levering out the intervening splinters, a highly characteristic technique and one which had been inherited and transmitted over a long period of time. The groove and splinter technique was apparently first applied to stag, as well as possibly to reindeer antler, by the Aurignacians of south-western France during the first interstadial of the last glaciation.[48] In the territories over which red deer was replaced by reindeer during the ensuing Late Glacial phase basically the same technique was applied, both by the Magdalenians[49] and also by the Hamburgians,[50] but in each case it was modified in practice to suit the differing character of reindeer antler, the splinters stopping short at the brow tine instead of continuing down to the root of the antler. When, with the onset of Post-glacial conditions the red deer regained and extended their old territories, the technique was once more practised in its original form: the Azilians of north Spain[51] and south-west France, as well as the proto-Maglemosians of the north (as exemplified at Star Carr), removed splinters down to the lower end of the beam in precisely the same fashion as the Aurignacians of France and the early Magdalenians of eastern Spain had done in Late Pleistocene times.

If, however, one turns to the Maglemosians proper, as known from so many sites of Boreal age from eastern England to west Russia,[52] one finds on the one hand a more catholic use of the skeletal parts of game animals and on the other a radical change from antler to bone as the material preferred for fabricating barbed points. Red deer was still the commonest game animal, but the antlers were now used almost, though not quite,[53] exclusively for mattock-heads and holders for flint adzes. Uniserial spearheads were an outstanding feature of material equipment, but these were now as a rule cut from the ribs of red deer or the metapodials of roe deer,[54] both materials abundantly available to, though conspicuously neglected by, the hunters of Star Carr. This change in the use of raw materials is all the more striking since the flint component of the Boreal Maglemosian culture, on which the possibility of working antler and bone depended, is so evidently in the same tradition as that represented at Star Carr. How then are we to interpret this? Does it reflect simply an advance in technical dexterity – barbed points being more difficult to work in bone than in antler, though for some purposes more effective – or is it that the finished products were intended for different uses? It is not my present purpose to suggest a solution, but simply to point to the existence of a problem of a kind which ought to abound in prehistoric archaeology. The choice of raw materials is worthy of research precisely because it prompts questions which might otherwise remain unasked, and it is only by questing that we can hope to discover.

The adoption of farming affected the choice of raw materials drawn from organic nature in much the same way as it did the supply of food: it increased their volume and availability and it led to the development of new substances. It was for instance the eliciting of *Linum usitatissimum* and the domestication and selective breeding of fleecy sheep that made possible the rise of textile crafts based on the weaving of linen[55] and wool.[56] Further, it is relevant to recall that sheep-breeding, and consequently a woollen industry, could not be carried on over extensive territories of temperate Europe until permanent deforestation had proceeded far enough to provide adequate open pasturage.[57] This is only another illustration of the need to view the various aspects of economic life in relation to the ecosystems which comprehend human societies.

The adoption of farming was associated with a progressively more extensive and effective use of the inorganic resources of the habitat. The greatly increased use of fired clay among peasant communities, epitomized above all by the craft of potting, though of great value as an archaeological indicator, was not in itself of any marked significance. It was the adoption of the working of copper and its alloys, and later of iron, that brought about major increases in control over physical environment,[58] not only in working such organic materials as wood and bone, but even more significantly in helping to improve the food-supply through more effective felling and clearance and through the provision of such things as pruning- and lopping-knives, plough-shares, coulters, and the like. The cheaper and the more effective metal tools became, the greater must have been their impact on food-production and so on population. Conversely, every increase in the density of population made possible a finer subdivision of labour, a most essential condition for further technical improvements. The interaction between food-production, population growth, and the ability to use more effective materials for implements and gear was both intimate and continuous, and it is certain that a more adequate understanding of economic prehistory waits on a much fuller and more precise knowledge about the growth of population during prehistoric times than we at present possess.

The importance attached to obtaining the most effective materials from which to make the tools needed to win a better living from the physical environment – and for that matter to forge the weapons for competing with neighbouring groups – is reflected in the care with which they were sought out and if necessary traded over great distances. The size of the territories over which primitive hunters had commonly to range in quest of food meant that in the normal course they were able to gather raw materials from different parts of what might be a variegated habitat. One effect of adopting agriculture was, as we have seen, to tie communities more closely to the soil, even if at first temporarily, so that the area from which raw materials could be gathered was much more restricted. The contraction in living-area, which was only one aspect of the increasing density of population made possible by the new economy, came at a time when advances in technology were making great calls on raw materials of uneven and often very restricted occurrence. This development of bronze metallurgy in regions lacking either tin or copper depended on trade – but this is a subject altogether too important to embark on at the close of a lecture.

At an early stage I made it clear that I was concerned with prehistoric economy primarily as an approach to prehistory. I ought not to conclude without reminding you that ways of approaching this subject are as

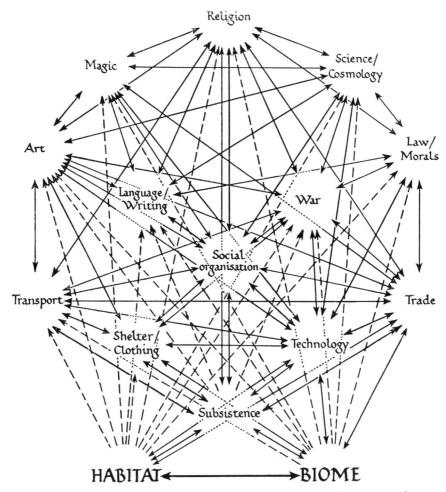

9.6 Interactions between different aspects of the socio-cultural component of ecosystems comprehending agriculture

numerous as culture and indeed as man himself is many-sided, and further that no aspect of culture, by which I mean everything acquired by individuals as members of societies, can be fully understood in isolation (fig. 9.6). Thus, not even the most prosaic activities of daily life can be adequately interpreted solely in terms of economic factors: even the selection of animals for food or of the skeletal remains of these for implements or weapons may depend on traditional beliefs in the field of law, magic, or religion, or on some circumstance of social organization, as much as upon such material factors as the means available for hunting or manufacture. Conversely, it is no less true that the influence of economic factors permeates all levels of social life, so that a knowledge of these is necessary for the understanding even of such apparently remote spheres as art or religion.

My theme has been the interaction between subsistence and technology and between each of these and habitat and biome. The thesis I have sought to sustain is first that even at this basal level, at which economy so to speak interlocks with ecology, the decisive factor has been social choice, and second that every advance in the control of the natural environment has enlarged the scope within which this choice could operate. In other words, economic progress in the sense of a growing capacity to utilize natural resources, such as we can trace in prehistory, marks stages in the liberation of the human spirit by making possible more varied responses and so accelerating the processes of change and diversification over the whole realm of culture. Advances in the means of production have indeed determined history, but only in the sense that they have widened the range of choice open to human societies.

Notes

1 *Proc. Brit. Acad.*, 1951, pp. 199–217.
2 *Op.cit.*, pp. 207–8.
3 *Britannia*, 1695 edn, p. 95.
4 *Britannia*, 1695 edn, p. iii.
5 Cf. A. M. Tallgren, *Eurasia Septentrionalis Antiqua*, x, pp. 16–24, and *Antiquity*, 1937, pp. 152–61.
6 Cf. J. G. D. Clark, 'Archaeological Theories and Interpretation: Old World', *Anthropology Today* (Wenner-Gren Symposium, A. L. Kroeber Chairman), Univ. of Chicago Press, 1952, pp. 343–60.
7 Papers of the Peabody Museum of American Archaeology and Ethnology, Harvard University, vol. xlvii, no. 1, Cambridge, Mass., 1952.
8 *Ibid.*, pp. 97–8.
9 F. Boas (ed.), *General Anthropology*, New York, 1938, p. 4.
10 Cf. J. G. D. Clark, *Prehistoric Europe. The Economic Basis*, London, 1952, pp. 7–8 *et passim*.
11 Donald F. Thomson, 'The Seasonal Factor in Human Culture illustrated from the Life of a Contemporary Nomadic Group', *Proc. Prehist. Soc.*, 1939, pp. 209–21; see p. 211.
12 *Ibid.*, p. 216.
13 Paul A. Vestal, *Ethnobotany of the Ramah Navaho*, p. 57. Papers of the Peabody Mus. of Am. Arch. and Ethn., Harvard Univ., vol. xl, no.4, Cambridge, Mass., 1952.

14 E. Peters, *Die altsteinzeitliche Kulturstätte Petersfels,* Augsburg, 1930; E. Peters and V. Toepfer, 'Der Abschluß der Grabungen am Petersfels bei Engen im badischen Hegau', *Präh. Z.,* XXIII, pp. 155–99.

15 W. Krause in A. Rust, *Das altsteinzeitliche Rentierjägerlager Meiendorf,* Neumünster, 1937, pp. 48–61; W. Krause and W. Kollau in A. Rust, *Die alt- und mittelsteinzeitlichen Funde von Stellmoor,* Neumünster, 1943, pp. 49–105.

16 F. C. Fraser and J. E. King, *Proc. Prehist. Soc.* XV (1949), pp. 67–9, and XVI (1950), pp. 124–9; also ch. 3 in J. G. D. Clark, *Excavations at Star Carr, An Early Mesolithic Site in Yorkshire, England,* Cambridge. 1954.

17 J. G. D. Clark, 'Die mittler Steinzeit', *Historia Mundi* (Fritz Kern), Bd. i, Munich, 1952, pp. 318–45; see p. 325.

18 Clark, *Prehistoric Europe,* p. 172.

19 E.g. the pre-ceramic levels at Jarmo (R. and L. Braidwood, *Antiquity,* 1950, pp. 189–95) and Jericho (Anon., 'The Archaeology of Palestine', *Occasional Paper no. 10,* pp. 10–12, London Univ. Inst. of Archaeology, 1953).

20 Pottery was for instance used in a late Mesolithic milieu in the west Baltic area (see especially T. Mathiassen, *Dyrholmen En Stenalderboplads paa Djursland,* Copenhagen, 1943, pp. 62–3), as well as much more extensively in the later hunter-fisher cultures of the circumpolar region northern (see G. Gjessing, *Circumpolar Stone Age,* Acta Arctica, Fasc. II, Copenhagen, 1944, pp. 40–6).

21 E.g. by the Mesolithic Natufians of Palestine: see D. A. E. Garrod and B. M. A. Bate, *The Stone Age of Mount Carmel,* Oxford, 1937, i, pl. xiii. The technique of setting flint flakes in slotted hafts was widely employed for weapon-heads by Mesolithic hunter-fishers from north-western Europe to inner Siberia.

22 Clark, 'Man and Nature in Prehistory, with special reference to Neolithic Settlement in Northern Europe', *Occasional Paper no. 6,* London Univ. Inst. of Archaeology, 1945, pp. 20–8; 'Farmers and Forests in Neolithic Europe', *Antiquity,* 1945, pp. 57–71; 'Forest Clearance and Prehistoric Farming', *The Economic History Review,* xvii (1947), 45–51.

23 J. Iversen, *Landnam i Danmarks Stenalder,* Dan. Geol. Unders. ii R. nr. 66, Copenhagen, 1941; K. Faegri, *Studies on the Pleistocene of Western Norway, iii. Bømlo,* Bergens Mus. Årbok, 1943, Naturvitensk. r. Nr. 8; H. Godwin, *Nature,* CLIII, p. 511, and CLIV, p. 6; F. Firbas, *Spät-und nacheiszeitliche Waldeschichte der Alpen,* Jena, 1949, pp. 353–66.

24 E.g. M. Bloch, *Les caractères originaux de l'histoire rurale française,* Oslo, 1931, pp. 27–9.

25 E.g. C. Schott, 'Urlandschaft und Rodung. Vergleichende Betrachtungen aus Europa und Kanada', *Z. d. Ges. f. Erdkunde zu Berlin,* 1935, pp. 81–102.

26 E.g. I. Manninen, *Die finnisch-ugrischen Völker,* Leipzig, 1932, pp. 274–5.

27 P. D. R. Williams-Hunt, 'A Technique for Anthropology from the Air in Malaya', *Bull. Raffles Museum Singapore,* Ser. B, no. 4 (1949), pp. 44–68.

28 Information from Dr. H. Godwin, F.R.S., who observed crops growing in the experimental clearing in the Draved forest, south Jutland.

29 V. G. Childe, *The Danube in Prehistory,* Oxford, 1929, pp. 46–7; Clark, *Prehistoric Europe,* pp. 95–6, fig. 45.

30 E.g. Köln-Lindenthal (W. Buttler and W. Haberey, *Die bandkeramische Ansiedlung bei Köln-Lindenthal,* Leipzig, 1936) and Brześć Kujawski (K. Jażdżewski, *Wiadomości Archeologiczne,* xv (1938), p. 93 and pl. ii).

31 V. G. Childe, *op. cit.,* 1929, p. 29 *et passim.*

32 P. V. Glob, *Acta Archaeologica,* 1939, pp. 131–40.

33 I. Manninen, *op. cit.,* 1932, p. 30.

34 A. Rieth, *Prähistorische Zeitschrift,* 34/35 (1949/50), pp. 230 ff.

35 Hay-making was developed only at the end of the prehistoric period and roots and other fodder crops came in quite late in the historical period. During prehistoric times livestock depended mainly on what they could secure by grazing on natural vegetation.

36 *Prehistoric Europe,* pp. 100–3. An important work, not available to me in time for my own book, is P. V. Glob's *Ard og Plov i Nordens Oldtid,* Jysk Arkæologisk Selsk. Skr., Bd. i, Aarhus, 1951.

37 Corresponding to Cyril Fox's primary area of settlement as defined in his *Archaeology of the Cambridge Region,* pp. 313–14, Cambridge, 1923.

38 *Prehistoric Europe,* pp. 105–7.

39 O. Heer, 'Die Pflanzen der Pfahlbauten vi. Pfahlbautenbericht', *Mitt. d. Antiqu.-Ges. in Zürich,* Bd. xv, pp. 310–17, Zürich, 1866.

40 E.g. the proportions between cattle and swine on one hand and sheep on the other in relation to the progress of deforestation. See Clark, 'Sheep and Swine in the Husbandry of Prehistoric Europe', *Antiquity,* 1947, pp. 122–36.

41 K. Jessen and H. Helbaek, *Cereals in Great Britain and Ireland in Prehistoric and Early Historic Times,* Det Kong. Danske Vidensk. Sels. Biol. Skr., Bd. iii, nr. 2, Copenhagen, 1944; H. Helbæk, 'Early Crops in Southern England', *Proc. Prehist. Soc.* xviii (1952), pp. 194–233.

42 The basic research was done at the turn of the century by G. L. F. Sarauw. His Danish results are set out in G. Hatt, *Landbrug i Danmarks Oldtid,* Copenhagen, 1937, pp. 20–3.

43 K. Thorvildsen, 'Moseliget fra Tollund', *Aarbøger,* 1950, pp. 302–9; H. Helbæk, 'Tollund Mandens Sidste Maaltid', *ibid.,* pp. 311–28.

44 G. Hatt, *Aarbøger,* 1938, pp. 221–5 and fig. 91.

45 H. Shetelig and H. Falk, *Scandinavian Archaeology,* Oxford, 1937, pp. 149 and 313.

46 C. J. Thomsen, *Ledetraad til Nordisk Oldkyndighed,* Copenhagen, 1936; Sven Nilsson, *Skandinaviska Nordens Urinvånare,* Lund, 1838–43. Cf. G. E. Daniel, *The Three Ages,* Cambridge, 1943, and *A Hundred Years of Archaeology,* London, 1950, pp. 42–51.

47 J. G. D. Clark, *Excavations at Star Carr,* Cambridge, 1954, ch. v.

48 A fine example of the base of a stag antler, from which at least four longitudinal splinters have been detached as far down as the burr, is illustrated by P. Girod (*Les Stations de l'Âge du Renne dans les vallées de la Vézère et de la Corrège,* Paris, 1906, pls. xcv–xcvi), from a deposit at Gorge d'Enfer B in association with characteristic split-base bone points. Other evidence for the still sparing use of this technique in Aurignacian times may be cited from Les Cottés l'abri Blanchard, and Isturitz.

49 Most notably at Meiendorf (Rust, *op. cit.,* 1937, pp. 90–8) and Stellmoor (1943, pp. 143–4), but also on stray finds, e.g. from the Havel Lakes (*Mannus Z.,* 1917, Bd. viii, Taf. iv, 8).

50 The lower parts of reindeer antlers showing traces of the groove and splinter technique have, for instance, been noted at La Madeleine, Laugerie Basse, St Marcel, Badegoule, and Montgaudier in south-west France; at Petersfels and Schussenquelle in south Germany; and in central Europe at Pekárna in Moravia. It is significant that the barbed harpoon-heads, recognized type fossils of the later Magdalenian, are almost invariably made from reindeer antler, as are also the lance-heads (*sagaies*) of earlier stages of this culture.

51 M. W. Thompson, *Proc. Prehist. Soc.* xix (1954).

52 J. G. D. Clark, *The Mesolithic Settlement of Northern Europe,* Cambridge, 1936, ch. iii.

53 Only isolated barbed points made from stag antler have been found on Maglemosian sites of Boreal age, e.g. *Danske Oldsager,* i, no. 173.

54 The great majority of the barbed points from Mullerup were made from ribs (*Aarbøger,* 1903, pp. 245–6). From Sværdborg only 40 of the 213 found during the 1917–18 excavations were made from ribs, the remainder from metapodial bones, mainly of roe deer (*Mém. des Antiq. du Nord,* 1918–19, pp. 320–4). The proportions from Holmegaard were similar to those from Sværdborg (*ibid.,* 1926–31, p. 58).

55 E. Vogt, *Geflechte und Gewebe der Steinzeit,* Basel, 1937; also *Ciba Review,* no. 54, pp. 1938–64, Basel.

56 H. C. Broholm and M. Hald, *Danske Bronzealders Dragter,* Nordiske Fortidsminder, ii. Bd., 5/6 Hft., Copenhagen, 1935; cf. A. Geijer and H. Ljungh, *Acta Arch.* viii (1937), pp. 266–75

57 J. G. D. Clark, *Antiquity,* 1947, pp. 122–36.

58 V. G. Childe, 'Archaeological Ages as Technological Stages', *J. Roy. Anthr. Inst.* lxxiv (1944), pp. 1–19.

CHAPTER 10

TRAFFIC IN STONE AXE AND ADZE BLADES

A basic condition for understanding the past is to avoid applying categories of thought and shades of meaning inappropriate to the period under review. This applies with special force to the study of the prehistoric past, by definition the phase of history most remote from the present and for this very reason most likely to be misunderstood. As Martin Jahn has well said,[1] much of the controversy between those who write about prehistoric trade and those who deny its existence is semantic: it arises from the different meanings they attach to the word trade. If one takes a definition of trade proper to a society with an advanced division of labour and an economy based on money – if one chooses, for example, to define trade as an activity carried on by a class of traders for financial gain, it is understandable that no evidence for trade can be found in societies functioning at a simpler level, societies in which there is a bare minimum of specialization and to which the notion of profit in the sense we understand it may be quite foreign. Yet, if one sees it as, in the last resort, no more than the peaceful and systematic exchange of goods, one has no difficulty in recognizing that trade of a kind is practised among even the most primitive societies known to ethnologists; and, by implication, one is entitled to seek for traces of it in the archaeological record of prehistory.

The present contribution, offered to a scholar whose lively mind ranges widely but penetrates at all times to the physical realities of existence, will concentrate on the interpretation of a specific archaeological phenomenon in terms of primitive trade, namely the manufacture and distribution over extensive territories of the blades of axes and adzes made from particular kinds of stone. The evidence will be reviewed under two main heads, namely that from north-western and northern Europe between the fourth and the second millennia B.C. and that from Australia, New Zealand and Melanesia down to the nineteenth and even, in the case of New Guinea, to the mid-twentieth century A.D. In conclusion some brief attempt will be made to collate these two sources of information and see how the prehistoric data appears in the light of ethnography.

The principle of the adze was well established among the mesolithic hunter-fishers for thousands of years before farming penetrated north-west Europe; and these people had even begun to apply polishing, a technique

169

devised long previously for shaping antler and bone, to stone tools.[2] Yet archaeologists have surely been right to see in the polished axe or adze blade a very symbol of neolithic culture.[3] The neolithic farmers of temperate Europe could only practise their way of life at the expense of the forest; and it must be remembered that neolithic farming in this part of the world involved, not just a once-and-for-all felling and burning, but the clearance and reclearance of zones of temporary cultivation.[4] Then again, a more settled economy and the need to provide shelter for livestock meant larger and more substantial buildings and the most obvious material for these, not to mention fences and palisades, was timber. In such a context it is easy to see why men went to the trouble of polishing flint blades, a laborious process, but one which provided more effective tools.[5] Again, the enhanced importance of the axe and adze laid a premium on selecting the best material for the blade and this in turn underlies the traffic which forms the subject of this essay.

I

Great Britain & Ireland

The documentation is particularly thorough for Great Britain and Ireland. Glaciation and the activity of rivers and tides distributed suitable materials quite widely and no doubt blades were made from pebbles spread over the country by natural forces. On the other hand systematic petrographic analysis has shown beyond doubt that stone of particular merit was often won from narrowly defined sources and distributed by human activity in the form of finished or almost finished blades. Again, excavation has revealed the existence of mines, quarries and working-floors and chance discoveries have brought to light hoards of completed axe or adze blades.

Care has always to be taken, even when dealing with a material of strictly local origin, to take account of the possibility of natural transport. On the other hand, when axes or adzes of such a stone are found distributed over more or less extensive territories with little or no regard to the movements of ice-sheets or the flows of rivers, the presumption is that the distribution was effected by man. The case is even more definite when traces of more or less intensive quarrying and manufacture are located at the sources of rock particularly suited for axe blades. Indeed, the very notion of a stone axe trade in prehistoric Britain arose from observation of the apparent widespread geographical distribution of axe-heads of the fine-grained augite-granophyre from Graig Lwyd on the slopes of Penmaenmawr in North Wales.[6] The first essay was based on the mere inspection of hand specimens,[7] but during the last three decades many hundreds of stone axes have been subjected to petrographic analysis.[8] This has shown that several other sources of stone contributed axe blades to the population of neolithic Britain. Among these should be mentioned the porcellanite from Tievebulliagh and Rathlin Island, Ulster,[9] and the greenstone from Great Langdale in the Lake District,[10] at each of which localities veritable factories have been identified in the form of wasters, axes fractured in the making and quantities of flakes. At each of the three main factory sites, it should be emphasized, an adequate supply of raw material was ready to hand in the form of surface scree and no mining or deep quarrying was necessary; only at Mynydd Rhiw, Caernarvonshire,[11] the importance of which as a source cannot yet be precisely assessed, are there signs that a particular seam, in this case of altered shale, was quarried to some depth below ground surface. The petrological evidence also points unequivocally to west Cornwall as the source of several different kinds of stone used for axes. The reason why axe factories have not yet been found there may be that the sites have been submerged by the rise in sea-level that has certainly taken place in southern England since neolithic times.

A feature common to the stone axe factories and to the flaking floors associated with the flint-mines is the absence or extreme rarity of polished blades; and, conversely, roughed-out but as yet unfinished blades are normally confined to the immediately surrounding area. The process of roughing out had generally to be done at the source of the stone, since it would otherwise have been necessary to transport needlessly quantities of material removed in the process of manufacture, a proceeding hardly likely to commend itself to people lacking wheeled transport or animal traction. The final stage of manufacture, the polishing of the blades, was evidently carried on at the settlements in more congenial surroundings, where spare time could be utilized for this purpose; and it was in the polished state that blades were distributed far and wide.

Although the petrographic analysis of stone axes has not been carried out with equal completeness over different parts of the country, enough has been done to throw valuable light on the areas over which the products of different factories were distributed as well as to establish their historical contexts. At least four west Cornish sources were apparently being drawn upon by the earliest neolithic inhabitants of south-west England by the end of the fourth millennium B.C.[12] and axe blades have been recovered from three out of four of the neolithic settlements so far excavated in Devon and Dorset, notably Hembury, Hazard Hill and Maiden Castle. Indeed, the discovery of pebbles of Cornish origin at the mesolithic settlement at Farnham, Surrey,[13] suggests that contacts, however indirect, between the extreme south-west and the south of England may have been established before the neolithic way of life had spread to these islands. It is still uncertain precisely when the sources in North Wales, the Lake District and Northern Ireland were opened up. Graig Lwyd axes from the Somerset and Cambridgeshire Fens show that the north Welsh factory was already active before the end of the first half of the third millennium B.C.;[14] and finds of Craig Lwyd and Langdale axes at the settlement on the course of the West Kennet Avenue at Avebury and in the upper silting of the nearby Windmill Hill, as well as at the sacred site of Cairnpapple in West Lothian, suggest that both factories were still in production during Later Neolithic times.[15] The evidence from Ulster suggests that the porcellanite factories were flourishing more or less contemporaneously with those at Graig Lwyd and Langdale; it may be noted that the porcellanite axes from Ulster have flattened sides like those from Great Langdale.

Whereas axes made from rocks obtained in west Cornwall during the initial phase of neolithic culture in Britain are confined in distribution to south-west England and do not extend further east than Wessex, those from the factories just mentioned, together with ones from an unidentified locality between Penzance and Mousehole in west Cornwall, spread over extensive parts of Britain even penetrating regions well supplied with flint. As might be expected the distribution of axe blades from particular factories (fig. 10.1) is strongly influenced by geography. If for instance we consider the axes listed in the *Fourth Report* and exclude those from the territories in which they were made, we find that Wessex and the south-west absorbed 87 per cent of Cornish (Group 1), 76 per cent of Graig Lwyd, 63 per cent of Ulster porcellanite and only 47 per cent of Langdale axes. Conversely, Scotland, the northern counties, and the east Midlands between them took 38 per cent of the Langdale axes, but only 10 per cent of those from Graig Lwyd and 4 per cent of those from Cornwall (Group 1). Even so it is striking how far afield axes travelled. Water presented no barrier, but on the contrary a ready medium for transport and it may well be significant that all the known factories are near the coast. Thus, it should be no surprise that porcellanite should have traversed the North Channel to Ayrshire, Arran and the Firth of Clyde and even reached the Hebrides, as well as crossing the Irish Sea to the Mersey and so by the Midland Gap to Gloucester and Dorset and even to London and north Kent; or, that axes from Great Langdale should have crossed Solway Firth and moved round Galloway to Arran and the Clyde,[16] as well as crossing to the Isle of Man. That Cornish axes (Group 1) should have reached as far east as Essex and as far north as north-east Yorkshire shows on the other hand that much traffic went on overland, even if some of it took advantage of rivers.

It is particularly striking how many stone axes from known sources converged on the cretaceous area of Wessex: evidently the pull of tradition – it will be remembered that the earliest neolithic settlers of the south-west used stone axes – or of other, possibly ritual, considerations was strong enough to override the abundance of flint in the region. On the other hand, the fact that stone axe blades from Graig Lwyd and Langdale failed to penetrate to the chalk zone of Sussex may in part reflect its remoteness from the sources of these axes. The forces responsible for the transmission of axe

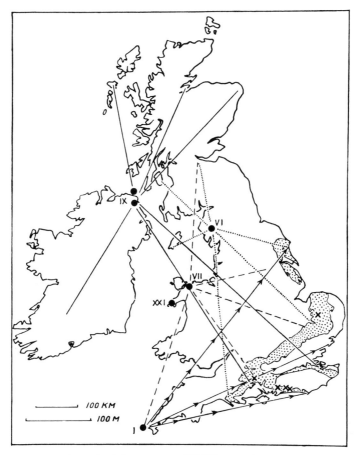

10.1 Some elements in the flint and stone axe blade traffic in the British Isles. The
maximum extension of products is indicated in each case by radial lines

blades of particular types of stone over hundreds of miles among neolithic
peasant communities will be considered in the final section of this paper. In
the meantime there is no substantial evidence that the manufacture of stone
axes formed a whole-time occupation for specialists. As we have seen, it was
only at Mynydd Rhiw that there is evidence for real quarrying and even there
the workings were quite shallow: elsewhere the material had merely to be
picked up from surface scree. It is likely enough that some men showed
particular skill, but there is no evidence for anything in the nature of the
permanent settlements one would expect if a group of specialists had made a
livelihood exclusively from knapping and shaping axe blades for export. It
has already been emphasized that only the basic work was done at the source
of the stone, the blades being dispersed to nearby settlements in roughed-out

form and there subjected to polishing. No doubt it is by analogy with the so-called merchants' hoards of the Bronze Age that the groups of polished flint or stone axe blades recorded from different parts of the British Isles have sometimes been taken as evidence of organized trade, but many doubts surround their interpretation. The one certain thing they remind us of is that such objects represented an important source of wealth: and the natural storage place for wealth, whether dedicated to unseen powers in the form of votive offerings or intended for the use of its owner, would in the prevailing state of society have been the soil.

That flint was mined in neolithic times in the cretaceous zone of southern Britain has long been known.[17] The most extensive mining area to be tested by excavation is that of Grimes Graves, Norfolk,[18] which extends in all over some 34 acres. About half this was mined by sinking shafts – over 360 are visible as well-defined depressions – through the overlying glacial deposits and the two uppermost layers of flint in the chalk down to the desired 'floorstone', which was gained by sending out radiating galleries, so that the whole region was honeycombed leaving only sufficient rock in place to avoid collapse. Where a shallow valley brought the 'floorstone' nearer the surface, the workings were shallower, comprising bell-shaped or even open-cast pits, leaving no clear surface indication. The comparatively narrow belt of chalk forming the Sussex Downs was intensively mined and five sites have already been tested by excavation:[19] of these the largest, that of Cissbury, probably had nearly 300 deep shafts and those at Harrow Hill and Blackpatch, not far away, around 100 each. Wessex, on the other hand, despite its great extent of chalk, has only yielded evidence for one mining site, that at Easton Down, Winterslow,[20] a fact not so surprising when one remembers that it absorbed a high proportion of the stone axe blades from the Cornish Group 1 source and took substantial numbers from the principal stone axe factories of the north-west.

Precisely when flint began to be mined from the chalk in southern England is as yet unknown, but it seems that the mines of East Anglia, Sussex and Wessex reached their peak comparatively late. In the case of Grimes Graves, Norfolk, samples taken from four different shafts gave radio-carbon dates clustering around 2000 B.C.[21] One at least of the Sussex mines, Church Hill, must have been active about the same time, since an ovoid beaker of early type was placed with a burial inserted in a shaft during the period of mining activity. Again, it was considered by the excavator of Easton Down that the mines had reached their zenith at a time when beaker pottery was used in Wessex.

Quite plainly the mining of flint requires far more expert knowledge and a much greater investment of labour than the mere selection of material from scree and it seems evident that for the handful of men, who are all we need suppose to have been active at any one time, even at the larger mining centres so far known in England, the work must have been full-time during the season when it was carried on. Yet we have no means of telling how long this was or of estimating the extent to which the mining of flint and the roughing-out of axe blades represented the full-time work of specialists. What does nevertheless seem to be true is that so far as England is concerned there is no sign of any traffic in flint blades of a kind different from that which accounted for the distribution of the stone axes. Although mined flint lacks features which allow one to diagnose its sources with real certainty and one cannot as a rule hope to trace the movement of flint axe blades from their workshops, as is sometimes possible in the case of stone axes, the existence of hoards of axes in mint condition and having every appearance of having been made from fresh, unbruised flint like that obtained from mines, suggests that flint blades travelled considerable distances from the sources of their raw material. As might be expected Norfolk is rich in hoards of flint axe blades, including one from Lound Run with a quartzite polisher; and others are known from Kent, Sussex, Surrey and Essex.[22] Hoards such as these, comprising a number of blades packed together in the soil, are to be distinguished from funerary finds,[23] like those found under burial mounds at Howe Hill, Duggleby and Seamer in the East Riding, Liffy Low (Derby) and Upton Lovell (Wilts.), in which flint axes feature alongside other elements, in the personal possessions of an individual man.

So far we have been considering axe and adze blades manufactured from materials obtained at certain localities, whether from surface deposits or as a result of mining, and distributed over more or less extensive areas of the country. It remains to mention a class of highly finished axe blades made of jade, almost all of which were made from jadeite, a material held to be definitely absent from Britain in its natural state.[24] Since no unfinished examples have been noted in this country it seems reasonable to suppose that the objects were brought here in a finished form. It was once considered that they were imported from Brittany, but this has lost some of its force from the recent discovery that none of the Breton axes tested have been found to be of local material. It seems much more likely that both Britain and Brittany alike received blades from the lower Rhenish area, since jadeite is considered to have come most probably from Piedmont or the Swiss Alps and finished specimens occur in Germany and Belgium. Dr Campbell Smith's map of the comparatively thin triangular specimens that stand closest to ones from the continent shows them to occur in each of their varieties over almost the whole of Great Britain, as well as to have spread into Ireland. It seems more likely that the jadeite axes were introduced to this country by one or another of the Beaker groups to reach us from the lower Rhineland, than that they reflect trading activities.

Continental Europe

Although nothing comparable in thoroughness to the petrographic work carried out on British stone axes has been done in Europe, the documentation which does exist enlarges our knowledge of the context in which a traffic in these objects occurred during prehistoric times. In particular there is evidence for traffic in stone adze blades among hunter-fisher communities living beyond the zone of neolithic peasant farming; and even for the passage of flint ones hundreds of miles into the circumpolar zone of Scandinavia. One may begin by quoting two examples of traffic within the ambit of hunter-fishers, one from the extreme west of southern Norway, the other from Russian Carelia.

The Norwegian evidence was recovered by investigating the source of stone used for large-scale axe manufacture on the southern part of the island of Bømlo south of Bergen.[25] This very dense and homogeneous greenstone was found to be identical with that outcropping on the minute island of Hespriholmen, at present just under 2½ miles west of Bømlo; and since glacial movements were from east to west, it would seem to follow that the stone must have been brought by man. At the present day traces may be seen on Hespriholmen of a well-defined quarry, having a flat floor some 30 metres long and 5.8 m. above modern sea-level; and it is assumed that this was worked when the sea was around 5 m. higher so that canoes could easily have been loaded direct from the source of raw material. On Bømlo the axe factory sites are concentrated on and between narrow fjord-like inlets that appear to mark the route by which raw material was brought from Hespriholmen and axe blades shipped to the mainland. Pollen analysis in bogs between the inlets suggests that the high-water mark of the manufacture in Bømlo of greenstone from the Hespriholmen quarry fell in the period when the area was still occupied by hunter-fishers in the Nøstvet tradition and declined or even passed out of existence by the time farming was established in the area. Although its scale implies that the axe manufacture on Bømlo must have been carried on very largely for use elsewhere, no detailed evidence is available as to the extent of the territory over which axe or adze blades of Hespriholmen stone were used, beyond the fact that they occur at Lego in Jaeren, some 70 miles to the south; nor do we know whether the axe manufacture was carried out by people who lived on Bømlo for any length of time or whether it was done by parties of temporary visitors. It has always to be remembered that hunter-fishers were both sparser and more accustomed to move about in pursuit of food and raw materials than peasants; and those living in coastal territories had a ready means for doing so by means of boats and canoes.

Much more is known about the distribution of the Olonetz green slate adzes and chisels manufactured at a source near Petrosavodsk on the north-east shore of Lake Onega in Russian Carelia.[26] To the south-east the rock was distributed in boulder trains by the Pleistocene glaciers, but the spread of finished objects made from the material over extensive territories to the west can only be explained in terms of human agency. Over a zone extending north to Lake Seg and west to the Gulf of Finland artefacts of Olonetz slate are so numerous that they must have been in common use among the inhabitants. Beyond this they were distributed (fig. 10.2) over a radius from Petrosavodsk of *c.* 500 miles; north of the Gulf they occur fairly commonly in Finland up to latitude 65° and more rarely up to 68° north; and to the south they are abundant in Esthonia and rather more sparse in Latvia.

The users of Hespriholmen greenstone and Olonetz slate were hunter-fishers, the contemporaries of peasant farmers to the south. The Nøstvet people of Jaeren exemplified by the earliest inhabitants of the Viste rock-shelters,[27] were largely contemporary with the Early Neolithic farmers of Denmark and south Scandinavia; and the Carelian hunter-fishers responsible for the adze factories of Petrosavodsk continued into a period contemporary with the Middle and Late Neolithic of Denmark. In many ways the circumpolar hunter-fishers were at least as well off as their peasant neighbours, who were, after all, among the most marginal in Europe. Favourable conditions for hunting and catching made it possible to settle down at least seasonally and the tribes of north-west Russia, Finland and south and middle Sweden made large coil-built pots, which they decorated with pits and comb-impressions.

When we move south into the farming zone of the north European Plain we find widespread evidence for flint-mining reminiscent of that already encountered from southern England. In Poland[28] it seems that a certain type of chocolate-coloured flint was already being mined in the central regions by Upper Palaeolithic hunters, as it continued to be by the group of Neolithic peasants defined by Funnel-neck Beakers. Nevertheless there was in Poland a marked intensification in flint-mining at a time when, during the last stage of the local Neolithic, copper axes were beginning to become available, though too expensive for general use. To quote one instance, the attractively banded flint of the Opatow district of central Poland was exploited during the final phase of the local Neolithic on such scale that at the Krzemionki mines alone about 1000 surface depressions, marking the position of filled up shafts, are visible over an area of rather more than 800 acres.[29] The mines, about 6 metres deep, are of a complex type like the deep workings at Grimes Graves or Spiennes in Belgium, having at the bottom radiating galleries from the floors of which the desired flint was extracted. The axe-blade factories with their quantity of waste flakes and spoiled rough-outs are sited close to the shafts. The blades themselves were distributed among the Złota and Globular Amphora peoples over an extensive territory from the Upper Oder, Upper Vistula and San to the Lower Oder and almost as far east as the Bug and the Niemen.

Although it is likely enough that the virtues of the excellent cretaceous flint of Belgium at the western margin of the plain of northern Europe were recognized quite early, intensive mining of the kind seen at Spiennes, Obourg, and St Gertrude, with shafts in the first mentioned as much as 9 or 10 metres deep, passing through thick deposits of quaternary gravels and a zone of tertiary sands before striking the flint-bearing chalk, was apparently first carried on by the Michelsberg people,[30] whose close relatives in Switzerland were already acquainted with flat copper axes. Although it is rarely possible to identify certainly the artefacts from any particular source of flint, axes of Michelsberg type, apparently roughed out at workshops close to the Belgian mines, have been recognized from the Meuse to the Rhine as far up as Coblentz.

One of the few kinds recognizable at sight is the wax-coloured flint of Grand Pressigny, the main area of working of which extends for a distance of some 12 kilometres in the departments of Indre-et-Loire and Vienne.[31] Although worked by the Late Palaeolithic Magdalenians, this source of flint was first systematically exploited on a large scale for wide distribution during the closing phase of the local Neolithic when copper tools and weapons were still very expensive. In this respect Grand Pressigny falls into line with the intensification of flint-mining already described. It differs in that axes were a relatively unimportant product. The flint of Grand Pressigny was outstanding for the fine regular blades it was capable of yielding and a prominent feature of the sites is the long core from which such blades have been struck. Some of the finest blades were converted into knife or dagger forms with shallow pressure flaking on the convex face, forms which, like the more elaborate ones made in Denmark and south Sweden about the same time, were in some sense cheap symbols or substitutes for copper ones. From central France Grand Pressigny blades spread west to Morbihan and the Channel Islands, north to the Paris Basin and east, on the one hand to the Low Countries and north-west Germany and on the other to Switzerland. In the course of this Grand Pressigny flint traversed cultural boundaries and was used indifferently by the makers of Late Chassey, Seine-Oise-Marne, Corded Ware and Bell Beaker pottery.

The finest flint axes and adzes of Europe and indeed of the whole world were made from material derived ultimately from the chalk found in restricted zones of Denmark and Scania (fig. 10.2). Comparatively little of the raw material was obtained by mining. The nature of the cortex still visible on some specimens, no less than the strongly coastal distribution of hoards of flint adze blades in Denmark and south Sweden, argues that the sea-shore was in itself a main source. Flint-mines are comparatively rare and, indeed, re-examination of the supposed flint-mines at Kvarnby near Malmo in Scania suggests that they were sunk to win chalk and may not be very old.[32] Nevertheless, recent excavations in Denmark have shown beyond doubt that flint was mined on the island of Thy and converted on the spot into thin-butted axe blades,[33] and, again, mines investigated near Aalborg, north Jutland, have been shown to have provided the flint needed to make daggers and crescentic dagger blades,[34] which dated from a period of Danish prehistory contemporary with the Early Bronze Age of south Germany.

The flint of Denmark and the extreme south of Sweden found its way, in the wake of farming, over extensive territories, where the indigenous hunter-fishers were accustomed to using polished slate and stone for piercing and cutting implements and weapons. This is well seen in Norway. The earliest farmers, confined to territories round Oslo Fjord and along the coastal strip as far west as Jaeren,[35] were marked in the archaeological record by thin-butted axes and many of these were of flint imported across the Skaggerak from north Jutland.[36] Again, when farming, carried on no doubt in varying combinations with fishing and hunting, spread as far as the Trondelag, as it did by Later Neolithic times, we find the zones of peasant occupation neatly defined by two-edged knives or daggers and crescentic sickle-like blades:[37] many of these were of darkish flint, often with white flecks, most probably derived from the Senonian deposits of north Jutland and imported in the form of almost completely finished artefacts.

That the Norwegian farmers should have ensured a supply of the flint to which they were accustomed is in no way remarkable. What is more surprising is evidence for the intrusion of southern flint into territories well beyond those into which farming penetrated.[38] Two main waves have been detected. First of all there was the spread of axe and adze blades and chisels during the closing phase of the Middle Neolithic of Denmark and south Sweden, almost certainly made of flint from Zealand or Scania. This is marked by stray objects that had apparently been taken into use and above all by hoards of objects, most prominent among them adzes with concave working edge, in almost mint condition, situated on what would then have been the coast of Västerbotten, as a rule close to the mouths of rivers flowing into the Gulf of Bothnia.[39]

The existence of these hoards of fresh adze blades, more than 900 miles north of the source of the flint from which they were made, poses several problems. The situation is quite different from that of the Olonetz slate adzes of Finland and the East Baltic, which spread more or less continuously from their centre of origin; instead, we have hoards deep in hunter-fisher territory and not merely far from their place of origin, but separated therefrom by a blank zone hundreds of miles across. What we appear to have is evidence for return journeys, presumably by sea in skin boats,[40] journeys which may well have taken a month in each direction. As if to complement these, objects of red slate that must have come from Norrland have been found in south Sweden either side of the flint area. It now seems likely that the people defined in the archaeological record by pit and comb ware, rather than the

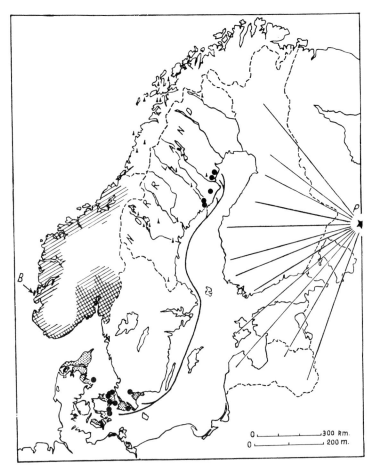

●   Hoards of flint adzes with hollow edge.

▲   Flint 'daggers' in Nord Norge and Norrland.

     Thin-butted flint axes in Norway.

     Flint 'daggers' in Norway.

     Cretaceous zone.

10.2 Traffic in certain groups of flint and stone artifacts in Scandinavia and the Baltic area. B = stone axe factory on Bømlo; P = the Petrosavodsk factory

battle-axe people, were those who undertook these trips. Certainly the pit-ware people, who penetrated south Sweden and the coasts of Denmark during late Middle Neolithic times, showed a marked interest in the good quality flint of the area.[41] Yet, even if hunter-fishers were more mobile than farmers, journeys between south Sweden and Norrland still require some explanation. How in the first place did the voyagers know about the remote shores of the Bothnian Gulf? One answer may lie in the very important role played by seal-hunting in their economy, an activity which must have involved considerable use of boats.[42] Evidence of seal bones on their sites shows that the pit-ware people of Gotland, the West Baltic and the Kattegat were able to take Atlantic, Spotted, Ringed, and Harp seals in some profusion in their home waters; and it may be considered likely that they pursued the two last-mentioned in the more distant hunting grounds of the Gulf of Bothnia. Despite the sparseness of modern settlement and relatively slight opportunities for chance finds or purposive archaeological research, evidence for seal-hunting has already been found on the northern shore of what is now Lake Malar, on the Aaland Islands and on the Finnish side of the Gulf of Bothnia as far north as latitude 65°. Since the hunting of these seals is seasonal, it does not seem fanciful to imagine that seal-hunters might from time to time have worked their way up in their skin boats into these northern waters, loaded up with seal-meat, blubber and skins and paddled home. On such expeditions they might be expected to have encountered indigenous hunters from the interior at the mouths of great rivers flowing down from the mountains; and such meetings would have provided opportunities for peaceful exchange. The northward movement of flint adze blades and the southward movement of red slate, and doubtless of other things besides, could be explained more easily in terms of seasonal hunting trips than of far-flung trading ventures.

The second wave of southern flint to the northern provinces of Scandinavia stemmed ultimately from north Jutland and marks an extension of the route up the west coast of Norway, by which the Late Neolithic farmers were supplied with their knives and daggers. Isolated flint daggers are found on the coasts and islands of Norway as far north as the Lofotens and the Vester Ålen; and they apparently penetrated Norrland through gaps in the mountains behind Trondheim and Narvik Fjords, passing down the rivers and lakes towards the Gulf of Bothnia. In this case there is no sign of organized traffic. The thinly scattered specimens are isolated except for one from near Renträsk in Lapland; and that was found with what appears to have been the personal equipment of a circumpolar hunter.

I I

Australia

As white explorers and settlers penetrated different parts of the Australian mainland they found stone axes with ground working-edges in widespread use, mounted on comparatively light handles and held in position by resin.[43] They were employed as general-purpose tools for cutting opossums out of cavities in trees; splitting open branches for extracting honey, grubs and the eggs of insects; removing sheets of bark for canoes; cutting down trees and shaping wooden artefacts; and dismembering large animals. The axe was not used formally as a weapon and the aborigines had no pressing need to clear

forest or construct timber buildings; even so the aborigines found it worth
while to obtain axe blades from a distance.

Although the edge-ground axe may not have been of high antiquity in all
parts of Australia, there is evidence that it was taken into use relatively early
in the eastern part of New South Wales: parts of four came from a deposit
with blades and microliths at Glen Davies;[44] and Isabel McBryde[45] found an
incomplete one in the lowermost deposit of Seeland's Cave near Grafton in
northern New South Wales, dated by radio-carbon analysis to *c.* 1920 B.C.
When large-scale axe factories began in Australia is still an open question,
although the well-known one at Mount William near Melbourne was still
active until the 1830's; nor can we expect to know in detail how far axes
travelled until systematic petrographic analyses have been undertaken.

What is certain is that substantial quarries and factory sites occur over
much of Australia; and that definite traditions exist about the distance over
which trade would run. Thus, rough-outs taken from quarries of a greenish
diorite at Cloncurry in north-west Queensland are said to have been traded
south, just as the products of a factory site at Parachilna Gorge were traded in
the opposite direction along more or less the same line.[46] Further east, axe
blades from quarries on isolated hills rising from the alluvial plain of the
Lower Macquarie river are said to have been traversed 50, 75 or 100 miles;
and some spectacular quarries have been noted in an outcrop of rock some
300 yards long and only 15–20 feet wide on the crest of a hill at Moor Creek
on the New England range between Tamworth and Armidale in northern
New South Wales.[47]

The best-known quarries are those at Lancefield, near Melbourne, where a
diabase rock outcrops between 1800–2000 ft. above sea-level on the north-
east slope of Mount William.[48] The stone, which varies in colour from light
green to nearly black, has been described as being probably the best example
of high-quality axe stone in Australia. The positions of the quarry areas are
clearly marked on the ground by mounds of waste flakes and splinters,
showing that the axes were roughed out in the immediate area of the outcrop.
Among the flakes it is still possible to recognize preliminary rough-outs for
axes, which because of some defect had been rejected, but, as in Europe,
finished specimens with ground edges are conspicuously absent. It is
tantalizing that, though the quarry was in operation when the white man
arrived (1835–6) and though the aborigines did not finally disappear from the
region until fifteen years later (1850–1), we have no first-hand contemporary
description of how the quarry worked or how its products were distributed.

The account given by A. W. Howitt in 1904[49] must be read in the light of
the fact that it was written two or three generations after the quarries had
ceased to operate, and can hardly have been based on notes compiled by
observers with anthropological training. Even so, with all reservations made,
Howitt's account is suggestive. The Mount William quarries were situated in

the territory of the Wurrunjerri tribe, but immediate control of operations seems to have been vested in the head of a particular family, the last of whom was Billi-Billeri (d. 1846). When Billi-Billeri went away for any reason the day-to-day supervision of the quarries passed to his sister's son, a reminder of how, under the social structure prevailing in aboriginal Australia, proprietary rights might in the course of generations of marriages come to involve numbers of people, extending even outside the Wurrunjerri tribe. It fell to whoever was in immediate charge to prepare roughed out axe blades for those who came for them bringing gifts. We have no information about the proportion of his time Billi-Billeri put into the work of shaping axes, but, since the stone out-cropped on the surface and required no mining or other heavy work and in view of the limited, though still impressive extent of the flaking-floors, it seems unlikely that he can have been anything like a whole-time specialist.

According to Howitt: 'When neighbouring tribes wished for some stone they sent a messenger to Billi-Billeri saying they would send goods in exchange for it, for instance, such as skin rugs. When people arrived after such a message they encamped close to the quarry, and on one occasion Berak heard Billi-Billeri say to them, "I am glad to see you and will give you what you want, and satisfy you, but you must behave quietly, and not hurt me or each other".' The transaction was, then, essentially peaceful involving some reciprocity; any attempt by visitors to obtain stone without leave caused trouble and was likely to result in a fight.

The true extent of the trade in Mount William axe blades cannot be determined from the few rather vague memories of early settlers and could indeed only be discovered as a result of systematic petrological surveys of the kind carried out in the British Isles. Albert A. C. Le Souef, a resident Protector of Aborigines in the Murray District in the early days, whose recollections were recorded by R. Brough Smyth in 1878,[50] expressed the opinion that 'the Mount William stone found its way from tribe to tribe for hundreds of miles', but the only specific instance about which he informs us in detail involves a distance as the crow flies of under 100 miles. Le Souef considered that 'there was a regular system of barter going on' between the aborigines of the Lancefield area and those of the Murray and Lower Goulburn rivers, 'large quantities of greenstone, for making tomahawks' being exchanged for the supplies of spears made from the reeds growing in the river valleys.

One is grateful for records like Le Souef's and those summarized so long after the event by Howitt, but the ineluctable fact is that, though the production of stone axes and their distribution over considerable areas in the form of blanks from localized quarry sites was in full swing down to the nineteenth century in the parts of Australia most intensively settled by white men, we do not know substantially more about the organization of the trade and the drive behind it than we do in the case of the axe trade that flourished four or five thousand years ago in north-western Europe: indeed, in default of systematic petrological determinations, our knowledge about it is less exact. It is only for the northern parts of the continent in such a territory as Arnhem Land, where aboriginal culture has persisted down to the ethnographic present, that there is any real hope of gaining formidable insights into the nature of primitive 'trade'.

Even here there are some difficulties. It is true that we may profit from Professor Donald Thomson's brief though exceedingly illuminating monograph[51] on the ceremonial exchange but, as this brilliant ethnographer has so clearly brought out, the system he was able to observe and interpret cannot be accepted without very strong reservations as in any sense primitive. The coastal regions of Arnhem Land have in fact stood in the full current of influence of seafarers from the north and this has been brought to bear on the culture of the aborigines over a period of at least two centuries and possibly longer. As Thomson has so clearly shown, the impact of Macassar trade goods, such as iron knives, axes and nails, fish hooks and lines, glass bottles and beads, smoking pipes, calico, blankets, string and wool, was enormous. The question must even be asked whether it was this that stimulated or even generated the whole elaborate cycle of exchange described by Thomson; and whether we ought not to view this as a product of culture contact rather than as an aspect of primitive aboriginal life. Yet Thomson's clearly expressed view is that the gift cycle was deeply embedded in aboriginal society, and that contact with a more advanced technology through the medium of Macassar seafarers did no more than intensify and give direction to a process of great antiquity.

Thomson was led to formulate his theory of the ceremonial gift cycle to account for the way goods circulated so freely among social groups that occupied well-defined territories and adhered closely to traditional cultures invested with all the sanctity of ancestral inheritance. He found on close investigation that every individual was born into a complex nexus of relationships that involved making gifts of goods (*gerri*) to persons of different groups connected by marriage. One result of this was to cause *gerri* to move over distances of hundreds of miles by a series of gift exchanges without any individual moving more than a short distance, so that, for example, bundles of spear-heads (*nambi*), made of tapered stone blades and wrapped in paperbark, moved overland from the quarries at Nillipidje in the hills behind Blue Mud Bay on the east coast and, conversely, Macassar goods, instead of being hoarded by coast-dwellers, were widely disseminated over the whole territory. The beauty of Thomson's insight is that it reveals the interlocking, almost self-regulating nature of human culture. Socially, the function of ceremonial gift-exchange was to emphasize and reiterate the existence and precise nature of relationships and so help to validate the structure of society, while at the same time doing something to counteract the enmity between groups that their sense of separate identity and their intense solidarity might otherwise have encouraged. Moreover, it was by satisfying his obligations in this respect that a man experienced his full sense of identity; it was not merely that non-fulfilment might involve reprisals and even death through magic or social ostracism, but a man's prestige and self-esteem depended in a positive sense on accumulating the necessary *gerri* and discharging his kinship obligations by means of gifts. Conversely, the giving of gifts was intensified at periods when social solidarity was in particular need of intensification, for instance in connexion with rites of initiation, death or the ceremonial display of totemic objects. Thus the gift cycle emphasized the solidarity of particular groups, while at the same time maintaining good relations with neighbouring ones and heightening the self-esteem of every active member of society. From an economic point of view the system served two great purposes. It gave an incentive not merely to work but to excellence in the production and finish of the broad range of artefacts that entered into the exchange cycle and reminds us that in all human societies emulation in giving is at least as important as a drive to action as emulation in consumption. Again, and more directly relevant to the matter in hand, it provided a mechanism for disseminating products of local skills and traditions of workmanship and distributing over an extensive territory artefacts made from materials that might occur exclusively in the territory of a single community.

Melanesia

The polished stone axe or adze played an immensely important role among the early agricultural peoples of east and south-east Asia and of the Pacific islands, both for clearing the ground for cultivation and for shaping timbers for fences, houses and boats; and over Melanesia and much of Polynesia they were still in use at the time of European colonization. Among the first to attract detailed attention from ethnographers were those of the small Melanesian islands immediately east of New Guinea. Even so, when Seligman described the axe trade in 1906,[52] iron tools had already displaced stone axes for some thirty years and when Malinowski contributed an essay on this topic to a volume in honour of Seligman published in 1934[53] it was hardly any longer even a living memory. Something can be learned nevertheless from their descriptions. In agreement with what we met with in prehistoric Europe and in aboriginal Australia the axe blades were roughed out and trimmed into shape, though not polished, at the source of the raw material, a volcanic ash and lava that outcropped below Suloga peak in the island of Murua or Woodlark Island, some 140 miles E.N.E. of the eastern tip of New Guinea. It was unnecessary to quarry the stone which could be got in pieces of suitable size from the bed of a creek and its side branches. The axes in their chipped state must have been traded to the Marshall Bennett and Trobriand Islands, the latter some 90 miles to the W.N.W., by boat, another analogy with prehistoric Europe. The stone blades were apparently polished on arrival at the islands; and on Kiriwana, the main island of the Trobriand group, this work was apparently concentrated on five villages. There appears from Seligman's account to have been some trade in polished axes from the Marshall Bennett Islands to Kiriwana and from Kiriwana to the D'Entrecasteaux Islands intermediate with the mainland.

Although Malinowski was twice as far removed in time from the stone axe trade, he gives a much fuller account of its cultural significance and must be presumed to have gained his information from oral traditions. Before iron axes were taken into use, about three-quarters of the way through the nineteenth century, stone axes and adze blades provided the only tools for 'cutting, planing scooping-out, or chiselling' available to the Trobriand islanders. A number of different forms adapted to particular functions were clearly recognized by name: thus, for cutting down the large trunks needed for making canoes heavy felling axes (*utuviya*), thick almost to the cutting edge, were needed; lighter, straight-edged adzes (*kasiwi*) were used for shaping or trimming canoes or boards or logs needed for building; for hollowing out the insides of canoes a stout, but fairly narrow blade (*kavilali*) was used, which might be mounted either as an axe or an adze to suit the requirements of the work; narrow chisels (*ginesosu*) were used for cutting the grooves and holes required in building canoes or houses; and, lastly, there were the *utukema*, resembling the *kasiwi* and no doubt in some cases worn-out examples of these, used for clearing scrub for gardens.

Over and above these utilitarian tools, Malinowski was at pains to emphasize the existence of a category of ceremonial blades 'so well finished, so large, so thin and streaked and well-polished, that they were too good to be used technically, too big even to be carried as everyday ornaments, though they might still be placed in specially beautiful handles and carried by a man of high rank during a ceremony'; some, indeed, were too valuable even to risk carrying on ceremonial occasions. Yet these technically useless blades played an essential role in Trobriand society, which was largely based on the power and authority of chiefs, 'leaders in war, organisers of big feasts, masters of the gardens, leaders of overseas trading expeditions, and supervisors of economic magic which controlled to a certain extent public life and production'. The basis of chiefly power was wealth and wealth, if it was to be wielded when required, had to be concentrated in some durable, condensed form. Axe blades provided one of the few media for storing wealth; and the more elaborate, highly polished and useless in a technical sense they became, the more effective they were for locking up and symbolizing the consumption of labour and surplus food. Malinowski summarized the position by

writing that: 'The production of polished axe blades was in the Central
Trobriands the main process by which accumulated food was transformed
into an object of condensed wealth and thus made available for purposes for
which it would have been useless in the form of perishable goods.' One of the
great advantages of the polished stone blade was that it was imperishable. It
could therefore serve as an heirloom and help to buttress and symbolize the
power and lineage of the chief. They played an important part in under-
pinning the social structure of the Trobriand Islanders: their ceremonial
display on such occasions as important burials or visits helped to enhance
social solidarity; and relatives might even comfort a dying man 'by rubbing
axe blades against his chest or belly'. The high value set on such blades is
reflected in the care taken to prevent their loss by theft and it is significant for
archaeologists that the most important hiding place was a hole in the ground.

The opening up of the highlands of Australian New Guinea during and
after the Second World War provided the last opportunity to observe
neolithic cultivators in their uncontaminated state and it is tragic that it
should have been so largely missed: many anthropological research workers,
indeed, went there, but these concentrated mainly on certain aspects of social
structure and kinship and neglected to make a complete and balanced study
of these last communities of neolithic type. Even so their records of the New
Guinea highlands are of value simply because they were made by actual
witnesses. The highlands, which occupy an area of *c.* 28,000 square miles and
carry an indigenous population of some three-quarters of a million, which
lives predominantly by intensive agriculture within a zone of between 4,000
and 8,000 feet above sea level, were ecologically both homogeneous and
isolated until the very recent past from overseas influences.

Dr and Mrs Bulmer[54] state that the stones most often used were fine-
grained greywackes and argillites and that these were obtained either from
quarries or, as we noted from Woodlark (Murua) Island, from stream beds.
At least eight sources have been located in the western and one in the eastern
highlands, but precise information about the range over which axe blades
from the different sources were traded is not yet available. Meanwhile, R. F.
Salisbury's work[55] on the eastern highlands points to the existence of some
form of the gift-exchange cycle observed by Donald Thomson in Arnhem
Land. Salisbury suggested that axes, at any rate in their roughed out forms,
may well have entered into cycles in which food and salt played a
predominant part. As in Arnhem Land, the existence of marriage relationships between individuals in neighbouring clans ensured that axe blades, like
other elements in the cycle, would have been able to move easily from one
group to another. As has so often been reported by those who also have had
the opportunity of observing primitive people, the highlanders of New
Guinea by no means adhered to the model perfected by prehistorians and
blades hafted strictly at right angles to (adzes) or parallel to (axes) the handle

were in the minority; as a rule the blades were mounted at an angle of around 10° to the handle in the western zone, but in parts of the south and east this might be up to as much as 45°; indeed, they might even be used unhafted as knives, chisels or scrapers. The predominant role of horticulture in subsistence means that axes were in great demand for clearing forest trees, the climax vegetation of this area, as well as for preparing timbers for house-building and fencing for keeping pigs out of the gardens. In parenthesis the Bulmers note that the axe was also an important aid to hunting, both in facilitating movement through the forest by clearing obstacles and in making it easier to climb trees. From his first-hand account of the stone axe agriculturalists of the Belim valley on the northern slope of the Snow Mountains of what was then Dutch New Guinea, immediately after their discovery by a flying boat in 1938, L. J. Brass noted[56] that adzes were used mainly for felling and dressing timber and axes for splitting it to form the kind of billets needed for fencing and house-building.

The fact that the transition has been made so recently means that it has been possible to observe closely and precisely the effect of substituting steel for stone axes and adzes. When the prospectors Leahy and Dwyer first entered the eastern highlands in 1930 the natives had no metal equipment of any kind, but between 1933 and 1945, when Europeans finally entered the territory, the people had managed to acquire a few steel axes by means of the long-standing exchange relationships. R. F. Salisbury's study[57] shows that the effect of the substitution was already profound. By reducing substantially the work traditionally undertaken by men, it put them in a relatively privileged position in relation to women. Just how substantial the reduction was can be shown by a few calculations. Cultivation of the sweet potato involved frequent forest clearance, since plots were only as a rule cultivated for eighteen months before being left fallow for a fifteen-year period; and the area freshly cleared every eighteen months, which in itself involved plenty of axe work, had to be fenced against wild pigs. By systematic questioning Salisbury found that, whereas during the Stone Age it needed visits every day for two months to clear a plot, the same area could be dealt with by means of steel tools by working every second or third day for about one month only. The matter could be expressed in a nutshell by saying that with stone axe-heads, a man had to expend about four-fifths of his working days on axe work, whereas with the introduction of metal blades the proportion sank to one-half. Moreover the advantages did not rest there: a steel axe cost more in the first instance – it took 12 days of casual labour for Europeans to buy one against the 6 days to make a stone axe and mount it on its handle – but, on the other hand, the steel blade lasted so much longer (c. twelve years against one and a half years), that, balancing initial cost and durability, it was four times as economical as a stone one. To sum up, a steel axe was not only three or four times as effective as a stone one, it was also more economical by about the same factor. No wonder the neolithic stone industry failed to stand up to the impact of steel.

New Zealand

In common with other Pacific peoples the Maori had a particular need for the cutting tools required for felling trees and shaping the canoes that are basic to their way of life, as well as for clearing the forest for horticulture and building the stockades and entrances for their defended *pas*, not to mention their often elaborately decorated houses. Since so much of men's work depended on the effectiveness of adzes, it is not surprising that they went to great trouble to secure the best stone; and this means, as elsewhere, seeking out the best sources, roughing out the blades at the quarry site and distributing them, freed from waste, but not yet finally polished. Some of the most sought-after adze-heads in the northern two-thirds of the South Island, that is above the Haast and Waitaki rivers, were of an altered, fine-grained and easily flaked argillite that outcrops at numerous points in the Richmond Range from Red Hill to D'Urville Island. The massive heaps of waste at quarry sites have led some authors to suppose that the rock must have been shattered by pouring water on surfaces heated by fire, but R. S. Duff's examination[58] of the Whangamoa quarries on the slopes of Red Hill brought to light stone hammer-stones up to 125 lbs. in weight that had evidently been hurled down from a large boulder with the object of cracking the outer, weathered surface so as to gain access to the fresh rock needed for adze-heads. Comparable quarry sites are known from the northern hinterland of Dunedin and in the extreme south of the Island at Riverton.[59] Although systematic petrological identifications of adzes have yet to be made, it is evident that quarries of favourable stone served considerable areas of country.

Even more remarkable and illuminating was the trade in nephrite, a precious greenstone harder than steel,[60] that was prized above all other substances by the Maori people of both islands, but which was confined by nature to a few narrowly defined localities in the South Island.[61] The early sources of translucent nephrite available to the Maori were the gravels of the Arahura and Taramakau rivers in Westland, though an opaque greyish-green variety was evidently obtained from the river Dart that flows into the northern end of Lake Wakatipu, and a clear, translucent serpentine (or bowenite) came from Anita Bay, Milford Sound. The importance attached to hard greenstone by the Maori is shown in several ways, beyond the obvious one that they sought out the very rare sources of the material and disseminated it over distances of hundreds of miles. To begin with there is the wealth of myths surrounding the material, myths which centre on the west coast and associate nephrite with the original migrations to New Zealand, not to mention the stories surrounding individual objects made from nephrite, or the fact that it was considered *tapu* and spells had to be recited before looking for it. The really passionate concern of the Maori with their favourite raw material is further evinced by the fact that according to Raymond Firth[62] they distinguished 'nearly a score of different qualities . . . by name' according to 'variation in colour and texture'. Among them may be noted:[63]

*tangiwai	Translucent serpentine or bowenite.
*pounamu	Dense, bluish-green nephrite.
*kawakawa	Dark green, often with 'tear' markings, named after the dark green leaf of the *Kawakawa*.
*manga	Whitish or pale milky green – named after the translucent and whitish whitebait.
*kahûrangi	Bright green, hard and clear – sometimes described as apple green. The name suggests that this variety was especially precious and distinguished.
*totowera	Olive green.
*pipiwharauroa	Silvery green, mottled – named after the plumage of the shining cuckoo.
ahunga	Opaque or frosty green.
*kahotea	Green, spotted or streaked with black.
raukaraka	Yellowish tone, cf. leaf of the *Karaka*.

The importance of greenstone to the Maori is shown again by the variety of uses to which they put it. Its extreme hardness and ability to take a smooth, sharp edge made it ideal for the fine adzes used for dressing timber as well as for the quite small and narrow chisels used in carving designs on wooden objects. The same properties made it a perfect material for the *mere*, a kind of hatchet used for smashing in the side of the skull, the weapon firmly grasped in one hand secured by a thong passed through the butt, the other hand being used to seize the enemy's hair. Again, it was no doubt the smoothness and colour, as well as the rarity of nephrite and the fact that it was so difficult to work, that made it so keenly sought after as a material for personal ornaments, notably lobe-shaped ear-pendants, *hei-tiki* pendants[64] in the form of conventionalized human figures and imitations of shark's teeth. Lastly, there was the sheer difficulty of shaping the material, which had first of all to be sawn out of a block by cutters of stone or wood, aided by sand and irrigated by water, and then laboriously ground smooth: the preliminary task of getting out a rough adze form might take a month and the finishing another six weeks; and more elaborate tasks, like the perforation of a *mere* butt, would have taken correspondingly longer. A man might work at the final polishing almost indefinitely to fill in time. It seems to follow that, however practical this exceedingly hard material was for hewing, cutting or carving, its real importance was as a store of value and a badge of rank. Conversely, the desire to gain nephrite was a main cause for the bloody raids of the Nga-ti-toa into the South Island; and an idea of its value can be gained from the fact that when Tuhuru, chief of the Poutini-Ngaitahu was captured during a raid on the west coast of the South Island by the Nga-ti-toa chieftain Rauparaha, he was ransomed for a greenstone *mere*.[65]

Individual *mere*, like the one used by Te Wherowhero on a single occasion to smash in the heads of 250 prisoners, became famous, acquired names of their own and passed as heirlooms from father to son. Ornaments and weapons of nephrite indeed served as veritable symbols of social prestige and rank, and many of them remained underground with the dead owner only for brief periods before being recovered and treated with even greater esteem.

One way of finding nephrite in pieces of convenient size was to wade in the river bed and this may account for the story told Captain Cook that it was originally a fish and only became a stone when dragged ashore. Boulders too heavy to carry were broken up into convenient size, but the stone was so precious and took so long to saw into blanks that it was transported in the rough; even small pieces of waste were used for ear-pendants. Indications that this was so are given by references in the mythology, such as the story that the adzes used by the Hawaiki people to make the canoes for getting to New Zealand were made from the block of stone brought back to Hawaiki by Nagahue on returning from her reconnaissance; by Captain Cook's observation that the talc, as he termed it, was traded in unworked lumps; and by the discovery of workers' caches like that from the mouth of the Rangitata river on the east coast of the South Island, comprising a portion fractured from a boulder and two pieces on which work had begun in the form of grooving.[66]

In a country like New Zealand, having an aboriginal population with well-preserved oral traditions and of which many accounts survive from early explorers, missionaries and settlers, it is possible to view the trade in stone adze blades and nephrite, like that in the obsidian from Mayor Island and Taupo on the North Island,[67] in a fuller context than is possible for instance in north-west Europe. Although Maori society was formed of substantially self-supporting communities in which specialization was not carried very far, the exchange of commodities between one group and another, despite their bellicosity and rivalry, was well-developed. The fuller sources available show that this exchange was by no means confined to commodities likely to survive in the archaeological record. There was, for instance, a brisk exchange in foodstuffs between coastal and inland communities, cray fish, for example, being swapped for potted forest birds. Interchange between North and South was carried on in an even more notable scale, since of the basic vegetable crops *taro* was confined to the North Island and *kumara* was absent from the South Island below Canterbury. Among the foodstuffs flowing in the opposite direction was the flesh of mutton birds from Stewart Island in the extreme south; and feathers and string of *Dentalium* sheels were other commodities known to have entered into the system of exchange.

This worked mainly by the reciprocal exchange of gifts between individuals united by kinship but living in different communities, a system which, as explained earlier in connexion with Arnhem Land, made it possible to circulate goods among groups that might on other grounds be at daggers drawn and to do so without any individual having to make a lengthy journey. Yet, nephrite seems to have proved an exception to the general rule and purposive journeys, often under a man of rank, were made from the North to the South Island to ensure a supply. Wherever possible water was used for preference, but in the interior it was sometimes necessary to carry goods for long distances by a system of paths worn smooth by the passage of feet and which traversed the forest along the crests of ridges or the courses of river beds. Raymond Firth[68] has drawn a harrowing picture of the rigours of the passage along the west coast of the South Island down to the nephrite rivers and it may well be that the precious stone was more often carried down the main rivers to the main east coast harbours at Banks Peninsula. In this connexion it is suggestive that house-ruins at Murdering Beach, a village on the northern arm of the Otago Peninsula, abandoned by the Maori most probably after its burning by the whaler James Kenny in December 1817, are estimated to have yielded some 3½ cwt. of worked nephrite and near-nephrite to collectors during the last half of the nineteenth century alone.[69] Indeed, it seems evident that greenstone from the Dart Valley and Anita Bay, together possibly with some from the Westland sites by way of Haast Pass, was worked up for market – a long and difficult process – by the people of Murdering Bay before being shipped north. The elaborate network by which greenstone reached the North Island is only another index of its importance in Maori society.

III

Although nuances of form and style differentiate the stone axe and adze blades of temperate Europe, Australia, New Guinea and New Zealand, and despite wide variations in hafting, their technological function was basically the same, that is to say to fell timber and shape it to the needs of man. Similarly there was a basic similarity in the methods by which they were produced. Non-siliceous rocks could as a rule be got from scree or river-beds, where pieces of convenient size were available in nature: the solid rock was only quarried when it was important to obtain fresh, unweathered material and especially when this occurred in a narrow seam in the parent rock. Both factors operated in the case of flint, which commonly occurs in narrow, more or less horizontal seams in the chalk; and the great galleried mines of parts of Europe find no parallel in Australasia.

The sequence of manufacture seems to have followed the same pattern. Highly precious and exceptionally hard stones like jadeite or nephrite, that could only be shaped by sawing and rubbing down, were collected in the form of easily portable pebbles and worked up at settlements. Flakeable flint or stone, on the other hand, was shaped as close as possible to the source of raw material, whether at an open quarry or round the head of a mine shaft, so as to avoid needless carrying of a great load of waste material. The final process of grinding and polishing, as has so often been observed, was normally carried out at the places of settlement. No doubt men preferred to carry on this slow work where they lived rather than on the exposed scree of a mountain slope, but this is hardly adequate to account for a similar treatment of blades made from mined flint, since the shafts were sunk through the very chalk formation that was so attractive to neolithic man in countries where it was present. The separation of the processes of knapping and polishing is in fact much more significant: if the production of axe and adze blades had been a full-time activity, one might have expected the process of manufacture to have been carried to completion on the same site, at least in the case of the flint-mines. The fact that only the preliminary phase was gone through at the manufacturing sites argues that, so far from being a full-time activity, the fabrication of axe and adze blades was carried on by men who for much of the year at least shared in the daily round of work.

It is when we come to the factors underlying distribution that the prehistoric archaeologist of Europe turns with highest expectation to the evidence from Australasia. Where there is similarity of form, function and methods of production, it might be argued, distribution would be likely to have proceeded on similar lines. It is all the more disappointing that, though the traffic was carried on so recently in parts of Australasia, relatively little is certainly known. Nevertheless, even if anthropologists in Australasia have had to work too much on virtually archaeological data, there remains a kernel of direct observation. The most valuable outcome of this is perhaps Professor Donald Thomson's theory of ceremonial gift-exchange developed in the context of Arnhem Land, in much of which indigenous culture was a going concern down to our own times. One of the most important items entering into the gift-cycle, it may be remembered, were bundles of stone spearheads, fabricated at open quarries close to the east coast and disseminated by this means over much of the territory as far as the west coast. When one reads the surviving accounts of the Mount William stone axe quarries near Melbourne with Thomson's study in mind, it is hardly possible to avoid concluding that a principal motive for the production and distribution of the axes may have been the desire to satisfy kinship obligations.

Malinowski and Seligman have emphasized, in the case of Melanesia, the importance of polished blades as stores of wealth, in particular the ceremonial ones too large and delicate for use. We are reminded that trade and votive offerings are not the only alternative explanations for the hoards of stone axes found in the soil: the ground has always been an obvious place for hiding treasure. Then, again, with reference to New Zealand greenstone, Raymond Firth in his thorough-going study of Maori economy has emphasized that this was only one element, albeit the most permanent, in a complex system of interchange operated by individuals united by kinship but living in separate communities.

In each of these territories there is evidence for the widespread diffusion of axe and adze blades made at places where particular materials were present without the intervention of any class of traders or even the movement of individuals over more than modest distances. The European is bound to ask himself, whether the production and diffusion of, say, Graig Lwyd axes or Petrosavodsk adzes, could not be accounted for in similar terms. In the nature of things one cannot prove what happened four or five thousand years ago, but one can and should adopt a hypothesis and the most likely one is that much of the traffic was carried on to satisfy the claims of kinship; and we may be fairly sure that many other things entered the cycle that have long since perished.

When the distribution of axes or adzes of particular kinds of stone is plotted on the map they may show a simple pattern like that of the adzes of Olonetz slate, which spread radially, north and south of the Gulf of Finland, from the factory at Petrosavodsk; or that of axes from the earliest Cornish sources,[70] which fan out predictably from the extreme south-west to Wessex. It is even more interesting to see what happens when, as in Middle and Late Neolithic Britain, several sources were being exploited in different parts of the country: instead of a number of fan-like distributions occupying well-defined regions, we find a much more complex situation with lines of diffusion crossing in a bewildering manner and the products of two or more factories converging on particular sites at the same time,[71] something which seems much more likely to have happened as a result of gift-exchange than of purposive trade. Evidence for lengthy journeys certainly exists for prehistoric Europe, as it does for Maori New Zealand: the discovery of hoards of a particular kind of adze of east Danish or Scanian flint in Västerbotten, some 900 miles north of their nearest analogues has already been discussed and linked hypothetically with seasonal seal-hunting expeditions to the Gulf of Bothnia; or, again, one might quote the few sherds of Plaidt and Hinkelstein ware from the famous neolithic site at Köln-Lindenthal as indicative of the movement of individual parties down the Rhine from the districts of Coblentz and Worms.[72] In any case such instances are isolated by comparison with the vast and complex movement and cross-movement of artefacts and commodities, of which only a small trace survives and the whole of which could, by analogy with the Arnhem Land evidence, have occurred without any lengthy journey other than sea-passages by so much as a single individual.

The evidence from Australia confirms what we had already learned from the hunter-fishers of circumpolar Europe that the manufacture of axes or adzes at sources of particular materials and their diffusion over substantial areas was no monopoly of peasant farmers. On the other hand, that from New Guinea and New Zealand confirms that the practice of agriculture powerfully emphasized the importance of this traffic. Again, flint or stone blades were everywhere superseded by ones made of metal, even though there were important differences both in circumstances and immediate outcome. In Australasia steel hatchets, or iron objects that could be fabricated into blades, were introduced so rapidly and were so manifestly superior that they very soon replaced stone ones, except for ceremonial purposes, as they permeated successive territories. In temperate Europe, on the other hand, the transition was more gradual: copper was less markedly superior than steel and it was to begin with very expensive for the Late Neolithic natives; and in point of fact the most obvious impact of copper was often to stimulate and inspire the production, especially in territories into which metallurgy spread relatively late, of substitute forms in flint, notably of daggers or two-edged knives; and it is even likely that the most intensive phase of flint-mining for axe blades, and locally also for daggers, reflects the stimulus and competition of copper.

It would be to step outside the limits of this essay to discuss how far the beginnings of commerce in the sense of a specialized occupation developed in the context of early metallurgy. If we deny that trade in anything like our modern sense existed among Stone Age farmers and even hunter-fishers, this is only another way of saying, what we already know, that modern society differs profoundly from Stone Age ones, whether of third or fourth millennium Europe or of nineteenth or, locally, even of twentieth-century Australasia. This does not alter the fact that, by whatever name we call it or on whatever basis it was conducted, peaceful interchange took place, even across the boundaries of 'archaeological cultures', and thereby axe and adze blades of different materials found their way into the hands of people living at a distance from their sources. In the end we have to admit that the basic economic function of trade, to make rare materials or skills more generally available, may be accomplished whether or not a society is sufficiently developed to support highly specialized extractive or manufacturing, let alone mercantile activities.

Notes

1 Martin Jahn, 'Gab es in der vorgeschichtlichen Zeit bereits einen Handel?', *Abh. d. Sächs. Akad. d. wissensch. zu Leipzig*, XLVIII (Berlin, 1956), 5–40.

2 J. G. D. Clark, *The Mesolithic Settlement of Northern Europe* (Cambridge, 1936), p. 105.

3 The polished stone axe was accepted as an element in the Neolithic as this was defined by Sir John Lubbock in his *Pre-historic Times* (1865); and there was even a period when it was common form to speak of the Polished Stone Age.

4 For a general account with references, see Grahame Clark, 'Farmers and Forests in Neolithic Europe', *Antiquity*, XIX (1945), 57–71.

5 Experiments have repeatedly been made to show the effectiveness of prehistoric stone axe blades in felling trees. Prof. Jacob-Friesen's demonstration that a polished blade is capable of cutting down a stem of equal girth more rapidly (by a factor of 5 : 7) than a chipped one is particularly relevant. For references, see *Antiquity*, XIX, 68 and S. A. Semenov, *Prehistoric Technology* (London, 1964), pp. 128–30.

6 S. Hazzledine Warren, 'A stone axe Factory at Graig-Lwyd, Penmaenmawr', *J. Roy. Anthrop. Inst.*, XLIX (1919), 342–65, XLI (1921), 165–98.

7 T. A. Glenn, 'Distribution of the Graig Lwyd axe and its associated cultures', *Arch. Cambr.* XC (1935), 189–218.

8 A sub-committee of the South-western Group of Museums and Art Galleries on the Petrological Identification of Stone Axes was originally set up under the chairmanship of the late Mr Alexander Keiller in 1936. The First Report, under the names of Alexander Keiller, Stuart Piggott and F. S. Wallis, was published in the *Proc. Prehist. Soc.* VII (1941), 50–72. Three more Reports have since been issued: *ibid.*, XIII (1947), 47–55; XVII (1951), 99–158; and XXVIII (1962), 209–66. The Fourth Report lists some 1200 axes.

9 E. M. Jope, 'The Porcellanite Axes of North-east Ireland: Tievebulliagh and Rathlin', *Ulster J. of Arch.*, XV (1952), 31–60.

10 B. Bunch and C. I. Fell, 'A Stone-axe Factory at Pike of Stickle, Great Langdale, Westmorland', *Proc. Prehist. Soc.*, XV (1949), 1–20.

11 C. H. Houlder, 'The Excavation of a Neolithic Stone Implement Factory on Mynydd Rhiw in Caernarvonshire', *Proc. Prehist. Soc.*, XXVII (1961), 108–43.

12 For the extended chronology of Neolithic settlement in Britain based on radio-carbon dating, see J. G. D. Clark and H. Godwin, 'The Neolithic in the Cambridgeshire Fens', *Antiquity*, XXXVI (1962), 10–23.

13 W. F. Rankine, 'Pebbles of Non-local Rock from Mesolithic Chipping-floors', *Proc. Prehist. Soc.*, XV (1949), 193–4.

14 A specimen from Shapwick Heath, Somerset, has been dated by radio-carbon (Q–430) to 2580 ± 130 B.C. Another, from Upware, Cambs., immediately precedes the formation of the fen clay somewhere during the first quarter of the third millennium B.C. (Q–31, 499, 580–1). Cf. E. H. Willis, 'Marine Transgression Sequences in the English Fenlands', *Annals N.Y. Acad. of Sciences*, XCV (1961), 368–76.

15 Stuart Piggott, *Proc. Prehist. Soc.*, XXVIII (1962), 234.

16 See R. G. Livens, 'Petrology of Scottish Stone Implements', *Proc. Soc. Ant. Scot.*, XCII (1958–9), 56–70.

17 For an outline, see G. Clark and S. Piggott, 'The Age of the British Flint Mines', *Antiquity*, VII (1933), 168–83.

18 W. G. Clarke (ed.), *Report on the Excavations at Grimes Graves, Weeting, Norfolk, March-May 1914* (London, 1915). See also A. L. Armstrong, 'The Grimes Graves Problem in the Light of Recent Researches', *Proc. Prehist. Soc. E.A.*, V (1926), 91–127; 'Report on the Excavation of Pit 12', *ibid.*, VII (1934), 382–94.

19 See E. C. Curwen, *The Archaeology of Sussex*, ch. VI (2nd edn, London, 1954).

20 J. F. S. Stone, 'Easton Down, Winterslow, S. Wilts., flint mine excavation', *Wilts. Arch. Mag.*, XLV, 350–65; XLVI, 225–42.

21 The published radio-carbon dates are as follows: BM-87, 2310 ± 150 B.C.; BM-88, 2090 ± 150 B.C.; BM-93, 1940 ± 150 B.C.; BM-97, 1870 ± 150 B.C.; BM-99, 2080 ± 150 B.C.

22 R. L. S. Bruce-Mitford, 'A Hoard of Neolithic Axes from Peaslake, Surrey', *Ant. J.*, XVIII (1938), 279–84.

23 Stuart Piggott, *Neolithic Cultures of the British Isles* (Cambridge, 1954), p. 355 ff.

24 W. Campbell Smith, 'Jade Axes from sites in the British Isles', *Proc. Prehist. Soc.*, XXIX (1963), 133–72.

25 K. Faegri, 'Studies on the Pleistocene of Western Norway. III. Bømlo', *Bergens Mus. Arbok, Naturvitensk. r.*, Nr. 8 (1943), 51 ff.

26 J. G. D. Clark, *Prehistoric Europe: the economic basis* (London, 1952), p. 245f.

27 H. A. Lund, *Fangst-Boplassen i Vistehulen* (Stavanger, 1951), pp. 120–3.

28 T. Sulimirski, 'Remarks concerning the distribution of some varieties of Flint in Poland', *Swiatowit*, XXIII (Warsaw, 1960), 281–307.

29 T. Zurowski, 'Flint-mining on the Kamienna River', *Swiatowit*, XXIII 249–79.

30 I. Scollar, 'Regional groups in the Michelsberg Culture', *Proc. Prehist. Soc.*, XXV (1959), 52–134; see p. 57.

31 J. de Saint-Venant, *Tailleries de silex du sud de la Touraine. Inventaire des produits exportés aux temps préhistoriques et carte de leur aire de diffusion* (Le Mans, 1911).

32 C. A. Althin, 'The Scanian Flint Mines', *K. Hum. Vetenskap. i Lund Årsber.*, IV (1950–1), 139–58.

33 C. J. Becker, '4000-aarig minedrift i Thy', *Nationalmuseets Arbejdsmark* (1958), pp. 73–82.

34 C. J. Becker, 'Late-Neolithic flint-mines at Aalborg', *Acta Arch*, XXII (1951), 135–52.

35 G. Gjessing, *Norges Steinalder* (Oslo, 1945), pp. 350 f.

36 There is evidence that axes of polished schist were traded in the reverse direction from south-west Norway to Vendsyssel in northern Jutland. See P. V. Glob, 'Norske Skifeokser i Danske Fund', *Aarbøger* (1939), pp. 296–301.

37 Gjessing, *op. cit.*, 414 ff.

38 J. G. D. Clark, 'Objects of South Scandinavian flint in the northernmost provinces of Norway, Sweden and Finland', *Proc. Prehist. Soc.*, XIV (1948), 219–32. But see the fuller and more recent paper by C. J. Becker, which should be followed: 'Die Nordschwedischen Flintdepots', *Acta Arch.*, XXIII (1952), 31–79.

39 The most important hoards are those from: (1) Bjurselet – *c.* 170 concave-edged adzes, 2 thick-butted axes, 2 chisels; (2) Kusmark – 56 adzes (only 10 polished), 8 thin-butted axes: (3) Kallbäcken – 17 adzes, 3 axes, 3 chisels; (4) Overboda – 5 unpolished adzes; (5) Dalsjo – 6, probably 7, adzes with concave edge.

40 G. Gjessing, *Nordenfjelske Ristninger og Malinger av den artiske gruppe* (Oslo, 1936), pp. 112–16.

41 C. J. Becker, 'Den Grubekeramiske kultur i Danmark', *Aarbøger* (1950), pp. 153–274.

42 J. G. D. Clark, 'Seal-hunting in the Stone Age of North-western Europe', *Proc. Prehist. Soc.*, XII (1946), 12–48.

43 F. D. McCarthy, *The Stone Implements of Australia* (The Australian Museum, Sydney, 1946), pp. 44ff.

44 D. J. Mulvaney, 'The Stone Age of Australia', *Proc. Prehist. Soc.*, XXVII (1961), 94.

45 I. McBryde, 'Archaeological Field Survey Work in Northern New South Wales', *Oceania*, XXXIII (1962), 12–17; see p. 17.

46 Information from Norman B. Tindale, South Australian Museum, Adelaide.

47 McBryde, *op.cit.*, p. 15; W. J. E. Webster, *ibid.*, pl. VI; and F. D. McCarthy, 'An Axe Quarry at Moor Creek, Tamworth District, New South Wales', *Records of the Australian Museum*, XXI (1941), 19–20 and pl. IV.

48 J. T. Guthridge, *The Stone Age and the Aborigines of the Lancefield District* (Lancefield, 1910); also, S. R. Mitchell, 'Victorian aboriginal axe stone', *The Victorian Naturalist*, LXXVIII (1961), 71–5. I have to thank Mr Dermot Casey for kindly showing me over the site in company with Mr John Mulvaney.

49 A. W. Howitt, *The Native Tribes of South-east Australia* (London, 1904), pp. 311–12.

50 R. Brough Smyth, *The Aborigines of Victoria: with Notes Relating to the habits of the Natives of other Parts of Australia and Tasmania* (Melbourne and London, 1878), II, 298–9 (Appendix C).

51 Donald Thomson, *Economic structure and the ceremonial exchange cycle in Arnhem Land* (London, 1949), esp. ch. 5.

52 C. G. S. Seligman, *The Melanesians of British New Guinea* (Cambridge, 1910); also, Seligman and Strong, *Geogr. J.* (1906), 348ff.

53 B. Malinowski, 'Stone Implements of Eastern New Guinea', *Essays presented to C. G. Seligman*, ed, E. E. Evans-Pritchard (London, 1934), pp. 189–96.

54 Susan and Ralph Bulmer, 'The Prehistory of the Australian New Guinea Highlands', *Am. Anthrop. Special Publ.* (1964): *New Guinea*, pp. 39–76.

55 R. F. Salisbury, *From Stone to Steel* (Cambridge, 1962).

56 L. J. Brass, 'Stone-age agriculture in New Guinea', *Geogr. Rev.*, xxxi (1941), 555–69.

57 *Op. cit.*, p. 145.

58 R. S. Duff, 'Native quarries of baked argillite (N.Z.)', *Records of the Canterbury Museum*, v (Christchurch, 1946), 115–24.

59 Information from Mr Leslie Braude of the Department of Anthropology, University of Otago.

60 According to Mohs' scale of hardness, nephrite = 6½ as compared with 6 for steel and 10 for diamond.

61 F. J. Turner, 'Geological Investigation of the Nephrites, Serpentines, and Related "Greenstones" used by the Maoris of Otago and South Canterbury', *Trans. Roy. Soc. of N. Z.* lxv (1935), 187–210; H. D. Skinner, 'New Zealand Greenstone', *ibid*. 211–20; E. Best, 'Pounamu or Greenstone (Nephrites)' *Dominion Museum Bull.* iv (1912), 156–96; F. R. Chapman, ' On the Working of Greenstone or Nephrite by the Maoris', *Trans. N.Z. Inst.*, xxiv (1891), 479–539. I have to thank Dr Duff for taking me to examine the boulders of the Arahura river in the company of some of the surviving Maori proprietors of the nephrite.

62 R. Firth, *Primitive Economics of the New Zealand Maori* (London, 1929), ch. xii, see p. 388.

63 This list is based very largely on the display in the Canterbury Museum, Christchurch, N.Z. The varieties mentioned in H. W. Williams' *A Dictionary of the Maori Language* (6th ed. 1957) are marked by an*.

64 H. D. Skinner, *The Maori Hei-Tiki* (1946).

65 W. T. L. Travers, *Trans. N.Z. Inst.*, v, 19ff.

66 Canterbury Museum, Christchurch, E. 99. 54. 14–18.

67 R. C. Green, 'Sources, Ages and Exploitation of New Zealand Obsidian. An interim report', *N.Z. Arch. Assoc. Newsletter*, vol. 7, no. 3 (Auckland, 1964), 134–43.

68 *Op. cit.*, p. 437.

69 H. D. Skinner, 'Murdering Beach. Collecting and Excavating. The first phase: 1850–1950', *J. Polynesian Soc.*, lxviii, 219–38 (Wellington, 1959); P. Gathercole, 'Murdering Beach, Otago – a suggestion', *N.Z. Arch. Assoc. Newsletter*, vol. 5, no. 3 (Auckland, 1962), 194–6. I have to thank Mr Gathercole for taking me to see this site.

70 Groups iaa, iva, xvi and xvii; see *4th Report*, pp. 233–40.

71 Thus, the Avebury district attracted axes of groups i, iia, vi–viii, xi and xiii; Stonehenge, groups i, ia, iii and xiii; Irchester, Northants, i, vi and xv; Bridlington, Yorks., i, iii and vi; and N. Deighton, Yorks., and Cairnpapple, W. Lothian, vi and vii.

72 Clark, *Prehistoric Europe*, p. 251.

CHAPTER 11

THE ECONOMIC CONTEXT OF DOLMENS AND PASSAGE-GRAVES IN SWEDEN

In a volume offered to Hugh Hencken to mark his unobtrusive but long sustained and formidable contributions to archaeology it may be appropriate to touch upon one of the most numerous and prominent categories of field monument surviving from the prehistory of Mediterranean and Temperate Europe, namely megalithic tombs. In doing so it is not my primary object to seek to reconstruct the history of their diffusion, still less to speculate about the character or motives to be attributed to those engaged in this process.[1] My first concern is rather to consider these monuments as social products. The time is indeed long overdue to consider megalithic and associated tomb structures as sources of information about the societies which in obedience to ideas of whatever kind or origin in fact erected them. Paradoxically it is by considering such monuments in functional and ultimately social terms that there lies the best chance of returning with greater hope of success to the historical problems which they undoubtedly pose.

In an admittedly speculative essay published in honour of another eminent prehistorian, Professor R. J. C. Atkinson[2] helped to point the way by considering some of the demographic and social implications of the earthen and megalithic long barrows of neolithic England. In the present essay I propose to examine the earlier forms of megalithic tombs, namely dolmens (dysse) and passage-graves, in economic terms and to do so in relation to an ongoing project of research into the early settlement of Scandinavia.[3] Although by far the larger number of these tombs is concentrated in Denmark (fig. 11.1), I intend for present purposes to concentrate on south Sweden, a territory on the very margin of megalithic distribution and one which for this very reason might be expected to throw light on the particular problem I have in mind. It has only been possible for me to do so because of the careful scholarship and helpfulness of Swedish colleagues. Much of their work is acknowledged in the usual manner by reference to their publications, but I would like especially to thank Dr Lili Kaelas, Director of the archaeological museum at Göteborg to whom I am especially indebted for the up-to-date and precise information about the tombs in Bohuslän, incorporated in fig. 11.5.

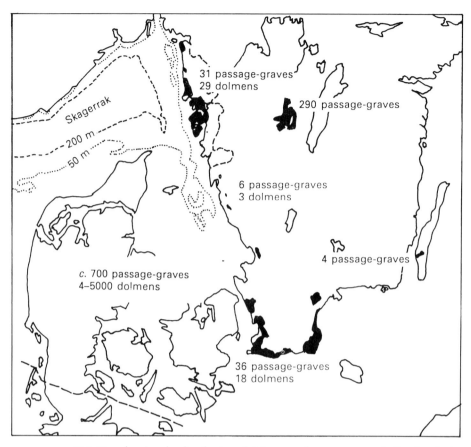

31 passage-graves
29 dolmens

290 passage-graves

Skagerrak

200 m
50 m

6 passage-graves
3 dolmens

4 passage-graves

c. 700 passage-graves
4–5000 dolmens

36 passage-graves
18 dolmens

11.1 Map showing the distribution of dolmens and passage-graves in Sweden. Scale: 1:5,000,000

A basic premise of this paper is that megalithic tombs were costly to erect in terms of man-power, more especially in terms of the demographic circumstances which we may suppose to have obtained in neolithic times, in south Scandinavia. By way of illustration, reference may be made to certain calculations in relation to English long barrows. Taking due account of such factors as the amount of lifting and fetching the necessary chalk and soil, Paul Ashbee calculated[4] that the construction of the Fussell's Lodge long barrow, Wiltshire, would have consumed something near 5,000 man days of labour, for the mound itself. Even when it is conceded that this barrow is rather larger than the average of its kind, this is a striking figure. The implications, for our own problem, become even more formidable if we accept Professor Atkinson's further estimate[5] that the construction of a megalithic chambered long barrow, of the type found on the Cotswolds, would have required, at least, three times as much labour as an earthen and chalk one, of comparable size. Even if we discount this, in respect of the Swedish tombs, on the ground that their covering mounds were relatively small and were made from materials available on the surface, the assembly and erection of the megalithic slabs, used in the erection of their chambers, and the obtaining and erection of the barrow materials, imply, between them, a formidable input of human labour. This implies the existence of a fund of labour, capable of being diverted in emergency, to purposes other than mere subsistence. In other words, the erection of the tombs seems to indicate the attainment of a certain level of prosperity, on the part of the people who built them. A question to be answered is what was the basis of subsistence which allowed so great an expenditure of economically unproductive labour?

Direct information about the settlements of the megalith builders being as scarce as it is, it remains to be asked what can be learned from the distribution and location of tombs. To answer this, we need to decide to what extent the pattern of settlement can safely be inferred from the distribution of tombs. Plainly a question of this kind is not one to be answered dogmatically. There is hardly any length to which men are not prepared to go in the face of ordinary economic forces under the impulse of ideology, as we are so well reminded in a megalithic context by the implications in terms of human labour of the assembly of bluestones and sarsens at Stonehenge.[6] What can nevertheless be said is that the same forces, which ensure that under a subsistence economy most food is obtained within an hour or so's radius of the focus of settlement, apply equally to the disposal of the dead and all the more so when this involved the periodical erection of tombs requiring a substantial volume of human labour. If the great events of history are proof in themselves that the forces of inertia do not invariably prevail in human affairs, they by no means alter the fact that human beings in most circumstances and for most of the time tend to conserve their energies. The hypothesis that burials are likely to reflect the propinquity of settlement is one which at least merits first consideration. Weight has been added to this argument that megalithic tombs were not erected once and for all. As recent investigations in Jutland and Scania have shown they were foci of ritual and cult observance carried on over lengthy periods of time. This fact alone suggested to Strömberg[7] that the people who maintained these observances whether funerary or otherwise lived close at hand.

Where actual settlements as well as burials can easily be discerned the hypothesis is not difficult to test. This commonly applies in the Mediterranean. The most famous example in the Aegean world is probably Mycenae where nine princely and many more numerous private tombs are concentrated within some 600 m. of the citadel and even closer to the outer town.[8] The same situation is found in Iberia. The hundred or so tholoi at the third millennium settlement of Los Millares for example are crowded within 500 m. of the outer defences of the township[9] and a similar situation exists at

Almizaraque. So much was this the case that Childe[10] felt no compunction in inferring the existence of similar townships from the existence of cemeteries at such sites as Belmonte, Puchena and Tabernas, even though these had not been precisely identified on the ground. Nearer home, from northwestern Europe, the evidence is more difficult to come by. Megalithic tombs are plentiful enough along parts of the Atlantic seaboard of western Europe, but settlements attributable to their builders are much more rare. Two suggestive conjunctions of tombs and settlements are known from hill-top sites surrounded by rich farm land in Co. Sligo, namely Carrowkeel and Knocknashee,[11] but in neither case has contemporaneity been proved between the megalithic tombs and the circular walls of drystone construction which probably sheltered tents or light huts. In the case of Carrowkeel the site has largely been eroded down to the limestone rock. The situation at Knocknashee is much more promising due to peat formation having blanketed much of the site. The obvious way of settling the matter is by excavation. Even if it should turn out that analogies from Greece and Iberia fail to hold good in Ireland, this would have little application to south Sweden, an area of relatively mild relief in which there were no prominent hills to influence in a decisive way the choice of locations for either settlements or tombs. A converse of this is that the most relevant evidence from western Europe is that derived from lowland sites. Three suggestive occurrences may be noted from Ireland. Thus, Sean O'Riordain found three megalithic tombs, one wedge-shaped and two ruined, within a radius of half a mile of the Knockadoon settlement near Lough Gur, Co. Limerick, and recovered Beaker pottery alike from the intact tomb and from the settlement,[12] clear indication of archaeological contemporaneity. In the other two cases megalithic tombs have been found overlying traces of settlement; thus tomb 8, adjacent to the great mount at Knowth, Co. Meath, overlay pits and trenches containing 'western neolithic' pottery;[13] and at Ballyglass, close to Bunatrahir Bay, Co. Mayo, Sean O'Nuallain found the well-preserved plan of a rectangular neolithic house underlying at an oblique angle the mound of a centre-court cairn. A further indication of the close juxtaposition of tombs and settlement comes from the long barrow of South Lodge near Avebury, Wiltshire, which was found to overlie directly traces of ard cultivation.[14]

Striking confirmation that megalithic tombs were closely linked to settlement comes from south Sweden itself and specifically from Scania, where as Mats Malmer has shown thin-butted flint axes relate to soil types in a similar way to megalithic tombs.[15] Even more to the point Dr Märta Strömberg is beginning to show that settlement traces adhere closely to actual tombs. Hearths and culture-layers have been found within a kilometre's radius of the Trollasten dysse[16] and systematic testing of the neighbourhood of four megalithic tombs clustered in the neighbourhood of Hagestad[17] revealed traces of no less than nine settlements in the immediate area of three of them.

The type of land taken up for settlement and its biological resources provide between them by far the best clue to the economic basis of the people responsible for the tombs. In the case of Sweden, with one important exception to which I shall return for detailed analysis, there is a marked degree of correlation between the distribution of the early types of megalithic tomb considered in this paper and the most productive farming land. This in turn coincides in south Sweden to a remarkable degree with the distribution (fig. 11.2) of lime-rich and by consequence strongly alkaline soils. This has indeed been so since farming first began in Sweden. Whether one examines the distribution of cultivated land at the present day or the density of rural population during the mid-18th century the same general pattern emerges. It has always been lime-rich soils that have supported the wealthiest and densest farming populations. Lime is not merely in itself a plant food. Even more important it helps to make soils more tractable as well as serving to liberate other plant foods. So long as equipment was rudimentary ease of working was an essential requirement. By no means all lime-rich soils meet this specification. For instance many of the soils enriched with lime by glacial action, as happened when advancing ice passed over lime formations and incorporated this material in moraines, were too stiff and intractable for

11.2 Map showing the extent of the lime rock formations in south Sweden

primitive ards. It was not until iron had become sufficiently inexpensive to arm ploughs and other implements of tillage that the heavier, potentially rich lime-bearing soils could be taken into systematic cultivation. The soils of eastern Sweden for instance, enriched though they were by lime derived by glacial action from rock formations at present under the Baltic off the east coast of Gästrikland, were not seriously tackled until the early Middle Ages during which they sustained the Viking power centered on the Mälar-Uppland region.

A striking example of the attraction of lime-rich and tractable soils is provided by the Cambro-Silurian region of southern Skaraborgs Iän. Västergötland, still to this day notable for the prosperity of its farming population. This narrow territory carries no less than 290 passage-graves[18] or about four-fifths of those known from the whole of Sweden. The concentration (fig. 11.3) is all the more striking in that part of the territory is occupied by

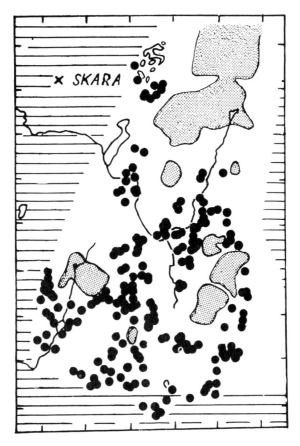

11.3 The distribution of passage-graves in Skaraborgslan, Västergötland. The reserved area coincides with the lime-rich Cambro-Silurian formation and the stippled zones with outcrops of dolerite. Scale: 1:250,000.

prominent outcrops of dolerite and that other areas were occupied by lakes, many of them now peat-bogs. Since these monuments belong to a comparatively brief period of time their density, around one per square kilometre, is impressive. It is a reasonable hypothesis that in this case the surplus output of food symbolised by and utilised in such an outstanding constructive effort was derived substantially at least from farming. At the same time it is worth noting that Magnus Fries' pollen-analytical investigation[19] of lake deposits near Varnhem in this area suggests that cereal cultivation was still only of minor importance during Middle Neolithic times and that even when this was increased somewhat during the Stone-Bronze age it was still insignificant by comparison with the position during the Iron Age. Presumably stock-raising and ancillary sources of food were relatively important, though until adequate material from settlements is available no certain conclusions can be drawn.

Turning next to the dolmens and passage-graves of southernmost Sweden in south Halland, Scania and Öland, the monuments are almost invariably situated on rock-formations rich in lime (fig. 11.4). On the other hand when the situation in Scania is examined more closely the significance of surface soils assumes a greater weight. Of very great importance for agriculture is the distinction drawn by Ekström[20] between the relatively stone-free Baltic

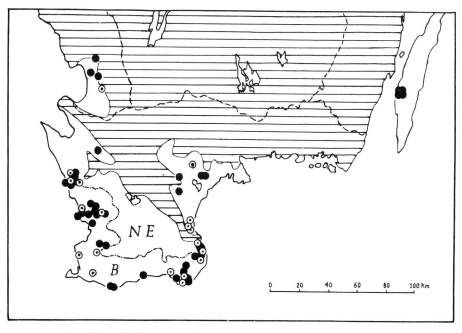

11.4 Map of dolmens (○) and passage-graves (●) in Scania, south Halland and Oland in relation to lime-rich soils (reserved). Within the latter the boundary between the soils of the Baltic end-moraine (B) and of the north-east moraine (NE) is marked by alternate dots and dashes

moraine with a clay component but relatively easy to work and the north-east moraine with its sandy soils practically free of clay and all too plentifully endowed with stones and boulders. No less significant is the fact that, whereas the soils of the Baltic moraine are alkaline or neutral, those of the north-east are mostly acid, except for part of the north-east corner of the province where the moraine is impregnated with lime from the underlying rock. The fact that dolmens and passage-graves and for that matter thin-butted flint axes are concentrated, as Malmer pointed out so clearly in 1962,[21] on this latter zone and on the Baltic moraine, that is on the agriculturally most favourable areas, argues that the economy of the builders was based primarily on farming. Confirmation in respect of crop-growing is indeed forthcoming from grain impressions on pottery from the megalithic tombs of Trollasten and Ramshog in Scania. According to Hjelmqvist[22] wheat pre-dominated strongly over barley as shown in table 11.1.

On the other hand there is some suggestion from the location of many sites[23] that coastal resources played some part in the subsistence of the megalith builders of this part of Sweden.[24] As the following table shows, slightly over 3/5th of dolmens were erected within 3 km. of the sea, that is within the potential daily catchment area. The fact that only a third of the passage-graves and transitional dolmens are within the coastal zone may

TABLE 11.1. Table showing predomination of wheat over barley from grain impressions on pottery from megalithic tombs in Scania

	Trollasten	Ramshog
Einkorn (*Triticum monocccum*)	20	6 or 7
Emmer (*T.dicoccum*)	6	3
Einkorn or emmer	14	1
Wheat (Club ?) (*T.compactum ?*)	2	3
Spelt (*T.spelta*)	–	1
Total wheat	42	14/5
Naked barley (*Hordeum* sp.)	5	2
Percentage of wheat	89	82/88

TABLE 11.2. Table showing distances from coast of dolmens and passage graves in Scania

	3 km.	3–9 km.	10 km.	Totals
Passage-graves	12	15	9	36
Transitional dolmens	2	2	1	5
Dolmens	8	3	2	13
Totals	22	20	12	54

perhaps suggest that coastal resources came to play a less important role during the full Middle Neolithic in this part of Sweden. The main attraction of this south coast during the stone age was probably the seal. To judge from the finds at Siretorp[25] seals were already being taken from the final stage of the local mesolithic and in substantial quantities during successive stages of the neolithic. The fact that seal bones accounted for 84 per cent of the total sample of 1,469 bones suggests that the site was essentially a sealing station. Of the three species represented, Greenland and grey seals were strongly represented and spotted seals rather less so. The first species was also present at the neighbouring site of Mollehausen,[26] though at this site seal-hunting was evidently only a subsidiary occupation. Although it looks very much as though the megalith builders in the coastal zone of Scania profited from seal-hunting, the importance of this in relation to farming ought not to be over-emphasised. It should be recalled that the Baltic moraine which carried the great majority of the Scanian megaliths formed only a comparatively narrow coastal girdle and on the other hand that over a sixth of dolmens and nearly a quarter of passage-graves were situated ten or more kilometres from the shore.

Analysis of the distribution of the third main group of early megalithic tombs in Sweden, those of Bohuslän, reveals a radically different pattern. So far from coinciding with areas of agricultural wealth the dolmens and passage-graves of Bohuslän diverge from this in a quite spectacular manner. From an agricultural point of view the province as a whole is poor: there is an absence of lime-rich soils, the distribution of cultivated ground is thin and the rural population as this is first known in the mid-eighteenth century is equally sparse.[27] Further, as our map (fig. 11.5) shows,[28] the early megalithic tombs with which we are here concerned are confined to a narrow coastal strip which from an agricultural point of view is the poorest zone of a poor province. The dolmens and passage-graves are confined to the coastal strip in which more than half the land is officially classified as unproductive from a farming point of view against figures of 40 per cent for the middle zone and 30 per cent for the inner or eastern zone.[29] What, then, was the economic basis of this important group of megalithic tombs? A closer look at their pattern of distribution and location provides a clue. In discussing the Scanian tombs attention was drawn to the numbers sited within daily range of the coast and the suggestion was made that seal-meat may have supplemented to an important extent the income derived from farming. The coastal orientation of the Bohuslän tombs of these early groups of tomb is much more marked and contrasts with the inland distribution of the much younger gallery graves of the same province as pointed out by Moberg.[30] The proportion of the early monuments erected within daily reach of the coast was greater and the degree of propinquity closer and each by a substantial margin. In table 11.3 propinquity is measured in relation to existing sea-level. Despite a certain

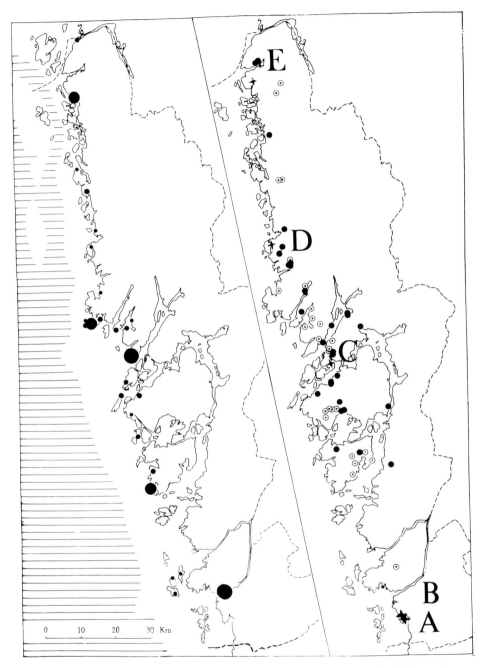

11.5 Dolmens (○) and passage-graves (●) on the Bohuslän coast in relation to known midden sites (+)

fluctuation in the height of sea-level this was not sufficiently pronounced during the later half of the Stone Age to affect topography to any major extent.

TABLE 11.3. Table showing distances from the existing coast of early megalithic tombs in Bohuslän.

	1	1–2	2–3	3–4	4–5	5–6	6–7 km.	
Passage-graves	14	6	6	3	–	1	1	31
Dolmens	16	8	5	–	–	–	–	29
Totals	30	14	11	3	–	1	1	60

A number of facts stand out from this. To begin with it will be noted that 100 per cent of the dolmens and 84 per cent of the passage-graves in Bohuslän are within 3 km. of the coast by comparison with 60.5 per cent and only 33.3 per cent respectively in the case of the Scanian tombs. Even more striking is the fact that no less than half the Bohuslän monuments are within 1 km. of the shore. A third thing to note is that as in Scania there was a tendency for passage-graves to be less closely associated with the shore than dolmens, though in the case of Bohuslän the indications of this are rather weaker.

Apart from Göteborg and its immediate neighbourhood and then only during the historic period, the coastal tract of Bohuslän has always depended on fishing as a main source of subsistence and wealth. The explanation for this is not hard to seek. The Bohuslän coast lies at the eastern extremity of the Skagerrak, the deep waters of which front almost precisely the zone of early megalithic tombs (fig. 11.5). Even today it is significant that the fish canning and conservation factories of Sweden are concentrated almost solely on this single stretch of coast. The degree to which this is so may readily be seen by tabulating the centres on the three main coastal zones of Sweden.[31] In doing so symbols of graded size have been used to designate the relative importance of the various factories.

TABLE 11.4. Table showing relative sizes of modern fish canning and conservation factories in Sweden.

Swedish coastal zones	●	●	●	●	•	Totals
West (Bohuslän)	2	3	5	5	8	23
South	–	–	–	–	2	2
East	–	–	–	–	2	2
Totals for Sweden	2	3	5	5	12	27

Note. The factories are listed according to size, the largest in the left-hand and the smallest in the right-hand column.

Close comparison of the maps shown on fig. 11.5 will show that the modern factories occupy the sites most accessible from the outer sea, whereas the megalithic tombs and presumably the settlements associated with these are found in more sheltered situations. Yet the agreement over all is extremely striking. It suggests at least the hypothesis that the megalith builders gained much of their wealth from the sea and above all from fish.

The most obvious way of testing this hypothesis is to examine the faunal remains from Stone Age sites on the Bohuslän coast. In doing so regard must be had to the fact that this particular coast was subject, by reason of its position along the margin of the zone of isostatic displacement, to a complex series of changes in relative land and sea levels. Although since mid-Atlantic times these were not of great magnitude in absolute terms, they were still sufficient to impair the archaeological record of coastal settlement in this part of Sweden. According to Mörner's paper of 1969[32] the oldest coastal sites one could expect to find above sea-level would be those dating from his second PTM (Postglacial transgression maximum) that is from the centuries immediately either side of *c.* 5000 B.C. Thereafter one must expect to find gaps in the surviving evidence corresponding with each of his main phases of regression, excepting only for lucky chances, as for example the coincidence of a deep dock or other excavation on the foreshore striking an actual settlement. We have for this reason to reconcile ourselves to an incomplete record. It is particularly unfortunate that the period of the earliest megalithic tombs in Bohuslän coincided with Mörner's sixth Postglacial regression (PR 6) and that by the onset of PTM 6 (2300–2000 B.C.) passage-graves had neared or even passed the point at which they continued to be built. Yet even if the coastal settlements of the earliest megalithic phase are no longer available for study the pictures of resource utilization for the preceding and immediately succeeding phases of settlement agree so closely that it seems reasonable to assume that they obtained during the intermediate and most directly relevant period.

The sites which by reason of their faunal remains are able to throw light on the utilization of coastal resources are lettered A–E from south to north of fig. 11.5 right. They may here be briefly listed in chronological sequence:

A. *Bua Västergård, Göteborg.*[33]
   Occupied when sea-level was not more than 25 m above that of today. Radiocarbon analyses by two laboratories (St. 3566–70 and U 851–2; 2444–6: 2520; 4016) suggest a date (uncorrected) in the first half of the sixth millennium B.C. The occupation could well relate to Morner's PTM (Postglacial Transgression Maximum) 2.

C. *Rottjärnslid, Dragsmark.*[34]
   Flint core axes and stone stump-butted and Lihult axes suggest a late Mesolithic context in archaeological terms. The site stands between 34–36 m above present sea-level and was occupied when the sea stood around 32–34 m higher than it does at present. Its (uncorrected) radiocarbon age (St. 2421: 3650±140 B.C.; St. 3878: 3620±300 B.C.; St. 3879:3505±300 B.C.) suggests that this site relates to Mörner's PTM 4.

B. *Hasslingehult, V. Frölunda, Göteborg.*[35]

Archaeologically this site features tanged flake arrowheads of Becker's class A with only odd specimens of later forms. In conventional terms this would relate the site to a middle stage of MN III, that is to a time when passage-graves were no longer being constructed. The main occupation belonged to a time when sea-level was between 13–16 m. above its present level and presumably related to Mörner's PTM 6.

D. *Rövik, Hamburgsund.*[36]

Archaeologically the finds from this site indicate that it belongs to the same period as Hasslingehult. It is situated on a shellbank *c.* 15 m. above present sea-level and presumably also relates to Mörner's PTM 6.

E. *Anneröd, Skee.*[37]

Archaeologically this points to a phase slightly younger than B and D. It is situated on a sandy strand deposit at 18.5 m. above present sea-level and in view of the number of discarded mollusc shells this suggests that sea-level stood only slightly below this level at the time of the occupation.

Analysis of the animal remains from these sites shows that land mammals made a certain contribution to diet. Red and roe deer are represented on the first three sites and pig at all but the third (B: Hasslingehult), the sample from which is in any case too small for absences to be at all significant. In addition elk occurred possibly at the first and certainly at the last site. The striking thing about the faunal remains on the other hand is unquestionably the

TABLE 11.5. Table showing the contribution of sea-food at different periods of the Stone Age in Bohuslän as shown by the faunal content of five coastal sites.

	A PTM 2 5000 B.C.	C PTM 4 3800/3700 B.C	B	D PTM 6 2300/2000 B.C.	E
Cod	●	●	•	●	●
Haddock		●		●	●
Ling	●	●		•	
Seals	•	•	•	•	•
Whales				•	•
Sea-birds	•	•	•	•	•
Shellfish	•	•	•	•	•

emphasis on coastal and marine resources. As our table shows, these invariably included shell-fish, except at Anneröd, where 13 species occurred alongside numerous edible mussels and abundant oysters; these played only a subsidiary role and may well in some cases have served for bait, rather than food. Sea-birds were present on all sites other than Hasslingehult, but in no case was there a marked concentration on any particular species, nor were birds as a class strongly represented in the fauna. Seals of one species or another, including Greenland, grey and spotted seals, were present among each assemblage and presumably contributed significantly to diet. Toothed whales on the other hand were much more sparingly represented. A leading role, at least in respect of numbers, was played by fish and notably by three species of bottom feeder: namely cod, haddock and ling, the first and third of which run to a very considerable size.

Closer analysis of the fish represented in the refuse from the five sites reveals a remarkable consistency over a period spanning around three thousand years. The first fact to be noted is the complete absence of herring, which at the present day predominates over cod in the annual catch on the Bohuslän coast (50 per cent against 30 per cent).[38] Evidently fishing, which for seven thousand years at least has been a major source of wealth in the coastal tract of Bohuslän, depended during the Stone Age primarily at least on fishing with line and hook for cod and other bottom-feeders. It is significant that bone fish-hooks (fig. 11.6) were present on the three of our five sites where bone artifacts survived in any quantity. Those from Rottjärnslid (C) have straight shanks with head expanded rearwards and points having one or in the case of the larger ones two barbs. The hooks from Rörvik had single barbs and the shanks had thickened heads grooved to secure the line. A second point to note is that, although the odd eel, flat-fish, mud-fish, pollack,

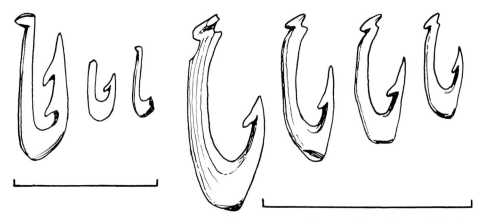

11.6 Bone fish-hooks from middens at Rottjarnslid (1–3) and Rorvik (4–7), Bohuslän, Sweden. Linear scales of 5 cm

whiting and wrasse were landed, the only species to be caught in sufficient quantity to indicate an organized fishery were cod, haddock and ling. At Bua Västergård (A) cod and ling accounted for no less than 140 out of 142/3 of individual fish identified, at Rottjärnslid (C) the three species accounted for 47 out of 49 individual fish and at Rörvik (D) for 146 out of 151. Thirdly, as if to confirm this, individual fish of these species were sometimes of exceptional size. Already in mesolithic times cod over 1 m. long were being caught both at Bua Västergård and at Rottjärnslid where the largest attained 1.5 m.; haddock up to 0.8 m. were caught at the latter; and ling up to 1.45 m. at the former and 1.7 m. at the latter. Large fish were also identified at the latter sites, cod of 0.97 m. occurring at Rörvik and 1.0 m. at Anneröd, though at both these sites it is fair to add that smaller fish were also present. The significance of large bottom-feeding fish is that for most of the year these keep to deep waters such as those of the Skagerrak or the Atlantic itself. On the other hand as Ekman pointed out[39] in respect of Hasslingehult and Henrici[40] in respect of Rottjärnslid, cod come into water as shallow as from 3 to 8 fathoms at spawning time. Yet even at this season ling rarely come into water much shallower than 20–25 fathoms and haddock seldom come above 12 fathoms. Either therefore the fishermen ventured out into the Skagerrak or they operated only during the spawning season, that is predominantly during the winter. In mesolithic times they may well have had to exercise both options, but during neolithic times it is likely enough that fishing was a seasonal activity that fitted into the farming year as it still did in Norway down to modern times.

Analysis of the location of early megalithic tombs in Bohuslän, taken in conjunction with the evidence of the potentialities of the province in early times, thus suggests that the exploitation of coastal resources contributed in a significant fashion to the wealth that made possible their erection. This has gained some support from an analysis of faunal remains relating to periods of relatively high sea-level before and immediately after the phase of marine regression (Mörner's PR 6) contemporary with the erection of the monuments. Although for this reason no information is or can be available from coastal middens of the actual builders the consistency of the pattern prevailing beforehand and immediately after is such as to make it a fair presumption that coastal resources were similarly exploited at the relevant time, as they certainly were being in Denmark.[41] Prominent among these resources, other than the seals which were also being exploited round the Scanian coast, were bottom feeding fish like cod, ling and haddock, the first two of which ran to a very large size. In order to catch these bottom feeders boats would have been needed. What kind they were can only be guessed at. The earliest direct evidence for the boats used on the Bohuslän coast is the Bronze Age rock-engraving from Kville[42] which shows two men line-fishing from a boat with upturned prow and projecting keel, almost certainly a craft with planks or strakes. Such a vessel can hardly have been made by the people who originated the fishery several thousand years earlier. The most likely boat employed in this fishery would have been made of skin stretched over a light frame, the kind of craft known down to recent times over a vast extent of the circumpolar zone, depicted on the late Stone Age rock art of the north-west Norwegian coast[43] and which significantly still remains active in the form of the curragh on the Atlantic sea-board of Ireland. The indications are, however shadowy,[44] that skin boats of this kind were active on the sea-ways between Ireland, Scotland and Brittany during the early Christian period and such could well have been descendants of those which linked these lands three or four thousand years earlier. Boats like the Eskimo *umiaq* were capable of carrying upwards of twenty people[45] across the open sea.

A main outcome of this enquiry into the economic basis of megalithic tombs in Sweden has been to emphasize the importance of the exploitation of coastal resources during the initial phase and in respect of Bohuslän to underscore the role of a line fishery for bottom feeding Atlantic fish, notably cod, haddock and ling, a fishery already established for a hundred generations or so in the Skagerrak before ever a passage-grave was built in Scandinavia. The relevance of this to the concept embedded in the literature of a dichotomy between 'megalithic farmers' and 'pit-ware hunter-fishers' during the latter half of the third millennium will only be mentioned in passing.[46] I would like to end this brief tribute by returning to a topic hinted at in the opening paragraph and consider the bearing of this study on the process of megalithic diffusion.

The coastwise distribution of megalithic tombs has long been accepted in conventional terms as evidence for the passage along the Atlantic sea-ways of 'megalith-builders', variously inspired according to the predilection of the writer by a thirst for metals, by missionary zeal or by sheer zest for adventure. The suggestion is worth considering whether fishermen may not have explored and opened up remoter territories as well as helping to feed the builders and even themselves assisted in the new cult. This applies not merely to south Scandinavia where the existence of the fisheries of the Skagerrak and the Kattegat and the seal and porpoise resources of the Swedish and Danish coasts make it easy to understand the close analogies in ceramic ornament and tomb form between N. Jutland and Bohuslän and between Zealand and Scania,[47] but also to the Atlantic sea-board of western Europe where the pursuit of fishing serves to knit together coasts and islands which to a landsman may seem far apart.

When Hugh Hencken first turned his attention many years ago to the archaeology of the extreme south-west of England he was immediately struck by the disproportionate number of megalithic tombs on the Scilly Islands, three times as many as in the whole of Cornwall even though the present land area of the islands only amounts to 3,500 acres.[48] Even if we allow for the possibility that the land in this region still stood sufficiently higher in relation to the sea than at present for the Scilly Islands to be joined together, 45 megalithic tombs is still a very large number; and the disparity is even greater when it is appreciated that all the Scilly monuments belonged to the category of V-shaped or Entrance Graves as opposed to only 4 or 5 of the Cornish monuments. Hencken was much in advance of his time when he found it 'hard to understand how such an island, which could scarcely have supported much of a population, came to have on it such a profusion of burials'.[49] He realized that in economic terms there was a problem: the land area was too restricted to support the investment. But the 'Western Seaways' syndrome was still too strong and it was felt sufficient to recall that Scilly was 'an obvious place for a sea-borne culture to strike deep root'. A generation and a half further on we may prefer to respond to his initial insight and find an economic explanation that really answers the question how sufficient resources were in fact available for the monuments to be constructed, never mind whence the inspiration came. In the light of our analysis of the situation in Bohuslän the most likely source is the sea. And this accords entirely with what we can observe within a radius of 300 km. or so of the Scilly Islands.

The distribution of entrance graves, of the type described by Hencken, extends from the Land's End district of Cornwall[50] to the area of Tramore Bay, on the coast of Waterford, in the south of Ireland,[51] east to the Channel Islands (Herm, Alderney and Guernsey, but not Jersey),[52] and south to Finistère and Morbihan, Brittany.[53] The one unifying factor in such a distribution is the sea and the most likely underlying cause of this activity is surely fishing. In his popular account of *Britain and the Western Seaways*,[54] Prof. Emrys Bowen considered the maritime distribution of megalithic tombs in the west, in the light of mediaeval traffic, notably that inferred from the distribution of Ogham inscribed stones, church dedications, traditional journeys of Celtic saints, and known pilgrim routes, like those converging on Santiago de Compostela. He assumed that these journeys were accomplished by means of skin-boats, resembling the still-existing curragh of western Ireland, a gold model of which exists in the Broighter hoard, dating, in all probability, from the dawn of the Christian era.[55] Prof. Bowen ended on a suggestive note:

While we have concentrated on travelling in pursuit of some great objective, or for health or religious reasons, we must not forget that the cause of travelling in every age and in every land is primarily, but not exclusively economic . . . There is in this context one reason for travelling by sea which is not often mentioned, but which must have had an influence on movement over the western seas from the earliest times, and that is the pursuit of fish.[56]

Whatever the factors that have led men to traverse the sea-ways of Atlantic

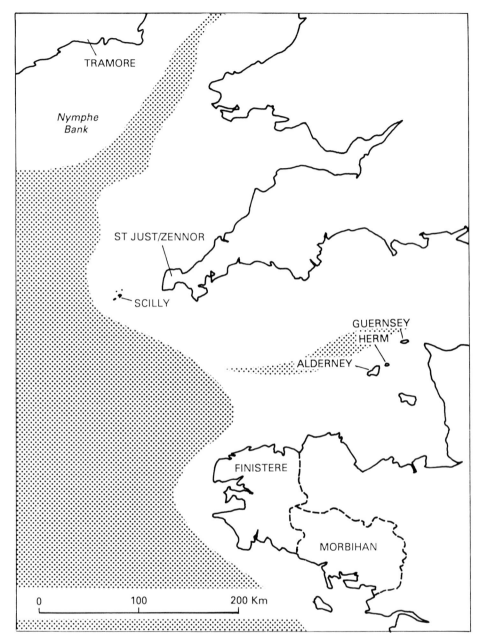

11.7 Map showing relation of V-shaped or entrance graves to the fishing zone between Brittany and southern Ireland. Shaded areas mark sea over 100 m deep.

Europe it seems safe to assume that the routes were first opened up by men intent on catching fish. Crustacea may locally have been a useful source of food during the Stone Age, as the crab claws from Obanian sites in south-west Scotland and from the midden at Skara Brae, Orkney, bear witness.[57] On the other hand it is migratory fish and the seasonal movements of fishermen that these imply which provide the most likely clue to the coastwise distribution of megalithic tombs in Portugal, Brittany, the Celtic Sea, north-west Ireland and south-west Scotland. In the context of south-western and western Europe four main species have been the object of commercial fisheries during historic times, namely pilchards, tunny, mackerel and hake. Of these the first two are mainly taken by drift nets of a size beyond the capability of early man, nor is it conceivable that primitive line tackle could have stood up to catching tunny in the manner of modern sportsmen. The most likely prospects remain hake and mackerel.

The distribution of hake (gen. *Merluccius*) as given by C. F. Hickling[58] and B. W. Jones[59] is highly suggestive in the light of that of megalithic and related tombs. It extends from the west Mediterranean, round the Atlantic coasts of Iberia, western France up to Brittany, south-west England, south and west Ireland, south-west and west Scotland and the Isle of Man. In the course of modern commercial trawling these fish are taken from deep water, but in earlier times they were caught on hook and line when they came into shoal water for spawning. According to Hickling the time of the year when this happens may vary within a range of three months, but the important point to note is that it occurred earlier in the Celtic Sea for instance than further north off the west coast of Ireland or south-west Scotland. Thus fishermen were able to extend the catching season by moving north during the course of the summer. The spawning cycle of the fish provided a mechanism for the northward movement of fishermen.

The importance of the Irish hake fishery between 1504–1824 has been well brought out by Arthur Went.[60] In connection with the pattern of distribution of entrance-graves it is interesting to note that in the area of the Celtic Sea there were two fishing grounds of key importance, namely the Melville Knoll off Scilly and the Nymphe Bank south of Co. Waterford. According to a mid-18th c. record quoted by Went a six-man boat might expect to take 1000 hake on hook and line in the course of a single night. It is small wonder that during the centuries covered by Went's survey the Celtic Sea should have attracted fishermen from Fance and even from Biscayan Spain, as well as England and Ireland, or that the fish whether wet or dried and salted should have found its way to the markets of Iberia and France as well as England. Again, it is significant, when viewed in the context of Ruadhri de Valera's idea that the impulses which led to the construction of court and allied cairns in Ireland entered by way of the west coast,[61] that Oliver St John should have noted in his *Description of Connaught* (1614) that a great trade in hake, cod, ling and conger from this coast was carried on by merchants from Brittany and Portugal as well as England.[62]

The other fish most likely to have played a significant part in prehistoric times in western as distinct from northern Europe is the mackerel (*Scomber scombrus*).[63] On this side of the Atlantic this is found mainly in the west Mediterranean and the warmer seas of western Europe. Since this fish moves near the surface in shoals, which off the coasts of N. America may be as much as 20 miles long and a ¼ mile wide, it is commonly taken in drift nets, but even in commercial fisheries it is still caught in large numbers on hook and line and is locally taken in small seine nets, both methods within reach of prehistoric man.[64] As with hake it is worth stressing seasonal movements linked with spawning: in winter the fish remain in deep water only to rise in the spring and make for their spawning grounds. Detailed information about the seasonal movements of mackerel is beginning to accumulate as a result of systematic recovery of tagged specimens. Thus according to experiments conducted by G. C. Bolster[65] fish tagged off the Atlantic shelf south-west of Cornwall and west-south-west of Co. Cork expanded over the whole extent of the Celtic sea in a matter of months and, still more interesting, individuals tagged off the south-west coast of Co. Cork found their way up the west coast of Ireland[66] and as far as south-west Scotland.

It is the more regrettable in view of these suggestive facts that the drowning of neolithic shore-lines in south-west Britain and Brittany makes it impossible to confirm the existence of hake and mackerel fisheries at this time in the way it was possible to demonstrate the existence from early times of the West Swedish line-fishery. The presence of accumulations of limpet shells offers one of the few clues, but this is unfortunately ambiguous: whereas Martin wrote of the inhabitants of St Kilda at the close of the 17th century that 'their common bait is the lympets or patellae', it is no less the case that these shell-fish were eaten directly in parts of Britain.[67] Dr Hencken himself recorded 'enormous quantities of limpet shells' from the midden at Halangy Porth on St Mary's, Scilly,[68] a midden which also yielded sherds resembling ones from entrance-graves and thick layers of limpets were noted in the chambers of the large-passage-graves of La Varde and Le Dehus, Guernsey[69] and of the gallery-grave of Ville-es-Nouaux, Jersey.[70]

Although stopping far short of proof it is at least a tenable hypothesis that the opening up of routes along the Atlantic sea-board of Europe was accomplished by fishermen. Moreover the superior cosmopolitanism of fishermen remarked by T. C. Lethbridge,[71] coupled with the god-fearing qualities of men accustomed to entrusting themselves to the unknown, further suggests that they may even have played some part in determining the maritime and coastal distribution of megalithic tombs in western Europe. Yet it has equally to be recognized that megalith builders were also farmers and that in many cases fishing was ancillary to stock-raising and cultivation, just as previously it had been carried on in a context of hunting and foraging. A final point to observe is that to judge from Dr John Coles' work at Morton, line fishing for cod was already well established on the coast of Fife, as on the west coast of Sweden, well before megalithic tombs began to be built in north-west Europe. [72]

Notes

1 Dr Glyn Daniel sensibly concluded a review of rival views on this matter by writing in *The Megalith Builders of Western Europe*, 1962, 125 that 'we may go on arguing for ever about the historical role of the megalithic builders'.

2 See his 'Old Mortality: some aspects of burial and population in neolithic England', in *Studies in Ancient Europe: Essays presented to Stuart Piggott*, J. M. Coles and D. D. A. Simpson, eds.1968.

3 *The Earlier Stone Age Settlement of Scandinavia*, Cambridge University Press, 1974, to be followed by a volume on *The Later Stone Age . . .*

4 P. Ashbee in *Archaeologia* c (1966) 35.

5 *Ibid.*, 91. Cf. Glyn Daniel, *ibid.* 22.

6 R. J. C. Atkinson, *Stonehenge* London 1956, 98–107.

7 M. Strömberg, *Der Dolmen Trollasten in St Köpinge, Schonen* Lund 1968, 227.

8 A. J. B. Wace and F. H. Stubbings, Eds., *A Companion to Homer*, London, Macmillan 1962, fig. 26.

9 M. Almagro and A. Arribas, *El Poblado y la Necropolis Magaliticos de los Millares*. Madrid 1963, folding plan.

10 V. G. Childe. *The Dawn of European Civilization*, 6th ed. London 1957, 170.

11 R. A. S. McAlister *et al*, *Proceedings of the Royal Irish Academy* xxix, sect. c. (1910–12), 311ff.; E. R. Norman and J. K. S. St Joseph, *The Early Development of Irish Society* Cambridge 1969, 20–3.

12 S. P. O'Riordain, *Proceedings of the Royal Irish Academy*, lvi sect. c. (1954) 443–56.

13 G. Eogan, *Proceedings of the Royal Irish Academy*, lxvi, sect. c. (1968) 299–400; *Antiquity* 41 (1967), 203–4.

14 Sean Ó Nualláin, *Journal of the Royal Society of Antiquaries of Ireland*, 102 (1972) 49–57; P. J. Fowler and J. G. Evans, *Antiquity* (1967) 290, fig.1.

15 M. Malmer, *Jungneolithische Studien*, Lund 1962, cf. abb. 117 and 120.

16 M. Strömberg, *op. cit.* (1968), 231–2.

17 M. Strömberg, *Die Megalithgräber von Hagestad* abb. 156, 370–1.

18 Our map (fig. 3) is based on that by G. A. Hellman in 'Västergötlands gånggrifter', *Falbygden* 18 (1963), 3–12. The geological basis is taken from *Sveriges Geologiska Undersökning* Sveriges Berggrund, Ser. B. nr. 16 (S. Sheet), controlled by outlines of the dolerite areas on Hellman's map.

19 M. Fries, 'Vegetationsutveckling och odlingshistorie: Varnhemstraken.' *Acta Phytogeographica Suecia*, 1958.

20 G. Ekström, 'Skånes moränområden', *Svenska Geografist Arsbok* 12 (1936) 70–7; 'Skanes akerjordsomraden', *Socker*, 6 (1950): 53–61.

21 *Op.cit.* 1962: 692ff.

22 In Strömberg. *op. cit.* (1968) 243–9; *ibid.* (1971) 138.

23 Strömberg, *op. cit.* (1971) 195, noted the coastal situation of many Scanian passage-graves, but drew no conclusions from this about the economic basis of their builders.

24 From the small scale maps in Dr Strömberg's books (1968; 1971) it is hardly possible to measure distance as accurately as those I have been able to obtain from Bohuslän. It is nevertheless possible to see that certain tombs (notably Strömberg 1971, nos. 4, 11–13 and 32–4) are sited within 1 km of the coast, although it is equally plain that the proportion is very substantially lower than in the case of Bohuslän.

25 A. Bagge and K. Kjellmark, *Stenåldersboplatserna vid Siretop i Blekinge,* Stockholm 1939. See E. Dahr, 242–5,

26 J. E. Forssander, 'Den sydsvenska boplatskuturen', *Medd. Lunds hist. mus.* 1940–41, 276–98.

27 See *Atlas över Sverige,* Stockholm 1953, maps 10, 66 and 49–50 (fig. 3).

28 I am much indebted to Dr Lili Kaelas for kindly supplying me with a detailed plot of Bohuslän passage-graves and *dysse* on the scale of 1: 200,000.

29 *Op. cit.,* map 67(1).

30 C. A. Moberg, *Bohusläns forntid,* map p. 33. From *Bohusläns Historia,* E. Lönnroth, ed.

31 Based on map 110 of *Atlas över Sverige.*

32 N. A. Mörner. *The Late Quaternary History of the Kattegatt Sea and the Swedish West Coast, Sveriges Geologiska Undersokning, ser.* C. nr. 640, Stockholm 1969.

33 J. Wigforas, Arkeologisk Rapport and J. Lepiksaar, Zoologisk Rapport in *Stenåldersboplatsen Bua Västergård Goteborg,* 1972.

34 J. Alin, 'En bohuslänsk kokkenmödding på Rotekärrslid, Dragsmark', *Göteborgs och Bohusläns Fornminnesforenings Tidskrift,* 1935, 1–38: P. Henrici, 'Benfynd fran boplatsen på Rotekärrslid', *ibid.* 38–42; S. Welinder. 'The Chronology of the Mesolithic Stone Age on the west Swedish coast', *Studier i nordisk arkeologi* 9, Göteborg 1973.

35 C. Culberg, 'Hasslinghult, Göteborg', *Fynd* 1972: 373–448. Also Jan Ekman on the bone material, *ibid.,* 571–7.

36 S. Janson, 'En boplats fran yngre stenåldern vid Rövik i Kville sn. Bohuslän.' *Göteborgs och Bohusläns Fornminnesforenings Tidskrift.* 1936: 57ff.; P. Henrici. *ibid.*

37 O. Frödin, 'En svensk kjokkenmödding. Ett bidrag till de postglaciala nivåförändringarnas.' *Ymer,* 1906, 17–35.

38 Axel Sømme, *A Geography of Norden,* London, Heinemann, 1968, p.314.

39 In C. Culberg. *op. cit.,* 1972, 576.

40 In J. Alin, *op. cit.,* 1935, 41–2.

41 This was recognized as early as 1900 in the report of the third commission on the Danish kitchen-middens by A. P. Madsen et al., *Affaldsynger fra Stenalderen i Danmark,* 176. Three of the six middens investigated were assigned to the period before megalithic tombs, but three (Aalborg, Ørum Aa & Leire Aa) were recognized to span the dolmen/passage-grave transition as this was then conceived.

42 J. G. D. Clark, *Prehistoric Europe: the economic basis,* London, Methuen 1952 and 1974, fig. 41.

43 G. Gjessing, *Nordenfjelske Ristninger og Malinger av den arktiske* Gruppe, Oslo 1936, 197; J. G. D. Clark, *Prehistoric Europe: the economic basis,* London, 1952, 283.

44 James Hornell, *Water Transport. Origins and Early Development,* Cambridge 1946, 136–42.

45 K. Birket-Smith, *The Chugach Eskimo,* Copenhagen, 1953, 49.

46 This very broad topic will be dealt with in *The Later Stone Age Settlement of Scandinavia,* now in preparation.

47 L Kaelas, *Den äldre megalitkeramiken under mellan-neolitikum i Sverige,* Stockholm 1953, passim; M. Strömberg, *op. cit.,* 1971, 199.

48 H. O'N Hencken, *The Archaeology of Cornwall and Scilly,* London, 1932, 17.

49 *Ibid.* 33.

50 E.g. Giant's House, Pennance, Zennor; Treen near Gurnard's Head; Carn Gluze, St Just; and Tregaseal, near Carn Gluze.

51 T. G. E. Powell. 'A new passage grave group in South Eastern Ireland.' *Proceedings of the Prehistoric Society,* 1941, 142, 143.

52 T. D. Kendrick, *The Archaeology of the Channel Islands,* 1, London, 1928, Figs. 86 and 113.

53 Glyn Daniel, *The Prehistoric Chamber Tombs of France,* London, 1960, 85–7, Fig. 35, Nos. 3 and 4.

54 E. G. Bowen, *Britain and the Western Seaways,* London, 1973.

55 Against A. Mahr's claim (*Proceedings of the Prehistoric Society,* III: 410) that 'the greater part of the objects is Indian', Rainbird Clarke argued (*Proceedings of the Prehistoric*

Society, xx, 42) that the Broighter hoard was in fact Irish and dated from around the time of Christ.

56 *Op. cit.*, 113.
57 J. G. D. Clark, 'The Development of Fishing in Prehistoric Europe,' *The Antiquaries Journal*, xxviii (1948), 45–85.
58 C. F. Hickling, *The Natural History of the Hake*, Fishery Investigations. Ser. ii, Vol. x, No. 2. H.M.S.O., London, 1927.
59 B. W. Jones, 'World resources of hakes of the genus *Merluccius.' Sea Fisheries Research*, F. R. Harden Jones, ed., London, 1974, 139–166.
60 Arthur E. J. Went, 'The Irish Hake Fishery, 1504–1842', *J. Cork Historical and Antiquarian Society*, li (1946), 41–51.
61 *Proceedings of the Prehistoric Society*, xxviii (1961), 243 and 250, map.
62 Quoted by Went, *op. cit.*, 43.
63 E. S. Russell, *Fishery Investigations*, ser. ii, Vol. iii, No. i.
64 B. & E. Megaw, *Proceedings of the Isle of Man Natural History & Antiquarian Society* v, No. iii (1952), 250–260. The seine nets used from yawls in the 19th *c.* were only *c.* 20 yards long and had a ¾ inch mesh.
65 G. C. Bolster, 'The Mackerel in British Waters', *Sea Fisheries Research*, F. R. Harden Jones, ed., London, 1974, 101–16.
66 Arthur Went noted a flourishing mackerel and pilchard fishery in Cleggan Bay, Co. Galway. *See Proceedings of the Royal Irish Academy*, li (1946), Sect. B, No. 5, 81–120.
67 M. Martin, *A Description of the Western Isles of Scotland c.* 1695, reprinted Stirling, 1934, 417; M. S. Lovell, *The Edible Mollusca of Great Britain & Ireland*, London, 1884, 178–9.
68 *Op. cit.* 29.
69 T. D. Kendrick, *The Archaeology of the Channel Islands*, i, London, 1928, 79–80.
70 Jacquetta Hawkes, *The Archaeology of the Channel Islands*, ii, 262.
71 *Boats and Boatmen*, London, 1952, 84.
72 John M. Coles, 'The Early Settlement of Scotland; excavations at Morton, Fife', *Proceedings of the Prehistoric Society*, xxxviii (1971), 284–366. See esp. pp. 351–2.

References

Almagro, M. and Arribas, A., 1963 El Poblado y la Necrópolis Megalíticos de los Millares, *Bibliotheca Praehistorica Hispana*, iii, Madrid.
Ashbee. P., 1966 The Fussell's Lodge Long Barrow Excavations 1957, *Archaeologia* c, 1–80.
Atkinson, R. J. C., 1956 *Stonehenge*, London, Hamish Hamilton.
    1968 Old Mortality: some aspects of burial and population in neolithic England, *Studies in Ancient Europe. Essays presented to Stuart Piggott*, J. M. Coles and D. D. A. Simpson, eds., Leicester University Press.
Birket-Smith, K., 1953 *The Chugach Eskimo*. Nationalmuseets Skrifter Etnografisk Raekke 6. Copenhagen.
Bolster G. C., 1974 The mackerel in British waters. *Sea Fisheries Research*, F. R. Harden Jones, ed., London, pp. 101–16.
Bowen, E. G., 1972 *Britain and the Western Seaways*, London, Thames and Hudson.
Childe, V. G., 1931 *Skara Brae*, London, Kegan Paul.
    1957 *The Dawn of European Civilization*, 6th ed., London, Kegan Paul.
Clark, J.G.D., 1948 The development of fishing in Prehistoric Europe, *Antiquaries Journal*, xxviii, 45–85, London.
    1952 *Prehistoric Europe: the economic basis*, London, Methuen.
    1975 *The Earlier Stone Age Settlement of Scandinavia*, Cambridge University Press.
Coles, J. M., 1971 The Early Settlement of Scotland: excavations at Morton, Fife. *Proceedings Prehistoric Society*, xxxviii, 284–366.
Daniel, G., 1960 *The Prehistoric Chamber Tombs of France*, London, Thames and Hudson.
    1963 *The Megalith Builders of Western Europe*, London, Hutchinson.
De Valera, R., 1961 The 'Carlingford Culture', the Long barrow and the Neolithic of Great Britain and Ireland, *Proceedings Prehistoric Society*, xxvii, 234–52.

Ekström, G., 1936 Skånes moranområden, *Svenska Geografisk Årsbok*, 12, 70–7.

1950 Skånes akerjordsområden, *Socker* 6, 53–61.

Eogan, G., 1968 Excavations at Knowth, Co. Meath, 1962–65 *Proceedings Royal Irish Academy*, 66 c, no. 4, 299–400.

1969 Excavations at Knowth, Co. Meath, 1968, *Antiquity*, XLIII, 8–14.

Fowler, P. J., and Evans, J. G., 1967 Plough-marks, Lynchets and Early Fields. *Antiquity*, XLI, 289–301.

Fries, M., 1958 *Vegetationsutveckling och odlingshistorie: Varnhemstrakten*. Acta Phytogeographica Suecia.

Gjessing, G., 1936 *Nordenfjelske Ristninger og Malinger av den arktiske gruppe*, Inst. f. Sammenlignende Kulturforskning. Oslo, Ser. B, no. XXI.

Hawkes, J., 1939 *The Archaeology of the Channel Islands*, II, London, Methuen.

Hellman, G. A., 1963 Vastergötlands gånggrifter, *Falbygden* 18, 3–12.

Hencken, H. O'N., 1932 *The Archaeology of Cornwall and Scilly*, London, Methuen.

Hickling, C. F., 1927 The Natural History of the Hake, *Fishery Investigations*, Ser. II, X, no. 2, London, H. M. Stationery Office.

Hornell, J., 1946 *Water Transport Origins and Early Development*, Cambridge University Press.

Jones, B. W., 1974 World resources of hakes of the genus *Merluccius*, *Sea Fisheries Research*, F. R. Harden Jones, ed., London.

Kaelas, L., 1953 Den äldre megalitkeramiken under mellan-neolitikum i Sverige. Kungl. Vitterhets Historie och Antikvitets Academiens Handlingar. Del. 83, *Antikvariska Studier*, V: 9–77.

Kendrick, T. D., 1928 *The Archaeology of the Channel Islands*, I, London, Methuen.

Lethbridge, T. C., 1952 *Boats and Boatmen*, London, Thames and Hudson.

Lovell, M. S., 1884 *The Edible Mollusca of Great Britain and Ireland*, 2nd ed., London, L. Reeve.

Macalister, R. A. S. et al., 1912 Report on the Exploration of Bronze-Age Cairns on Carrowkeel Mountain, Co. Sligo, *Proceedings Royal Irish Academy*, XXIX, C, 311–47.

Mahr, A., 1937 New Aspects and Problems in Irish Prehistory, *Proceedings Prehistoric Society*, III, 261–436.

Malmer. M., 1962 Jungneolithische Studien, *Acta Archaeologica Lundensia*, Octavo Ser., No. 2.

Martin, M., 1934 *A Description of the Western Isles of Scotland* (c. 1695), reprinted, Stirling.

Megaw, B. and E., 1952 The Development of Manx Fishing Craft. *Proceedings Isle of Man Natural History and Antiquarian Society*, V. no. III, 250–60.

Norman, E. R. and St Joseph, J. K. S., 1969 *The Early Development of Irish Society*, Cambridge University Press.

Ó Nualláin, S., 1972 A Neolithic House at Ballyglass near Ballycastle, Co. Mayo, *Journal Royal Society Antiquaries Ireland*, 102, 49–57.

Ó Riordain, S. P., 1955 Lough Gur Excavations: the Megalithic Tomb. *Journal Royal Society Antiquaries Ireland*, LXXXV, 34–50.

Petrie, G., 1867 Notice of ruins of ancient dwellings at Skara, Bay of Skaill, in the parish of Sandwick, Orkney, recently excavated, *Proceedings Society Antiquaries Scotland*, VII 201–19.

Powell, T. G. E., 1941 A new passage grave group in South Eastern Ireland, *Proceedings Prehistoric Society*, VII: 142–3.

Russell, E. S., 1914 Report on Market measurements in relation to the English Haddock Fishery during the years 1909–1911. *Fishery Investigations*, Ser. II, Vol. III (1), London, Board of Agriculture and Fisheries, H.M.S.O.

Strömberg, M., 1968 Der Dolmen Trollasten in St Köpinge, Schonen, *Acta Archaeologica Lundensia*, Octavo Ser. 7.

1971 Die Megalithgräber von Hagestad, *Acta Archaeologica Lundensia*, Octavo Ser. 9.

Wace, A. J. B. and Stubbings, F. H., 1962 *A Companion to Homer*, London, Macmillan.

Went, A. E. J., 1946a The Irish Hake Fishery, 1504–1824, *Journal Cork Historical and Antiquarian Society*, LI, 41–51.

1946b The Irish Pilchard Fishery, *Proceedings Royal Irish Academy*, 51, B, No. 5, 81–120.

CHAPTER 12

SOME REMARKS ABOUT THE INTER-RELATIONS BETWEEN ARCHAEOLOGY AND NATURAL SCIENCES

The work of this symposium and of its predecessors exemplifies the modern trend towards interdisciplinary research as a way of bringing increasingly specialized interests and fields of study to bear on particular topics. On the one hand we have the possibility, so well exemplified in the present case by the group excavating in Rijckholt, of combining the special knowledge of amateurs with the often more theoretical knowledge of professional archaeologists. On the other there is the possibility of bringing specialized natural science to bear on the solution of human problems. I would only like to stress that co-operation between specialists must be genuine, that is to say that specialists must maintain their integrity.

Here in the Netherlands you have a fine example in the Biological-Archaeological Institute at Groningen of what I mean by genuine creative co-operation, as distinct from the bogus co-operation which exists when an archaeologist seeks to justify preconceived ideas by the selective use of scientific data.

The author of a recent work on the history of molecular biology has recently commented that politeness is the death of scientific converse. What he meant I think was deference, deference to seniority, deference to established views. We have to pursue the insight of our specialisms and in doing so must not be afraid of conflict. If we disagree politely but firmly, who knows, but that in the end, we reach conclusions of a durable kind.

In the present case we find a combination primarily of the Earth Sciences, Physics and Chemistry on the one hand and of various studies focussed on human society on the other. It is perhaps understandable that during its initial stages a series of symposia dedicated to the study of flint should focus on its physical character, on the history of its formation, its mode of occurrence in nature and its properties as a potential source of implements for shaping other materials. A knowledge of such matters is plainly essential if we are to understand correctly the winning, dissemination and utilization of flint by man.

The converse is no less true. If research is to be effective its aims need to be defined and brought into focus. To seek to learn more about flint purely as a substance is of course a perfectly valid aim. I would certainly not subscribe to

223

the view popular with some politicians and nearly all tax-payers that scientific research ought only to be supported to the extent that it can be shown to be directed to the satisfaction of perceived social needs. Research into the nature of flint needs no more extraneous justification than the scientific study of any other phenomenon or for that matter writing poetry, painting pictures or even pursuing archaeology. On the other hand it is surely right in the presence of distinguished archaeologists from several countries to consider what light such studies can be expected to throw on prehistory and in particular on the nature of prehistoric societies. Perhaps I am right to assume that the organizers of this conference invited me to address you in expectation that I would emphasise precisely this.

The information to be won from flint in respect of technology is in several respects more precise than that afforded by the igneous and metamorphosed rocks that were also favoured by early man for axe and adze blades. The fact that flint occurs in seams in the parent chalk called for greater skills and a more complex technology in the process of mining than the quarrying of rocks from surface exposures. Descriptions of the method used in particular localities were offered at the Second Symposium and we look forward to hearing more on this topic in the coming days. Again, the dense texture of flint offers the maximum promise for studying the techniques used in shaping it to form artefacts, the manner in which it was used to shape other materials and not least the nuances by which prehistorians are able to distinguish the products of particular social groups. For a time igneous and metamorphosed rocks appeared to give more specific information about the dissemination of products from extractive centres, since they lent themselves to petrological determination. As we now know thanks to the work of the British Museum team even the advantage conferred by this will not hopefully continue for very much longer. The fact still remains that a large volume of work on the determination of stone-axe blades already exists in the literature so I make no apologies for drawing upon this as an earnest of what we may hope to learn from flint when more definitive results have been obtained and published.

In a brief talk one has to choose between offering a comprehensive but necessarily superficial review or going slightly deeper on a narrower front. I intend on this occasion to emphasize the social rather than the technological or even the purely economic aspects of early man's relationship with flint. In respect of the winning of raw materials the social dimension is guaranteed by the fact that the lead in establishing this symposium was after all taken by a group with direct experience of mining as an organized team activity. To view a site like Grimes' Graves as the outcome of group activity of a specialized kind is in itself an education in social archaeology. By the same token every archaeologist knows that the forms into which flint was worked by prehistoric man need to be viewed as expressions of the identity and solidarity of social groups, in other words as expressions of ethnicity and occasionally of hierarchy as much as adaptations to economic needs. I propose therefore to concentrate on the dissemination of products. I shall argue that the patterns produced by plotting axe or adze blades made of materials from particular foci of mining or quarrying reflect social as well as economic forces and, conversely, that the systematic attribution of artefacts to the sources of the materials of which they are made is capable of throwing light on the social life of early man unobtainable by other means and vital to the correct interpretation of archaeological data as a whole.

In doing so I shall draw upon primary data from two sources:
a) the British Isles, mainly from the third millennium B.C.
b) aboriginal Australia dating in part from the ethnographic present or recent past.
One of the most valuable outcomes of being able to trace the sources of raw materials and map the distribution of artefacts made from them is to gain an insight into the dynamics of the communities among which they were disseminated and used. To illustrate this we may begin by considering the information accumulated in Britain since systematic work began in 1936 on the sources and distribution of stone axes made from igneous and metamorphosed rocks.[1] The evidence for seven provinces of the British Isles is here summarized:

Table showing proportions of axes of igneous and metamorphosed rocks in different parts of Great Britain and Ireland identified from quarries in Cornwall, North Wales, Northumberland, the Lake District and Antrim, N. Ireland

Sources	South-west (1972)	E. Anglia (1972)	Lincs., Notts., Rutland (1973)	Derby, Leics. (1974)	Yorks. (1971)	Scotland (1968)	Ireland (1962)
Cornwall							
I–IV	163	52	16	8	14	–	–
XVI	49	–	1	2	–	–	–
XIX	3	–	–	–	–	–	–
Total	215:68.5%	52:35.6%	17:6.5%	10:8.0%	14:8.6%	–	–
N. Wales							
VII–VIII	31	15	40	26	18	1	2
XII–XIII	2	–	–	–	–	–	–
Total	33:10.5%	15:10.3%	40:15.2%	26:20.8%	18:11.0%	1:1.6%	2:2.9%
Lake District							
VI	52:16.6%	72:49.3%	196:74.5%	84:67.2%	103:63.2%	3:4.9²⁄₃	1:1.5%
Northumberland							
XVIII	3:1.0%	–	7:2.7%	3:2.4%	26:16.0%	–	–
Antrim							
IX	11:3.5%	7:4.8%	3:1.1%	2:1.6%	2:1.2%	57:93.4%	65:95.6%
TOTALS	310:100.1%	142:100%	262:100%	125:100%	163:100%	61:99.9%	68:100%
Other groups	14	16	15	23	–	–	–

If the distribution patterns of stone axes had been determined by purely economic factors, one might expect to find the products of each factory concentrated in relatively compact and mutually exclusive territories. What we see in fact is very different. This is not to say that the economic factor was unimportant. The cost of transport, at any rate over land, ensured that axes occurred more densely in areas nearer their sources. Thus axes from Cornish quarries, at present presumed to be submerged by the sea, account for more than two-thirds of those identified from the south-western counties and around half even for East Anglia, but for very much less further north. Again, axes from the Graig Lwyd quarries in North Wales were common in proximate parts of England, but markedly scarcer in East Anglia and the southwestern counties. Similarly, axes of dolerite from the Whin Sill, situated mainly in Northumberland, are well represented in Yorkshire, less so in the Midlands and only rarely further afield. The fact remains that although in different parts of the country axes originating from one source predominated, small and in some instances quite considerable elements invariably occurred from all but one of the English sources and isolated specimens of the one exception. Whin Sill, reached as far south as Southampton. In the case of Ireland and Scotland small components were present from North Wales and the English Lake District. Again, although the distribution of axes from the factory of Creag na Caillich near Killin, Perthshire, has yet to be systematically plotted, an example has already been identified as far south as Lincolnshire. The evidence shows decisively that factors other than purely economic ones must have been at work to account for the distributions established by petrological determinations. To pick out only one of the most evident features the concentration of sacred monuments in the Avebury-Stonehenge region of Wessex attracted stone axes from Cornwall, North Wales, the English Lake District, Northumberland and even Co. Antrim. More generally the evidence of the axes brings home the truth that whatever the regional variations of culture existing in Neolithic Britain the province as a whole was in fact knit together by an intricate pattern of interchange, a network held together rather than sundered by the sea.

The ethnographic evidence strongly confirms that the patterns of dissemination of stone axe blades from known sources was in large measure determined by social rather than purely economic factors.[2] It will be convenient to turn for examples to the results of systematic work on the petrological determination of the sources of stone axes carried out by R. A. Binns and Isabel McBryde in the New England province of New South Wales and in Victoria, Australia.

In neither case can the patterns of distribution be explained convincingly in economic terms. Thus in the case of northern New South Wales[3] axes of Group 2B from quarries in the Baldwin formation are concentrated mainly on the tableland. Whereas they expanded west along the Darling river to the

Paroo between 500/600 km. to the west, they failed to penetrate the much nearer coastal zone to the east. By contrast axes of Groups 4 and 7 were concentrated in the northern half of this same coastal zone. In the case of Victoria[4] the evidence from distribution is even clearer and in this case is confirmed by ethnographic observations. Thus although axes from the Mount William and Mount Carmel quarries were evidently carried over considerable territories it was noted that they failed to reach either the extreme north-west or, despite its proximity to the sources, the district of Gippsland in the south-east. Since Gippsland in particular had relatively high potential and was in fact relatively densely inhabited, the absence of Mount William axes can hardly have been due to economic causes. Ethnographic studies show that the Gippsland aborigines belonged to a language group (Kurnai) quite distinct from that (Kulin) spoken by the people in whose territory the axe factories were situated. Again, studies of other forms of social interaction show that the axe blades were being redistributed within a well defined social territory. In this connection Dr McBryde recalled the Nillipédji quarries of Arnhem Land studied by D. F. Thomson.[5] These produced a material that was esteemed at a technical level for fabricating effective spearheads, but even more for the prestige value that made it desirable as a medium of exchange and thus a potent agent in generating obligation and debt. Even in societies restricted to a lithic technology and a mode of subsistence resting on various forms of catching and foraging the dynamic factor behind the widespread dissemination of products from localized sources related to prestige as much as to utility. From this it follows that the patterns of distribution ought to reflect the intensity and extent of social interaction and offer clues to social structure and relations. The extensive movement of artefacts of stone and doubtless of flint[6] is only a particular instance of what became even more sharply apparent as societies acquired a more vertical, hierarchical structure, namely that prestige came to attach to materials and artefacts by virtue of their exotic origin.[7] It is not difficult to appreciate why control of traffic in exotic resources should have become so important in the process of acquiring and safeguarding power, whether political as during later prehistoric times or, as seems more likely in Neolithic Britain, sacred. The progress of the British Museum team in defining the movement of axes made of flint from specified mining areas is all the more keenly awaited and will need to be closely studied in relation to the patterns already established by plotting axes made from igneous and metamorphosed rocks.

Notes

1 For identification of the sources of stone axes from Neolithic Britain, see 1st to 5th Reports of the Sub-Committee of the South-western Group of Museums and Art Galleries on the Petrological Identification of Stone Axes, in *PPS*, VII (1941), 50–72; XIII (1947), 47–59; XVII (1951), 99–158; XXVIII (1962), 209–66; and XXXVIII (1972), 235–75.
   Reports for other regions of England include those for Yorkshire (*PPS*, XXXVII (1971), 16–37), East Anglia (*PPS*, XXXVIII (1972), 108–57), Lincs., Rutland and Notts. (*PPS*, XXXIX (1973), 219–55), and Derby and Leicester (*PPS*, XL (1974), 59–78). For Ireland, see E. M. Jope, *Ulster J. Arch*, XV, 31–60, and XVI, 31–6; and for Scotland, P. R. Ritchie, in *Studies in Ancient Europe*, ed. J. M. Coles and D. D. A. Simpson, 1968, 117–36.

2 G. Clark, 'Traffic in Stone Axe and Adze Blades', *Economic History Review*, XVIII (1965), 1–28.

3 'Preliminary Report on the Petrological Study of Ground-edge Artefacts from North-eastern New South Wales, Australia', *PPS*, XXXV (1969), 229–35; *A Petrological Analysis of Ground-edge Artefacts from Northern New South Wales*, Canberra, 1972.

4 I. McBryde and A. Watchman, 'The Distribution of Greenstone axes in South-eastern Australia: a Preliminary Report', *Mankind*, X (1976), 163–74; L. McBryde, 'WIL-IM-EE-MOOR-RING: or, Where Do Stone Axes Come From?' *Mankind*, XI (1978), 354–82.

5 D. F. Thomson, *Economic Structure and the Ceremonial Exchange Cycle in Arnhem Land*, Melbourne, 1949.

6 G. de G. Sieveking, P. Bush, J. Ferguson, P. T. Craddock, M. J. Hughes and M. R. Cowell show in 'Prehistoric Flint Mines and their Identification as Sources of Raw Material', *Archaeometry*, XIV (1972), 151–75, that under certain conditions flint can be linked with its source.

7 S. Frankenstein and M. J. Rowlands cite a number of useful references in their article, 'The Internal Structure and Regional Context of Early Iron Age Society in South-west Germany', *Bull. London Univ. Inst. of Archaeology*, XV (1978), 73–112.

CHAPTER 13

COASTAL SETTLEMENT IN EUROPEAN PREHISTORY WITH SPECIAL REFERENCE TO FENNOSCANDIA

I

Although this paper is restricted to European prehistory, I have contributed it to the present symposium in the hope that it may illustrate the importance of coastal resources in the history of human settlement, at least in respect of peoples living at a subsistence level of economy. For this reason it seems appropriate to open on a theoretical note. It is only in so far as coastal settlement offered tangible advantages to early man that it is capable of yielding significant insights into what really happened in the prehistoric past. Conversely, a study of coastal settlement can be expected to advance understanding of the processes that shaped prehistory only if we first offer hypotheses for testing against the empirical data of archaeology. The problem may be generalized by seeking to identify the key factor influencing settlement preferences on the part of communities constrained to subsist on food derived to an overwhelming extent from local resources. It is surely not extravagant to adopt the hypothesis that this was none other than subsistence. This is not to maintain that subsistence determines settlement patterns – the reverse might apply under certain circumstances – or that subsistence is the only factor influencing choice in respect of settlement. All we can be sure of in interpreting any archaeological record is that the community responsible for it was successful enough to leave a deposit, that it can have achieved this only through a successful routine of acquiring food, and that, in other words, its settlement pattern must at least have been consistent with success in the food quest. Further than that, it may be affirmed in the light of evolutionary theory that the more perfect the match between subsistence and settlement pattern, the better adapted for survival a community would have been. One has every reason, therefore, to expect that study of settlement patterns will provide clues to the process of change, as well as help us to understand particular phases.

Turning next to coastal territories in particular, one may begin by considering what advantages these would have offered, at least in theory, over inland ones, first and foremost in respect of subsistence. Most important, it may be suggested, is the fact that they offered a greater abundance and diversity and above all a greater degree of security against dearth. Although it is true that the inland zone within convenient reach of coast dwellers would on average have been only half that available to settlers in the hinterland, its biomass is likely to have exceeded the norm at least in the temperate zone through the moderating effect of the sea on temperature and thus on vegetation, on grazing and browsing animals, and on their predators. To this may be added the advantage of low-lying soils acquired, in the case of Scandinavia, through the progress of isostatic recovery. Of far greater importance, on the other hand, was the availability of the resources of the seashore and coastal waters, not to mention the limitless potential of the open seas, given the use of boats and – in circumpolar regions – of sledges. Resources like seabirds and their eggs, crustacea, sea mammals including different kinds of whales and seals, and fish with a wide range of habits and breeding seasons, were not merely diverse in character, but offered a range of seasonal food-stuffs that together with inland resources were capable of being combined in an intricate scheduling of seasonal harvests, as well as affording reserves for times of difficulty in the form of mollusks, limited in bulk yet having the supreme advantage of being always available.

One outcome of a successful harnessing of coastal and maritime resources in combination with those of the immediate hinterland that might reasonably be anticipated would be that people previously constrained to move seasonally over more or less extensive annual territories might find themselves able to meet their needs all the year round without moving their habitations. In other words, coastal settlement could well have led to the adoption of a sedentary mode of life. This, if it occurred, would have enlarged the possibilities of subsistence, and house building and technology, including the production of pottery. Other concomitants of marine-catching activities, namely navigation and – in northern territories – devices for moving over fast ice, would have increased mobility, facilitated economic interchange between relatively remote areas, and thus favoured the spread of other cultural attributes. The intensification of coastal settlement might thus be expected to have exerted a dynamic influence on cultural development.

II

Although for reasons discussed in this section, the evidence is and is likely to remain incomplete, even the known distribution of prehistoric sites in Europe offers plenty of empirical evidence that the Mediterranean, Atlantic, and Baltic coasts exerted a powerful attraction on early man. Indeed, the empirical evidence argues that the demographic situation of northern Europe during the later Stone Age resembled that of aboriginal North America. According to A. L. Kroeber's estimate (1939: 145), the density of population in the coastal territories of that continent was between 5 and 10 times that of the interior and was even twice as much as among agricultural groups away from the coast. Before analyzing the data from northern Europe to test the ideas set out earlier, it seems important to stress some of its more noteworthy limitations. To begin with, it is possible to assess the extent to which settlement was attracted to the coast only when the shoreline in question is available for study. Effectively, this means in the case of almost the whole of Europe that nothing can be said about when the emphasis on coastal settlement widely evident for the Mesolithic phase began, since the Upper Palaeolithic shorelines of the Atlantic and Mediterranean zones were submerged by the Neothermal transgression.

Even in respect of Neothermal times, there is a wide variation in the quality of evidence bearing on coastal activities and settlement. The most complete documentation comes from Scandinavia, a territory that has the added advantage of long-established schools of Quaternary research and a tradition of systematically salvaging and identifying organic refuse from archaeological deposits. Even so, there are wide variations in the quality of the evidence from different parts of even this highly favoured territory. For instance, there is a much more complete series of prehistoric strandlines available for study above modern sea level in Fennoscandia, the territory most powerfully depressed by the weight of the Pleistocene ice sheet, and therefore the one that experienced the strongest isostatic recovery of the land as the ice melted during Neothermal times, than in a peripheral region like Denmark, where the sea rose only for brief periods above the level at which it has settled today. Again, there are marked local variations in the degree to which organic refuse that makes it possible to test the utilization of coastal and marine resources has survived. Whereas the rocks of extensive parts of the Fennoscandian shield were acidic and hostile, those of Denmark and the rest of the west Baltic area, west Sweden, southwest Norway, and Varanger Fjord in the far north were often exceptionally favourable. Despite such local variations, on the other hand, the evidence from Scandinavia provides by far the best insight into the role of the seacoast in the later prehistoric settlement of Europe.

The only European territory outside Scandinavia where isostatic recovery eventually brought shorelines from the later Stone Age above modern sea levels was north Britain and Ireland. Elsewhere and notably round the Atlantic coasts of southwest Europe and in the Mediterranean basin, the eustatic rise of sea level that accompanied the melting of the Pleistocene ice sheets was the predominant factor in geographical transformation. As the widespread submerged forests exposed at low tide and the occasional submerged monument remind us, the process of marine transgression continued through much of the Neothermal Period (Reid 1913; Hencken 1932). Although the rise of sea level since the later Stone Age has been comparatively slight, whether in southern Britain[1] or the Aegean,[2] it was enough to deprive archaeology of ready access to the coastal middens that incorporate the most decisive evidence for the subsistence economies of coastal settlers. This is not to exclude the possibility of exploring submerged middens by means of the techniques devised by submarine archaeologists (Bass 1966; Muckelroy 1978); indeed, the thrust of the present paper points to the need to make this investment when suitable sites are located. The fact remains that in default of such investigation, detailed information about the subsistence activities of Stone Age coast-dwelling populations is mainly confined to territories where the relevant coastlines exist above present sea levels.

III

That Scandinavia, and Fennoscandia in particular, is better endowed with old strandlines above modern sea level than other parts of Europe is not the only reason why it is best adapted for testing the hypothesis that coastal settlement during prehistoric times was closely linked with the systematic exploitation of coastal and marine resources. It happens to be a territory in which hunting and catching of sea mammals and fish have continued to play a significant role down to modern times. Three components of coastal economies may serve to test our hypothesis: the cod and associated fisheries of north and east Denmark, and more particularly of the west coast of Sweden and the coasts of Norway from Stavanger in the west to the extreme north; the hunting of toothed whales off the coast of Norway; and the seal-hunting activities of the Baltic and the Gulf of Bothnia in particular.

The cod that form the backbone of the Bohuslän and Norwegian fisheries leave the depths of the Atlantic in great shoals around mid-February and come within reach of hook and line as they enter shallower waters to spawn. The harvest is not only rich but predictable. To quote from Hjort, the migrations 'take place with periodical regularity, each of the great fisheries being bound to a certain time of the year and, in all main features, the one year is but a repetition of the other' (1896:6). The most evident way to test the prehistory of the Scandinavian fishery is to scrutinize archaeologically-dated midden deposits for the bones of fish like cod, haddock, and ling, as well as for the hooks by which they were caught and hauled up from the seabed. Since my original study made over 30 years ago,[3] new discoveries have made it possible to fill in some of the main gaps. Excavations at Bua Västergård near Göteborg (Lepiksaar 1972: 72–81) show that cod over 1 metre and ling up to 0.45 metre in length were being taken in a specialized line fishery from the coast of Bohuslän at the eastern end of the Skagerrak as early as the sixth millennium B.C. in radiocarbon years.

The line fishery based on shoals of cod, ling, and haddock moving in from the Atlantic to spawn in shallower waters has continued to play a role of economic importance down to modern times in Bohuslän, despite being overlaid by the commercial and industrial wealth of Göteborg. Even today the fish canning and conservation stations of the whole of Sweden are overwhelmingly concentrated on this tract of coast (Lepiksaar 1972: table 4).

Evidence that the fishery continued through the rest of the Stone Age is documented in series of middens, including Rottjärnslid from a late phase of the local Mesolithic (Alin 1935: 1–38; Henri 1935: 38–42; Welinder 1973) and three from the closing phases of the Middle Neolithic (Cullberg 1972: 373–448; Ekman 1972: 571–7; Janson 1936: 57–81; Henrici 1936: 82ff.; Frödin 1906: 17–35). The latter, each of which yielded pottery, and one, Rörvik, the bones of domestic sheep or goat and pig, raises a significant theme in northern prehistory, namely, the relation between catching and farming activities. In the marginal zones of farming, the contents of coastal middens are particularly instructive. Here the stadial notion of a clear-cut transition from hunter-forager to farmer breaks down. The evidence from Scandinavia shows that in 'Neolithic' times, the various activities of the food quest were combined in the manner best adapted to local conditions.

A concomitant of the hunting of porpoises and seals and the conduct of line fisheries from settlements around the Atlantic coast of Scandinavia from west Sweden to the far north of Norway must have been the use of seagoing boats capable of coping with winter conditions. That boats were certainly being used even during Mesolithic times off the coast of Norway is shown by plentiful evidence of traffic between the islands and mainland. The only indications of their nature are provided by representations in the Stone Age rock engravings between the Trøndelag and Finnmark. The well-known engraving at Rødøy in Helgeland, for instance, shows rather clearly the profile and projecting ends of the frame of the type of keeled skin-covered boat used down to recent times in the circumpolar zone. The engravings also give useful hints about the activities pursued from boats. The Rødøy boat (Gjessing 1936), for instance, is shown in close proximity to a small-toothed whale, probably a porpoise, and a seal, an animal whose skin (because of its toughness) was particularly well suited for covering such craft. On the other hand, one of the two representations of similar boats at Evenhus is shown overlaid by a line to which a halibut is attached (Gjessing 1932). A more detailed representation of a fishing scene, though in this case dating from the Late Bronze Age, is depicted on the well-known rock engraving at Kville, Bohuslän, which shows two anglers plying hook and line and seated in an anchored boat of uncertain construction (Clark 1952: fig. 41). The use of seaworthy boats for fishing and marine hunting provided a means of establishing and maintaining contact between territories separated by sea. In particular, it helps to account for the northward diffusion of cultural elements originally developed by farmers among communities of settled hunter-fishers occupying coastal territories. The spread of perforated stone battle axes (Hagen 1967: fig. 2) as far north as Varanger Fjord is a simple case in point, even though these most probably reached northwest and north Norway directly by traversing Sweden. The adoption of stock raising by at least one hunter-fisher community on the Bohuslän coast has already been noted. More surprising is the case argued in detail elsewhere for supposing that the Middle Neolithic passage graves of the barren coastal strip of Bohuslän were erected by the maritime hunters and cod fishers of the region (Clark 1977) in contact with Jutland farmers. There is plenty of lithic evidence for coastal traffic in southwest Norway. Already during the Mesolithic Nøstvet phase, fine-grained greenstone was being quarried on the small Atlantic island of Hespriholmen and flaked into axe blades on the larger island of Bømlo (Faegri 1943), whence they were traded over the islands and mainland certainly as far as Jaeren some 120 kilometres to the south. The volume of the traffic may be gauged from the fact that the quarries still visible on Hespriholmen must have yielded some 35,000 cubic feet of material. Again, as Egil Bakka has shown,[4] artifacts of the kind of veined quartz (*årekvarts*) exposed in the rock on Bømlo have been found, mainly on the coasts and islands, from Jaeren in the south to the islands of Ålesund some 300 kilometres to the north of Bømlo, a range of nearly 4° of latitude.

The earliest traces of human settlement in northernmost Norway, defined by the stone industries of Fosna and Komsa in the Trøndelag and Finnmark respectively, adhere closely to the coasts of the fjords and islands and point to a sea-based economy and the widespread use of boats.[5] Thanks to Povl Simonsen's investigation of settlement on the south shore of Varanger Fjord (1961) and the systematic study of Haakon Olsen (1967) of the rich animal remains from the Gressbakken site at Nesseby, much more is known about the situation in the far north, more particularly during the second millennium B.C. (Simonsen's third and fourth periods). For the first time, apart from the rectangular houses recorded by Gjessing at Hellarvikjae on Traena immediately south of the Arctic Circle (1943: pls. 4–10), we have archaeological evidence for actual houses and settlement patterns (fig. 13.1). Although the plans vary, with round and oval as well as rectangular ones in period II and mainly rectangular ones having two, three, or even four entrances from period IV, their general structure is similar, with thick earth walls enclosing semisubterranean floors, stone-set hearths, and narrow entrances. Again, the same settlement plan persists with houses strung out along the shorelines as if to give their inhabitants the readiest access to boats. Although it is hardly possible as yet to estimate the number of dwellings occupied at any one time, it is already clear that we have to deal with communities made up of several households, reflecting the need for teamwork among a number of men for hunting sea mammals.

The most direct evidence about the economy of the later Stone Age inhabitants of the north Finnmark coast comes from the period IV houses at the Gressbakken site and comprises a very substantial sample of animal

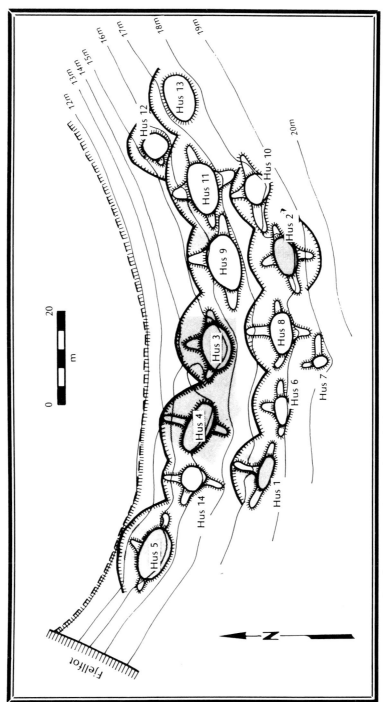

13.1 Plan of Stone Age settlement of Gressbakken, Nesseby, Finnmark (After Simonsen)

skeletal remains. These cast a useful light on the fish and meat components of diet.[6] They reflect a strong emphasis on maritime species, amounting to all the fish, 85 per cent of the birds, and 93 per cent of the mammals. While it is evident that fishing and hunting were each important, their relative contribution to diet is problematic: if fishbones, despite their greater fragility, account for well over half the items identified, it must be remembered that a given number of mammal bones, which amounted to over one-third of the total, implies a substantially larger amount of food than an equivalent number of fishbones. The fact that over three-quarters of the fishbones comprised cod suggests that a main attraction of this coast was, as in the present day, the annual arrival of vast shoals of this species.

It is clear that sea mammals also contributed to the food supply. The evidence of rock engravings argues that whales were more important than seals on the Norwegian coast. Care should, of course, be taken when seeking to draw economic inferences from iconography. One may agree with Anders Hagen (Simonsen 1965:400) that the motifs of Norwegian rock art may 'inform us about the hunter's eating habits,' but recognize at the same time that the hunter's art is more a measure of anxiety than a direct index of the proportions in which different species were taken for food. For instance, there is no clear representation of cod even though we know that it played a key role in subsistence, presumably because catching this fish was a matter of routine. The art depicts rather those animals that were a matter of exploit, notably large herbivores and marine mammals. In the latter case, it may be noted that whales are depicted on rock engravings at 18 localities, whereas seal were shown only at 2, in each case with whales.

Although by no means prolific, because of adverse conditions for survival over much of the territory, bone refuse confirms that a number of species of toothed whales were taken. No fewer than six species were represented in the middens associated with later Stone Age settlements on the south shore of Varanger Fjord (Olsen 1967:181), and remains of some of the same species have been identified at several localities on the west coast (fig. 13.2).

A feature of the sea birds is the evident preference accorded to various species of auk, which account for two-thirds of the total bird bones by comparison with less than 3 per cent for gulls, even though these two groups occur in nature in more or less equal numbers. Similarly, land birds were made up substantially of one species, the willow grouse, which normally comes down from the mountains in the autumn and lends itself to snaring during the period of snow cover. The mammalian fauna from the interior is also unevenly represented and so throws significant light on human preferences. Although nearly four-fifths of the finds are of reindeer, extremely few of the bones were of the nature of meat refuse, and those few related to joints detached from carcasses. The vast majority had been shaped elsewhere into artifacts including fishhooks and harpoon heads (Simonsen 1965:400).

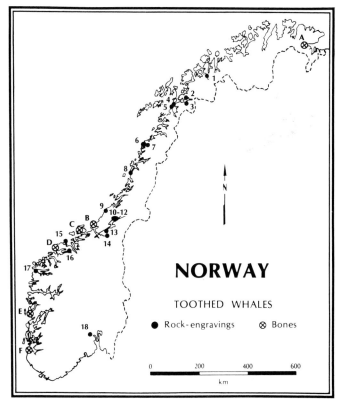

13.2 Evidence for whaling during the Norwegian Stone Age
  Rock engravings: 1 Tennes; 2 Sletfjord; 3 Forselv; 4 Valle; 5 Leiknes; 6 Klubben;
  7 Fykanvatn; 8 Rødøy; 9 Strand; 10 Hammer; 11 Buavika; 12 Bardal; 13
  Evenhus; 14 Hommelvik; 15 Søbstad; 16 Bogge; 17 Vinge; 18 Skogerveien
  Bones: A Varanger Fjord; B Dalen; C Dolm; D Bjornerem; E Ruskenesset; F
  Viste

Among the remainder there is a strong representation of fur-bearing animals including arctic fox, bear, beaver, ermine, hare, and marten, a fact which may connect with the emphasis on auks, the skins and plumage of which were adapted to making exceptionally warm linings for fur garments (Olsen 1967:181). The occurrence of a few traces of sheep and ox argues that the settlers on the Varanger shore were already maintaining domestic livestock, if only on a restricted scale.

The overwhelming importance of catching, and more particularly of marine-catching activities, in the economy of the Gressbakken settlement is reflected in the emphasis on polished slate knives, and weapon heads, and above all in the range of antler and bone harpoon heads and of fishhooks. The short, stoutly-made harpoon heads, provided with two unilateral barbs or a single one, occasionally on either side of the tip, and normally short tangs with ears to engage the line, resemble those closely associated with seals and small whales over extensive tracts of Scandinavia including the Baltic basin. Fishhooks ranged in size from those designed for large cod down to those suited to haddock and coalfish and included composite as well as single-piece forms; the latter, though mostly barbed, were sometimes unbarbed. The effort of hauling in heavy fish on long lines was evidently mitigated by bone attachments (*Vabein*) grooved for up to four lines and fitted to boat gunwales. Among other artifacts made from animal materials particular note may be taken of finely-eyed needles of a kind suited for sewing furs or skins for clothing.

A key factor in the adoption of settled life is the ability to store food and so make seasonally harvested resources available for consumption over extended periods of time. This is especially relevant in the case of a resource like the shoals of cod that annually approach the coasts of Norway and afford a harvest of immense richness but short duration. As the etymology of the Norwegian word for cod (*torsk* from *tørrfisk*, dried fish) suggests, the method of preserving this fish by drying is of considerable antiquity. Although artificial means are increasingly used, the old method can still be observed of hanging the fish on wooden racks of the kind employed for drying cereals and hay. At the present day, cod dried in this way (*klippfisk*) is exported as far afield as West Africa. The probability is that it served as a medium of exchange for the exotic products that found their way across Fennoscandia to the northwest coast of Norway during the later phases of prehistory. In order to avoid transporting waste, cod heads are removed in processing klippfisk and converted into fishmeal for cattle. This, like the common use of drying racks, is an interesting illustration of the symbiotic relations that still exist between catching and farming activities on the west coast of Norway. It also affords a means of checking when distant trade began. Haakon Olsen's analysis of cod bones from Gressbakken refuse (1967:173) argues that the inhabitants had not yet begun to process the fish for long-range export, since head bones were proportionately as frequent as those from the pectoral girdle. Cod may, of course, have been dried for local consumption, but in a region where the snow habitually lies until the end of May, it might have been simpler to depend on refrigeration.

The solid construction of the Varanger houses and their aggregation in hamlets, together with evidence for the use of pottery, comb ware of the Säräsniemi type from the period II midden at Nordli (Simonsen 1965: figs. 28–30), and asbestos pottery from period IV (Simonsen 1965), argue for some degree of sedentariness based on an assured supply of seafood. On the other hand, Olsen's analysis of the fauna argues for seasonal and specifically winter occupation of the coastal sites. Thus, cod could mmost readily be caught as the shoals approached the coast (February, March) and the seals were killed when they were young (February–May). The birds also pointed to the winter. Willow grouse are habitually snared during the season of snow cover, and the High Arctic species would have been present between October and May. By contrast, the complete absence both of young birds and of salmon suggests that the inhabitants had moved inland from the coast by the beginning of June. Again, the reindeer, represented almost entirely by artifacts shaped from their antlers and bones, were presumably culled in the interior while on their autumn migration routes (September–October). A positive hint that the people began to move inland to take the salmon as these ran upstream is provided by traces of temporary settlement from the same period along the course of the Pasvik River, at least one of which (Noatun) (Simonson 1963, 1967) yielded pottery of the Säräsniemi style. The temporary nature of the sites is shown by the light construction of the dwellings, consistent with summer use, and by the evidence in their stratigraphy of frequent abandonment and return. Unfortunately, the absence so far of deposits of organic material makes it impossible to check whether their occupation was in fact linked with the salmon run. This nevertheless remains a likely hypothesis. A natural progression might then have been to predate the reindeer routes returning to winter on the coast gaining a supply of antler gear for fishing and hunting sea mammals.

IV

The Finnish and Swedish coasts of the north Baltic basin resemble those of Norway in the sense that they extend far beyond the temperate zone to which predominantly farming economies were confined in early times. They afford a second opportunity to test the extent to which a concentration on coastal settlement rested on exceptionally favourable conditions for subsistence, as well as the degree to which it favoured the growth of sedentary life and so made for a greater openness to diffusion from the south. On the other hand, the geographical environment differed in one particularly notable way. Whereas the warm currents of the Gulf Stream ensured that the coast of Norway remained open as far as Varanger Fjord throughout the year, the lower salinity of the Baltic meant that in a normal season, the gulfs of Bothnia, Finland, and Riga must have frozen more or less completely. During an extreme winter, ice extends today over almost the entire Baltic, the Kattegat, and the east end of the Skaggerak as far as east Norway. Even in a mild season, a zone of fast ice forms round the entire coast of Finland and that of Sweden north of Öland Island. This had a considerable influence in respect of communication and subsistence. The indications are that sledges had already come into use by Suomusjärvi times and that these had been joined by skis at a time when comb ware was widely used in Finland (Clark 1952: 293–301).

Distribution maps make it clear that settlement concentrated on the coast of Finland, although supplemented to varying degrees by occupation and exploitation of the interior, throughout prehistoric times. This was already the case during the Suomusjärvi phase, when substantial parts of the country were still submerged: there was a marked concentration of settlement on contemporary strandlines (Luho 1967; Clark 1975: maps 15–16). During the comb ware phase, when pointers to actual settlements were better defined, the attraction exercised by the coast was still marked, although there are clear signs of increased interest in the interior as time went on.[7] Much the same situation obtained during the opening centuries of the second millennium B.C., as documented by the distribution of stone axes of perforated shaft hole type attributed to the Kuikais culture (Meinander 1954b:44).

The earliest monumental evidence for the distribution of settlement on either side of the Gulf of Bothnia comprises numerous stone cairns (fig. 13.3) covering earth or stone-lined graves and a few elongated boat settings. Although these inform us strictly only about the location of burials, it is fair to assume as a working rule that the dead were buried within easy reach of settlements. The only way of dating the great majority of the cairns, either unexcavated or lacking in grave goods, is by reference to their relations to sea level: at least this can provide minimum dates in a territory of rapid isostatic adjustments in which the land gained progressively from the sea. On the Swedish side, Evert Baudou (1968, 1977) and Noel Broadbent (1979), in Ångermanland and in north Västerbotten and south Norbotten respectively, found that the cairns were concentrated between 50 and 30 metres above modern sea level, that is, within a zone restored to dry land through continued isostatic recovery in the course of the Bronze Age. Confirmation of their Bronze Age date is shown archaeologically by the grave groups excavated from a number of examples. Baudou concluded that the funerary cairns of Ångermanland were the outcome of the impact of a knowledge of Bronze Age burial rites from the south on the indigenous Stone Age population. In his study of the Bronze Age in Finland, C. F. Meinander (1954a) noted that stone cairns were concentrated on former coasts of the gulfs of Bothnia and Finland and concluded that these were the outcome of influence from Swedish bronze-using communities. At that time, Meinander refrained from assigning the cairns north of Oravais some halfway up the coast of the Gulf of Bothnia to the Bronze Age on the score that none of them had yielded grave goods dated to that time. On the other hand, Ari Siiriainen's analysis (1977:13–25) of the heights of cairns above sea level argues that the proportion assignable to the Iron Age was in fact lower to the north rather than to the south of Oravais. It seems safe to conclude that the distribution of the cairns on either side of the Gulf of Bothnia argues for a concentration of settlement on the coast during the latter part of the second and the earlier part of the first millennium B.C. Indeed, the indications are that this continued into comparatively recent times. North of the Vaasa region of Finland, for instance, medieval churches were almost confined to

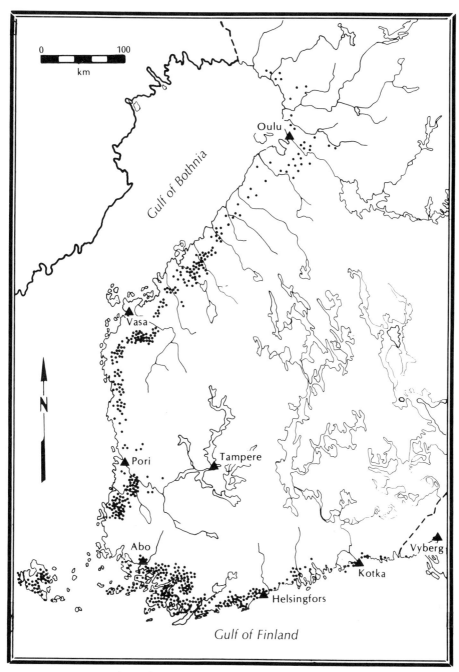

13.3 Map of (mainly) Bronze Age cairns in Finland (After Meinander)

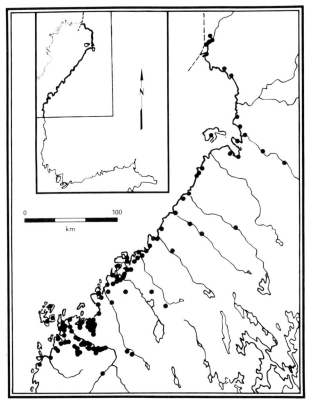

13.4 Settlement in Ostrobothnia in mid-sixteenth century AD showing villages with 10 or more farms (After Jutikkala)

the coastal strip (Somme 1968: fig. 9.7). The distribution of villages including more than 10 farms each (fig. 13.4) was also markedly coastal (Jutikkala 1959: map 7), though with more examples in the hinterland, mainly on the courses of rivers flowing down to the gulf.

It is commonly accepted, and indeed proved by the distribution of monuments and the facts of historical demography, that human settlement in the northern part of the Baltic and notably on either side of the Gulf of Bothnia was concentrated in the coastal zone from prehistoric down to modern times. It is also widely agreed (Broadbent 1979; Engelmark 1978) that the biomass of the coastal zone was substantially greater than that of almost all inland areas, due in part to the moderating effect on temperature of the gulf waters and in part to the greater fertility of soil recovered from the Baltic by the rise of land levels. On land this was reflected in the richer vegetation and better conditions for grazing and browsing animals and helps to explain why when agriculture ultimately spread so far north, it did so in the coastal zone and the river valleys debouching on it. But the main advantage of coastal settlement in respect of subsistence was, of course, access to marine resources. In this respect, the Gulf of Bothnia was and still is particularly well endowed with seals, in themselves easily caught and rich in protein and raw materials. This can be neatly illustrated from the records of seals killed for the bounty between 1902 and 1906.[8] Significantly, the largest numbers per 10 kilometres of coast are recorded from the Bothnian provinces ice-bound for upward of 100 days a year, viz., Norbotten (230), Västerbotten (283), and Västernorrland (195). The numbers of seals killed on the coasts of east Sweden (Gävelborg 106, Uppsala 57, Stockholm 103, and Södermanland 69) were still relatively high, but in the southern provinces sank to between 15 and 37.

Definite proof of the use actually made of resources by prehistoric communities can be obtained only from systematic analysis of food refuse from archaeological sites. As in all archaeological evidence, this has been filtered, among other things, by the factor of differential conservation. In the case of the coastal lands of the gulfs of Bothnia and Finland, acidic soils have been highly destructive of the animal bones needed for reconstructing catching activities, as well as of much of the gear used in securing them. In too many cases, we are left with fragments that have survived through having been calcined. Even so, surprisingly full information can be obtained from such data if adequate means of recovery are used and skill developed in the interpretation of fragmentary samples. Further, information from sites where conditions for the survival of unburnt animal bones were highly unfavourable and reliance had to be placed on calcined fragments can fortunately be calibrated against assemblages from districts with more calcareous soils and with occasional exceptional finds like the skeletons of seals that, though mortally wounded, managed to escape their hunters and become incorporated in marine sediments.

One result of the systematic analysis of animal bones from coastal settlements has been to suggest that in certain cases, we have to do with temporary occupations at a time when the predation of particular species of seal was in full swing. For example, no fewer than 98 per cent of the mammalian bones from Lundfors in Västerbotten[9] were identified as seal, of which all those attributable to a particular species were found to be ringed seals (*Phoca hispida*). At Jettböle in the Åland Islands,[10] all the mammals other than dogs were of marine species, comprising 2 common porpoises, 1 ringed seal, and no fewer than 39 harp seals (*Phoca groenlandica*). None of the 4 species of fish or the 7 of birds was represented in a manner suggesting that they had been the object of specialized catching activities. In contrast, the faunal remains from more permanently occupied sites show that seal hunting was only one among a number of catching activities. The rather exiguous calcined material relating to the coastal settlements of the Suomusjärvi and Comb Ware inhabitants of Finland (Clark 1975: table 19) showed that apart from keeping dogs and catching seals, the people also hunted elk, bear, and beaver as well as engaged in fishing and fowling. Fuller information has survived on some of the pitware settlements excavated in east Sweden, notably Äs in Västermanland[11] and Åloppe in Uppland (Almgren 1906:1–19, 101–18). At each, the inhabitants drew heavily on elk and pig, as well as bear, beaver, and smaller fur-bearing animals. From Äs, the bone material of which has been subject to modern scrutiny, there is evidence that fishing contributed usefully to diet, perch being overwhelmingly represented among the remains of some 15 species, although there is no sign that birds contributed otherwise than casually to the food quest.

Although the refuse from sites occupied more permanently reflects the degree to which coastal populations exploited the game resources nourished by the richer vegetation of the coastal zone, the fact remains that marine resources and above all seals (fig. 13.5) were an added bonus and must surely

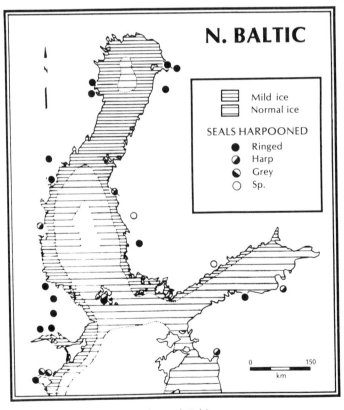

13.5 Stone Age seal hunting in the north Baltic
Sweden (south to north): Norköpping, Sater, Djupvik, Äs, Ålope, Sotmyra, Torslund, Måartsbo, Skarvtjärn, Overveda, Anundsjön, Lundfors, Bjurselet
USSR (Estonia): Pernau, Kunda, Narva
Finland: Jettböle (Åland I.), Kerava, Säräsniemi, Honkajoki, Närpes, Wihanti, Muhos, Oulu

have been a significant attraction. Seals combine in compact form an unusually wide range of resources:[12] their skins are capable of providing outstanding material for clothing, tents, coverings for frame boats and sledge harness; the teeth made decorative, and doubtless also symbolic ornaments for clothing, and seal bones were certainly used in the Baltic Stone Age for harpoon heads and awls; and above all, their blubber, meat, and blood were invaluable sources of nourishment and, in the former case, also of heating and lighting. Seals were not merely a highly valuable resource. They were also readily caught under the ice conditions prevailing in the northern part of the Baltic. In particular the ringed seal, although able to maintain itself under fast ice, needed to come to breathing holes for air and customarily brought forth its young on the ice. On the other hand, the harp, or Greenland, seal was at home on the margin of fast ice.

From recent descriptions (Gustafsson 1971) it appears that despite the introduction of rifles, the basic methods of hunting and catching seals rest on observation of the habits and life cycle of the different species. The varying degree to which particular methods are likely to be reflected in the archaeological record is difficult to evaluate. In recent times both harp and ringed seals, the species with which we are primarily concerned in the Gulf of Bothnia, were readily taken in nets and traps. The numerous stone weights recovered from the Stone Age sealing station of Lundfors (Broadbent 1979) recall those found at Tuorsniemi, Pori, west Finland, with remains of over 20 nets, each some 30 metres long, together with floats and seal bones (Luho 1954). The very abundance of remains of ringed seals on Stone Age sites in the north Baltic region in itself suggests that they were mainly caught in nets that could be worked through holes in fast ice as well as in open water. On the other hand, both ringed and harp seals were also caught during the Stone Age by harpooning either from open boats or, in the case of ringed seals, by the *maupoq* method still practised by Askimos, by which the hunter waited to strike when the seal came up to breathe at its hole. The most conclusive evidence[13] that seals were in fact harpooned during the Stone Age in the north Baltic is the recovery of skeletons accompanied by barbed bone harpoon heads from clay deposits formed under the Litorina Sea, with each of harp and ringed seal from both east Sweden and the west Finnish province of Österbotten. Direct evidence of this kind is reinforced by the frequent association of harpoon heads with remains of harp and ringed seals in the refuse deposits of Stone Age settlements.

For several reasons, including the relative robustness of their bones and the fact that their carcasses would normally have been dismembered and exploited at the sealing station or permanent settlement as the case might be, the role of seals in the Stone Age economy of northern Sweden is relatively well documented. A good deal is also known about the role of important land mammals, notably elk and pig, and it is symptomatic of the way coast dwellers combined inland and marine resources that each of the three harpoon heads recovered from seal skeletons of which the raw material could be diagnosed were found to have been made from the metacarpal or metatarsal bones of elk. A third major source of animal protein exploited in north Sweden during historic times was the anadromous fish that year by year move upstream to spawn, salmon (*Salmo salmo*) that run in June–July, and white-fish (*Corregonus* sp.) in August. We know from representations. (Hallström 1960: 327 and fig. 127) of salmon pecked on the rock surfaces of the Nämforsen rapids on the Ångerman River that the Stone Age population was well aware of the fish, which still ascend as far upstream as approximately 115 kilometres from the mouth (Hertting 1965: 256). It is hard not to think that this rich and dependable source of protein was not harvested in prehistoric times, more especially since basket traps of the kind that, built into weirs, would have been fully adequate to the task were certainly available in northern Europe since at least the sixth millennium B.C. (Clark 1975:182 and pl. 2). It is significant that the wealth of the salmon fisheries of Norrland has been advanced as a main factor in the colonization of the region by Swedish farmers during the Middle Ages (Hertting 1965:256).

The amplitude of food resources available to the inhabitants of the Bothnian coastal zone was sufficient to make for a notable degree of stability of settlement during the Stone Age, a process that began, according to Broadbent's researches, well before the end of the fourth millennium B.C. Since the economy of the coast-dwellers involved the use of boats and sliding devices, they were equally well equipped to exploit the interior, notably in regard to fish and furs, and at the same time to profit from sea-borne contacts with the south. The degree of sedentariness achieved through success in catching activities, combined with the greater availability of favourable soil and a marginally more favourable local climate, made the inhabitants of the Bothnian coastal zone notably receptive to the northward spread of agriculture. Although pollen analysis points only to a retarded and tentative introduction of cultivation, it shows nevertheless that barley and wheat were already being grown in the coastal zone of Medelpad (Engelmark 1978:45), Ångermanland (Huttunen and Tolonen 1972), and even as far north as Bjurselet on the Byske River in Västerbotten (Christiansson 1965; Königsson and Christiansson 1970; Broadbent 1979:206) by the early centuries of the second millennium B.C. Further, although ringed seal remained a main source of animal protein for the inhabitants of Bjurselet, they had nevertheless begun, like their counterparts the codfishers of Varanger Fjord, to maintain domestic cattle and sheep. Similarly, they too had adopted pottery that, though presumably the outcome of diffusion, was of local manufacture. An even more palpable sign of contact with Neolithic communities far away to the south is afforded by the occurrence in the coastal zone of large numbers of adze blades and some axe blades, occurring singly or in hoards like the 175 or so from Bjurselet, made of flint derived from south Scandinavia and probably from Zealand well over 1,000 kilometres distant (Clark 1948b; Broadbent 1979:226). Their form (thick-butted and in the case of adzes, commonly with hollow cutting edge) and their proportions compare so closely with those from graves with stone battle axes from south Sweden (Malmer 1962) as to denote the cultural context within which they spread. Even if we accept that their introduction to the coastal zone of Norrland was a concomitant of the spread of farming into the richer soils of territories where settled life was already developing on the basis of maritime resources, it is no less true that south Scandinavian flint, as an exotic substance of high practical utility is likely to have become a prized component of exchange networks (fig. 13.6).

A significant feature of the south Scandinavian flint imports into Norrland is that whereas the several hundred adze blades were concentrated in the coastal zone, smaller objects like scrapers and arrowheads made from the

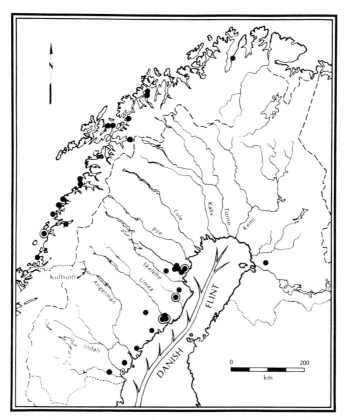

13.6 Exchange network of northern Fennoscandia illustrated by the expansion of axes and adzes of Danish flint by way of the Gulf of Bothnia and the river system of north Sweden to the Norwegian coast. Hoards are indicated by larger circles enclosing black spots

same flint and sometimes from actual adze blades occur along river courses and on lake margins sometimes deep in the interior (Königsson and Christiansson 1970:9). Evidently such pieces reflect the economic penetration of the interior from the coastal zone. Animal bones from two such localities, the Storavan Lake area at the head of the Skellefte River and the site of Garaselet 100 kilometres upstream from the mouth of the Byske, showing a predominance of elk and beaver respectively, argue that meat and furs may have attracted hunters and trappers into the interior. It is even possible, though the evidence is still too slight to prove the case, that the fur trade, which, together with hunting and salmon fishing, did so much to open up Norrland in later times, may already have begun at a time when boat axes were still in current use. Indeed the import of flint and battle axes from south Scandinavia to the Bothnian coast may have found its counterpart in the export of furs from the interior. One might even go further and suggest that the concentration of flint adze and axe blades and boat axes found on the coasts of Helgoland and Troms and, in the latter case, even on Varanger Fjord are most likely to have reached their destinations by traversing Norrland up the river and lake systems, anticipating the seasonal migrations of the Lapps during recent centuries. It is even possible, despite Olsen's negative evidence from Varanger Fjord (1967), that bundles of cod dried under the more favourable conditions of the northwest may have reached the Bothnian coastal zone in exchange for flint adze blades and prestigious boat axes from south Scandinavia. At least the stone plaque from the Kultsjön (Clark 1948a: fig. 3) in the lake system of the upper Umea River, with its engraving of a pilot whale, offers tangible evidence of contact between Jämtland and the Fosna coast of Norway where this kind of whale was not merely at home but engraved by Stone Age man on the living rock.

V

Even a brief survey of northern Fennoscandia has been enough to confirm, first, that both on the Atlantic and Arctic coasts and in the north Baltic, coastal settlement has been clearly linked with the utilization of maritime resources, including fish and sea mammals, as well as in the former case, sea birds; second, that, combined with the heightened potential of terrestial resources in coastal territories, this favoured the development of sedentary settlement on the coast, while at the same time permitting expeditions into the interior to secure seasonal harvests of high value; third, that sedentary settlement, once attained, to a certain degree favoured the reception of, and was itself further intensified by, the spread of elements of farming economy; fourth, that techniques, artifacts, and materials accompanying and promoting the new element in subsistence economy themselves stimulated exchange networks and so furthered contacts between geographically remote populations; and, fifth, that such contacts stimulated developments not merely in economics and technology but also in the realm of ideas, visibly displayed in the stone burial cairns erected on the coasts either side of the Gulf of Bothnia at a time when bronze technology was flourishing in south Scandinavia. To sum up, in Fennoscandia, as indeed on the Atlantic and Mediterranean coasts, the intensification of coastal settlement during Neothermal times played an outstandingly dynamic role in the later prehistory, as in the early history, of the European continent.

Notes

1 Thus the Early Neolithic level in the Ely fens has been established in the lower peat between 3 and 4 metres below mean sea level. See Clark and Godwin (1962).
2 Ian Morrison's study of the topography of the Antiparos–Paros region suggested that sea level had risen a matter of some 3½ metres since the Neolithic occupation. See App. 1 (pp.92–8) to Evans and Renfrew (1968).
3 Clark 1948a: 45–85. See especially 74–9, fig. 18, and App. 2.
4 Bakka 1974. I have to thank Dr Bakka for plotting a distribution map of kinds of *arevarts* for me.
5 For maps, see Clark 1975: figs. 13–14.
6 The results are tabulated diagrammatically in fig. 57 of Clark 1975.
7 Compare for instance the maps in figs. 11, 19, and 21 showing the distribution respectively of Suomusjärvi, and Early and Typical Comb Ware in Kivikoski 1964.
8 Cited by Broadbent 1979:186, from Ekman 1910.
9 Identifications by Dr Johannes Lepiksaar of the Natural History Museum, Gothenburg, assisted by Jan Ekman. See Broadbent 1979:1974ff.
10 The identifications were made by Dr Herluf Winge of Copenhagen. The bones also included small numbers of each of four species of fish and seven of birds. I am grateful to Professor C.F. Meinander of Helsingfors University for abstracting this unpublished information from his master's thesis.
11 The results of Dr Lepiksaar's bone analysis are published in his contribution 'Djurrester från den mellanneolitiska (gropkeramiska) boplatsen vid As, Romfartuna sn, Västmanland': see Löfstrand 1974: 140–56.
12 These are set out with references on pp. 37–9 of Clark 1946:12–48.
13 For full documentation see Clark 1976.

References

Alin, J., 1935. 'En Bohuslansk Kokkenmodding pa Rotekarrslid, Dragsmark', in *Gotesborgs och Bohuslans Fornminnes*, pp. 1–38.

Almgren, O., 1906. 'Upplandska stenaldersboplatser', *Fornvannen*, 1–19, 101–18.

Bakka, E., 1974. 'Steinaldergranskingar i Nordhordland 1960–63', *Arbok for Nord- og Midhordland Sogelag* 17, pp. 3–36 (Bergen).

Bass, G. F., 1966. *Archaeology Under Water* (London: Thames and Hudson).

Baudou, E., 1968. *Forntida Bebyggelse i Angermanslande Kustland: Arkeologisks undersokningar av angermanlandska kustrosen* (Harnosand).

Broadbent, N., 1979 *Coastal Resources and Settlement Stability: A Critical Study of a Mesolithic Site Complex in Northern Sweden* (Uppsala).

Christiansson, H., 1965. 'De Arkeologiska Undersokningarna vid Bjurselet i Byske', *Vasterbotten*, 191–202.

Clark, J. G. D., 1946. 'Seal-hunting in the Stone Age of North-Western Europe: A Study in Economic Prehistory', *Proceedings of the Prehistoric Society* 2: 12–48 (Cambridge, England).

　　1948a. 'The Development of Fishing in Prehistoric Europe', *Antiquaries Journal* 27: 45–85.

　　1948b. 'Objects of South Scandinavian Flint in the Northernmost Provinces of Norway, Sweden, and Finland', *Proceedings of the Prehistoric Society* 4: 219–32 (Cambridge, England).

　　1952. *Prehistoric Europe: The Economic Basis* (London, Methuen).

　　1975. *The Earlier Stone Age Settlement of Scandinavia* (Cambridge: Cambridge University Press).

　　1976. 'A Baltic Cave Sequence: A Further Study in Bioarchaeology', in *Archaeologica Austriaca*, vol. 13, pp. 113–23 (Vienna).

　　1977. 'The Economic Context of Dolmens and Passage-graves in Sweden', in *Ancient Europe and the Mediterranean*, ed. V. Markotic, pp. 40–2 (Warminster: Phillips).

Clark, J. G. D., and H. Godwin, 1962. 'The Neolithic in the Cambridgeshire Fens', *Antiquity* 36: 10–23.

Cullberg, C., 1972. 'Hasslingekult, Gotberg', *Fynd*, pp. 373–448.

Ekman, J., 1972. 'On the Animal Bones', *Fynd*, pp. 571–7.

Ekman, S., 1910. *Norrlands Jakt och fiske* (Uppsala).

Engelmark, R., 1978. 'The Comparative Vegetational History of Inland and Coastal Sites in Medelpad, N. Sweden, during the Iron Age', *Early Norrland* 2: 48.

Evans, J. D., and C. Renfrew, 1968. *Excavations at Saliagos near Antiparos* (London: Thames and Hudson).

Faegri, K., 1943. 'Studies on the Pleistocene of Western Norway', *Bergens Museum Arbok, Naturvitenskap*, no. 8: 7–100.

Frödin, O., 1906. 'En Svenska Kjokkenmodding. Et Bidrag Till de Postglaciala Nivaforandringarnas', *Ymer*: 17–35.

Gjessing, G., 1932. *Arktiske Helleristninger i Nord-Norge* (Oslo).

　　1936. *Nordenfjelske Ristninger og Malinger av den Arktiske Gruppe* (Oslo).

　　1943. *Traen-Funnene* (Oslo).

Gustafsson, P., 1971. 'Om Vasterbottnisk Saljakt', *Vasterbotten*, 66–119.

Hagen, A., 1967. *Norway* (London: Thames and Hudson).

Hallström, G., 1960. *Monumental Art of Northern Sweden from the Stone Age: Namforsen and Other Localities* (Stockholm).

Hencken, H. O'N., 1932. *The Archaeology of Cornwall and Scilly* (London: Methuen).

Henri, P., 1935. 'Benfynd Fran Boplatsen pa Rotekarrslid', in *Gotesborgs och Bohuslans Fornminnes*, pp. 38–42.

Henrici, P., 1936. *Gotesborgs och Bohuslans Fornminnes*.

Hertting, V., 1965. *Hunting and Fishing: Nordic Symposium on Life in a Traditional Hunting and Fishing Milieu in Prehistoric Times and up to the Present Day*, ed. H. Hvarfner (Lulea: Norbottens Museum).

Hjort, J., 1896. *Hydrographic-Biological Studies of the Norwegian Fisheries* (Christiania).

Huttunen, P., and M. Tolonen, 1972. 'Pollen Analytical Studies of Prehistoric Agriculture in Northern Angermanland', *Early Norrland* 1: 9–31.

Janson, S., 1936. 'En boplats frna yngre stenaldern vid Rorvik i Kville sn. Bohuslan', in *Gotesborgs och Bohuslans Fornminnes*.

Jutikkala, E., ed., 1959. *Suomen Historian Kartasto* (Atlas of Finnish History), 2nd rev. ed. (Helsinki: Werner Soderstrom OY).

Kivikoski, E., 1964. *Finlands Forhistoria* (Helsinki).

Königsson, L. K., and H. Christiansson, 1970. *The Bjurselet Settlement I: Traces of Neolithic Human Influence upon the Landscape Development at the Bjurselet Settlement, Vasterbotten, Northern Sweden* (Umea).

Kroeber, A. L., 1939. *Cultural and Natural Areas of Native North America* (Berkeley: University of California Press).

Lepiksaar, J., 1972. *Stenaldersboplatsen Bua Vastergard Goteborgs*, ed. J. Wigforss, J. Lepiksaar and P. Wedel (Gotesborgs Universitet).

Löfstrand, L., 1974. *Yngre Stenalderns Kustboplatser* (Uppsala).

Luho, V., 1954. *Porin Tuorsniemen Verkkoloyto*, no. 61, Suomen Museo.

1967. *Die Suomusjarvi-Kultur: Die Mittel- und Spatmesolithische Zeit in Finnland*, no. 19 (Helsinki).

Meinander, C. F., 1954a. *Die Bronzezeit in Finland* (Helsinki).

1954b 'Die Kuikaiskulture', *Finska Fornminnesfor* 53: 1–192.

Muckelroy, K., 1978. *Maritime Archaeology* (Cambridge: Cambridge University Press).

Olsen, H., 1967. *Varanger-Funnene IV: Osteologisk Materiale* (Tromso).

Reid, C., 1913. *Submerged Forests* (Cambridge).

Siiriäinen, A., 1977. *The Bronze Age Site at Anttila in Lastijarvi and the Dating of the Coastal Cairns in Middle Ostrobottnia, Finland*, Suomen Museo, pp. 13–25.

Simonsen, P., 1961. *Varanger-Funnene II: Fund og Udgravninger pa Fjordens Sydkyst* (Tromso).

1963. *Varanger-Funnene III* (Tromso).

1965. 'Settlement and Occupation in the Younger Stone Age', in *Hunting and Fishing*, ed. H. Hvarfner, pp. 397–406 (Lulea: Norrbottens Museum).

1967. 'Bopladsene ved Noatun i Pasvikdalen', *Finska Fornminnes Tidskrift* 58: 233–67.

Somme, A., ed., 1968. *A Geography of Norden* (London: Heinemann).

Welinder, S., 1973. *The Chronology of the Mesolithic Stone Age on the Swedish West Coast*, Studier i Nordisk Arkeologi, no. 9 (Goteborg).

PART II

WORLD PREHISTORY

CHAPTER 14

AUSTRALIAN STONE AGE

In offering this contribution on the Australian Stone Age to a distinguished Polish prehistorian I make no apologies, because prehistory embraces even the remotest continents and underlies human realities in every part of the world. The substance of prehistory is no less than the emergence and self-realisation of humanity itself. Among prehistorians no modern ideologies or political divisions have any meaning when they engage professionally in their task of revelation, the true splendour and significance of which are only now being more widely appreciated and utilised in the process of education and enlightenment. All honour, therefore, to the pioneers of prehistoric archaeology, among whom we salute our senior colleague and eminent exponent Professor Joseph Kostrzewski.

Australia is at once the last of the continents to be brought within the purview of prehistorians and that in which prehistory prevailed most recently. The huge size of the country – about equal to that of the United States of America without Alaska – and the fact that colonisation by white men did not begin until 1788 and only broadened out towards the middle of the 19th century explains why scientific study of the aborigines did not seriously begin until nearly the close of the century; such descriptions as we have from early explorers and administrators,[1] precious as they sometimes are, are hardly more sophisticated than were those of Captain Cook himself. The publication of W. Baldwin Spencer's and F. J. Gillen's *The Native Tribes of Central Australia* in 1899 really marked the beginning of scientific anthropology in Australia.

Systematic attempts to reconstruct the prehistoric antecedents of the aboriginal inhabitants were even more recent. Many individuals collected stone implements and the museums made some attempt to classify the huge assemblages that converged upon them,[2] but as Mulvaney has pointed out[3] it is highly significant that such broad groupings as were observed were as a rule explained as the outcome of utilising different sources of raw materials. There was to begin with no appreciation that the aborigines might have entered Australia many thousands of years ago and that their culture might have passed through several phases of development. Australian prehistory had to wait on scientific excavation and above all on the observation of stratigraphic sequences.

The first advance was pioneered by the South Australian Museum at Adelaide, which between 1925 and 1928 had carried out a systematic survey of aboriginal camping-places in the Lower Murray River, a region that had been described in the last phase of relatively undisturbed aboriginal culture by E. V. Eyre in 1845[4] and illustrated in the following year by G. F. Angas.[5] In the course of the recent survey the last scraps of information were obtained from the handful of (Europeanised) aborigines then surviving. The site chosen for excavation was Devon Downs, a rock-shelter overlooking the Murray River, that was marked as a site of recent occupation by tell-tale smoke-marks on the overhanging cliffs. The section cut in 1929–30 by H. M. Hale and Norman B. Tindale[6] was historic in the sense that it revealed a succession of twelve distinct strata giving a total depth of 6 metres and revealing evidence of distinct cultural changes.

Invaluable as this excavation was as a pointer to the most promising line of advance – the stratigraphic excavation of carefully selected rock-shelters and caves – Australian prehistorians lacked any key for locking together sequences established in different parts of the continent. The provision of such a key in radiocarbon dating by W. F. Libby at Chicago opened up an era of rapid discovery, one which is in full spate and about which it would be premature to write except in the most general terms. In the first major list of dates published in 1951[7] Libby included determinations from samples taken from the Victorian middens. Even if the older of these (c.600. A.D. 773±175) only went back to the first millennium A.D. it was a portent of things to come. The next objective was to attempt to date the human cranium found in 1940 at a considerable depth in the Keilor Terrace near Melbourne. The publication in 1955 of a determination (W 169. 6550±250 B.C.) for a sample supposedly from above the level of the cranium immediately opened up new vistas; and in 1959 came the issue from Wellington, New Zealand, of a substantially earlier date (NZ 207. 13,050±1500 B.C.) for a sample from the presumed level of the cranium.[8] Radiocarbon dating imparted a stimulus to scientific prehistory in Australia as decisive as it did to that of the New World.

The new period that began in 1956 with John Mulvaney's excavation of shelter 2 at Fromm's Landing,[9] a few miles below Devon Downs, showed beyond doubt that since man reached Australia well back in the Late Glacial Period his culture has undergone substantial changes, even if his economy and way of life remained substantially the same. Already it is possible to discern three main phases of Australian prehistory (fig. 14.1). Fromm's Landing and Devon Downs between them showed that, underlying deposits relating to comparatively recent aboriginal settlement, were strata containing well-defined microlithic crescents and projectile points known as *pirris*, leaf-shaped flakes having the butt thinned by secondary flaking and the convex face wholly or in part retouched by flat scale-like flaking.[10] The next

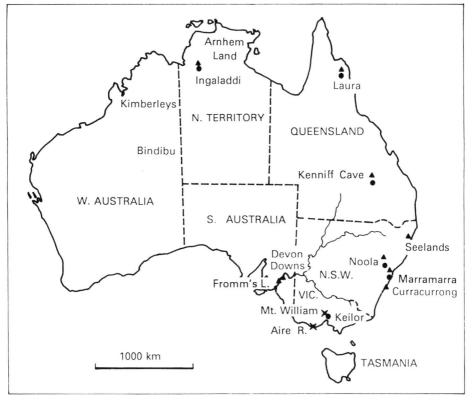

14.1   Map of Australia showing key sites of the Early, Middle, and Recent Stone Age
mentioned in the text.

decisive excavation was that undertaken by Mulvaney at Kenniff Cave[11] in
southern Queensland between Charleville and Rockhampton, where, strati-
graphically below Middle Stone Age levels, the upper of which yielded
microliths, he found a succession of layers containing a relatively crude flake
industry, layers which yielded a succession of dates going back to
14,180 ± 140 B.C., that is further back than Keilor man. Even so, the earliest
sample at Kenniff Cave came from ¾ metre above the floor; and it is
improbable that this was the first cave occupied by the original immigrants to
Australia.

Still earlier dates may confidently be expected. The important thing to
emphasise at this stage is that dates of this order are those most credible when
geographical conditions are taken into account. If Australia had been settled
recently or, indeed, since the Late Glacial Period, it could only have been
entered by people able to navigate considerable stretches of open sea and this
is something for which the recent aborigines at least have not been
conspicuous. On the other hand during Late Glacial times sea-levels were
low enough to allow access to people only capable of crossing comparatively

narrow stretches of open sea: at a time when the Sunda and Sahul shelfs were still dry land the longest sea-passage between Asia and Australia was hardly more than 40 miles across: Borneo, and most of Indonesia, were joined to south-east Asia in a solid land mass; and New Guinea still formed part of Australia. It is interesting to note in this context that, whereas the later Stone Age assemblages of Australia were confined to the continent, the early flake industry from Kenniff Cave and other mainland sites can be closely paralleled from Tasmania to which it presumably penetrated during the mainland period of lower sea-levels.[12] Comparable Early Stone Age stone industries have been excavated by a number of prehistorians over a wide extent of Australia from deposits overlaid by Middle Stone Age strata, notably by Mulvaney himself at Ingaladdi in the northern part of the Northern Territories, at about latitude 150±s; by Richard Wright of the University of Sydney at Laura near Cooktown, about the same latitude on the east coast of northern Queensland,[13] and again at Marramarra, north of Sydney;[14] and by Norman Tindale at Noola[15] in northern New South Wales from a level dated by radiocarbon to 7000 B.C. Although the early industries from these sites have yet to be systematically studied, their general character is not in doubt: they comprise flakes, frequently with plain platforms at an obtuse angle to the main line of the flake, and include thick plane-like tools, hollow scrapers and spurred tools, types that can plausibly be associated with shaping wooden artifacts (fig.14.2). The crude and rather colourless nature of this

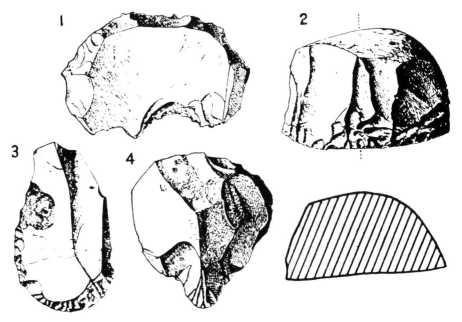

14.2   Stone implements from Tasmania.

industry may serve to remind us that the original Australian aborigines issued from one of the most unenterprising parts of the Late Pleistocene world. In keeping with this is the further circumstance that no obvious or striking development appears to have taken place in the successive layers at Kenniff Cave between approximately 14000 and 3000 B.C., even though metrical analysis may be able to demonstrate changes hardly perceptible on first inspection.

No doubt one reason why rather static conditions prevailed in Australia for so great a length of time is that the continent was cut off from Indonesia and south-east Asia by the eustatic rise of sea-level that gained in momentum as the ice-sheets melted. It was not until these territories were occupied by people capable of negotiating considerable stretches of open water – and this does not appear to have happened until the beginning of the third millennium B.C. – that there is evidence for new contacts and for the exotic influences that characterised the Middle Stone Age of Australia.

The diagnostic feature most widely represented in Middle Stone Age assemblages is the occurrence of the small, rather highly specialised forms noted in the earlier deposits of the Lower Murray shelters, where they first appeared at Fromm's Landing near the beginning of the third millennium B.C. (NZ 456/1: 2900 B.C.±100), and in one form or another in deposits overlying Early Stone Age flake industries at the sites mentioned in the previous paragraph. A point to emphasise is that by this stage marked regional differences had begun to appear in Australia. Thus *pirri* points (fig. 14.3, no. 12), which in Northern Territories may occur together with bifacial points as at Sleisbeck rock-shelter excavated by Jack Golson and in the upper level at Ingaladdi, also abound in South Australia west of the Lower Murray river and even extend into the Darling and Paroo valleys of New South Wales.[16] East and south of the Murray River, in Victoria, and east of the Great Divide up into Queensland, on the other hand, is the territory *par excellence* of industries marked by backed blades and which may include crescents and other geometric microliths (fig. 14.3, nos. 1–10) and on occasion true burins, industries which nevertheless occur also in the extreme south-west of Australia and in the arid centre.[17] It needs to be emphasised that neither *pirris* nor microliths nor backed blades were known to recent aborigines, who may be said to have lived in the Late Stone Age of Australia.

The largest collections of microliths have been made at coastal sites in Victoria and to a lesser degree in New South Wales, but it is on excavations in caves and rock-shelters that we depend for precise information about their context in Australian prehistory. The earliest date we have so far is that of 2900 B.C. from Fromm's Landing No. 2. Radiocarbon dates already available suggest that the Middle Stone Age tradition spanned about four millennia. At the Curracurrang shelter in the Royal National Park south of Sydney, excavated by Mr Vincent Megaw of the Department of Archaeology at

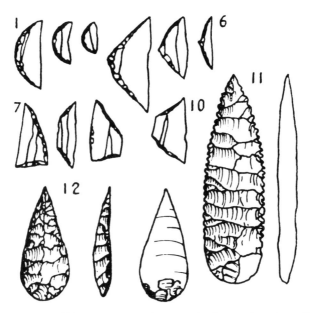

14.3   Middle Recent (No. II) Stone Age implements from Australia: 1–10, crescentic, triangular trapeziform microliths; 11, Kimberley point; 12 Pirri point.

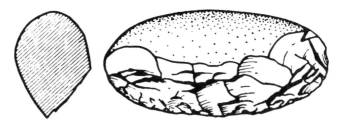

14.4   Uniface pebble tool from Kangaroo Island, South Australia.

Sydney University, a black charcoal layer containing backed blades and microliths gave a radiocarbon date of c. 200 B.C.; and Miss Isabel McBryde has obtained still more recent dates for backed blade and microlith levels in rock-shelters in the Grafton district of northern New South Wales, notably one of A.D. 310±120 at Whiteman's Creek and for a comparable assemblage from Seeland's dates of A.D. 750±40 and A.D. 1040±80.[18].

Among other types of stone implement to appear in this context were heavy chopping tools made by striking flakes from one face of a smooth pebble (fig. 14.4), a form which appeared at Seeland's in a deposit that gave a radiocarbon date of 1920 B.C. ± 120, but at Whiteman's Creek appeared in a backed blade horizon dating from 2000 years later; and edgeground stone axes, which were found by Dr Tugby's expedition to Cathedral Cave in the Carnarvon National Park, Queensland, well down in microlithic levels.[19]

Other innovations include the dingo, the earliest dated skeleton of which came from level 11 at Fromm's Landing shelter 6, dated by radiocarbon to 1220 B.C. ± 94.[20] Although essentially feral in habit and comparable with the pariah dog of southern and western Asia, the dingo must have been introduced to Australia by man; this could hardly have happened at the time of the first immigration well back in the Late Pleistocene and, significantly, the dingo was not known to the Tasmanian aborigines. The same applies to the art engraved and painted on the walls of rock-shelters. Although of course rock art remained very much a feature of recent aboriginal culture in Australia and it is notoriously difficult to relate appearances in inhabited rock-shelters to any particular phase of occupation, its occurrence at shelters occupied by Middle Stone Age man is frequent enough – Kenniff Cave and Miss McBryde's shelters are notable examples – to suggest that it was introduced at the same time.

Disturbed conditions in Indonesia have impeded research projects planned in that area by the Australian National University and the sources of information available in the publications of Dutch archaeologists of the colonial era are in many cases tantalisingly imprecise. Nevertheless, it is already plain that analogies for many of the innovations of the Australian Middle Stone Age exist in different parts of Indonesia. For instance stone industries containing backed blades and crescents, together with points reminiscent of *pirris*, having thinned bases and some flat flaking on the surface, have been collected in the highlands of Bandung in Java[21] and from the middle levels of the cave of Panganreang Tudea in South Celebes.[22] Again, uniface pebble chopping-tools are a prominent feature of Hoabinhian middens in eastern Sumatra;[23] and edgeground stone axe-heads could well have been inspired by the polished stone axes of New Guinea. The dingo must have passed through this area and rock-paintings featuring stencilled hands, a common motive at Kenniff Cave and elsewhere, are known from Celebes and New Guinea.[24]

The Recent Stone Age, which prevailed everywhere among the aborigines when white settlement began in 1788 and which still survives, albeit in degenerate form in Arnhem Land[25] and in remote parts of west-central Australia,[26] is characterised more by the loss of cultural traits – notably the manufacture of backed blades and microliths – than by the acquisition of new ones. In the northern part of the continent a high standard of stone-knapping was maintained. The production of bifacially flaked spearheads (fig. 14.3, no. 11) in the Kimberley region, which may well be thought of as marking the culmination of the tradition already noted from the Middle Stone Age contexts in northern Australia, survived so vigorously that heaps of bottle-glass had to be placed at the foot of telegraph posts to discourage the aborigines from using the insulators. Another form of spearhead (*nambi*), comprising a regular blade with tapered point, was observed in manufacture at a quarry behind Blue Mud Bay in eastern Arnhem Land by the anthropologist Donald Thomson, who described how this and other local products were diffused over the territory by means of ceremonial gift exchange.[27] The edge-ground stone axe (fig. 14.4, no. 1), introduced in the Middle Stone Age, was still being manufactured at the Mount William quarries at Lancefield[28] north of Melbourne down to the eighteen-thirties and may well have been distributed from this and many other factories by similar means. For obvious reasons the wooden equipment of the Recent Stone Age has survived much more completely and one of the most important items even down to the present day in the desert region of west central Australia is the wooden spear-thrower.[29] This also served as parrier, scoop and carrier, as well as holding a stone flake inset in resin at the end of

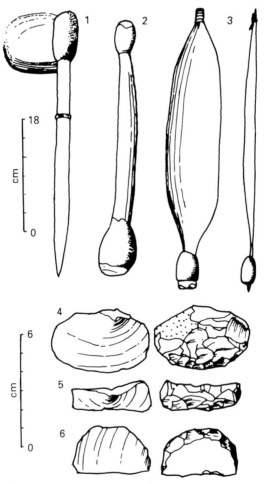

14.5   Recent Stone Age axe scraper-adze equipment from Australia: 1, mounted edge-ground stone axe; 2–3, scraper-adze flakes mounted on stave spear thrower; 4–5, Tula flakes, fresh-worn; 6, Elouera flake.

the handle, which acted as a scraper-adze for shaping the many wooden artifacts, on which the aborigines so largely depended, notably spears, throwing-sticks, boomerangs and digging-sticks. The flakes that formed the working edges of scraper-adzes, whether on spear-throwers (fig. 14.4, no. 3) or at one or both ends of stout staves (fig. 14.4, no. 2), were of two main kinds, forms resembling convex scrapers known as *tula* (fig. 14.4, nos. 4–5) and others, the so-called *elouera* (fig. 14.4, no. 6) recalling segments of a tangerine in their general shape, struck from one of the narrow ends and having the convex back steeply retouched. How far back in Australian prehistory these forms go is still uncertain, but both were present in the Middle Stone Age. The existence of analogous forms in Indonesia is to be noted.[30]

The dominant fact of the Australian Stone Age as a whole was its continuity. For ten and possibly fifteen thousand years, indeed, the original immigrants, cut off by rising sea-levels, were virtually stranded on an island of continental size and isolated from all stimulus imparted by cultural contacts. During the Middle Stone Age, indeed, Australia was enriched by a number of new elements of culture and by the dingo; but the aborigines experienced no basic change in their way of life as a whole. Finally, as we have seen, the Recent Stone Age, covering the last few hundred years down to the ethnographic present and the period of white settlement, was marked if anything by cultural loss, notably visible in the decline of flint-work in the southern part of the continent. It is to be noted above all that the aborigines failed to take over any of the food crops grown by the Indonesian and Papuan peoples with whom during the Recent Stone Age they came into contact.[31]

During their long period of isolation the Australian aborigines achieved a remarkably perfect adaptation to the diverse environments of their continent within the limits of their restricted cultural endowment, but the very perfection of their adjustment made them disinclined to change. The web of social obligations, mythology and beliefs that ensured the perpetuation of traditional modes grew so rigid, in default of the questioning arising from cultural contacts, that it – so to speak – cocooned the native Australians in their existing culture. The result was that they were quite unable to adjust to the radically changed conditions that came with settlement by Europeans. Despite the most persistent attempts by administrators and missionaries alike it proved impossible to wean the aborigines from their own ways and not one of the attempts to get them to settle and adopt agriculture succeeded for more than the briefest period. The greater the pressure to 'civilize' them, indeed, the more rapidly the aborigines declined in numbers, so that for instance the 40,000 or so existing in New South Wales in 1788 had sunk to under 12,000 in 1881, 4,000 in 1901 and 800 in 1939; in Victoria, where the policy of education and kindness was pursued most relentlessly, the 10,000 of 1835 had sunk to 3,000 by 1850, 565 in 1891 and only 49 by 1931. Disease, brushes with settlers and intertribal conflict caused by the displacement of groups from lands taken up by the white man all helped to account for this demographic decline. On the other hand the Maori of New Zealand, despite losses from disease and bloody fighting, survived and are now multiplying twice as fast as Europeans, because they were able to adapt themselves to new ways of life; and the tribes of the New Guinea highlands, Neolithic when brought under Australian administration in 1945,[32] are already being educated in democratic electoral procedures and may even achieve independence within little more than a generation since stepping out of the Stone Age.

It is only when we view the varying fate of these Australasian peoples in the perspective of prehistory that we find the explanation. All three peoples were technologically still in the Stone Age when they came into contact with European civilisation, yet there were fundamental differences: whereas the Maoris and Papuans stand the same side of the Neolithic transformation as we do, and in this respect are far closer to us than to the Australian aborigines, the Australians were still subject to most of the limitations of Palaeolithic man and indeed preserved traditions that stemmed from a particularly backward part of the Late Pleistocene world. They paid a fearful penalty for their isolation.

Notes

1 D. J. Mulvaney, 'The Australian Aborigines 1606–1929. Opinion and Fieldwork', in *Historical Studies*, vol. 8 (1958), 131–51.
2 An outstanding publication in this field is F. D. McCarthy's *The Stone Implements of Australia*, Sydney, 1946.
3 In his valuable survey 'The Stone Age of Australia', *Proc. Prehistoric. Soc.* VII (1961), 56–107; see pp. 59f.
4 E. V. Eyre, *Journals of Expeditions of Discovery*, vol. 2, London, 1845.
5 G. F. Angas, *South Australia Illustrated*, London, 1847.
6 H. M. Hale, N. B. Tindale, 'Notes on Some Human Remains in the Lower Murray Valley, South Australia', *Rec. S. Aust. Mus.*, IV (1930), 145–218.
7 W. F. Libby, *Radiocarbon Dating*, Chicago, 1951.
8 E. D. Gill, 'Radiocarbon Dates for Australian Archaeological and Geological Samples', *Aust. J. Sci.*, 18 (1955), 49–52; Mulvaney, *op. cit.*, 107.
9 D. J. Mulvaney, 'Archaeological Excavations at Fromm's Landing on the Lower Murray River, South Australia', *Proc. Roy. Soc. Victoria*, 72 (1960), 53–85.
10 T. D. Campbell, 'The Pirri – An Interesting Australian Aboriginal Implement', *Rec. S. Aust. Mus.*, XIII (1960), 509–24.
11 The Kenniff Cave sequence gave the following radiocarbon dates: 61 cm (600 B.C.±90); 76–84 cm (1880 B.C.–90); 122–9 cm (3070 B.C.–90); 170–3 cm (10,660 B.C.±110); 178–203 cm (10,950 B.C.−170) and 226–34 cm (14,180 B.C.−140). Geometric microliths occurred at 61 cm and below 122 cm there occurred an Early Stone Age flake industry. Information from Mr Mulvaney and personal inspection of the lithic material.
12 A useful account of lithic material collected from Tasmania is that by Henry Balfour, 'The Status of the Tasmanians among the Stone-Age peoples', *P.P.S.E.A.*, V (1925), 1–15. Scientific excavation is now being conducted on the island by Mr Rhys Jones of the Department of Anthropology at Sydney University.

13 Information from Mr Richard Wright.

14 *Ibid.*

15 N. B. Tindale, 'Archaeological Excavation of Noola Rock Shelter: A Preliminary Report', *Rec. S. Aust. Mus.*, 14 (1961), 193–6.

16 Mulvaney, *The Stone Age of Australia*, fig. 8–9.

17 *Ibid.*

18 I. McBryde, 'Archaeological Field Survey Work in Northern New South Wales', *Oceania*, xxxiii (1962), 12–17.

19 Information from Dr Tugby and from Mr John Clegg of Brisbane University.

20 D. J. Mulvaney, G. H. Lawton, C. R. Tindale, 'Archaeological Excavations of Rock-Shelter No. 6, Fromm's Landing, South Australia', *Proc. Roy. Soc. Vict.*, 77 (1964) 479–516.

21 H. G. Bandi, 'Die Obsidianindustrie der Umgebung von Bandung in West Java', *Südseestudien (Felix-Speiser-Gedenkschrift)*, Basel, 1951.

22 H. R. van Heekeren, *The Stone Age of Indonesia*, 1957, fig. 17.

23 *Ibid.*, pl. 20.

24 *Ibid.*, pl. 32.

25 D. F. Thomson, *Economic Structure and the Ceremonial Exchange Cycle in Arnhem Land*, London, 1949.

26 D. F. Thomson, 'Some Wood and Stone Implements of the Bindibu Tribe of Central Western Australia', *Proc. Prehist. Soc.*, xxx (1964), 400–22.

27 Thomson, *Economic Structure*.

28 A. W. Howitt, *The Native Tribes of South-East Australia*, London, 1904, pp. 311–12; I. T. Guthridge, *The Stone Age and the Aborigines of the Lancefield District*, Lancefield, 1910.

29 Thomson, 'Some wood and stone implements', 409ff.

30 E.g. Bandi, *op. cit.*, Abb. ii, 15–19 and Abb. iii, 13–14.

31 F. D. McCarthy, 'Habitat, Economy and Equipment of the Australian Aborigines', *The Aust. J. Sci.*, 19 (1957), 88–97; see p. 94.

32 L. V. Brass, 'Stone-Age Agriculture in New Guinea', *Geogr. Rev.*, 31 (1941) 555–69; R. F. Salisbury, *From Stone to Steel*, Cambridge, 1962.

CHAPTER 15

THE EXPANSION OF MAN WITH SPECIAL REFERENCE TO AUSTRALIA AND THE NEW WORLD

It seems appropriate that any tribute to M. Varagnac should take account of his genius for treating in broad lines topics of wide significance to mankind, topics which transcend the boundaries not only of races and civilizations, but also of periods of human history. Of the many themes that lend coherence to prehistory and history, and permit us to view in perspective the current strivings of mankind, few are of greater significance than the expansion of human settlement. In the most literal sense it was only by emerging from the old primate homelands that man was able to inherit the whole earth and it was only when he had accomplished this that he began to seek new worlds to conquer in extra-terrestrial space.

Man has been able to break out from his ancient homeland and settle progressively more remote territories by making appropriate adjustments in the field of culture. Conversely the enlargement of his territory illustrates in a conspicuous manner the dynamic possibilities inherent in human culture. It is after all, one of man's most notable characteristics when compared with other animals, that he has shown himself able to transcend the limitations of particular habitats and biomes. At any particular stage it is true that he is restricted in his range of colonization, just as he is limited in his ability to utilize natural resources, by the knowledge and technical means available to him by virtue of the cultural traditions in which he happens to exist. But it is of the essence of cultural traditions that they are capable of enrichment and transformation, so that the possibilities open to men in their capacity as organisms are in truth indefinitely extendible.

Before considering the extension of human settlement the point should first be made, that throughout the Lower and Middle Pleistocene, a period of perhaps two million years, man underwent his biological and cultural evolution within the territories occupied by the great apes and the Old World monkeys, namely Africa, southern Europe and Asia south of the Himalaya and east of the Central Asian plateau: it has only been during the last fifty thousand years or so that he began to break out of this ancient homeland of the Primates. The second thing to bear in mind is that prehistory was first developed in the north-western part of this ancient cradle of mankind and specifically in western Europe, so that knowledge of the expansion of prehistoric man has had to wait on the spread of scientific prehistory to

Russia, North America and Australia. Thirdly it may be emphasized that research on this problem has been given special impetus and precision since the nineteen fifties, when facilities for radio-carbon dating first became available.

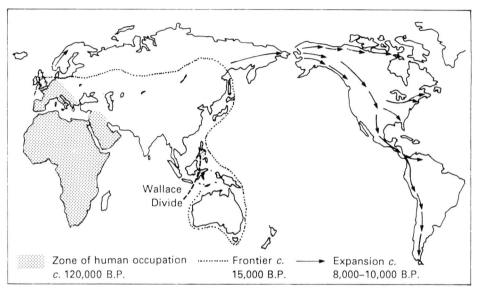

15.1 Map showing the expansion of human occupation

The researchers of Soviet prehistorians have shown that the northward spread of human settlement was initiated in Eurasia by men of Neanderthaloid type equipped with a lithic technology of Middle Palaeolithic and specifically Mousterian character. Numerous sites in the Ukraine and contiguous parts of the south Russian plain and in Uzbekistan, Central Asia,[1] have produced large numbers of Mousterian scrapers, an implement significantly resembling those used by Eskimo for preparing skins. The fact that formalized side-scrapers emerged in the northern parts of the Middle Palaeolithic world, is suggestive in view of the importance of animal skins for clothing and as a covering for tent-like dwellings. In the last connection special significance attaches to the discovery by A. P. Chernysh at Molodova I[2] on the Dniester of traces of a substantial house containing hearths and surrounded by a perimeter of heavy animal bones of a kind that might well have held down a tent-like covering of animal skins. Even more conclusive evidence for cultural adaptation to cold conditions has been obtained from rather younger settlements of Advanced Palaeolithic character, from the Ankara basin west of Lake Baikal explored by Okladnikov and Ephimenko. The imperforate needles from Mal'ta[3] and still more the mammoth ivory carving of a human figure from Buret,[4] apparently clothed in a hooded fur garment resembling those worn by the Eskimo, reflect the importance of protective clothing in settling Inner Siberia. Again one may note the occurrence at the Buret site of plans of semi-subterranean dwellings approached by passages of the kind widespread in the Arctic zone in recent times and valued for the protection they afford against the cold; and at Mal'ta we have well-preserved plans of circular and subrectangular dwellings with slightly sunken floors, walls defined by stone-slabs and roofs apparently weighted down with reindeer antlers.

Although useful progress has been made in the investigation both of north-east Siberia[5] and of Alaska[6], it would be incorrect to claim that a continuous dated trail has been defined between the Old World and the New. Yet the work of the last forty years has established, beyond reasonable doubt, that early man was active on the High Plains of North America before the end of the Pleistocene[7] and that he must have reached this area ultimately by way of the land-bridge across the present Behring Strait that existed during the periods of low ocean level in the course of the Ice Age. The first reliable clue was the discovery in 1926 near Folsom, New Mexico, of the skeleton of an extinct form of Bison associated with fragments of a flint projectile head of fluted type. During the ensuing years many more kill-sites were investigated including that at Lindenmeier in Colorado (1934–8) having points of Folsom type, leaf-shaped with maximum width about a third of the way down and a thinning-flake struck from the concave base and running almost to the tip, giving an overall fluted appearance. Concurrently, kill-sites were found at Clovis and elsewhere associated with remains of Mammoth and flint points of allied but distinct type, having a maximum width about mid-way and a thinning-flake confined to the lower end.

These and other discoveries stimulated a driving interest among American prehistorians in the problems of early man. This took three main forms. Some concentrated on trying to extend the range of human occupation as far back as the evidence would allow; others were mainly concerned with tracing the expansion of the Palaeoindians over different parts of the continent by means of their characteristic projectile points; and latterly some attempt has been made, though it has not yet been pressed as far as it might have been, to broaden knowledge of the early hunters' equipment and so obtain a more adequate basis for assessing their connections with the Old World.

The attempt to date the spread of man into and over the New World was greatly helped by W. F. Libby's[8] opportune discovery of the possibilities of radio-carbon dating and it is significant that Folsom was among the first archaeological sites to benefit from the application of his method. Since the main results have been so accessibly summarized by Vance Haynes[9] it need only be recalled here that, give or take the standard deviations determined for each sample, Folsom points go back to the ninth and Clovis to the tenth millennium B.C. In other words, we get a whole cluster of reliably dated kill-finds dating to the thousand years or so, immediately following the opening of a passage to the High Plains as the Cordilleran and Laurentide ice-sheets parted soon after the final major advance of glaciation. Of itself this does not dispose of the possibility that men passed through the passage, when it was previously open before 27000 B.C. Meanwhile it is fair to say that we have no evidence of human occupation of north-east Siberia at anything like so early a date, and that no claims for the presence of man at this time in the United States itself have stood up to close scrutiny: in far too many instances they rest on high dates for burnt patches interpreted as hearths but equally well to be explained as the products of conflagrations produced by natural agencies without the intervention of man; and in others, of which Tule Springs, Nevada,[10] is the most notorious because the most expensive of cost and effort, large-scale investigation has shown that artifacts were not in fact contemporary with the deposits with which they were associated because of what turned out to be defective exploration.

The chance that the first Paleoindian sites to be discovered were of a particular kind, namely the kill-sites of large mammals, set a pattern and led to undue concentration on projectile points and to begin with even on the special kinds marked by more or less prominent fluting. Yet it is obvious that since the fluted point was indigenous to North America it was hardly the best pointer to Old World origins. More interest in this respect attached to the leaf-shaped points that began to turn up in different parts of America, from the Old Cordilleran culture, extending from the Yukon to California and from the Lerma complex of Mexico and the Ayampitín of parts of South America, since these compare with points known from different parts of the Old World. The ancillary tools that were in due course recovered from Paleoindian sites pointed in the same direction, especially the magnificent blades of Clovis[11] and the undoubted burins recognized from many localities in California.

Finally, it soon came to be recognized that the concentration even of fluted points on the High Plains was another accident of discovery. It is of course true that this region provided among the best grazing for the herds on which the Paleoindian hunters depended. On the other hand search among collections of flint implements from different parts of the United States soon showed how widespread these type-fossils in fact were. Stray specimens were found as far east as the Atlantic seaboard; investigation of sites like Bull Brook, Mass., and Debert, Nova Scotia, showed that this had been reached by the eighth or even the ninth millennium B.C. It is also known that, by about the same time, Paleoindian hunters had penetrated Mesoamerica and traversed South America. To mention only one Mesoamerican site one might point to the famous lake-bed of Santa Isabel Iztapán in Mexico Valley, where mammoth skeletons were found with Lerma points. Occurrences in South America extend from El Jobo in Venezuela to Chivateros on the coast of Peru, Ayampitín in the Argentine and Fell's Cave on Magellan Strait, a site that yielded a particular form of projectile head, having a fish-tail tang. The most striking thing about this expansion is the speed with which it was accomplished, since the occupation of Fell's Cave dates in terms of radio-carbon to the ninth millennium b.c.[12] This in turn is a useful reminder that man shared with other animals the drive to explore his environment: the propensity to spread was there and, provided that geography imposed no insuperable barrier, insuperable that is to the people concerned, expansion of settlement might be expected. Plainly the New World could hardly have been occupied until Advanced Palaeolithic man was able to penetrate and traverse north-east Siberia and Alaska and until a suitable passage was effected by the parting and contraction of the Cordilleran and Laurentide ice-sheets. It seems, according to radio-carbon dating, that the High Plains were pene-trated as soon as this was possible, and that within a few centuries the Paleoindian hunters had spread to the Atlantic seaboard and the Magellan Strait.

The dominant factor limiting expansion from south-east Asia was on the other hand the sea. During periods of glaciation in the temperate zones, when sufficient water was locked up in the ice-sheets to lower ocean levels by several hundred feet, Sumatra, Java, Borneo, Palawan and several smaller islands were of course joined to Malaya by the now-submerged Sunda shelf; and it is hardly surprising that Java should have yielded some of the most important Middle Pleistocene fossils of man, not to mention early stone industries,[13] or again, that the caves of Nia in Sarawak[14] and Tabon on the Philippine island of Palawan should have yielded traces of human occupation comparable in age to the beginning of the Advanced Palaeolithic in Europe. The only barrier to the further expansion of man, as of other animals, to New Guinea and Australia was the depth of water in the Macassar Strait and the gap between Bali and Lombok islands, a line recognized over a hundred years ago by A. R. Wallace as marking a significant faunal break. Precisely when early man first crossed this barrier by using floats or boats only future research will exactly define. Since the sea-crossing would have been notably shorter at times of low ocean levels, it is more than likely that these would have been undertaken during a glacial phase rather than during an interglacial or post-glacial one; and as we shall see in due course the radio-carbon dating of a number of sites in Australia itself has already made it certain that the continent was occupied well back in the Late-glacial period, several thousand years earlier than the New World is known to have been settled by man.

The idea that man had occupied their continent for any great length of time came even more recently to the Australians than to the Americans. The underlying reason for this was the same in both cases : both continents were after all occupied in relatively modern times by men of high civilization who in large measure dispossessed and despised the aboriginal inhabitants and who, when they did begin to study them, did so in the context of anthropology rather than of archaeology.[15] The aborigines were a given fact like the fauna or the climate and they were studied as a present responsibility. When collectors found flint and stone tools in different parts of Australia they tended to interpret differences more in relation to varying environments than as evidence for changes in the course of time. It is hardly surprising, given this climate of thought, that the first systematic archaeological excavation aimed at securing a sequence of cultural material, that undertaken by Hale and Tindale under the rock-shelter of Devon Downs on the lower Murray river near Adelaide,[16] did not occur until 1929–30. Although this excavation marked a veritable water-shed in Australian prehistory it did not provoke immediate imitators: instead, and as it turned out unfortunately, the sequence of cultures found in the shelter and in the near neighbourhood was used as a yardstick for ordering the prehistory of the whole continent. Yet, even if analogous sites had been dug in other parts, it is doubtful whether much progress could have been made until radio-carbon dating had been introduced, since it would otherwise have been almost impossible to synchronize sections, over such wide territories as Australia provides. It was the impact of radio-carbon dating that did more than anything else to stimulate interest in Australian prehistory and at the same time to make rapid progress possible.

The first clue to the high antiquity of man in Australia came with the publication of radio-carbon determinations from the site of the discovery in the course of commercial activities of the fossil cranium from Keilor near Melbourne. A sample (NZ 336) from the estimated level of the cranium gave a determination of 13050 B.C. ± 1500 and another (NZ 207) from an underlying burnt area interpreted as a hearth one of 16050 B.C. ± 500 years. Admittedly the precise stratigraphic horizon of the original Keilor find is open to some conjecture, but whether or not these dates are confirmed by the analysis of samples of the more recent finds from this site made under more propitious circumstances, only publication will show. What is sufficiently plain, is that nothing can alter the impact of the original findings on the outlook of Australian prehistorians. The suggestion that man had reached Australia at a much earlier date than had hitherto been imagined, a date moreover that could be expressed in round if only probable figures, was just the stimulant needed to provoke an exciting outburst of excavation over a territory extending from New Guinea and the Northern Territories to South Australia and Tasmania.

This is not the occasion to summarize the findings of Australian prehistorians, which are in any case only partly published. Yet one cannot conclude this tribute to the vision and sympathetic appreciation of the world-wide ramifications and implications of prehistory displayed by M. Varagnac without indicating some of the discoveries which point to an early occupation of the Australian continent.

As the results of excavating rock-shelters and caves over a broad tract of the eastern half of Australia appear in published form, it is becoming evident that industries from the lower levels of a number of sites conform to the relatively simple patterns long known from early collections made in Tasmania. The bulk of the artifacts comprise flakes and the relatively unspecialized cores from which they have been struck; where these have been subjected to further work this was most commonly to convert them into convex scrapers, hollow scrapers and pointed or spurred forms, many of them heavy and apparently suited to shaping wood. At Kenniff Cave in south Queensland, perhaps the most important and completely published cave among those recently explored,[17] such an industry was found stratified below one containing smaller artifacts of kinds that must have been hafted; and a similar succession has been noted at many other sites, notably at Noola,[18] Murramarra[19] and Capertee in New South Wales,[20] Laura in North Queensland[21] and Ingaladdi in Northern Territories.[22] Radio-carbon determinations already available from some of these sites suggest that the earlier industries go well back into the Late-glacial era. Thus, the three samples processed from early levels at Kenniff Cave by the National Physical Laboratory, London, gave the following results:

Depths		B.C.
170–173 cm	NPL 67	10660 ± 110
178–203	NPL 33	10950 ± 170
226–234	NPL 68	14180 ± 140

Even the discrepant Tokyo determinations from samples taken below these, namely – in descending order – GaK 526 (13200 ± 300), GaK 645 (9650 + 100) and GaK 527 (9300 ± 200), fall within the Late-glacial period as this is defined in the Northern Hemisphere. A broadly analogous industry excavated by Tindale from the Noola shelter in the interior of New South Wales was also dated to the same period by radio-carbon (GaK 334: 9650 B.C. ± 400). An eroded hearth exposed on an ancient shore-line of Lake Meninde, South Australia, gave a date of the same order as that for the Keilor cranium, namely 16850 B.C. ± 800 (GaK 334). More recently another date in the seventeenth millennium B.C. (16250 B.C. ± 500: GaK 5111) has been determined for an implementiferous deposit in a deep cavern at Koonalda, South Australia. So far the earliest dates published from Tasmania go back no further than the seventh millennium B.C. (I 323: 6750 B.C. ± 200; GXO 266: 6170 ± 120), but since many sites belonging to the period when Tasmania was still joined to the mainland are submerged this is perhaps not so surprising.[23]

The elementary nature of the lithic technology introduced to Australia makes it difficult to determine either its source or the route which it followed. Even if it can be assumed that the first immigrants to Australia came from Indonesia, it is still to be established whether they came by way of New Guinea, from which a radio-carbon date of 8400 B.C. ± 140 (Y 1366) is available for a sample from near the base of the deposits in a rock-shelter at Kiowa;[24] or whether they may not have arrived by way of Timor or the easternmost islands of Indonesia and the Sahul shelf. What seems in any case to be established is that man entered Australia substantially earlier, on present evidence, than he did the New World.

A final point to make, is that early man had occupied almost the whole world before he had learned to farm, still more before he had developed even the earliest civilizations. From a spatial point of view, man expanded his dominion almost to the uttermost limits, while still gaining his living as hunter, fisher and gatherer. The Circumpolar tracts of northern Eurasia and North America, in fact, could only be penetrated and occupied by food-producers in quite recent centuries and then only with the support of home bases in Europe or North America.[25] One of the few extensive zones to be occupied for the first time, by people accustomed to grow their own food, or at least a proportion of this, was the Pacific Ocean,[26] the scattered islands of which could only be settled by people equipped technically and socially to traverse great expanses of sea. To judge by radio-carbon dating this last major territory was appropriated during the first millennium A.D.

Notes

1 Hallam L. Hovius, 'The Mousterian Cave of Teshik-Tash, southeastern Uzbekistan, Central Asia', *Am. School of Prehistoric Research*, Bull. 17 (1963), 11–71.
2 A. P. Chernysh, *Kratkie Soobshscheniya Inst. Archaeol.* (Kiev), vol. 10 (1960), 4–6.
3 M. M. Gerasimov, 'The Paleolithic site Mal'ta: excavations of 1956–57', *The Archaeology and Geomorphology of Northern Asia* (ed. H. N. Michael), 3–32, Toronto, 1964.
4 A. P. Okladnikov, *Kratkie Soobscheniya o Doklad in Polevykh Issled* (Moscow-Leningrad), vol. 10 (1941), 16–31; *Mat. i. Issled po Arkh. SSSR*, vol. 2, 104–8, *ibid.*, vol. 79, 137.
5 A. P. Okladnikov, 'Palaeolithic remains in the Lena River Basin', *The Archaeology and Geomorphology of Northern Asia* (ed. H. N. Michael), 33–79. For a useful survey of conditions during the Quaternary period in Siberia east of the Lena River, see A. P. Vaskovskiy, *ibid.*, 464–512.
6 For a personalised account with a good bibliography, see J. L. Giddings, *Ancient Men of the Arctic*, New York, 1967. A useful article by Henry C. Collins may be found in Jennings and Norbeck, cited in n. 7 below.
7 Useful references with ample bibliographies are: H. W. Wormington, *Ancient Man in North America*, Denver, 1957; H. M. Wormington and Richard G. Forbis, *An Introduction to The Archaeology of Alberta, Canada*, Denver, 1965; Gordon R. Willey, *An Introduction to American Archaeology*, vol. I, ch. 2, New Jersey, 1966; and Jesse D. Jennings and Edward Norbeck (eds.), *Prehistoric Man in the New World*, Chicago, 1964.
8 W. F. Libby, *Radio-carbon Dating*, 2nd edn., Chicago, 1955.

9 C. Vance Haynes, 'Fluted Projectile Points: their age and dispersion', *Science* 145 (1964), 1408–13.

10 R. Shutler, 'Tule Springs Expedition', *Current Anthropology*, vol. 6 (1965), 110–11.

11 F. E. Green, 'The Clovis Blades', *American Antiquity 29* (1963), 145–65.

12 W. 915 8770 ± 300 B.C.

13 M. R. van Heekeren, *The Stone Age of Indonesia*, The Hague, 1956.

14 T. Harrison, 'The Great Cave of Nia', *Man*, 1957, No. 211.

15 D. J. Mulvaney, 'The Stone Age of Australia', *Proc. Prehist. Soc.*, xxvii (1961), 56–107; see esp. pp. 59–60 and 65.

16 H. M. Hale and Norman B. Tindale, 'Notes on some human remains in the Lower Murray Valley, South Australia', *Rec. South Austr. Mus.*, iv (1930), 145–218, Adelaide.

17 D. J. Mulvaney and E. B. Joyce, 'Archaeological and Geomorphological Investigations on Mt Moffatt Station, Queensland, Australia', *Proc. Prehist. Soc.*, xxxi (1965), 147–212.

18 Norman B. Tindale, 'Archaeological Excavation of Noola Rock Shelter: A Preliminary Report', *Rec. South Austr. Mus.*, xiv (1961), 193–6, Adelaide.

19 By Richard Wright of the Department of Anthropology, University of Sydney.

20 F. D. McCarthy, 'The Archaeology of the Capertee Valley, New South Wales', *Rec. Australian Museum*, 26 (1964), 197–246, Sydney.

21 By Richard Wright.

22 By Jack Golson and John Mulvaney of the Institute of Pacific Studies, Austr. Nat. Univ., Canberra.

23 As Rhys Jones has recently emphasized, stone age sites are concentrated in the existing coastal zone; if this has always been the case, settlements from the mainland period would now be submerged. See *Rec. Queen Victoria Mus.*, No. 25 (1966), 1–12, Launceston.

24 S. and R. Bulmer, 'The Prehistory of the Australian New Guinea Highlands', *Am. Anthrop.: Special Publ. New Guinea*, 1964, 39–76.

25 The relative importance of the various factors in the demise of the short-lived Norse settlement of West Greenland is still debated, but the significance of the breakdown of contact with Norway is generally admitted.

26 See Robert C. Suggs, *The Island Civilizations of Polynesia*, New York, 1960.

CHAPTER 16

THE ARCHAEOLOGY OF STONE AGE SETTLEMENT

Survival technique. Does this not summarise what we study in archaeology? On the one hand the physical environment, on the other the material equipment which the art of museum men may contrive to display to the best advantage, but which still seems pitiful – or would do if we were dumped down in some territory away back in time with these bits and pieces of flint, stone, bone or fired clay in our hands. Of course, there is one factor of a technical kind which distorts the picture. That is the distortion brought about by the remorseless, but also selective workings of the second law of thermodynamics. We all know that some materials revert to a lower order of organisation very much more rapidly and completely than others. What we have in the archaeological record are assemblages, not of the artifacts of early man, but of those components of his tool-kit, weaponry and gear that have survived and which we have succeeded in finding. If we get depressed at times by how little we have of the equipment of many prehistoric groups in temperate Europe, imagine our state of mind if we had to depend on the materials likely to survive from that of many recently extant primitive peoples. Ethnographic collections can be a snare for uncritical archaeologists, but at least they remind us that the tool-kits of many peoples, who adapted satisfactorily to their surroundings and formed viable communities, were composed almost entirely of organic materials that in the normal way would perish without leaving the slightest trace for the archaeologist. All one could expect to find if one were to excavate the material equipment, say of an Australian aboriginal group after a few hundred years from a site where normal conditions obtained, would be the stone armatures of predominantly wooden artifacts. The fact that by and large mineral materials survive much better than organic ones – and that primitive man depended to a large degree on the latter – is something we all recognise, but emphatically it is not something to which we need submit. The pessimistic school of archaeologists rejoice in the poverty of the material data which they tell us is all we have; let us cherish it, typologise it, date it, exhibit it, embalm it in expensive catalogues – but don't imagine for a moment that it can tell us anything about what happened in the past. I will say no more of these postage stamp archaeologists than that it grieves me as a taxpayer to have to share in paying their salaries.

If I am an optimistic archaeologist it is partly that I see no future in pessimism, but partly because if we look at it the right way the possibilities of learning something – or at least of framing hypotheses – about what happened long ago are much greater than might at first seem likely. Even at the very lowest level – that of the actual artifacts – the situation is transformed once we realise that by taking thought and not very much thought at that – by exercising even the most elementary discrimination, we can enormously enlarge the range of material. That is why when I first wrote a small book addressed to students I made a great point of emphasising the importance of understanding the factors that slow down or even arrest the disintegration of the primary data and control the survival of the all important organic component. At the time, I believe, this was regarded as little more than a gimmick, a device for relieving the tedium of pots and stones by illustrating structures, clothing and a wide range of other artifacts preserved by refrigeration, desiccation or, in the temperate zone, by water-logging. I was never more serious. Perhaps I had had a surfeit of microliths and burins. At any rate I resolved to attempt to do something practical about what had up till then been my own special field. I felt that the time had passed for stopping short at dating artifactual assemblages and refining the study of a negligible component of the industrial equipment of mesolithic man.

After the war there were many things to do, but I had a very clear idea what I wanted – a mesolithic site immediately contiguous to water-logged deposits – deposits that is which offered the possibility of recovering the organic materials that have so generally vanished. If this could be found one might hope for:

(a) a much more complete range of material equipment, including objects of antler, bone and hopefully also of wood;

(b) food refuse, animal bones, plant remains;

(c) evidence for the environmental conditions prevailing in the immediate locality at the time it was occupied;

(d) clues as to the scale of social unit represented.

Anyone who specialises on a particular class of archaeological material is likely to hear from keen amateurs. I used frequently to receive small packets through the post. I did what I could, but always firmly resisted the temptation to invest time on sites whose potential was limited to the multiplication of microliths. It was a parcel of flints from Mr John Moore of Scarborough that first made me excited. These were recognisably Maglemo-sian and they came from the Vale of Pickering. The possibility was there of recovering this industry in early Post-glacial deposits. The vital clue would be animal bone. Mr Moore responded by systematically exploring ditches on the northern margin of the alluvium. Sure enough, he was able to lead me on my first visit to a site where decayed bone and antler were visible in a dike profile at the same level as the flints. This site was Star Carr (fig. 16.1).

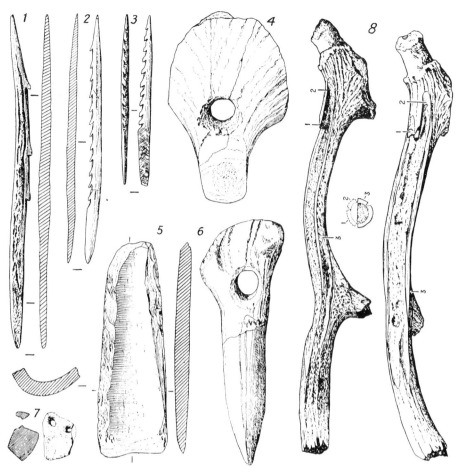

16.1   Objects of antler, bone and amber (7) from Star Carr, Yorkshire, England.

Those who may be interested in this particular site can consult not only the original monograph[1] but also the Addison-Wesley Module.[2] I do not want, therefore, to spend time on any extensive treatment of this particular site. It does, however, offer a convenient illustration of some of the topics I want to discuss. The first is the elementary one that if material equipment offers a main key to the way in which prehistoric man managed to survive by utilising the resources of his environment, then it follows that we must as a first requisite maximise the range of our knowledge of his equipment. This needs emphasising again and again. It applies to all periods of archaeology. How often in the quite recent past have we watched archaeologists going through the familiar motions and Committees voting resources to excavators to go on finding the same categories of object, the same kind of information. The ritual is an established one and it is only necessary to turn over the pages even of the contemporary periodical literature to see that those who participate in the self-validating routines still belong to a goodly company.

To illustrate how even the excavation of one site with the right conditions for the survival of organic materials can transform our knowledge of the material equipment of a particular phase of prehistory, I have prepared a table in which the artifactual components found at Star Carr and at other Early Mesolithic sites in England respectively have been tabulated.

British early Mesolithic assemblages

Categories of artifact	Starr Carr	Other sites
Flint assemblages with microliths, burins, end scrapers and core axes/adzes with tranchet edge	×	××××
Stone macehead with hourglass perforation	–	×
Barbed points: antler/bone	191	6
Antler mattock-heads (elk)	6	–
Bodkins (elk metapodial)	4	–
Skin-working(?) tools (aurochs bone)	11	–
Stag frontlet masks (red deer)	21	–
Wooden paddle	1	–
Wooden mattock handle	1	–
Birch bark rolls	×	–
Birch pitch resin mounting	1	–
Beads: amber	3	–
perforated shale	×	–
tubular bone	1	–

Two things need stressing about this. To begin with, although half a dozen barbed antler or bone points had previously been found, they had almost without exception been discovered in isolation. It was only inference from Continental finds, backed by a few finds from the Skipsea mere-bed, that allowed us to associate these with lithic assemblages like those from Broxbourne, Kelling, Thatcham (before of course the Wymer excavations) and Uxbridge, none of which had produced artifacts made from organic materials. Star Carr confirmed that a form of culture analogous to that known from Denmark, South Sweden and North Germany really did exist in Britain. Second, and more relevantly, I want to emphasise how greatly it enlarged the number of traits previously known even in isolation. If priority is given to the task of increasing the range of primary data by taking account of this factor of differential conservation, then at least we may hope to secure a much more complete picture of the range of equipment available to early man and – another point – of the techniques by which he shaped his equipment, something only to be understood from a systematic study of by-products and waste.

Now, if equipment is important as an aid to survival, food is the medium. Like any other animal, man can only exist and perpetuate his kind by ingesting plants or other animals. Biologically he may stand at the top of the food chain, but he is still a part of the web of life and from time to time the predator in chief falls a victim to his fellows and even his prey. In the sum total of his diversity, man is an omnivorous animal, but it is one of his basic characteristics, something that follows from the mere fact of culture, that particular populations conform to selective patterns. A main aim of the archaeology of settlement must be to discover the precise pattern followed by the populations living at different periods in the territory under study. Here, again, it will not have escaped you that the same conditions, which favour the survival of organic components of equipment, will necessarily favour that of food residues – in fact, so far as animals are concerned, the skeletal materials utilised for artifacts will almost invariably come from animals taken for food. Assemblages of animal remains are of archaeological interest, not merely to the extent that they may have been utilised for tools or weapons, but even more because they reflect cultural selectivity in respect of subsistence. In parenthesis an important difference is worth noting in respect of the interpretation of animal and plant remains from archaeological settlements. It is a fair working assumption, because of their mobility, that most animals were brought to the settlement by man, even if others may have been predators or merely incidental visitors, whereas without indications to the contrary, the presumption must normally be that plants were growing there independently of man. When it comes to proof, the skeletal remains of animals have the great advantage that they may be expected to display palpable signs in the form of wounds (or even embedded projectile heads) or signs of butchery, whereas it is very much more difficult to offer convincing proof that traces of plants recovered from an archaeological site were brought there by man in the course of his food-quest and eaten. It has been part of archaeological routine since the original investigation of the so-called 'Swiss lake-villages' well over a hundred years ago, for excavators to pick out the more obvious bones and even cereal grains and charcoals and pack them off to zoologists and botanists with a request for reports which duly get consigned to appendices. If they frequently deserve no other fate, this is due in part to poor sampling and in part to inadequate briefing by the excavator. After all, we spend our time interrogating data. Unless we ask intelligent questions we are unlikely to get useful answers; and it is a waste of time to ask intelligent questions of data that has not been systematically collected with intelligent questions in mind.

The manner in which communities acquire their food is basic to any appreciation of early settlement. Subsistence, like technology, is one of the main hinges which articulate communities to their environments. Men detach materials from their habitats to make their most crucial tools. They eat components of their biome (fig. 16.2). There is no need to emphasise here that early settlement can only be adequately studied in the context of Quaternary Research. It is not our business as archaeologists to trace the course of climatic, geographical, botanical or faunal history. This is some-

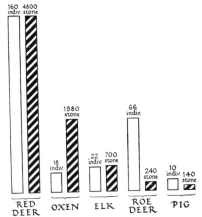

16.2   Histogram illustrating the proportions by numbers and weight of the larger game animals represented at Star Carr.

thing we leave to specialists in the Earth and Life sciences. It *is* our business to fit the communities we study into their correct slot in environmental history, to ensure in other words that we can assess their performance in an ecological context. We cannot interpret the archaeology of human settlement with any hope of success unless we are appraised both of the options open to human populations and of the constraints which at any particular juncture set limits to these.

At this point it is well to remember that in concerning themselves with men, archaeologists face a task of another order of complexity from that confronted by botanists or zoologists. Animal and plant ecology each have their problems, but human ecology has to face an extra variable and one which in the course of social evolution grew in pervasiveness and complexity – the variable of cultural inheritance transmitted to men by virtue of belonging to specific social groupings. This was a major fact in deciding which options were in fact chosen by a particular community. There must in the long run have been a bias in favour of choices that were adaptive in an evolutionary sense, but it should be remembered that competition has become progressively less perfect with every advance in social evolution. When social value attaches to some particular way of doing things this will not necessarily be displaced even when demonstrably less efficient: up to a point it may, if society continues to feel that way, be maintained even at some economic cost – in our own society Beefeaters, dockers and many others are employed at some social cost to perform functions which in some cases are no longer necessary. When considerations of value enter in, simplistic explanations, whether economic or ecological, cease to be adequate. In studying human settlement, we are concerned with societies which manipulate their natural environments in terms of social values, that is, values acquired by belonging to communities constituted by history. The notion that the Natural Sciences are somehow more difficult than the Humanities is one of the most preposterous confidence tricks of the century immediately following the Great Exhibition. The bluff has only recently been called. Please don't misunderstand me. I'm certainly not attacking the procedures of natural science. The complexity and difficulty of the human sciences, which I have intended to emphasise, call insistently for the application of every kind of scientific procedure that can be brought to bear upon them. Indeed, one way of bringing out the diversity and complexity of human societies is precisely to deploy procedures designed to define and account for basic regularities.

We return to the point that men have to live by exploiting natural resources, even if the methods they use – and in this I would include social as well as technical means – are conditioned by factors some of which are extraneous to the natural environment. In practical terms this means exploiting territory. In relation to human societies it is convenient to think in terms of three categories of territory:

(1) the home territory, the land exploited from the individual settlement, whether this consists of one household or many;

(2) the annual territory, that habitually used in the course of the year by the community in question;

(3) the social territory, that drawn upon by a given community for supplies by virtue of belonging to a larger social grouping.

The need for some form of nest, shelter or home base to which food can be brought and where the immature can be kept secure and warm is essential for animals whose young are born defenceless and unable to fend for themselves. This applies particularly to men. It is not merely that the process of maturation and the period of weakness is long: even more important is the time it takes the human young to absorb their cultural heritage and equip themselves for life in human society – around thirty years in the higher echelons of our own society. The acquisition of culture, which in human society provides a basic source of group identity and includes particular articulate languages, technologies, subsistence patterns and value systems, involves a prolonged period of learning and the basis of this is laid in the home that shelters mother, siblings and at least from time to time, father.

In investigating settlements, therefore, we are exploring the very cradles of humanity. Investigation of the grouping and form of structures can be a means of gaining information about the size and organisation of social units, even if in practical terms the subject bristles with difficulties. By uncovering the whole site – and this, rather than the time-honoured practice of sampling many, must surely be our ideal once we are past the initial sorting phase in archaeology – and plotting the distribution of finds, we were able at Star Carr to establish that not more than three or at least four primary biological units can have lived there at once. If traces of the actual shelters had survived – we found only the basic platform – we would have to have faced the problem what these implied in terms of population. Did each structure imply a biological family? and were they all occupied at the same time? are only two of the most basic questions. In investigating the basic but extremely difficult problem of population density there would seem to be two complementary ways of approach:

(a) the direct way, involving the mapping of settlements and/or cemeteries and the total excavation of representative ones. This is not merely arduous. It is full of problems. If it is difficult to infer population size from individual settlements it is no simple matter to determine with precision which settlements were occupied contemporaneously;

(b) the indirect way of estimating the resource potentials of territories known from the plotting of loose finds to have been exploited.

The basic requirements of the home base territory are water and food. In the case of people whose only means of travel is their own feet, the territory normally exploited for food from any particular base is likely to be that within a radius of one or two hours' walking, something which in terms of distance would, of course, vary according to topographical circumstances. Fairly plainly for people dependent on gathering and on hunting or culling wild animals this circumstance limited rather narrowly the size of social group able to live together for any other than a brief period. Indeed, for most people so dependent it was necessary to exploit territory seasonally, to shift the home base and its attendant territory over a more or less extensive annual territory in order to maximise the yield of food. This might conceivably under certain conditions involve an almost continuously peripatetic home base. As a rule, though, there are one or more seasons which may last several months, during which the home base remains at one place. This is something we can only hope to learn with precision from organic data from archaeological settlements. In the case of Star Carr one of the key questions put to Drs Fraser and King was precisely this: what do the animal remains have to tell us about seasonality? Of course, to get a full answer one needs to consider a site of this kind in the context of annual territory. This I tried to do when rethinking Star Carr. The most economical hypothesis seemed to me that the movements of the Star Carr people were conditioned to a significant degree by those of their chief quarry the Red Deer. In north-west Europe these animals tend to leave high ground at the approach of snow and shelter during the winter on low ground. Almost all the Red Deer from Star Carr were adult males killed during the winter while still carrying antlers. Quite evidently the inhabitants of Star Carr were culling adult stags at the time of the year when, having completed the rut, these were concentrated in their own yards. Clearly it would have been improvident to kill hinds at a time of the year when they were carrying young and the few hinds represented may well have been sterile. From an industrial point of view, the outstanding feature of Star

Carr was evidence for intensive utilisation of stag antler. Some four-fifths of all those from the site have been subjected to the groove and splinter technique and all but an insignificant proportion of the barbed points had been made from blanks obtained in this way. In this respect it is significant that burins were the commonest flint tool.

Calculations of the yield of meat on an area basis show that if the deer had stayed put, there is no reason why their human predators should not also have done so, provided, that is, that they lived in micro-bands of not more than three or four biological families. But herbivores tend to follow the grazing as it re-appeared first on the lower slopes and at the height of summer at higher altitudes. The microlithic industries on the crests of the North Yorkshire moors and high up on the Pennines may well relate to summer hunting grounds. Here we come up against the kind of gap in the evidence which makes prehistory so tantalising. By and large the chances are good for finding other Star Carrs – the recent discovery of barbed points in the skeleton of an elk in an Allerød deposit at Poulton-le-Fylde near Blackpool,[3] west of the Pennines, is a pointer. The chances of finding a site with the right conditions for conservation on the high ground hypothetically used during the summer are much slighter – but should be all the more eagerly sought.

In the meantime, it is of interest to note a main difference between the lowland and upland flint industries in northern England – the abundance of burins in the former and their relative scarcity in the latter. If we are right in linking burins with antler and bone working, their comparative scarcity on the uplands is consistent with the exploitation of these territories during the summer when stags were still growing their antlers.

Two other examples may be worth a brief reference. Examination of the skeletal material from Late-glacial stations in Schleswig-Holstein, where reindeer account for 99% or so of the prey, showed that they were only occupied intermittently. When first examined the fauna from the sites of Stellmoor[4] and Meiendorf[5] were held to indicate occupation during the summer months: the reindeer herds were supposed, according to this hypothesis, to have moved south during the winter to shelter in the forest zone. Recent hardness tests conducted on the reindeer antlers by Dr D. A. Sturdy[6] have argued that the reindeer on these sites were killed predominantly in autumn and spring with the main emphasis on the former. This agrees very neatly with the observation by Degerbøl and Krog[7] that the vast proportion of reindeer antlers from Late-glacial Denmark as far north as northern Jutland were shed, a clear indication so far as male animals are concerned that the animals were able to winter far to the north of Schleswig-Holstein. This in turn agrees with the presence in Danish Late-glacial deposits noted by Iversen[8] of a number of plants that 'do not tolerate more than a thin and transient snow cover'. It looks as though the reindeer herds were thinned on the way north and south in autumn and spring respectively. The fact that the main kill was in the autumn makes sense if the community had to sit it out during the winter – under Arctic to sub-Arctic climate meat could easily have been stored and drawn upon at leisure.

As a third example, let us consider the beautiful results obtained by Haakon Olsen from a study of the bird and fish bones obtained from Stone Age earth-houses on the south coast of Varanger Fjord in north Norway.[9] Both point unambiguously to the winter: for instance, four-fifths of the fish bones belong to cod, whereas there were no salmon and few coalfish, and the birds include winter migrants that breed in the Arctic. Large quantities of whale and seal bones also point to winter sea-hunting and suggest why at this time of the year people were living in aggregations of band size. During the summer the bands apparently broke up into micro-bands or even biological families and penetrated inland to take the seasonal run of salmon upstream and engage in land hunting. Here again the evidence is still defective. The recovery of pottery of identical character from both coastal and inland river sites is certainly consistent with seasonal movement. Proof could only come by finding inland river sites with adequate assemblages of animal bones pointing to exclusively summer occupation.

Site and annual territory only coincided when settlements were occupied all the year round and under primitive conditions this could only happen when assured sources of food were available within easy reach. This explains the importance from a settlement point of view of the adoption of effective farming, a form of economy that depended in north-western Europe at least in some measure on the introduction of animal and plant species; these certainly included sheep and goat, wheat and barley and perhaps also certain breeds of ox and pig. We must, however, beware of over-simplification. In territories with extensive areas suited to mixed farming we certainly find evidence for settled communities of another order of magnitude from those prevailing among mesolithic peoples. Indeed, sites like Bylany[10] show that on the fertile areas of central Europe the neolithic peasants were able to live in communities of the same scale as their descendants some six thousand years later. Even as far north as Jutland we find in Barkaer[11] evidence for a community of 52 housing units arranged in two opposing terraces dating from the mid IIIrd millennium. But nucleated settlements were by no means general in temperate Europe. In areas where grass rather than cereals was the main crop and cattle-keeping the main activity, settlement was likely to be dispersed in single farmsteads or small hamlets. The same applied to Scandinavia outside Denmark and southernmost Sweden, where farmland, at least of a kind capable of being cultivated by primitive equipment, tended to occur as small patches and where supplies of water were widely dispersed.

Again, in the marginal territories of Scandinavia no clear lines can be drawn between communities who lived mainly by catching and gathering either without or with a bare minimum of planting and stock-raising and those in which the latter activities were predominant. By and large, people gain their living by exerting the minimum of effort. Another point to remember is that the adoption of a settled mode of life by no means precluded the exploitation of more extensive territories by segments of the population. The most familiar illustration of this lies in the Norwegian *seter* or the Swedish *fäbod* system by which parties of young girls accompany cattle to upland pastures for summer grazing and return with the cheese from their dairying. More striking and perhaps less well known is the Finnish *erämaan* custom[12] by which peasant communities in the agricultural zone were able to exercise rights of hunting and fishing in the interior over a radius of up to 250 km.

Certainly the Stone Age peoples of Scandinavia would have been surprised to know that archaeologists of a later date categorised them as advanced or retarded – neolithic or mesolithic (or as a compromise sub-neolithic) – according as their economy approached that of modern western society. What archaeologists have to do is to forget simplistic typologies and discover how in fact prehistoric communities gained a living. The most direct clues to this lie in the organic refuse from their settlements and in the evidence for the shaping of the cultural landscape recoverable above all by palaeobotanical research. In interpreting such clues, I need not emphasise the enormous importance of recent folk usage in the identical region, whether recorded in early historic sources or by modern ethnologists.

Economic prehistory[13] and indeed economic archaeology, the archaeology that concerns itself first and foremost with the productive forces of society, has grown very greatly in importance in recent years in territories where the preliminary stage of establishing spatial and temporal frameworks has been accomplished or at least carried to a stage at which something more interesting becomes possible. But economic archaeology can form its own routine. We must not forget that economy is only a means to an end and that is the maintenance and perpetuation of society. There are already welcome signs, certainly at Cambridge, that bright graduates are beginning to turn to what we might term Social Archaeology. We must never forget that all archaeological data is the product of men who not merely lived in society but owed their very patterns of behaviour by virtue of belonging to social entities. We would be wrong, I think, to dismiss entirely the idea entertained by the early Soviet prehistorians that the terminology of the basic periodisation of archaeological data ought to be based on social structure rather than on technology or subsistence patterns. It may well be that Ephimenko and the rest were merely conforming to propaganda directives in the categories they used. This does not alter the fact that they may have attempted something we too might aim at. And the introduction of new conceptual tools,[14] many of them sharpened and honed by American anthropologists, makes the emergence of Social Archaeology much less far-fetched than might at first appear.

The extent of social territories can be determined in two ways. One is through the geographical patterning of idiosyncratic traits. Here it seems to me is the continuing justification for studying the minutiae of style and form. As indicators of community taste these have the same kind of interest as the plumage of different species of birds. It is through such features as hair-styles, the patterning in a whole range of artifacts, whether utilitarian or decorative, as well as through behavioural patterns, language, value-systems, mythology and the like, that human populations achieve a sense of identity. This appears with particular clarity in the archaeology of elementary societies, societies that is which lack the social stratification which sets up another and complicating range of identity and status patterns. Thus, if we observe the archaeology of the North European plain during the final stages of the Late-glacial, we find, as might be expected, a broad community corresponding to a common ecological setting with reindeer as a principal food resource. Over the whole territory from the Lower Rhine to S. Scandinavia and Poland (fig. 16.3) we find the same type of flint industry, characterised by end-scrapers, burins and tanged points, the same way of utilising reindeer antlers for clubs and a stylistically identical form of biserially barbed harpoon head with triangular base. Yet, as Wolfgang Taute has shown[15] in his meticulous study of the lithic assemblages, there is a pronounced regional patterning in the form and mode of production of the

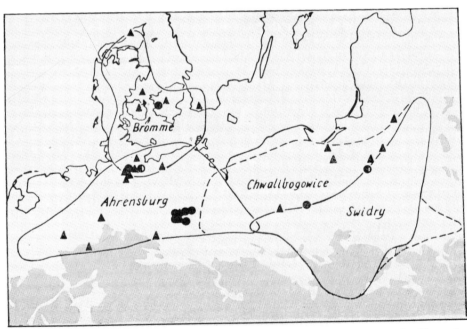

16.3 Map showing Lyngby–Bromme–Segebro, Ahrensburg and Swidry–Chwalibogowice territories. Stippled areas are over 500 m above sea level.

most specialised trait, the tanged point (fig. 16.4). Three main territories can be defined having only minor overlaps:

(a) *Ahrensburgian*. From Belgian Limbourg and Anvers to Schleswig-Holstein, Mecklenburg and Brandenburg.

(b) *Swiderian*. From the Warta to the Neman, but only sporadically on their lower courses. The points, which vary widely in the degree of definition of the tang, resemble those of the Ahrensburg assemblages in lightness and delicacy but differ in that the tangs have been partly shaped by flat flaking on the bulbar surface. No hafted specimens known.

(c) *Bromme*. From Schleswig-Holstein and Mecklenburg over Denmark to South Sweden (Scania with possible extension up the west coast). The points are larger – up to 12 cm (*c.* 5 in.) long – and are as a rule made on flakes from cores so carefully prepared that little or no retouch was often needed for the tip. The tangs have been made exclusively by flakes struck from the bulbar flake surface as in the case of Ahrensburgian points.

To give an idea of the extent of these social territories, the Ahrensburgian covers approx. 120,000 sq. km; the Swiderian approx. 100,000 sq. km; and the Bromme (excluding the possible west coast extension) approx. 70,000 sq. km.

To judge from the distribution of various categories of artifact shaped into animal forms, comparable territories apparently existed among the predominantly hunter-fisher groups of the coniferous forest zone of North Scandinavia and European Russia (fig. 16.5).[16] Thus:

(a) *Two-edged knives of slate with elk-head terminals.*
The distribution in Swedish Norrland covers *c.* 75,000 sq. km but seasonally

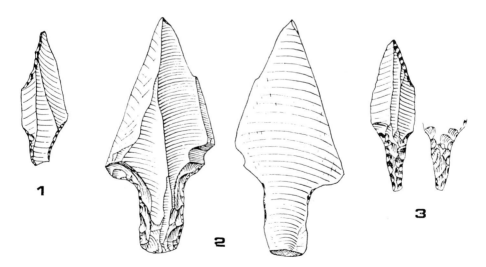

16.4   The leading forms of flint tanged-point in use during the Late-glacial of the N. European Plain. 1 Ahrensburg; 2 Brome–Lyngby; 3 Chwalibogowice (actual size).

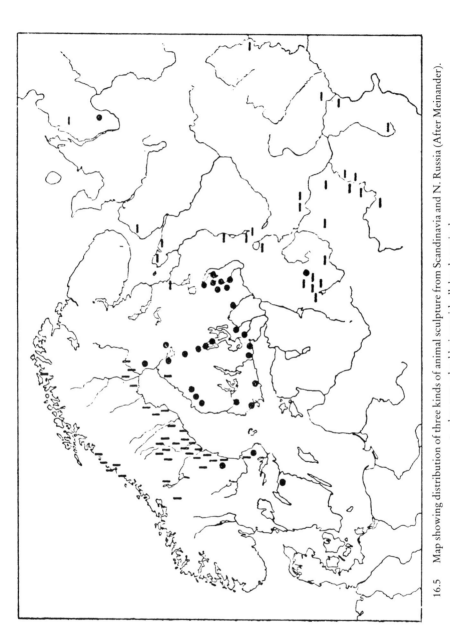

16.5   Map showing distribution of three kinds of animal sculpture from Scandinavia and N. Russia (After Meinander).

| slate two-edged knives with elk head terminals
● perforated stone objects with animal heads
– flints chipped with animal profiles

at least the cortical area must have extended to the north-west Norwegian coast, which would give an area of *c.* 120,000 sq. km.

(b) *Perforated 'maces' and 'axes' with animal head terminals.*
The cortical area includes much of Finland and Carelia and extends over *c.* 170,000 sq. km.

(c) *Flints chipped into the profiles of animals.*
Centred on the Upper Volga-Oka basins with outliers on the White Sea and the Middle Volga. The central area comprises *c.* 120,000 sq. km, but if the territory is extended to include both outliers and the intervening blank zones, this would have to be doubled.

The rather larger size of these territories, especially if account is taken of outliers in the first and third cases, is probably to be linked to the widespread use of sledges and skis.

Now I am well aware that my last example involves the second factor I want to consider, namely, that of redistribution. All human societies known to history are founded on the complementary institutions of the sub-division of labour and the redistribution of products and scarce materials. This applies even to primitive societies among which the sub-division of labour has hardly been carried further than that between the sexes. That this should be so is hardly surprising when it is remembered that societies are at bottom constituted by the existence of reciprocal obligations among and between their members. When the unit normally living together was a microband of no more than three primary families, it must be obvious that some form of exogamy would have been necessary in the long term for bare survival. The web of kinship set up by interchange in marriage, and the fact that every individual had obligations that extended far beyond his immediate circle, taken in conjunction with the fact that relationships were normally recognised and validated by this interchange of gifts and services, was of the highest adaptive value: on the one hand it reinforced social solidarity far beyond the range of territory known to any individual and on the other it had the effect, like trade in our own type of society, of spreading raw materials and skills more evenly over extensive zones. Although redistribution may have served much the same purpose as trade, it was in some respects fundamentally different: whereas trade is carried on by specialists with a narrow economic end in view, the mechanism of redistribution as activated, for example, by the aborigines of Arnhem Land was primarily ceremonial[17] and social and followed the intricate web of kinship obligation without the intervention of any extraneous merchant or trader. For this reason material objects subject to redistribution can serve, whether they were the product of specialised skills or embodied some locally restricted or scarce material, as so to say trace elements which serve to delineate social territories, territories with which people identified and within which they acknowledged kinship and obligation. It is in this light, I suggest, that we ought to interpret the distribution, for example, of axe-blades made from particular factories.[18]

There are many reasons why we cannot expect sharply defined results from studying particular distributions. One I would like to mention arises from the fact that redistribution was by no means limited to particular social territories. The same factor that made redistribution within a territory so advantageous applied also to redistribution as between territories. The alternative to establishing relations between friendly territories would have been damaging conflict and friendly relations were likely to be symbolised by interchange.

We may find examples of this on our map of circumpolar products featuring animal motifs: perforated stone objects with animal heads, for instance, occur in East Sweden, in the Oka-Volga basin and far to the north-east in the basin of the Pechora river.

Again, as appears very plainly in the distribution of stone axes in Britain, centres of outstanding socio-ceremonial importance such as Avebury-Stonehenge attracted examples from several widely separated sources. It has to be remembered that exotic objects, objects derived from outside redistribution systems, were by that very fact endowed with extra value and might be expected to re-enter systems, ceremonial or otherwise, at an enhanced value.

The final topic I wish to touch upon arises from the fact that human settlement occurs through time and is therefore subject to change. This applied even to the last few thousand years of the Stone Age in temperate Europe; and the Stone Age after all does not mark the end, but rather the beginning of the process that has brought us to our present situation. In the early days of archaeology the changes which unfolded in prehistory and provided the very basis for its periodisation were treated rather in the same manner as the writers of the Old Testament treated the creation of the world. Some of the chief figures in the mythology of British Archaeology were invaders.[19] Each change in the way people fastened their safety-pins, each innovation in ceramics, each variation in the hilts of 'leaf-shaped swords' was ascribed to a different group of invaders, who because they were anonymous were thoughtfully provided with the names of the artifacts they were held to have introduced. The ensuing pantomime would have been harmless enough if some people had not proceeded to accept it as corresponding to historical fact.

Today we are accustomed to the notion that archaeological data is best understood as the residue of social systems and to seek for explanations of change in terms of social change. The social anthropologists have accustomed us to think of human societies as working systems which comprise every-thing from value systems to the ecology of the social territory. In the short term the leading feature of such systems is their stability: cohesion, coherence, conformity and continuity are ensured by a plenitude of sanctions. Cultural patterns survive because they are of high adaptive value. Conversely, it is only societies that achieved stability for a sufficient period of time that feature in the archaeological record. Again, one has to remember that the law of the conservation of energy applies to man as much as to any other component of the universe. The force of inertia institutionalised in custom was even more powerful in prehistory than it is today.

The reverse of the medal is that in modern times the rate of change has speeded up very greatly. Yet change has been active since the earliest times. Had it not been there would be no such thing as prehistory. Social systems, so long as they function effectively, are able to withstand pressures making for change rather as organisms are able to adjust to passing changes in the environment without undergoing structural change. The homeostatic principle only breaks down when the effort involved in maintaining equilibrium passes a certain threshold beyond which it becomes economic to undertake a rapid and quite radical re-adjustment of a kind we recognise as a major change. In seeking to account for major changes, whether in the field of human society or of the habitat or biome, a distinction has to be made between proximate causes and the underlying pressures that impair the resistance of systems. If social systems can be considered as in any sense structured to maintaining equilibrium at any moment of time, it follows that when pressures for change have built up beyond a certain point the upset could be quite sudden and be brought about by any one of a number of immediate causes, including mere historical contingency, few if any of which may be reflected in the archaeological record.

Two main classes of underlying pressure need to be distinguished. First, there is what may be termed economic dynamism. For example, when land is occupied it is likely to be taken up selectively in accordance with social preferences and technology up to the limits imposed by environmental constraints: some tracts will be ignored, others occupied and within these certain kinds of site will be preferred. During this pioneer stage the total population, though not of course the density of population, will increase until the point is reached where its needs can no longer be met by customary means from the available preferred land. What happens next will depend on reaction to the closing of the frontiers. If social constraints are used to maintain population at its existing density, the economic and social life may continue without changes of a kind likely to be reflected in the archaeological record. The converse is true, that if any one or more of a number of ways of increasing the food supply are adopted – for instance, through the more effective use of areas already settled, through the taking in of poorer secondary land areas or through increased exploitation of sea-foods – then more or less marked changes are likely to occur in economic and social structures allowing increased densities of population; and this in turn may precipitate significant changes in settlement and social hierarchy. It goes without saying that the story is likely to be greatly complicated if account is taken of environmental change.

Next there are pressures from the environment, both the immediate natural environment and the cultural environment. As to the former, if social systems are hinged into ecosystems, it follows that changes, whether in the habitat or the biosphere, are likely to make for change in the system as a whole. On the other hand, environmental changes are not in themselves either favourable or hostile. They are both. By altering the conditions to which social systems are adjusted they impede some choices and facilitate others. Natural conditions impose constraints, but they also offer opportunities. Thus in south Scandinavia, the onset of warm climate during the early Post-glacial brought a rather sudden end to regimes based on reindeer, but at the same time opened up the possibility of adapting to an environment dominated by forest, an adaptation that marks for prehistorians the transition in this part of the world from Advanced Palaeolithic to Mesolithic. When temperatures rose sufficiently for the oak-mixed forest to dominate and spread beyond its present northern limits, it at the same time made it possible to adopt a mixed farming economy at least in the more favoured areas. Again, the decline of temperature towards the close of the prehistoric period, if it disadvantaged mixed farming in northern and extreme western territories, was on the other hand favourable to a regime based on hay-making and cattle husbandry.

Another main threat to the stability of established systems came from the socio-cultural environment and in particular from contact with other systems. This can only be considered apart from the natural environment for purposes of analysis. It must frequently have happened that shifts in population were linked with changes in the habitat and/or biosphere, which, as we have seen, were influential in undermining systems on their own account. Movements of people in competition for land, such as are documented from the historical period, whether caused by environmental change or some historical contingency, were only one of the mechanisms by which contact was established with systems exercising different options and informed by different values. To judge from the experiences of modern primitive peoples, it seems likely enough that ideas and concepts could also move across socio-cultural divides. A factor that came to play a part of special importance when communities at different levels of economic achievement came into contact was social emulation. This grew in importance as societies became more stratified, since it is characteristic of elites that they should seek to emphasise their separate identity by displaying exotic possessions; and innovations acquired by the few would have filtered down the social scale by virtue of prestige. Another way of putting the matter would be to say that contacts with neighbours were capable of and in fact normally did generate new appetites and frequently the know-how by which to realise them, something illustrated with particular clarity in the spread of copper and bronze metallurgy.

The final point which comes out of settlement archaeology, when studied in one region relative to a long period of time, is the basic fact of continuity. Whatever the changes, whether representing adjustments to changes in the natural environment or whether the result of contact with other systems brought about by the spread of ideas, of redistribution between social territories or indeed by actual movements of population, we return to the essential fact that systems continued to operate under the dead weight of millennia of custom. We ought not to be surprised by continuity in lithic or ceramic traditions. Let me end by quoting a couple of sentences from the Introduction to Professor Lawrence Stone's distinguished book on *The Crisis of the Aristocracy 1558–1641:*

Words like 'crisis' and 'revolution' should not come tripping too lightly from the historian's pen. History lumbers jerkily on with few real breaks from the past. The forces of inertia ensure an amazing degree of continuity in human affairs, whatever the strength of the pressures for change that are brought to bear.

Let us remember this when we draw hard lines across period tables, even when we draw them obliquely.

Notes

1 J. G. D. Clark, D. Walker, H. Godwin, F. C. Fraser and J. E. King, *Excavations at Star Carr* (Cambridge University Press, 1954, 1971).

2 Grahame Clark, 'Star Carr: a Case Study in Bioarchaeology', *Addison-Wesley Modular Publications in Anthropology*, No. 10 (Reading, Mass., 1972).

3 B. Barnes, B. J. N. Edwards, J. S. Hallam and A. J. Stuart, *Nature*, 232 (1971), 488–9.

4 A. Rust, *Die alt- und mittelsteinzeitlichen Funde von Stellmoor* (Neumünster, 1943).

5 A. Rust, *Das altsteinzeitliche rentierjägerlager Meiendorf* (Neumünster, 1937).

6 D. A. Sturdy, 'Reindeer Economies in Late Ice Age Europe.' Ph.D. Thesis, Cambridge, 1972.

7 M. Degerbøl and H. Krog, 'The Reindeer (*Rangifer tarandus L.*) in Denmark', *Biol. Skr. Danske Videnskab. Selskab.*, 10, nr. 4 (Copenhagen, 1959).

8 J. Iversen, 'The Late-Glacial Flora of Denmark and its Relation to Climate and Soil', *Danmarks Geologiske Undersogelse*, 11 R., nr. 80 (Copenhagen, 1954).

9 Haakon Olsen, 'Varanger-Funnene. IV. Osteologisk Materiale', *Tromsø Museums Skr.*, 7, hft. 4 (Tromsø, 1967).

10 B. Soudsky, *Bylany* (Prague, 1966).

11 P. V. Glob, 'Barkaer, Danmarks aeldste landsby', *Fra Nationalmuseets Arbejdsmark* (Copenhagen, 1949), 5–16.

12 *Suomen Historian Kartaso*, map 4 (Helsinki, 1959).

13 Grahame Clark, 'The Economic Approach to Prehistory', *Proc. British Acad.*, 39 (1953), 215–38.

14 D. L. Clarke (ed.), *Models in Archaeology* (London, 1972).

15 W. Taute, *Die Stielspitzen-Gruppen im Nördlichen Mitteleuropa* (Köln, 1968).

16 C. F. Meinander, 'Die Kiukaiskultur', *Finska Fornminnesföreningens Tidskrift*, no. 53, abb. 51 (Helskini, 1954).

17 Donald Thomson, *Economic Structure and the Ceremonial Exchange Cycle in Arnhem Land* (London, 1949).
18 Grahame Clark, 'Traffic in Stone Axe and Adze Blades', *Econ. Hist. Rev.*, 18 (1965), 1–28.
19 Grahame Clark, 'The Invasion Hypothesis in British Archaeology', *Antiquity*, 40 (1966), 172–89.

CHAPTER 17

SEASONALITY AND THE INTERPRETATION OF LITHIC ASSEMBLAGES

In adding to the tributes offered to Professor Luis Pericot, I wish to touch upon a theme which bears directly on our understanding of the life of prehistoric man, a subject to which our distinguished and beloved colleague has dedicated so much of his life. Seasonality is a topic which confronts anyone concerned with living communities in a direct fashion whatever their stage of technology. It is therefore fair to assume that it played a significant role in prehistoric times and not least among stone age peoples whose economy was based wholly or completely on hunting and gathering.

Even today, the revenues of great commercial enterprises are affected by seasonal vagaries affecting the consumption of ice-cream or of oil for heating. Until comparatively recently, the lives of even the most advanced European societies were regulated by the rhythms of the farming year. Among societies lacking the means for bulk transport or the prolonged and large-scale conservation of food, the effect of seasonal change on the tempo of social life was even more pronounced. Even so seasonal changes were less marked in the case of peasant societies, able to occupy the same settlements all the year round, than they were among hunter-fishers or pastoralists who had to change not merely their occupations but their settlements in the course of the year in order to maximise the return from their territories.

As ethnographers have been at pains to emphasise, even people as primitive in respect of their technology as the Australian aborigines have a remarkably intimate and detailed knowledge of natural resources. Indeed it is only by this means that people like the Wik Monkan of Queensland or the Arnhemlanders of the Northern Territories have managed not merely to survive but to live well, sometimes under conditions which we would regard as extreme. Their very survival and well-being depends one might say on their ability as empirical ecologists. Such people may well and generally do occupy a home base for a longish period – the Wik Monkan for example shelter in bark huts at a fixed site through the season of heaviest rainfall – but in the course of the year they habitually move over an extensive territory, camping for varying periods at different spots, but essentially moving from one seasonal source of food to another. People like the Wik Monkan are sometimes referred to as though they were parasitical or exploitive by contrast with the productive or manipulative stance of more settled communities. An alternative way of viewing the matter would be to see hunter-gatherers as people who depended on cropping or harvesting a broad range of natural products, not haphazardly or randomly but systematically and in an orderly manner. The more deficient the technology, the greater the dependence on understanding the properties and habits of animals and plants of the territory from which they had to gain their living. The movements of such peoples over their respective territories were far indeed from the random wanderings of popular fiction; they were on the contrary a direct outcome of the knowledge they had of the availability of different sources of food at various times of the year.

The bearing of this on the interpretation of archaeological data was fully appreciated by Donald Thomson (1939) in his classic paper 'The Seasonal Factor in Human Culture illustrated from the life of a contemporary nomadic group'. As he implied, archaeologists, more especially those concerned with traces of hunter-fishers, should always bear in mind that the material from any particular site or level may only reflect a range of activities carried on at a particular season or seasons. The ethnologist observing living 'people at different seasons of the year' might 'find them engaged in occupations so diverse, and with weapons and utensils differing so much in character, that if he were unaware of the seasonal influence on food supply' he might be 'led to conclude that they (belonged to) different groups' (Thomson, 1939, 209). Conversely, when the prehistorian is confronted by varying facies of the same basic industry he does well to remember that one explanation may relate to the seasonal activities of the same group rather than to the cultures of different groups.

The study of seasonality like that of prehistory in general can be approached from either of two directions. The conventional way, which also happens to be the more laborious and the less rewarding, is to focus on or be captivated by the vast mass of flint and stone which represents the ultimate detritus of early hunter-gatherer societies. Morphological analysis of lithic industries, especially when based as it is today on the assessment of total assemblages, is an essential tool for prehistorians. The danger lies in its fascination as a sphere of activity sufficient to itself; and this danger is enhanced by the almost limitless supplies of material and the increasing possibilities opened up by electronic facilities and ever more sophisticated analytical techniques. The development of more objective methods of categorising lithic data and of more effective methods of displaying differences and convergences, for instance, whether by cumulative graphs (Bordes, 1950) or by comparative histograms (Bohmers, 1953), laid a firm foundation for further advance towards understanding the life of prehistoric man, but this advance could only come by positive action. An essential question posed by Freeman (1966) and the Binfords (1966) was precisely what do variations in the composition of lithic assemblages portend? If assemblages of flint and stone artifacts reflect in some way the preoccupations of the people who made them, it must be true that the more narrowly these can be defined the more precisely problems for research can be formulated. The only question is whether these problems are likely to be solved by continuing to pursue a single thread of evidence with the aid of ever more refined means – or whether results could not more easily be obtained by working in the opposite direction and seeking to bring as many kinds of evidence as can be found to bear directly onto the central concern of prehistory, that is the kind of life lived by prehistoric man? The Binfords in the final section of their fascinating 'Preliminary Analysis of Functional Variability in the Mousterian of Levallois Facies' (1966) suggested a trifle coyly that 'kinds of data not available for our study such as animal bone . . . pollen and plant remains, etc., might be profitably investigated'. Indeed they might.

If we accept, as we surely must, that the object of prehistory is to discover how men lived in the prehistoric past, it would seem to follow that we might consider making a more direct, bioarchaeological approach. If we are concerned with life, there is much to be said for studying the fossils of life. The Binfords were of course right to accept that flint implements were made to be used and that in consequence the make-up and profile of lithic assemblages may be accepted as indications of the activities of those responsible for them. But what precisely were flint tools for if not to utilize the environment, secure and prepare food and shape the organic substances needed for a broad range of equipment? If we want to understand why lithic stages or facies vary from one another, a question which from a bioarchaeo-logical point of view is perhaps framed the wrong way round, then surely we need to view the flints and stones in the context of the organic substances that they were designed to manipulate? Within the limitations of a cave – and limestone after all is exceptionally favourable for the survival of animal bones – McBurney has shown (1968) in respect of the sequence of Ali Tappeh, north-east Iran, how much can be learned by plotting fluctuations in the make-up of successive lithic assemblages in collation with changes in the environment and in the utilization of resources abstracted from this environ-ment. Viewed in the context of bioarchaeology changes in artifact assem-blages need no longer be viewed conventionally as evidence for the replacement of one 'culture' by another, but rather as the outcome of changes in the utilization of natural resources in the course of time, changes which may of course be highlighted or dramatized by intermissions in occupation.

If we accept that the most resistant and therefore most widespread residues of prehistoric communities can best be understood in the light of the maximum information about organic materials, and if these only survive where particular conditions obtain, then it might be argued, as I implied many years ago (1939, ch. III) in a text-book designed for students, that prehistorians might do well to pay more attention to problems of survival.

Whether or not, pace Lord Snow, a knowledge of the Second Law of Thermodynamics is a valid criterion of an educated man in the mid-twentieth century, it is an unquestionable fact that an understanding of the practical implications of this law is vital to an intelligent practice of archaeology. If physical processes proceed in the direction of degradation, if the material evidence on which the very possibility of archaeology depends disintegrates and disappears in the course of time, then an understanding of the circumstances under which this process is delayed or even temporarily inhibited is likely to prove rewarding. It is surely the beginning of wisdom to concentrate attention on sites or finds where such physical processes as desiccation, refrigeration or water-logging have permitted the survival of the maximum range of organic materials. From this point of view it is a mistake to look upon such things as the bog finds of Jutland (Glob, 1969), the dry caves of Mexico (MacNeish in Byers (ed.), 1967), Peru (MacNeish, 1969–70), and Nevada (Heizer and Krieger, 1956), or the frozen tombs of the Altai (Rudenko, 1970) as peripheral curiosities. On the contrary they are not only mines of information, but reminders of what we ought to look for. Returning to seasonality, Freeman (1966, 235) was surely correct to think that a possible explanation of Mousterian facies lay in the practice of seasonal activities. What is on the other hand sure is that proof of what these may have been is not to be sought in the first instance from the lithic assemblages themselves: it is to be found in the organic residues which under certain verifiable conditions accompany them; and these residues can only be recovered where they survive.*

Star Carr (Clark, 1954/1971) is a case in point. For years the only traces of early Post-glacial hunter-gatherers known from England comprised assemblages of worked flint and scattered finds of barbed spearheads made of bone or antler. In a few instances these could be tied into the record of environmental change by means of pollen-analysis, but in no case could lithic assemblages be linked with food refuse or even with artifacts of antler or bone. No doubt intensive collecting might have resulted in the recovery of more assemblages of flint artifacts; and of course all available lithic assemblages, whether or not newly recovered, could be subjected to intensive analysis. For the reasons given I preferred to take the other course and wait for a site offering reasonable prospects of recovering an adequate sample of animal remains, including artifacts, debris of working and food refuse. The discovery of the site of Star Carr on the northern shore of the lake that once occupied the eastern end of the Vale of Pickering in East Yorkshire offered precisely the right conditions, since the water-logged deposits on its lakeward side contained a lithic assemblage together with abundant traces of animal and plant remains.

Palynology and radio-carbon analysis between them showed that it was occupied, almost certainly on several occasions, during an early phase in the development of Neothermal forests in northern England towards the end of the birch phase in the mid-eighth millennium B.C. (C 352: av. of two runs 7538 B.C. ± 350). As a result of almost complete excavations, it could be seen that the site can hardly have carried more than three or four hunters and their biological families, corresponding in scale to a 'micro-band' in MacNeish's terminology (MacNeish, 1971). Examination of the animal skeletal material which was present in quantity and in a fine state of preservation gave an insight into the main basis of subsistence and provided the evidence needed to establish seasonality. It seems that herbivorous animals were the main quarry and it is estimated that these provided meat in the following proportions:

Species	%
Red deer *(Cervus elaphus L.)*	61
Roe deer *(C. capreolus L.)*	3
Elk *(Alces alces L.)*	9
Aurochs *(Bos primigenius Boj)*	25
Wild Pig *(Sus scrofa L.)*	2

The most telling source of information about the season of occupation was provided by the antlers of red deer, roe deer and elk, since, though being shed and renewed at varying dates from year to year, these were nevertheless keyed into the annual cycles. The mere fact that the great majority (65 out of 106) of red deer antlers had been broken out of or were still attached to their skulls argues that they were killed during the winter. It is highly relevant that red deer were represented almost exclusively by adult stags of four years or older: of the 106 antlers only 2 came from an animal in its second year and 6 in an animal in its third year. The fact that there were only two skulls of hinds is consistent with a wide use of resources, since it would plainly have been improvident to cull hinds at a time of the year when most of them were carrying young. Quite evidently the inhabitants of Star Carr were culling adult stags at a time of the year when, having completed the rut, these were concentrated in yards on their own, congregating for the winter on sheltered ground in the east end of the Vale of Pickering. The fact that the material from Star Carr relates to the intensive culling of adult stags on low ground is in itself another strong pointer to winter occupation.

How late in the year did the encampment last? A point to note is that shed antlers of red deer, although in a minority, were nevertheless numerous. It cannot be stated dogmatically that because these are shed in April they necessarily imply occupation until that time of the year, since shed antlers might have been carried to the site. Yet it hardly seems likely that they were carried throughout seasonal migrations and back to the winter base; and in any case the presence of three crania and two frontlets from which antlers had been cast argues for occupation into if not beyond the period of casting. The presence of considerable numbers of well developed roe deer also indicates occupation until the spring, since these animals do not discard the velvet from their antlers until April. When the occupation began is less well defined. It could be argued that the complete absence of shed roe deer antlers argues against occupation as early as October, since these animals cast their antlers in that month, but this would be to imply that shed antlers were necessarily collected by man. In the case of red deer we know that antler was keenly sought and used, but there is no evidence that they in fact had any interest in roe deer antlers: not a single cut has been noted on any single one of the numerous specimens still attached to or broken out of the skull. Another clue is provided by the elk antlers from Star Carr. These consisted almost equally of shed and unshed specimens. Since these animals normally shed their antlers during January, this seems to suggest that the site was occupied for some months before this time.

The evidence for industrial activity at Star Carr agrees very well with the idea that the site was occupied at a time of the year when it was convenient and consistent with good herd maintenance to concentrate on culling stags. The most outstanding feature of the site from an archaeological point of view is the abundance of stag antler and the intensity with which this material was exploited. Among red deer, it is of course only stags that carry antlers and it was during the winter that these were most compact and suitable for use as a raw material. Something like four-fifths of the mature antlers from the site had been subject to the process by which splinters of the hard outer surface layer had been isolated by deep grooves and prised out for use as blanks for making the barbed spearheads which were by far the commonest artifacts made from antler or bone from the site. Again it is significant that the flint burin, the tool commonly associated with the groove and splinter technique (Clark and Thomson, 1953) was by a small margin the commonest single type of finished flint implement from this site. In other words there is abundant artifactual evidence that while they camped at Star Carr the inhabitants took the opportunity to manufacture the spearheads they needed during the whole year. Thus industrial activity fitted admirably with the food quest.

If the animal remains from Star Carr itself give a clear indication that the site was occupied during the winter, it may next be asked, where the inhabitants spent the warmer time of the year. To answer this we must consider a wider range of evidence than that contained in the actual finds from Star Carr itself. Most important are the seasonal movements of the herbivorous animals on which the hunters depended and notably of the red deer which provided more than two-thirds of their meat; and these have to be considered in relation to the topography of the north of England and of Yorkshire in particular (fig. 17.1). The evidence of animal ecology (Ingebrig-

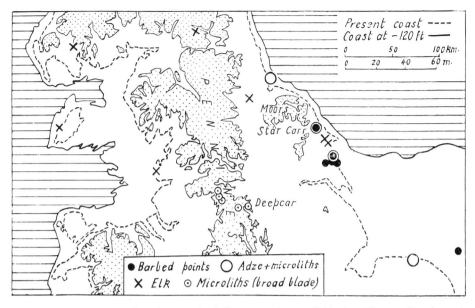

17.1 Map of northern England showing Early Mesolithic sites. The coastline shown is that existing at the transition from Late-glacial to Post-glacial. The stippled zone denotes land at present 152.5 m above sea level

sten, 1924; Darling, 1969) allows us to assume that the deer responded to seasonal change by shifting their feeding grounds. In areas of marked surface relief the highest ground would have been cropped at the peak of summer and in winter refuge would be taken on low sheltered ground. Movement from low-lying winter yards onto the moors must have been gradual since the vegetation on which red deer and other herbivores depended appeared first on the lower slopes and reached its climax on the higher ground only during the summer. According to Darling the deer were started on their move to shelter by their anticipation of snow at which they are particularly apt. Shelter and sunlight are two key factors in the choice of winter refuge areas. This makes it easy to understand why the eastern end of the Vale of Pickering should have been chosen and in particular why its northern side with a gradual slope exposed to the sun and penetrated by valleys carrying small streams and rivers should have been favoured.

When camp was broken in the spring this was doubtless connected with the seasonal movement of deer and other herbivores. The lie of the land and the availability of extensive feeding grounds at mounting altitudes on the North Yorkshire Moors argues for a northward movement; and it is significant that not merely Star Carr itself, but all other finds of comparable material in the Vale of Pickering, are situated on the north of the Derwent river and of the lake which once existed, in the neighbourhood. That mesolithic microbands or individual households exploited this high ground is shown by the many assemblages of mesolithic flints including microliths and an occasional stray find of a chipped flint axe or adze, from sites up to 320 m (1250 ft) on the Moors. The presumption is that this occupation of the high moors occurred at a time when herbivorous animals were feeding on the upland vegetation.

There is fuller and more directly relevant evidence from the high Pennines, the mountain backbone of northern England, that analogous groups, who may have wintered either side on the Cheshire and Morecambe Plains and in the Vale of York, similarly followed herbivorous animals onto high ground during the summer. Lithic assemblages of mesolithic type, including microliths, flake scrapers, a few burins and occasional axe or adze blades, have long been known from sites on the high ridges and crests of the Pennines up to 426 m (1400 ft) above sea-level in situations too exposed to have been habitable in this latitude without substantial protection except during the summer. Exposures of the old surface revealed by the erosion of overlying ombrogenous peat have been intensively searched by flint collectors and failed to reveal any trace of substantial structure. All Francis Buckley and others have found (Clark, 1932, 23) were small patches of flint and occasional traces of burning indicating transitory visits by small numbers of people. Traces of a more substantial encampment of people making the same type of industry have recently been found on a low spur of the Pennines at Deepcar (Radley and Mellars, 1964) a few miles north-west of Sheffield overlooking the Vale of York at a height of 152 m (500 ft). The presumption is that Deepcar dates from an intermediate period between winter and summer and since deer move down rather rapidly to winter shelter at the first premonition of snow it seems more likely that this encampment relates to the spring than to the autumn.

It was for long the orthodox view (e.g. Clark, 1932) that two distinct groups of cultures co-existed in England during the earlier part of the Post-glacial period: one had a predominantly microlithic aspect, was mainly based on the highland zone and was once considered to be closely analogous to microlithic industries from Belgium; the other, enriched by an axe-adze component and by artifacts of antler and bone, which made it comparable to the Maglemosian of northern Europe, was confined to the lowland zone, predominantly to the Thames basin and Holderness, Yorkshire. This picture was first modified when Wainwright (1960) showed that such a 'Maglemosian' component as the axe or adze with transversely sharpened cutting edge in reality interpenetrated the microlithic province as far as Wales and south-west England. A further advance was made by Radley and Mellars (1964), who, in publishing the results of their excavation of a hut-emplacement at Deepcar on a low spur of the Pennines, undertook a revision of the relationship between the microlithic industries of northern Britain and those associated with the 'Maglemosian' group.

The lithic assemblage at Deepcar was compared in the first instance to one of the two groups of microlithic assemblages recovered by Francis Buckley from the crests of the Pennines. Buckley distinguished (Clark, 1932):
(a) a 'broad-blade' industry made from grey flint, probably from the chalk of the Lincolnshire or Yorkshire Wolds, with microliths over 1.5 cm long and mainly of elementary forms;
(b) a 'narrow-blade' industry of translucent flint, including micro-geometric forms under 1 cm in length.

On purely typological grounds and by comparison with European assemblages I maintained in 1932 (Clark, 1932, 27) that the 'broad-blade' assemblage was the earlier of the two. Since then pollen-analysis has confirmed a late date for the 'narrow blade' group: the assemblage from Stump Cross, Yorkshire, was dated by Walker (1956) to zone VII a (Atlantic) and an analogous industry from Peacock's Farm, Shippea Hill (Clark, 1955), East Anglia has been dated to zone VI c (Late Boreal) with a radio-carbon age of 5650 B.C. ± 150. No pollen-analytical or radio-carbon date is yet available for the 'broad-blade' microlithic assemblage. The analogy still rests with the microlithic component of assemblages dating from early in the Post-glacial period. The achievement of Radley and Mellars was to bring out that in fact the 'broad-blade' microlithic industries of the Pennines from such sites as Lominot, Warcock Hill and Windy Hill found their nearest analogues in the microlithic component of British 'Maglemosian' assemblages.

When the 'broad-blade' microlithic assemblages of the high Pennines are compared with total 'Maglemosian' assemblages, such as the one revealed most completely at Star Carr, the most obvious distinguishing feature lies in the organic component and more particularly in the antler and bone artifacts; whereas neither Pennine microlithic assemblage yielded a single artifact of these materials, Star Carr (fig. 17.2) produced 191 barbed spearpoints, 9 bevelled tines and 21 masks of red deer antler, as well as 5 mattock-heads and 8 bodkins of elk antler and bone and 11 scraping tools made from the metapodials and femora of bos, not to mention miscellaneous forms and a great quantity of waste products and debris resulting from the exploitation of antler and bone. But this is only a distinction of museological relevance. If Star Carr encampment had been situated on the high Pennines not a single trace of this organic component would have survived. It is simply that the low-lying, and according to our hypothesis winter, bases were in some instances sufficiently water-logged to inhibit or reduce bacteriological activity and so permit the survival of the organic component.

If we turn to the lithic assemblages (fig. 17.3), the observable differences can be explained for the most part as well in functional as in 'cultural' terms. A feature of British Maglemosian industries on which a good deal of emphasis has been laid in the past (Clark, 1932) is the presence of axes and more often of adzes flaked down from nodules or thick flakes and sharpened

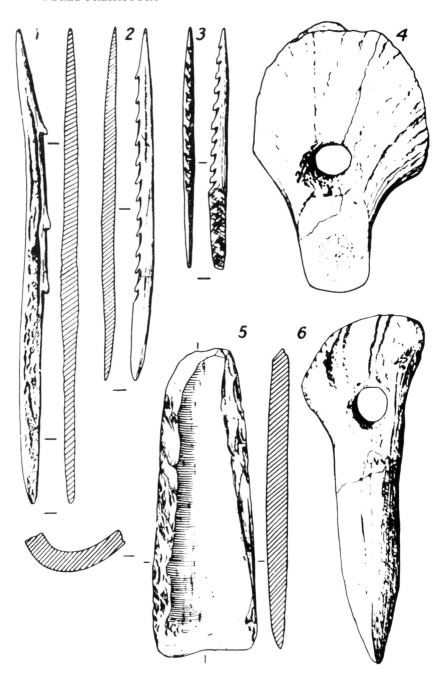

17.2 Antler and bone component of the Star Carr assemblage (2/3)

Table showing composition of lithic assemblages from Star Carr and Deepcar

	Star Carr	*Deepcar*
Burins	334	7
Scrapers (flake)	326	37
Microliths	248	68
Core scrapers	122	–
Narrow awls	107	–
Truncated flakes	48	5
Miscellaneous	23	23
Axes, adzes	7	1?
(Axe/adez sharpening flakes)	(26)	(–)
Totals	1,215	141

by a transverse blow producing a characteristic sharpening flake. That these were no longer found exclusively on the lowland sites is shown by the recovery of rare but typical specimens on the Pennines and the Moors, not to mention a single sharpening flake from Pike Low (Radley and Mellars, 1964, fig. 10). On the other hand there was evidently much less call for the use of axes or adzes on the highland sites. At Star Carr the occurrence of 7 specimens and still more eloquently of no less than 26 sharpening flakes can readily be accounted for when it is realized that the encampment was situated on a birchwood platform resting directly on the reed swamp bordering the lake: the felled birch trees on the lakeward side of the platform (Clark, 1954, pl. IV) showed evident signs of the use of axes or adzes. The marked difference in the occurrence of these tools on the lowland and highland sites respectively relates in part to the nature of the vegetation – Star Carr was immediately environed by birch woods – and in part to differences in the character of the settlements, the one a fixed winter base on a swamp, the others presumably comprising tents or light shelters relating to transitory occupation of the mountain uplands during the summer.

Two of the main components numerically speaking, namely flake scrapers and microliths, were strongly represented in each assemblage. This is hardly surprising since animals must have been hunted and skinned at all times of the year. The lack of core-scrapers, abundant at Star Carr, but apparently absent from Deepcar, goes hand in hand with the scarcity of cores at this site, a fact relating to the absence of locally available flint and consequently to the industrial activities carried on there. Two remaining groups of flint artifact, namely burins and awls on steeply edge-blunted flakes, are much less strongly represented on the upland sites than at Star Carr. Awls on narrow flakes with steep flaking appear to be absent from Deepcar, though examples are known from the Pennines (Radley and Mellars, 1964, fig. 9, 82). The relative importance of burins is well seen by their ratios to the other largest groups, namely flake scrapers and microliths at the two sites:

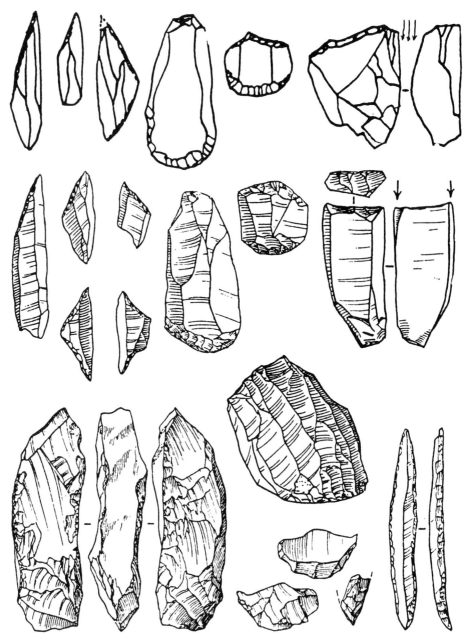

17.3 Lithic component of Early Mesolithic assemblages from Deepcar (top row) and Star Carr, Yorkshire (actual size)

	Star Carr	Deepcar
Burins: scrapers	1.02	0.19
Burins: microliths	1.35	0.10

In the case of the former and conceivably also the latter this may well relate to the working of antler. The very high representation of burins in the Star Carr assemblage – they were marginally the most numerous class – has been linked (Clark and Thompson, 1953) with some reason to the task of cutting blanks for spearheads from stag antlers by the groove and splinter technique, an activity understandably important during the winter when the antlers were fully developed and tough. Conversely the much lower representation of burins at Deepcar and on the sites on the Moors and the High Pennines reflects the fact that during the summer the stags were not carrying antlers at a stage of growth that made them suitable for working.

To sum up, there is no need to accept that differences in the mesolithic assemblages in Northern England during the earlier part of Post-glacial time imply the co-existence of two 'cultures'. They could equally well reflect seasonal aspects of the same population. On the basis of the flints themselves no definite answer could be provided however sophisticated the analytical procedures employed. Analysis of the biological materials, even when this has only so far proved possible for lowland assemblages, argues on the other hand convincingly that the seasonal explanation is the correct one for the observed difference.

*Much more can be recovered than often meets the eye, through the use of appropriate equipment. The apparatus for recovering plant residues from archaeological deposits developed by Eric Higgs' unit concerned with the Early History of Agriculture at Cambridge is a case in point.

References

BINFORD, L. K., and BINFORD, S. R. (1966). 'A preliminary analysis of functional variability in the Mousterian of levallois facies', in *Recent Studies in Paleoanthropology*, ed. J. Desmond Clark and F. Clark Howell, American Anthropological Association, pp. 238–95.

BOHMERS, A. (1956). 'Statistics and graphs in the study of flint assemblages', in *Paleohistoria*, v, I, 38. Groningen.

BORDES, F. H. (1950). 'Principes d'une méthode d'étude des techniques de débitage et de la typologie du Paléolithique Ancien et Moyen', in *L'Anthropologie*, 54, 19–34.

BYERS, DOUGLAS S. (ed.) (1967). *The Prehistory of the Tehuacan Valley. Vol. I. Environment and Subsistence*. University of Texas Press, Austin and London.

CLARK, G. (1939, 1957). *Archaeology and Society*, ch. III. Methuen, London.

CLARK, J. G. D. (1932). *The Mesolithic Age in Britain*. Cambridge, University Press.

   (1954/1971). *Excavations at Star Carr, an Early Mesolithic Site at Seamer, near Scarborough, Yorkshire*. Cambridge, University Press.

   (1955). 'A microlithic industry from the Cambridgeshire Fenland and other industries of Sauveterrian affinities from Britain', in *Proceedings of the Prehistoric Society*, XXI, 3–20.

   (1971). *Star Carr: a case study in bioarchaeology*. Addison-Wesley Modular Program in Anthropology, Reading, Massachusetts.

CLARK, J. G. D. and THOMPSON, M. W. (1953). 'The groove and splinter technique of working antler in Upper Palaeolithic and Mesolithic Europe', in *Proceedings of the Prehistoric Society*, XIX, 148–60.

DARLING, FRASER. (1969). *A Herd of Red Deer*. Oxford, University Press.

FREEMAN, LESLIE G. (1966). 'The Nature of Mousterian facies in Cantabrian Spain', in *Recent Studies in Paleoanthropology*, ed. J. Desmond Clark and F. Clark Howell, American Anthropological Association, pp. 230–7.

GGLOB, P. V. (1969). *The Bog People: Iron-Age Man Preserved*. Faber and Faber, London.

HEIZER, R. F., and KEIEGER, A. D. (1956). *The Archaeology of Humboldt Cave, Churchill County, Nevada*. University of California Publications in American Archaeology and Ethnology, vol. 47, no. 1. Berkeley and Los Angeles.

INGEBRIGSTEN, O. (1942). *Hjortens Utbredelse i Norge*. Bergen: Naturvidenskabelige rekke. No. 6.

MACNEISH, R. S. (1969–70). *1st and 2nd Annual Reports of the Ayacucho Archaeological-Botanical Project*. Peabody Foundation for Archaeology, Andover, Massachusetts.

——— (1971). 'Speculation about how and why food-production and village life developed in the Tehuacan valley, Mexico', in *Archaeology*, 24, 307–15.

McBURNEY, C. B. M. (1968). 'The Cave of Ali Tappeh and the Epi-Palaeolithic in N. E. Iran', in *Proceedings of the Prehistoric Society*, XXXIV, 385–413.

RADLEY, J., and MELLARS, P. (1964). 'A Mesolithic Structure at Deepcar, Yorkshire, England, and the Affinities of its Associated Flint Industries', in *Proceedings of the Prehistoric Society*, XXX, 1–24.

RUDENKO, S. I. (1970). *Frozen Tombs of Siberia: the Pazyryk Burials of Iron-Age Horsemen* (transl. M. W. Thompson). Dent, London.

THOMSON, DONALD, R. (1939). 'The seasonal factor in human culture illustrated from the life of a contemporary nomadic group', in *Proceedings of the Prehistoric Society*, V, 209–21.

——— (1949). *Economic Structure and the Ceremonial Exchange Cycle in Arnhem Land*. Macmillan: London and Melbourne.

WAINWRIGHT, G. J. (1960). 'Three microlithic industries from south-west England and their affinities', in *Proceedings of the Prehistoric Society*, XXVI, 193–201.

WALKER, D. (1956). 'A Site at Stump Cross, near Grassington, Yorkshire, and the age of the Pennine microlithic industry,' in *Proceedings of the Prehistoric Society*, XXII, 23–8.

CHAPTER 18

A BALTIC CAVE SEQUENCE:
A FURTHER STUDY
IN BIOARCHAEOLOGY

In this brief but sincere offering to Professor Richard Pittioni I would like to pay tribute to one particular aspect of his work as a prehistorian, namely his realistic approach to specific problems. In particular I am thinking of his sustained attack on problems concerned with the mining and production of copper in the Austrian Tyrol carried out in conjunction with Ernst Preuschen and other specialist colleagues. By focussing on the activities of early man rather than on the formal attributes of certain of his artefacts Pittioni set an inspiring example of what can be achieved by a realistic rather than a schematic approach. This way of approaching archaeology has recently developed on a wide front, but so far it has mainly been tried out in synchronic studies. It is the aim of this paper to apply the Bioarchaeological approach[1] to a diachronic problem, that posed by the sequence of cave deposits and their contents.

When archaeologists observe changes in the artefacts recovered from successive levels in a cave, or for that matter in any stratified site, they have long been accustomed to interpreting these in abstract cultural terms: stratigraphic changes are commonly held to indicate a succession of 'cultures'. A more realistic explanation may be suggested, namely that the artefacts found in a particular deposit relate to the activities pursued by the occupants of the site at that particular time and by consequence that variations in the archaeological content of a sequence of deposits reflect changes in the activities of the human population. While it may be agreed that activities, even at the level of subsistence, may be patterned to some extent by tradition and that in consequence changes in the pattern of activities may on occasion reflect the replacement of one population by another, this is something that needs to be tested for each particular case, rather than accepted as a rule of thumb. One way of doing this is to see how far changes in artefacts correspond with changes in the patterns of subsistence and how far this in turn relates to changes in the external environment.

Charles McBurney[2] undertook an interesting experiment on these lines in respect of the mammals, molluscs and artefacts from successive levels in the cave of Ali Tappeh near the southern shore of the Caspian at the foot of the Elburz mountains in northern Iran. Thus seals were found to attain a marked peak at the maximum of a warm phase corresponding in age with the Allerød of northern Europe, whereas gazelle abounded in the preceding cold phase and recovered somewhat during the ensuing one, though not on the scale found by Carleton Coon[3] at the Belt Cave in the same region. In respect of artefacts it was noted that mesolithic flint triangles and other geometric forms correlated positively with gazelle and negatively with seal.

The seals from Ali Tappeh and the other Caspian caves apparently belonged to a local variety of the ringed seal (*Phoca hispida*). This essentially circumpolar species presumably entered the waters of the Caspian and Aral Seas, as of Lake Baikal, the Carelian lakes and the Gulfs of Bothnia and Finland in the Baltic, at a time when these communicated with the Arctic ocean. To judge from the complete absence of harpoon-heads from the seal-bearing deposits at Ali Tappeh, deposits which were clearly favourable to the conservation of animal skeletal materials, the inhabitants must surely have used some other method of catching the seals. Since ringed seals may take to the water only two or three days after birth,[4] they can hardly have been clubbed while still on their breeding grounds as was frequently done with grey seals. In this regard it is significant that Coon[5] states that the ringed seals from the Belt Cave were 'fully adult in most cases'. On the other hand since seals are peculiarly sensitive to anyone approaching from the landward, they can easily be stampeded into coarse-meshed nets set on the seaward side of favoured sleeping places. It may well be that this method was used by the Caspian seal-hunters. It was observed by Linnaeus[6] on the Baltic island of Gotland and was employed recently to take ringed seals on Fåro island off the north coast of Gotland[7] as well as in Finland.[8]

The case into which I intend to enter in some detail in the present paper is that presented by the sequence of some 4 metres of stratified deposits in the cave of Stora Förvar situated on the islet of Stora Karlsö some 6.5 km off the south west coast of the large Baltic island of Gotland. Much of the perimeter of the islet, which extends at present to c. 2.5 sq.km., is formed by cliffs and the cave lies on the east side of the inlet on the north coast which forms one of the few easy landing places. The quantities of animal remains, pottery and other archaeological objects show clearly enough that it was visited by man throughout the period represented by the accumulation of deposits during Middle and Late Neolithic times. It is unfortunate that an interval of nearly half a century intervened between the final season of excavations in 1893 and the publication of the archaeological finds.[9] This and the fact that the cave which penetrated the rock on a narrow front was excavated in sections over a period of five seasons means that by no means all the finds can be ascribed to their correct relative position. As against this we have the valuable study of the stratigraphy of seal remains by Pira[10] which makes it possible to plot fluctuations in the occurrence of remains of the three species, represented in the cave (fig. 18.1).

In the lower seven of Pira's levels (F13–G8) only two species of seal were represented and of these the grey seal (*Halichoeris grypus*) predominated, amounting to between 71% and 94%. A marked change occurred at level G7 in which Middle Neolithic sherds of Säter III style began to appear. At this point the ringed seal (*Phoca foetida*), which had been present from the beginning, rose markedly in importance and at the same time was joined by

| Layers | PHOCINAE | | | Numbers | ARTEFACTS | | |
	GREY SEALS %	RINGED SEALS %	HARP SEALS %		HARPOONS %	FISH-HOOKS	CERAMICS
B 1	100			6			
H 2		100		1			
B 2	75	25		4			
H 3	66`6	33		3			
G H3	100			1			STONE CIST
B 3	100			2			
I 4		89	11	9	3		
G 4		86	14	14	3		
I 5	14	71	14	14	3		
G 5	11	76	13	38	32		SÄTER IV
B 6		86	14	43	53		
H 7	57	42	1	74	53		SÄTER III
G 7	37	54	9	59	53		
G 8	71	29		55	3		
G 9	73	27		86			
F10	88	12		32			
G11	94	6		34			SÄTER II
A11	75	25		40	3		
F12	92	8		38			
F13	85	15		39	Total 34		

18.1 Diagram illustrating changes in the representation of different species of seal and of certain types of artefacts in the deposits at the cave of Stora Förvar, Stora Karlsö, Gotland. (Based on data from Pira, *Acta Zool.*, 8 (1926), 123–7, and Schnittger and Rydh, *Grottan Stora Förvar på Stora Karlsö* (Stockholm, 1940).

the harp seal (*P. groenlandica*) even if in modest proportions. By B6 grey seals had sunk to insignificant proportions and ringed seals rose to unquestioned dominance. In the upper levels of the cave containing pottery from the Stone Cist period the number of individual seals fell rapidly away until in the top six they represented no more than a few strays in a predominantly domestic fauna. In this succession Pira saw evidence for two profound changes, first of all a swing of grey seal plus a few harp seals and second a phase setting in just before the Stone Cist period when seal hunting evidently became quite subsidiary to stock raising, but in which grey seals returned to importance, amounting to 82% of the total number of individual seals from these levels.

In considering why it was that grey seals gave place to ringed seals Pira discussed whether this was due to human activities and specifically to the extinction of a grey seal breeding ground or whether on the contrary it might be accounted for rather in terms of a decline in temperature. The fact that the change-over was accompanied by the appearance of another circumpolar species, the harp seal (*P. groenlandica*), suggested to him that the latter was the more likely. A specific explanation is that the change was due not to some major climatic fluctuation but to an alteration in the conditions of ice-formation.

Whereas in the Baltic the grey seal only takes to the ice during the breeding season, the ringed seal is able to exist under fast ice for long periods of time. An expansion of the area over which fast ice endured for any considerable length of time would therefore favour the ringed as against the grey seal. Even today, as can be seen from our map (fig. 18.3), there are very considerable annual variations in the area and duration of fast ice.[11] It is by no means improbable that during the Litorina Sea phase the contrast between the surface layer of freshwater and intruding saline water may have favoured ice-formation in the Baltic and so have created conditions suitable for the ringed seal.

In his study of the seal remains of the cave Pira interpreted the initial dominance of the grey seal as an indication that the island was a breeding place for this species. Particular significance attaches to the abundance of young individuals in the levels marked by a predominance of grey seal, since the pups of this species habitually stay on their breeding grounds for three weeks and do not finally take to the sea until they are six or seven weeks old. Since the pups put on considerable weight – they may yield 20/30 kilos of blubber and 12/18 kilos of meat at three weeks[12] – they are highly desirable as well as most vulnerable immediately before they become mobile. The easy way to take grey seals is to approach them on their breeding grounds and slaughter both cubs and adults by clubbing or by jabbing with a pike. This method is attested for the Faroes,[13] the western isles of Scotland,[14] the Frö island off Trondheim[15] and, for many parts of the Baltic

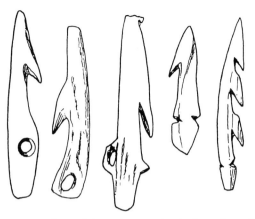

18.2a Antler and bone harpoon-heads from Stora Förvar, Stora Karlsö, Gotland, Sweden

18.2b Finnish hunter standing by the breathing hole of a ringed seal waiting to strike with his iron-headed harpoon (After Schwindt, *Finsk Ethnografisk Atlas I, Jagt och Fiske* (Helsingfors, 1905))

including Östergötland and Gotland[16] and the Gulfs of Riga[17] and Bothnia.[18]

On the other hand the habits of the ringed seal are rather different. In the Baltic both species breed on the ice. On the other hand whereas grey seal cubs do not take to the water until they are three weeks old, the young of ringed seal are able to do so within two or three days of birth. Again, the fully grown ringed seal, unlike the grey seal, is able to maintain itself under fast ice by making and maintaining a number of breathing holes. This means that there was a markedly different emphasis in the methods used to hunt them. A particular feature of ringed seal hunting was the máupoq method employed over broad territories by the Eskimos, whereby the hunter stopped up all but one breathing hole, stationed himself at this and harpooned the animal as it came to breathe.[19] The self-same method is amply attested for modern Finland[20] (fig. 18.2b) and the Bothnian coast of Sweden.[21] Another point to emphasise is that whereas the slaughter of grey seals at their breeding grounds is a brief episode, the máupoq method can be carried on during a period limited only by the duration of fast ice.

The time has now come to test our hypothesis in terms of the content of the successive deposits at Stora Förvar. The first point to note is the observation made by Schnittger and Rydh[22] that whereas pottery and remains of domestic animal bones occurred down to the bottom of the section, they were notably sparse in the lower levels dominated by grey seals. Such indications of more prolonged occupation on the other hand were notably more abundant in levels dominated by ringed seals, confirming that at the time longer periods were being spent on hunting. Another sign that more time was spent at Stora Förvar during the ringed seal period is that fish-hooks were concentrated at this level. More decisive perhaps is the evidence of hunting gear. If our hypothesis is correct one might expect to find evidence of the máupoq method appearing at the time when ringed seal rose decisively in importance. This is indeed what we do find, even if for the reasons already mentioned, it is hardly possible to attain absolute precision on this point.

Of more than 50 harpoon-heads (fig. 18.2a) known to have been found only some 34 can be related to Pira's[23] stratigraphic sequence on the basis provided by Schnittger and Rydh, but this is a substantial enough proportion to give a fairly accurate idea of their context (fig. 18.1). Only two specimens can be tied into the earlier phases of the sequence, one from A11/12 in which ringed seals accounted for a quarter of the seals represented and one from G8 when they accounted for nearly 3/10. More than half the harpoon-heads were found in deposits yielding pottery of Säter III style, but since about 19 of these came from layer G16 whose precise context in Pira's sequence cannot be accurately determined, the most acceptable course has been to average them over the three deposits G7 to B6, deposits in which ringed seals accounted for between 42% and 86% of the total seal content. The proportion of harpoon-heads in level G5, corresponding to an early phase of the Säter III style is about one third of the total from the site. Thereafter the number of harpoon-heads drops markedly. Nevertheless it is worth noting that they continue to the level at which the harp seal finally disappears and the ringed seal declined drastically with the return of the grey seal. In this last connection the number of individuals represented is so low that the percentages for individual layers may be discounted: a more impressive statistic is that 14 out of the 17 (i.e. 82%) of the seals represented in the harpoonless layers B3 to B1 are grey seals. Evidently ice conditions had reverted to the situation prevailing during the initial phases in the occupation of the cave.

The time has now come to make a further test, to see how far the prehistoric evidence for the Baltic as a whole (fig. 18.3) confirmed the varying emphasis on different types of hunting in respect of the kinds of seal found in the deposits at Stora Förvar. The contextual evidence is of two kinds. First there is the testimony of seals that have sunk down to the sea-bed complete with harpoon-heads after escaping their hunters. Next one may examine the evidence of harpoon-heads found loose in archaeological assemblages containing seal-bones. And lastly there is the negative evidence provided by the non-occurrence of harpoon-heads in deposits dominated by particular species of seal.

Analysis of the associations of harpoon-heads with remains of seals

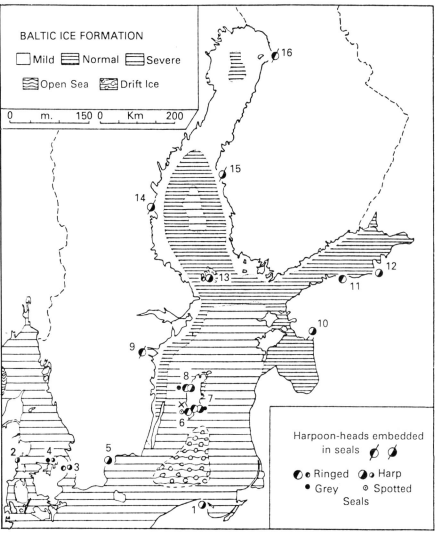

18.3 Map showing sites at which harpoon-heads have been found in association with different kinds of seal. X marks the site of Stora Förvar, Stora Karlsö. The maximum extension of fast ice is shown for mild, medium and severe winters

Table showing occurrences of different species of seals from Stone Age sites in the Baltic region yielding harpoon heads: see map (fig. 18.3). Underlining denotes seals with harpoon heads embedded; large crosses denote abundance.

Finding places	Spotted seal	Grey seal	Harp seal	Ringed seal	References
16. Oulu, Österbotten, Finland				X	Sauramo 1938
15. Närpes, Österbotten, Finland			X		Sauramo 1938
14. Skarvtärn Hälsingland, Sweden			X		Cederschiöld 1959
13. Jettböle, Åland I.			X	X	Meinander n.p.
12. Narva, Esthonia, USSR			X		Gurina 1967
11. Kunda, Esthonia, USSR				X	Indreko 1948[24]
10. Pernau, Esthonia, USSR			X		Leppäaho 1936[25]
9. Norrköping, Östergötland, Sweden				X	Lönnberg 1908
8. Visby, Gotland, Sweden		X	X	X	Holmqvist 1912[26]
7. Hemmor, Gotland, Sweden		X	X	X	Holmqvist 1912[26]
6. Gullrum, Gotland, Sweden	X			X	Holmqvist 1912[26]
5. Möllehausen, Gualöv, Scania				X	Berlin 1944[27]
4. Sølager, Sjaelland, Denmark		X	X		Winge 1904[28]
3. Bloksbjerg, Sjaelland, Denmark			X	X	Westerby 1927[29]
2. Flynderhagen, Jutland, Denmark			X		Andersen 1971[30]
1. Rzucewo, East Prussia (former)		X	X		Kostrzewski 1931[31]

suggests that during the Stone Age there was a positive correlation in the Gulf of Bothnia with harp and ringed seals and a negative one with grey and spotted seals.

It should first be stated that on the four occasions on which harpoon-heads have been found embedded in skeletons, two related to harp seals and two to ringed seals:

(1) Norrköping, Östergötland, Sweden.
Found 4.5 m deep in Litorina clay. At present the site is only c. ¼m below sea-level. At its maximum the Litorina sea stood c. 60 m above present level. The fairly young ringed seal evidently sank in fairly deep water.
E. Löhnberg, Om Någro fynd i Litorina-lera i Norrköping 1907, *Arkiv f.g. Zoologi* 4/24 1908 1–27; SHM 13476.

(2) Skarvtjärn, Harmangers sn., Sweden.
The harpoon-head, probably made from the left metatarsal of an elk, was found at a depth of 1.10 m in the skeleton of a harp seal.
L. Cederschiöld, Om två sålharpumer från Hälsinglands Stenålder, *Fornvannen* 1959 36–40; SHM 24675.

(3) Oulu, Österbotten, Finland
Harpoon-head made from a metacarpal or metatarsal bone of an elk, found with the skeleton of a ringed seal in Litorina clay. The seal is calculated to have sunk in c. 62 m of water about 30 km from the contemporary coast on which was situated the comb ware site of Muhos, a site rich in remains of ringed seal.

M. Sauramo, Ein harpunierter Seehund aus dem Litorina-Ton Nordfinn-lands, *Quartär* 1 1938 28; E. Kivikoski, *Finlands Förhistoria*, Helsingfors 1964 57.

(4) Närpes, Österbotten, Finland
Harpoon-head of elk bone from Litorina clay associated with skeleton of harp seal. It has been calculated that this seal sank in 42 m of water at a distance of c. 20 km from the Litorina coast.

M. Sauramo, Ein harpunierter Seehund aus dem Litorina-Ton Nordfinn-lands, *Quartär* 1 1938 28; E. Kivikoski, *Finlands Förhistoria*, Helsingfors 1964 57.

Next one may consider the twelve occasions on which harpoonheads have been found loose on Stone Age sites with remains of seals (see table, p. 316). The first point to note is that in each case these included harp or ringed seal or both. And the second that in no single instance were remains of either grey or spotted seal found alone or in combination at sites yielding harpoonheads. Thirdly, on the one occasion on which spotted seal occurred on such a site the dominant species was ringed seal. Fourthly, it may be noted that of the three sites yielding harpoonheads at which grey seal remains were present, in one harp seal occurred and in two harp and ringed seal occurred in predominant quantities.

The only hypothesis which fits these observations is that the Stone Age inhabitants of the Baltic area and Denmark used harpoons for hunting harp and ringed seals, but did not do so for grey or spotted seals.

As a test of the correlation between harpoon-heads and predominantly harp seals it is worth quoting the results recently obtained[32] for the three Narva sites in Esthonia on the south coast of the Gulf of Finland towards its eastern end. The ratios between the two are convincingly close more especially when allowance is made for the fact that an unknown number of seals belonged to one or more different species.

	I	II	III
Seals (no. of individuals)	27	3	9
Harpoon-heads	13	–	3

A final test is to review the situation at the numerous sites which have yielded seal remains comprising grey seals only. Of the 29 recorded from Denmark up to Sub-boreal times[33] not a single one appears to have produced a harpoon-head.

To sum up, the most notable artefacts other than pottery from Stora Förvar, namely the harpoon-heads of antler and bone, were controlled by economic and ecological rather than cultural factors. The changes in human activity presupposed by the artefacts represent responses in the first instance to changes in the type of seal predominating at different periods; and these changes in turn are most probably to be explained as functions of changes in ice-formation. We have here in fact an instructive example of the interaction of habitat, biome and culture. Yet it is of course true that the cultural response depended in this case on social inheritance. The harpoon-head was as much a component of the Kunda culture of the East Baltic as the barbed point and it is worth noting that remains of ringed seal were found at the name site and that those of harp seal occurred among the material recovered from the Pernau river. Again it is interesting to observe that the precise form of harpoon-heads were subject to social selection. Thus, whereas all eight of the most elementary form having a hole drilled through the middle of the base illustrated from Stora Förvar had only one barb, the eight complete ones illustrated from the site of Västerbjers on the east side of Gotland invariably had two.[34] The samples are not large, but the contrast is sufficiently clear cut to suggest that a feature which might at first glance be dismissed as idiosyncratic may in fact have served to identify distinct social groups and their hunting gear.

Notes

1 For a development of this concept see J. G. D. Clark, *Star Carr: a Case Study in Bioarchaeology*, Module in Anthropology, 10, 1972; *idem*, The Archaeology of Stone Age Settlement (Oliver Davies Lecture 1972), *Ulster Journal of Archaeology*, 35, 3–16; *idem*, 'Seasonality and the Interpretation of Lithic Assemblages', *Estudios dedicados al Prof. Dr L. Pericot*, 1973, 1–13; *idem*, 'Prehistoric Europe: The Economic Basis', *Arch. Researches in Retrospect*, Cambridge, Mass., 1974, 33–57; *idem*, *The Earlier Stone Age Settlement of Scandinavia*, Cambridge, 1975; *idem*, 'The Economic Context of Dolmens and Passage-graves in Sweden', *Essays presented to H. Hencken*, 1977.

2 C. B. M. McBurney, 'The Cave of Ali Tappeh and the Epi-Paleolithic in N. E. Iran', *PPS*, 1968, 385–413.

3 C. S. Coon, *Cave exploration in Iran*, Pennsylvania, 1951; *idem, Seven Caves*, London, 1957.

4 O. Nordqvist, 'Beitrag zur Kenntnis der isolierten Formen der Ringelrobbe (*Phoca foetida* Fabr.), *Acta Soc. pro Fauna et Flora Fennica*, 15/7, 1899, 28.

5 Coon, op. cit., 151 49.

6 Linnaeus, *Ölandska och Gothländska Resa*, Stockholm, 1745, 184–6.

7 N. Lithberg, *Gotlands Stenålder*, Stockholm, 1914, 118–22.

8 U. T. Sirelius, *Die Volkskultur Finnlands I, Jagd und Fischerei*, Berlin, 1934, 91–2.

9 B. Schnittger, H. Rydh, *Grottan Stora Förvar på Stora Karlsö*, Stockholm, 1940.

10 A. Pira, 'On bone deposits in the cave "Stora Förvar" on the isle of Stora Karlsö, Sweden', *Acta Zoologica*, 7, 1926, 123–7.

11 K. A. Sjodahl, 'Isförhallånden, vintersjöfart och isbrytning i Sverige omgivan de farvatten', *Ymer*, 1967, 41–55; O. Hook, A. G. Johnels, 'The breeding and distribution of the grey seal (*Halichoerus grypus* Fab.) in the Baltic Sea, with observations on other seals of the area', *Proc. Royal Soc. London*, 182, 1972, 39.

12 Sir H. Johnston, *British Mammals*, London, 1903, 205.

13 L. J. Debes, *Faeroe et Foeroa reserta: That is a description of the Islands and Inhabitants of Foeroe*, London, 1676, 168.

14 M. Martin, *A description of the Western Isles of Scotland*, Stirling (1704), 1934, 134; H. Pritchard, *Sport in Wildest Britain*, London, 1936, 15–17.

15 R. Collett, 'On *Halichoerus grypus* and its breeding on the Fro Islands off Trond-hjems-fjord in Norway', *Proc. Zool. Soc. London*, 1881, 385.

16 G. Berg, S. Svensson, *Svens Bodenkultur*, Stockholm, 1934.
17 F. Leinbock, *Die materielle Kultur der Esten*, Tartu, 1932, 10.
18 Olaus Magnus, *Carta Marina et descriptio septentrionalium terrarum*, Rome, 1939; see J. G. D. Clark, 'Seal-Hunting in the Stone Age of North-Western Europe: A Study in Economic Prehistory', *PPS*, 1946, fig. 8.
19 K. Birket-Smith, *The Eskimos*, London, 1936.
20 T. Schwindt, *Finsk Ethnografisk Atlas I, Jagt och Fiske*, Helsingfors, 1905, fig. 144–6.
21 Berg-Svensson, ref. 16, 54–5.
22 s. ref. 9.
23 s. ref. 10.
24 R. Indreko, *Die Mittlere Steinzeit in Estland*, Stockholm, 1948, 229–43.
25 J. Leppäaho, 'Narpiön ja Oulujoen Kivikauden hyljelöydöt', *Suomen Museo*, 43, 1936, 31.
26 O. Holmqvist, 'Tierknocken aus den steinzeitlichen Wohnplätzen in Visby und bei Hemmor sowie aus einem Öländischen Ganggrabe', *Kgl. Vetenskap. Handl.*, N. F., 49, 1912, 75–5.
27 H. Berlin, 'Benfynden från stenåldersboplatsen i Gualöv', *Medd. LUHM*, 1941, 151–2.
28 H. Winge, 'Om jordfundne Pattedyr fra Danmark', *Vidensk. Medd. fra Dansk nat. Foren*, 1904, 193–304.
29 E. Westerby, *Stenalderbopladser ved Klampenborg*, Kopenhagen, 1927, 33.
30 S. H. Andersen, *Ertebøllekulturens harpuner*, Kuml, 1971, 73–125.
31 J. Kostrzewski, 'Über die jungsteinzeitliche Besiedlung der polnischen Ostseeküste', *Acta Congr. Sec. Arch. Balticorum Rigae*, Riga, 1931, 55–64.
32 N. N. Gurina, 'Iz Istorii Drevnikh Plemen Zapaldnikh Oblastey SSSR', *Mat. i. issledov.* 144, 1967.
33 U. Møhl, *Fangstdyrene ved de Danske strande. Den zoologiske baggrund for harpunerne*, Kuml, 1970, table, 320–1, nos. 3–6, 9–12, 14–16, 19, 23, 24, 26, 27, 34, 37, 40, 41, 43, 44, 46–48, 54, 57, 59, 61.
34 M. Stenberger, *Das Grabfeld von Västerbjers auf Gotland*, Stockholm, 1943, figs. 17, 29, 37, 38, 58.

CHAPTER 19

DOMESTICATION AND SOCIAL EVOLUTION

In their preface to the volume issuing from the first joint discussion meeting in the present series Lord Blackett and Sir Kenneth Wheare emphasized that 'The range of knowledge and research remains, as it has always done, continuous.' It would be hard to find a topic to which this applies more aptly than the one down for discussion over the next two days. Agriculture occupies a key position. Its fruitful study – and for that matter its most profitable pursuit – depends on combinations of disciplines drawn from both camps. It calls for a synthesis of natural scientific and humanistic insights and techniques. Furthermore it enshrines a truth we ought never to forget, namely that the acceptance of research, and so in the long run its success, depends on reconciling the exploration and manipulation of natural forces with the nature and aspirations of men.

One way of making clear the centrality of agriculture is to identify the main fields of study within our two bodies which converge upon it. To take first the Royal Society. The physical sciences bearing most directly on the habitat discussed by Professor Dimbleby all fall within the purview of a single section (table 19.1). Those bearing on different aspects of the biome on the other hand involve, though to a markedly varying degree, disciplines grouped under each of the six sectional committees which together form the biological sciences (table 19.2). We shall be hearing Dr Pickersgill on genetics, Professor Jope on biophysics, Professor van Zeist and Dr Evans on palaeobotany, Mr Jarman on palaeozoology and animal husbandry and Professor Harlan on the problem of domestication as a whole.

No doubt it was partly because of the range of interests served that the Early History of Agriculture Project was the first to be adopted by the British Academy under the policy adumbrated by Lord Robbins in his Presidential Address for 1965. It is no wonder that it should have emanated from the archaeology section, since so large a proportion of the material data recovered by excavations relates to people who supported themselves by means of farming. But the importance of investigating the economic and in the first instance the subsistence base of human societies (table 19.3), as a means of understanding how they functioned and why they were structured in the way they were, applies not merely to the prehistoric communities among whom farming first developed, but to all societies which obtained their food substantially from agriculture. The history of agriculture is

Table 19.1 The main fields of study bearing on the habitat of early farmers within the scope of sectional committee 5 of the Royal Society

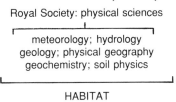

Royal Society: physical sciences

meteorology; hydrology
geology; physical geography
geochemistry; soil physics

HABITAT

Table 19.2 The main fields of interest bearing on the biome of early farmers within the scope of sectional committees 6–11 of the Royal Society

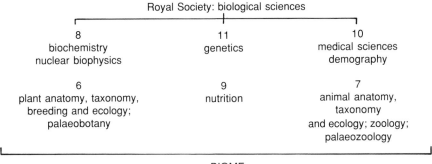

Royal Society: biological sciences

8	11	10
biochemistry	genetics	medical sciences
nuclear biophysics		demography
6	9	7
plant anatomy, taxonomy,	nutrition	animal anatomy,
breeding and ecology;		taxonomy
palaeobotany		and ecology; zoology;
		palaeozoology

BIOME

Table 19.3 The sections of the British Academy bearing most directly on the social dimension of early agricultural systems

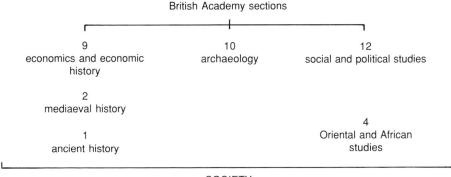

British Academy sections

9	10	12
economics and economic	archaeology	social and political studies
history		
2		
mediaeval history		
		4
1		Oriental and African
ancient history		studies

SOCIETY

important not merely for archaeologists, but for historians, economists, anthropologists and all those concerned with the socio-cultural dimension of human affairs, not excluding literature and the arts.

The study of the early history of agriculture not merely requires the attention of many disciplines from both sides of the fence between the arts and sciences (fig. 19.1). Above all these have to be brought to bear in an ecological context. The relations of the various disciplines are a mirror image of the way in which human societies themselves function in their natural settings. We need to think of them in terms of systems, systems constituted

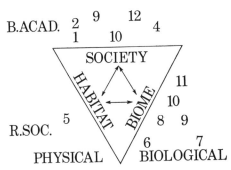

19.1 Diagram illustrating the sectional committees of the Royal Society and the British Academy most relevant to an understanding of ecosystems comprehending agriculture

by the reciprocal interaction of a variety of physical, biological and socio-cultural forces. Each system is to a degree unique (fig. 19.2). The great civilizations of mankind were each based on varieties of farming, but the species of animal and plant domesticated, the relative importance of animals and plants, the degree of fixity of settlement and many other factors varied within wide limits. It is right that we should hear in this meeting about the type of farming with which most of us are familiar in the west. We look forward to hearing from Professor Harlan and Professor van Zeist about the formative stages in southwest Asia and no less from Mr Higgs, the Jarmans and Mr Boardman about the varying forms of husbandry practised in different parts of Europe. On the other hand contributions such as those by Dr Bushnell on Mesoamerica, by Sir Joseph Hutchinson on the crops of India and from Dr Chang on the rice cultures, which today support so large a part of the world's population, should help us to appreciate that wheat and barley and the range of domesticated animals familiar in the west are only a small part of the story. Time alone restricts us to only a few of the numerous systems devised by mankind.

Another reason why I have emphasized the partnership between the humanities and the natural sciences in the study of agriculture is that its practice, which we recognize as a necessary foundation of societies capable of formulating abstract scientific theories, implies at least an empirical know-ledge of science based ultimately on observation. In a recent issue of *Daedalus* (Summer 1974, p. 83) André and Jean Mayer went so far as to claim that: 'When human beings first learned the cycle of plants and seeds, they were scientists. As they learned when and how to plant, in what soil, and how much water each crop needed, they were extending their understanding of nature. This knowledge was not less scientific for having been discovered and transmitted by people who could not read or write. No scientist performs a greater act of faith in the predictability of the operation of natural laws than the farmer who plows a part of this year's harvest back into the earth.'

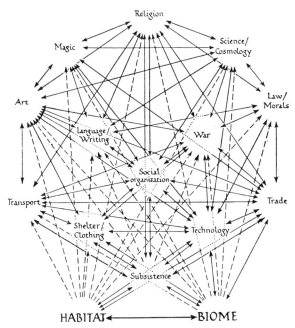

19.2 Diagram illustrating some of the interactions between different aspects of the sociocultural component of ecosystems comprehending agriculture

If peasants are to be accounted scientists by virtue of apprehending natural forces well enough to be able to manipulate them for predictable ends, what of reindeer? Do these not display intense discrimination, exploit their environments effectively and by the way in which they regulate their seasonal movements evince a capacity for successful prediction? But we are not here to discuss the differences between genetically and socially acquired behavioural patterns. Two things only need to be said:

(1) By contrast with other animals men employ a more or less complex material apparatus of their own making to aid them in the acquisition and processing of food, apparatus which involves both technical know-how and social organization for effective deployment. Professor Steensberg's contribution will illustrate this in respect of tillage.

(2) Whereas mammals, if we exclude parent/young relationships and the symbiotic relationships established between members of certain species, are self-sufficient units, 'a large proportion of a man's energy expenditure' to quote Richard B. Lee in respect of Bushmen 'goes to feeding others, and a large percentage of an individual's consumption is of food produced by others'. The social structure of primitive societies is directed as much to distributing as to securing food.

The fact that Lee based his observations on Bushmen reminds us of something which has emerged strikingly from the work of the Cambridge

Unit of the Early History of Agriculture Project, notably in that of Mike Jarman and Eric Higgs, namely that the same fundamental regularities underlie the food quest of human societies whether these are classified as hunter/foragers or agriculturalists. Semantic considerations have helped to obscure this truth. Words like crop, harvest or husbandry are so closely linked in our minds with the agricultural basis of our own society that we are only too prone to overlook the fact that human societies of whatever kind depend for their subsistence, directly or indirectly, on cropping, harvesting, and husbanding animals and plants. The viability of any society rests upon its success in feeding its members. Under primitive conditions this in turn depends directly on knowledge of the distribution, habits, life cycles and properties of available animals and plants, on the technical means available for exploiting these, on the social mechanisms involved in the quest for food and in its distribution and not least on the ideology that ensures the coherence of society and a correct balance between population and food supplies. The convention by which economies based on such activities as foraging and hunting are considered to be merely predatory, whereas those based on farming are held to be productive in a sense begs the question. Both systematically exploit natural resources. If they do so at different intensities, this is mainly because they are attuned to supporting human populations at different densities and standards of social life.

From a historical point of view indeed the essential difference between hunter/foragers and farmers resides precisely in the much greater potential in respect of both population density and social development of societies whose economies are based substantially on domesticated animals and plants. Whereas no society restricted to exploiting the natural increase of animals and plants living under wild conditions could enhance its efficiency more than marginally, farming, as we can see with the benefit of hindsight, held the promise of a continuing expansion of yields and so of population. The process of domestication entailed the creation of an artificial, that is of a man-made environment in which animals and plants were protected from predators (other than man himself) and advantaged in relation to competitors. It also implied that the preferred animals and plants were raised and tended in the more or less immediate area of the homestead (as the term domestication itself suggests). On the other hand where conditions favoured pastoralism stock might be grazed over annual territories as extensive as those required for some hunter/forager economies. In so far as effective control over breeding could be established domesticated animals and plants became sexually isolated and this, together with the differing conditions under which livestock were maintained, may well explain why in course of time many species diverged genetically from their wild prototypes sufficiently to be readily distinguished among the refuse found on early settlements.

It follows from the premise that human societies are components of interacting systems which comprehend habitat, biome and all the several dimensions of economic, social and intellectual life, that a change in the relationship between men, animals and plants as fundamental as that implied by domestication was bound in the long run to entail changes of a thorough-going nature in the socio-cultural dimension, whether in respect of settlement, population, technology, social structure or ideology. Gordon Childe summed these up by claiming that together they constituted a veritable 'Neolithic revolution'. In what respect was he justified in speaking in such terms? Let me emphasize at the outset that no one has effectively denied that the domestication of animals and plants was revolutionary in its implications. No society we could term civilized has ever developed on any other basis. The debate centres only on how far the change was revolutionary in the sense of being catastrophic and sudden. The answer as with so many questions depends on one's point of view.

To anyone concentrating on the food refuse from prehistoric settlements there can be no question that the process was gradual and long drawn out. This can be seen with special clarity in the case of plants in the remarkable sequence obtained from the Valley of Mexico by R. S. MacNeish described by Dr Bushnell or, again, in the progressive intensification of methods of cultivating rice described by Dr Chang. The differences between foraging and reliance on fully domesticated and elaborately cultivated plants may be obvious enough, but the transition may extend over thousands of years and be barely perceptible in the short term. The process can as a rule only be broken down into phases by statistical means in much the same way as the development of forest history has been by pollen-analysis.

To anyone more concerned with the socio-cultural outcome of changes in the pattern of subsistence things do not always appear in the same light. Admittedly the archaeological record when studied in quantitative terms is often found to reveal a much more gradual process of change than that which appears when more subjective methods are used. Even so there are occasions, even if much rarer than appeared in an earlier stage of archaeological research, when abrupt changes appear to have occurred. To understand why socio-cultural systems were able to maintain coherence and form in the face of changes in the pattern of subsistence over long periods of time and then at infrequent intervals undergo more or less marked and rapid periods of readjustment it may be helpful to bring into play the principle of homeostasis. According to this, any system, whether this be a body or a social order, responds to threats by drawing on its own resources. It is only when a critical threshold has been passed that systems break down. Just as when vital organs cease to function the body dies and disintegrates, so when pressures and contradictions build up in a society to a point at which the cost of maintaining the *status quo* exceeds the advantages of doing so, one social pattern or system gives place to another better adapted to existing circumstances. If we adopt this model we might expect archaeologists, who deal after all with no more than the material detritus of former states of society, to reveal well defined faults in their stratigraphic sequences, faults coinciding with crises when one system gave place to another. It was his recognition of these in the archaeological sequences of different parts of southwest Asia that led Gordon Childe to formulate his concept of the Neolithic revolution. If we allow for the time lag inherent in the homeostatic process, there is no essential contradiction between regarding domestication as a long drawn out and barely perceptible transition and accepting that under certain conditions consequential social changes might appear as comparatively sudden.

The question must next be faced why this process unfolded apparently independently in different parts of the world and why farming and its correlates spread from such innovating centres over extensive territories until they reached their ecological limits. After all people like the aborigines of Cape York, so lovingly recorded by Donald Thomson, or the Eskimos of Hamilton Inlet, Labrador, observed by Fitzhugh, maintained self-regulating and socially fulfilling systems with a minimum of equipment solely by appropriating the natural increase of animals and plants. And such people, like their analogues in Ice Age Europe, had leisure for ceremonial, ritual and artistic activities of some complexity. A point to be emphasized is that all this was accomplished on a low input of work. Richard Lee's observation of Bushmen with similarly limited technology is that they satisfied their needs on the equivalent of a 2½ day week. By contrast farming involved heavy burdens, markedly greater input of technology and hard labour to produce supplies of food which, if more assured, had to be shared among larger numbers. Professor Wolf Herre expressed it mildly in relation to livestock when he wrote that to offset its many advantages, 'with domestication man took on responsibilities as well . . . The more man aims at [this] higher quality in his domestic animals, the greater the attention they must receive, so that man becomes the servant of his animals. A remarkable psychological adjustment was necessary to bring this about, entailing a readjustment of social structure.' Agriculture was even more onerous. Wholesale forest-clearance, land-terracing and irrigation are only a few of the calls made by different environments. The blunt fact is that the process of domestication involved man himself quite as much as his animals and plants. The milk-stool and the mattock were forerunners of the conveyor-belt and the punch-card. When Adam ate that apple he did so not from hunger but from a desire to know. We can only understand domestication if we remember that foragers were scientists too. Farming was one fruit of their experiments.

It is hardly necessary to look beyond Darwin's insight to account for the widespread acceptance where ecological conditions were appropriate of innovations which improved the quality and bulk of food supplies and at the same time made them more accessible and more certain, even if for individuals they imposed a more irksome discipline. The adaptive value, from a social viewpoint of a more reliable subsistence base, more especially when muscled by a more effective technology, requires no emphasis. As to the mechanism by which farming economies spread widely over territories peripheral to the main centres of innovation, I would remind you that ecosystems only exist as isolates for purposes of analysis. In reality the existence of other systems and not necessarily only proximate ones is an ever-present factor in the environment of any one of them. In the case of systems including men the need to adapt to ideas derived from elsewhere must always have been a factor in promoting radical change at critical times. It is a matter of observation that farming made its appearance in peripheral regions in new socio-cultural settings conventionally termed 'Neolithic'. On the other hand new systems might be expected to expand only so far as they proved more effective than older ones based on foraging and hunting. In northern Europe for example farming expanded only marginally beyond the temperate zone in early times. Further north and locally even within the temperate zone food was most economically obtained by foraging, fishing and trapping.

What I have sought to emphasize in this opening talk is that modes of subsistence and in particular the methods used to exploit animal and plant resources form so to speak a hinge between human societies and their physical and biological environments. That is why they can only be understood in terms of systems comprehending human societies and by means of humanistic as well as natural scientific disciplines. The very structure of societies depends upon and constrains methods of securing food. These in turn are both constrained by but increasingly in the course of social evolution have come to mould the various habitats and biomes occupied by men.

References

Fitzhugh, W. W. 1972. *Environmental Archaeology and Cultural Systems in Hamilton Inlet, Labrador.* Smithsonian Contributions to Anthropology, no. 16. Washington.

Herre, W. 1969. 'The science and history of domestic animals', in *Science in Archaeology* (ed. Brothwell and Higgs), 2nd ed., London, pp. 258–9.

Higgs, E. R. and Jarman, M. R. 1972. 'The origins of animal and plant husbandry', in *Papers in Economic Prehistory* (ed. Higgs), Cambridge, pp. 3–13.

Lee, R. B. 1969. 'Kung bushman subsistence: an input-output analysis', in *Environment and cultural behaviour* (ed. A. P. Vayda), New York, pp. 47–79.

Mayer, A. and J. 1974. *Daedalus. J. Am. Acad. Arts and Sci.*, Cambridge, Massachusetts, p. 83.

Robbins, Lord. 1965. 'Presidential address'. *Proc. Br. Acad.* 51, 43.

Thomson, D. F. 1939. 'The seasonal factor in human culture illustrated from the life of a contemporary nomadic group'. *Proc. Prehist. Soc.* 5, 209–21.

CHAPTER 20

NEOTHERMAL ORIENTATIONS

The ambiguity of my title is more apparent than real. If we are concerned with the way the prehistoric inhabitants of temperate Europe reorientated their lives in the context of environmental change, the way they adapted their economy, their technology and their society to the manifold changes implied by the onset of Neothermal climate, the contraction of ice-sheets, the spread of forests and so on, we must at the same time orientate our thoughts – hopefully reorientate our thoughts – about the role these people played in European prehistory.

I do not wish to dwell at length or in detail on the history of European prehistory, but I must make the point that our attitudes to the prehistory of the Neothermal have been largely distorted by the attitudes of our predecessors. If one compares the situation in the northern hemisphere in the Old and New Worlds, it is evident that there is a certain disadvantage in living in the continent that invented prehistory, just as there is in living in the country that invented the Industrial Revolution: one has to put up with the aftermath of crude and often uncouth beginnings. Above all, we in Britain have had to live with the consequences of Sir John Lubbock, the Victorian evolutionists and their Marxist aftermaths. During the formative days of prehistory the definition of the Palaeolithic and Neolithic Stone Ages appeared to mark a palpable advance. Why then am I implying that some of the consequences were unhappy? It is understandable, but nonetheless unfortunate, that the distinction should have been over-emphasised – the point had to be made and made emphatically – and we must remember the context of Lubbock's book, *Prehistoric Times* (1865). It appeared within six years of the publication of Darwin's *On the Origin of Species by means of Natural Selection* (1859) – that is, in the first flush of applying the doctrine of evolution to human affairs. Again Lubbock was writing as a young man (31), and at a time when the finds of Lartet and Christy were coming fresh from the Dordogne caves and contrasting mightily and palpably with the fortuitous revelation a decade earlier of the Swiss lake dwellings.

Perhaps it was not so surprising that G. de Mortillet's *Musée Préhistorique* (1881), the first great systematisation of the French sequence (issued within seven years of Lubbock's first definition of the Palaeolithic/Neolithic dichotomy: cf. Mortillet (1872)) should have incorporated that, to us, preposterous doctrine of the hiatus between the cave sequence and the Robenhausian.

I have described the hiatus theory as preposterous. Hugo Obermaier, writing in the immediately succeeding generation (1924), put the matter more mildly by objecting that 'it would be strange indeed if man should have deserted [the continent of Europe] at the very moment when its climatic conditions were becoming increasingly favourable'. This did not prevent the dogma (it was hardly advanced as a hypothesis) being fiercely held at the time. When Allen Brown ventured to write *On the Continuity of the Palaeolithic and Neolithic periods* (1893) and suggested the term Mesolithic to designate 'those objects in stone which neither belong to the drift period nor to that of polished stone', a designation which had already been proposed by Westropp (1872: 102–4) before the hiatus theory had been enunciated and one which comprehended a much more extended range of time than present usage, he was heavily jumped upon by Boyd Dawkins. As is so often the case the convert was more convinced than the originator. Dawkins emphasised the environmental as well as the cultural differences: in addition to the 'great gulf' in cultural terms there was 'a zoological break of the first magnitude' between the Palaeolithic and the Neolithic and, on an insular note, he recalled that Britain had become an island during this interval. He (rightly) dismissed the surface industries quoted by Brown as 'waifs and strays . . . worthless for the purpose of archaeological classifications', and correctly discounted the primitive appearance of material from the flint mines. Dawkins concluded his furious broadside by stating that 'the progress of discovery had not yet bridged over the abyss separating the Palaeolithic age of the Pleistocene period from the Neolithic age of the Prehistoric period in any part of the world' (1894: 251). He was prepared to admit that there must somewhere have been continuity, though 'probably not in Europe', but emphasised that 'the intermediate stages by which he passed from the Palaeolithic to the Neolithic stage of civilisation still remain to be discovered'.

I have referred to the hiatus theory, not because there is any danger of its being revived, but because I believe it can be shown to have warped much of our thinking. When it was discovered that the early postglacial period was far from empty (I refer to the Azilian and Tardenoisian levels in cave sequences but above all to the successively earlier Stone Age industries brought to light in south Scandinavia) this did not change attitudes overnight. Mesolithic finds tended to be depreciated as mere gap-fillers, not as providing evidence for ongoing continuity or even as restoring, so to say, the seamless garment of prehistory. They were neither fish nor fowl. They represented a decline from the period of cave art and failed to anticipate the imagined lake villages of the Robenhausian, still less the megaliths of western and northern Europe. It seemed happily symbolic that the new age should be represented by microliths, whose diminutive size neatly suggested their historical insignificance.

In the first Presidential Address to the Prehistoric Society in 1935, Professor V. Gordon Childe was studious in avoiding any reference to the Mesolithic. 'What,' he asked, 'is to become of the hallowed terms Palaeolithic, Neolithic, Bronze Age, Iron Age? I would suggest that the classification Old Stone Age, New Stone Age, Bronze Age and Iron Age draws attention to real revolutions that affected all departments of human life' (1935a:7). Childe was clearly not unaware of the existence of archaeological material intermediate in age between the Palaeolithic and Neolithic: a few years earlier, the first chapter of *The Dawn of European Civilization* (1927) had, after all, been entitled 'The Transitional Cultures'. On the opening page he admitted that the Palaeolithic and Neolithic could no longer be regarded as epochs 'standing over against one another sharply contrasted and separated by an impassable gulf. The Neolithic arts were not suddenly introduced complete and fully developed into an empty continent as our forefathers imagined. A whole series of intermediate stages have come to light to fill the old hiatus.' Yet it was clear that Childe was still captivated by the Palaeolithic/Neolithic dichotomy. For him the newly-found cultures of early Neothermal Europe did no more than fill an awkward temporal gap. On page 20 he wrote in so many words: 'Though the Epipalaeolithic cultures do fill a gap of time and prove the continuous occupation of parts of Europe from the Old Stone Age, they do not in any real sense constitute points of transition from the Palaeolithic to the Neolithic cultures.'

Childe preferred the term 'Epipalaeolithic' to 'Mesolithic' because he chose to regard the newly-found material as mere survivals of no real historical interest. After discounting the notion of indigenous domestication in Europe or of Palaeolithic pottery, he concluded that 'the contribution of the former age to European culture is negligible. The hiatus is only recreated. The traditional position may then be retained.' In *The Dawn*, as in *The Prehistory of Scotland* (1935b) he went through the motions of describing Epipalaeolithic finds, but relegated everything of importance to later prehistory as the outcome of diffusion from outside. So, for Childe, the only interest of the early Neothermal in temperate Europe was the evidence it provided for the adaptation of surviving hunter-fishers to environmental change – notably the onset of temperate forests. In passing, this adaptation was surely of significance not merely to the Mesolithic population, but also to its successors. In temperate Europe it was Mesolithic man who came to terms with the Neothermal environment, and for the first time sought out its resources. The subsistence and technology of the Neolithic, and indeed of later stages of European prehistory, rested on this foundation. For Childe, though, the Neolithic way of life on which subsequent history rested was seen as the outcome of a revolution – the 'Neolithic Revolution' – which was conceived of as taking place outside Europe. European society was thought of as the product of transformation by impulses from the most ancient east. If there had been no hiatus in settlement in Europe, then according to this view there might just as well have been. The Mesolithic phase of settlement was of so little relevance to the main course of prehistory.

What of the Russians? Here we can see very plainly the link between ideology and terminology. To begin with they followed the same antique model of mid-Victorian evolutionism followed by Childe. For thirty years or more after the Revolution attitudes were determined by the obligatory use of a book by Engels entitled *The Origin of the Family, Private Property and the State*, first published in 1884, a work itself based, as Michael Thompson has pointed out, on Lewis H. Morgan's *Ancient Society* (1877), and on Karl Marx's notes thereon. Prehistory had a special fascination in Soviet eyes because primitive society was held to have been classless, exemplifying communism in all its pristine pre-class and pre-civilised glory. As such, the findings of prehistorians took on something of the character of a sacred writ, or rather they could do so if the findings were correct. And correctness in a totalitarian society is what its leaders find most conducive to perpetuating their ideology and consequently their power. So careful guidance was needed. During N. Y. Marr's dictatorship of the Russian (State) Academy of History of Material Culture (1930–4), prehistory was divided into five periods equated with supposed stages in social evolution, rather than based on the classification of material data:

Primitive Herd (Lower Palaeolithic)
Primitive Community (Upper Palaeolithic)
Matriarchal Class Society (Neolithic)
Patriarchal Class Society (Bronze Age)
The period of break-up of tribal society (Iron Age) immediately preceding the emergence of the State

Note the clean break between the Upper Palaeolithic and the Neolithic: such a system presupposed a quantum jump, and for 'the transformation of the Primitive Community into the Matriarchal Clan Society' read Childe's 'Neolithic Revolution'.

The effect of Hitler's assault, like that of Napoleon's, was to stimulate patriotic feelings in Russia. One form taken by the upsurge of Russian patriotism was the revision, indeed the destruction, of Marrism, reviewed by Michael Thompson in his foreword to the Penguin edition of Mongait's *Archaeology in the U.S.S.R.* (1961). Stalin, in his *Marxism and the Problems of Philology* (1950), denounced Marr as non-Marxist. Marr's name was expunged from the title of the Institute and in 1951 leading archaeologists rushed to contribute to a book entitled *Against the Vulgarisation of Marxism in Archaeology* in which the errors of 'vulgar sociology' were denounced as leading to 'the decolourisation of the historical process'. What was needed was the replacement of abstractions by concrete archaeology and the enrichment of prehistory by taking less account of theory and more of national and racial variations. In other words prehistory was to help build a consciousness of Russian history. But it is of the essence of any national or regional history that it should be continuous and that, so far as possible, its course should be explicable in terms of indigenous development.

As Mongait expressed it in his book: 'Marr's followers [had] fitted the data of material sources to ready-made, prepared schemes. Works were published in which it was asserted that, as a result of a leap, by means of a miraculous transformation, one people changed into another . . .' (1959: 57). In the same way, one could no longer explain the change from the Palaeolithic to the Neolithic in terms of a single leap. It is significant that in his book Mongait envisaged (p. 85) that 'the transition to a new historical epoch . . . gradually took shape in the postglacial age'. The fact that he gave only 23 lines out of 429 pages to this transition he explained by the simple statement that 'much less is known in the world about the Mesolithic than about the other periods of the Stone Age.'

Since then, Mesolithic studies have undergone a rapid growth in the Soviet Union, from the east Baltic to the Caspian. Already in 1966 a whole volume of *Materialy i issledovaniya po Arkheologii S.S.S.R.* was consecrated to twenty-two studies on Mesolithic topics, under the editorship of N. N. Gurina. With a wholesome logic V. M. Masson's map of Mesolithic sites in south-west Asia includes not merely Natufian but also some of those grotesquely designated 'Pre-Pottery Neolithic' in some western literature. As if to underline the point, the aceramic artefacts of flint, stone, antler and bone from sites like Jarmo, Palegawra, Djeitun, Eynan, Jericho or El Khiam could be lost in early Neothermal assemblages over a large part of Europe.

Our colleagues in the New World were spared both the hiatus and the Mesolithic because they were equally spared the Palaeolithic and the Neolithic. There never has been any doubt that New World prehistory was continuous. In plotting its history our American colleagues have been helped immensely by radiocarbon dating. Indeed it may not be generally known that it was Willard Libby's belief in the remote antiquity of man in the New World (a belief still largely unfounded) that spurred him on to investigate the potential for dating purposes of the precise measurements of residual radiocarbon. It so happens that one of the classic applications of radiocarbon dating relates to our main theme, the continuity of prehistory. I refer to the investigations in the Tehuacan valley of central Mexico, sponsored by the Peabody Foundation for Archaeology, and directed by Richard S. MacNeish. Although subject to revision and supplementation by subsequent research, the volumes edited by Douglas S. Byers (1967) remain of particular therapeutic value to prehistorians trained in the broken-backed European tradition. Here the arid environment has preserved a stratigraphic sequence of plant remains in cultural contexts which provides invaluable clues to the changing pattern of man/plant relationships throughout almost the entire Neothermal period. Here we can see fossils of the key process saluted by Childe as the 'Neolithic Revolution'. In fact, this proved to have been gradual and protracted, though at critical points giving rise to decisive changes in the nature of the adjustment between human societies and their parent ecosystems. Indeed, one might go further and emphasise how much we have to learn from New World prehistory, not merely in relation to originative foci, but also and no less to an understanding of the twin processes of slow expansion depending on the need for genetic adaptation, and that of independent cultural developments in territories with differing ecologies.

Nearer home it has been not the least of the services rendered by the British Academy's Major Research Project on the Early History of Agriculture, under the direction of Eric Higgs, to treat the relationship between man and the animals and plants on which he depends as an ongoing, continuous one (Higgs 1972, 1975). To mention only one example, the study of transhumance, which after all is based on the simple biological fact that men predate herbivores which in turn go where the food is to be found at different times of the year, has yielded its best insights by being pursued across the period divisions of prehistory. We learn not merely about 'Palaeolithic' or 'Mesolithic' man, but also about the men of later prehistoric and indeed historical times. Such themes as Sangmeister's beaker reflux movements or the Hallstatt migrations into south-west Europe, inferred from correspondences in pots or metal forms, may often be illuminated in the same terms as the distribution and location of early Stone Age sites.

What is perhaps not so well understood is that the continuities revealed in economic life exist also, and in some ways more significantly, at a conceptual level, at least for the forty thousand years or so since the final emergence of *Homo sapiens sapiens* with the physical attributes of modern man, including his brain and nervous system. The notion that man suddenly acquired a new dimension, the possibility of becoming civilised, at the moment he started to grow wheat, barley, rice or beans as controlled crops, is as absurd as the contemporary fallacies which attempt to equate consumption with well-being.

The fact that cave art is twice as old as the oldest cultivated crops is familiar enough. Herbert Read was not trying to be funny when he wrote: 'Some of the painters of Greek vases, some of the medieval illuminators of manuscripts, the great painters of the Renaissance, certain painters of the nineteenth century – all of these have perhaps reached the level of aesthetic quality present in the cave paintings of Lascaux or Altamira, but they have not exceeded that original standard' (1951: 12). Alexander Marshack (1972) is beginning to show with the aid of microphotography that the makers of this art were also practising a form of notation which in some instances appears to relate to the passage of the moon. Again, detailed observation of still living peoples, who, to judge from their material equipment and the fact that they subsisted by hunting and foraging, would in archaeological terms be judged Mesolithic or even Palaeolithic, has shown that they enjoyed a rich conceptual and ceremonial life, richer in many respects than that of most members of modern metropolitan communities. What may not always be realised is that such people engaged in an activity we are often prone to associate exclusively with communities whose economies were based on agriculture – namely the construction of monuments. Naturally, when the size of the day-to-day community was rarely more than fifteen or twenty persons a limit was set on the nature and scale of monumental constructions. That such were nevertheless made may be illustrated by the stone constructions made by the Australian aborigines in different parts of the continent. Although, as might be expected, the stones used in these were small by comparison with monuments set up in more populous societies, the structures are often quite extensive. The curvilinear alignment terminating in a spiral at one end observed by Richard Gould at Lake Moore, Western Australia, for instance, was over 200 feet long and made up of some 437 stone slabs, most of which stood about two feet high (fig. 20.1). The *bora* grounds, where initiation rites involving circular dancing were being carried out in parts of Australia into the nineteenth century, were frequently enclosed by low earth banks (Howitt 1904: 593). Where there were two circles, as at Samford site, west of Brisbane, these might be connected by a straight avenue. No less evocative to a British archaeologist were the funerary mounds and their associated earthworks noted by early observers in New South Wales. That shown in my illustration (fig. 20.2) was recorded by John Oxley when exploring the Lachlan river in 1817. The mound stood like the tump of a disc barrow in the midst of a flat area defined by a penannular bank. The arc-shaped banks opposite the gap were interpreted by Oxley as seats for the spectators at the funerary rites (Oxley 1820). Analogies could be multiplied; for instance, the carvings made on trees surrounding burials compare remarkably in some instances with those pecked on the stones of some Irish passage graves. The danger of drawing parallels between the artefacts of communities far removed in time, space and culture needs no emphasis. It is still legitimate to point out that the construction of monuments connected with burial and other ceremonial activity, like the practice of symbolic art, is no monopoly of communities founded on farming. Nearer home, indeed, it has recently been argued that at least two groups of Mesolithic tombs in Europe – the *dysse* and passage-graves of Bohuslan, western Sweden, and the entrance graves of the Celtic Sea – were constructed by people whose economy rested on fishing rather than farming (Clark 1977). This is perhaps something to remember when radiocarbon dating confronts us with the likelihood that megalithic monuments, whether funerary or ceremonial, are indigenous to western Europe. To generalise, the recognition that parts of Europe were inhabited during early Neothermal times by adaptable indigenous Mesolithic commu-

20.1 Rock alignments and sacred rock-piles figure as important archaeological monuments in Australia. This serpentine alignment occurs on Lake Moore, Western Australia.

20.2 Burial mound and associated earthworks recorded by John Oxley (1820) on the Lachlan River, New South Wales

nities makes it easier to accommodate ourselves to the findings of radiocarbon dating. As Colin Renfrew has recently been emphasising, a number of key innovations of later Neothermal times need not and in some cases (even without the aid of recalibration) cannot any longer be explained, as Childe would once have had us believe, as mere emanations from the orient.

References

Brown, J. A., 1893. 'On the continuity of the Palaeolithic and Neolithic periods'. *Journal of the Royal Anthropological Institute*, 22: 66–98.

Byers, D. S. (ed.), 1967. *The Prehistory of the Tehuacan Valley*. Austin and London, University of Texas Press.

Childe, V. G., 1927. *The Dawn of European Civilization*. London, Kegan Paul. (2nd edn).
    1935a. 'Changing methods and aims in prehistory'. *Proceedings of the Prehistoric Society*, 1: 1–16.
    1935b. *The Prehistory of Scotland*. London, Kegan Paul.

Clark, G., 1977. 'The economic context of Dolmens and Passage-graves in Sweden'. In V. Markotic (ed.), *Ancient Europe and the Mediterranean*. Warminster, Aris and Phillips: 35–49.

Darwin, C., 1859. *On the Origin of Species by the Means of Natural Selection*. London, Murray.

Dawkins, W. B., 1894. 'On the relation of the Palaeolithic to the Neolithic Period'. *Journal of the Royal Anthropological Institute*, 23: 242–57.

Engels, F., 1884. *The Origins of the Family, Private Property and the State*. English translation by E. Untermann, 1902. Chicago, Kerr and Co.

Gould, R. A., 1969. *Yiwara: Foragers of the Australian Desert*. London, Collins.

Gurina, N. N. (ed.), 1966. *U Istokov Drevnikh Kul'tur. Epokha Mezolita*. Materialy i Issledovaniya po Arkheologii S.S.S.R., No. 126. Moscow and Leningrad, Academy of Sciences.

Higgs, E. S. (ed.), 1972. *Papers in Economic Prehistory*. London, Cambridge University Press.

Higgs, E. S. (ed.), 1975. *Palaeoeconomy*. London, Cambridge University Press.

Howitt, A. W., 1904. *The Native Tribes of South-east Australia*. London, Macmillan.

Lubbock, Sir J., 1865. *Prehistoric Times*. London, Williams and Norgate.

Marshack, A., 1972. *The Roots of Civilization*. New York, McGraw-Hill.

Mongait, A. L., 1959. *Archaeology in the U.S.S.R*. English translation by M. W. Thompson (1961). London, Penguin Books.

Morgan, L. H., 1877. *Ancient Society*. New York.

Mortillet, G. de, 1872. 'Classification des diverses périodes de l'âge de la pierre'. *Comptes Rendus du Congrès International d'Anthropologie et Archéologie Préhistorique*, 6: 432–44.

Mortillet, G. de, and Mortillet, A. de, 1881. *Musée Préhistorique*. Paris.

Obermaier, H., 1924. *Fossil Man in Spain*. New Haven, Hispanic Society of America.

Oxley, J., 1820. *Journal of Two Expeditions into the Interior of South-East Australia*. London.

Read, H., 1951. *Art and the Evolution of Man*. London, Freedom Press.

Stalin, J., 1950. *Concerning Marxism in Linguistics*. London, Soviet News.

Westropp, H. M., 1872. *Prehistoric Phases*. London, Bell and Daldy.

CHAPTER 21

PRIMITIVE MAN AS HUNTER, FISHER, FORAGER AND FARMER

Since much of the primary data surviving from prehistory relates directly or indirectly to the quest for food, and since in any case the only communities to leave archaeological traces were those successful in securing food, it would be perverse to overlook or indeed to fail to concentrate very considerable attention on the early history of subsistence. But let there be no misunderstanding, this is emphatically not to argue for a reductionist view. The mere fact that man like other animals has to eat in order to survive does not mean that he need or should be judged primarily as an organism. Man is of supreme interest not so much because he is an animal that has to eat or even, I would submit (for I am no gastro-archaeologist), as one whose highest purpose is to eat, as for the aspirations he is able, having eaten, to entertain. The real reason why early subsistence is of interest is that the manner in which men secure their food to some extent conditions (and is, of course, conditioned by) the kind of cultural environment in which such aspirations can be entertained and realized.

You will hardly need to be reminded of the constraints traditionally held to have applied to societies that depend exclusively on hunting, fishing, and foraging, still less perhaps of the liberating effect widely supposed to have issued from the adoption of farming. All the same, it hardly seems appropriate to treat as a mere backdrop the period during which men survived entirely by what they were able to appropriate from wild species of animals and plants, considering that this encompasses all but a small part of human history anywhere and until modern times the entire history of quite extensive areas of the world. It is surely essential if we are correctly to assess our existing situation to appreciate and fully digest the fact that by and large the experience of mankind has been that of an omnivorous predator. Less than ten generations have experienced the heavy constraints of industrial society, and then only in confined territories, and hardly more than a few hundred the less burdensome, though still considerable, ones of farming. If the object of history is to widen perspectives and in this way to deepen understanding, it is strange to find this subject increasingly equated in the schools with the history of industrial society and hardly less so, if a visitor may be pardoned the comment, to find the Oxford Chair of European Archaeology restricted to so narrow a slice of time as that since men first engaged in farming.

Our knowledge of the economy practised by the earliest man (*Homo erectus*) has been won to a substantial extent from the exploration of Lower Pleistocene deposits in East Africa carried out by the late Louis Leakey, his wife Mary, and their associates. The key information comes from occupation levels in beds I and II in Olduvai Gorge, northern Tanzania, dating from between *c.* 2.0 and 0.7 million years ago.[1] The animal bones from bed I show that meat was already providing a significant component of diet. Although, as we know from recent observation of chimpanzees and baboons in the wild, these animals were not by any means averse to meat, it remains a fact that this was invariably obtained from animals smaller than themselves and remained an extra rather than a basic component of diet. The regular eating of meat, including that of prey as large as or larger than the hominids themselves, is widely recognized to define 'a highly significant adaptive shift' in diet.

The notion that Lower Pleistocene man confined his predation to small species and concentrated on young individuals can no longer be sustained. Although remains of medium-sized antelopes predominated in the food refuse investigated from the East African sites, it appears certain that much larger species were also represented.[2] This is shown by the bones scattered in general refuse and most strikingly at kill sites featuring the partly broken-up carcasses of individual animals. These included such large forms as hippopotamus from the KSB tuff at East Rudolph and the elephant and dinothere from Olduvai locus FLK N. The frequent presence of stone artefacts both on kill sites and among refuse scatter emphasizes the adaptive advantages these things conferred on man as distinct from other primates. This was so despite the extreme simplicity of the earliest stone industries. The artefacts fell into two main categories, sharp flakes and the crude core-tools and discoids from which these had been struck. Even with such equipment it would have been possible to shape wooden weapons including spears and at the same time to cut and dismember slaughtered animals whether for meat or as sources of raw materials. When fire first came into use as an aid in making artefacts, for rendering dwellings more habitable, in hunting and in cooking, remains an open question. Although present in the earliest deposits to be examined in any volume both in western Europe and north China,[3] it is absent from Middle Pleistocene as well as Lower Pleistocene deposits in the African continent. On the other hand, Desmond Clark may well be correct in attributing this to the greater speed at which charcoal is broken down in tropical soils.[4]

The hunting of large mammals depended on social as well as technological factors. It involved among other things an organized system of co-operation among hunters who, to judge from ethnographic observation, would have been exclusively men. The reason for this is not far to seek. Hunting involved movements that might be extensive and of long duration. In this respect the role of women was complementary, that of staying close to the home base,

21.1 Australian woman of the Wik Monkan tribe of Cape York, Queensland, with vegetable foods of the peak season and the utensils used in gathering them

nourishing, tending, and bringing up the young during the increasingly long period of dependence during which they had to acquire learned behaviour of ever-increasing intricacy and scope. Guarding the home base and looking after the family by no means excluded women from the food quest. As we know from observation of people like the recent Australian aborigines (fig. 21.1)[5] or the Bushmen of South Africa,[6] domestic duties could readily be combined with foraging for plant food and small animal products, activities, it may be added, through which young children could most readily be initiated into the food quest by their mothers. The partnership of the sexes was from the beginning quite as much economic as sexual and in each regard focused on the home base. It is a matter of some moment that what may have been the stone footings of the kind of artificial shelter that might have served as the focus of a primary biological family were observed at the very base of the Olduvai sequence[7] along with bone refuse and stone artefacts. The earliest human economies are likely to have been based on a subdivision of functions between the men who concerned themselves with hunting, and had to be prepared to operate at a distance from the home base, and the women who watched over the young, cooked, maintained the home base and

21.2 Bushman hunter distributing meat to members of the other band sharing the same waterhole

engaged in foraging in the near neighbourhood. Hunting large animals with primitive equipment must for its part have involved active co-operation between the males. The basis of this rested if we may judge from ethnographic parallels on institutionalized sharing of the meat (fig. 21.2), a social bond that held together complete bands, just as the division between hunting and foraging cemented individual family units. The system by which the earliest communities lived was thus based throughout on co-operation and sharing rather than struggle. Once established it was self-regulating and, until replaced by competitively more effective ones, long enduring. This may well help to explain why it was that the earliest cultural patterns were so slow to change.

The archaeological evidence recovered from the Middle Pleistocene (c.0.7 to 0.1 million years ago) continues to reflect a way of life resembling that of the phase just reviewed. The importance of hunting as a component of the food quest and the prowess of those who pursued it are particularly manifest in the material preserved in the limestone fissure of Choukoutien near Peking.[8] The fact that men equipped with stone tools no more elaborate than those from the lower beds at Olduvai were able to master animals as large as the elephant and the rhinoceros and as fierce as the sabre-toothed tiger and other carnivores, as well as herbivores of widely varying habit, testified to their adaptability and the effectiveness of their social co-operation. Large animals like the elephants at Torralba, Spain,[9] continued to be butchered where they finally succumbed, and their meat distributed among those sharing the same hunting territory. On the other hand, to judge from the proportions in which different parts of their skeletons were represented on human settlements, it appears that smaller animals were as a rule dismembered and carried to the home base in convenient joints. Analysis of stones from settlement sites suggests that most were obtained within a radius of 5 km, with occasional exceptions extending to 65 km, which argues that home base territories were comparatively restricted. The fine stratigraphy at Kalambo Falls, Zambia,[10] extending in time well into the earlier part of the Upper Pleistocene in Sub-Saharan Africa, suggests that the site was frequently revisited. This in turn argues that dense accumulations of artefacts are at least as likely to indicate frequent returns to the same location as its use by large numbers of people at once.

The use of fire is now for the first time positively documented at sites as widely distributed as Hoxne and Torralba in England and Spain and Choukoutien in north China, all in the northern part of the zone occupied by man during the Middle Pleistocene. Indeed the evidence of fossil pollen pointing to forest clearance and the expansion of open vegetation when the site at Hoxne[11] was occupied by Acheulian man argues that fire may well have been as useful to the Middle Pleistocene hunters of England as it was to the recent aborigines of Australia. A noteworthy innovation at this time in respect of flint and stone technology was the emergence of cleavers and bifacial hand-axes. On the other hand, it needs to be stressed that these forms were confined to Africa and proximate parts of Asia and Europe, and supplemented rather than replaced earlier forms. Butchery probably continued to be carried out by the flake component, but the precise roles of bifaces and cleavers remain enigmatic. It was nevertheless the latter which provided the dynamic element. Broadly speaking the direction of evolution was towards the production of forms with more regular working edges while reducing the quantity of raw flint or stone used. On the other hand the new Acheulian forms displayed a uniformity over immense territories so great that the origins of individual specimens could often only be guessed at by identifying the material from which they were flaked.

It was only with the emergence of different variants of the large-brained *Homo sapiens* during the Upper Pleistocene that the first noteworthy advances in conceptual life, technology, and economy can be detected in the archaeological record. Indeed these first became really marked with the appearance not much more than 35,000 years ago of men of modern type (*Homo sapiens sapiens*). Even so, certain notable advances may be attributed to the archaic form represented in Europe from Iberia to south Russia, in north Africa and from south-west to central Asia by Neanderthal man (*Homo sapiens neanderthalensis*). The most notable development in the conceptual field was unquestionably the practice of careful burial with the

implication this carries of a personal awareness of death. The contrast with
the situation at Choukoutien is particularly marked. There not one of the
forty or so individuals of the species *Homo erectus pekinensis* was accorded
burial. On the contrary the bones showed clear signs of the practice of
cannibalism: the long bones were split as if for the extraction of marrow and
the foramen magnum, the aperture at the base of the skull, was in some cases
enlarged to allow the removal of the brain. In certain instances, as witnessed
by discoveries in the cave of Krapina in Croatia or again at Monte Circeo in
Italy, Neanderthal man continued to practise cannibalism.[12] On the other
hand, he generally buried his dead as we are forcibly reminded by the
cemetery of ten graves in front of the Mugharet es-Skhūl, Mount Carmel.[13]
Often the lower limbs were drawn up, sometimes so closely as to suggest that
the corpse had been bound tightly before it stiffened. One of the Mount
Carmel burials, that of a man of forty-five, clasped the two lower mandibles
of a large boar, and a child burial from Teshik-Tash, Uzbekistan[14] (fig. 21.3),
was ringed by goat skulls held in position by ramming their horns into the
sub-soil.

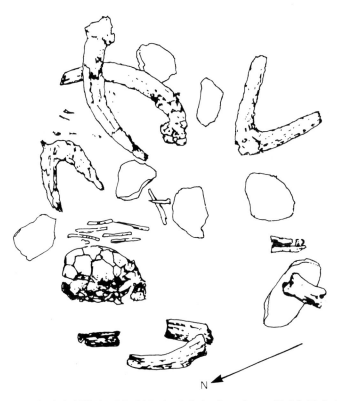

N

21.3 Neanderthal child's burial within ritual circle of goat horns, Teshik-Tash, Uzbekistan, USSR

One of the most noteworthy achievements of Neanderthal man was to break out of the frost-free zone to which previous hominid populations had been confined[15] and initiate the process by which during the later Upper Pleistocene and recent ages man extended his domain over the rest of the world (fig. 21.4). The northward expansion into the territories of the USSR was all the more striking in that it seems mostly to have occurred during the earlier part of the Würm glaciation. Although the main weight of settlement was concentrated between the Don and the Bug in south Russia, smaller numbers of settlers equipped with Mousterian artefacts are now known to have advanced along the corridor between the eastern margin of the Scandinavian ice-sheet, which then extended over much of the north part of European Russia, and the northern Urals reaching as far as Krutaya Gora well beyond latitude 65° N.[16] In keeping with this we now have evidence, notably from Molodova in the Dnestr Valley,[17] for more elaborate dwellings, which take the form of oval settings of animal bones and teeth. These enclosed fireplaces and cultural debris and are generally considered to have served to weight the perimeters of skin coverings stretched over timber supports. Clothing must also have been needed in such relatively cold conditions at least for wear out-of-doors, and this can hardly have been made of anything else at that time than animal skins. The preparation of these for

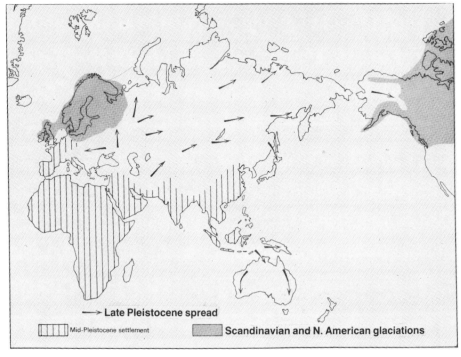

21.4 Late Pleistocene expansion of human settlement

clothing and shelter would have been a heavy task and it is suggestive that well-made flint scraping tools were a leading component of most Mousterian industries.

There are many signs that artefacts were adapted more sensitively than previously to local needs. Although it would be easy to exaggerate the trend, there is little doubt that the Upper Pleistocene was marked by an increasing acceleration in the rate of technological change and conversely in the degree of cultural diversity.[18] Every advance in our knowledge of the Levalloiso-Mousterian industries associated with Neanderthal man from western Europe and north Africa to south-west Asia and the inhabited zone of the USSR helps to define more accurately their diversity, both as regards size and still more as regards the techniques and forms of implement represented. South of the Sahara the stone industries of this time reflect above all a broad ecological distinction between those adapted to the grasslands and savannah and those encountered when colonization began to extend into the forest.[19] Whereas industries in the continuing Acheulian tradition continued in the former, the latter elicited quite distinctive configurations in the Sangoan and Lupemban.

The final emergence of *Homo sapiens sapiens*, having all the attributes of modern man and to which without exception all the existing races of men belong, ushered in a period of increasingly rapid change and diversity in respect of culture. Archaeology suggests that the decisive threshold was crossed around 35,000 years ago in terms of radiocarbon dating. Since men have diverged from other primates most strikingly, from a biological point of view, in the size and organization of their brains, it is appropriate to emphasize the conceptual advances documented in the artefacts surviving from prehistory. In the first place one may note a marked elaboration in the ritual of interment. The ceremonial burials dating from the closing stages of the Upper Pleistocene, found in caves and rock shelters as well as at open sites over a broad tract of Eurasia, already displayed many of the features that prevailed down to the onset of Christianity. The dead were commonly clothed and accompanied by personal ornaments and accoutrements. The provision of ornaments was in itself a notable innovation. Despite the number of Neanderthal burials excavated, many of them under scientific conditions, not one has yielded so much as a single bead. By contrast the Upper Palaeolithic burials investigated in Europe were normally enriched by ornaments. Sometimes these were extremely numerous. The burials at Sungir (fig. 21.5) in central Russia,[20] for example, were smothered under some 8,000 perforated ivory beads, some of which were found to delineate outlines of the garments, presumably of skin, in which they had been laid to rest. Taken together also the ornaments placed with the dead at this time reveal a rich diversity in respect of materials, forms, and workmanship.

An even richer insight into the aesthetic awareness of the early representa-

21.5 Ceremonial Upper Palaeolithic burial, Sungir, Central Russia. Note the large number of personal ornaments.

tives of modern man is provided by the works of art displayed on the walls and ceilings of caves and rock shelters and incorporated in archaeological deposits over a territory extending from Spain to the Urals.[21] Whatever motives inspired the Quaternary artists and whatever may have been their role in social life, it is evident that some of the earliest representatives of modern man created works of art capable of holding their own against the products of later ages and more sophisticated cultures. In addition to the exact observation, manual dexterity, and aesthetic sensibility which they exhibit, detailed study under magnification indicates that some of the engravings incorporate evidence of a system of notation that may well have served some of the functions performed by writing and mathematical symbols in more complex societies.

Several of the trends already established by Neanderthal man and his relatives were carried further by their immediate successors. Modern man still sought the shelter of caves and rock shelters. Similarly in territories like the Ukraine or the loess areas of central Europe (fig. 21.6), where natural shelters were absent or scarce, he continued to construct dwellings sufficiently robust to make warm home bases. Whether due to an accident of survival or to a genuine advance it is too early to say, but the more numerous structures dating from the closing phase of the Upper Pleistocene in Europe include examples more elaborate than anything surviving from earlier periods. Good instances are provided by the dome-shaped houses from

21.6 Upper Palaeolithic house floor defined by stone boulders and mammoth tusks under a thick loess deposit, Dolni Veštonice, Czechoslavakia

Mezhirich near Kiev,[22] the walls of which were built of interlocking mammoth jaws supporting skulls and the roofs of which were presumably formed of animal skins weighed down by mammoth tusks. From this time also eyed needles and representations like the mammoth ivory figurine of a fur-clad man from Buret, Siberia,[23] provide reliable evidence for the first time of skin clothing.

Expansion of the geographical territories settled by man which had already been begun by Neanderthal man was notably advanced. New lands were colonized in northern Europe as the Scandinavian ice-sheet contracted,[24] but expansions of much greater significance were carried forward from the Far East and south-east Asia. The Japanese islands were certainly occupied at this time, if not before.[25] There is evidence that the Yukon on the Asian side of the North American glaciated zone was already occupied by around 30,000 years ago.[26] When this barrier was breached towards the close of the Ice Age by the parting of the Laurentide and Cordilleran ice-sheets, the Paleo-indians spread south to inherit game reserves of immense wealth. Within a remarkably short time they had reached the Atlantic and had moved southwards, through Middle America, to the southern tip of South America. Another territory hardly less vast in extent was colonized from south-east Asia. The relatively low sea-level prevailing during the last glaciation meant on the one hand that Borneo and most of Indonesia were joined to south-east Asia and on the other that New Guinea and Tasmania formed part of the continent of greater Australia. This meant that at this time the continent could be approached mainly over dry land leaving only a few sea breaks, none of them very formidable, to be crossed by boat or float. Precisely when the first entry was made has yet to be decided, but though this certainly occurred more than 20,000 years ago it is suggestive that all the human remains so far identified in Australia are of *Homo sapiens sapiens* character.

A basic role in the quest for food continued to be played by hunting. Indeed in more than one respect this activity seems to have been carried on in a more sophisticated and specialized manner. Attention seems frequently to have been focused on particular species of animal as with mammoth in south Russia and parts of central Europe. A highly gregarious species like the reindeer seems to have invited a particularly close relationship in western and northern Europe during the Late-glacial period,[27] involving a certain degree of seasonal movement on the part of its human predators. Many new types of weapon were introduced, including spears, darts, and harpoons with detachable head, as well as in some contexts bows and arrows. The manufacture of hunting equipment as well as of the implements used in preparing skins and making clothes and ornaments was associated with the use of a wider range of materials and a more sophisticated technology, including in particular the fabrication of many composite artefacts. The flint worker for instance had to produce a wide range of specialized tools for gutting, grooving, piercing, sawing and scraping, as well as the armatures, points, barbs and cutting edges, of a variety of weapons (fig. 21.7). A far more varied and sophisticated use was made of antler, bone, and ivory, materials that for most purposes could only be used in the form of blanks detached by ringing or grooving by means of burins and other flint tools.[28] The wider range of materials employed and the greater degree of specialization in respect both of function and technique of production made for more rapid change and a greater diversity both in space and time.

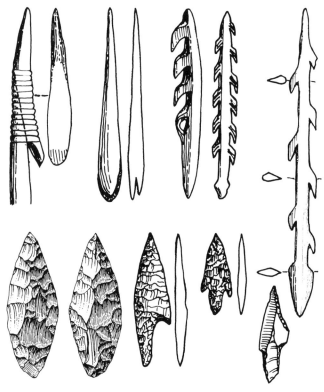

21.7 Some of the many varieties of projectile head of flint, antler and bone made by Upper Palaeolithic man in Western Europe

Analysis of the materials used for ornaments, tools, and weapons shows that these were sometimes obtained from a considerable distance. The amber and shells used for personal adornment by the inhabitants of the Mezhirich dwellings for example must have come from distances of between 350 and 500 km.[29] Again, the chocolate-coloured flint mined from a district *c.* 80 km south of Warsaw was used over a radius of some 180 km by the makers of Swiderian industries during the Late-glacial period,[30] just as the Zarzians of the Zagros mountains flaked obsidian derived from the region of Lake Van in eastern Anatolia.[31] Whatever the mechanism, whether seasonal movement, exogamy, or the straight exchange of exotic substances, or some combination of these, it is plain that desirable materials were being distributed over wide territories by late Upper Pleistocene hunters. Like the Australian aborigines of recent times the Pleistocene hunters thus benefited from a redistributive process that wrought the same kind of purpose as trade was to do among settled societies with a relatively advanced subdivision of labour.

Despite his success in expanding his settlement, diversifying and elaborating more effective material equipment, and ultimately developing and exploring new areas of self-awareness, modern man was held back in his social development for at least twenty-five millennia and in some cases down even to modern times. Precisely what was limiting the realization of his potential? It was surely not, as has so often been suggested, that hunting and foraging were so demanding that they left neither time nor energy for progress. On the contrary, systematic study of hunter-gatherers as these could recently be observed in action has shown repeatedly that they manage to supply their needs at the cost of a surprisingly low input of energy. Richard Lee's model study has shown for instance that the Kung Bushmen of South Africa[32] make do on the equivalent of a two-and-a-half day week. This helps among other things to account for the fact that people like the Australian aborigines, while depending entirely on what they could grub, catch, or forage, nevertheless maintained decorative arts, ritual observances, mythology, and a web of social obligations whose intricacy and richness continues to fascinate modern anthropologists. Similarly it helps to explain how it was that as early as the Middle Pleistocene Palaeolithic man was already fabricating artefacts, notably bifacial hand-axes, to standards of perfection far beyond what was required from a merely functional stand-point. Even more it allows us to account for the cave art of the late Upper Pleistocene, including such things as the rock-paintings of Altamira, Lascaux, or Le Portel, the relief carvings of Cap Blanc or Le Roc, the modelled or sculptured female figurines extending from France to the USSR or the designs engraved on small objects from innumerable cave deposits (fig. 21.8). The archaeological data from this time already reflects an amplitude of leisure. It was this and the pleasurable way of life that went with it, rather than penury and a day long grind, that explains why social life remained so static. Is it really so surprising that a self-regulating mode of life returning rich satisfactions for little work should have perpetuated itself for so long?

What then were the factors that held back hunter foragers and conversely

21.8 Spiral designs carved on bone objects of Upper Magdalenian age from Isturitz, Basses Pyrénées, France

made possible the dynamic progress that followed on the adoption of farming? Before attempting to answer this it is important to look more closely at what we mean by farming. As the work of Eric Higgs and Mike Jarman and their team at Cambridge has emphasized in recent years,[33] the distinction between hunter-forager and farmer is much less clear-cut than might be imagined from the dialogue of cultural evolutionists. In part this is a question of semantics. As I indicated in my contribution to the symposium on early agriculture held jointly by the Royal Society and the British Academy in 1976:

Words like crop, harvest or husbandry are so closely linked in our minds with the agricultural basis of our own society that we are only too prone to overlook the fact that human societies of whatever kind depend for their subsistence, directly or indirectly, on cropping, harvesting and husbanding animals and plants . . . The convention by which economies based on such activities as foraging and hunting are considered to be merely predatory, whereas those based on farming are held to be productive, in a sense begs the question. Both systematically exploit natural resources.[34]

Although it is vital to an understanding both of the origins of the new economy and of the complexity of subsistence systems operating at any particular time that the dichotomy between hunter-foragers and farmers should not be overdrawn, it remains an inescapable fact that, however gratifying a life they were capable of affording, no society depending exclusively on hunting and foraging has ever entered upon the wider experience of civilization. And the converse is no less true. All those who share in the consciousness of civilized existence have up to the present depended in the last resort on the cultivation of crops and/or the maintenance of animal herds. Since those who follow me in this series will be speaking on the archaeology of civilized societies, it is necessary, therefore, to consider what was really involved in the transition from hunting and foraging to farming. The more so in that it helps to explain the rich diversity of the several civilizations of mankind as this is encountered in the archaeological record.

The essential change in the transition to farming lay in the greater degree of control over the animals and plants contributing to sustenance. It is important from the outset to emphasize the dynamic element in the new relationships. Control by its very nature invites intensification, since the more effectively it is exercised the more productive and, therefore, the more adaptive it becomes. The key to farming was domestication and the essence of domestication is that the animals and plants subject to it were attached to the home bases of those who controlled them. The relationship was mutually advantageous. Livestock were protected from all but one of their natural predators, had their food supplemented when necessary by fodder, and were

21.9 Forest clearance for agriculture: (a) Man attacking tree with stone-bladed adze, New Guinea, 1964; (b) Fire in use for clearance in the course of swidden agriculture in nineteenth-century Finland

afforded shelter when conditions were too inclement in the open. Plants were advantaged by removing or at least reducing competition from weeds or grazing animals, and positively through cultivation of the soil, drainage or irrigation as the case may be, and sometimes also enrichment through the addition of manure. The farmer for his part gained by having reasonably assured supplies of preferred foods virtually on his doorstep. Naturally there was a price to pay for greater security and convenience. The practice of farming involved the domestication of the farmer himself as well as of his crops and his herds. Quite apart from the need to adjust to the social requirements of larger and more complex communities, the new economy was in itself more demanding. Looking after livestock, not least milking them, involved a rigid daily timetable and meant that in effect the farmer became a servant of his animals. The practice of agriculture was even more onerous, more particularly when this involved the clearance (fig. 21.9) and taking into cultivation of virgin lands (fig. 21.10) terracing or irrigation. The adoption of agriculture, though a decisive step, was only one on the lofty and seemingly endless ladder of progress, the attainment of each rung of which imposed an extra burden. Why then did not our forebears rest content on the lower rungs? If progress exacted such a price, why did men embark on it? The short answer is that this was the price of survival. Economic, technological, and intellectual, not to mention social advances were by nature adaptive, favouring those who adopted them, penalizing those who failed to do so.

21.10 Clay model of the Cypriot Early Bronze Age showing two pairs of oxen yoked to ards or light Mediterranean scratch-ploughs.

Only in the remote backwaters that once gave scope for anthropologists was it possible to stay for a time unregenerate. Today almost the last refuge has been engulfed. On the highlands of New Guinea[35] men who hardly more than a generation back were happily polishing their stone axes are busy putting crosses on ballot papers and qualifying for income tax.

The practice of farming certainly involved risks. So long as men lived in bands of hardly more than twenty persons and had the freedom of extensive territories they were able to select from a large number of seasonal resources and stood in little danger of starvation. The greater density of population made possible by farming on the other hand presented hazards all the more serious when we remember the low yields of crops in antiquity and the liability of herds to pestilence. Yet to some degree the risks of farming were counterbalanced by the relative ease with which crops could be stored and by the fact that livestock herds constituted in themselves living reserves from which dairy products, meat, and such products as hides, horn, and wool could be obtained at will. A further resource was open to early farmers. Foraging and hunting, not to mention fishing, continued to provide ancillary sources of foodstuffs, though ones that ceased to be quantitatively significant with each increase in the density of population. Another consideration, particularly relevant to prehistory, is that fully sedentary settlement and a marked increase in the density of population were neither of them achieved suddenly. The distinction between nomadic and fully sedentary settlement was not clear-cut. The home base was peripatetic before it became permanently static and there were many gradations between the two. In particular it need not invariably follow that hunter–foragers were nomadic or farmers fully sedentary. Under certain conditions the opposite might have obtained in the past as it certainly has done in the ethnographic present. Above all, whatever their main source of food, the same people might be sedentary at one time and nomadic at another time of the year.

Yet there is no question that for a number of reasons the practice of farming conferred advantages. For one thing, in so far as it made it possible to obtain all that was needed within a narrow radius of a permanent home base, it freed men from the need to range over extensive territories and made it possible to occupy the same settlement not merely throughout the year but over a period of years. This in turn made possible a marked increase in both the density of population and in the potential size of groups able to live together, giving them marked advantages in the competition for land and resources. Indirectly also the enlarged size of settlements for long restricted in most territories to villages permitted an increase in the subdivision of labour which in turn favoured advances in technology. Another dynamic outcome and accompaniment of domestication was the way it increased productivity through its impact on the genetic composition of favoured animals and plants.

This can be documented rather neatly from the sample of 1,248 maize cobs recovered from successive levels of the San Marcos cave in the valley of Tehuacan, Mexico:[36]

	Strata	Average length	Average number of spikelets	Settlement phase
		mm		
AD 800	B	55	163	Cities served by irrigation
BC 200	C¹	47	134	
900 1500	C	45	120	Villages and ceremonial centre
2300 3500	D	43	113	Semi-permanent villages
c.5000				

It is because such genetic changes ensured higher yields from the same input of energy and in this way provided the economic base for the emergence of peasant societies and ultimately of imposing civilizations that they are of such diagnostic significance. In principle they can only have come into existence as an outcome of human selection working on biological mutations. This could in large measure have been exercised unwittingly. The mere act of growing preferred plants close to the home base in soil enriched by organic waste would alone have exerted some influence and this could only have been increased by assisting such plants by removing or reducing competitors. Again, once the notion of growing preferred plants in concentrations, as distinct from foraging, took root, the convenience of harvesting crops at one time would have operated selectively in the case of such cereals as wheat, barley, or maize. Whereas in wild species those specimens with a brittle rachis gained an advantage by achieving a wider dispersal of seed, in the case of cereals harvested at one time variants with a relatively tough rachis were more likely to feature in the seed corn. Again, the process of threshing would certainly have favoured mutant maize with relatively soft glumes. None of this in the least detracts from the likelihood that when farming had attained a certain importance in subsistence its practitioners would have begun to influence the character of herds and crops in a directly purposeful though, of course, empirical fashion by favouring the breeding of more productive strains.

The process of establishing closer relations between human societies and preferred species of animal and plant must by its very nature have been gradual, worked out in the context of prevailing ecological systems. To think of farming as if it was an abrupt invention capable of being diffused like some new gadget is hardly possible today when so much is known about its development in different territories. Systematic investigations in the Tehuacan Valley (fig. 21.11) and the district of Oaxaca, Mexico,[37] backed up by radiocarbon dating shows that for several thousand years domesticated

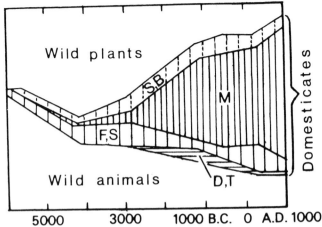

21.11 The transition from wild to predominantly domesticated sources of plant and
animal food in the valley of Tehuacan, Mexico, between 6000 BC and AD 1000.
M = maize; S,B = squash and beans; F,S = fruit and seeds; D,T = dog and
turkey

species like avocado, beans, maize, and squash remained quantitatively
inconspicuous by contrast with a multitude of foraged plants.

The decisive turning-point is usually marked in the archaeological record
by a number of closely linked changes, notably a sharp upturn in the
proportion of domesticated animals and plants accompanied by a reduction
in the number of species, together reflecting a more intense concentration and
a heavier investment in the form of cultivation and maintenance. With this is
associated a greater degree of sedentarism, a markedly greater overall density
of population and the possibility of larger numbers of people living together
in single settlements. In technology a common, though by no means
invariable innovation is the appearance of pottery containers and cooking
vessels[38] to supplement and in part replace those made of organic materials.

Cultivated plants and domestic animals might be introduced in territories
beyond the range of their original prototypes, as we know happened in
temperate Europe and North America or again in the Pacific. Their diffusion
was subject only to ecological constraints which imposed limits and involved
genetic adaptations that slowed it down. On the other hand, it is certain that
domesticated species can only have been developed in territories where their
wild prototypes were available.[39]

Given the advantages that accrued to communities that succeeded in
developing closer relations with animals and plants to the point of domestication, it is hardly to be wondered at that the process should have unfolded
in so many parts of the world. Whether this occurred completely independently or whether in some instances it was stimulated from outside is of no
great moment. What is important is that the process unfolded in territories

with widely different ecologies. One of the clues to the astonishing diversity of human civilizations is that they rest on the cultivation and raising of such a wide variety of species. The raising, harvesting, and preparation of plants as various as rice, beans, maize, manioc, potato, wheat, barley, rye, or yams, would alone have served to promote diversity not merely in subsistence and technology, but also in settlement and social organization. Even within the cereal zone of Europe widely differing regimes adjusted to regional ecosystems are reflected in the archaeological record of early peasant communities. One has only for example to compare the dry farming regime of the Mediterranean zone, complemented by the cultivation of almonds, figs, olives, and vines, with the mixed farming of the deciduous zone based on year-round rainfall or again with the regime of the marginal economies of much of Scandinavia and north Russia, where the growing season was too short for cereals to play more than a subsidiary role, to appreciate the importance of the ecological factor.

In view of the lectures which follow I would only conclude by emphasizing that if farming provided the economic base for civilization it hardly accounts for it. For this we must look to social dynamics. Prehistoric farmers, no less than hunter-fishers, were severely limited by their egalitarian nature as evinced for example by the plans and contents of their houses (fig. 21.12). Such social structure as they did display was strictly segmental. There were distinctions of age and sex, but hardly yet of hierarchy. By contrast, the high cultures or civilizations considered by later lecturers in this series were invariably the product of vertically or hierarchically structured societies. Hierarchy and social inequality were not merely the invariable accompaniment but the formative factor in the emergence of high cultures. And by high cultures I mean those whose upper classes observed, or failed to observe, canons of behaviour furthest removed from those of the lower animals. In terms of archaeology high cultures are those whose noblest artefacts diverge most notably from the sticks and stones of *Homo erectus* and in so far as they relate to the higher levels in the hierarchy transcend most clearly the homely products of prehistoric societies in respect of complexity, diversity, and sophistication. It is a matter of fact based on stratigraphy that the material embodiments of high culture invariably appear in the context of hierarchically organized societies. Again, the archaeology of the lower levels in hierarchical societies normally approximates more closely to that of earlier phases in the history of the same tradition. Whereas the peaks of cultural achievements, the finest products of human craft, were exclusively associated with and indeed helped to define and signal the highest levels in hierarchical societies, the objects and structures used by the mass of the population, including the very craftsmen who made the noblest insignia and built the grandest monuments, were often comparable with those of their prehistoric forebears. The conclusion is surely inescapable that without a hierarchical

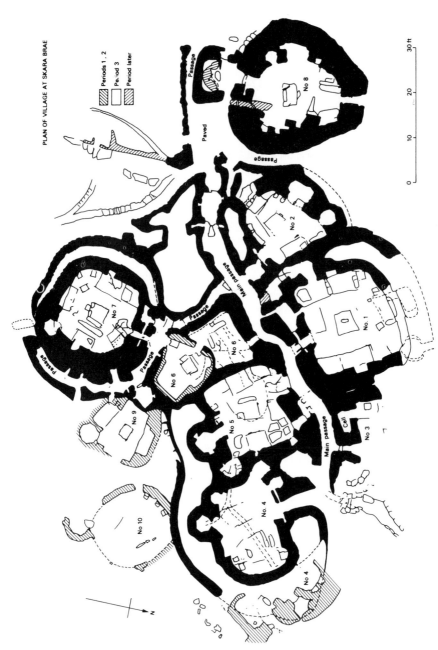

PLAN OF VILLAGE AT SKARA BRAE

Periods 1, 2
Period 3
Period later

No 8

No 2

No 7

No 1

No 6

Main passage

Passage

No 6

No 9

No 5

Cell

No 3

No 10

No. 4

No. 4

Passage

Paved

Passage

Passage

Passage

N

0   10   20   30 ft

21.12 Cluster of Neolithic dwellings at Skara Brae, Orkney, Scotland. The equal status of the inhabitants is suggested by the similarity both in the character and scale of the dwellings and in the regular pattern of their furnishings.

structure, without a marked degree of inequality in consumption, the astonishing diversity and perfection of Chinese, Egyptian, Anglo-Saxon, or indeed any other civilization could hardly have been achieved. When the organizers of the recent Chinese exhibition denounced the luxury and depravity of the feudal classes they never stopped to ask themselves whether the superlative jades, silks, porcelains, and paintings would ever have been fabricated unless to exhibit and proclaim a status superior to that of the artificers. Archaeology tells us what the cultures of China, Egypt, or Britain were like before class societies developed in these lands. The prehistoric peasants were egalitarian. They were illiterate. Their products were more vital, but in many respects as dull as those used by the lower levels in say Shang China, Pharaonic Egypt, or Anglo-Saxon England. Archaeology tells that the finest artefacts made by man, the most superb and diverse embodiments of his humanity, were made to celebrate social systems founded on hierarchy and inequality.[40]

References

1 L. S. B. and M. D. Leakey, *Olduvai Gorge, 1951–1961. Excavations in Beds I and II* (Cambridge, 1971); G. Isaac and E. R. McCown (eds.), *Human Origins: Louis Leakey and the East African Evidence* (Benjamin, California, 1976).

2 Isaac and McCown (eds.), *op. cit.*, 497ff.

3 K. P. Oakley, *Frameworks for Dating Fossil Man* (3rd edn, London, 1969), 237, 239.

4 J. D. Clark in Isaac and McCown, *op. cit.*, 43.

5 D. F. Thomson, 'The Seasonal Factor in Human Culture illustrated from the life of a contemporary nomadic group', *Proc. Prehist. Soc.*, v (1939), 209–21; M. J. Meggitt, *The Desert People* (Sydney, 1962).

6 R. B. Lee, 'Kung Bushman Subsistence: an input-output analysis', *Environment and Cultural Behaviour*, ed. A. P. Vayda (New York, 1969).

7 Mary D. Leakey in Isaac and McCown, *op. cit.*, 437f.

8 D. Black, P. Teilhard de Chardin, C. C. Young and W. C. Pei, 'The Choukoutien Cave Deposits . . .', *Mem. Geol. Surv. China*, Ser. A, no. 11 (Peking, 1933).

9 F. C. Howell, 'Observations on the earlier phases of the European Lower Palaeolithic', *American Anthrop.* 68 (1966), 88–201.

10 J. D. Clark, *Kalambo Falls Prehistoric Site*, i, ii (Cambridge, 1969, 1974).

11 R. G. West and C. B. M. McBurney, 'The Quaternary Deposits at Hoxne, Suffolk and their Archaeology', *Proc. Prehist. Soc.*, xx (1954), 131–54; see p. 135.

12 F. M. Bergounioux in G. H. R. von Koenigswald (ed.), *Hundert Jahre Neanderthaler* (Cologne, 1958), 152f.

13 D. A. E. Garrod and D. M. Bate, *The Stone Age of Mount Carmel,* i (Oxford, 1937), 97–107.

14 H. L. Movius, 'The Mousterian Cave of Teshik-Tash, South-eastern Uzbekistan, Central Asia', *Am. School of Prehistoric Research Bull.*, xvii (1953), 11–71.

15 G. Clark and A. Piggott, *Prehistoric Societies* (New York, 1965), 59f.

16 C. B. M. McBurney, *Early Man in the Soviet Union. The Implications of Some Recent Discoveries*, Reckitt Archaeological Lecture, British Academy, 1976.

17 O. P. Chernish, *The Palaeolithic Site Molodova V* (Kiev, 1961).

18 C. B. M. Mc Burney, 'The Geographical Study of the older Palaeolithic stages in Europe', *Proc. Prehist. Soc.*, xvi (1950), 163–83; esp. pp. 173ff.

19 J. D. Clark, *The Prehistory of Africa* (London, 1970), ch. IV.
20 O. N. Bader, *Quartär* bd. 18, 191 and 21, 103; C. B. M. McBurney, *op. cit.* (1976), pls. VI–VIII.
21 A. Leroi-Gourhan, *Préhistoire de l'art occidental* (Paris, 1965).
22 I. G. Pidoplichko, *Late Palaeolithic Dwellings of Mammoth Bones in the Ukraine* (Kiev, 1969).
23 A. P. Okladnikov, *Yakutia* (Montreal, 1970), 30f.
24 G. Clark, *The Earlier Stone Age Settlement of Scandinavia* (Cambridge, 1975), ch. I.
25 G. Clark, *World Prehistory in New Perspective* (3rd edn, Cambridge, 1977), 321ff.
26 C. R. Harington, R. Bonnichsen, and R. E. Morlan, 'Bones say man lived in Yukon 27,000 years ago', *Canadian Geogr. J.* 91 (1975), 428.
27 Clark, *op. cit.*, (1975), ch. I.
28 J. G. D. Clark and M. W. Thompson, 'The Groove and Splinter Technique of working antler in Upper Palaeolithic and Mesolithic Europe', *Proc. Prehist. Soc.*, XIX (1953), 148–60.
29 Pidoplichko, *op. cit.*, fig. 56.
30 S. K. Kozlowski, 'The System of Providing Raw Flint Materials in the Late Palaeolithic in Poland', *Second International Flint Symposium, Maastricht 1976*, 66–9.
31 C. Renfrew, J. E. Dixon, and J. R. Cann, 'Obsidian and Early Cultural Contact in the Near East', *Proc. Prehist. Soc.*, XXXII (1966), 30–72.
32 Lee, *op. cit.*
33 E. S. Higgs (ed.), *Papers in Economic Prehistory* (Cambridge, 1972); *Palaeoeconomy* (Cambridge, 1975).
34 G. Clark, 'Domestication and Social Evolution' in *The Early History of Agriculture*, 5–11, ed. Sir J. Hutchinson, British Academy, 1977.
35 L. J. Brass, 'Stone Age agriculture in New Guinea', *Geogr. Rev.*, XXXI (1941), 555–69; G. Lerche and A. Steensberg, 'Observations on spade-cultivation in the New Guinea Highlands', *Tools and Tillage* II (1973), 87–104.
36 P. C. Mangelsdorf, R. E. MacNeish and W. C. Galinat, 'Prehistoric Wild and Cultivated Maize' in *The Prehistory of the Tehuacan Valley*, I, ed. D. S. Byers (Univ. of Texas Press, 1967).
37 For a useful summary, see N. Hammond, 'The Early History of American Agriculture: recent research and current controversy' in Sir J. Hutchinson, *op. cit.*, 120–8.
38 Clark, *op. cit.* (1977), 61f.
39 J. R. Harlan and D. Zohary, 'Distribution of Wild Wheats and Barley', *Science* 153 (1966), 1074–8.
40 The implications of this are spelt out in an essay entitled 'Archaeology and Human Diversity' due to appear in the *Annual Review of Anthropology* (Palo Alto, California) 8 (1979).

CHAPTER 22

WORLD PREHISTORY AND NATURAL SCIENCE

In this Jacobsen Memorial Lecture my aim is to convey two interlocking ideas:

first, that the concept of world prehistory as a study concerned with the emergence of man, the growth and differentiation of his cultural heritage has developed as part of the shift from a traditional to a more rational view of man, society and the natural universe and is only capable of being realised through the application of many branches of natural science,

second, that human history, even the prehistoric parts is not amenable to explanation in the same terms as natural history – in other words that archaeology is above all a method of studying the emergence and realisation of what it means to be human. Indeed that the consequences of the advance of a rational world view combined with modern technology, to which we owe the possibility of conceiving world prehistory, offer threats to our humanity as powerful as those they are recognised to offer to our environment. Whereas *Homo sapiens* has realised his humanity through enriching and diversifying his culture, the advances of science, technology and not least of 'progressive' ideas have already gone some way to impoverishing our heritage through a relentless and accelerating process of homogenisation.

In accepting your invitation I have chosen a topic which involves disciplines within each of the two main classes of the Academy. In doing so I follow the example of the Carlsberg Foundation which has won international acclaim for the support it has given to interdisciplinary research in this field. I would recall in particular investigations directed to the way in which the earlier Stone Age hunter-fisher-forager populations adapted to environmental changes since the Late-glacial period and, again, those bearing on the introduction of a Neolithic economy. As in the case of modern agriculture, indeed of modern Danish society, the key has lain in co-operation.

To the archaeologists, even to some of the historians among you, it must be sufficiently plain that no firm interpretation of archaeological evidence can be given without the kind of exact knowledge of the environment and of raw materials and techniques that only natural scientists, often of a highly specialised kind, can provide. It took longer for the converse to be admitted, namely that the benefits should be mutual, that in contemporary jargon there ought to be a two-way feed-back or pay-off and that natural science has something more substantial than improving its image to gain by co-operating with the humanities. Yet, surely, this is basic to the concept of ecology. Human societies must needs interact with each of the other components of the systems in which they operate. Here again Danish science, notably in the person of the late Johannes Iversen, gave a decisive lead. It was Iversen's genius that, while prepared to follow the routines of palynology as if vegetational change could be explained wholly in terms of such natural factors as climate and plant succession, he was always on the watch for anomalies as challenges to the conventional wisdom. It was for instance precisely because this failed to account for the sudden increase in the pollen of birch, immediately following a temporary decline in forest trees and a corresponding increase in non-tree pollen, that he sought alternative explanations. The hypothesis[1] that all three phenomena were due to temporary clearance followed by recolonisation on the part of rapid spreading birch trees effectively introduced the idea of prehistoric man as an active agent in ecological change. This opened up new perspectives for palaeo-botanists and archaeologists alike and further advertised the over-riding need to pursue Quaternary Research on the basis of intimate co-operation. Recognition that economic forces played a significant, in some cases a dominant role in shaping the environment even during prehistoric times, carried with it the possibility that economic history could be read as much from pollen diagrams, soil profiles, molluscan and faunal assemblages and the like as from the artefacts of early man.

The experience of those actively engaged in research was soon reflected in the attitude of bodies concerned with the allocation of funds. If I speak of the situation in Britain this is partly because it is one with which I am most familiar but partly also because until very lately it is a country in which the provision for science and the humanities has been more widely separated than in most others. Whereas in Denmark your Academy presides over the whole field of learning, in Britain, as is well known, responsibility has been divided between the Royal Society and the British Academy, the former overseeing the equivalent of your Mathematical-Physical, the latter that of your Historical-Philosophical class. In Britain the division has been further exaggerated by a marked difference in public financial provision. Whereas the Natural Sciences have long been recognised to be expensive but acceptable as a form of national investment, research in the humanities has been and still is to some extent regarded as a luxury.

Understandably it was the archaeologists who felt most emphatically the need for more than a quiet place to sit. The mere expense of recovering their basic data by excavation and survey, has soared with the rise of wages, not least in overseas territories. Moreover, the more scientifically archaeologists have sought to operate and the more closely they have sought to work with colleagues over a wide range of natural sciences in the analysis of their data, the more closely their financial needs approximate to those at least of the less expensive sciences. Although financial needs were important – and archaeologists were by no means the only group of humanistic scholars to call for more adequate provision – I would not wish to exaggerate their influence. Nor would it be right to over-emphasise the extent to which scientific leaders have come to accept the need to display a more positive attitude to society and its concerns over and above satisfying its material, medical and defence needs. The discontents of humanists and the apprehension of scientists have certainly played a part, but I would prefer to stress the growing awareness on both sides of what they have to gain from cooperation. This has already found practical expression in the series of symposia designed to illustrate the outcome of joint humanistic and natural scientific research organised by the British Academy and the Royal Society.[2] More than one of these dealt with areas of research in which the Carlsberg Foundation has long displayed a special interest and it is significant that Danish scholars made leading contributions to the symposia. In introducing[3] that devoted to *The Early History of Agriculture*, I specified in some detail the Sections within the organisation of the two bodies involved: no doubt this analysis could have been worked out in more detail, but it is plain that many lines of study are needed to effect serious advances, an operation that is bound to be costly.

In this connection the Department of Scientific Research, the main organisation for channelling public funds to scientific research in Britain, has recently recognised its concern for humanistic studies by setting up a Science Based Archaeology Committee.[4] One of the arguments to carry conviction was the prospect that intensive application of natural science to archaeology might benefit both sides.

When I began to think about this lecture I was inclined to the view that World Prehistory could usefully be thought of as in a sense an artefact of Natural Science. It is true enough that the prime stimulus to the idea of prehistory came from geology, biology and palaeontology and further that the advance of archaeology in the case of all periods has owed much to the application of scientific techniques and procedures. Yet on reflection prehistory can hardly be regarded as a product, still less as itself a branch of natural science. Since communities are human to the extent that they conform to patterns of behaviour shaped to an increasing degree by cultural rather than genetic inheritance, they can only be regarded in the final analysis as products of the historical process. If prehistory has to be categorised it can only be as an historical discipline.

History itself is part of the cultural inheritance of all peoples. Even the most primitive of men, when questioned by explorers, traders, missionaries, administrators or anthropologists, attribute their adherence to particular customs to the example of ancestors. An awareness of history, however this is conceived and expressed, has consistently served to promote and deepen the sense of humanity that informs communities of men.[5] It does so in three distinct though interlocking ways. It enhances the confidence of which men feel the need as they embark on increasingly artificial modes of life in the face of natural forces, by legitimising and validating their institutions. Secondly, it intensifies the cohesion and in consequence the effectiveness of communities by emphasizing their common inheritance. Thirdly, and complementarily, the possession of a unique history enhances the sense of identity of human societies vis-à-vis their neighbours. In each of these ways a sense of history is of adaptive value by making human societies more effective and at the same time more enduring. Conversely every advance in culture, every increase in the degree to which behaviour is conditioned by historical rather than merely biological factors, may be assumed to involve an increase both in the range and depth of human awareness. In a general sense it can be admitted that man's awareness of history as much as his economy or technology is subject to the selective processes of evolution.

It seems to follow that human societies are likely to entertain a sense of history appropriate to their circumstances. In terms of space the range of historical awareness is and must necessarily be restricted to territories known to a society either directly through its annual exploitation cycle or indirectly through exchange or other social networks. Similarly the temporal range of historical awareness can be expected to be confined to what is relevant to a particular society and permitted by its intellectual attainments. Thus a community restricted to oral communication would hardly be as capable of transmitting the kind of detailed history open to a literate one, even supposing that this would have served any useful purpose to people who had not yet attained the degree of organisation that required literacy. On the other hand, as we are reminded by the oral literature of the Greek, Celtic or Teutonic peoples of Europe or the wealth of lore enshrined in the stories, riddles, dances, mimes, representations, decorative designs, social structure and customs and not least in the religious beliefs, rituals and symbols of the preliterate peoples until recently beyond the direct influence of the industrial world, the written word is by no means the only medium for transmitting history. The fact remains that in preliterate societies everywhere the dimensions of historical awareness were more or less narrowly confined both in time and space. By the same token, the possibility of envisaging history as comprehending the whole world and the entire span of human existence depended on the spread of western civilisation equipped with means of transport and communication that reduced the world to readily comprehensible proportions and informed and propelled by scientific modes of thought.

The first constraint to go was the geographical one.[6] Five hundred years ago Christendom, with few exceptions like those offered by the reports of travellers and missionaries to the Mongol court, was less well informed about territories within immediate reach than the peoples of Classical antiquity.

Indeed it was the translation into Latin in *c.* 1406 of a Greek manuscript of Ptolemy's *Geographia* that provided a base and one of the main stimuli for the voyages of discovery which as much as anything defined the onset of the modern age. Paradoxically, although inspired by Ptolemy, the Portuguese navigators who rounded the Cape of Good Hope and within fifteen years had not merely crossed the Indian Ocean to the Malabar coast but made contact with the western terminus of the China trade and even reached Canton, by exposing the error of his Southern Continent and a land-locked Indian Ocean, helped to break the grip of ancient book-learning on the imagination of western man. Similarly the navigators who in the final decade of the fifteenth century voyaged west across the Atlantic imagined themselves to be heading for the eastern extremity of Asia. When Columbus sighted the Bahamas he thought he must be encountering the outliers of Japan and when John Cabot encountered Greenland and Labrador he identified these as peninsulas of north-east Asia. As renewed voyages brought more clearly into view the true outlines of the world, the limitations of traditional book-learning were rammed home by the very prows of the exploring vessels. Even more important than the stimulus to astronomy and magnetics involved in navigation was the lesson that new knowledge of the world could only be won by observing and testing nature herself; as has recently been pointed out,[7] 'unlettered seamen, travellers and merchants by simple observation gave the lie to the greatest philosophers of Antiquity'.

The age of reconnaissance made Europeans aware of more than new territories. It brought them face to face with peoples having previously unknown racial characteristics and social customs. Indeed when Europeans first encountered the inhabitants of the New World they doubted whether to classify them as apes or accept them as men. When the Pope solved this particular problem in 1512 by pronouncing them true descendants of Adam and Eve,[8] this only raised another question. If all the peoples encountered in the course of geographical reconnaissance were indeed descended from the same pair, how could one account for the diversity of race, language and cultural level? It is symptomatic of the theological patterns of thought still prevailing in the 16th–17th centuries and persisting sporadically through the 18th and even into the 19th century, that the diversity encountered by explorers was squared with the doctrine of monogenesis by reference to the dispersal of the sons of Noah[9] or even the builders of the Tower of Babel.[10] The fact that all men, however much they differed from Europeans, were acknowledged to be descendants of Adam and Eve stimulated missionary zeal and in so doing led to the intensive observation of the indigenous inhabitants that laid the basis for systematic ethnology.[11]

The temporal limits to the span of human history inferred from literal interpretation of the Old Testament were scarcely threatened during the initial phase of the scientific revolution. As Stephen Toulmin and June

Goodfield have brought out so clearly[12] the model of the world and the universe devised by Galileo, Descartes and Newton was essentially timeless: the world-machine was conceived of as operating continuously on self-evident principles or at least on principles demonstrable in mathematical terms as these were conceived of in western Europe at the time, and it should be remembered that Isaac Newton himself displayed a profound concern for theology. It was much the same with the biological sciences. Physiology was marked above all by Harvey's studies in the circulation of the blood and in botany and zoology, as with archaeology, the emphasis lay above all on classification as exemplified in the work of Ray (1627–1705) and Linnaeus (1707–78).

The notion that the universe and everything therein was the product of a still unfolding evolutionary development did not appear effectively until the middle of the 18th century. The first systematic attempt to give an evolutionary account of cosmic history was provided not by a physicist or a mathematician but by a philosopher. In his *General History of Nature and Theory of the Heavens* (1755) Immanuel Kant[13] held that 'The creation is never finished or complete. It did indeed once have a beginning, but it will never cease. It is always busy producing new scenes of nature, new objects, and new Worlds. The work which it brings about has a relationship to the time which it expends upon it. It needs nothing less than an Eternity to animate the whole boundless range of the infinite extension of Space with Worlds, without number and without end.' One of Kant's pupils, J. C. Herder,[14] in a four volume work *Ideas towards a Philosophy of Man* applied his master's system to the earth and the species that lived upon it, including man and his history. Geology which like archaeology began with collections of curiosities entered on an intensive phase of classification largely to meet the need for minerals and means of communications generated and sustained by the Industrial Revolution. Faced with sequences of rocks containing fossils of widely differing character, geologists of the late eighteenth and early nineteenth century were divided into those like the eminent French authority Cuvier who explained them in terms of recurrent catastrophes and those who like John Hutton of Edinburgh preferred to see them as outcomes of processes similar to those still operating at the present time. The most influential proponent of Hutton's transformist thesis, Charles Lyell (1797–1875), confirmed in his *Principles of Geology*[15] that the sequence observed in the rocks could be explained as products of processes similar to those operating today. All that the uniformitarians needed was a sufficiency of time. If men clung to the chronology inferred by Archbishop Ussher from Old Testament genealogies only six thousand years or so were available. So when flint artefacts began to be recognised in the same layers as remains of extinct animals the catastrophic hypothesis was invoked: as late as 1823 William Buckland, Professor of Geology as well as Dean of Christchurch, Oxford, did not hesitate to attribute discoveries made during the excavation of caves to the operation of the Biblical Flood.[16]

For many people, including Charles Darwin, the publication of Lyell's *Principles* was decisive, but it was the combination of biological and geological evidence that finally destroyed the credibility of a traditional chronology and convinced the educated world that man and his culture had developed over immensely long periods. Jean B. Lamarck based his view that existing species had emerged from earlier ones by a process of slow transformation on his observation that there was a clear palaeontological succession, the older rocks containing the simpler fossils and the younger ones progressively more complex ones. Again, Charles Darwin acknowledged his debt to Lyell who was one of the foremost in urging publication of *The Origin of Species by Means of Natural Selection* (1859).

The publication in 1863 of Lyell's *The Geological Evidences of the Antiquity of Man* and of Huxley's *Evidence as to Man's Place in Nature* made it crystal clear that Darwin's hypothesis applied to man himself. The notion that existing races had diverged from the parent stem by a process of gradual transformation was already half a century old when Huxley published his essay. Indeed in his *Researches into the Physical History of Man* (1813) J. C. Prichard had to some extent anticipated Darwin by stressing the role of selection in the process of diversification. What was new when Huxley addressed himself to the problem was that the evolution of man could then be viewed in the dimension of geological time. In this respect the discovery in the Neanderthal[17] between Düsseldorf and Elberfeld, West Germany, in 1857 of a human cranium displaying features of a notably more primitive character than those of modern man was providential, since it gave Huxley just what he needed to stimulate the development of Human Palaeontology. I shall not be touching on the physical and neural evolution of early man, beyond reminding you that this not only limited but was to a significant degree conditioned by his cultural history.

The Darwinian revolution further impelled research into the cultural and social history of man along paths blazed in the course of the previous hundred years. The most immediate, though ultimately fallacious results were claimed by ethnologists. The first impact of encounters with peoples living in remote parts of the world outside the scope of European civilisation lay with political economy. For one thing it led men like Hobbes, Locke and Rousseau to conceive of a time when men lived in or close to a State of Nature. For another it prompted speculation into the stages by which men advanced from this basal level to that reflected in classical literature or that of the *philosophes*. Montesquieu's *L'Esprit des Lois* and Condorcet's *Progress of the Human Mind* drew data from as far afield as North America and the South Seas.[18] The speculations of political philosophers about the progress of mankind were systematised by ethnologists on the basis of the much fuller knowledge of so-called primitive peoples available by the latter half of the nineteenth century. Lewis H. Morgan, American author of the most influential work in this now discredited genre, *Ancient Society or Researches in the Lines of Human Progress from Savagery to Civilization*, admitted that he only changed his views 'respecting the relation of savages to barbarians and of barbarians to civilized man' in the face of the new evidence for the high antiquity of man brought forward by the Victorian evolutionists. If there was time enough to account for the diversity of rocks, of plants and of animals, there was more than sufficient to explain the emergence of human societies at differing levels of cultural attainment. In the euphoria of evolutionary doctrine Morgan was prepared to state as a matter of certainty 'that savagery preceded barbarism in all the tribes of mankind, as barbarism is known to have preceded civilization' and furthermore that 'since mankind were one in origin, their career has been essentially one, running in different but uniform channels upon all continents'.[19] In specifying the seven phases through which he supposed human societies had passed in the course of social evolution Morgan was even helpful enough to provide clues for archaeologists:

Lewis H. Morgan's stages in social evolution (1877)

	Stages	*Material Clues*
VII	Civilization	Inscriptions
VI	Upper Barbarism	Iron
V	Middle Barbarism	Domesticated animals & plants
IV	Lower Barbarism	Pottery
III	Upper Savagery	Bow
II	Middle Savagery	Fishing, fire
I	Lower Savagery	

Although unilinear schemes of social evolution were transmitted down to modern times embalmed in Marxist dogma by Engels and enforced by Marr as head of the Institute of the History of Material Culture at Moscow,[20] they were doubly fallacious. They rested on the false assumption that human cultural traditions evolved as though they were natural organisms instead of in the context of unique historical processes. Again, they assumed that by arranging societies in order of their cultural complexity they had found an infallible guide to the evolutionary sequence in time. If such was indeed the case, archaeology would have been reduced to a method of recovering fossils of an already known course of unilinear evolution. Conversely the pioneers of social anthropology who dismissed the writings of the early ethnologists as hypothetical history were fighting for space in which to cultivate the new discipline concerned with how the societies still functioning beyond the range of the world industrial economy in fact operated.

The alternative and only reliable way of exploring the remote past was to deploy the proven methods of archaeology. From the nature of their calling archaeologists were accustomed to the notion that for them there was no easy way. For the prehistoric period at least there was no other source, apart from a few texts from contemporary records bearing on the final phases, than ancient monuments and the vestiges buried in the soil. The idea that understanding of the past could be achieved through the medium of its material as well as its written records is much older than the discipline of archaeology as this has developed in the course of the last two centuries. Again, it is not peculiar to western civilisation. As early as the Han dynasty Chinese scholars engaged in careful and respectful study of the antique bronzes relating to their ancestors and it is significant that Chinese products have ever since displayed archaising tendencies based on a close understanding of ancient prototypes.[21] Although the Classical Greeks and Romans seem to have speculated about the remote past more in a philosophical and poetic than in a scholarly vein, Hesiod was well aware that the use of iron was preceded by bronze and, as is well known, Lucretius anticipated the sequence embodied in the Three Age system.[22] Again, in importing and copying the works of Greek sculptors wealthy Romans of imperial times anticipated the practice of a future age. The renewed interest in Classical Literature that marked the Renaissance was accompanied by a growing concern with the art of the Greeks and Romans. The fashion for assembling collections of sculpture, vases, coins, medals quarried from ancient sites first developed by Italian magnates of the fifteenth century spread north of the Alps to former provinces of the Roman Empire. Apart from the direct and immediate impact on taste, this helped to provide the basis from which two distinct branches of archaeology ultimately developed. On the one hand the recovery of Classical artefacts made it possible for Winckelmann and his successors to devise the stylistic criteria on which Classical Archaeology was founded.[23] On the other study of classical writers in itself directed attention to the non-classical barbarians at the very moment when the new nations stemming from the break up of medieval Christendom were actively concerned with establishing their identities. Indigenous antiquities were cherished as symbols of identity as they still are among newly emergent nations.

Initially interest was primarily topographical. Before the end of the 16th century William Camden was illustrating Stonehenge[24] in the original edition of *Britannia*.[25] Careful field studies of monuments like Avebury and Stonehenge were undertaken by John Aubrey not long after the foundation of the Royal Society and even more detailed surveys of the same monuments were carried out during the first half of the 18th century by the antiquary William Stukeley.[26] On the other hand, Stukeley's views about the meaning and context of the monuments accorded ill with the excellence of his field records and published illustrations. His preoccupation with the Druids shows for one thing that he belonged to an age, although as it happened to its final stage, when it was normal to rely for explanations on the authority of the written word, even as was more commonly the case on more or less far-fetched conjectures based however speciously on classical or biblical texts. The first adequately recorded attempt to recover information by the excavation of ancient monuments in Britain in the spirit of experimental science was in fact begun by the Rev. Bryan Fausset in 1754,[27] the year before Stukeley's death. Resort to scientific excavation by leading to the recovery of an ever-increasing number of artefacts of varying age in turn emphasised the need to classify data. It is hardly surprising that the Three Age System should have been devised and applied by a museum curator embarrassed by an ever growing mass of materials.[28]

A point to be emphasised at this juncture is that the change from a conjectural to a more scientific approach to the study of archaeological monuments and relics since the middle of the 18th century formed part of a major shift in European thought from reliance on authority and traditional procedures to a greater readiness to apply new techniques in the rational understanding and manipulation of nature and society. Seen from this point of view archaeology was a by-product of the Age of Enlightenment,[29] an age that witnessed not merely the Industrial and French Revolutions but also the genesis of the main disciplines of natural and social scientific research, not to mention a radical transformation of historical scholarship extending even to the Bible. As might have been expected in view of the key role played by geology in the genesis of transformist ideas the early prehistorians turned to stratigraphy as a way of gaining the initial objective of a temporal frame of reference. It was largely due to its rich endowment of Quaternary sequences in river terraces and caves that the extended chronology opened up by the victory of the evolutionists was first effectively documented in France. Within months of the key papers of Darwin and Wallace the archaeologist John Evans accompanied by the geologist John Prestwich visited Abbeville in the Somme Valley and returned convinced that Boucher de Perthes was justified in his claim to have found hand-axes in true association with the fossils of Middle Pleistocene Elephant and Rhinoceros.[30] Systematic investigation of the Late Pleistocene deposits in the Dordogne caves was begun by the French palaeontologist Edouard Lartet and the Englishman Henry Christy as early as 1863.[31] By 1865 enough primary data had been recovered from western Europe for John Lubbock to distinguish between the Palaeolithic and the Neolithic phases of the Stone Age, the former represented by the material from diluvial deposits and the infill of caves, the latter by finds from megalithic tombs and the settlements exposed round the margins of the Swiss lakes during the drought of 1853–4.[32] The accelerating tempo of excavation made it possible by 1881 to publish a scheme of classification for the Stone Age in France based on a conflation of detailed stratigraphical observations.[33]

Within France and adjacent regions de Mortillet's scheme as modified by Breuil[34] still retains some validity. Its main fault lay with those who sought, like the Soviet prehistorians of a certain period,[35] to apply the French local terminology to their discoveries in quite a different territory. A more egregious but also a revealing error was perpetrated by a geologist, W. J. Sollas, who by a strange irony occupied the same chair at Oxford as that from which Dean Buckland had urged the scriptural merits of his cave researches on the Lord Bishop of Durham. Sollas equated the Eskimo with the Magdalenian phase of the French sequence and even went so far as to opine that the Tasmanians might 'be regarded with great probability as representing an ancient Mousterian race which cut off from free communication with the surrounding world had preserved almost unchanged the habits and industrial arts which existed during the later days of the Lower Monastirian age',[36] for all the world as though the Mousterian was the equivalent of a geological stratum buried deep in Europe but outcropping in Tasmania. As Gordon Childe was to stress in his inaugural address to the Prehistoric Society in 1935,[37] prehistorians had had to waste much time during the preceding half century in clearing away misconceived analogies between cultural and geological sequences. I would only add that the need to keep clearly in mind the historical nature of archaeological data grows the more insistent as more effective scientific procedures are brought to bear on its decipherment.

The prerequisites for even an outline of world prehistory, in particular the world-wide spread of archaeological research and the application of geophysical methods of dating, have only been available during our own generation. The world-wide spread of archaeology and its scientific aids was due in the first instance to the expansion of European thought and technology, in part through colonisation, trade and administration and increasingly during the 20th century under the impulse of research in North America. The process began already during the first phase of disciplined archaeology.[38] When in 1784 Thomas Jefferson addressed himself to the excavation of a burial mound on his estate in Virginia he was acting in quite the same way as a country gentleman of his period on this side of the Atlantic. His special quality showed through in his strict observance of stratigraphy and in his appreciation of the public importance of the study of antiquity. As president of the American Philosophical Society he held that the members had 'always considered the antiquity, changes and present state of their own country as primary objects of their research'. The first volume of the *Transactions and Collections of the American Antiquarian Society* appeared in 1820 and the first issue of the *Smithsonian Contributions to Knowledge* was devoted to the classic account of the earthworks of the Mississippi Valley by E. G. Squier and E. H. Davies.

Professional archaeology based on university training and involving the employment of full-time specialists and the funding of major research projects developed earlier in the United States of America and on a more comprehensive basis than in most European countries. Whereas in Europe archaeology grew up in the main as a leisure hobby within the polite ambience of history, the classics or oriental studies, in North America it developed as a branch of anthropology at a time when the American Indian was still a vivid memory when not indeed a feature of daily life. In 1866 George Peabody founded the first of the great university power houses of archaeology in the Museum of Archaeology and Ethnology at Harvard. This was followed in 1875 by the first session of the still active Congress of Americanists and in 1879 by the foundation in the Bureau of Ethnology at Washington and the Department of Anthropology of the American Museum of Natural History at New York of two of the main institutions devoted to advancing knowledge of the Amerinds and their origins and early history. The foundation that same year of the Archaeological Institute of America served notice that the ambitions of American scholarship were by no means confined to the New World as was soon to be demonstrated in the founding of the several American Schools working overseas.

So long as western Europe remained the economic and political focus of the world it retained the lead in expanding the range of archaeological research. This was pursued in a variety of ways. Much of the pioneering work was accomplished by individuals, wealthy men such as Schliemann, Arthur Evans or Maudslay or experts working on overseas assignment like J. G. Anderson who single-handed opened up the vista of Stone Age China extending from the cave-dwellers of Chou-kou-tien to the peasant cultivators who prepared the ground for the Shang. As archaeology grew in complexity it began to require full-time professionals, large scale expeditions and long term programmes of research. Although in the case of Europe these requirements did not begin to be met at all adequately until 1918, Funds and Schools for furthering training, research and the all-important dialogue with the scholars of host countries had already been set up by several European countries in respect of Biblical, Classical and Egyptological scholarship.[39] Since then British scholars for example have set up institutes in territories of the former Ottoman Empire, Iran and territories outside the Hellenistic world as far away as East Africa and South-East Asia.[40]

The advance of learning and higher education were by no means the only factors behind the spread of archaeology from its European base. The pursuit of national prestige and the expansion of overseas empires have also been potent factors. Napoleon's inclusion of scholars in his expedition to the Nile[41] effectively gave birth to Egyptology and incidentally resulted in the discovery of the Rosetta stone, now by the spoils of war safely lodged in the British Museum. The French colonisation of Algeria set in train the effective beginning of systematic research into the older stone age of Africa[42] and that of Indo-China revealed South-East Asia as an early focus of high civilisation[43] just as French ambitions in Persia and Syria contributed mightily to opening up the archaeology of these key territories in the archaeology of South-West Asia.[44] In the long term European involvement in Africa and southern Asia contributed most to archaeology by imparting modern traditions of research and leaving behind trained personnel and institutions. It was a recurring theme of the British administrators in India to care for ancient monuments. The first Director-General of Archaeology was appointed in 1868 only thirteen years after the proclamation of the Empire in India. One of Lord Curzon's first acts as Viceroy (1899–1905) was to reconstruct the Survey and charge it 'to dig and to discover, to classify, reproduce and describe, and to cherish and conserve'.[45] In the work he did for India's past as much as in his planning of the architecture of New Delhi as an integrating and symbolic focus Lord Curzon was, as we know, looking beyond the Raj to a time when as he hoped the sub-continent would be united under its own regime. The recall of Mortimer Wheeler from active service in North Africa during the depth of the last war at the personal request of the penultimate viceroy falls into place as the final act in a long continued policy.[46] When Wheeler had completed his period as Director-General he left behind not merely apt pupils, but as their brilliant achievements have since demonstrated pupils of a kind every teacher dreams of – they applied the methods they had been taught and came up with fresh answers.[47]

Interest in Nigerian art and antiquities, first aroused by the bronzes and ivories removed from Benin during the punitive expedition of 1897, was strongly revived by the life-like heads of fired clay recovered during tin workings on the plateau of Jos in 1929.[48] One outcome was the appointment in 1943 of an Antiquities Officer. Another was that disciplined excavations were undertaken in both Ghana and Nigeria in 1943–4.[49] The immediate post-war years saw a rapid build-up of the infrastructure of archaeology in both states against independence which came in 1957 and 1960. Particular stress was laid on the building of museums for public instruction and on the creation of chairs of archaeology in the universities of Ghana[50] and Ibadan[51] with a strong emphasis on research. During Thurstan Shaw's tenure of the chair at Ibadan he and his chief colleague at the Institute of African Studies, Graham Connah, introduced several of the main techniques of science-based archaeology to West Africa, including the diagnosis of disease by X-ray analysis of bones, the determination of bronze composition and not least systematic radiocarbon dating.[52] In cutting through the 11.50 m mound of Daima in the *firki* south of Lake Chad and interpreting the section as a key to the early settlement of a little known part of the continent, Connah acknowledged[53] cooperation from colleagues in many departments of the University, notably Forestry, Botany, Zoology, Geology, Chemistry, Arabic Studies and History, confirmation from what was then a dark part of Africa of the value of interdisciplinary research and the role of archaeology in stimulating interaction between academic disciplines.

Although Europe, increasingly strongly reinforced since the war of 1914–18 by the United States acting mainly through university institutions like the Peabody at Harvard, the Oriental Institute at Chicago, the University of Pennsylvania Museum and latterly the University of California at Berkeley, took the lead in mediating archaeology to extensive tracts of Asia, Africa and Australasia, the rise of Japan and the Soviet Union to the front rank of industrial powers broadened support for the advance of world archaeology. Prehistoric archaeology first reached the Japanese homeland as part of the apparatus of Western knowledge adopted in the wake of the Meiji restoration of 1868 and from the beginning the leading role was taken by the (then) Imperial University of Tokyo. The progress of archaeological research within Japan can be seen in the number of 'Neolithic' sites, as defined by the presence of pottery and the absence of metallurgy, officially listed by the university: c.3500 in 1900, c.4000 by 1911 and c.10,000 by 1928.[54] Japanese archaeological enterprise first broke out of the Far East on the flood tide of prosperity that followed the war of 1939–45. Among its outstanding contributions to world prehistory are the campaigns mounted by the Institute for Oriental Culture in Iran and Iraq[55] and excavations at Kotosh which have thrown new light on the early development of civilisation in Peru.[56] Although archaeology had been vigorously pursued under the old regime in Russia more especially in the south and in the East Baltic states, it received strong aid from the Soviet state on account of the support it was thought to offer for the materialist interpretation of history. Intensified industrialisation and a notable shift of economic development to the east after the war of 1939–45 led to notable excavations in the circumpolar and inner Asian territories of the Soviet Union. It has been shown for example that the bearers of Mousterian culture had extended the range of settlement up to c.65° N. in the Pechora basin and that Upper Palaeolithic groups had colonised well beyond the Arctic Circle in Siberia as well as penetrating as far east as Kamchatka. They were only able to do so on account of the elaborate houses which in themselves form one of the main contributions of Soviet archaeology to prehistory.[57] In central Asia major advances have been achieved in our knowledge of nomads contemporary with the Scyths of South Russia through excavation of frozen tombs in the Altai,[58] and exploration of arid territories further west has thrown important light on the rise of early states in Chorasmia.[59]

The eclipse of European hegemony in the aftermath of the 1939–45 war assisted the advance of archaeology in two main ways. The newly emergent states for their part were anxious to reinforce their identity but were deficient in historical records beyond orally transmitted genealogies, myths and legends. For such archaeology was providential, since although many of their people were unable to read they were still responsive to the traditional forms and styles of artefacts. No wonder that the governments of so many of the new nations were prepared to invest in archaeology. On the other hand Europe's loss not merely of Empire but of economic and even intellectual dominance brought about a radical change in attitudes to history. Europocentricism was out and with it European systematisations of archaeology. There was still concern for the origins of man, but there was a growing interest in the emergence not merely of European but of all the other civilisations of mankind. Since archaeology has been so widely recognised as the only means for achieving this, local efforts have been enhanced and supplemented by internationally conceived projects aimed at solving specific problems. The quest for identity has indeed proved as infectious as it is demanding, calling as it does for scientific and technical skills, sensitivity to form and style and above all historical insight.

A key factor in the advance of the last three decades, one that has at the same time stimulated research and made it possible to write prehistory, has been the devising and systematic application of geophysical dating methods. Even those like potassium-argon capable only of yielding dates within a wide range of error were of value for periods as remote in time as the lower beds at Olduvai[60] when the tempo of change was still extremely slow. It is all the more fortunate that the radiocarbon method[61] capable of establishing within certain limits of probability a much finer chronology extends neatly over the more dynamic phases of prehistory enacted by *Homo sapiens sapiens*. The utility of radiocarbon chronology is only marginally affected, notably in linking late prehistoric with historically dated sequences, by its deviations from solar chronology due to fluctuations in solar radiation. The prospect has already opened up of adjusting radiocarbon to solar chronology by measuring and plotting the curve of its deviations through time.[62] In any case, as Libby himself has recently emphasised,[63] these fluctuations do not affect the simultaneity principle which permits the correlation of local sequences in different parts of the world. A clear sign of its value is its rapid spread. When the first issue of *Radiocarbon*, the international vehicle for publishing results, first appeared in 1955 the original laboratory in Chicago had already been supplemented in North America, and in Western Europe, though elsewhere only at single stations in Japan and New Zealand. By 1977 New World stations had expanded north to Canada and south to the Argentine, many stations were operating in central and eastern as well as in western Europe and, more strikingly, radiocarbon samples were being processed in Africa, India, Australia and the Pacific.

Among the many services rendered by radiocarbon analysis to archaeology one of the most obvious is that of tracing man's expansion over northern Eurasia and into the New World, as well as from south-east Asia into Australia and more recently his settlement of islands scattered over the

Pacific ocean. In achieving this natural science has in effect added new provinces to world prehistory. The impact of the new method was felt most decisively precisely in the new territories. For instance in the case of Australia, a continent in which the first stratigraphic demonstration of a cultural succession was made as recently as 1929, radiocarbon dating extended the range of its prehistory within a few years to twenty, perhaps more than thirty millennia. Australian archaeologists were presented with a challenge almost as urgent as that with which Darwin and Huxley had once confronted the British and French pioneers of prehistory. An Australian midden sample was among the determinations in the first corrected list issued in 1951[64] alongside as it happens ones from Aamosen and Star Carr. Examination of the lists of Australian dates published by Mulvaney between 1961 and 1975[65] illustrates the rapid tempo of this research and its increasingly international involvement as well as the stimulus it gave to Australian archaeology and natural science:

Location of laboratories	1961 (16) %	1969 (81) %	1975 (108) %
Australia	–	40.8	60.0
New Zealand	27.7	9.9	4.6
Japan	–	23.5	16.7
UK	–	11.1	6.5
USA	72.3	14.8	12.2

Changes in the participation of radiocarbon laboratories from different areas in the determination of prehistoric samples from Australia.

Radiocarbon dating has also been of exceptional value in building up the chronology not merely of the new but also of the old territories which pioneered prehistory. One of the first concerted tests of the new method indeed was that directed at the Upper Palaeolithic sequence in Europe.[66] The method has also proved itself in the investigation of specific problems in cultural history, in some cases by compelling revision of existing views. For instance the high radiocarbon dates obtained even without calibration for megalithic tombs in western and for metallurgy in eastern Europe[67] suggest that the continent was far less retarded in relation to the Near and Middle East than had once been thought. Again, the radiocarbon testing of Chalcolithic sites in India carried out by Agrawal in the Tata Institute of Fundamental Research at Bombay[68] has provided clear terminal dates for the Harappan civilisation while at the same time placing the termination of this efflorescence in a less dramatic light than it has previously been viewed. In particular the testing of many sites in central and northern parts of south India has gone far to restoring the continuity of Indian history by showing that a similar tradition persisted though at a humbler level through most of

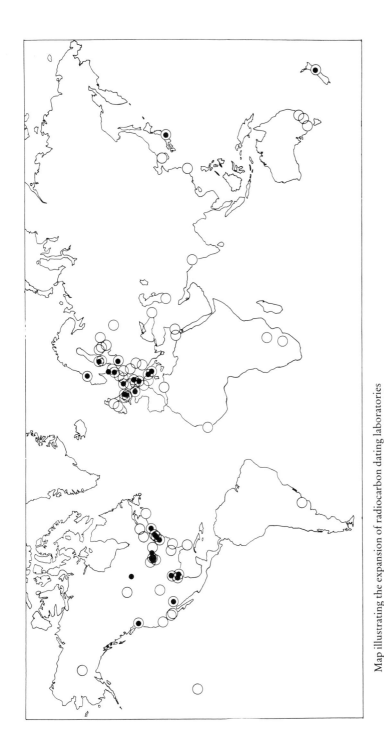

Map illustrating the expansion of radiocarbon dating laboratories

● The original station in the Institute of Nuclear Physics, Chicago

• Stations operating at the time of the first issue of *Radiocarbon* (1955)

□ Stations operating in 1977

Note: In certain cases symbols represent more than one station.

the second millennium B.C. For a final example one may turn to Japanese prehistory. Although the high radiocarbon dates from the early ceramic levels of Japanese middens were at first received with incredulity, their consistency with the internal development of Jomon pottery[69] has since brought widespread acceptance and with this the rejection of the doctrine, prevalent since the time of Lubbock, that the making of pottery appeared at the same 'stage' as farming economy.

The value of a precise method of relative chronology like radiocarbon dating thus extends far beyond refining the mere framework of prehistory into its very dynamics. In particular it is capable of defining foci of innovation and rates and zones of diffusion. One area in which it is proving itself is the crucial one of subsistence. Systematic radiocarbon dating carried out in association with the detailed assessment of territories, careful stratigraphic excavation and the critical sampling and specialist examination of food refuse has achieved classic results in the case of two key areas. In respect of the Valley of Mexico[70] and parts of south-west Asia[71] it has already shown that the shift from hunter-forager to farming economies was in each case a slow process and one that however profound in its implications is better understood as a gradual transformation than as a revolution.[72] This suggests among other things that one might expect farming to emerge among hunter-foragers wherever the right ecological and social conditions obtained. Radiocarbon dating is already defining foci of plant domestication in the New World[73] other than that already known in the Valley of Mexico and in the Old is serving as a probe to define the original focus of rice cultivation,[74] one of the key objectives of prehistoric research at the present time. Again, if farming was slow to develop, it is only to be expected that the expansion of domestic crop plants should also have been a gradual process more especially when it involved the penetration of territories beyond the range of the wild prototypes. Here again radiocarbon dating soon began to make its contribution.[75]

Another application of radiocarbon dating has been to link archaeological sequences more closely with the evolution of the natural environment and in this way make it possible to view economic systems in their precise ecological contexts, the only way in which such historical processes as the genesis and diffusion of cultivated crops can be adequately understood. The quest for such understanding in turn implies new strategies in archaeological research and the close association of archaeologists and biologists in the recovery and analysis of data. Thus, whereas a limited range of relatively imperishable artefacts from stratified deposits suffices to define archaeological cultures and establish local sequences, any attempt to understand how the societies concerned were structured and functioned involves an altogether more sophisticated approach and the application of techniques drawn from a variety of disciplines. There is already an impressive literature bearing on the new approaches to archaeology,[76] on data recovery,[77] and on the analysis and interpretation in ecological terms of the artefactual and organic materials recovered in the course of excavation.[78] Here I will only touch upon two areas in which Danish scientists and scholars have made conspicuous contributions, namely Quaternary Research and Experimental Archaeology.

Quaternary Research, although now concerned with investigating the history of ecosystems since the first emergence of human societies and applied with varying degrees of success wherever prehistory is studied,[79] was originally devised by Scandinavian and not least by Danish scientists for advancing knowledge of the comparatively brief period since the Scandinavian ice-sheet began to contract. There are several reasons why Scandinavia should have taken the lead. For one there are the stark facts of geography. It was not only that the mere possibility of a Scandinavian history depended on the freeing of its territory from ice but that the lives of the prehistoric inhabitants were conditioned by the changes of climate, geography, vegetation and animal life inherent in the dynamics of deglaciation. Then the development of economic life in recent times had placed a premium on geological and biological research and the formation of strong institutional and professional bases for precisely the branches of expertise required for effective Quaternary Research. Again, it is worth emphasising that the region is exceptionally well endowed with the recent formations on which this type of research depends. Finally it should not be overlooked that the very brevity of recorded history in the north focussed attention on prehistoric settlement and provided a favourable environment for archaeological research and the provision of institutions dedicated to it.

At least it is a matter of history that the first systematic essays in Quaternary Research were undertaken in Scandinavia and I need hardly remind this audience that it was the Royal Danish Academy of Sciences which pioneered group research in this field by setting up a Commission to investigate the kitchen middens of the Danish Stone Age as long ago as 1848, composed of the archaeologist Worsaae, the geologist Forchhammer and the zoologist Japetus Steenstrup, and publishing the results in its *Proceedings*. When the attack was renewed towards the close of the century (1893–8) the lead was undertaken by the National Museum, the institution that in the very early days of prehistory had seen the genesis of the Three Age System, and the range of specialists was extended to include a botanist.[80]

The third campaign, that brought to focus the excavations at Dyrholmen in 1938–9, was interdisciplinary both in its sponsorship and at a research level. It was led by the National Museum assisted by the Danish Geological Survey and the University Zoological Museum, financed by the Carlsberg Foundation and published by the Royal Danish Academy.[81] In respect of research it was aimed first and foremost to refine the history of coastal settlement by subdividing its history in relation to the fourfold recurrence of Litorina marine transgressions demonstrated by Iversen in 1937 at Søborg Sø on the basis of fluctuations in the pollen of *Chenopodiaceae* and of parallel variations in the frequencies of salt-demanding diatoms.[82] Mathiassen's careful excavations made it possible to distinguish the artefact assemblages and animal refuse discarded immediately prior to the second, third and fourth transgressions. Supplemented by observations from elsewhere this archaeological sequence confirmed those based on geology and palaeontology and at the same time provided new insights into cultural history. Among other things it demonstrated the continuity of coastal settlement in Denmark during Atlantic and Sub-boreal times and reflected the introduction during the latter period of the elements of farming economy.[83]

Possibly the most important single technique to emerge from Quaternary Research in northern Europe was pollen analysis, developed originally as a way of zoning deposits but applied in due course in an increasingly sophisticated manner to gaining insights into the ecological setting of early cultures. Pollen grains were first recognised from geological deposits as far back as the early half of the nineteenth century in Germany but the possibility of using their survival as a way of reconstituting the nature of early vegetation was not appreciated until the early years of the twentieth century. Indeed the first diagram to illustrate fluctuations in vegetation through time in terms of percentage changes in the pollen of different species was constructed by the Swedish state geologist Lennart von Post as recently as 1916.

The standard text-book[84] on the technique of pollen-analysis was understandably written by Scandinavian botanists, Kurt Faegri of Bergen and Johs. Iversen of Copenhagen. Dedicated to the Swede van Post, it made special acknowledgements of the work of Knud Jessen and J. Troels-Smith and was published by a Copenhagen publishing-house with subventions from Norwegian and Danish funds, including the Carlsberg Foundation. At the same time it is one of the beauties of natural science that wherever its techniques were invented they are capable of worldwide application provided the right conditions obtain. Already in 1950 the authors were able to cite original contributions from central and western as well as northern Europe, and also from many parts of the New World from Greenland and Labrador to Patagonia and even from New Zealand and Hawaii in the Pacific zone. Pollen-analysis had already been applied in the USSR[85] and since then has been adopted as far afield as India,[86] Australia[87] and the Far East (China[88] and Japan[89]).

It is understandable that the first essays in Experimental Archaeology should have been made by amateurs[90] since the few professionals, mainly in the museum profession, were preoccupied with chronological and cultural classification. Professional work in this field[91] arose from a more critical approach to the retrieval of the primary data[92] and above all from a growing concern with interpreting this in terms of functioning societies. Description or systematic analysis of the spheres to which Experimental Archaeology has been applied, including subsistence, technology, defence or ideology, would call for a lengthy course of lectures. Two points of general application may be made. The first is that the most successful essays in experimental archaeology are interdisciplinary, involving practical men as well as experts in particular branches of natural science and humane scholarship. Early agriculture is a case in point. Danish archaeology has been well forward in this field in respect both of excavation[93] and of expert determination of samples. Going back only a few decades one may recall the fine stratigraphical work, in many cases involving pollen-analysis, carried out by Knud Jessen,[94] Johs. Iversen and Jørgen Troels-Smith, or the labours of Magnus Degerbøl[95] on the animal remains from Late-glacial and Postglacial deposits, or again the virtuosity of Hans Helbæk in identifying grain imprints and plant refuse.[96] The initiative for undertaking the experimental work in the forest of Draved in South Jutland on the clearance cultivations of forest land and the reaping and preparation of crops in fact stemmed in Denmark predominantly from palynologists and in particular from Dr Johs. Iversen.[97]

As part of the controlled experiments conducted in the forest of Draved in South Jutland between 1953–5 two main agencies of clearance were tested for their impact on vegetation, namely the axe and fire. For the former Iversen obtained the co-operation of Svend Jørgensen and Jørgen Troels-Smith of the National Museum. Using polished flint axe-blades hafted in the style known to have been employed by Neolithic man in Denmark, Jørgensen soon discovered that to minimise breakage he had to use a gentler technique than that suited to steel ones.[98] In the case of burning Iversen was fortunate in being able to call upon Professor Kuusta Vilkuna of the University of Helsingfors with direct experience of *Brandwirtschaft* as recently practised in parts of Finland. The use of ethnographic expertise alongside simulation has all along been a fruitful aspect of experimental archaeology. This has been particularly true where comparisons are taken from the same or a closely analogous culture area.[99] In this respect Scandinavia is happily endowed not only with the possibilities arising from a comparatively late industrialisation but no less with active scholars. In this connection I would cite Professor Axel Steensberg's work, strongly supported by the Carlsberg Foundation, on the implements and techniques used in the practice of every aspect of agriculture.[100] The value of wide comparative knowledge in this field is well exemplified in his well known study 'Med bragende flammer. Braendingskulturens metoder i fortid og nutid'.[101]

A second point is that, although modelled on the standard procedures of natural science, experimental archaeology cannot promise answers of the same order of precision or certainty. The historical dimension in human culture and its manifestations in the archaeological record introduce variables which quite simply are not amenable to explanation solely in terms of natural science. No matter how impressive the analytical expertise, the technical apparatus or the degree of statistical manipulation brought to bear on archaeological data the prehistorian has to rely in the final resort on historical insight. Experimental archaeology remains a valid and useful approach. It can sometimes limit but more often widen the range of possible alternatives. A major barrier to inferring historical conclusions from experiments lies in the very ingenuity, adaptability and manual dexterity of men. The same forms can be made and used in diverse ways. The method chosen by members of a particular society is commonly itself a cultural attribute, even in some cases an identifying mark of a particular culture. In such cases success in the experimental reproduction of a particular type does not of itself prove that the method chosen was in fact used in antiquity. For proof, or at least the high order of probability which is the closest to proof attainable in respect of past events beyond the range of direct observation, one needs to have recourse to physical tests. As Dr M. W. Thompson phrased it in his translator's preface to S. A. Semenov's major work on Prehistoric Technology[102] 'in modern experiments one can do practically anything with flints:[103] the only reliable guide to the original purpose of a tool is the traces of wear that it bears'.

An illustration familiar to northern prehistorians is C.-A. Moberg's experiments on Rovaniemi stone picks.[104] Suitably mounted, these could with ingenuity and practice have been used for any of a number of the purposes suggested, among them hoeing the soil, wood-working, breaking the ice for winter fishing or even removing or preparing the hides of hunted animals. Such demonstrations would prove nothing beyond the extent of human adaptability and ingenuity. Of the four possibilities Moberg concentrated on hoeing as the only one amenable to scientific testing. By mounting a stone pick on an electrically operated apparatus simulating the action of hoeing soil, Moberg showed that after a spell of 142,000 blows the stone blade was marked by clearly visible striations. The absence of these from ancient specimens argued that whatever else they had been used for it could hardly have been for hoeing. As between the other three hypotheses the prehistorian has to be guided by historical judgement, that is in effect by context.

To take another even more familiar example, Thor Heyerdahl's[105] experiments in testing primitive craft against the hazards of long-distance navigation in themselves demonstrate only what is physically and psychologically possible to sophisticated men of the twentieth century, not what happened in history. The voyage of the Kontiki from South America across Polynesia of itself proves nothing about the drift of culture in antiquity. The test of an historical question can only be historical, in this case archaeological evidence. The fact is that so far no artefacts of certainly South American origin have been found further west than the Galapagos Islands.[106]

Experimental archaeology also has potential for investigating social structure and demography. One way it can do this is to simulate the construction of cult monuments or defensive works or the manufacture of such things as personal ornaments and from this estimate the time needed to make them. While it gives no direct guidance how the work was organised, experiments are capable of illustrating the order of effort involved. Calculations of the cost in labour of constructing barrows, megalithic tombs,[107] ceremonial monuments[108] or defensive works, and alternatively, of shaping and perforating and stringing the necklaces of upwards of 15,000 beads of minute size found with Pueblo cremations in Arizona[109] or carving the nephrite *Hei tiki* worn by Maori[110] are valuable as clues to political integration and social hierarchy. It must be equally evident that information of this kind needs to be interpreted in terms of history, and at the same time suggests objectives for research. If the mere presence of personal ornaments embodying high concentrations of labour cannot prove the existence of social hierarchy, at least it points to the need to analyse the associations of such things with other kinds of artefact and where possible with large numbers of burials of individuals of widely varying ages and of either sex.[111]

In the final analysis archaeology, by widening the sources of history and enlarging its geographical and temporal range to embrace all territories occupied by man and all periods since his emergence from the Primate stem, has transformed the context of our existential concerns. We have of course to accept that what history can tell us is limited by the nature of its sources. Since individuals are lost to us from prehistory we can hardly evaluate their moral choice. If our interests lie in that direction we must turn to literature or recorded history. This does not mean that because archaeology depends on material data it need be wedded to a materialist interpretation of history or that its concern with *Homo faber* precludes it from throwing light on *Homo sapiens* and his problems, any more than its reliance on natural science and modern technology for the retrieval and analysis of its basic evidence implies that it is limited to the kind of conclusions attainable by the Natural or Social Sciences. On the contrary, by one of those paradoxes in which history abounds the doctrine of evolution, once considered a threat to our humanity, has in practice served to underline the community of men of all races and cultural levels. Further, in promoting anthropology, animal ethnology and prehistoric archaeology, it has helped to indicate where the essential differences between men and other forms of primate in fact lie.

The gradualness inherent in the evolutionary process and its immense duration in time, making even the most expanded estimate of human prehistory seem brief, confined as it is to the outer crust of the geological sequence, should warn against expecting sharp definition. As the palaeontological record becomes more complete it is reasonable to expect that it will reveal a continuous development between the physique of the earliest fossil men at present known to us and fossils of the common ancestors of anthropoids and hominids. Again, we hardly need the elaborate studies of animal behaviourists to tell us that the appetites and desires of men are hardly to be distinguished by any abrupt line from those which animate apes, monkeys and indeed a wide range of our fellow creatures: we have only had to live through decades of the twentieth century, visit the cinema or even glance at film reviews to know that. The uniqueness of man lies surely in the extent to which his behaviour is conditioned or at least influenced by cultural patterns transmitted by the fact of belonging to communities constituted not by genetic inheritance but by history. The prime and overriding interest of archaeology is that the artefacts which form its stock in trade are in themselves embodiments of the cultural patterns in and through which we can hope to trace the progress of humanisation.

One of the keys to archaeology's appeal lies in what it has to tell us about our identity. If it be true that we are human to the degree that we channel our animal appetites through cultural forms and if the artefacts recovered by archaeology provide the only continuous record of these, then prehistoric archaeology should provide us with a scale for measuring degrees of humanity. Viewed in the perspective prehistory allows, two main phases may be detected in the process of humanisation. The first, which endured throughout the million years or so of the Lower and Middle Pleistocene, was marked by the simplicity of the lithic industries, almost the sole cultural traces to survive from this time, by a rate of change so slow that it can only be measured in geological terms and not least by the large degree of homogeneity that prevailed over the warmer parts of the world to which human settlement was then confined. In contemplating Middle Pleistocene hand-axes one is struck equally by the immensity of the gap between them and anything within reach of the cleverest ape and on the beauty and economy with which they have been shaped to forms standard over large parts of Europe, Africa and peninsular India.

By contrast the second phase was featured by an increasingly complex cultural endowment, a progressive increase in the tempo of change and an accelerating diversity of culture that culminated in the high civilisations of the literate societies recorded in history.

The process of cultural diversification[112] began during the Upper Pleistocene with the appearance of *Homo sapiens*. Regional specialisation took off with the colonisation of new territories, including the forest zones of sub-Saharan Africa, extensive tracts of northern Europe and Asia and ultimately of the Americas and Australia. The adoption of settled life and the domestication of a wide variety of animals and plants in different regions gave a further thrust to the process of diversification. Sedentary life favoured the accumulation of property and apparatus and more certain supplies of food. Even more potent was the shift from relatively homogeneous social groups structured on a segmental basis to vertically structured hierarchies. This not merely gave rise to social diversification but also heightened the sense of identity in communities more highly integrated by the very fact of their hierarchical structure. The artefacts and styles by which archaeologists are so readily able to distinguish between the cultures of Celtic and Anglo-Saxon Britain or Dynastic Egypt and Minoan Crete or Imperial Rome and Han China were enhanced and indeed elicited in large measure by their ruling classes if not indeed by their rulers. The compilers of books issued in connexion with the recent Exhibition of Archaeological Finds of the People's Republic of China wrote in ambivalent terms of some of the richest finds. For instance admiration for the patience and skill of the workers who fabricated the jade plate funeral clothes of a princess of the Han period was combined with severe condemnation of 'the feudal class's luxury and depravity at the expense of the labouring people'. Really one cannot have it both ways. If not made for superiors in hierarchies silks, porcelains, fine metal work and lacquers as well as jades which lend lustre to the very name of China would never have been made.

The shift from homogeneity to increasing diversity in the archaeological record was a move away from a condition common to the genetically determined patterns that restrict the scope of other animals. The growth of cultural diversity at a later stage of prehistory symbolised the progress of humanisation. It has been truly said that archaeology and the natural sciences between them have helped to recover the kind of history appropriate to our world of shrunken space, standardised products, egalitarian sentiment and generalising modes of thought. Certainly we may agree that in an age of nuclear fission we need to nourish a sense of community. Equally surely, though, we need to hold fast to our identity, in other words to our cultural integrity, remembering that we achieved our full humanity as members of the species *Homo sapiens* by subscribing to the traditions of particular cultures.

The forces making for homogenisation are indeed formidable, all the more so that they march under the banner of progress. Let us make no mistake. What is at stake is nothing less than the humanity we have attained, if only very partially, in the course of the last few thousand generations. The feeling is entertained in the wilder regions of the far west and even nearer home that culture is in some respect discriminatory, elitist and only fit in this progressive day and age to be displaced by nature. No one who has spent his life studying the arts, literature or history of mankind would feel inclined to take such a charge seriously to heart. If our forebears of the Pliocene or Lower Pleistocene had been content with equality or rested content solely with what was needed to support their biological needs, our species would never have emerged, let alone created the heritage salvaged by archaeology. Certainly we ignore nature at our peril. As the Chinese long ago understood and expressed in their arts as well as in life, the artificial life of culture still depends as it has always done on maintaining harmony with the natural world. But harmony can only reign between parties. Mankind cannot be saved by reverting to nature. Allow me to conclude this lecture by quoting a couple of sentences from a work by Karl Popper.[113]

The choice of conformity with 'nature' as a supreme standard leads to consequences which few will be prepared to face; it does not lead to a more natural form of civilization, but to beastliness.

Or again, and this time printed in italics:

There is no return to a harmonious state of nature. If we turn back, then we must go the whole way – we must return to the beasts.

Notes

1 Johs. Iversen, *Land Occupation in Denmark's Stone Age. A pollen-analytical study of the influence of farmer culture on the vegetational development.* Danmarks Geol. Unders. II R. Nr. 66. Copenhagen, 1941. of. *Det Kgl. Danske Videnskabernes Selskab Oversigt* 1972–3, 142–3.

2 According to the Preface of *The Impact of the Natural Sciences on Archaeology.* (ed. T. E. Allibone, Sir M. Wheeler *et al.*, Oxford Univ. Press, 1970), the first joint symposium held in the rooms of the Royal Society in December 1969 marked a conscious 'decision of the Royal Society, and the British Academy to work together in the many fields of learning where their interests overlap'. It is significant that at the working lunch held in the previous year to consider ways of forwarding co-operation between the two bodies it 'was felt by all present that a joint enterprise was called for and that there could be no more appropriate subject, linking science with the humanities, than archaeology'. The first symposium, which included a celebration of the first twenty years of radiocarbon dating, was followed in 1972 by one on *The Place of Astronomy in the Ancient World* (ed. D. G. Kendall, S. Piggott *et al.*, Oxford Univ. Press, 1974) and in 1975 by a third on *The Early History of Agriculture* (ed. Sir J. Hutchinson, G. Clark *et al.*, Oxford Univ. Press, 1977).

3 In the opening paper 'Domestication and Social Evolution', see esp. pp. 5–7.

4 The Committee was established by the Science Research Council in July 1976 on the recommendation of the Advisory Board for the Research Councils following an expression of concern by the British Academy and other bodies over the inadequacy of the funds available for the development and application of scientific methods in archaeology. A valuable insight into the work of the Committee can be obtained from the *Annual Report 78/79* of the Science Based Archaeology Committee of the Science Research Council.

5 For a fuller exposition see ch. 1 'The Relevance of World Prehistory' in my *Aspects of Prehistory*, Univ. Cal. Press, 1970 and 1974.

6 J. H. Parry, *The Age of Reconnaissance. Discovery, Exploration and Settlement 1450 to 1650*, Weidenfeld and Nicolson, London, 1963.

7 By R. Hooijkaas, 'Humanism and the voyages of discovery in 16th-century Portuguese science and letters', *Med. d. kon. Nederlandse Akad. v. Wetenschappen, Afd. Letterkunde, N. R.*, deel 42, no. 4, p. 106.

8 T. K. Penniman, *A Hundred Years of Anthropology*, Duckworth, 1935, p. 41.

9 Margaret H. Rubel, 'Savage and Barbarian. Historical Attitudes in the Criticism of Homer and Ossian in Britain, 1760–1800', 105. *Verh. d. Kon. Nederlandse Akad. v. Wetenschappen, Afd. Letterkunde, N.R.*, deel 96. Amsterdam, 1978.

10 *Ibid.*, 109f.

11 A. C. Haddon, *History of Anthropology*, Watts & Co., 1943, pp. 102–3; Penniman, *op. cit.*, 39ff.

12 *The Discovery of Time*, Hutchinson, 1965, p. 80.

13 Quoted from Toulmin and Goodfield *op. cit.*, 130ff.

14 *Ibid.*, 135–9.

15 3 vols., London, 1930–3.

16 The full title of the book in which the Rev. William Buckland F.R.S. summarised his researches was *Reliquiae Diluvianae; or, Observations on the Organic Remains contained in Caves, Fissures, and Diluvian Gravel, and on other Geological Phenomena, attesting the Action of an Universal Deluge.* London, 1823. In the dedication inscribed to the Lord Bishop of Durham from his Deanery of Christchurch the Professor of Geology at Oxford University expressed the hope that 'by affording the strongest evidence of an universal deluge . . . it will no longer be asserted, as it has been by high authorities, that geology supplies no proofs of an event in the reality of which the truth of the Mosaic records is so materially involved'.

17 Penniman, *op. cit.*, 68. This stimulated a spate of new discoveries in western and central Europe: *ibid.*, 225ff.

18 *Ibid.*, 50ff.

19 See p. liv of the Introduction to the Meridian Book edition of 1963.

20 See M. W. Thompson's foreword (p. 29) to his translation of A. L. Mongait, *Archaeology in the U.S.S.R.*, Penguin Books, 1961.

21 Cheng Te-K'un, *Archaeology of China*, vol. 1, Heffer, 1959, p. xvi; G. Clark, *Aspects of Prehistory*, Univ. Cal. Press, 1974, p. 6 n.6.

22 G. E. Daniel, *A Hundred Years of Archaeology*, Duckworth, 1950, pp. 14–16.

23 *Ibid.*, 16–21.

24 Reproduced in G. Clark, *op. cit.*, 1974, fig. 1.

25 For a perceptive study of Camden's contribution to antiquarian studies in Britain, see Stuart Piggott's Reckitt Lecture, 'William Camden and the Britannia', *Proc. Brit. Acad.*, xxxvii (1951), 199–217.

26 Stukeley entitled his most notable publication *Abury, a Temple of the British Druids, with Some Others, Described*, London, 1743.

27 Unfortunately the Rev. B. Faussett died without publishing his results. We have testimony to the systematic manner in which he recovered his data from the late 18th-century antiquary and excavator the Rev. James Douglas, in his well illustrated *Nenia Britannica* (1793), 37 fn. Douglas who dedicated his volume to his royal master, the Prince of Wales, began his Preface with a sentence which reflects the transition from the acquisition of curiosities to the systematic salvage of the materials for reconstructing the past. 'If the study of Antiquity [he wrote] be undertaken in the cause of History, it will rescue itself from a reproach indiscriminately and fastidiously bestowed on works which have been deemed frivolous.'

28 This is well brought out by G. E. Daniel, *The Three Ages. An Essay in Archaeological Method*, Cambridge, 1943, pp. 6–8.

29 Jean Starobinski, *Bull. Am. Acad. of Arts and Sciences*, xxxii (1979), 5–9.

30 Daniel, *op. cit.*, 1950, 60ff; Joan Evans, *Time and Chance*, Oxford, 1943, pp. 100f.

31 In 1863 Lartet was joined by Henry Christy. Owing to the death of Christy in 1865 and Lartet in 1871 their joint publication, *Reliquiae Aquitanicae; being contributions to the Archaeology and Palaeontology of Perigord and the adjoining provinces of southern France*, edited by Prof. Rupert Jones, did not appear until 1875. The volume is distinguished both by the accuracy of its illustrations and by the attention paid to animal remains.

32 In his *Prehistoric Times, as Illustrated by Ancient Remains, and the Manners and Customs of Modern Savages*.

33 G. de Mortillet, *Musée préhistorique*, Paris, 1881.

34 Abbé H. Breuil, 'Les Subdivisions du Paléolithique Supérieur et leur Signification'. *Cong. Int. d'Anthrop. et d'Archol. Préhistoriques*, C.R. xiv Sess., Geneva, 1912. A revised edition (pp. 5–78) was issued by the Abbé in 1937.

35 E.g. E. A. Golomshtok, *The Old Stone Age in European Russia*, Am. Phil. Soc., Philadelphia, 1938. See index entries under 'Aurignacian', 'Solutrean' and 'Magdalenian'.

36 W. J. Sollas, *Ancient Hunters*, third edition, 1924, pp. 131–2.

37 V. G. Childe, 'Changing Methods and Aims of Prehistory', *Proc. Prehist. Soc.*, I (1935), 1–15.

38 Gordon R. Willey and Jeremy A. Sabloff, *A History of American Archaeology*, London, 1974.

39 The Palestine Exploration Fund was founded in 1865, the Egypt Exploration Fund in 1883, the British School of Archaeology at Athens in 1886 and the British School at Rome in 1901.

40 *A Handbook to the British Schools & Institutes Abroad*, British Academy, 1977. It is significant of the changed relation of Europe to the third world that the last School was that of Iraq in 1932. Since the war of 1939–45 only Institutes have been founded as if to emphasise co-operation and dialogue.

41 Glyn E. Daniel, *A Hundred Years of Archaeology*, London, 1950, pp. 21–2.

42 L. Balout, *Préhistoire de l'Afrique du Nord*, Paris, 1955.

43 B. R. Groslier, *Indochina: Archaeologia Mundi*, London, 1966.

44 In 1897 the French bought the right to excavate antiquities in Persia and sent out the Délégation Française en Perse to dig at Susa under de Morgan. Work resumed after the 1914–18 war by de Mecquenem.

45 G. Clark, *Aspects of Prehistory*, Univ. Cal. Press, 1970, p. 23.

46 Mortimer Wheeler, *My Archaeological Mission to India & Pakistan*, London, 1976.

47 Among others: D. P. Agrawal, S. B. Deo, A. Gosh, V. N. Misra, H. D. Sankalia, B. Subbarao, B. K. Thapar & M. S. Vats.

48 B. Fagg, 'The Nok terracottas in West African art history', *Actes du 4 Congr. Pan-Africain de Préhistoire*, II, 445–50. Tervuren, 1959.

49 Thurstan Shaw, *Proc. Prehist. Soc.*, x (1944), 1–67; Fagg, *ibid.*, 68–9.

50 The first holder of the chair (1951–7), A. W. Lawrence of Cambridge, established museums, created a Monuments Board and undertook the restoration of Portuguese trading posts and forts. His successor P. L. Shinnie arranged for Ghanaian participation in the Unesco Nubian Monuments Campaign. A useful insight into the position of archaeology in Ghana is given in Prof. Merrick Posnansky's inaugural lecture *Myth and Methodology – the archaeological contribution to African History*, Ghana Univ. Press, Accra, 1969.

51 Thurstan Shaw's inaugural lecture at Ibadan provides a useful survey: *Archaeology and Nigeria*, Univ. of Ibadan Press, 1963.

52 Thurstan Shaw, *Radiocarbon Dating in Nigeria*, Univ. of Ibadan Press, 1968.

53 Graham Connah, 'Settlement Mounds of the Firki – The Reconstruction of a Lost Society', *Ibadan*, no. 26 (1969), 48–62.

54 N. G. Munro, *Prehistoric Japan*, Yokohama, 1911, p. 14; J. E. Kidder, *Japan before Buddhism*, London, 1959, p. 28.

55 Under Prof. Namio Egami's leadership the Institute has published 15 magnificently illustrated volumes, including series on *Marv-Dasht* (3 vols. 1962–73), *Dailaman* (4 vols. 1965–71) and *Telul Eth Thalathat* (3 vols, 1958–74).

56 Gordon Willey, *An Introduction to American Archaeology* vol. 2, Prentice-Hall, New Jersey, 1971, pp. 102–4.

57 For a well illustrated and critical summary, see C. B. M. McBurney, *Early Man in the Soviet Union*, Reckitt Archaeological Lecture, 1975, British Academy, 1976.

58 S. I. Rudenko, *Frozen Tombs of Siberia* (transl. M. W. Thompson), London, 1970.

59 A. L. Mongait, *Archaeology in the USSR*, Penguin Books, London, 1961, pp. 235–44.

60 Glynn Ll. Isaac and Elizabeth R. McCown (eds.), *Human Origins. Louis Leakey and the East African Evidence*, W. A. Benjamin Inc., California. 1976, pp. 126ff.

61 W. F. Libby, *Radiocarbon Dating*, Chicago, 1955; E. H. Willis, 'Radiocarbon Dating', *Science in Archaeology* (ed. Brothwell and Higgs), 2nd ed., London, 1969, pp. 46–57.

62 W. F. Libby, 'Radiocarbon Dating', *The Impact of the Natural Sciences on Archaeology* (ed. T. E. Allibone), British Academy, 1970, pp. 1–10.

63 *Ibid.*, p. 9.
64 Dates assembled in February 1951 and released in June were listed in Table I of Frederick Johnson, *Radiocarbon Dating*. Mem. 8, Soc. American Archaeology. Supplement to *American Antiquity* XVII (1951).
65 J. D. Mulvaney, 'The Stone Age of Australia', *Proc. Prehist. Soc.*, XXVII (1961), 101; *The Prehistory of Australia*, London, 1969, pp. 178–82; *ibid.*, Penguin Books, 1975. The lists of 1969 and 1975 are of selected dates, but this does not affect the trend.
66 H. L. Movius, 'Radiocarbon dates and Upper Palaeolithic archaeology in central and western Europe', *Current Archaeology*, I (1960), 355–91.
67 Colin Renfrew, 'The autonomy of the East European Copper Age,' *Proc. Prehist. Soc.*, XXXV (1969), 12–47.
68 D. P. Agrawal, *The Copper Age in India*, New Delhi, 1971.
69 J. E. Kidder and T. Esaka, *Jomon Pottery*, Tokyo, 1968.
70 For useful summaries, G. H. S. Bushnell, 'The beginning and growth of agriculture in Mexico', *The Early History of Agriculture* (Hutchinson and Clark, eds.), British Academy, 1977, pp. 117–20, and N. Hammond, 'The early history of American agriculture: recent research and current controversy', *ibid.*, 120–8.
71 G. Clark, *World Prehistory in new perspective*, 3rd ed., Cambridge, 1977, pp. 41–61.
72 G. Clark, 'Neothermal Orientations', *The Early Postglacial Settlement of Northern Europe* (ed. Paul Mellars), Duckworth, London, 1978, pp. 1–10.
73 Hammond, *op. cit.*, fig. 3.
74 Te-Tzu Chang, 'The Rice Cultures', *The Early History of Agriculture* (ed. Hutchinson and Clark), pp. 143–57.
75 G. Clark, 'Radiocarbon dating and the expansion of farming culture from the Near East over Europe', *Proc. Preh. Soc.*, XXXI (1965), 58–73. Subsequent work has modified this particularly in relation to the Mediteranean basin: see J. Guilaine, 'The earliest Neolithic in the West Mediterranean: a new appraisal', *Antiquity*, LIII (1979), 22–30.
76 K. C. Chang, *Rethinking Archaeology*, New York, 1967; Sally R. and Lewis R. Binford (eds.), *New Perspectives in Archaeology*, Aldine, Chicago, 1968; D. L. Clarke, *Analytical Archaeology*, London, 1968; M. P. Leone (ed.), *Contemporary Archaeology*, Illinois Univ. Press, 1972; E. S. Higgs (ed.), *Papers in Economic Prehistory*, Cambridge Univ. Press, 1972.
77 See, notably, *Archaeometry*, the annual review of progress in techniques of data recovery and analysis issued since 1968 by the Research Laboratory for Archaeology and the History of Art, Oxford. There is an extensive literature on particular fields, e.g. George F. Bass, *Archaeology under the Water*, Thames and Hudson, London, 1966; Lerichi Foundation, *A Great Adventure of Italian Archaeology, 1955/65. Ten Years of Archaeological Prospecting*; D. Brothwell and E. Higgs (eds.), *Science in Archaeology*, sect. VII, 2nd ed., Thames and Hudson, London, 1969.
78 *Archaeometry, op. cit.*; Brothwell and Higgs (eds.), Sect. II–IV; M. S. Tite, *Methods of Physical Examination in Archaeology*, Seminar Press, London, 1972; T. R. Hester and R. Heizer, *Bibliography of Archaeology, I: Experiments, Lithic Technology and Petrography*, Addison-Wesley Modules in Anthropology, no. 29, Reading, Mass., 1973.
79 E.g. Karl W. Butzer, *Environment and Archaeology. An Introduction to Pleistocene Geography*, Chicago, 1964.
80 A. P. Madsen, S. Müller *et al.*, *Affaldsdynger fra Stenalderen i Danmark undersøgte for Nationalmuseet*, 3, Copenhagen, 1900.
81 T. Mathiassen, M. Degerbøl and J. Troels-Smith, *Dyrholmen. En Stenalderboplads på Djursland*, Kong. Danske Videnskab. Selsk., Ark.-Kunsthist. Skr., Bd. 1, Nr. 1, Copenhagen, 1942.
82 Johs. Iversen, *Undersøgelser over Litorina transgressioner i Denmark*, Dansk Geol. For., Bd. 9, Hft. 2, Copenhagen, 1937.
83 For a discussion see Grahame Clark, *The Earlier Stone Age Settlement of Scandinavia*, Cambridge, 1975, ch. 5.
84 Kurt Faegri and Johs. Iversen, *Textbook of Modern Pollen Analysis*, Munksgaard, Copenhagen, 1950.

85 See A. J. Brjussow, *Geschichte der neolithischen Stämme im europäischen Teil der Ud. SSR*, Moscow, 1952, pp. 52 and 176f.

86 Gurdeep Singh, 'A preliminary survey of the post-glacial vegetational history of the Kashmir Valley', *Palaeobotanist* 12 (1963), 73–108.

87 D. M. Churchill, *Australian J. of Botany*, 1968, 125–51.

88 Kwang-chih Chang, *The Archaeology of Ancient China*, 34, Yale, 1968.

89 Shoichi Hori in N. Matsumato *et al., Kamo: a study of the Neolithic site and a Neolithic dug-out canoe discovered in Kamo, Chiba Prefecture, Japan*, Arch. and Ethn. Ser. no. 3, Hist. Dept., Keio Univ., Tokyo, 1952, ch. xi.

90 Examples include: the experiments made in the manufacture and use of polished flint and stone axes by N. F. B. Sehested (*Archaeologiske Undersøgelser* 1878–1881, 1, Copenhagen, 1884); the investigation of silica gloss on flint sickles by F. C. Spurrel (*Arch. J.* 49, 1892, 53–69); and the testing of bronze trumpets from Ireland by MacAdam (*Ulster J. of Archaeology* 8 (1860), 99–110).

91 J. M. Coles, *Archaeology by Experiment*, Hutchinson, London, 1973.

92 The first archaeologist to test the erosion and silting of earthworks appears to have been Gen. Pitt-Rivers in respect of Wor Barrow: see *Excavations in Cranborne Chase*, vol. iv 1898, 24. More exhaustive tests are those set up by a Research Committee of the British Association based on the experimental earthwork built for the purpose on Overton Down, Wiltshire: see P. A. Jewell (ed.) *The Experimental Earth-work on Overton Down, Wiltshire, 1960*, London, 1963. For studies in data retrieval, see Sect. ii of *Papers in Economic Prehistory* (ed. E. S. Higgs), Camb. Univ. Press, 1972.

93 Notably by Gudmund Hatt as summarised in his *Landbrug i Danmarks Oldtid*, Copenhagen, 1937. See also the same author's monograph 'Oldtidsagre', *Kong. Danske Vidensk. Selskab, Ark.-Kunsthist. Skr.*, Bd. 11, Nr. 1, Copenhagen, 1949.

94 Acknowledged among other ways in *Studies in Vegetational History in honour of Knud Jessen* presented by an international body of colleagues in 1954 and edited by Johs. Iversen, Danmarks Geol. Unders. IIR. Nr. 80. Copenhagen.

95 See for example his magisterial *Danmarks Pattedyr i Fortiden i Sammenligning med recente Former*, Vidensk. Medd. Dansk naturh. Foren., Bd. 96, 2, 357–641. Copenhagen, 1945. Or, again, his work jointly with Bent Fredskild of the Danish Geological Survey on *The Urus (Bos primigenius Bojanus) and Neolithic Domestic Cattle (Bos taurus domesticus Linné) in Denmark*, Kong. Danske Vidensk. Selskab. Biol. Skr. 17, 1, 1–224.

96 In addition to specialised reports for excavators in Denmark and many countries of Europe and South West Asia, including an exceptionally elegant 'Botanical Study of the Stomach Contents of the Tollund Man' in *Aarbøger* 1950, 311–41, Dr Helbaek contributed a comprehensive treatment of prehistoric cereal imprints for the British Isles up to 1952 in *Cereals in Great Britain and Ireland in Prehistoric and Early Historic Times*, Kong. Danske Videnskab. Selskab. Biol. Skr., Bd. III, Nr. 2. 1944; and in 'Early Crops in Southern England', *Proc. Prehist. Soc.*, 1952, 194–233.

97 Johs. Iversen, 'Forest Clearance in the Stone Age', *Scientific American*, 1956, vol. 194, no. 3, 36–41.

98 Svend Jørgensen, 'Skovrydning med flintøxse', *Fra Nationalmuseets Arbejdsmark*, 1953, 36–43.

99 Grahame Clark, 'Folk-culture and the study of European Prehistory', *Aspects of Archaeology in Britain and beyond* (ed. W. F. Grimes), London, 1951, pp. 49–65, esp. 55f.

100 The wide range of Steensberg's interests has been reflected in the periodical *Tools and Tillage* since its appearance in 1968. See also his contribution 'The husbandry of food production' in *The Early History of Agriculture* (ed. Sir Joseph Hutchinson, Grahame Clark, *et al.*) British Academy, 1977, pp. 43–54.

101 *Kuml*, 1955, 65–130.

102 S. A. Semenov, *Prehistoric Technology. An Experimental Study of the Oldest Tools and Artefacts from traces of Manufacture and Wear*, English edition, London, 1964.

103 *Ibid.*, x.

104 C. A. Moberg, *Studier i Bottnisk Stenålder*, Stockholm, 1955, fig. 49–55 and pp. 108ff.

105 Thor Heyerdahl, *American Indians in the Pacific: the theory behind the Kon-Tiki expedition*, London, 1953.

106 Thor Heyerdahl and Arne Skjolsvold, *Archaeological evidence of Pre-Spanish visits to the Galapágos Islands*, Mem. 12 Soc. American Archaeology, Salt Lake City, 1956.

107 For references to estimates based ultimately on military experience of earthwork see Grahame Clark, 'The Economic Context of Dolmens and Passage-Graves in Sweden', *Ancient Europe and the Mediterranean* (ed. V. Markotic), Warminster, 1977, p. 35.

108 One may cite as examples the experiments conducted to simulate the transport of the bluestone components of Stonehenge by water and overland summarised by Prof. R. J. C. Atkinson, *Stonehenge*, London, 1956, pp. 98–110.

109 It was shown by experiment that Pueblo necklaces might embody as many as 480 eight-hour days of work. E. W. Haury, 'Minute beads from prehistoric pueblos', *American Antiquity, 33* (1931), 80–7.

110 Using only those techniques available in Maori technology it was found that it took some 350 man hours to carve a *hei tiki* from nephrite: T. Barrow, 'An experiment in working nephrite', *J. Polynesian Soc.*, 71 (1962), 254.

111 As carried out recently by Dr Susan E. Shennan in her analysis of the social hierarchy represented in cemeteries dating from the Early Bronze Age in Czechoslovakia. See her Ph. D. thesis on 'Social Organisation in the earliest Bronze Age in Czechoslovakia: a study based on the Cemeteries of the Nitra Group', Cambridge University Library Ph. D. thesis no. 10767, December, 1978.

112 G. Clark, 'Archaeology and Human Diversity', *Ann. Rev. Anthropology*, 8 (1979), 1–20, Palo Alto, Cal.

113 K. R. Popper, *The Open Society and its Enemies*, vol. 1, Routledge & Paul: London, 5th ed., 1966, pp. 70 and 200.

PART III

ARCHAEOLOGY AND SOCIETY

CHAPTER 23

ARCHAEOLOGY AND THE STATE

The interest of the State in the ancient monuments and civilizations of Britain is recent in origin and limited in extent.[1] It is the purpose of this paper to trace in outline the growth of State interest, the limits of State control at the present time, and the main *lacunae* which appear to exist in the mechanism for the preservation of our national antiquities. Before embarking on this topic it might be well to point out the two chief reasons why, before 1882, the State undertook little or no responsibility within a sphere now generally recognized as the proper concern of any civilized state. In the first place the study of British Archaeology has only within the last fifty years reached a degree of accuracy and discipline worthy of the expenditure of public funds; it is of the utmost significance in this connection that the first scientific British archaeologist, General Pitt-Rivers, was appointed as first Inspector of Ancient Monuments under the Act of 1882. Subsequent students of the subject, no less than the tax-payers of the day, may congratulate themselves that certain of the earlier figures of British archaeology were not invested by the State with powers that might well have increased the extent of those devastations which we have good reason to mourn at the present time. In the second place the whole conception of the State exerting its power for the conservation of a national heritage at the expense of a narrowly conceived view of private property is of itself a product of recent constitutional changes, reflected in the successive extensions of the franchise between 1867 and 1918. The various Ancient Monuments Acts, etc. may be considered as manifestations of the same social conscience that successfully demanded such measures as the regulation of conditions of employment, insurance for work-people, provision for unemployed persons, compulsory education, suitable housing for the poor, and the nationalization of certain resources such as petroleum.

We shall consider the question of the relations of the State to archaeology under four separate heads:

1 The preservation of monuments.
2 The mapping of antiquities.
3 The preservation of loose antiquities.
4 Museums.

I. THE PRESERVATION OF MONUMENTS

It will be convenient first of all to pass in review the successive Acts of Parliament by which the State has recognized, and to a large extent assumed, its obligations in respect of the preservation of monuments of national importance.

The Ancient Monuments Protection Act, 1882, is chiefly important in that it constitutes the earliest recognition by the State of its responsibility for national monuments. Some 68 monuments in the British Isles were specified in a schedule as being of national importance, and among them were numbered such famous sites as Stonehenge, Avebury, Arbor Low, and New Grange. The Act provided that anyone, *the owner excepted*, convicted of damaging or defacing any of these monuments would be liable to a fine not exceeding £5 or one month's imprisonment. Secondly it provided that *owners should have power* to constitute as guardians (of any of the monuments on the schedule) the Commissioner of Works, who would thenceforth be responsible for their maintenance; in this event the owner would become liable to the same penalties as any member of the general public for any damage he might do. Thirdly the Commissioners could *with the consent of the owner* and of the Treasury purchase any monument on the schedule, and fourthly they could accept as a gift or bequest any such monument. Finally it was provided that one or more inspectors be appointed by the Commissioners of the Treasury 'to report . . . on the condition of such monuments, and on the best mode of preserving the same'.

As previously intimated the Act is important more as an indication of dawning responsibility than for any real power that it bestowed on the State for the implementing of its intentions. The authority of an owner over his property, even where expressly stated by the Act to be of national importance, remained unimpaired unless of his free will he placed it under the guardianship of the Commissioner of Works, or sold, gave or bequeathed it to the same authority. It is no surprise, therefore, that the first Inspector appointed under the Act, General Pitt-Rivers, soon wearied of his task and felt compelled to offer his resignation after seven years' experience of Government inactivity.[2] In actual fact, the Act being almost entirely permissive in character, the Government enjoyed no authority to act even assuming it felt the desire or the responsibility.

More elasticity was secured by the Act of 1900, which empowered the Commissioners of Works to become guardians at the request of the owner of *any* monument (as opposed to scheduled monuments only) when its preservation was considered to be 'a matter of public interest by reason of the historic, traditional or artistic interest attaching thereto'. The only exceptions to the scope of the Act were dwelling-houses occupied by anyone other than a caretaker and family. This Act is interesting in that it empowered County

Councils to purchase by agreement, to become guardians of, and to contribute towards the cost of maintenance of, monuments within their counties 'or in any adjacent county'. Another important principle that was to survive was that of public access to monuments within the ownership or guardianship of the Commissioners or of the County Councils; in the latter case the permission of the owner was necessary. For the purposes of the Act 'monument' was defined as 'any structure, erection, or monument of historic or architectural interest, or any remains thereof'.

The Act of 1910 empowered owners to give or will monuments within the meaning of the Act of 1900, thus remedying a careless omission from that Act.

The Acts of 1900 and 1910 did little to lessen the essential weakness of the original Act. A memorandum by the First Commissioner of Works, published in the Annual Report of the Inspector of Ancient Monuments for 1912, is worth quoting in this context; 'existing Acts', it stated, 'are purely permissive in character. The State cannot undertake the guardianship, or arrange for the protection, of any monument, except with the consent, and indeed by the desire, of the owner'. The First Commissioner went on to point out that many monuments were falling into decay, declaring in conclusion . . .'it is, in my opinion, most desirable that the State should have power to intervene in such cases'. The result was the new Act of 1913, which repealed the previous Acts, consolidated their main provisions relative to purchase and guardianship, and added in the Preservation Order a potent weapon in the struggle to prevent the destruction and decay of monuments of national importance.

The Commissioner of Works was empowered to constitute an advisory board, known as the Ancient Monuments Board, and composed of representatives drawn from the Royal Commissions on Historic Monuments, the Society of Antiquaries of London, the Society of Antiquaries of Scotland, the Royal Academy of Arts, the Royal Institute of British Architects, the Trustees of the British Museum, and the Board of Education. It was on the advice of this Board that the Commissioners were enabled by the new Act to place under the protection of the State by means of a Preservation Order any monument of national importance declared to be in danger. In order to ascertain the state of any monument the Board were empowered to carry out an inspection. The Preservation Order would be effective for 18 months unless confirmed by Parliament, and if unconfirmed at the end of that time it could not be applied to the same monument for a period of five years. When in force the Preservation Order placed a monument under the protection of the State, carrying with it penalties of a fine of £5 or for any damage or alteration one month's imprisonment. Moreover if any monument, the subject of a Preservation Order, appeared likely to fall into decay, the Commissioners were empowered to make an order constituting themselves guardians of the monument for the duration of the Preservation Order *without the consent of the owner*. The Commissioners were further enabled to take measures for the protection of a monument, the subject of a Preservation Order, *with or without the permission of the owner*.

The 1913 Act provided a second important check on the destruction of monuments. The Commissioners of Works were instructed to publish a schedule from time to time of 'such monuments as are reported by the Ancient Monuments Board as being monuments the preservation of which is of national importance', and to inform owners when fresh monuments were added to the list. It then became the duty of owners to give one month's notice of their intention 'to demolish or remove in whole or in part, structurally alter, or make additions to, the monument', so allowing time for a Preservation Order to be issued. The penalties for failing to give such notice as the Act required were a fine of £100 or imprisonment for three months or both.

From the provisions of this Act, as of previous Acts, all inhabited dwelling-houses other than those occupied by a caretaker and family, were excluded as well as buildings at present in ecclesiastical use. The definition of 'monument' was, however, somewhat widened to include 'any part of the adjoining land which may be required for the purpose of fencing, covering in, or otherwise preserving the monument from injury', and further 'the means of access thereto'.

A major defect of the 1913 Act was revealed in a dramatic manner when a Company was formed for quarrying the rock in the immediate neighbourhood of the Roman Wall. The Wall itself and its subsidiary constructions were protected under the Act and many people assumed that the protection would extend to such parts of their immediate surroundings as gave them their character and meaning. This assumption, however, proved groundless when tested by this practical case and the grandeur of the Wall was only saved to the Nation by the munificence of a private individual. The outcome of the scare was the Act of 1931.

The new Act introduced the principle of the 'controlled area' by which the Commissioners were empowered to delimit such an area contiguous to a monument as will ensure the full preservation of its amenities. Within the area controlled buildings can be prohibited or restricted and their design and appearance prescribed, excavations and tree felling can be prohibited and any other restrictions imposed that may be necessary. The owner can be compensated for any loss he may sustain through the restrictions, but for any contravention of the scheme he may be fined up to £20 a day. In various other ways the Act of 1913 was tightened up and in some cases its provisions were extended considerably in scope.

The Act of 1931 has been in force for too short a period for its full weight to be felt; it would, however, be safe to say that the legislative powers at present possessed by the Commissioners of Works for the preservation of ancient monuments of national importance are greater than is generally realized. Financial considerations are bound to curb development to a certain extent and it is certain that the Commissioners will not exert their powers too much in advance of public opinion. With these reservations, however, it remains a fact that by the exercise of powers already legally entrusted to them the Commissioners could control the whole of the archaeological excavation of the country: not only are the Commissioners themselves empowered to carry out excavations, but by including 'any cave *or excavation*' within the definition of 'monument' they are able to employ the Preservation Order and other weapons to stay undesirable excavations by others. Legally, indeed, it would seem that the Commissioners of Works could bring to an end all excavation by individuals or societies, and themselves exercise a complete monopoly. Present practice, as well as the traditions of the country, indicate that in fact the Commissioners will co-operate with individuals and bodies of proved competence; meanwhile it is satisfactory to know that powers exist which may curb the inefficient, uneconomic, and therefore anti-social, excavation that is still responsible for the steady destruction of ancient monuments. The only tragedy is that the necessity for these powers was not earlier appreciated. The extent and rapidity of the destruction of ancient monuments by agriculturalists and archaeologists during the last hundred years has been appalling. We illustrate (fig. 23.1) the distribution of megalithic monuments in a district of Hannover, which happens to have been accurately surveyed in 1846 and again in 1914; the destruction revealed by a comparison of these surveys is probably not abnormal.[3] The powers

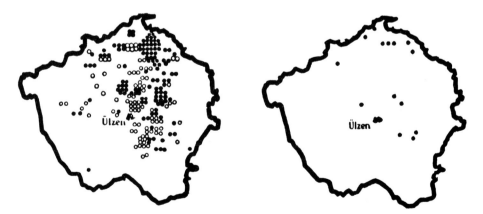

23.1 The left-hand map illustrates the distribution of megalithic tombs in the *Kreis* of Ülzen in the province of Hannover, as surveyed by C. von Estorff in 1846, when 129 survived relatively intact and at least 90 survived in a damaged condition. That on the right shows the distribution of the same class of monument as observed by Dr Jacob Friesen in 1914, when no more than 14 examples survived.

possessed by the Commissioners may appear dangerous on paper, but in the face of such menaces they are certainly not too great; we feel confident that in practice the English tradition of co-operation between State and individual will assert itself and nullify the possibility of any centralized bureaucratic control.

The Inspectorate of Ancient Monuments

In describing the gradual development of the legal control by the Commissioners of Works over ancient monuments of national importance we have necessarily referred constantly to the machinery by which the Acts are enforced. The original Act of 1882 provided for the appointment by the Treasury Commissioners of 'one or more inspectors of ancient monuments, whose duty it shall be to report to the Commissioners of Works on the condition of such monuments, and on the best mode of preserving the same'. General Pitt-Rivers was appointed in 1882 and held the position until his death in 1900, though disgust at the futility of the Act prevented him from drawing his salary or taking any very active interest after 1890. After the death of the General, indeed, the office fell into abeyance. A good deal of work was done unofficially by Mr J. Fitzgerald, who had overtaken the arrears of work by 1908, only to die in the following year. In 1910 Mr (now Sir) C. R. Peers was appointed and it was under his leadership, as Inspector to 1913 and Chief Inspector from then till 1933, that the Inspectorate as it exists today was built up. It not only controls in practice the machinery for the preservation of ancient monuments, but in the person of its late Chief Inspector, it did much to mould the course of the necessary legislation. Moreover the same annual report (1912) of the Inspector which exposed the inadequacy of the then existing Acts also laid down the fundamental principles which have in practice guided the Commissioners of Works in the actual work of preservation. The Commissioners were to avoid 'as far as possible . . . anything that can be considered in the nature of restoration' and were 'to confine themselves rigorously to such works as may be necessary to ensure their stability, to accentuate their interest, and to perpetuate their existence in the form in which they have come down to us'. Up till the end of 1933 the total number of monuments in England scheduled for protection had reached 2205.

The Royal Commission (England)

As a necessary preliminary to the extensive preservation of monuments of national importance by the State an authoritative survey of all existing monuments of a certain antiquity was and is a paramount necessity. A Royal

Commission was therefore appointed in 1908 'to make an inventory of the Ancient and Historical Monuments and Constructions connected with or illustrative of the contemporary culture, civilization and conditions of life of the people in England, excluding Monmouthshire, from the earliest times to the year 1700, and to specify those which seem most worthy of preservation'. The first Secretary to the Commission was the late Sir G. E. Duckworth (1908–33), during whose term no less than fifteen volumes were published notwithstanding the interruption caused by the Great War. The volumes have set and maintained a standard of accurate scholarship which is widely recognized, yet they are so written and illustrated as to appeal to the general educated public. They thus serve not only to provide the accurate information required for a comprehensive policy of preservation by the State, but also to broaden interest in the antiquities of the country and to stimulate that public opinion which is so necessary to the satisfactory operation of the Acts. Considering the attention to detail and the wealth of the material dealt with the output of the Commission has been astonishing. During the first period of activity between 1908 and 1915 the English Commission investigated no less than 5,631 monuments in 462 parishes, while on resuming its activities from 1919 until 1923 it dealt with 3,554 monuments in 314 parishes. In this way the investigation of the monuments of the counties of Hertfordshire, Buckinghamshire and Essex was completed. The Commission next turned its attention to the difficult area of London, on which it published five volumes between 1924–30 in addition to a sixth volume for Huntingdonshire. From 1930–2, 2,480 monuments in 169 parishes were investigated in Herefordshire, the third and final volume on which has been published recently. Whilst engaged on counties the Commission has investigated well over 700 monuments annually, a truly amazing record of achievement when one considers that many of the monuments concerned are of considerable size and complexity. The cost to the tax-payer is, owing to the speed with which the work is done, almost negligible. Working on the basis of the average number of monuments investigated and the total estimate of annual expenditure it costs about £8 to have each of our English monuments investigated, truly a small enough sum to secure such a birthright.

2. THE MAPPING OF ANTIQUITIES: THE ORDNANCE SURVEY

It is a truism of modern archaeology that one of the most significant facts about antiquities is their exact provenance, and the State in the guise of the Ordnance Survey has contributed handsomely to British archaeology in this respect. Although at present a department under the Ministry of Agriculture and Fisheries, the Ordnance Survey was military in origin and is still mainly staffed by Royal Engineers. Owing, however, to the antiquarian interests of General Roy (1726–90), author of *The Military Antiquities of the Romans in North Britain* and virtual founder of the Survey, archaeological information has from the beginning been incorporated on its published sheets. We illustrate (fig. 23.2) part of a sheet of the original 1-inch survey on which archaeological features were marked. Roy's tradition was ably maintained by subsequent Directors, notably by Sir Charles Close, and ultimately resulted in 1921 in the appointment of an Archaeology Officer to the staff. The primary task of this Officer is to ensure the accuracy of the archaeological features printed on the maps issued to the public, to revise the information for new editions and, so far as is practicable, to incorporate fresh discoveries as they are made. In this way the State is able to ensure the adequate cartographic record of its antiquities at a negligible cost, and the general public is given accurate information on its maps. There is no doubt that the practice of marking the sites of antiquities on the ordinary official maps has done much to broaden general interest in the subject, and for this reason alone the institution of an Archaeology Officer has been invaluable; but already there is a growing public with a special interest in archaeology and to serve this the Ordnance Survey is producing Period Maps, which are models of their kind. Those already published include Roman Britain, 17th century England, two sheets of a Megalithic Survey, and the first sheet of a survey of the Celtic Earthworks of Salisbury Plain. The staff can hardly be regarded as commensurate to the magnitude of its task, but it is important that the accurate mapping of national antiquities has been recognized in principle as a legitimate charge upon public resources.

It will be convenient to note under this heading the contribution made to British archaeology by the Royal Air Force, since in practice the air-photographs of archaeological interest taken during the course of training are dealt with at the Ordnance Survey. The air-photographs are filed at Southampton and prints may be bought by the general public (crown copyright being reserved). It is interesting to notice that the survey of Celtic Earthworks on Salisbury Plain has largely been based upon air-photographs taken by the R.A.F. in the normal course of duty.

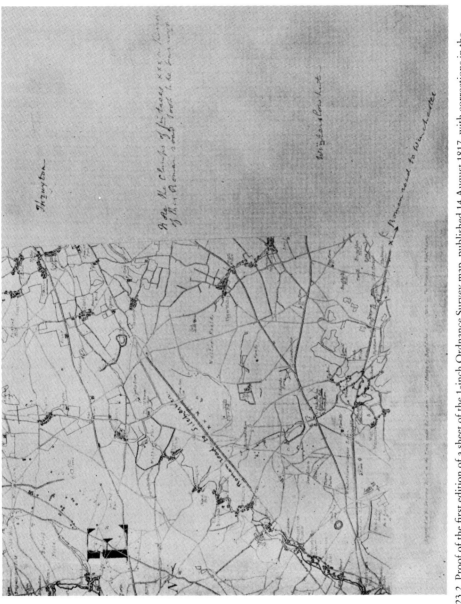

23.2 Proof of the first edition of a sheet of the 1-inch Ordnance Survey map, published 14 August 1817, with corrections in the handwriting of Sir Richard Colt Hoare. It shows the district to the northeast of Salisbury with the valley of the river Bourne. Figsbury can be seen in the left-hand bottom corner. Numerous tumuli are also indicated.

3. PRESERVATION OF LOOSE ANTIQUITIES

When we come to examine the powers exercised by the State over moveable antiquities we find ourselves confined to a consideration of the law of treasure trove, since apart from its jurisdiction within this extremely narrow sphere the State appears to have no powers over antiquities found in its own soil, unless within the area of a National Monument within its ownership.

Fortunately one more qualified in every way to discuss the subject has recently published an important paper on 'The law and practice of Treasure Trove' (*Antiquaries Journal*, 1930, pp. 228–41), so that it will be unnecessary to enter into any detail. As is the usual case with the laws and institutions of our island the origins of the law of treasure trove are lost in the mists of antiquity, mists into which we have no desire to stumble. Sir George Hill has given us the key to the proper understanding of the law when he bids us consider it as no more than 'a specific application of the common law of the land, which provides that the estate of a person dying intestate with no known heirs becomes the property of the Crown'. We feel incompetent to define the law in a manner likely to commend itself to a lawyer, and confident that if we succeed we should fail in the more important task of conveying information to the general public. We shall rest content, therefore, with stating the fundamental facts which determine whether or not a given find falls within the category of treasure trove. In brief the law applies only to treasure that has been hidden and of which neither the owner nor his representative can be found, the treasure itself being either of gold or silver. It does *not* apply to treasure that has been abandoned,[4] *nor* does it apply if the owner can be found, *nor* does it apply to any objects other than those of gold or silver.

In origin there is no doubt that treasure trove was solely designed to secure revenue to the Crown and to this day the concealment of treasure trove remains a misdemeanour. It is, therefore, the police who are responsible for seeing that treasure trove is properly reported, and it is by a Coroner's inquest that it is decided whether or not a given find is in fact treasure trove. The attitude of the Treasury, however, to whom the treasure is ultimately delivered, has undergone a welcome change, and the law of treasure trove as today administered forms part of the machinery by which the national antiquities are preserved by the State. This change of attitude can be summarized quite briefly by considering the position of the finder of treasure trove. Up till 1871 his chances of receiving any reward at all were doubtful and until 1886 he was paid only the bullion value of his find. The Treasury Minute of 13 July 1886, however, marks a new step forward, and taken in conjunction with the Ancient Monuments Act of 1882 can be taken as a definite indication that the State was no longer indifferent to the fate of its antiquities. The minute stated: 'My Lords have stated that the Crown right to treasure trove, regarded financially, is valueless, and that special cases excepted, they would not assert the Crown's claim at all. They, in fact, only interest themselves in the matter to assist the efforts of Antiquarian Societies for the preservation of objects of general interest.' In order to further this desirable object finders of treasure trove who properly reported their finds were from this date rewarded on the basis of the antiquarian value of their discoveries, subject only to a deduction of from 10 per cent to 20 per cent. Finally within very recent years the Treasury has waived its right even to this small deduction.

In practice, once the Crown's right to the treasure has been established by a Coroner's inquest, its administration is delegated by the Treasury to the British Museum. At the British Museum the treasure is examined and valued by experts on the basis of its market value. Any objects not retained by the British Museum, the Royal Mint, local museums or the owner of the land on which they were found, are returned to the finder, who receives in addition the full value of any objects retained. In this way every encouragement is given to anyone who finds treasure trove to report to the police without delay, in order to qualify for a reward fixed by impartial and expert opinion. Meanwhile the penalties for intentional concealment still remain, and the alternative to receiving a financial reward is a fine and imprisonment with hard labour.

Admirable in its limited scope though the law of treasure trove may be in these latter days, when it works for ends entirely foreign to those which inspired the evolution of its mechanism, it can hardly be regarded as an efficient method for the safe-guarding of moveable national antiquities as a whole. The insufficiency of a law which takes into account only objects of gold and silver (and even those only when found under certain circumstances) is well illustrated by the maxim of General Pitt-Rivers, the father of modern British field-archaeology, that 'the value of relics, viewed as evidence, may . . . be said to be in inverse ratio to their intrinsic value'.[5]

At the present time antiquities other than those coming within the scope of treasure trove belong to the ultimate owner of the land upon which they are found. It is a curious anomaly that while monuments and constructions of national importance have been to a very large extent socialized by the Acts and the machinery which implements them, loose antiquities, including in some cases the very objects which give indication of the date or associations of a monument of national importance, are left unprotected to be bought and sold, collected or lost, or intrigued for by museums. The anomaly is brought home the more when we consider that the archaeological objects in monuments placed under the protection of (but not the property of) the Commissioners of Works belong to the land-owner and not to the State, even though they alone might lend any meaning to the monument in question. The attitude adopted by the modern State that ancient monuments are in effect the heritage of the nation and not the playthings of individual land-owners seems to demand some measure of protection for loose antiquities found in the soil. The enlightened manner in which the law of treasure trove is now administered is so much to the good, but it is totally insufficient to ensure the proper preservation of what ought to be regarded as part of the national heritage.

Before leaving the subject of loose antiquities it might be useful to mention the Geological Survey, since for the earlier periods of archaeology monuments and constructions tend to give way to geological sections. Much has been done in the past by individuals on the staff of the Survey, such as Skertchley and Jukes-Browne, and much is now being done to notice features of archaeological interest in the course of geological work. We suggest, however, that an archaeological staff officer similar in status to the one attached to the Ordnance Survey might save a vast amount of information about the earlier periods of British Archaeology that is now lost.

4. MUSEUMS

An essential part in the preservation of antiquities is played by museums, and it is therefore necessary to consider how far those in this country are organized and how far they are in themselves equipped for the services they ought to render to the community. In actual fact there is very little to consider, since there is an almost total lack of organization and system for the museums as a whole, and with very few exceptions the individual institutions lack the first elements of a proper equipment.

In his most admirable Report on the Public Museums of the British Isles prepared in 1928 for the Carnegie United Kingdom Trustees, Sir Henry Miers stated that 'one of the peculiarities of the present museum system in England, Northern Ireland and Scotland is the almost entire absence of any form of co-operation'. This is perhaps partly due to the fact that the museums have grown up or rather struggled into existence singly and unrelated to any plan. Some museums are private, others belong to Societies of various kinds, others are attached to Universities and Schools, a great number are run by municipalities, and a few are of national character. Over the first three categories there is no kind of public control. The municipal museums maintained by the rates came into being as a result of the Museums Act of 1845 and subsequent Acts, all of which were mainly concerned with empowering local authorities to appropriate public money to the upkeep of museums. Legislation on the subject of museums has been concerned almost solely with the purely financial aspect of the situation, and the management of each institution is left in the hands of a committee of the local council. The only national museum with which we are concerned here is the British

Museum, which is still run along the lines laid down by the British Museum Act of 1753, vesting the museum and collections in a Board of Trustees, and laying down the principle of free access for the public. Strictly speaking the British Museum is the only museum in England containing substantial collections of British antiquities for which the State is responsible. There are no formal relations between the British Museum and other museums in the country of any kind whatsoever, except in so far as the British Museum is authorized under certain conditions to distribute duplicate specimens. An organized system of museums in this country simply does not exist. Their distribution is 'of the most haphazard nature', they have no defined spheres of influence, and they are linked by no connection either with one another or with any central institution.[6]

No intelligent person reading Sir Henry Miers' report could fail to be shocked by the glaring inadequacy of the equipment of the museums dealt with. As regards staff Sir Henry Miers found that in only 14 per cent of the museums of the British Isles was there a full-time paid curator, while in only 4 per cent was there an assistant curator. He further found that in many instances the curators appointed lacked 'any previous training or experience', while one of the chief facts disclosed by his enquiry revealed a 'disgracefully low standard of salaries', salaries falling on the average 50 per cent below the minimum recommended by the Museums Association. As to buildings he found that 'only 10 per cent of the museums in the country are housed in a separate building (good or bad) designed for the purpose', while 'very few of the museums in the country are provided with the storage rooms or work-rooms which are essential'. Small wonder is there 'that almost all museums contain collections . . . consisting to a great extent of mere curios'!

With the educational aspect of museums, important though it is, we are not here concerned, but rather with the bare preservation of antiquities, which should be a national interest. If the State is to extend its interest from monuments and constructions to the objects which so often date them and invest them with meaning and associations, it seems clear that it will also have to take in hand the whole problem of the proper organization of museums. It would appear that there are certain drastic changes necessary, and we suggest that there are certain elementary pre-requisites for efficiency:

(*a*) Museums should be set up where they are required.
(*b*) They should no longer exist as isolated and in some cases competing units. They should in some way be related to the National Museum, and they should each serve a recognized territory.
(*c*) They should be staffed by trained curators, who should be paid salaries bearing some relation to their attainments and social value.
(*d*) The buildings in which collections are housed should be designed as museums, and should be equipped to meet the needs of the various classes of person using a museum.

These requirements are simple enough and their cost quite trivial when compared with the millions spent on other 'services', social and otherwise. Moreover a State policy for museums seems to be the logical conclusion of the policy for the preservation of national antiquities, to which the State is already partly committed. With the museums in their present state any effective control of antiquities, other than monuments or constructions, would appear to be difficult if not impossible. Conversely it must also be clear that so long as the private ownership of antiquities from English soil is tolerated by the State it must remain difficult for the museums to help themselves. The necessity of negotiating for objects with private individuals imposes an intolerable burden upon museum staffs, and frequently means the acceptance of junk, hampering restrictions on the proper utilization of objects, and even the temporary suppression of provenance.

In conclusion it would be true to say that while the State has been eminently successful in the limited spheres of archaeology into which it has entered, much is lacking before a comprehensive policy for the preservation of the national heritage of antiquities can be said to exist. While the preservation of monuments and the mapping of antiquities are both on a sound basis, there is no organization for the preservation of loose antiquities other than treasure trove, and no organization of museums in which to house and exhibit them.

Notes

1 We are dealing here with England only.
2 *Vide* Third Annual Congress of Archaeological Societies, 23 July 1891.
3 E.g. Dr Fox's remarks on the destruction of round barrows in *The Archaeology of the Cambridge Region*, pp. 28–9.
4 In the words of Judge Baylis, writing in the *Archaeological Journal* (1886, XLIII, 342) and quoted by Sir G. Hill, the treasure 'must be found hidden *in* the earth or in the walls, beams, chimneys, or other secret places above the earth, but affixed to the soil'. 'If found *on* the earth or in the sea' it is not hidden, but abandoned and therefore outside the scope of the law.
5 Preface to volume III of *Excavations in Cranborne Chase*, p. ix.
6 This reflects in no sense on the work of the Museums Association of which Sir Henry Miers stressed the importance and value.

Archaeological publications of the Ordnance Survey

Map of Roman Britain, 1928.
Map of XVII Century England, 1930.
Megalithic Survey:-

Professional Paper, 6. The Long Barrows and Stone Circles of the Cotswolds and the Welsh Marches. (Sheet 8, ¼ inch map), 1922.

Professional Paper, 8. The Long Barrows and Megalithic Monuments of Kent, Surrey and Sussex. (Sheet 12, ¼ inch map), 1924.

Map of Neolithic Wessex. (Sheet 11, ¼ inch map), 1933.

Map of the Trent Basin. (Sheet 6A, ¼ inch map), 1933.

Professional Papers:-

No. 7. Air Survey and Archaeology, 1924.

No. 10. The Work of the Ordnance Survey: Archaeology and the Ordnance Survey, by O. G. S. Crawford, 1926.

No. 12. Air Photography for Archaeologists, 1929.

Celtic Earthworks of Salisbury Plain: Old Sarum, 1934.

N.B. The Megalithic Survey will be completed in eleven sheets, and the survey of Celtic Earthworks of Salisbury Plain in six. It should be noted that the first two sheets of the Megalithic Survey (numbers 8 and 12 in the Old Series) were published as Professional Papers (numbers 6 and 8 above), so that four sheets have been dealt with. Three more sheets are rapidly nearing completion and publication. East Anglia contains no megalithic monuments so that no map of this area will be published. The precise position of the Survey cannot be stated concisely, owing to the fact that, since it was begun in 1924, the sheet-lines of the ¼ inch map, which was then adopted for convenience as the publication unit, have twice been altered. But it may be said that only two whole sheets (7 and 10 in the present series) and one half-sheet (the eastern, or mainland, portion of Sheet 2) have not yet been touched. When the Megalithic Survey is complete, the combined results will be published on a single Period Map on the scale of 1 : 1,000,000 uniform in style with the maps of Roman Britain, XVII Century England and the forthcoming Map of Britain in the Dark Ages.

CHAPTER 24

EDUCATION AND THE STUDY OF MAN

Education as a subject for post-war planning is on everyone's lips today. Public interest has never been higher. Yet it may be doubted whether even now the full measure of its importance is realized. Next to winning the war, nothing is of greater moment than the battle for enlightenment, for if this is lost the 'victory' will be vain and we may all prepare for an ordeal more terrible than the present, because fought out among still larger aggregations of political and military power. The whole of history bears witness to the corruption of power, the struggles of the few for spoil of the many, the ignorance of the peoples and its lethal consequences to themselves. Today, thanks for the most part to the heroism of the common man, whether citizen of a bombed city, defender of Stalingrad, peasant of China, inhabitant of oppressed Europe or member of the forces of liberation, we stand on the threshold of what could be a new world: whether we cross that threshold or are elbowed back into the dark passage that leads to another holocaust depends primarily on our attitude to education, on the steps taken during the next few years to bring to the common man everywhere a realization of his inheritance as a citizen of the world and an awareness of his power to mould his own destiny. What is needed above all is an overriding sense of human solidarity such as can come only from consciousness of common origins. Divided we fall victims to tribal leaders: united we may yet move forward to a life of elementary decency.

Extension of facilities for education in the post-war era may be anticipated with confidence, identified as it is in the public mind with equality of opportunity. The machinery for achieving this – raising the school leaving age, securing entry to places of higher education for those most fitted to profit, and the provision of extended education for wage-earners – should not of itself be difficult to devise and once in operation should even go some way to solve the problem of leisure, which a social utilization of productive capacity would render acute. The problem is not one of means so much as of ends, for an extension of educational facilities is to be welcomed only in so far as the education to be provided is of itself sound. Were it a case merely of extending to the masses an education hitherto confined to the rich, the problem would be comparatively simple, but there can be few who see the going so easy as that. Propagation on a wider basis of a system of education with limitations lethal to the well-being of the world constitutes, indeed, one of the outstanding dangers of the post-war period. It may easily happen that the looked-for blessing may in fact turn out to be a curse. The prospect of a substantial broadening of educational facilities makes it more than ever necessary to reconsider the nature and purpose of education. The opportunity is great, the menace real.

The most sweeping criticism levelled against modern education is that it lacks coherence and direction, other than those imparted by sectional interests or the ambition of the individual to further his success in a chosen career. To quote Mr Walter Lippmann:[1] 'Modern education has renounced the idea that the pupil must learn to understand himself, his fellow men and the world in which he is to live as bound together in an order which transcends his immediate needs and his present desires. As a result the modern school has become bound to conceive the world as a place where the child, when he grows up, must compete with other individuals in a struggle for existence. And so the education of his reason and of his will must be designed primarily to facilitate his career.'

The consequences of this educational void, which we now call education, are, as we know too well, economic misery in domestic affairs, total war in foreign. If educational reform meant no more than that larger sections of the population are to be drawn into this void for a longer portion of their lives, then we might well despair of the future; the only result could be a still further undermining of the prospects for a healthy, social and international existence in the years ahead. The democratic drive for education might easily create conditions mortal to democracy.

It is not the purpose of the present essay to review the various remedies proposed, to discuss the value of this or that dead language or this or that system of belief, but rather to urge the thesis that human well-being should be the overriding aim of education, that its value should be judged primarily by the extent to which it promotes human solidarity; in a word, that education should be truly anthropocentric. Now it so happens that the progress of the human sciences during the last hundred years has accumulated the material for integrating education on the level of world citizenship for the first time in history. Within the territories of Medieval Christendom, before the Reformation, there was certainly a system of education generally accepted and in itself coherent, but this church education was confined to a very small part of the world and within the narrow confines of Christendom itself was restricted to but a small section of the population. During the secularisation of education which followed one has to reckon with disintegration along two distinct lines: on the one hand 'professional' subjects over and above religious and legal training began to disturb the unity of education, a process greatly accelerated during the last hundred, and particularly during the last fifty years; on the other, national allegiances began to undermine the solidarity of civilized men, so that the virtues of citizenship came to be confined in their scope to the limits set by the exigencies of national policies. The result we all know – warfare fought out by the most advanced specialists, the highest achievements of human ingenuity turned to the destruction of civilization. If in the political sphere it has become obvious that national and even regional allegiances must be abated in favour of a world allegiance, so cramped has science made our human living-space, it must be equally clear that some scheme of education is required, common to the whole human race, understandable by all and tending to a common norm of conduct, being based fundamentally on the biological unity and the cultural inheritance of mankind. In a word education must be re-integrated on the broadest possible basis, nothing less than the universal experience of man.

It is a fact, which may explain many of the ills from which the world has suffered, that science turned her attention last upon human kind – the sun, the moon and the stars, the structure of the earth, the rocks, plants, insects, fishes and beasts of the field, all were subjected to the scrutiny of men of science, while Man, perhaps because made in the image of God, was accepted like a sacrament and set apart. Darwin's great achievement was to bring man down to earth, to draw him within the field of scientific observation and so to make possible his own emancipation. Anthropology, like the idea of evolution itself, was older than Darwin, but it was the publication of *The Origin of Species* that made it a subject of widespread interest and concern. In the same way Prehistory achieved a new meaning in the light of the extended vistas of human existence opened up by acceptance of the new doctrines. Together they have unfolded in the last eighty years a story of human development and achievement which ought to rank high in the heritage of every human being capable of receiving education. Yet it is a fact that, up to the present, educationists as a body have ignored the study of men as completely as did the scientists of the pre-Evolutionary era. While the study was still in its formative stages and before students had produced an agreed body of doctrine concerning the evolution and development of man and society, it is understandable that its claims to rank as a subject for general education were held in check. Today the position is different: the labours of the last two or three generations have produced a coherent picture, the broad outlines of which are generally accepted as valid, not only by anthropologists and prehistorians, but by workers in many branches of knowledge.

The key position of the study of man in the field of knowledge was early appreciated by that father of British Anthropology, E. B. Tylor, who in the preface to his *Anthropology: an Introduction to the Study of Man and Civilization*, outfaced the criticism that the educational curriculum was already too overloaded to make room for yet another 'subject' by the claim that the new science would lighten rather than increase the student's burden. Tylor put his finger on the integrating role of the human sciences when he wrote:[2] '. . . the science of Man and Civilization . . . connects into a more manageable whole the scattered subjects of an ordinary education. Much of the difficulty of learning and teaching lies in the scholars not seeing clearly what each science or art is for, what its place is among the purposes of life . . .'

Now it is precisely in this respect that anthropology and prehistory have most to offer. One of the major ills of education today is that from the point of view of the majority, both of pupils and teachers, the curriculum appears to be made up of a bundle of 'subjects' abstracted from their context in life and bearing little or no relationship to one another. At best these 'subjects' are graded brands of intellectual pabulum done up in conventional packets; at worst they are degraded into media for the acquisition of marks in competitive examinations. An education based on such a parody of knowledge is bad, not only intellectually, but also socially; it breeds barbarians possessed of a little knowledge in restricted fields, but unaware of its relation to life in human society, individuals fit only for regimentation by bureaucrats, themselves among the most accomplished and therefore the most deplorable products of the system. Between them anthropology and prehistory, functional and historical aspects of the same basic study, give a complete picture, both of man's place in nature and of the emergence, development and functioning of human society. By focussing all upon man and his development, they and they alone can bridge the gap between the arts and the sciences, the humanists and the technicians. In this respect the secular study of man may yet, if it can break the crust of academic conservatism, resolve the chaos brought about by the disintegration of Christendom.

Practical details as to the manner in which the elements of anthropology and prehistory can best be introduced into the educational curriculum I do not propose to debate in this place, but there is one question which can hardly be avoided even in a general discussion. At what age should this teaching be given? Should it be reserved for adult education? Ought it to be introduced in secondary education? Or, should it form one of the foundations of primary education? My own reply would be that it could not be started too early or continued too late. The subject is precisely as all-embracing as life itself. At every stage of the individual life it is capable of integrating impressions received on any particular topic and relating them to the wider purposes, not only of the particular society, but to society and human well-being in general. In favour of beginning the teaching at an early age I would urge that interest in origins is deeply embedded in the childhood both of peoples and of individuals. As Reinach has written,[3] 'the problem of the origin of the world and man, to which anthropology, geology and the kindred sciences are now systematically seeking a clue, confronted humanity the moment it became self-conscious'. The earliest efforts to supply an answer took the form of cosmogonies – 'poetic attempts at reading the riddle'

– the best known of which among the white races is that formulated among the Hebrews and handed down in the Book of Genesis. When interest is aroused by cosmogonies is surely the time to begin imparting an outline of the story pieced together by modern research, an outline which later education should progressively expand and into which all knowledge acquired in later years could comfortably be fitted without conscious break. Thus would knowledge evolve gradually and naturally, patterned by the evolution of humanity itself.

Man's Place in Nature	
(i) The world and the Universe	*Astronomy*
(ii) The structure and recent history of the earth and its climate	*Geology and climatology*
(iii) The antiquity of life and the emergence of man	*Biology and natural history*
(iv) The human family, the distribution of its principal varieties and the meaning of race	*Ethnology, anatomy and psychology*
(v) The symbiosis of man and nature	*Geography and anthropogeography*
Man and society: the development of civilization	
(vi) Modes of subsistence, utilization of natural resources, exchange, measurement and counting	*Economics and mathematics*
(vii) The evolution of industrial processes and techniques	*Handicrafts, technology, chemistry and physics*
(viii) Transport and habitations as functions of economic and social development	*Engineering and architecture*
(ix) Clothing, personal adornment, decorative and pictorial art, music, dancing	*Aesthetics*
(x) The power of the unseen in the world of the living and of the dead	*Theology*
(xi) Social organization and the traditional regulation of communal life	*Sociology, law and linguistics*
(xii) The development of human society – Savagery, Barbarism and Civilization	*History*

In the present essay I am concerned only with emphasizing the importance of making education everywhere anthropocentric, of putting man as such in the very centre of the picture, and of relating all other studies to human rather than to group interests or to purely individual needs. The table given above is designed to show how a study of human development in its broad outlines can be made to introduce all the main fields of knowledge, at the same time focussing them on the requirements of man and society. Such a table could easily be amplified, but even in its present simplified form it should help to substantiate the claim that between them Anthropology and Prehistory form an introduction to knowledge which ought on the one hand to make its assimilation easier to the individual and on the other to promote its social utilization.

But the study of man should be more than a primary introduction to education: it should itself constitute a framework for education throughout life. Moreover it cannot be stressed too strongly that education is not merely or even mainly a process of imparting information. Far more important is its function of training the will and supplying motive power. The conception of pure 'subjects', abstracted from life and injected into students at stated periods during their course of academic instruction, is surely as outmoded as that of the untrammelled operation of pure 'economic law'. Education acquires dignity and value only in so far as it contributes to the larger purposes of life, among which that of living in society is foremost.

Now it is the thesis of the present essay that by society we mean human society at large, and that by consequence education should have for its prime purpose the training of the individual to live in the world as a human being, rather than as an individual or as the member of any particular association. Such a conception has, indeed, been forced upon us by modern technics. By reducing space through means of communication vastly superior to any previously known, aeronautical science and wireless have in effect made the world a unit in a sense never previously known. The world of the Greeks and the Romans was essentially a Mediterranean world: that of medieval Christendom was only slightly less constricted. Until the advent of the steamship, the new continents opened up by the great discoverers of the fifteenth and ensuing centuries served merely to enlarge the known world, and reduce its cohesion. The steamship went far to knit together those parts of it accessible by sea, but it is the long-distance airplane in our own day that has created a situation in which the whole world has become for practical purposes a single unit. Today, as Mr Wilkie has recently emphasized in his *One World*, 'there are no distant points in the world any longer'. It is as easy to traverse the Continents today as it was to journey from parts of Scotland to London at Victoria's accession. Thanks to wireless, words can travel round the world almost as they are spoken. It must be sufficiently evident that the conquest of space holds of itself no promise of a better future: whether wireless and the airplane knit men together in a world community or assist in the mutual destruction of rival associations of nations depends precisely on whether constructive thought in our generation becomes world-wide in its scope or follows its old tribal grooves. If men everywhere only hang together there seems no limit to the possibilities of human betterment: if they allow their differences to be exploited nothing is more certain than that in the name of this 'cause' or the other they will be herded to destruction with an accomplished efficiency and a perfection of technique hitherto unknown. The dilemma is not to be avoided: it has never been easier to build or to destroy and we are too much in each other's way to be neutral. Mr Wilkie concludes that if there is to be any hope of evolving a decent order 'our thinking in the future must be world-wide'. One would go further and add that our feeling likewise must be world-wide.

As the leaders of Christendom and of the national states that succeeded its dissolution appreciated, community of sentiment is founded not upon race or language, but upon tradition – in other words upon the appreciation of a common past. The transmission of this tradition and the kindling of this appreciation in the minds of succeeding generations is the historic role of education. By analogy, therefore, the realization of a world community depends on the existence of a common human past on which a common tradition may be founded. As archaeologists and anthropologists know, this common past, this common tradition, has been rescued from oblivion during the last hundred years. It is a matter of urgent and imperative importance that education everywhere should be grounded and based on the common experience of humanity, its emergence from the world of the beasts, its age-long struggle for betterment. Here, providentially, we have placed in our hands the key to a fuller world in which all men everywhere appreciate their innate community, their persistent indebtedness one to another, their fundamentally common interests. Such a world is hardly likely to be attained by those eminent educationists who advocate for humanity whatever course of instruction was esteemed in the days of their youth in the particular society in which they happened to find themselves. The author of a recent book on education recommends a blend of Hellenism and Christianity as a panacea.[4] Had he been writing exclusively in respect of the British middle classes his thesis might have had more relevance, but on the showing of the title of his book he has the whole world in mind, a world composed of the most diverse elements in the tradition of many of which neither Hellenism nor Christianity have played an important part. To the peoples of the world generally, the peoples who willy nilly must in future co-operate and build or fall out and destroy, I venture to think that Palaeolithic Man has more meaning than the Greeks. Dig up a Greek vase in the suburbs of Pekin and you bring to light a mere freak, the discarded treasure perhaps of some collector from the West: excavate Pekin Man and his crude implements and you establish ground of common interest to educated men of every race, something which concerns them all equally as men.

It follows, if we approach education from an evolutionary point of view, that instruction should first be given in those subjects of broadest concern to mankind at large, the special characteristics and problems attaching to particular societies and cultural traditions being reserved for later stages in the educational process. Primary education the world over should thus be concerned first and foremost with broad outlines of the human story, viz.:

(a) The relation of man to the universe, stages in his evolution, the definition of his principal varieties, their distinctive features, their distribution, their common origin and their common nature.

(b) The outlines of world prehistory from the earliest times to the period of the discoveries basic to civilization, broadly speaking from Palaeolithic times to the Bronze Age, from Savagery to Barbarism.

Introductions both to the natural sciences and to the problems and experiences of human life, economic, social, aesthetic and religious would follow easily from such a grounding. Thus would the whole field of knowledge be brought gradually into view, not as a congeries of abstract 'subjects', but as a natural and necessary extension of the life of humanity at large. Brought up in such a primary education one might have some grounds for hoping that mankind would be immune from some of the more outrageous deceptions of its leaders. Had the German, Italian and Japanese peoples of the present generation received a grounding in the natural and cultural history of mankind, it seems impossible that they could have been mesmerized by the crazy dreams of racial and cultural domination which today are sweeping them to ruin. Illusions as fatal as these will not be dispelled in any final sense by military defeat alone. Sanity and a better disposition can be made to return only after a lengthy period of education. Let us hope that a liberal dose of elementary anthropology and prehistory will be prescribed, rather than the history of modern states, perverted in its national guise, but suspect in any other.

When the common basis of understanding has been laid, then comes the time for building an edifice in accordance with whatever cultural tradition prevails in the society concerned. Diversity of cultural inheritance is a fact highly persistent and at the same time of the highest value to humanity at large, even if in the recent past it has been exploited in the interests of power-maniacs to lever great communities into destructive conflict.[5] Properly handled, diversity in the inheritance of communities, like that of individuals, should redound to the general advantage. Right education is and must always be the only insurance worth taking out against the destruction of our inheritance, and the basis of this must surely be that all men are brought to realize that their community goes deeper than their diversity. It is, thus, the highly responsible task of secondary education to introduce adolescents to the distinctive features of their own particular cultural inheritance in such a way as to promote rather than impede the larger aim. The distinctive genius and traditions of peoples and national communities should be a joy and a glory to every individual in them, something to be treasured, but also something to be dedicated to the purposes of all humanity – if not so dedicated they will sooner or later be exploited to subserve the purposes of tribal policies and in due course impoverished, if not destroyed, by war.

It follows logically from the evolutionary position that modern history and current affairs, which have come to play an ever-growing part in teaching, ought to be reserved for the closing stages of secondary or even for higher and adult education. Modern history, the more it approaches our own times, approximates to discussion of modern problems and such discussion, if not used to give currency to some form of propaganda, can only serve to confuse minds not sufficiently equipped to grapple with them. There is much to be said for school history books stopping short at 1789, provided that further instruction is forthcoming either at the University, or in the course of some form of extension teaching. The child and the young scholar should learn his lessons in an epic school in which whole eras can be comprehended. In the primary school he should learn of the childhood of the race, in the secondary of the birth and growth of his own peculiar civilization; only on the threshold of adult life should he be plunged into the complexities of modern history, the problems of which are in many cases contemporary.

Insistence on the universal aspects of the study of Man should not be in the least inconsistent with enjoyment of traditions shared in common by nations or smaller associations of individuals, held together it may be by no more than common residence in an administrative county or borough. On the contrary, since the young learn most easily by illustration, it must be evident that even the elements of world prehistory will in practice be taught in terms of the local hill-fort, gravel-pit, or museum. Moreover, any tendency to dull uniformity should be finally dispelled at the secondary stage, when the individual is brought to a study of the upgrowth and development of his own cultural background from Barbarism to Civilization, and the era of recorded history. Then the subject matter of teaching will vary broadly according to local or national tradition. Whereas the young European will learn of the Aryan-speaking peoples, in particular of the Celts, the Teutons and the Latins, of the achievements of Greece and Rome, of medieval Christendom, of the Renaissance and of the rise of national consciousness, the young Indian will be more concerned, *pace* Macaulay, with the development of his own civilization from Mohenjo-Daro to the European encroachments. The Indian's interest in Greece and Christendom will be secondary: the former he will study mainly for the effects of Alexander on his own history, the latter for the light it throws on the European conquerors and overlords of the last two centuries.

Realization of a world order based on the extinction of diverse national traditions would be Dead Sea fruit indeed, for it is only by the cultivation of their diverse traditions that national communities can contribute anything of value to the international comity. From this point of view domination of the world by the concepts of Hebrew prophets or Greek oligarchs would be every bit as bad as subjection to any one of contemporary ways of thought. If as individuals or peoples we have contributions to make, let them be genuinely our own, welling up from the springs of our own being. Traditions rooted in remotest antiquity, form a heritage of incalculable worth, valuable alike to the society, its individual members and the 'One World'; their cultivation and perpetuation should be a prime concern of society in general and of educationists in particular. As trustees of a world empire the responsibilities of the British people in this sphere are immense. The stimulation of interest in their own cultures is something we owe, both to the indigenous peoples themselves and to the well-being of the Empire. In this respect we have something to learn from the USSR, the constituent peoples of which have been encouraged in the study of their own specific cultures, with results which not only enrich their own lives but also strengthen their will to preserve the Union in time of trial. No amount of political or economic well-doing can compensate for lack of appreciation of, and sympathy for, native culture. Recognition of anthropology in the training of Colonial Probationers, while doubtless intended to promote smooth administration, is a step in the right direction, but there is room for an even more positive attitude to indigenous culture; specialized archaeological and anthropological services and the education of peoples in their indigenous history are urgently needed.

Throughout my argument emphasis has lain on the role that anthropology and particularly prehistory must play in education if the new world order is to have more than an ephemeral existence. But it has further been suggested that if life is to be worth living we must be careful to maintain and, indeed, to develop that diversity of cultural tradition by which peoples are distinguished and through which alone they can enrich humanity. The absolute value of cultural tradition needs to be stressed today as never before, since conditions of life in the dominant nations of the world, engendered by the Industrial Revolution that brought them to the position they now occupy, threaten to dry up its very well-spring. The drift to great cities, the decay of craftsmanship, the impoverishment of family life and the sweeping away of standards of traditional behaviour are only a few of the symptoms of a process of mass deculturalization.[6] The pattern of life, even its very fabric, has been sacrificed in great industrialized communities to the pursuit of economic efficiency. The mass satisfaction of artificial wants, stimulated and standardized by advertisement, may 'raise the people's standard of living', may increase the size of their bodies, may even prolong the duration of their lives, but can hardly of itself enrich them in any genuine sense. In a world of economic and political anarchy everything must be sacrificed to industrial efficiency in the interests of bare survival, and education must be geared to the production of administrators and technicians and the schooling of the grey masses. The reversal of these trends depends primarily on the realization of a world order under which it will cease to be necessary to concentrate on the mere preservation of society. But international security, while it might lessen the drive, cannot of itself cure the ills of society. Intelligent readjustment of the relations of town and country, by bringing town-dwellers into closer contact with the rhythm of rural life, might go some way to restore the balance. But from a long-term point of view it is only by tapping the accumulated treasures of human experience that successive generations can be restored to a full measure of life. From the traditions and achievements of the race we may yet draw inspiration and, refreshed from the deep springs, we may yet shake free from the nightmare of vicarious existence.

Man, it has been said, differs from the beasts in the possession of culture. As a cultural being he can lead a full and satisfying life only in so far as he conforms to cultural patterns. It is a tragedy of our time that millions, possessing equal political 'rights' in the most advanced states and 'enjoying' a standard of life beyond the wildest dreams of the emperors of antiquity, are ceasing even to be conscious of culture. The 'cultural orphans', who proliferate in our great cities, constitute, like the infiltrating barbarians of antiquity, a fifth column of portentous dimensions. If civilization is to survive, the process must be reversed, decisively and on the broadest front. The process of deculturalization must be arrested and men made conscious once again of their heritage as cultural beings.

Notes

1 From his Address to the American Association for the Advancement of Science, 29 December 1940, printed in *The American Scholar*, Spring, 1941. From lack of access to the original the passage has been quoted from Sir Richard Livingstone's *Education for a World Adrift* (Cambridge, 1943), p. 111.
2 *Op. cit.* (London, 1881), p. 1.
3 S. Reinach, *Cults, Myths and Religions* (London, 1912), p. 157.
4 Livingstone, *op. cit.*
5 See the present author's *Archaeology and Society* (London, 1939), ch. VII. It is fair to add that this would have been stressed differently if written today.
6 During the evacuation of urban centres in the present war the country has realized with something of a shock the progress of deculturalization among the population of industrial cities. Thus a speaker in a recent House of Lords debate, a former professor of anatomy, is reported (*Daily Telegraph*, 6 May 1943) as remarking that 'these people who came from the cities – women and mothers – seemed quite unable to do anything very much for themselves, and . . . were quite obviously without any effective social tradition'. The children were like untrained puppies and about 10 per cent of the evacuees, he estimated, were 'deplorably and absolutely cultural orphans'.

CHAPTER 25

PREHISTORY AND HUMAN
BEHAVIOUR

The American Philosophical Society carries in its title two potent epithets. The word American summons up above all an image of human ingenuity and practical achievement: the world is impressed not merely by the speed with which you have tamed a continent and made wealth to flow in the wilderness, but even more I believe by the new kind of society you have created. How does this image of achievement consort with the epithet Philosophical? It most certainly doesn't go with resignation or the acceptance of conditions as they are; nor I think, despite highly distinguished contributions made by Americans, does technical academic philosophy, or the kind of problems with which philosophers in the technical sense concern themselves, occupy a very central place in American thinking. The impression I carried away from Daniel Boorstin's first volume is that all the circumstances of your earlier history combined to emphasize the role of experience and diminish that of speculation as a guide to conduct. You may remember that he wrote of the Puritans that 'like many later generations of Americans . . . [they] were more interested in institutions that functioned than in generalities that glittered',[1] a sentence that reminds one that the Americans share with the British quite a deal more than their language. I'm going therefore to assume that by philosophy is meant in the present context the cultivation of knowledge in the highest sense useful to man: in that case the conjunction of American and Philosophical makes sound sense.

The American Philosophical Society, like the Universities of Oxford and Cambridge, has reached an age at which its precise antiquity no longer matters. What is quite certain is that the Society, established on its present foundations in 1768, still retains the imprint of the man who by more than one line of descent must be reckoned its founder and begetter. Benjamin Franklin was throughout his long and active life impelled by a basic desire to effect improvements. We do not picture him as a man wracked with doubt or over-much concerned with defining the ideal; he was occupied with what was self-evident and he regarded himself and his young companions as among the first subjects for improvement. Having profited by the Junto's program of self-improvement he and his friends sought to promote and propagate knowledge useful to the world at large. The Founder had no doubt the best results would flow from the co-operation of individuals adept in particular fields of knowledge – you will remember how in his prospectus of 1743 he proposed that the nucleus of his Philosophical Society should include 'a physician, a botanist, a mathematician, a chemist, a mechanician, a geographer and a general natural philosopher'.[2] But he never forgot for a moment that the object of such a society was to harvest the results of their labours for the common good, not merely of themselves but of men in general. Benjamin Franklin would surely have approved the way the Society has, through succeeding centuries, refrained from dividing itself into sections and staunchly maintained the human relevance of its diverse interests. Again, it is not fanciful to see Franklin's inspiration in the policy of opening the membership not merely to scientists concerned with natural phenomena but also to students of man and not least to contemporary leaders in law, government, and affairs. If Franklin was a philosopher in the generous sense of that term he was also, in the words of the *Encyclopaedia Britannica*, 'printer, author, publisher, inventor, scientist, public servant and diplomat', not to mention instigator and founder of all the most important institutions of public utility in this city. Now that so much intellectual activity has come to be focussed on and cloistered in universities, I venture to think that Franklin's message and the message of this Society is more than ever important. We must never forget that knowledge is valuable in proportion as it is relevant and as a human being I can only mean relevant to our human condition.

I would not have accepted your kind invitation to speak here this evening if I did not believe that archaeology was relevant in the sense I have just indicated and I am encouraged by the mere fact that you are holding this symposium to believe that you share this view. Turning back to the records of the speeches made at your bicentenary banquet on April 30, 1927, I was particularly struck by some remarks made by John C. Merriam in proposing the toast of 'Our Sister Societies'.[3] Recalling that from its beginning the Society had concerned itself above all with the 'linking of those aspects of science which touch accumulation and interpretation of facts to the group of problems concerning human interest', Mr Merriam went on to specify the special need to 'obtain scientific foundation for study of characteristics peculiar to man'. I don't imagine for one moment that the speaker had archaeology in mind when he made these remarks, but he might almost have been defining what I believe archaeology to stand for. And this uncanny feeling of anticipation returned to me when the speaker went on to say of the need for co-operation that 'in the universe of human beings [this] involves not merely all men in all places, but all men at all times'. These are the very topics on which I want to enlarge this evening. I want to suggest that within our own lifetimes archaeology has brought within reach new possibilities for defining and assessing the attributes and behaviour we can regard and value as specifically human; and at the same time that it has opened up new historical perspectives which allow us to view our situation in the world in terms peculiarly relevant to our age and times.

It has done so in part by making us more fully aware of the civilization reflected, often rather dimly and always incompletely, in the earliest written sources. Revelation of the cities and ziggurats of Mesopotamia, of the pyramids and royal tombs of Egypt, of the historic structures of Jerusalem, of the Palace of Minos, of the precincts of Olympia, or of the Roman forum has allowed us to see with our own eyes memorials of civilizations on which our own is based. We look, we touch, and we believe. It all becomes real. And archaeology has plenty to tell us of our own quite recent past. Industrial archaeology – the archaeology of the Industrial Revolution – is currently the rage in Britain, a land which also specializes in social and, I might add, political archaeology. The world's best-selling writer on archaeology, C. W. Ceram, has, I see, just published *The Archaeology of the Cinema*. Here in America you have shown your customary ingenuity by reversing the time machine and creating monuments to remind you of your history – I am thinking not only of set-pieces like Williamsburg, Plymouth, or films like *The Covered Wagon*, but also of the ingenious and teasing little touches which bring home to British visitors the exploits of Paul Revere and his Minute Men.

Even more important is the way archaeology has allowed us to reconstruct prehistory, the age-long history of the preliterate past of all mankind. For in prehistory we see, not merely the source of the great literate civilizations, but the emergence of everything we signify as human. If history gives us an insight into the main civilizations through which men have expressed their genius, prehistory tells us of the phenomenon of man himself. Through the ages seers, thinkers, preachers, artists, writers and philosophers have sought to convey in their various idioms the answer to a question which interests us as men (as distinct from the two-legged animals to which advertisers and politicians too often address themselves), the question who and what are we? From my list of explainers I omitted to mention biologists. Darwin may have told us where we came from, but he still did not establish our identity, any more than his successors have done. Human paleontology can tell us much about our physical antecedents even if our more immediate predecessors are represented by no more than scarce and fragmentary fossils. From a behaviouristic point of view the existing primates offer a more promising source, more especially since primatologists have taken to studying animals living in the wild instead of concentrating on the frustrated denizens of zoos; but we need to keep firmly in mind that the non-human primates that still survive are descended from those that diverged from the main line of evolution many millions of years ago. We must never forget that we are organisms of lowly descent – really there is very little possibility of that – but this is not after all the important thing about us as human beings; the significant thing is not that we are animals but that we are human. We must turn to prehistorians if we wish to learn how certain hominids become human and developed their humanity to the point of civilization, for the documents studied by prehistoric archaeologists are no more and no less than fossils of human behaviour.

If one wanted to characterize man's behaviour one would I suppose lay stress on the fact that it differs from that of other animals to the extent that it is conditioned by culture. One does not have to be an anthropologist to recognize this. That a man is human in proportion as he behaves in a cultured way has entered deeply into folk wisdom. This is the meaning of the motto 'Manners makyth man' devised by William of Wykeham and still treasured by the ancient school at Winchester. The converse is just as revealing and far more commonly expressed at the level of daily discourse. When we disapprove strongly of anyone's behaviour we are apt to term it bestial or label it with the name of some animal of particularly noisome smell or evil habit. But hogs and even skunks are quite nice animals at heart. I prefer the Russian term of opprobrium *nekulturny*, uncultured. When you come to think of it this is much more devastating than the phrase uncivilized, a libel on the preliterate folk of simple culture whose behaviour is as human in all essentials as our own. The important thing to stress is the link between humanity and culture. By implication and in parenthesis there is a clear moral here for protagonists of naturism, whether in literature or in life: human values are not natural; they are artificial, the creation of human society.

Studies of animal behaviour have shown indeed that not all of it can be explained in terms of genetic inheritance, that learning can be shown to play a certain role; and even that, as in local variations in bird-song, cultural patterning can sometimes be detected. The fact remains that in human societies culture is not only much more pervasive; it is much more rapidly and widely transmitted; and it is capable of being stored in a way that leads to accumulation and growth. Whereas among birds or apes we have to look for culture – PhD's are earned that way – in the case of men it is the dominating fact of their behaviour. By and large the study of prehistory shows that culture is not merely pervasive, but self-generating and, subject to whatever local setbacks, progressive. This is the essential message of Gordon Childe's *Man Makes Himself*. Man made himself by widening and deepening his culture. This is not something about which it is necessary to speculate or argue. Material traces of human culture have survived over thousands, indeed over hundreds of thousands of years, and by interpreting these archaeologists have been able to recover at least in outline what amounts to a veritable history of mankind, a history not written in words but wrought in labour.

Most abundant are the traces which tell us of man's biological success, shown by the fact that he has come to outnumber his nearest living relatives by a factor of two or three thousand times. Or, again, there is his ability to adapt to a variety of environments, breaking out of the warm cradleland, to which modern apes are still confined, and spreading first into temperate Eurasia and later to the New World and Australia and even to islands scattered far over the Pacific, so that when Europeans set out on their voyages of discovery, commerce, missionary endeavour, and conquest they found almost the whole world occupied by men. Another way in which early man demonstrated his biological dominance was his role in bringing about ecological change, more particularly since he first learned to domesticate animals and plants. That prehistoric man was able to inherit and dominate the earth was of course made possible by his physical endowment and most notably by the size and quality of his brain; but the means he employed were products of his culture.

The most palpable of these were tools, extra-corporeal limbs as Childe used to term them, by means of which he shaped the gear needed for the ever-increasing range of his activities. Indeed, man has often been classified as the tool-making primate. Of course apes and even animals much lower down the evolutionary scale are known to utilize inert objects to further their biological aims, but man is unique in fabricating tools to standard patterns and above all in his ability to make cumulative improvements in these. So much is this the case indeed that when archaeologists first tried to arrange their finds in temporal sequence one of their main clues was to identify lines of technological advance. As the founder of this Society so well understood, technological advance, by which mankind has been able to enlarge so significantly the possibilities of life, implies and depends upon a progressive increase both in knowledge and in manipulative skills. The evolution in techniques of flaking flint that at first proceeded so slowly as to be almost imperceptible over tens of thousands of years and the progressive discovery of how to work different kinds of metal ores so as to produce artifacts mark early but vital stages in the emergence of modern technology.

Quite as important, and closely linked with this, was early man's progress in making secure and increasing the sources of his subsistence. The discovery of how to domesticate and control the breeding of food plants and animals, a discovery which seems to have occurred independently in the two hemispheres, is surely one of the great turning points in human history and you will not need reminding that in the early days of your Society the improvement of farming was one of the principal objects of its endeavours. The ability to increase and ensure the supply of food had a direct effect on human populations by making it possible for men to live together in larger communities. This encouraged a finer subdivision of labour, which in turn accelerated technological progress. Better equipment made for more productive farming and so, like the cultural advance itself, the process was cumulative. It is hardly surprising that within a few thousand years of the initiation of farming we are able to see in successive levels of Mesopotamian settlement mounds the appearance of metallurgy, urban life, and writing.

What did the evolution of material culture imply and how did it come about? Here, again, we can learn something from Benjamin Franklin: he was himself a writer, he founded this Society to propagate useful knowledge and he also founded a university. He recognized, no one more clearly, the vital importance of transmission. If the fruits of learning had died with each generation, progress could hardly have occurred. It was only at a quite recent stage that human culture reached a degree of complexity that necessitated writing: the great achievements of prehistoric men were transmitted by oral tradition and precept, powerfully assisted by imitation. It is not for nothing that articulate speech has been taken as a criterion of humanity. The great apes, like all other animals, communicate with one another: they do so by emotive noises as of 'defiance, anger, fear, frustration and contentment', but they also employ a remarkably resourceful silent vocabulary: as A. H. Schultz has so graphically stated[4] 'crouching down, presenting buttocks, extending hands in pronation, exposing teeth partly or fully, raising eyebrows, protruding lips, shaking branches, pounding chest, dancing in one place, etc., are all actions full of definite meaning' . . . and of course not a few of them are indulged in under stress of particularly violent emotion by thwarted dictators and children in different phases of their immaturity. In the sense that they communicate, the great apes have a language, but they still lack anything that can be called articulate speech: they can convey emotions and desires, but, as Wolfgang Köhler has stated[5] emphatically, they 'never designate or describe objects' and it may be recalled that Dr and Mrs Hayes found during their famous experiment in rearing 'Viki' from the age of three days to three years that it was impossible even after eighteen months of intensive coaching to persuade this young chimpanzee to identify even her own nose, eyes, hands, or feet.[6] Primatologists seem to agree that it is this failure to achieve articulate speech that constitutes the greatest handicap of the apes, holding them back from anything approaching human culture.

Articulate speech after all is essential, not merely for transmitting acquired culture and storing up learning, vital though this may be: it is equally essential in securing social co-operation in the increasingly complex tasks of an evolving way of life. As the eminent physiologist, J. Z. Young, has phrased it,[7] 'we can compare the use of the words we speak with that of tools and other indirect means of satisfying need . . .' Again there is the role of language in intellectual development. As Young has put it, words help one to observe more closely and, by allowing men to see connections between things apparently separate, they help them to understand the causes of what goes forward in their surroundings. There is a vital link between speech and thought. According to Ernst Cassirer,[8] 'by learning to name things a child does not simply add a list of artificial signs to his previous knowledge of ready-made empirical objects. He learns rather to form concepts of those objects, to come to terms with the objective world.' Of course we cannot know much about language in the preliterate past, though the possibilities of linguistic palaeontology are not to be neglected. Yet the prehistorian cannot doubt when he observes his range of archaeological material that it was made by people capable of articulate speech; and it could well be, as Kenneth Oakley has suggested,[9] that the accelerated tempo of cultural evolution that set in between 35 and 40,000 years ago in a restricted zone of the Old World and found expression in Advanced Palaeolithic culture was connected with a break-through on the linguistic front. Similarly, although we should always remember that the main characteristics of man were developed during the preliterate phase of humanity, it remains true that the invention of writing had a profound effect on the quality of life by favouring precision and making possible a more objective and critical appraisal of the past. There has always been a close and reciprocal connection between talking, thinking, and, when it came, writing; and the maintenance of precision in these fields is more than ever needed today when the sheer accumulation of knowledge and complexity of social life make wise decision so much more difficult and so much more necessary. Precision in thought and self-expression is unhappily much rarer than the right to vote and it can hardly be an accident that the most populous free democracy should have produced, from Benjamin Franklin to Walter Lippmann, the clearest explicators of public issues. This still does not absolve universities, colleges, and schools from doing all they can to sharpen man's most precious tool, his ability to think and share his thoughts, at the expense if need be of factual information doomed in any case to early obsolescence.

The culture transmitted by articulate speech and materialized in the artifacts dug up by archaeologists was the product of individuals who owed their humanity to the communities in which they were reared. When we say that even the most elementary biological functions of man, like eating and reproducing, are regulated by culture, we mean that they are conducted in accord with the conventions of particular societies. But the converse is equally true. To live in society is normal in the world of living things, but there is a wealth of difference between human society and the societies of even the most advanced non-human primates available to study, a difference summed up by Marshall D. Sahlins in the statement[10] that 'human social life is culturally, not biologically determined'. Whereas among the non-human primates the position of an individual is determined mainly by sexual competition, among men it is defined by artificial concepts like kinship or law. The economic effect of kinship must indeed have been profound, since it not merely replaced confrontation by co-operation, in what were potentially the most disruptive areas of life, but by prescribing mutual obligations provided at once a motive for work and a basis for cohesion. The fact is that men are born into a cultural environment and only achieve human status as individuals through the process of socialization termed, in relatively complex societies, education. Study of the institutions that embody the values and reflect the organization of human societies is of course best conducted by social anthropologists operating on living communities, but much can be got in the light of their insights not only from historical sources but also from oral traditions of prehistoric origin. Even the archaeological data of societies entirely beyond the range of oral tradition can, as Gordon Childe showed in his *Social Evolution*, be made to yield vital information on this topic; and the recent concentration in the archaeologically more advanced countries on excavating complete settlements and cemeteries is aimed to document just such studies. Only a beginning has been made, but already it is plain that there has been a progressive increase in the maximum numbers of people living together and in the degree to which within individual communities economic functions become subdivided and specialized.

It is no paradox that the emergence of societies of human character should have been bound up with the appearance of self-awareness, since until a man is conscious of himself as a person it is hardly possible for him to be aware of obligations to others. Self-respect, as we well know, is a prerequisite for social usefulness. It might be thought that archaeology would have very little light to throw on such an internal matter, but this would be to fall into the common error of supposing, along with Professor Arnold Toynbee,[11] that because archaeologists are concerned with material data they are limited to the material aspects of culture. In reality the archaeological record can tell us more of the emergence of self-consciousness than might at first be supposed. To begin with the very manufacture and manipulation of tools made to standard patterns may serve as evidence for the power of continuous or at any rate of long-sustained objectification which the philosopher Francisco Romero rightly takes as the psychological equivalent of subjective awareness. Linking the manufacture of tools to the power of objectification, Romero states in so many words that:

the successful handling of things presupposes the capacity for objectification. To manipulate things to the degree necessary to derive knowledge from their handling presupposes the possibility of discerning them as things, of being aware of their relations, modes and properties . . . it is not the hands that know – it is the mind.[12]

We may assume in the light of this that the pebble tools of Olduvai indicate some degree of objectification as far back as the Lower Pleistocene. That self-awareness was nevertheless slow in developing is shown by the fact that it was not until the Late Pleistocene that we find the first explicit recognition of death in the form of the careful burials made by Neanderthal man. Indeed it was not until the appearance of Advanced Palaeolithic culture that we find much evidence of ceremony in the disposal of the dead. It is in the context of such ceremonial interments that we find the first evidence for an even more definite manifestation of self-awareness in the form of personal adornment by necklaces, headdresses, bracelets, and girdles made from such things as perforated shells, animal teeth, carved ivory, antler, bone, amber, and lignite. Personal ornaments continued to proliferate among the earliest peasant communities of the Old World and from this stage good evidence survives for the use of cosmetics. No doubt men and women – and archaeology shows that men were at least as fond of self-adornment as women – admired themselves first as reflections on water, but already in the sixth millennium B.C. the polished obsidian mirrors of Çatal Hüyük in Anatolia[13] anticipate the metal and glass mirrors of later ages. Like the plumage of birds, artificial finery must have played its part in sexual display, but it is a matter of common experience that this is not the whole story. We do not need advertising specialists to tell us that one of the main purposes of dressing up, grooming, and self-adornment is to reinforce self-esteem and incidentally to define rank and status as well as age and sex. What might be condemned by the censorious as vanity in fact serves a useful purpose in society as well as symbolizing the important role of self-awareness in the emergence of specifically human behaviour.

Evidence can be found even from quite remote periods of prehistory of active regard for others. One may quote as an example the skeleton of an arthritic cripple, whose right arm and shoulder had never fully developed, dug up by Ralph Solecki from a Middle Palaeolithic level in the cave of Shanidar in the Zagros Mountains in eastern Iraq.[14] The important point is that this cripple lived to the comparatively advanced age for that time of forty years. For this individual to have survived under fairly rigorous climatic conditions, he must have been the subject of active compassion on the part of what must have been a relatively small number of Neanderthal companions. The care and nurture he received from his fellows can only represent an extension of feelings originally called into play to protect infants during the long period needed to absorb the cultural heritage. Unquestionably it was the solidarity based on ethical considerations that in the final resort made possible the future achievement of man.

Another specifically human attribute was the ability to practise art. Desmond Morris has shown[15] that chimpanzees are perfectly suited emotionally and physiologically to manipulating paint and that when supplied with suitable equipment they are glad to do so. The fact remains that no non-human primate, when left to itself, has produced a work of art any more than it has described an object in words. Another way of putting this would be to say that man alone is able to communicate by symbols. The failure of apes to draw or use articulate language is only an aspect of a basic inability to symbolize or form the mental images necessary for creative activity of any kind. One of the most important realms for this was the manufacture of progressively more effective tools. It would be wrong to suppose that primitive man set out consciously to make his implements and weapons more efficient. That this in fact happened, as anyone can see by studying a series of Lower Palaeolithic hand axes, was no doubt due to the filtering effect of what might be termed economic selection, more effective tools driving out less effective ones. For the positive drive we must look elsewhere. I suggest that the prehistoric flint-knapper developed his technique primarily because he enjoyed doing so. Most individuals in a modern society have to seek in hobbies or personal relationships the emotional satisfaction obtained by prehistoric – or for that matter medieval and later – craftsmen in their daily work. Yet progress in the higher reaches of technology, in abstract science and in mathematics, on which industrial progress depends, is notoriously accomplished by men who gain their deepest satisfaction from more elegant machines, theories, or equations. I'm not suggesting that the achievement of aesthetic satisfaction on the part of originators was the only driving-force in the dynamic evolution of material culture to which archaeology bears such striking testimony – social emulation, for example, has played an increasingly important role, more particularly on the part of consumers – but I believe the aesthetic explanation is much more satisfying than the notion that early man set out consciously to improve his standard of living.

It is an interesting fact that the first indications of visual art as distinct from craftsmanship appear among Advanced Palaeolithic people in the same context as the earliest overt signs of self-adornment. Illustrated books have made us all increasingly aware of the capabilities of the cave artists of southern France. I will, therefore, confine myself to emphasizing one or two points of general application. One is that even in the rendering of animal or human forms there is a more or less strong element of symbolism.[16] This is even more marked in the emphasis laid on representations of such directing parts of the human body as sex organs or the hand, the limb that reaches furthest, shapes and uses tools and weapons, and makes gestures of command or supplication, obedience, or defiance. Enigmatic signs like the blazons of Lascaux remind us even more forcibly that in Dr Giedion's own words 'symbolization is the key to all paleolithic art'[17] just as it was to articulate speech. The other point I would make is that, whereas in technology we may legitimately pride ourselves in standing far ahead of other civilizations, in art our position is much more equivocal. Let me quote an appraisal offered by Herbert Read in his *Art and the Evolution of Man*:

Some of the painters of Greek vases, some of the medieval illuminators of manuscripts, the great painters of the Renaissance, certain painters of the 19th century – all these have perhaps reached the level of aesthetic quality present in the cave-paintings at Lascaux or Altamira, but they have not exceeded that original standard.[18]

By the same token modern artists have consciously sought out primitive art to help free themselves from nineteenth-century academicism. This in itself is a fascinating topic and I will have to content myself with an autobiographical fragment broadcast by the sculptor Henry Moore on the B.B.C. in 1941,[19] in which he told us how he sought to learn more about his calling by exploring the galleries of the British Museum. He went first to those which showed sculptures of the great civilizations of the past, to those which as he supposed would stand closest 'to the familiar Greek and Renaissance ideals'. He soon wearied of passing before the products of one academicism after another. It was not until he reached the prehistoric gallery that he felt himself at home and free. He was especially struck by a 'lovely tender carving of a girl's head, no bigger than one's thumbnail, and beside it female figures of very human but not copyist realism with a full richness of form . . .'. The lovely head was of course that known as the Venus of Brassempouy, perhaps 20,000 years old. We are reminded that, however superior our technology and wealth, there are still important areas of feeling and expression in which we are much closer to our Advanced Palaeolithic forebears or for that matter to our poorer brethren in the world today: art is a field of awareness in which all men are able to meet, regardless of their wealth or power.

One great field of human awareness in which progress has surely been made is that of time. Those who have studied non-human primates seem to be agreed that they have no real appreciation of the past or the future, but live almost entirely in the present. It is true that apes and lowlier animals are able to recall people and situations, but they do so by a process of mere association. Organized memory only became possible with articulate speech and conceptual thought, since we recall the past very largely through words or rather the kind of images that lie behind these. Again, the apparently forward-looking behaviour of animals like squirrels has been shown to be innate, a quasi-automatic response to seasonal change, rather than the outcome of learning through experience. Gaston Viaud has claimed[20] that 'apes simply prepare their implements – when they do – in order to solve immediate problems, while men use tools for tackling future contingencies and construct them accordingly'. Of course, when we speak of human foresight, this is not to be taken as implying that we exhibit this valuable quality every time we engage in activities directed to our future well-being. Most human behaviour, as we have emphasized, is social: to a larger degree our planning is as social as our sharing of memories of the past and the kind of timetable to which we work is determined largely by the role we play in our own particular society.

There has of course been an evolution in notions of time as of so many other things. To judge from what we know of Bushmen and comparable peoples, men dependent on hunting and gathering for subsistence were limited in their interest to diurnal and seasonal changes. On the other hand, societies depending to any significant extent on farming have to take account of years and periods of years, as in planning crops or livestock-breeding. The more highly organized society became economically the greater the need for precise awareness of the passage of time. This was especially true as the subdivision of labour proceeded, since production came increasingly to depend on synchronizing the work of people engaged in distinct crafts and vocations. The rise of a market economy and the growth in capital plant laid special emphasis on the need for accurate forecasting and phasing of investment. Similarly, transport as it developed required more and more accurate timing. Nor were economic forces the only ones to point in this direction. Scientific observation depended on the accurate measurement of time and space and scientists shared with astrologers an interest in the precise movements of the heavenly bodies. Again, the need to ensure regularity in the observation of rites and worship caused the priests of most religions to concern themselves with the measurement of time and it is no accident that the medieval church took the lead in developing mechanical clocks. Dynastic rulers were interested in vindicating their prescriptive right to rule and it is indeed significant that dynastic history began so soon after the invention of writing. As society developed in all its aspects, it became more and more important to maintain punctuality, to forecast trends, and to recapitulate what had happened in the past.

History, or rather man's awareness of it, is as old as mankind, since by definition human societies are constituted by sharing traditions held in common. Awareness of a common past has always been a main factor in maintaining solidarity; and primitive man with only the meanest equipment and the most meagre store of knowledge had need of all the moral reassurance he could get. By validating his environment and social customs, oral traditions and myths played as important a role in primitive society as history does in our own. Similarly, as they expanded their dominions, civilized peoples automatically enlarged the area comprehended in their historical records. The great literate civilizations of the world were subject to the same basic needs as each of the five hundred or so linguistically defined groups of aboriginal Australia: their adherents may have numbered millions rather than hundreds, but their sense of community on which the integrity of their culture depended was equally based on the exclusive sharing of common traditions about the past. The idea that history can be equated to all intents and purposes with the origins and doings of Europeans and their former dominions overseas, the point of view enshrined, if that is the right word, in the great Cambridge Histories, Ancient, Medieval and Modern, has been rendered out of date in our own lifetime. By one of those ironies in which history abounds the very success of western civilization has undermined its self-esteem or at least has altered the basis on which this can be justly based.

I have already stressed the dynamic quality of human culture, a quality amply documented by archaeology and one which has brought us to our current adventure of reaching out into space. Yet it remains impossible, even when we confine ourselves to archaeological fossils abstracted from past cultures by the inexorable process of time, to arrange what we dig up in any scheme of unilinear development. One of the most interesting measures of progress has been an increase in the range of choice – and hence of cultural expression – opened up by increases in material standards. In archaeological jargon we classify our data in terms of cultures as well as of periods; and we recognize that the interaction of distinctive cultural traditions has indeed been a major source of over-all advance. In a very real sense, therefore, the emergence of distinctive literate civilizations, each with its own script and each capable of perpetuating its own version of what constituted history, marked the culmination of an immensely long process. One of our major problems today is how to reconcile the spread of universal technology and of the whole apparatus and cast of thought accompanying this with the cultural diversity which adds so much to the flavour and texture of life.

One way in which we can reconcile our sense of community with an awareness of cultural uniqueness lies in developing an adequate notion of the past. That this is already happening is due above all to archaeology, which may in time come to be recognized as one of western man's most significant contributions to mankind. For let there be no mistake, it is by adding the dimension of prehistory that we are now able to view our own history in the context of oecumenical history; or if you like to put the matter in less academic terms, it is through prehistory that a new mythology of the past is beginning to appear, a mythology that is adequate to the times in that all men can find fulfilment in it.

Let me end by quoting a favourite passage of mine from a lecture by the great English historian, G. M. Trevelyan:[21]

Man's evolution is far more extraordinary than the first chapter of Genesis used to lead people to suppose. Man's history, pre-historic, ancient, medieval and modern, is by far the most wonderful thing in the Universe of which any news has come through to us. It contains religion; it contains science – at least it contains their history. It contains art and literature. The story of man is far more wonderful than the wonders of physical science. It is a mystery unsolved, yet it is solid fact. It is divine, diabolic – in short human.

Notes

1 Daniel Boorstin, *The Americans I: The Colonial Experience*, London, Penguin Books, 1965, p. 29.
2 A Proposal for Promoting Useful Knowledge among the British Plantations in America. Annually reprinted in *Year Book Amer. Philos. Soc.*
3 'The Record of the Celebration of the Two Hundredth Anniversary of the Founding of the American Philosophical Society Held at Philadelphia for Promoting Useful Knowledge, April 27 to April 30, 1927', *Proc. Amer. Philos. Soc.*, 66 (1927), p. 737.

4 A. H. Schultz in S. L. Washburn and I. de Vore (ed.), *Social Life of Early Man*, London, 1962, p. 62.

5 W. Köhler, *The Mentality of Apes*, London, Penguin Books, 1952, pp. 258–9.

6 Mrs Cathy Hayes, *The Ape in our House*, New York, 1951, p. 229.

7 J. Z. Young, *Doubt & Certainty in Science*, New York, Oxford Univ. Press, 1960, p. 91.

8 E. Cassirer, *An Essay on Man,* Yale Univ. Press, 1962, p. 132.

9 K. P. Oakley, *Man the Tool-maker,* 2nd ed., London, 1952, p. 79.

10 Marshall D. Sahlins, 'The Origin of Society', *Scientific American*, Sept., 1960, p. 77.

11 Arnold Toynbee, *A Study of History*, abridged by D. C. Somervell, Oxford, 1946, p. 193.

12 Francisco Romero, *The Theory of Man*, trans. W. F. Cooper, Univ. of Calif. Press, 1964, p. 18.

13 James Mellaart, 'Excavations at Catal Hüyük, 1962', *Anatolian Studies*, 13 (1963): p. 99 & pl. xxv (b).

14 Ralph Solecki, 'Shanidar Cave, a Palaeolithic Site in Northern Iraq', *Ann. Report of the Smithsonian Institution*, 1954, pp. 389–452.

15 Desmond Morris, *The Biology of Art*, London, 1962.

16 This has been strongly emphasized very recently by André Leroi-Gourhan in his *Préhistoire de l'Art Occidental*, Paris, Mazenod, 1965.

17 S. Giedion, *The Eternal Present: vol. I. The Beginnings of Art*, London, 1962, p. 79.

18 Herbert Read, *Art & the Evolution of Man*, London, 1951, pp. 12–13.

19 Henry Moore, 'Primitive Art', *The Listener*, 24th April, 1941, pp. 598–9.

20 Gaston Viaud, *Intelligence. Its Evolution & Forms*, London, 1960, p. 56.

21 G. M. Trevelyan, *History & the Reader*, London, 1945, pp. 24–5.

CHAPTER 26

ARCHAEOLOGY AND HUMAN
DIVERSITY

An invitation to contribute an essay to the *Annual Review of Anthropology* is flattering to the self-esteem of anyone engaged in the profession of Anthropology. Nevertheless, I intend to resist the temptation to reminisce or recapitulate. Instead, I intend to step out from my narrow corner and examine what experience of prehistoric archaeology leads me to think about the way we have all been heading since the Industrial Revolution. In particular, I would draw attention to the nature of the threats posed to some of the attributes which distinguish the archaeological from the merely palaeontological record, above all those epitomized in the cultural diversity of man. I would suggest that danger threatens not merely from the homogenizing pressures of natural science and mass production, but also and perhaps even more from an ideology that seeks to justify the destruction not merely of our heritage but of our very humanity in the name of economics and an ostensibly liberal political philosophy.

The esteem which archaeology has always enjoyed, particularly in the Old World, has derived in the main from its ability to dignify and validate the status quo by investing it with the sanction of antiquity, at the same time as providing the visual images needed to attract and sustain the adherence of the common man. The patronage traditionally accorded to archaeology by heads of state related not merely to the material symbols of their own sovereignty, but even more significantly to establishing, validating, and displaying the identity of peoples and their attachment to their native lands. Archaeology has been harnessed equally to ideologies distinct from, and in the long run inconsistent with, the maintenance of national identity. Much of the impetus behind the rapid development of archaeology during the nineteenth century came from the objective support it appeared to give to the idea of progress. Conversely, the dominance of this idea itself helped to determine the preoccupation of archaeologists with establishing an overall sequence of development from rude beginnings to the complexity and sophistication of modern industry, as first comprehensively displayed in the Great Exhibition of 1851. The idea of progress which archaeology appeared to validate not merely obscured or compensated for some of the less pleasing aspects of industrial society, but it also made possible and in a sense inevitable the conscription of nonindustrialized peoples both in Europe and overseas.

435

Archaeology has been no less esteemed by protagonists of another by-product of the Industrial Revolution. It has been accorded favoured treatment and systematically cultivated by the Institutes of the History of Material Culture maintained by the several academies of the USSR and its satellites in the simple faith that excavation, by recovering the material products of former states of society, automatically validates the central doctrine of Marxism.

According to the English summary of *Historical Relics Unearthed in New China* (Peking, 1972):

The remarkable achievements in the excavation of historical relics since the founding of New China have been due mainly to the emphasis the Party and government have laid on this work. At the same time, the active support and participation in the work by the masses of workers, peasants and soldiers has been very important. The broad masses of people fully understand that these priceless historical relics represent in essence the ancient working people's wisdom, their sweat and blood. They recognise these as the best teaching material in knowing their own history and creative power, *as well as in studying dialectical and historical materialism* (my italics).

In a sense this expectation is self-fulfilling. At the very least, the muteness of archaeological evidence ensures that it is hardly in a position to be contradicted.

It follows from the privileged position of their subject that archaeologists have tended to conform to the canons of the societies in which they operate. Protest in anthropology on such topics as racism or imperialism has issued exclusively from physical and social anthropologists. One of the main purposes of this essay is to suggest that archaeologists may also have something to say, not indeed on overtly political problems, but on matters of arguably greater importance bearing on the very quality of human life. Archaeologists base their claim to speak with professional authority on such key issues primarily on the unique perspective opened up by their subject. Archaeology not only ranges over the whole earth but spans the entire period of man's existence. The artefacts that provide its basic documents form a continuous network. They encompass and indeed provide the most reliable diagnostic evidence for the earliest manifestations of human culture, and they document progressive advances in man's ability to exploit and shape his environment in accordance with his desires up to and including the phase of literacy during which he has become increasingly aware of himself and his context in time and space. The mere fact that archaeology spans the gap between biology and recorded history, between primate behaviour and that of civilized man, helps to account for its ambiguous position in the hierarchy of knowledge. In the final resort, archaeology – and prehistoric archaeology in particular – is concerned with nothing less than the identity of man. The converse is also true. The way an archaeologist approaches his data, the view he takes of his subject in the hierarchy of knowledge, depends ultimately on the view he takes of man.

From one point of view, archaeology can be held not merely to document and validate the materialist interpretation of history, but to extend the range of this over the entire prehistory of man (4). It is true enough that, barring local vicissitudes, the archaeological record reveals a progressive growth in the complexity of material culture, that is, in the apparatus by which men supplement their limbs in manipulating and shaping their environment, from the most primitive stone industries to the most advanced products of modern science-based technology. To anyone satisfied to regard man as a mere animal, as a biological species that fulfills its highest destiny by utilizing its environment with ever greater efficiency in competition with other species, the archaeological record and the future of mankind can be contemplated with an equal measure of equanimity. It is only if he prefers to concern himself with the quality of life that an archaeologist may feel impelled to question the wisdom of succumbing unreservedly to the ideology and way of life envisaged by modern industrial society.

The position taken in this essay is humanist only in the sense that it accepts that the unique interest of man resides in the degree to which he diverges from the other primates and the rest of the animal world. Artefacts, as animal behaviourists are never tired of reminding us, are not entirely unique to man. Nor is man the only species whose behaviour is influenced by cultural patterns acquired by belonging to social groupings constituted by sharing common histories, rather than being transmitted by genetic inheritance. The uniqueness of man resides in the degree to which his behaviour is conditioned by culture and in particular in the way his artefacts have until quite recently displayed an ever greater increase in diversity as well as mere complexity. From this point of view the main interest of prehistory is the scope it offers for tracing the process of humanization. The artefacts which provide the basic archaeological record embody and exemplify the very attributes that enable us to recognize men as beings distinct from apes or monkeys.

There is no intention, on the other hand, of falling into the basic fallacy of liberal humanism and forgetting the animal nature of man. The zoological classification of modern man as *Homo sapiens sapiens* expresses more an aspiration than a commonly accomplished fact. When Teilhard de Chardin (8) spoke of the noosphere he merely hypothesized a new dimension that man is uniquely capable of inhabiting, surely not one that men automatically inherit by the mere fact of belonging to this species. From a palaeontological point of view, distinctions between fossils of *Australopithecus* and *Homo* and again between successive stages in the evolution of *Homo* are sufficiently blurred to occasion serious differences of view on matters of classification and nomenclature (12). The fact that the fossils in effect form continuous series should be enough to remind us that men, even of the most advanced culture, remain animals and inherit genes that issue from far up the stream of life. Without strong evidence to the contrary, it can hardly be supposed that the basic appetites of men are any more widely separated from those of his primate forebears than is his bodily structure. On the contrary, we must accept the fact that the basic drives and appetites of men are likely to resemble those of their closest relatives and are not likely to differ widely from those activating even lowlier organisms. It is at this level and only at this level that the findings of animal behaviourists are directly relevant to the study of man.

The Hebrews of old were so appalled by what they saw as the wickedness of man that they could only suppose him to have fallen from a former state of grace. Darwin and his followers have shown that the evidence suggests a more economical explanation. The hypothesis of biological evolution ought to have prepared us for the almost unimaginable horrors perpetrated by the Nazis or the masters of the Kremlin during the second quarter of the twentieth century, not to mention the atrocities still being practised in and by societies equipped with advanced technologies. Pain or at least surprise can only stem from ignoring the continuing role of our animal natures. Paradoxically, the converse also applies. If we sin, it is not because we are still animals, but because we are men with the faculty of self-awareness. As our own times so grimly emphasize, the mere elaboration of the cultural apparatus by no means ensures that human values prevail in our affairs. On the contrary, it may even amplify the scope and intensify the destructiveness of our animal appetites. The idea of automatic progress at any other than a material level is surely one of the silliest as well as among the most pernicious illusions of our time.

The case for culture is not that it can make us better unless indirectly by making us more acutely aware of the beastliness, in its most literal sense, of our uncontrolled natural appetites. It is rather that it is capable of making life fuller, richer, and more human in the sense of diverging increasingly from the primate prototype. Because archaeology depends for its main source on the material embodiments of cultures in the form of artefacts, it ought to be capable of assessing rather precisely the degree to which they embody human values. In this sense archaeology allows objective assessments to be made about whether at any particular juncture conditions are favourable or unfavourable to the further enrichment of human life in the sense of making it more or less possible to enjoy experiences accessible to men alone, whether in a word they enhance or impair the quality of life.

Archaeology shows very plainly that we have achieved our humanity only to the extent that we have constrained our animal natures by means of artificial conventions acquired in the course of history and incorporated in cultural traditions. The most palpable index of progression from mere animality is provided not merely by the increasing complexity but still more by the cultural diversity of the artefacts which constitute the archaeological record of human history down to quite modern times. If a main part of this essay is given to an examination of the process of cultural enrichment, this should not be taken to endorse the idea of progress as this has commonly been understood, still less the complacent doctrines of liberal humanism. On the contrary, it is offered as a reminder of the heritage that mankind stands in imminent danger of losing in the name of science and social justice. From this standpoint archaeology by no means stops short at validating contemporary trends and goals. Instead it poses questions more radical than those commonly asked by political science or sociology because they are framed in an ampler perspective.

The most palpable and also the most pervasive attribute of man featured in the archaeological record is his capacity to make artefacts. These artefacts owe part of their importance to the mere fact that certain of them, notably those made of stone, constitute a continuous network extending over the last two million years. Moreover, artefacts and the technology that informs them illuminate not only the way man has adapted to and manipulated his environment but also his ideology and social life. They preserve an unrivalled record of the way human culture has increased in complexity and diversity.

It is worthy of note that the earliest material equipment, that of *Homo erectus*, was not merely elementary and uniform but also remarkably static. The first significant change came in the Middle Pleistocene with the addition of bifacially flaked hand axes (mode 2) to the earlier repertoire of elementary flake and core tools (mode 1). These hand axes were so uniform in style over their entire territory that, short of recognizing local materials, an archaeologist might have difficulty in deciding whether individual specimens came from England, the Cape, or Madras. As Desmond Clark, our leading authority on this phase of prehistory, has so well expressed it:

One of the most striking things . . . about the broad cultural pattern of the Middle Pleistocene is its general 'sameness' within the limits imposed by the stone industries . . . Handaxes from Europe, South Africa, or peninsular India are all basically similar tools, and this is also true for the rest of the heavy duty and the light duty elements (7, p. 45).

Yet the appearance of these hand axes introduced for the first time an element of industrial diversity, since they never reached as far as East Asia. The inhabitants of Chou-kou-tien near Pekin, while capable hunters and well accustomed to the use of fire, continued to shape their stone tools in an earlier mode.

The first substantial signs of cultural dynamism and diversity appeared in conjunction with the earliest large-brained men of *Homo sapiens* type. Although the stone industries of Neanderthal man and his cousins north and south of the Sahara shared the same prepared core technique (mode 3), they displayed a wide range of regional differentiation and a more perceptible rate of change. To some extent this reflects a closer adaptation to ecological circumstances than had existed when generalized equipment was used over the total range of environments exploited by man. The grasslands and savannah of sub-Saharan Africa continued to support men equipped with Acheulian-type stone industries, but the colonization of forest zones in that territory elicited the adaptations displayed in the Sangoan and ultimately Lupemban traditions. Similarly, when in northern Eurasia Neanderthal man colonized periglacial territories as far north as the Lower Pechora basin close to the Arctic zone, ecological adaptation once again promoted distinctive changes in the industrial apparatus and so furthered cultural diversity.

The increase in cultural responsiveness evinced by the first sapient men was significant more for what it presaged than for what it achieved. The acceleration in cultural dynamism that found its ultimate expression in the rich diversity of the great historic civilizations of mankind was accomplished after all by the men of modern type who emerged as *Homo sapiens sapiens* only 40,000 years or so ago. The complexity, diversity, and sheer richness of cultural patterns were the achievement and peculiar glory of our own species.[1] The artefacts that archaeologists are privileged to study, and above all those least subject to the constraints of the physical world, such as works of art, insignia of social hierarchy, and symbols of religious cult and observance, are very embodiments and measures of our humanity.

There was scope for diversity even at the basic levels of subsistence and technology. The archaeological record shows an overall trend from a generalized to a more specialized and therefore more diverse quest for food. This can be discerned at the level of relatively advanced catching and foraging economies, as well as more notably in those based on different forms of farming. A large measure of diversity can be observed in the game and the hunting and catching gear used by the Upper Palaeolithic and Mesolithic communities of Eurasia and neighbouring parts of north Africa and, again, by the Paleo-Indian and Archaic inhabitants of different parts of the Americas. The adoption during the last 10,000 years of sedentary economies based on the cultivation of crops and the keeping of livestock lent a further strong impetus to the process of diversification. The mere fact of adopting settled life intensified adjustments to local conditions. Of greater importance is the fact that the great civilizations of mankind have grown up on wealth based ultimately on the cultivation of a variety of highly diverse crops. The raising, harvesting, and preparation of plants as various as rice, maize, beans, manioc, potato, wheat, or barley would alone have served to promote diversity, not merely in subsistence and technology, but also in settlement and social organization. Even within the cereal zone of Europe, widely differing regimes adjusted to regional ecosystems are reflected in the archaeological record of early peasant communities. One has only to contrast, for example, the dry farming regime of the Mediterranean zone, complemented by the cultivation of vines, almonds, figs, and olives, with the mixed farming based on year-round rainfall in the deciduous zone of Temperate Europe or again with the hybrid economies of the northern territories where the growing season was too short for the cereals available in prehistoric times to play more than a marginal role in relation to catching and foraging.

The adoption of settled life based primarily on farming also served to promote hierarchy in the organization both of settlement and of society. The increased yield of cultivated over wild crops and the fact that these could be stored in some cases over appreciable periods of time made it safe for substantial numbers of people to enjoy the benefits of urban life. For their part, the inhabitants of villages, hamlets, and farmsteads in the surrounding territories that supplied the city dwellers with food were able to secure not merely the products of specialized crafts but also such important services as protection against enemies, insurance against death through access to central granaries and, not least, the possibility of sharing in the intensified religious rites celebrated in the urban temples. Again the adoption of permanent settlement made it practicable to construct buildings more elaborate than mere shelters, as well as to accumulate movable property in the form of artefacts beyond what could readily be carried on the person. In this way, sedentary life made practicable the material embodiments of the varying status of individuals occupying different ranks in the emerging hierarchy.

Every advance in technology that allowed a more effective manipulation of natural resources conferred competitive advantages on those adopting it. Progress at a material level was therefore cumulative for ongoing communities (5). One sign of material progress was that artefacts served for progressively more specialized ends. So long as production was organized on a local preindustrial basis, increased specialization resulted in the use of a wider range of materials and the application of novel techniques, as well as in the development of artefacts calculated to attain better results for a smaller input of energy.

For almost the whole of his history, man's most effective tools were made from flint, stone, and wood. The utilization of an ever-wider range of raw materials necessarily made for greater diversity. The Upper Palaeolithic and Mesolithic hunter-fishers of Eurasia were distinguished in the archaeological record by their sophisticated use of animal skeletal material for a wide range of specialized gear. The adoption of fired clay pottery for receptacles, as well as serving to distinguish pottery making from aceramic communities, provided a medium peculiarly well adapted to a variety of modelling and ornamentation.

Another craft frequently taken up by settled peoples was weaving, and this also assumed a diversity of forms corresponding in part to the materials used in different territories, notably wool of different kinds, flax, cotton, and silk.

Metal working also served to distinguish those who adapted it, as well as providing a number of variants according to the kinds of metals and the techniques used in working them. And so it was with every new material, including some such as amber, jade, or jet, occurring only in restricted localities, and others, like faience, manufactured by special processes.

Although it was variation in subsistence and technology that was most readily documented in the archaeological record, the increasing diversity of artefacts was the outcome in reality more of social than of merely economic factors. Economic ones like the adoption of particular patterns of subsistence or the multiplication of crafts stemming from specialization and the use of an ever-widening range of materials implied a subdivision of labour far beyond that of age groups and sexes. On the other hand, purely social forces were also important. The larger and more complex communities became, the more insistent was the need to promote identity and cohesion. Conversely, there was the need to emphasize definition from neighbours, something that became more pressing with every increase in the permanence of settlement and the accumulation of wealth that accompanied successive improvements in farming. It is significant that when Gordon Childe first tried to define the frontiers of the early peasant communities of prehistoric Europe in his *Dawn of European Civilization* (3), he sought to do so by mapping cultures. These he defined by conformities in the whole range of social activities reflected in the archaeological record, notably subsistence patterns, productive techniques, tool and weapon forms, defensive systems, personal ornaments, art styles, religious observances, and funerary practices, stressing in each case abstentions as well as affirmative choices. In a word, his method depended on the extent to which the various communities of Europe had already developed richly divergent cultural expressions between the fifth and the second millennia B.C. This diversity was indeed sufficiently pronounced to make it reasonable to require a first-year undergraduate to assign assemblages of artefacts from this phase of European prehistory to their correct geographical provenance. And the same would go for any territory that supported peasant communities during early times.

Whereas the hunting bands and peasant kin groups described by Childe in *The Dawn* (3) were homogeneous and within the primary divisions of age and sex made up of individuals of equal status, the societies that experienced the explosive increase in diversity documented in the finest exhibits displayed in the great museums of the world were invariably of a more complex order. The climax of cultural achievement coincided in various parts of the world with the replacement of segmented by vertically structured societies. It is not my purpose here to examine the forms taken by vertical structuring, still less to propose a typology from chiefdoms and kingdoms to empires. I merely wish to emphasize that in every traditional society known to history, hierarchy and inequality, whatever forms these took in particular cases, were the invariable accompaniment, indeed the formative factor, behind the emergence of high cultures. And by high cultures I mean those most widely separated from the behavioural patterns of animals whose fossils in fact appeared at lower levels in the palaeontological record. In terms of archaeology, high cultures were represented by artefacts farthest removed from the sticks and stones of *Homo erectus* and far transcending the homely products of Gordon Childe's egalitarian peasants of prehistoric Europe. The material embodiments of high culture invariably appeared as a matter of stratigraphic fact in the context of hierarchically organized societies. Conversely, the archaeology of lower levels in stratified societies incapsulates earlier stages in cultural history. Whereas the peaks of cultural attainment, the finest products of human craft, were exclusively associated with and indeed helped to define and signal the highest levels in the social hierarchy, the objects and structures used by the mass of the population, including the very craftsmen who made the noblest insignia and built the most symbolic monuments, often compared with those made by their remote forebears.

In terms of early Britain, one might recall that the plainer pottery of the Celtic peoples, who created in the metal insignia of their chiefly class (1) one of the outstanding manifestations of decorative art known to man, hardly differs in appearance from that made by stone age peasants two or three thousand years previously in the same territory. Again, if the jewellery from the Sutton Hoo burial (2) or even some of the richest Kentish graves of the pagan Anglo-Saxon period (11) would tax the finest craftsmen of the present age, undecorated pottery of this archaeological phase has on occasion been assigned to the pre-Roman Iron Age or even to the Neolithic. Even more striking comparisons might be made by reference to the material equipment of the peasants who supported the elaborate structures of pharaonic Egypt or from recent times of princely India or Tsarist Russia.

It is no contradiction that the overall cultural patterns displayed by hierarchical societies should have been so much richer and more sharply defined than those of the humbler segmented societies from which they developed. Archaeology documents that, whereas in segmented societies settlements tended to be of approximately the same size and to comprise structures of more or less homogeneous form and scale, stratified societies are often marked by a hierarchy of settlement with major centres ministering to and drawing upon a number of lesser ones distributed over dependent territories and themselves sometimes of more than one order of importance. The precise role of such major centres varied in different societies. They might be primarily foci of religious observance, combining with this social functions and often playing a role in the redistribution of commodities. Alternatively, they might be cities containing rulers and their courts and bureaucracies, temples and their priests, specialized craftsmen and merchants, in fact everyone and everything that rendered specialized services of whatever kind to the communities of which the cities were capitals and foci. The frequent presence at such centres of granaries or other storage facilities reminds us of the redistributive functions implicit in hierarchy. Town dwellers who produced no food depended on rations derived ultimately from the surrounding countryside. Conversely, cities had responsibilities to their dependent realms in times of dearth. Temple stores were not, as some Marxists have implied, symbols of priestly exploitation so much as prototypes of banks and mutual assurance corporations, mechanisms of social well-being.

A counterpart to the concentration of wealth that more than anything distinguished stratified from segmented societies was a preoccupation with armament and defensive works. In the archaeological record it is a matter of observation that whereas it was exceptional for peasant communities to erect defensive works, this was normal practice among hierarchically structured groups more richly endowed with movable wealth. Moreover, the scale of defences matched the status of particular sites. Central sites housing leaders and the focus of specialized activities were more likely to be defended strongly than less important ones. Again, the finest personal armament, weapons, helmets, and body armour were concentrated on leaders and their immediate associates, and the same applies over much of Eurasia to equipment concerned with personal mobility. Mycenaean princes, Celtic chieftains, and Shang knights were conveyed to and from the thick of battle on splendidly accoutred chariots, just as the kings of Ur and the nomad leaders of the Altai were brought to burial in horse-drawn wagons for reasons of status as well as of convenience.

The archaeological record shows that in stratified societies the most specialized craftsmen worked primarily for the uppermost stratum. Foremost among the objects which denoted and enhanced status were personal weapons, helmets and shields and body armour, harness and chariot gear, personal jewellery and ornaments, not to mention mirrors and utensils relating to feasting and drinking. As well as displaying the highest technical expertise available, such things were frequently made of materials inherently precious or valuable because they were only obtainable from a distance and sometimes, as in the case of jade, also extremely expensive to work. Since they were thus precious in all measurable respects, they provided ideal media for conspicuous consumption and display. Exotic artefacts, particularly those originating in more advanced and prestigious cultures, provided another medium through and by which the higher ranks in stratified societies advertised their status. Appropriation of such attributes was not left as in a modern society to individual initiative, but, to judge from usage in historically known situations, was assigned to people occupying particular ranks by custom if not by explicit sumptuary laws. Although the prime purpose of this was undoubtedly to define and validate the hierarchic structure of stratified societies, it also played a significant part in cultural dynamics. Thus the use of exotic artefacts and materials as insignia of status was a potent factor in promoting change in communities marginal to the main foci of cultural development. Within societies, therefore, the degree to which the most skilled craftsmen were specialized and concentrated on the fabrication of the richest objects for comparatively few people acted like a forcing house of innovation and enrichment, not merely for the upper ranks but for all those to whom new types of artefact or decorative motif were in time devolved from above. The myth that the average man was likely to display cultural creativity or contribute to rapid innovation if only given the opportunity is much less dangerous but no less mistaken than the assumption that he would be good if only he were free from the constraints of social hierarchy.

Both the persistence of the myth and its falsity may be illustrated in the attitude towards the finest products of early civilizations adopted by modern communist states. Exhibits from the Han dynasty shown in the recent exhibition of Chinese archaeology on either side of the Atlantic were held, for example, to 'glaringly expose the luxury and decadence of the feudal ruling class'. In particular the funeral garments made up of jade plates linked by gold wire that formed a focus of the exhibition were singled out as exposing 'the feudal class's luxury and depravity at the expense of the labouring people'. The same could have been written of the jade vessels, the silks, porcelains, fine metal work, lacquers, and paintings of this and later periods of Chinese history or, indeed, the luxury products of any age. The fact is that such things, if not made for superiors in social hierarchies, would never have been made at all. If the ruling classes had not been luxurious and sophisticated and if they had not been in a position to enlist the skill of the artificers, these things which define and illustrate the essential qualities of Chinese art would never have existed. And the same applies to the treasures of Tutankhamen's tomb or the Sutton Hoo ship. Without a hierarchic structure, without a marked degree of inequality in consumption, the astonishing diversity of Chinese, Egyptian, or Anglo-Saxon culture would never have developed. This is not a matter of speculation. We know what the culture of China, Egypt, or Britain was like before class societies developed in these lands. Archaeology tells us much about their prehistoric peasant populations. They were egalitarian. They were illiterate. And their material products by comparison with the fine things produced in the ambience of class societies were as dull and boring as those used by the lower classes in Shang China, Pharaonic Egypt, or Anglo-Saxon England. Archaeology shows unequivocally that the finest artefacts made by man, the most superb and diverse embodiments of his humanity, were made to celebrate and render more effective the operation of social systems in which craftsmen exercised their most refined skills on the most precious materials in the service of the highest levels of social hierarchies.

In his slim but pregnant volume, *The Birth of Civilization in the Near East*, Henri Frankfort (10) strongly attacked the notion that the early civilizations of Egypt and southwest Asia – and by implication those of Europe, south and east Asia, and the New World – can be adequately appraised as mere representatives of a stage in social evolution. Instead he insisted on the autonomy of cultural manifestations. Each civilization, he believed, had its own peculiar genius and identity. In each, he wrote, we can recognize 'a certain coherence . . . a certain consistency in its orientation, a certain cultural "style" which shapes its political and its judicial institutions, its art as well as its literature, its religion as well as its morals' (10, p. 16). This elusive identity, which was nevertheless embodied in the material products available to archaeology, was termed by Frankfort its form. It was this form that 'is never destroyed though it changes in the course of time'. Although more clearly defined in the more advanced cultures of stratified societies, it needs to be emphasized that even the humblest cultures of *Homo sapiens sapiens* were marked by this precious quality of unique identity. It is cultural form that gives meaning and savour to human life, a savour only men can perceive and without which they revert to the status of the primates from which they evolved in the course of prehistory.

Much has been made in this essay of the contributions to cultural diversity and enrichment made by economic and social factors. It is important not to overlook ideology. As Henri Frankfort so clearly recognized, religion and the ideological attitudes associated with religious beliefs have played a role of great importance both in validating individual cultural systems and in promoting their distinctiveness. Ideology is important both because it motivates men over a wide range of their activities and still more, historically speaking, because of its key role in perpetuating and indeed deepening the coherence of social traditions. Religion and the ideas associated with it have not only been leading factors in promoting diversity among men. They also provide keys to defining this diversity since, though by nature incorporeal, they are nevertheless impressed on a wide range of archaeological data including shrines and temples, utensils used in ritual observance, and elements in the iconography of graphic art. Again, the diversity of literate societies is nowhere more beautifully exemplified than in the scripts used to communicate and perpetuate liturgies, histories, and laws (9).

What Frankfort discerned in the civilizations of antiquity available only from their archaeological and epigraphic remains, civilizations which included the Harappan, the Maya, and the Shang no less than the Egyptian or Sumerian, was present also in the cultural traditions known to us from the much fuller sources of recent history, those for instance of Ch'ing China, the France of Versailles, Georgian England, or Tsarist Russia. Anyone travelling through a territory as restricted as Europe as recently even as 1914 could have savoured a diversity not merely of material products but of social and political styles transcending that available today in the entire world. The texture of life was so immeasurably richer then that to experience even an inkling of it today people have to resort as they do in their millions to monuments, museums, illustrated books, or the theatre.

It is not difficult to see why an archaeologist should view the trends and some of the tenets of modern industrial society with a certain ambivalence or even disenchantment, nor is it surprising that this attitude should be widely shared by laymen. Whereas his studies have documented the attainment of humanity through the gradual emergence of hierarchically structured societies distinguished by patterns of ever-increasing distinctiveness and diversity, the archaeologist finds himself confronted in his daily life by an increasingly rapid reversion towards the intraspecies homogeneity of a prehuman situation. The brutal rapidity at which this process of cultural impoverishment has unfolded in the face of science and technology and the economic systems stemming from them explains why men everywhere are registering their dismay. In trying to understand his situation the ordinary person has received little help from the intelligentsia. Indeed, by a supreme irony the undermining of human values has been furthered rather than diagnosed, still less arrested, by those who would like to see themselves as leaders of opinion. The quality of human life is threatened not by some supreme cataclysm of nature or untoward social catastrophe so much as by the proponents of self-styled progressive philosophies.

An immediate cause of the homogenization of culture has been the incorporation of traditional societies within the nexus of a world-wide market in the products of machine industry. Whereas in preindustrial societies of the kind most commonly encountered in archaeology the elaboration of hierarchy and the enrichment and diversification of culture were adaptive and for that reason selected not merely for survival but for enhancement, in the case of industrial society the precise opposite applies. Standardized products of the kind most readily manufactured by machines, because of their greater cheapness, have a built-in advantage over hand-made ones reflecting local skills and the styles of diverse cultural traditions. Economic forces left to themselves increasingly ensure that hand-made products displaying regional diversity become too costly for daily use. Outside museums they can only survive as luxuries, but luxuries imply disparities in consumption which industrial societies serve to reduce. The trend towards uniformity applies not merely to different societies but to classes within them. Articles that deviate from the standard become too expensive to buy in the very societies in which it pays to spend the maximum amount in promoting the consumption of standard ones by means of advertising and persuasion in a variety of media.

The price mechanism is powerfully reinforced in this regard by ideology. The 'enlightenment' which generated natural science and in due course modern industrial economies itself seeks to promote equality as a desirable aim of society. Egalitarian notions affect patterns of consumption directly through the impact of steeply progressive taxation, but also indirectly through psychological constraints. Even the very rich are increasingly inhibited from consuming luxuries they can still afford for fear of appearing conspicuous. In striking contrast to their behaviour in hierarchically structured societies in which status is in a measure defined by conspicuous consumption, in industrial societies they strive to remain inconspicuous and so to avoid even heavier fiscal penalties for their success. Economic, social, political, and psychological forces thus combine to maximize the production and consumption of common things while penalizing that of uncommon ones. Indeed, the degree to which the common man dominates consumption has come to be accepted by capitalists and Marxists alike as an index of progress. Societies in which the production of exceptional things is matched by marked inequality in consumption have even come to be accepted as backward. The richer in economic and the more 'progressive' in political terms the world becomes the more relentlessly it is impoverished with respect to the very attributes that mark the emergence and cultural enrichment of mankind.

Another powerful force making for cultural homogenization has been the dramatic advance in systems of communication in the industrial world. Railways, motor vehicles, and aircraft have shrunk the world so that formerly remote territories have been brought within effective reach of a single market dominated by a comparatively few states which share a common technology and modes of thought powerfully influenced by the concepts of natural science. The installations and mechanisms that now girdle the earth not merely conform in all essentials to universal patterns but for the most part are themselves manufactured at a few centres. They bear no more relationship to modes of transport traditional in most parts of the world than they do to local ecological systems.

Even more important as a factor in the process of homogenization than the movement of men and goods is the communication of ideas. Printing and the electronic transmission of texts and the spoken word have brought the peoples of the world within range not merely of a single technology and market but even more significantly of concepts linked with the pursuit of economic profit, scientific comprehension, and notions of social justice. Again, the new facilities have conferred decisive advantages on those able to communicate directly with representatives of the dominant Western culture. Just as mass production involved the standardization of goods, so improvements in communication have promoted the domination of progressively fewer languages. Again, as modern business soon appreciated, television is an unrivalled medium for manipulating, standardizing, and so making more profitable the satisfaction of consumer tastes. More than that, its effect must be to undermine traditional modes of thought and values. The impact of electronics has been further amplified by computers, which by sorting data from the whole range of science and the humanities has helped still further to break down conceptual barriers while at the same time giving rise to a jargon common to all cultures and disciplines. Inevitably, modern media for the transmission of ideas operate to favour universal as opposed to local patterns of behaviour. In this way they serve to reinforce uniformity at the expense of diversity both within and between communities.

The process of impoverishment by homogenization, which has already done much to destroy the diversity and richness of the artefacts used in the physical activities of daily life, poses an even more lethal threat to the more spiritual dimensions of human experience. In the traditional cultures recovered by archaeology, the products of graphic and sculptural art and architecture mirror cultural diversity with all the greater sensitivity in that they are relatively freer from the constraints of utility than the generality of artefacts. The converse is no less true. The graphic and sculptural products of modern society reflect with startling clarity the degree to which the human spirit has already been impoverished by abstraction. In painting the process has taken two main forms but the outcome is essentially the same. At one extreme the artist resorts to elementary geometric forms or covers the whole of his picture with a single colour, as with Malevich's famous white on white series or Rodchenko's riposte in black on black. At the other extreme he depicts natural forms of artefacts with a fidelity that rivals the camera. The effect in either case is to deprive the work of cultural content. Geometry and photography operate, like the laws of natural science or the processes of modern technology, irrespective of cultural endowments. Furthermore, the practitioners of modern abstract art, while striving for originality as innovators as though they were scientists, often seek to eliminate personal as well as cultural diversity, if necessary by using spray guns or applying natural or ready-made materials.

Sculptors have equally sought to evade cultural affiliations or even personal identity. This has sometimes been achieved, as with Paolozzi, by combining parts of machines or, as with Vantangerloo or Caro, by using wire or standard products of machine industry. An alternative has been to adopt and improve upon natural forms such as Brancusi's eggs or Moore's animal bones. In architecture it is much the same. Modern structures recalling factory products betray their indifference to ecology by obtruding alike from Brazilian rain forests or Arabian deserts and display their contempt for man and his traditions by overshadowing without prejudice oriental mosques and pagodas or the classical, gothic, and neogothic structures of the Western world. As eloquent as the nature of its products in some respects is the fact that the very term 'architecture' has been abandoned by some progressives as in itself anachronistic because of discriminating in respect of quality. The substitute term 'built form' serves the dual purpose of advertising the divorce of building from culture and the devaluation of that very discrimination by which men emerged from the other primates and diverse civilizations developed in the course of ages from the base of primitive communism.

A similar process of homogenization deforms the ideas and concepts that once inspired and embodied the identities of the several civilizations of mankind. This is true most notably of the religions that more than anything inform the arts and enshrine the beliefs of these civilizations. The positivist temper until recently prevalent in natural science undermined traditional beliefs in whatever sphere primarily on the ground that their validity was incapable of proof. Religion of whatever description was regarded as incredible, irrational, and superfluous because all phenomena that were real were held to be susceptible to explanation by natural science. Religious belief indeed could even be condemned on the ground that it impeded the progress of natural science and was therefore not merely obscurantist but positively harmful to the prospects of mankind. If rationalism was hostile to religion in general, it was still more opposed to the notion of diversity of belief. It is of the nature of scientific laws to be universal in their application, whereas beliefs, codes of social behaviour, or artistic conventions are by their mere origin particular to historically constituted communities. The universalizing character of natural science has so conditioned modes of thought that even those who retain religious faith find themselves increasingly unable to tolerate religious differences. So far from proclaiming belief in the rightness of their own particular creed, religious leaders proclaim the need for ecumenical thought, not merely as a practical necessity but as desirable on its own account. Religions when not flatly repudiated are increasingly being homogenized not by their enemies but by their friends.

In many ways the most revealing manifestation of popular feeling in societies of collapsed hierarchy is the cult of what Karl Popper aptly termed 'biological naturalism,' manifested in diet, the immitigable growth of hair, nudism, sexual permissiveness, and even bestiality. It is encouraging to a prehistorian whose profession leads him to trace the emergence of man from a state of nature, whose subject rests on the assumption that men become human to the extent that they elaborate cultural modes of behaviour, to find the following appreciation of the implications of this vulgar heresy set out by this eminent philosopher, more especially since he finds himself unable to accept so much else of his message:

. . . it must be admitted that certain forms of behaviour may be described as more 'natural' than other forms; for instance going native or eating only raw food; and some people think that this in itself justifies the choice of these forms. But in this sense it is not natural to interest oneself in art, or science, or even in arguments in favour of naturalism. The choice of conformity with 'nature' as a supreme standard leads to consequences which few will be prepared to face; it does not lead to a more natural form of civilization, but to beastliness (13, p. 70).

As Popper wrote later on in the same work, emphasizing his meaning by italicizing the sentence: '*There is no return to a harmonious state of nature. If we turn back, then we must go the whole way – we must return to the beasts*' (13, p. 200). Indeed, the position of lapsed men is in many ways worse, since they have lost the instinctive guides to behaviour on which other animals are able to depend.

The course of history has been shaped less by popular heresies than by the original thinking of outstanding men. This is particularly true when the insights of successive pioneers are incorporated in an organized body of codified thought like that presented by the natural sciences. The importance of the sciences far transcends their contribution to advancing the technology of production, distribution, and communication. Of greater significance in the long run is their role in promoting abstract and universal modes of categorizing experience. Whereas cultural traditions by their very nature reflect the diversity of their parent cultures and favour historical modes of thought, scientific laws are abstract and necessarily universal if they are true. As modes of thought proper to the natural sciences spread over the world they serve to promote and intensify the process of homogenization exhibited in tangible form in the products of machine industry.

If the natural sciences operated to lessen diversity and impose homogeneity among different societies, another product of increasing human awareness, that of concern for others and specifically for the weak and unsuccessful, not only promoted a greater degree of equality and hence of homogeneity within societies, but made their attainment a talisman of philosophic and indeed political morality. In Karl Popper's rhetoric, the attainment of 'open' societies of the kind that stemmed from the experience of Classical Greece was held to be a self-evident aim in contrast with 'closed' societies of tribal character which were by the same token considered to be outmoded. What was regarded as particularly reprehensible about 'closed' societies is that they were hierarchically ordered and informed by traditional values invested with the sanction of history and even of the supernatural. By contrast, open societies, to the attainment of which all the previous experience of mankind was thought of as a mere preliminary, were held to be rational rather than magical, abstract rather than organic, equalitarian rather than hierarchical, and universal rather than tribal. It is paradoxical that Popper, who saw with such clarity of vision the fallacy of naturalism, should have failed to appreciate the contradiction implicit in the very notion of an 'open' society. The artificial values that constrain human behaviour and make it so distinct from that of the nonhuman primates are neither abstract nor necessarily rational. They are the product not of logic but of history, not the generalized history of mankind, but that of particular societies. To speak of abstract culture is a contradiction in terms. A society truly open would soon enough revert to a state of nature with all that that implies. Conversely, culture can only exist by constraining or at least moulding individual men, the sole way of ensuring the viability of traditional patterns and values.

The object of this essay is by no means to advocate reaction. On the contrary, the last thing archaeology should encourage is any disposition to believe that the historical process can safely be ignored. It would be suicidal as well as futile to dream of returning to a golden age before the 'enlightenment' spawned the natural science, machine technology, and egalitarian philosophies that between them threaten those diverse expressions of the human spirit that we term civilizations. The extended view of history made possible by archaeology is valuable above all for the improved perspective from which it allows us to view the present and indeed the future. If the past is embalmed in history, the future lies open before us. As we peer ahead, our knowledge of the past should nevertheless stand us in good stead by defining perils and reminding us of what we stand to lose if we ignore them.

It has been a main contention of this essay that whereas for long ages the course of social evolution was benign, in that it promoted diversity and so enriched mankind, we are now in a new phase of world history, one in which prevailing trends are malignant and even threaten to terminate the adventure chronicled by archaeology. Our future has been in peril since during our own times the concepts and techniques of modern science have engulfed the world. Unless we can hold fast to the values defined by our history, we shall be reduced not to a pristine and therefore still hopeful state, not to a prehuman so much as a subhuman condition. If our common aim is to enhance our lives, our guiding light must surely be quality rather than quantity, hierarchy rather than equality, and diversity rather than homogeneity. By the same token, we should not be afraid to count archaeology as a humane study. Since men necessarily derive their humanity by virtue of belonging to and sharing the heritage of social groups, it follows that archaeologists must concern themselves with, and where appropriate use methods developed by, the social sciences. Equally, since man is an animal and his societies can only exist in the context of nature, his history can only be fully understood by applying the insights and techniques of the biological and physical sciences. This is not to say that the natural and social sciences are to be worshipped, revered, or even mimicked. They are merely there to be used in order to promote understanding. The objective of archaeology is to elucidate the manner in which in the course of ages we have become human and in this way define what we mean when we declare ourselves to be men. By the same token, a prime objective of social policy ought surely to be not to undermine but to conserve and promote the values by which in the course of their long history men have managed to distance themselves from their primate relatives.

Notes

1 That is why I dedicated the illustrated third edition of *World Prehistory* to 'the diversity of men' (6).

References

1 Brailsford, J. 1975. *Early Celtic Masterpieces from Britain in the British Museum*. London: British Museum Publ.
2 Bruce Mitford, R. 1972. *The Sutton Hoo Ship Burial: A Handbook*. London: British Museum Publ.
3 Childe, V. G. 1925. *Dawn of European Civilization*. Sixth and last edition published in 1957. London: Routledge & Kegan Paul.
4 Childe, V. G. 1942. *What Happened in History*. London: Pelican Books.
5 Clark, G. 1970. *Aspects of Prehistory*, Chap. 2. Berkeley: Univ. California Press.
6 Clark, G. 1977. Dedication. *World Prehistory in New Perspective*. Cambridge: Cambridge Univ. Press. 3rd ed.
7 Clark, J. D. 1976. African origins of man the toolmaker. *In Human Origins: Louis Leakey and the East African Evidence*, ed. G. L. Isaac, E. R. McCown. California: Benjamin.
8 de Chardin, T. 1959. *The Phenomenon of Man*. London: Collins.
9 Diringer, D. 1962. *Writing*. London: Thames & Hudson.
10 Frankfort, H. 1951. *The Birth of Civilization in the Near East*. London: Williams & Norgate.
11 Jessup, R. 1950. *Anglo-Saxon Jewelry*. London: Methuen.
12 Le Gros Clark, W. E. 1955. *The Fossil Evidence for Human Evolution*, Chap. 1. Chicago: Univ. Chicago Press.
13 Popper, K. R. 1966. *The Open Society and its Enemies*, Vol. 1. London: Routledge & Kegan Paul. 5th ed.

PART IV
_____

RETROSPECTIVE

CHAPTER 27

THE INVASION HYPOTHESIS IN BRITISH ARCHAEOLOGY

THE BACKGROUND

One of the basic facts about England – from some points of view the basic fact – is that it faces east across the North Sea to a broad arc of territories from the Low Countries to Denmark and the Scandinavian Peninsula; south to northern France, the Biscayan seaboard and Iberia; and west to the Atlantic Ocean and the New World, the discovery of which was in due course, long after prehistoric times had been forgotten, to transform both its own destiny and that of Europe. The imperial adventures of their fellow-countrymen, in the course of which western civilization was mediated to the world at large, however much they may have coloured historical and political thought, have never so far as can be seen, distorted, unless in a negative sense, the vision of British archaeologists.

In this respect there is a strange contrast with Germany, where the growth of imperialism in the closing years of the 19th and the early years of the 20th century was marked by a veritable chauvinism of prehistory, a chauvinism tinged with racialism, of an exceedingly virulent and sinister kind. The British took the expansion of their power in the world almost as if providence rather than any qualities of their own was responsible. Was not the Empire acquired in a fit or series of fits of absence of mind? By the same token it would never have occurred to British archaeologists to vaunt British superiority in the Stone Age, to distort chronology and ascribe every glimmer of light in the cultural world, not merely of Europe but of Asia, to the tonic incursions of a morally superior and racially satisfactory weapon-bearing *Urbritischkultur-volk*. Quite the contrary has been the case: the ancient Briton may have been taken seriously during the romantic era, especially when clad in druidical garb, but ever since he has been a figure of fun, if not of scorn.

So little did British archaeologists of the era from Kipling to Winston Churchill feel the need to underpin the Empire with prehistoric props that they went out of their way to ascribe every good thing about their early past to foreign influences, if not indeed to foreign conquerors. So anxious were some of them to avoid ascribing any innovation to their own forbears that one might say that they were suffering from a form of invasion neurosis. For much of the first half of the 20th century British archaeologists felt themselves under strong compulsion to ascribe every change, every development to overseas influences of one kind or another. The more accessible parts of the Continent between Portugal and Norway, or more often the literature

457

bearing on these, were searched hopefully for analogies. So sure were prehistorians that every new thing must have come from the Continent that even quite vague similarities sufficed to define and denote not merely culture contact but actual invasion. In the final stage of the neurosis hypothetical invasions became so real that they, instead of the archaeological material itself, were actually made the basis of classification.

In behaving in this way British archaeologists were not of course without some measure of justification; after all, even the last 2,000 years have witnessed three major phases of invasion and numerous small infiltrations and there is every reason to think that prehistoric Britain must also have experienced incursions of a kind. Again it has to be admitted at a pragmatic level that the obsession with invaders has had its uses. The insular torpor that oppressed British archaeology during the late Victorian and Edwardian eras can only be fully savoured by turning over the periodical literature of the period. At least the anxiety to trace invaders led British archaeologists after the War of 1914–18 themselves to invade the Continent, to scour museums, investigate field monuments and even, as Sir Mortimer Wheeler, Professor Frere, Mrs Cotton, Mr Case and others have done, to undertake excavations in France or, like Professor Hawkes, in Portugal.

Today the invasion neurosis, if it can be called such, seems to be waning with imperial power itself. British archaeologists have begun once again to appreciate the achievements of their prehistoric forbears and value them, not as mere products of alien impact, but as in themselves manifestations of an age-long process of organic growth. It is not suggested that it would be a good thing if we returned to the fabulous notions of Geoffrey of Monmouth; or that British archaeologists should relapse into the stale nostalgia of a Celtic fringe. The imperial past made us citizens of the world and as such we have gained a sense of proportion that one trusts will always be retained. What is happening among the younger school of British archaeologists is a new attempt to re-examine the evidence so far as possible with an open mind. It is the contention of this article that preoccupation with invaders during the past generation has been obsessive and even dangerous. It has been dangerous because, like other obsessions, it feeds on itself and distracts attention from what is of much greater importance: when all is said the object of British archaeology is surely to tell us about the lives of the people who, generation by generation, age by age, in unbroken succession occupied and shaped the culture of the British Isles.

THE NEOLITHIC IN SOUTHERN ENGLAND: THE HISTORY OF THE PROBLEM

To develop this theme systematically for Great Britain and Ireland would need a substantial volume. I shall therefore confine myself to southern

England, the region closest to the Continent, and concern myself mainly with the period from the introduction of farming to the full establishment of bronze-working. Criticism of a construct so hypothetical as the current version of the prehistory of England during the earliest phases of settled life is not of course difficult; but in this article I want to go further and suggest a way of ordering the basic data more in accord with modern knowledge and ways of looking at the past. By common consent pottery is the most reliable guide to the vicissitudes of culture for those periods in which potting as a craft was still largely in the hands of women working in their own homes. The first study of Neolithic pottery from southern England was that published by Reginald Smith in 1910.[1] Smith, it will be remembered, compared the pottery found together with Beakers in the Peterborough pits with a well-known bowl from Mortlake in the Thames Valley; but he also went on to compare the English pottery with wares from east Sweden and Finland. In 1925 T. D. Kendrick distinguished two separate groups of Neolithic pottery in England and in so doing unwittingly set his successors on a course that was to lead them for years into a blind alley: he contrasted pottery from the Wexcombe Down long barrow, which he characterized as 'a primitive ware of the crudest kind ... exactly what the earliest attempts at potting in this country should provide', with that from the West Kennet long barrow in which he detected 'a slight improvement in potting' and 'a big advance in the matter of ornament'.[2] The Austrian prehistorian Oswald Menghin continued to recognize two distinct groups though he preferred to label them Grimston and Peterborough, and made explicit Kendrick's hint that the plain ware preceded the decorated one.[3] Meanwhile the need to classify the pottery from his own excavations at Abingdon led E. T. Leeds to consider terminology in greater detail.[4] In his report of 1927 he preserved the notion of duality and the terms he adopted have remained in use for a generation: he preferred Windmill Hill to Wexcombe or Grimston, but retained Peterborough, invented by Smith and followed by Kendrick, for the other group. Leeds considered that each class must have been brought to Britain from different sources, Windmill Hill ware being 'in the main linked with western France and the Iberian Peninsula', and Peterborough with northern Europe, Denmark and the Baltic, a conclusion broadly accepted by Harold Peake in the following year.[5]

This was the position when in 1931 Piggott[6] and Childe[7] published the papers which have been major points of reference ever since in any discussion of British Neolithic pottery. Piggott's chief contribution was to assemble a much larger body of material than had ever previously been considered and to subject this to a careful and comprehensive morphological study. In reviewing this he adopted Leeds's basic terminology, but suggested a useful shorthand reference to Windmill Hill and Peterborough, respectively as classes A and B. His main departure was to divide class A into two sub-classes. Class A1 comprised the simple undecorated vessels, based according to Schuchhardt on leather-bag prototypes, vessels thought at the time to make up the bulk of the pottery from the lowest level of the ditch at Windmill Hill. Class A2, which formed the main assemblage at Abingdon and was supposed, mistakenly as has since appeared, to occur higher up in the silt of the Windmill Hill ditches, is distinguished by thickened rims, shoulders, and incised decoration. The whole class might appear, following Schuchhardt,[8] to have been inspired by leather prototypes and Piggott[9] argued that all the novel elements in A2 ware might be accounted for in skeuomorphic terms by supposing that two withies were sewn into the prototypical bag, the decoration on rim and shoulder being suggested by the stitching. One of the beauties of this insight is that it provides for once a self-sufficient explanation for a marked change in pottery style.

Matters did not rest for long. In 1934 Piggott made a substantial change of ground;[10] the immediate stimulus to this was his examination of pottery excavated from the causewayed camp of Whitehawk on the Sussex Downs and in particular his recognition alongside 'typical Neolithic A2 pottery' of seven sherds decorated with motifs 'entirely characteristic of the second great family of British neolithic pottery – Neolithic B ware'. This led him to retract from his earlier conclusion that Windmill Hill ware antedated Peterborough and accept Leeds's notion of 1927 that the two were (in Piggott's words) 'broadly contemporary and geographically complementary'. Accordingly he explained the anomalous sherds from Whitehawk as hybrids; more than this he retracted his own skeuomorphic explanation as sufficient to account for the evolution of A2 ware. He now maintained that the Neolithic A potters would have needed 'some stimulus . . . to suggest . . . that they might modify and ornament their vessels' and he found in the presence of 'highly ornamented Neolithic B pots . . . a very plausible stimulus to the makers of the undecorated A ware'. The logic of this is hard to follow, since it is the essence of his own skeuomorphic explanation that there was a causal link between rim-form, carination and the character and positioning of the ornament. Again the mere fact that pottery happens to be the only form of container to have survived on the vast majority of Neolithic sites in north-western Europe ought not surely to lead us to suppose that potting was carried on in a vacuum: Schuchhardt's approach is soundly based on the realities of Neolithic life, in which there was little specialization and such crafts as potting and leatherwork would have been carried on in the same milieu and probably by the same people. The point to emphasize, though, in the present context is that in 1934 Piggott found it necessary to account even for the A2 pottery style in terms of contact with another pottery style from overseas. In the same paper, it is worth noting, Piggott sought to distinguish 'dual strains' in the A pottery, namely simple pots equated with Cortaillod (or Vouga I) and carinated bowls with widely everted lips (form G and its allies) which appeared to him, following Childe's suggestion of 1931, 'to have Michelsberg, or at all events "Germano-Belgic" affinities'.[11]

Meanwhile it was not long before Childe, perhaps in response to mild protests from colleagues in the Baltic countries, began to revise his views on the origin of Peterborough Class B ware. Already in 1935, after stating firmly that 'the affinities of Peterborough ware are admitted to lie in the great forest of north Europe. The nearest analogues . . . come from dwelling-places on Bornholm, in Sweden and round the Baltic', he proceeded to hint broadly that 'quite possibly the Peterborough folk reached eastern England from some now submerged tract from the north German or Dutch coast'.[12] This was in a sense carrying the invasion hypothesis to an ultimate point: if Peterborough ware had to come from somewhere, and if no really convincing analogies could be found in any existing part of Europe, it could only be supposed, so the theory ran, that it must have come from some area now submerged. One can see the logic of this, but only on the assumption that Peterborough ware must indeed have come from somewhere else. It is evident on the other hand that doubts were growing in Childe's mind about the self-evident truth of this, a truth which at bottom rested on another even more basic assumption, the notion first adumbrated by Kendrick and developed with increasing emphasis by his successors that there were in fact as well as in fancy 'two great families' of British Neolithic pottery. In 1940 Childe came out with the idea that invasion 'seems unnecessary' to account for Peterborough ware; instead he reminded his readers of the existence of a common Mesolithic tradition that formerly existed over extensive tracts of the north European plain and went on to suggest that 'the similarity between Peterborough and Baltic ware' might more satisfactorily be explained by treating them as 'parallel developments within that continuum of Forest cultures under the impact of the same Western and Megalithic societies'.[13] Indeed he went so far as to express the notion that Late Neolithic societies, characterized for example by Peterborough or Skara Brae ware, might 'result from the acculturation of . . . residual food-gathering groups'.[14]

It was this idea of Childe's that underlay the concept of the secondary Neolithic as this was developed by Piggott in 1954.[15] Piggott found the origins of the Peterborough and associated cultures, notably that denoted by grooved ware, to 'lie in the Mesolithic cultures of northern Europe, and of Britain in particular'.[16] He termed them 'secondary Neolithic in the sense that they represent the assimilation of Neolithic elements . . . by the indigenous Mesolithic hunter-fisher population after the first impact of the intrusive immigrants' who introduced agriculture and the culture traits that went with this.

With the validity of this thesis we are not for the moment concerned. The immediate point to emphasize is that by adopting this hypothesis Piggott fell into step with Childe in retracting the notion of an invasion across the North

Sea as a way of accounting for Peterborough and allied cultures. From this it followed logically, if we agree to dispense with the notion that pottery was independently invented in a part of Britain unoccupied by Class A ware, that 'Peterborough ware' must in some sense have developed from 'Windmill Hill ware'. This is precisely the conclusion reached by Isobel Smith in her Ph.D. dissertation for London University,[17] a work completed in 1956 and, regrettably, still unpublished. A notable convert was Professor Piggott himself, who in his important paper at the Prague Symposium in 1959 stated in so many words that in his opinion Dr Smith had 'conclusively shown that the whole of the Peterborough pottery series can best and most economically be explained as a continuous insular development starting in middle Neolithic times from evolved forms of Windmill Hill ware and continuing in late Neolithic times with contributions from the relatively newly intrusive pottery styles embodied in the Beaker cultures'.[18]

Dr Smith's thesis was of course formulated at a time when radiocarbon analysis was already opening up new perspectives of time. Since the impact of C14 on our concept of the Neolithic phase of British prehistory has been so recently reviewed,[19] only the salient facts need to be recalled here. When Piggott was composing his *Neolithic Cultures of the British Isles*, short chronologies were still the rule and he felt obliged to compress the whole phase between the 20th century and *c.* 1500 B.C. Now that we are able to envisage a maximum time span well over a thousand years longer, it is very much easier and more plausible to accept a long development of pottery styles. Moreover, radiocarbon has done far more than merely expand the time range; it has already made it possible to fix certain sites and categories in their correct context within what is now a lengthy span. To take only one example, it has shown that the concentric interrupted ditches at Windmill Hill were not cut until comparatively well on in Neolithic times, a matter of immense importance when it is recalled that Piggott structured his treatment of the material from southern England very largely on the supposed context of different elements in the fill of the ditches of this type-site. The qualification 'supposed' is used advisedly because Piggott was obliged to depend on what proved to be an imperfect record. Indeed the full report on Mr Alexander Keiller's excavations prepared for his widow by Dr Smith was not finally published until 1965.[20]

The publication of the Windmill Hill volume reminds us sharply that the implications of recent developments for the ordering and nomenclature of the British Neolithic have hardly yet begun to be appreciated.[21] It should surely be apparent that the new knowledge can no longer be expressed by the old formulation: something new must be attempted and a beginning must first be made with southern England, the cornerstone of Professor Piggott's stately but no longer habitable edifice. In so active a field it would surely be strange if a radical revision of a scheme set out in its fundamentals so long ago as 1931 was not by now necessary, and Professor Piggott's courageous statement at Prague in 1959 encourages us to make a beginning. What is the kind of picture we now see if we stand back from the material and try to visualize it with the clarity we need for the task of initiating students?

EARLY MIDDLE NEOLITHIC BOWL CULTURE

We have to begin by recognizing that farming economy and the whole complex of technology, practices and ideas that made up our Neolithic culture must have been introduced from overseas. No one can doubt that the invasion hypothesis is here essential and justified. Many problems of definition remain to be solved and will not here be discussed, but there is widespread agreement that France was the main source of our Neolithic invaders. What concerns us in the present context is that farming communities, having once been established here, developed continuous traditions over hundreds, indeed thousands of years. This continuity, though a basic fact of later British prehistory and indeed of the rest of British history, was not of course undisturbed; and the impact of ethnic and cultural intrusions in the opening centuries of the 2nd millennium B.C., marked in the archaeological record among other things by the introduction of Beaker pottery, copper metallurgy and the practice of single-grave burial, had a powerful influence not only on the Later Neolithic cultures of southern Britain but even more importantly on those of the ensuing Bronze Age.

Archaeologically the most persistent and widespread traces of Neolithic culture from the pre-Beaker era in southern Britain were round-based bowls and indeed it would seem legitimate to speak symbolically of a Round-based Bowl culture. Many varieties of bowl have been defined, some having chronological, others merely local significance. The first distinction to be made is between pottery assemblages in which all the bowls were plain and those in which some – at Hurst Fen, Mildenhall, it was about one in four – were decorated.

Of the plain-ware styles (Piggott's A1) the most important was that named after the causewayed-ditch site of Hembury in Devon.[22] Similar pottery occurred at Maiden Castle, Dorset,[23] and at Windmill Hill, Wilts., where it antedated the causewayed-ditch enclosure.[24] The radiocarbon dates for Hembury (B.M. 130, 3150 ± 150 B.C.) and pre-enclosure Windmill Hill (B.M. 73, 2950 ± 150 B.C.) suggest that this plain thin-rimmed pottery belonged to the earliest phase of farming settlement in Britain. Another find of plain Neolithic pottery from this early phase is that from the lower peat deposit at Peacock's Farm, Shippea Hill (Q 825/8 Av. 2950 + 120 B.C.).[25] It may be noted that rolled rims are rather more strongly represented at Shippea Hill than at Hembury and that no lugs were present at the former site; on the other hand the sample, only half a dozen pots, is too small for meaningful comparisons and we are hardly entitled to assume that we are dealing with two distinct wares.

Insufficient radiocarbon dates are available to make it certain when the thick-rimmed decorated pottery (Piggott's A2) made its first appearance. What is already known is that no less than five styles of this class of pottery have so far been recognized, three of which appeared in the fill of the Windmill Hill enclosure ditches:

(i) *Windmill Hill* style proper, in the sense of the pottery described by Dr Smith[26] as occurring exclusively at the name site. This includes bowls with vertical incisions running between rows of dots on rim and shoulder, as well as plain vessels with a well-defined thumb groove below the rim.

(ii) *Abingdon* style named after Mr Leeds's site in the Middle Thames Valley.[27] This comprises rounded and lightly carinated bowls with thickened rims, a sizeable proportion of which are T-sectioned, projecting internally as well as externally. Ornamentation in the form of oblique or transverse stroke-ornament or punctuations is concentrated on the rim, but also on or immediately above and below the shoulder, or in the case of smooth-profiled vessels at an equivalent position. When handles occur these take the form of perforate or imperforate lugs; strap-like handles are an occasional but notable feature.

(iii) *Whitehawk* style, after the site at Brighton on the Sussex Downs,[28] is marked by shouldered bowls, often with mouths wider than the carination, on which lugs, sometimes vertically perforated, may occur. Lines have frequently been incised on the shoulder; thickened rim, and stabs sometimes occur on the neck.

(iv) *Mildenhall* style (Piggott's East Anglian ware) is named from the prolific site of Hurst Fen, Mildenhall, Suffolk.[29] It differs from Abingdon ware in being more often more markedly carinated and in having relatively few of the T-sectioned rims. The carinated bowls of Mildenhall are often proportionately deeper than those from Whitehawk and the style of ornamentation is distinctive: vertical and oblique lines are common on the rim but also occur on the neck, and the shoulder is commonly marked by up to five rows of round to oval impressions, that could in most cases have been made by impressing the articular end of a bird bone. Lugs include some vertically perforated, but others of the Abingdon, strap-like form.

(v) *Ebbsfleet* style, first described by Piggott[30] from North Kent, includes carinated vessels with rim and shoulder picked out by a vertical or oblique linear decoration, but more common are weak-shouldered vessels with everted neck and thickened, sometimes T-sectioned rim. Ornamentation, confined to the upper part of the pot, includes lattice patterns made by incision, shallow pits made by the finger-tip on the neck and occasionally whipped-cord impression.

It is important to emphasize that both the main categories of pottery so far considered and each of their several styles were made by people who shared broadly the same culture. One may first remark the close association of four of these groups of pottery with causewayed enclosures. If at Windmill Hill itself the Hembury style predated the enclosure, it was identified with this at the name-site as well as at Maiden Castle. We have already emphasized that styles A2 (i, ii and v) occurred in the enclosure ditches at Windmill Hill. It is particularly revealing that Dr Smith satisfied herself that Ebbsfleet pottery occurred in the primary levels at Windmill Hill,[31] because, as recently as 1962, Piggott was still including this in his Peterborough family.[32] Nor does this instance stand alone. At Whitehawk Piggott himself described Ebbsfleet ware as being 'intimately associated with the primary occupation of the camp'.[33] Again, the occurrence of Abingdon ware (A2 ii) in the primary fill of the causewayed enclosures at the name-site[34] has more recently been confirmed lower down the Thames at Staines.[35]

The same homogeneity appears in the flint and stone equipment associated with the makers of the round-based bowls and the causewayed enclosures. The polished axe of flint or stone was a key symbol of Neolithic culture, because the early farmers had to introduce the new economy at the expense of the forest and they also needed timber to make more substantial houses and in some parts of the country their funerary monuments. It is worthy of note, as has been recently emphasized,[36] that the quarrying of particularly favourable stone and the traffic in stone axe-blades was so far from being a 'secondary Neolithic' trait or, alternatively, an element derived from some Scandinavian or Circumpolar source, as to be in fact an integral part of the Bowl culture. The quest for the best material for stone axe-blades was carried on already by the inhabitants of Early Neolithic Hembury who exploited several Cornish sources. Again stone axe-blades from the Graig Lwyd and Langdale factories in North Wales and the Lake District, respectively, were freely used by the makers of Decorated Bowls during the Middle Neolithic occupation of southern England: it is interesting for example to find fragments of Langdale axes at Windmill Hill with Decorated Bowls, styles i, ii and v, at Abingdon and Staines with style ii and at Hurst Fen with style iv. The commonest flint types were those needed for working organic materials – finely serrated flakes for ringing bone or possibly wood and convex scrapers for working skins and wood – and there is no apparent difference between those used by the makers of the different styles of decorated or undecorated bowls. The leaf-shaped arrowhead is another element in the flint component which, though showing minor variations in outline, is substantially homogeneous over the whole range of the Bowl culture. It has been argued by the present writer[37] that larger and heavier laurel-leaf forms were particularly favoured by the makers of Mildenhall pottery, but part of one occurred at Abingdon with style A2 ii pottery and Dr Smith has shown that they occurred in primary levels at Windmill Hill.[38]

Few of the bone forms are sufficiently diagnostic to be of much help, but the antler 'dehairing' combs[39] occur with Whitehawk pottery (style iii) and Abingdon (style ii) pottery, as well as at Windmill Hill with pottery styles i, ii and v; and the single specimen from Maiden Castle belongs on the face of it to the Hembury plain ware.

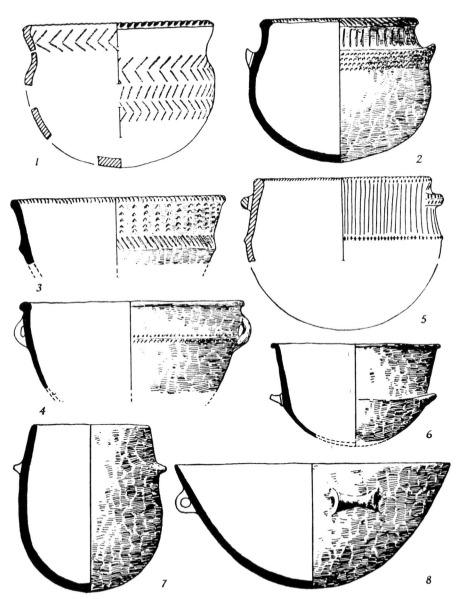

27.1 Pots of the Early/Middle Neolithic Bowl culture of Southern England. MN: 1 Ebbsfleet; 2 Mildenhall; 3 Whitehawk; 4 Abingdon; 5 Windmill Hill. EN: 6–8 Hembury. Scale 1 : 4

Again there is clear association between the bowl makers and long barrows.[40] Insufficient material has yet been obtained under scientific conditions to make close analysis profitable, but the link is already plain. Bowls, whether plain or decorated in style, occur in primary contexts both in earthen (e.g. Holdenhurst, Thickthorn and Nutbane) and in chambered long barrows (e.g. Pole's Wood East and Eyford, Cotswold; West Kennet, Wilts; and Coldrum, Medway).

There are also indications that makers of decorated bowls were responsible for at least two other kinds of sacred structure. The layout of cursus monuments alone indicates a clear association with long barrows, as Professor Atkinson[41] has shown particularly well in the case of the one on Cranborne Chase, Dorset, that incorporates and encloses long barrows as well as terminating close by such; and he has also recovered a polished flint axe and a leaf arrowhead from the primary, and Ebbsfleet pottery from the secondary, silt of a cursus at Dorchester, Oxfordshire.[42] Again, Abingdon Pottery has come from Site 1 at Dorchester, one of a group regarded by Atkinson as prototypical of the whole class of 'henge' monuments.[43]

LATE NEOLITHIC CULTURE

There is no intention to question that the appearance of Beaker pottery in this country, along with cultural innovations on a broad front, indicates some intrusion of actual people, more especially since burials disclose the presence of a new physical type with notably broader heads. Yet modern reseach has not only narrowed down the area from which Beaker-using invaders are supposed to have come, but has also shown that certain classes of Beaker and associated artifacts long interpreted as intrusive were in fact the product of indigenous growth. It is no longer believed that maritime Beakers reached Wessex from Brittany;[44] the immediate source of our earliest Beakers was almost certainly the Low Countries,[45] a meeting-place themselves of more than one group of Beaker-making people. Two of the most clearly defined groups to reach Britain were the all-over cord Beaker (van der Waals 2 IIB; Childe B3) and the Beaker with contracted zone decoration in hyphenated lines (van der Waals 2 IA), a type which with its smooth profile would equate with Childe's B1, but in its more angular short-necked form with Childe's C. The long-necked Beaker, Childe's A, along with such attendant forms as flint daggers, flat metal daggers with rivets, etc., are now seen to be indigenous products;[46] for instance the flint dagger, though inspired by the introduced metal form, was made possible by the native skill in flint-working, witnessed by the laurel-leaves of the Bowl culture.

Our main concern in the present context is with the impact of the intrusive culture on the continuing native tradition and in the first instance on pottery. Two main groups other than the Beakers themselves existed during our Late

Neolithic phase; on the one hand there is the pottery stemming from Middle Neolithic and specifically Ebbsfleet sources, notably the wares named after Mortlake and Fengate. *Mortlake* pottery continued to adhere to the round-based bowl form, but the neck was now more pronounced and the rim more heavily moulded – moreover ornament tended to cover the whole or at least most of the outside of the pot as well as the inner face of the rim. Decoration mainly took the form of such patterns as herringbones made by imprinting twisted cord, the articular ends of small mammalian or bird bones, or finger-nails, or occasionally of rows of pits sunk into the thickness of the wall. *Fengate* pots on the other hand had flat bases, presumably acquired from Beaker sources, as were some of the decorative elements, notably rustication by pinching the surface and the shaded triangles applied to the more heavily moulded and sometimes even overhanging rim of the pot. The other main group of flat-based pots which appears about the same time and sometimes in the same context as Mortlake and Beaker pottery is that characterized above all by the grooving technique used in decoration. In publishing the rich finds from the submerged land surface of the Essex coast at Lion Point, Clacton, Piggott[47] showed that similar pottery occurred over a wide tract of southern England as far west as Worcester, Somerset and Wiltshire. The *Grooved* ware,[48] as it may be termed, is not in fact a homogeneous entity. As seen at Clacton it takes the form of broad, flat-based bowls with flaring sides decorated on the one hand by grooves arranged in the form of horizontal lines, chevrons and large triangles and lozenges filled by shallow oval impressions, and on the other by relief decorations in the form of wavy bands, cable patterns and raised bands with transverse incisions. The pottery from Woodhenge,[49] on the other hand, showed much greater use of finger-nail rustication and the form of the pots was apparently bucket-shaped, some having collared rims. The flaring bowls of Clacton recall similar forms from the Dutch *hunebedden*, and rustication could well have come in with Beakers and in fact is found on large pot-Beakers like those from Somersham, Clacton and Arminghall.[50]

As Piggott brought out so well in 1954,[51] the flint industries of the Late Neolithic phase of southern England differ notably from, although showing some continuity with, those of our Bowl culture. Since the makers of Beaker pottery, Mortlake bowls and Grooved vessels frequently occupied the same sites, it is difficult to assign particular forms of flint tools to specific groups. Leaf-shaped arrowheads persisted, as did finely serrated flakes, but barbed and tanged triangular forms of arrowhead were introduced by the makers of Beaker pottery, and transverse and derivative forms of arrow were those most commonly found with both Mortlake and Grooved pottery.

Thus, the arrowheads from the Late Neolithic occupation site on the course of the West Kennet avenue[52] comprised 89 transverse and derivative forms, 7 barbed-and-tanged, 6 triangular and one leaf-shaped. Woodhenge[53] yielded 9 transverse derivative forms and only one leaf-shaped. Again, Smith noted[54] that none of the 24 transverse derivative forms found stratified in the ditches of Windmill Hill occurred below 2 ft from the surface. Among other flint forms to appear at this time one may particularly note plano-convex knives and edge-polished knives.

In common with other parts of north-western Europe the Late Neolithic phase in southern Britain was affected by the practice of metallurgy, introduced in this case by the makers of Beaker pottery who first opened up the copper resources of Ireland.[55] Yet in Britain as elsewhere copper remained at first a material too expensive for general use and one of the main effects of its introduction was to stimulate work in flint. Mention has already been made of the daggers developed by the makers of long-necked Beakers which find their counterparts in the daggers of Grand Pressigny flint and in the north European daggers. It may well be that it was the degree of specialization implied by metallurgy that favoured the development of more or less elaborate flint mines in the late Neolithic societies of Poland, Denmark, the Low Countries, northern France and southern England.[56] Although it has been claimed that flint-mining was an element of the earlier phase of Neolithic culture in the latter region, Dr Smith is quite definite[57] that in the silting of the Windmill Hill ditches 'the half-dozen large cores and flakes of flint-mine type were all found in upper or unrecorded levels, so there is no clear evidence for contact with this industry during the primary occupation'. Certainly there are signs that in Britain as in many parts of temperate Europe flint-mining was intensified during the last phase of Neolithic culture.

In respect of burial the Beaker-using intruders introduced, as Piggott has emphasized,[58] the practice of individual inhumation burial, whether in flat graves or under round barrows. The practice of other Late Neolithic groups is less clear-cut. Piggott hinted[59] that they followed, at least occasionally, the rite of inhumation under round barrows, but it seems clear also from observations at Dorchester, Oxfordshire, that they practised cremation. What is certain is that in relation to long barrows Mortlake pottery was secondary: it occurred in the secondary fill of the ditches of earthen long barrows like Holdenhurst and Thickthorn, and in the forecourt blocking of megalithic tombs (e.g. Notgrove, Nympsfield and West Kennet). In his report on West Kennet Piggott held[60] that with the 'phenomenon of a break in material culture' there was a continuing concern for the tomb. This continuity of concern is surely an indication that at a more fundamental level than the superficial changes in material equipment mirrored in the archaeological record the behaviour of the late Neolithic population was strongly influenced by still older, persisting traditions.

Other striking evidence of continuity may be found in sacred monuments of the 'henge' type which are found nowhere else outside Great Britain and which as we have already seen stem from the middle Neolithic prototypes in southern England. The fact that the great monuments of Avebury, Stonehenge 1 and 2, Woodhenge and Arminghall were erected by the late Neolithic population among whom the makers of Beakers mingled easily with those who made Grooved and Mortlake pottery, is hardly to be reconciled without grave qualifications with Piggott's 'secondary Neolithic' hypothesis; so far removed were these people from recently upgraded savages that they created sacred monuments without close parallel on the Continent, the two largest of which were to flourish well down into the full Bronze Age. This need not of course exclude the notion that Mesolithic survivors were incorporated in the Late Neolithic population – the intrusion of Beaker-using groups may well have caused additional land to be taken over for farming – but it does suggest that the influence of the hunter-fisher element was much less marked than that of the Beaker intruders or the continuing Middle Neolithic tradition. The complex monument at Avebury[61] with its great ditched and embanked area and its stone circles, the Sanctuary on Overton Hill and the connecting West Kennet Avenue, were erected by Late Neolithic people on land already frequented by people of the Bowl culture, but sherds of Long-necked Beaker and of Collared Urn from the secondary silting of the great ditch testify to a continuing concern for the site down to the time of the rich graves of the Early Bronze Age in Wessex. As with the West Kennet long Barrow, so at Avebury, to quote Dr Smith's words,[62] there was 'a continuity of ritual and ceremonial extending over a long period and through successive changes of material culture'. The case of Stonehenge is equally striking: sherds of Woodhenge ware from the primary silt of the ditch[63] and fragments of Beaker from the base of the Heel Stone[64] show that phase I of this site like the nearby Woodhenge was of Late Neolithic construction. The indications are that the original bluestone features of phase I were also erected by makers of Beaker pottery.[65] The third phase of construction, of which only the ruins of the last modification survive, is on the other hand plausibly attributed to the Early Bronze Age: rich burials of this time cluster round the monument and numerous engravings of axe-blades characteristic of the culture of this period in Wessex are visible on the sarsen uprights. Stonehenge has indeed been compared to a cathedral and the constructional changes through which it has passed bear witness to a basic continuity of tradition.

BRONZE-WORKING AND ITS IMPLICATIONS

With the onset of craft specialization and social stratification that accompanied the rise of a bronze metallurgy in southern Britain a new factor has to be taken into account. It is a matter of common observation that one way in which the more prosperous individuals in any community are liable to display their success is by consuming exotic products and adopting exotic styles. This is especially true of a society in which wealth and prominence come about, as it did in Wessex at the middle of the 2nd millennium B.C.,[66] largely through controlling trade in commodities of international importance, including in this case Cornish tin and Irish copper and gold. It is therefore hardly surprising to find in the richer burials of the Early Bronze Age in Wessex such things as bronze daggers and pins or even small ancillary pots of Continental style, jewellery displaying tricks known to Mycenaean gold-smiths or even trade beads of faience from the east Mediterranean; yet 30 years ago it seemed the most natural thing in the world to interpret such innovations as pointers, not to economic and social change, but to the source of the invasion that was assumed to have been responsible for their appearance. 'We are forced', wrote Stuart Piggott, 'to admit another wave of prehistoric immigration to Britain. Fortunately we have not far to seek the point of departure of these intruders, the real founders of our Bronze Age . . . Brittany supplies the answer . . . we have indeed no option but to regard the Wessex culture as the result of an invasion from Brittany'.[67]

A basic methodological error now generally admitted was to categorize a hundred or so rich burials as though these constituted a culture. It is only to be expected that, concentrating attention on the rich stratum of the popula-tion of the Early Bronze Age in Wessex, one should find indications of exotic fashions. Piggott, though continuing to designate these graves as constituting 'the Wessex culture', nevertheless went on to qualify his invasion hypothesis, stating that 'the archaeological evidence strongly suggests a dominant and

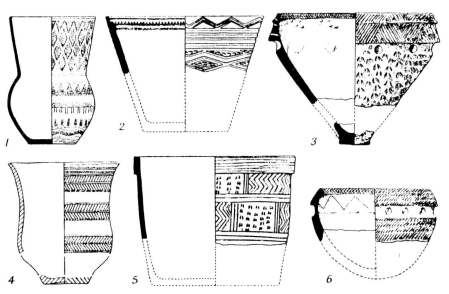

27.2 Late Neolithic pottery, Southern England: 1 'A' Beaker; 2 Clacton; 3 Fengate; 4 'B' Beaker; 5 Woodhenge; 6 Mortlake. Scale 1 : 5; no. 5 c. 1 : 7

intrusive aristocracy who for some centuries at least lorded it over the native element'. It was not a mass invasion so much as 'an annexation' by upper-class elements.[68] What of the 'native element'? It is strange that Piggott should have found this so 'elusive and difficult to assess',[69] since at least 17 of the graves on his list are shown as having cinerary urns and some of these, for instance no. 5 Bloxworth Down, no. 6 Clandon Barrow, no. 28 Tynings Farm East and no. 72 Normanton (Colt Hoare no. 156), were later to be classed by Dr Longworth[70] as among his Primary Series of Collared Urns.

Longworth has shown that the Collared Urn itself is an indigenous growth stemming in the main from Mortlake and Fengate sources, and so ultimately from the Middle Neolithic Bowl culture. On the other hand it also incorporated some elements from Beakers. In this connexion it is suggestive that one of the urns to show the most direct Beaker influences[71] is that from a Wessex grave (Piggott's no. 72), Colt Hoare's Barrow 156 at Normanton, especially since Normanton 164 (Piggott's 74) contained, according to Colt Hoare, a 'richly ornamented drinking cup'[72] and since Bulford (Piggott's 52) contained a grooved dagger noted by Piggott as being 'said to have been associated with a Beaker (now lost)'.[73] This basic dualism, which it is worth recalling in parenthesis is also reflected in the Food-vessel pottery further north, though in this case Beaker traditions were more evident,[74] is further reflected in the burial ritual of the Wessex Early Bronze Age: the round barrow (of which the bell barrow is merely an elaboration) and the rite of inhumation alike stem from the Beaker tradition; and the cremation rite, so far from supporting the invasion hypothesis, harks back, as we now know, to Late or even Middle Neolithic sources in southern England. Further evidence for continuity during the earlier part of the Bronze Age in southern England may be seen in the persistence of certain Late Neolithic flint forms. Derivatives of the transverse arrowhead have been found fairly commonly in barrows dating from the first half of the Bronze Age, for instance in a rich barrow at Martinsdown, Dorset (Piggott's no. 12), and with a Primary Series Collared Urn (Longworth's no. 143) in Tynings Barrow, Somerset. The plano-convex knife was a veritable type-fossil of the Food-vessel culture of northern England and in the south occurred with Primary Series Collared Urns both in barrows (e.g. Market Lavington, Wilts., and Snailwell, Cambs.; Longworth nos. 75 and 141–4) and on the open settlement at Plantation Farm, Cambs., with Longworth's urn no. 140.

The Middle Bronze Age in southern Britain was by general consent a time of peaceful consolidation and technical improvement in the sphere of bronze-working. Dutch prehistorians[75] have indeed come to accept that a group of urns, taking its name from Hilversum and found in the southern part of Holland either side of the Rhine-Maas Valley, were the product of an ethnic movement from southern England, where urns had by this time become bipartite and were sometimes ornamented by finger-printed cordons placed at the shoulder. Signs of their ancestry were at first retained by the Hilversum urns in the form of cord-imprinted chevrons and other linear patterns above the cordon, but in the Drakenstein urns derived from them this was abandoned. Glasbergen's thesis, now generally accepted, is especially relevant to our theme because the British archaeologists had long been accustomed to see in the Dutch urns a prototype for the finger-printed bucket urns that were supposed to have ushered in the late Bronze Age and to have reached Britain from the Netherlands. So soon as it was recognized the Dutch and British urns were merely cousins, British archaeologists began to see their own urns as indigenous developments. Already in 1956 we find J. J. Butler and Isobel Smith[76] arguing strongly for the indigenous origin of the cordoned urns of the British Middle Bronze Age. The same trend was followed by other of the younger workers in this field. Thus, in publishing the urnfield at Ardleigh, Essex, Longworth[77] remarked not on the exotic nature of the bucket urns, but rather on the 'strong local conservatism' displayed by it, and the late R. Rainbird Clarke wrote[78] of the pronounced change in the burial rites and pottery that marked the second main phase of the Bronze Age in East Anglia in the following terms:

Previously it has been held that these revolutionary innovations must indicate an invasion from the Low Countries . . . But the pottery of the Low Countries can no longer be regarded as ancestral to the East Anglian cremation urns, for the former had evolved from the pottery of British emigrants.

Hawkes in his valuable survey at the Hamburg Congress fully accepted the implications of Glasbergen's work as regards bucket urns, but continued to maintain that barrel urns and, still more, globular urns were alien to the British tradition and therefore presumably intrusive.[79] Even this reservation has not gone unchallenged and Ap Simon's derivation of the globular urns found in the settlement on Shearplace Hill, Dorset, from Cornish rather than Continental sources has received some support.[80]

Far more is of course involved than the intrusive or indigenous character of Deverel-Rimbury and analogous kinds of pottery. The invasion hypothesis, as this was applied to the Bronze Age, depended on the conjunction of changes across the whole range of culture from pottery and bronze-working to burial rite, agriculture and settlement pattern. As regards metalworking, advocates of the invasion hypothesis have in the past seized upon almost every innovation. Yet it would seem rash to accept changes of fashion or even of technique as evidence for invasion in view of the highly complex web of trade connections which closer study of the material is continually unfolding. Indeed, when one considers the bronzes themselves one is impressed above all by the imprint of native craftsmanship and tradition. When Cowen,[81] for example, takes such time-honoured invasion symbols as U and V leaf-shaped swords, what does he find but native products? And the introduced

prototypes, Hemigkofen and Erbenheim, amount to a mere handful. Superficially considered changes in burial custom might seem to offer a more
promising criterion for ethnic movement, were it not that there is plenty of
evidence in societies known to history that changes in burial fashion can
happen without changes in other departments of life and most certainly
without changes of population. Leaving this aside, however, the point has
already been made that cremation is a rite of Neolithic antiquity in Britain;
and any increase in the size of cemetery might surely be taken to reflect
economic rather than cultural change.

Really decisive evidence for immigration, if it could be sustained, would be
indications of the introduction of new regimes of farming and settlement.
Farmsteads with round houses set among Celtic fields and droveways were of
course an established feature of the late Middle Bronze Age in southern
England from the Sussex Downs (Itford Hill[82] and Plumpton Plain[83]) to
Dorset (Shearplace Hill[84]) and Dartmoor.[85] What is more to the point is that
excavations at Gwithian have shown that small lyncheted fields were being
cultivated by criss-cross ploughing in Cornwall already at the transition from
the Early to the Middle Bronze Age.[86] If this is accepted at its face value and
if we reject the hypothesis of a 'Wessex culture' invasion, this might suggest
that criss-cross cultivation by ards was introduced to Britain by the
Beaker-making intruders, a proposition that seems reasonable enough when
it is recalled that traces of similar agriculture relating to the Beaker culture are
known from the Dutch homeland.[87] It is also suggestive that Hans Helbaek
should have concluded from his study of grain impressions on pottery that
the Beaker-using invaders of Britain 'brought a marked change in agricultural
habits, in that they, contrary to the Neolithic farmers, were principally
barley-growers'.[88] While recognizing the importance of pastoral activities
Helbaek went out of his way to emphasize the importance of the part played
by agriculture during the Early Bronze Age. In particular he stressed with
regard to impressions of flax seeds on the B beaker from Handley Down,
Dorset, that they lead one to think in terms of a 'comparatively stable
agricultural occupation, at least over some years in succession'.[89] Finally, it is
significant that Helbaek should have noted that the pattern established by the
Beaker-using population continued apparently undisturbed throughout the
Bronze Age.

THE INCEPTION OF IRON METALLURGY

The invasion hypothesis reached its peak in relation to the Pre-Roman Iron
Age. In a recent paper Dr Roy Hodson[90] referred to 'the fundamental
problem that is ever present in British prehistory – the problem of distinguishing a native population from invaders'. Evidently this problem held no
terrors for those concerned with this period of our prehistory because, as Dr

Hodson has pointed out, they were so confident of being able to recognize invasions that they based their fundamental classifications upon them, as if they were established verities: the A of Hawkes's 'ABC of the British Iron Age'[91] was in effect defined by 'Hallstatt invasions', the B by the 'Marnian invasions', and the C by the 'Belgic invasions'.[92] Dr Hodson has questioned the methodological soundness of this procedure and asked whether in fact it might not have been a sounder principle to classify the material on its own merits.

The same author has recently taken a dispassionate look at the general body of material relating to Iron Age settlement in its early phase in southern England[93] and his conclusion, stated very briefly, is that it has as a whole a notably British look. If, for example, the Early Iron Age culture was essentially intrusive, is it not, he asks, very peculiar that its bearers shed, so to say, the rectangular houses of the Continent to step into round ones immediately on landing? More especially does this appear strange when we recall that the round house, like the 'Celtic fields' with which it was so often linked, was characteristic of the later Middle Bronze Age settlements and in this case almost certainly goes back to the time of the Beakers. The weaving-comb and the ring-headed pin equally have an indigenous back-ground. And so Hodson feels able to speak of a Woodbury culture rooted in the Bronze Age past, but carrying forward ultimately to the time of the Roman occupation. Plainly there have been many enrichments from the Continent, but down to the time of the Roman Conquest can we be sure of more than local intrusions?

Of course the leaders of the settled and increasingly numerous populations of the Iron Age were able to indulge in conspicuous consumption and this most often took the form of adopting foreign fashions or even merchandise. Even so when any particular class of prestige products is closely examined it is commonly found that, although inspired by Continental fashions, it nevertheless shows insular features and these features commonly reflect indigenous traditions continuing from a previous age. What did Jope find when he examined closely the earliest iron weapons from Britain, daggers made under the inspiration of Hallstatt and La Tène I models? He concluded, briefly, that 'those daggers were not imports, but were being made in Britain, the products of a coherent and complex workshop tradition operating continuously from the 6th through the 5th and 4th centuries B.C.'.[94] Among the features he found to be distinctively British were the twin-loops by which they were suspended, a device stemming from an indigenous Late Bronze Age practice.

Prominent among the traits characterizing 'Marnian invaders' was the practice of making pots with pedestal bases, but Hodson's re-examination[95] of supposedly early pottery from Eastbourne and his demonstration that some of the vessels had characteristic pedestal bases, convinced him that the hypothesis attributing this characteristic to the effects of a specific influence from the Marne between 300–250 B.C. must be wrong. One of the main arguments used by Hawkes in formulating the doctrine of a 'Marnian invasion'[96] was an apparent bunching of hillfort construction between *c.* 300 and 250 B.C. Yet, the correlation of hillfort construction with external menace is at best no more than a hypothesis and it is a hypothesis which is quite unnecessary to explain what we see. After all, if we take a region like the North Island of New Zealand we see that it was stuffed with defended settlements or *pas*, even though down to the white colonization the country was notoriously free from invaders after the original colonization. Here the construction of hillforts had during the pre-European phase nothing whatever to do with external enemies: on the contrary the hillforts were an expression of a particular form of society in which prowess in fighting conferred status on leaders and lent spice to the lives of their followers. Everything archaeology tells us of Early Iron Age society in southern Britain

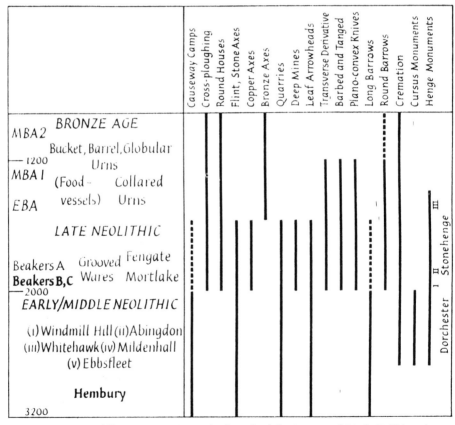

27.3 Middle Bronze Age in England south of the Severn and Wash. Bold lettering = intrusive

supports the notion of comparatively small units led by chieftains of warlike temperament, men given to conspicuous display and who paid particular regard to their weapons. Indeed Professor Hawkes has himself put us in debt for his demonstration of the way individual hillforts dominated small tracts of countryside. Under such conditions the presumption is surely that hillforts were the products of rivalry among the indigenous leaders and their followers. The invaders with la Tène culture for which a reasoned case has been made – and they are strictly speaking outside our area – were the offspring of the Parisii who introduced the Arras culture to East Yorkshire.[97]

The first wave of migrations into southern England since that associated with the introduction of Beaker pottery, metallurgy and single-grave burial, unreservedly accepted by the younger school of British archaeologists, is that associated with the Belgae. Even here there are doubts. In her recent review of the burial groups relating to the Aylesford-Swarling culture,[98] the most impressive evidence for 'Belgic' intrusion, Dr A. Birchall finds herself compelled to assign them to the time range of *c.* 50/30–10 B.C. When she turns to consider the material of pre-Caesarian age she finds herself in some embarrassment. Is this embarrassment really necessary? It is occasioned of course by the fact that shortly before she found it necessary to contract the age of the Aylesford-Swarling culture, Mr Allen had demonstrated the arrival in south-eastern England of successive waves of coins including a particularly strong one, his Gallo-Belgic 'C' coins, at *c.* 100 B.C. A question one asks oneself is why 'waves of important coinages', to quote Dr Birchall, should of themselves be 'taken to reflect the pattern of Belgic migration to Britain'?

CONCLUSION

To sum up, whereas for the first half of the 20th century it was common form to try to explain every change in the culture of the first 3,000 years or so of peasant culture in the south of England in terms of invasion, the younger school of prehistorians has been more inclined to seek the explanation for change in terms of indigenous evolution. When, for instance, rich exotic things occur in the archaeological record, these are likely to be interpreted as signs of increasing wealth on the part of native leaders rather than as in themselves signs of replacement by an invading aristocracy. Invasions and minor intrusions have undoubtedly occurred, even if far less often than other forms of culture contact, but their existence has to be demonstrated, not assumed.

Notes

1 R. A. Smith, 'The Development of Neolithic Pottery', *Archaeologia*, LXII (1910), 340.
2 T. D. Kendrick, *The Axe Age* (London, 1925), 14–15.
3 O. Menghin, in Hoernes, *Urgeschichte der bildenden Kunst* (3rd edn, Vienna, 1926), 717.
4 E. T. Leeds, *Ant. J*, VII (1927),456.
5 H. J. E. Peake, *J.R.A.I.*, LVIII (1928), 30.
6 S. Piggott, 'The Neolithic Pottery of the British Isles', *Arch. J.* LXXXVIII (1931), 67.
7 V. G. Childe, 'The Continental Affinities of British Neolithic Pottery', *Arch. J*, LXXXVIII (1931), 37.
8 C. Schuchhardt, *Alteuropa* (Berlin, 1919), 48 and 51.
9 Piggott, *op. cit.*, 81.
10 S. Piggott, 'The Mutual Relations of the British Neolithic Ceramics', *P.P.S.E.A.*, VII (1934), 373.
11 *Ibid.*, 379.
12 V. G. Childe, *The Prehistory of Scotland* (London, 1935), 80.
13 V. G. Childe, *Prehistoric Communities of the British Isles* (London, 1940), 83.
14 *Ibid.*, 80.
15 S. Piggott, *The Neolithic Cultures of the British Isles* (Cambridge, 1954), chs. X, XI.
16 *Ibid.*, 277.
17 I. F. Smith, 'The Decorative Art of Neolithic Ceramics in South-eastern England and its Relations', unpubl. Ph.D. thesis, London University, 1956.
18 S. Piggott, 'The British Neolithic Cultures in their Continental Setting', in *L'Europe à la fin de l'âge de la pierre,* ed. J. Böhm (Prague, 1961), 568.
19 J. G. D. Clark, 'Radiocarbon Dating and the Expansion of Farming Culture from the Near East over Europe', *P.P.S.*, XXXI (1965), 58.
20 *Windmill Hill and Avebury. Excavations by Alexander Keiller 1925–1939* (Oxford, 1965).
21 It is unfortunate that the terms 'Windmill Hill' and 'Peterborough' have been retained in this work, since they were devised to suit the 'two great families of Neolithic pottery' concept, effectively destroyed by Dr Smith. The term 'Windmill Hill', again, belongs to a time when it was thought that the ditches of the Windmill Hill enclosure preserved the whole Neolithic sequence of the area; and, in any case, Dr Smith has applied the term to a particular class of pottery (our group A 2 i) peculiar to the name-site. As for the term 'Peterborough ware', Professor Piggott has recently pleaded to retain this (*The West Kennet Long Barrow Excavations 1955–56* (London, 1962), 32) to denote small sherds too featureless to assign to any particular style within the series Ebbsfleet-Mortlake-Fengate: this hardly seems a valid reason for retaining a term which enshrines a discarded concept.
22 D. M. Liddell, in *Proc. Devon Arch. Expl. Soc.*, 1930–2 and 1936.
23 S. Piggott, in R. E. M. Wheeler, *Maiden Castle, Dorset* (Oxford, 1943), 137ff.
24 *Windmill Hill*, 57–9.
25 J. G. D. Clark and H. Godwin, 'The Neolithic in the Cambridgeshire Fens', *Antiquity,* 1962, 10; cf. *Ant. J*, XV (1935), 301.
26 *Windmill Hill*, 69.
27 *Ant. J*, VII (1927), 438; VIII (1928), 461.
28 E. C. Curwen, *Ant. J*, XIV (1934), 99.
29 J. G. D. Clark, E. S. Higgs and I. H. Longworth, *P.P.S.*, XXVI (1960), 202.
30 *Ant. J*, XIX (1939), 405.
31 *Windmill Hill*, 246.
32 *West Kennet*, 77.
33 *Ant. J*, XIV (1934), 118.
34 *Ant. J*, VII (1927), 438; VIII (1928), 461.
35 E. Robertson-Mackay, *Acts of the Sixth Congress of Pre- and Proto-historic Sciences,* II (Rome, 1965), 319–23.
36 G. Clark, 'Traffic in Stone Axe and Adze Blades', *Econ. Hist. Review*, XVIII (1965), 1 (esp. pp. 3ff.).
37 Clark, Higgs and Longworth, *op. cit.*, 223, 242.

38 *Windmill Hill*, 99f.
39 *Ibid.*, 83.
40 *Ibid.*, 50ff., 142ff.
41 *Arch. J*, CIV (1948), fig. 2, opp. p. 10.
42 R. J. C. Atkinson *et al.*, *Excavations at Dorchester, Oxon.* (Oxford, 1951), 63.
43 *Ibid.*, 108–9.
44 E.g. by Piggott, *P.P.S.*, IV (1938), 57–7, and W. F. Grimes, *Guide to the Collection Illustrating the History of Wales* (Cardiff, 1939), 49n. The correctness of this was queried as early as 1940 by Childe in his *Prehistoric Communities.*
45 J. D. van der Waals and W. Glasbergen, 'Beaker Types and their Distribution in the Netherlands', *Palaeohistoria*, IV (1955), 5–46. See esp. pp. 28–30, 34 and 36f.
46 Cf. Piggott, 'British Neolithic Cultures', 569.
47 *P.P.S.*, II (1936), 193ff.
48 This has come to be referred to in the literature as Rinyo-Clacton ware on the basis of analogies pointed out by Piggott (*P.P.S.*, II (1936), 201) between pottery from Clacton and Skara Brae, an analogy extended by Childe (*Prehistoric Communities*, 87) to his new Orkney site of Rinyo. Since the cultural links between Essex and the remote Scottish island are still in the realm of hypothesis, it might be better to rest terminology on established and verifiable facts. The term 'Grooved ware' refers to a leading method of decorating the pottery. If a site-name terminology is preferred. 'Clacton-Woodhenge' has the merit of spanning a broad range of variation.
49 M. E. Cunnington, *Woodhenge* (Devizes, 1945), 118–45.
50 *P.P.S.*, II (1936), 19–23.
51 *Neolithic Cultures*, 310–12, 358–9.
52 *Windmill Hill*, 237.
53 Cunnington, *Woodhenge*, pls. 23–4.
54 *Windmill Hill*, 104.
55 H. H. Coghlan and H. Case, 'Early Metallurgy of Copper in Ireland and Britain', *P.P.S.*, XXIII (1957), 91.
56 G. Clark, 'Traffic in Stone Axe and Adze Blades', 10.
57 *Windmill Hill*, 86.
58 *Neolithic Cultures*, fig. 64.
59 *Ibid.*, 307.
60 *West Kennet*, 74.
61 *Windmill Hill*, part II.
62 *Ibid.*, 249.
63 R. J. C. Atkinson, *Stonehenge* (London, 1956), 80.
64 *Ibid.*, 61.
65 *Ibid.*, 64, 157.
66 S. Piggott, 'The Early Bronze Age in Wessex', *P.P.S.*, IV (1938), 52.
67 *Ibid.*, 94.
68 *Ibid.*
69 *Ibid.*, 90.
70 I. H. Longworth, 'The Origins and Development of the Primary Series in the Collared Urn Tradition in England and Wales', *P.P.S.*, XXVII (1961), 263.
71 *Ibid.*, 280.
72 Piggott, 'Wessex', 106 (*Ancient Wilts.*, I, 205).
73 *Ibid.*, 105 (*Wilts. Arch.Mag.*, XXXVIII, 217.)
74 Longworth, 'Collared Urn Tradition', 283.
75 W. Glasbergen, *Barrow Excavations in the Eight Beatitudes* (Groningen, 1954). As Glasbergen points out, van Giffen was the first to compare Drakenstein and British urns and to hint that the Dutch vessels might indicate movement from Britain.
76 *12th Ann. Rep. Inst. of Archaeology* (London, 1956), 37–46.
77 *P.P.S.*, XXVI (1960), 178.
78 R. Rainbird Clarke, *East Anglia* (London, 1960), 87.

79 'The Southern British Bronze Age: Archaeology and the Ethnic Problem', *Report of the 5th Int. Congr. Pre- and Proto-historic Sciences* (Berlin, 1961), 379.

80 *P.P.S.*, xxviii (1962), 319.

81 *P.P.S.*, xvii (1951), 195.

82 *P.P.S.*, xviii (1957), 167.

83 *P.P.S.*, i (1935), 16.

84 *P.P.S.*, xxviii (1962), 289.

85 E.g. Kestor, described by Lady (Aileen) Fox in *P.P.S.*, xx (1954), 87. Unlike Lady Fox who wishes to attribute the site to the Early Iron Age, Dr C. A. Ralegh Radford maintained (*ibid.*, xviii (1952), 76–7) that the Dartmoor sites belonged to the Bronze Age.

86 J. V. S. Megaw, A. C. Thomas and B. Wailes, 'The Bronze Age Settlement at Gwithian, Cornwall. Preliminary Report on the Evidence for Early Agriculture', *Proc. W. Cornwall F.C.*, ii (1960), 200.

87 E.g. at Gasteren, Drenthe, by A. E. van Giffen, *Nieuwe Drentse Volksalmanak*, LIX (1941), 29–31. J. D. van der Waals also cites (*Prehistoric Disc Wheels in the Netherlands* (Groningen, 1964), 26) plough-marks under a barrow of the single-grave Battle Axe Culture at Aldrupgaarde in Jutland.

88 H. Helbaek, 'Early Crops in Southern England', *P.P.S.*, xviii (1952), 194–233, 204.

89 *Ibid.*, 207. This makes all the more strange Piggott's notion expressed in his Wessex paper (*op.cit.*, 91) 'that the structure of our Bronze Age was built on a Mesolithic rather than a Neolithic foundation'.

90 F. R. Hodson, 'Pottery from Eastbourne, the "Marnians" and the Pre-Roman Iron Age in S. England', *P.P.S.*, xxviii (1962), 140 (see p.147).

91 *Antiquity*, 1959, 170.

92 *Ibid.*, 153.

93 F. R. Hodson, 'Cultural Grouping within the British Pre-Roman Iron Age', *P.P.S.*, xxx (1964), 99.

94 E. M. Jope, *P.P.S.*, xxvii (1961), 320.

95 Hodson, 'Pottery from Eastbourne', 145.

96 *Sussex Arch. Coll.*, LIX (1939), 217.

97 I. M. Stead, *The La Tène Cultures of Eastern Yorkshire* (York, 1965).

98 Ann Birchall, 'The Aylesford-Swarling Culture: The Problem of the Belgae Reconsidered', *P.P.S.*, xxxi (1965), 241.

Acknowledgement: The drawings of Neolithic pottery are taken from quoted sources. In the majority of instances they will be recognized as the work of Professor Stuart Piggott.

CHAPTER 28

STAR CARR: A CASE STUDY IN BIOARCHAEOLOGY

If prehistoric archaeology is to contribute to anthropology as a serious discipline, it can do so only if its practitioners are ready to take account of conceptual as well as technical advances and the sometimes adventitious accumulation of data. The importance of technical developments stemming from empirical observation and of the mere accretion of new facts should not be minimized, and it is of course true that these new facts can and do arise from routine salvage excavations and even from discoveries made by chance in the course of day-to-day economic activities. Yet the progress of prehistoric archaeology as a discipline depends fundamentally on improvements in the quality of the concepts and theories which guide research and mold its interpretations. In this review of excavations undertaken by the Department of Archaeology and Anthropology at Cambridge between 1949 and 1953, the main emphasis will rest on the effect of conceptual advances on the interpretation of data published in *Excavations at Star Carr*.[1]

The author regards himself as having passed through three phases in his study of the Mesolithic settlement of northwestern Europe over a period of some 40 years.

1 *Typological*. The recognition and definition of artifactual assemblages distinct from those ascribed either to the previously defined Paleolithic or Neolithic Stone Ages.
2 *Stratigraphical*. The enlisting of Quaternary research as a means of establishing the age and environmental contexts of such assemblages.
3 *Functional*. The interpretation of assemblages, as thus defined and dated, in terms of the utilization of resources within the constraints imposed by physical environment, technology, and demography.

The opportunity to investigate Star Carr arose at the moment of transition from the second to the third of these phases. The book in which the results were made available, while written with the economic dimension very much in mind, was primarily concerned with presenting an exceptionally well-preserved archaeological and biological assemblage from an unusually well-defined chronological and environmental context. It was also concentrated on the results obtained from one particular site. The present monograph gives me an opportunity to engage in a functional or bioarchaeological interpretation of the data, something that involves looking beyond the actual site of Star Carr.

It will be convenient to divide the monograph into three parts: Part One explains why excavations were undertaken at Star Carr, what objectives were sought, and what human and conceptual resources were available. Part Two takes account of minor revisions and of discoveries in the same field made elsewhere in England and continental Europe since 1953. Part Three attempts to reinterpret Star Carr in the light of bioarchaeological concepts and in so doing to suggest new paths and new goals for research.

PART ONE: OBJECTIVES AND RESOURCES

Success in archaeological research depends on the formulation of significant problems and on the acquisition of the techniques, procedures, and organizations needed to resolve them. Yet success often depends at a crucial stage on opportunity. Where ancient sites are clearly defined by visible monuments it is often possible to set up a controlled experiment and undertake excavations with a clearly defined objective in fair certainty that a definite answer can be obtained. In the case of sites occupied by hunter-fishers there is as a rule no visible indication, unless the people occupied a cave or rock shelter or left behind them a well-defined midden, to show precisely where to dig. The archaeologist may narrow the area of detailed search by assessing the subsistence and conservation potentials of different localities, but in the end he has to depend on stray finds brought to light by cultivation or burrowing animals or exposed by field ditches or other excavations. He may exploit these opportunities himself by diligent search of the most likely localities, but in a country like England with a long tradition of archaeology, local observers and collectors are often the best source of clues. This was the case with discoveries in the Yorkshire Vale of Pickering (see fig. 28.16), of which the site at Star Carr was only the most dramatic example (Moore, 1950). The very possibility of locating and excavating Star Carr was due to the initiative of Mr John Moore, who for years past had systematically collected flint implements in the region. Yet the significance of Mr Moore's finds became apparent only in the light of specialized knowledge and in the context of a well-defined field of research.

A sample of Mr Moore's flints first came to me because the then Curator of the Scarborough Museum realized that they fell within my sphere of special interest at that time. It took only a glance to see that here was a clue to something I had been seeking for many years: that is, a flint industry, analogous to that first recognized by Danish archaeologists at Maglemose, Mullerup, on the island of Zealand, from a British locality offering promise of recovering a settlement site with organic as well as merely lithic data. The typological features of Mr Moore's finds were suggestive, since they confirmed a pattern already well established for the early Postglacial period in many parts of eastern and southern England. Their topographical provenance added greatly to their research potential. The fact that they came from the eastern end of the Vale of Pickering, a territory of alluvial deposits, offered the promise of finding a site favourable to the conservation of organic materials. Such a site would be likely to provide opportunities for discovering traces of an actual settlement, evidence for its date within the early Postglacial sequence, and precise clues to the manner in which the people who made the flint tools utilized their environment and gained a living. The fact that the Vale of Pickering was separated only by the open hilly region called the Yorkshire Wolds from Holderness, famous for having yielded finds of bone spearheads of Maglemosian affinities, only emphasized the possibilities. It was with such thoughts in mind that my first question on establishing contact with Mr Moore was whether he had found antler or bone on any of his sites. On hearing that he had, I lost no time in meeting him. At Star Carr Mr Moore was able to show me decayed antler and bone projecting from the side of a field drain at the same level as his flint industry. The indications were that by excavating on the lakeward side, where the alluvial deposits were likely to be waterlogged, we would find skeletal material in a good state of preservation as well as indications of wood and vegetation. And so it was to prove.

To understand my interest more fully, something more should be said both about the history of research into early Postglacial settlement in England and about my own preoccupations at the time. During the first phase of my interest, marked by the publication of *The Mesolithic Age in Britain* (Clark, 1932),[2] the only data available were typological. Certain flint industries were recognized in Britain that were comparable to some on the European continent. Some of them could be shown on stratigraphical evidence to date from the earlier phases of the Postglacial period before farming economy had spread into this part of the world. My book is now, of course, a fossil. Yet it does serve to illustrate one important truth: data that might be disregarded or even ignored at a more advanced stage of research may at an initial stage provide clues on which insight can operate in a creative way. The evidence available from England consisted basically of flint assemblages and a few isolated artifacts of antler or bone. It had mostly been collected from surface exposures by interested amateurs, and such excavation as had occurred had not as a rule differed markedly in technique from garden digging. There was no evidence of actual settlements as distinct from places where flint had been flaked, no faunal assemblage, no direct dating evidence, and no firsthand study of the history of the environment during the Postglacial period. And yet, in a curious way, as much because of the very defects in the quality of the material treated as by any illumination derived from its typological study, my book did open a new field for research in British prehistory.

The most coherent body of data, derived mainly from the low-lying parts of eastern and southeastern England, comprised on the one hand flint industries and on the other stray finds of antler and bone artifacts, each having affinities with Maglemosian[3] assemblages from northern Europe (Clark, 1936, chs. 3 and 4). These affinities had first been recognized in 1922 in connection with a flint industry at Thatcham in the valley of the Kennet, a tributary of the Thames (Peake and Crawford, 1922). Shortly afterwards barbed bone points found respectively at Skipsea in 1903 and at Hornsea in 1905, both localities in Holderness, Yorkshire, were described (Armstrong, 1923) as Maglemosian in character. The coincidence in time was hardly accidental. Peake, Crawford, and Armstrong were all members of the Prehistoric Society of East Anglia. As such they may be assumed to have read and digested the Presidential Address of 1918, in which a summary account was given (Smith, 1918, pp. 483–4) of the original discoveries made at Maglemose (Sarauw, 1903). Moreover, there had recently appeared an account in French of excavations at another Danish Maglemosian station, that at Svaerdborg (Friis-Johansen, 1918–19). From the references in the accounts of both the Thatcham and the Holderness finds we know that their authors were well aware of the Danish find. The controversy that arose about the Holderness spearheads, a controversy in which expert opinion pronounced in favour of their authenticity,[4] only had the effect of stimulating further interest in seeking traces of Maglemosian culture in England. Thus an analogous flint industry was excavated at Kelling, Norfolk (Sainty, 1924, 1925, 1927), and soon afterwards a Danish archaeologist observed three more unilaterally barbed points in public collections from eastern England, two from the Thames at Battersea and Wandsworth respectively, and one supposedly from the neighbourhood of Royston (Westerby, 1931, pp. 45–6).

These finds were supplemented by flint assemblages in the Maglemosian tradition from many localities in southeast England, notably from the Colne Valley and Hullbridge, Essex; Kimble, Buckinghamshire; Haslemere, Surrey; a number of places in Sussex, including Hassocks, Horsham, Peacehaven, Selmeston, Streat, and West Harting; and in addition from various sites in the Isle of Wight. Finally, there was the exciting discovery of a barbed bone point brought up by the trawler *Colinda* in September 1931 from a depth of 19–20 fathoms between the Leman and Ower Banks some 25 miles from the Norfolk coast (Clark, 1932, Appendix VII; Evans, 1932).

Just as the publication of *The Mesolithic Age in Britain* marked the end of one phase in this branch of study, the 'typological phase', so the recovery from the North Sea bed of a Maglemosian barbed point of deer antler ushered in the second or 'Quaternary research phase', during which the emphasis was to rest on recovering archaeological materials in its geological, botanical, and zoological context. The trawling of the Leman and Ower spearpoint from a depth of around 20 fathoms (120 feet, or about 36.6 metres) was a vivid reminder of the geographical changes that have taken place since early in Postglacial times. Scandinavian geologists and prehistorians had already established that, during an early phase of the Maglemosian settlement,

Jutland, the Danish islands, and southernmost Sweden formed a solid land mass separating the Ancylus Lake, which filled part of the Baltic basin, from the North Sea (Munthe, 1940). By this time also it was known (Reid, 1913) that the southern part of the North Sea supported a vast freshwater fen; and that the shore extended from the region of Yorkshire to that of northern Jutland, indented by the estuaries of great rivers stemming from the present river systems of eastern England and the area between the present-day Maas and Elbe. In such a context it is easy to see why a broad community of culture should have existed during early Postglacial times on either side of what is now the North Sea.

This was one good reason why I decided to study intensively the evidence for early Postglacial human settlement in the West Baltic area (Clark, 1936). Another was that by excavating sites formerly on the shores of lakes and since incorporated in waterlogged alluvial deposits, the archaeologists of this region had succeeded in recovering a broad range of Maglemosian technology in the form of artifacts made from organic materials, as well as significant information about subsistence. A third reason attracting me was that Scandinavian scientists had pioneered the detailed study of environmental change. Among other things they had developed a framework of geochronology by means of varve analysis, a system that made it possible to date stages in the progressive contraction of the Scandinavian ice sheet during the last 12,000 years or so (de Geer, 1910). They had also, as we have seen, worked out results of the sometimes complex interplay of isostatic land movement and eustatic changes in sea level[5] and had reconstructed the geographical evolution of the region during this period. Even more to the point, they had pioneered the technique of pollen analysis,[6] by means of which geographical change and successive periods of human occupation could be tied into a sequence of vegetational history reflecting the progressive warming of the climate during Neothermal times.

This concern with Scandinavian prehistory underscored the value of Quaternary research as a means of establishing a chronological and environmental framework for the study of early Postglacial human settlement, and emphasized the need to pursue this on an interdisciplinary basis. If the situation in England was to be remedied, the obvious course was to take advantage of the location of Cambridge and set about trying to establish the stratigraphic context of successive phases of human settlement in the sequence of alluvial deposits that filled the fenland basin (Skertchley, 1877), the area of marshy lowlands bordering the Wash. Since waterways have always been the key to settlement in the fenland, search was directed to 'roddons' or fossil watercourses in the archaeologically rich area in the southeast between the central drainage system and the chalk zone, overlaid in places by sand, that formed its southeastern margin.[7] Within this zone the most likely sites were hillocks rising above the generally flat surface. It was this fact that led me successively to sand ridges on either side of the Little Ouse roddon at Shippea Hill. The first one chosen, that on Plantation Farm, revealed abundant surface traces of Early Bronze Age material with a small admixture of Mesolithic flints. The first trial cutting undertaken in the summer of 1931 showed that the occupational scatter continued down the slope under an upper layer of peat (Clark, 1933). It was the promise of this peat that led me to the Botany School at Cambridge University and my first meeting with Harry Godwin.

Fortunately I was not the only person to have sought inspiration in the Scandinavian school of Quaternary research. Quite independently Dr and Mrs (later Professor Sir Harry and Lady) Godwin had equipped themselves to study the history of British vegetation (Godwin, 1955) by acquiring the Swedish technique of pollen analysis. The Godwins first became widely known to archaeologists through the classic paper in which they analyzed samples from two places where barbed points of Maglemosian character had been found, the Leman and Ower area of the North Sea bed and the merebed at Skipsea (Godwin, 1933). This demonstrated to British archaeologists the potentialities of pollen analysis for dating prehistoric remains in the context of environmental change. On the other hand, the possibilities arising from intensive investigation of one area through a period of time in conjunction with specialists in other fields were first demonstrated in England by work in the Cambridgeshire fens.

The catalyst that brought together the Botany School and the Department of Archaeology at Cambridge and shortly afterwards the Geography School and the Department of Geology, not to mention individuals and interests from outside, was the investigation at Plantation Farm to which reference has already been made. A combined operation was clearly needed if the best results were to be obtained, not merely at this site but at all the others that would require investigation. In the context of a residential university the easiest way to ensure co-operation was to form a committee large enough to cover a broad range of interests but not so large that it could not dine together. The Fenland Research Committee was accordingly formed on June 7, 1932 (Phillips, 1951) under the firm but genial chairmanship of Sir Albert Seward, the distinguished paleobotanist who held the chair of Botany in the University.

It so happened that several research workers having precisely the right interests were based in Cambridge or its neighbourhood at this time ready to take advantage of the peculiarly favourable circumstances offered by the fens. Because of the low altitude of much of the land between Cambridge and the Wash, the region was particularly sensitive to changes in the relationship of land and sea, changes accurately reflected in the foraminifera preserved in the fenland silts and clays; and it was a fortunate chance that Dr W. A. Macfadyen, who employed foraminifera as zoning fossils during his professional activities as an oil geologist, happened at this time to be attached to the Sedgwick Museum of Geology at Cambridge. Again, there was the coincidence that Gordon Fowler, by nature a highly observant man, happened to be appointed as Transport Manager to the Ely Beet Sugar Factory, a position that gave him a professional interest in waterways and not least in the predrainage waterways plainly visible as meandering silt banks or roddons (Fowler, 1932, 1933, 1934a, 1934b). By a further coincidence two Cambridge geographers happened at that time to be interested in problems for which the fenland offered scope, namely the geomorphologist J. A. Steers (1934, 1946), who had a special interest in problems of silting and coastal formation, and the historical geographer H.C. Darby (1932, 1940, 1952–67), who was then working on the history of the fenland drainage. The waterlogged nature of the fenland deposits, the fact that they included peat beds and 'buried forests,' and the likelihood of being able to relate geographical and archaeological episodes to specific stages in the development of the vegetational sequence, made them particularly suitable for Dr and Mrs Godwin as a field of application for pollen analysis and other paleobotanical means of research. Finally, the publication of Cyril Fox's classic and still unsurpassed essay on the changing pattern of occupation of a region from the introduction of farming down to the Domesday survey (Fox, 1923) had drawn attention to the wealth of the fenland in traces of early settlement and notably to the concentration of Neolithic and Bronze Age finds in the southeast (Clark, 1933, 1935) and of Romano-British settlement on the higher siltlands farther north (Hallam, 1964; Salway, Hallam, and Bromwich, 1970). The message was plain. Here, if anywhere, it should be possible to fix successive phases of early occupation in a succession of deposits capable both of throwing light on the evolution of the environment during Postglacial times and of defining the context of successive phases of human settlement within this period.

There is no need to chronicle the activities of the Fenland Research Committee during its brief life – its main task had been completed by 1936 and it faded out in 1940 with the dispersal of its members on war service – because these have been well described elsewhere (Phillips, 1951). Its importance was less what it did than how it did it. The lesson of studying successive phases of human settlement in relation to changing environment by means of interdisciplinary research was well learned. Its effectiveness was much enhanced by the fact that the wider implications of the fenland programme attracted individuals from outside Cambridge and its area as well as from many departments within the University. Among the younger members of the group were the present holders of the chairs of Archaeology at Oxford and Edinburgh, as well as Cambridge, not to mention successive holders of the chairs of Botany and Geography at Cambridge and the recently retired Archaeology Officer to the Ordnance Survey.

If the Committee itself was a casualty of the war, the continuity of

Quaternary research at Cambridge was maintained in the person of Harry Godwin and his co-workers in the Botany School at Cambridge. It was through the researches of this group that, with the support of the Royal Society, the range of investigation was extended over the British Isles as a whole. Already in 1936 we find Godwin reaching out to the bogs of Cardiganshire. By 1940 he was able to propose a zonation of forest history based on analyses from all over England and Wales (Godwin, 1940), and in his presidential address to the British Ecological Society in 1943 he surveyed the coastal peats of the British Isles and the North Sea area as a whole in relation to changes of land and sea levels (Godwin, 1943, 1945). Not the least of his services was to maintain continuity during the difficult period of the war and so to be in a position to bring up a new generation of young workers with the minimum of delay when peace was restored. Thus it was possible in 1948, with the imaginative support first of the trustees of the Nuffield Foundation and later of the University, to institutionalize the kind of co-operative approach pioneered at Cambridge by the Fenland Research Committee by setting up the University Subdepartment of Quaternary Research, administratively in the Botany School but designed also to serve the needs of the Departments of Archaeology and Anthropology as well as of Geology. The Subdepartment was thus available precisely at the right time to share in the investigation of the region of the Vale of Pickering and of the site of Star Carr in particular. The thread of continuity running from the Fenland Research Committee to the exploration of Star Carr is acknowledged in the Preface to *The History of the British Flora* (Godwin, 1955).

After recalling how his book grew out of the attempt made by himself and his wife 'to apply to the British Isles the technique of pollen analysis then newly worked out in Scandinavia', Godwin went on to refer to the way vegetational change had in the course of his researches 'become securely knit into the general fabric of Quaternary History, through numerous correlations with geological, archaeological and climatic events'. The third paragraph in his Preface may be quoted in full:

Considerable stimulus to such co-ordinated research was given to Cambridge workers by the establishment, under the chairmanship of the late Sir Albert Seward, of the Fenland Research Committee, which ultimately achieved an effective though obviously still incomplete outline of the history of the East Anglian Fenlands from Late-glacial times to the Romano-British period. The constant appeal to geological evidence in this work was repeated in the later Cambridge investigations of the Mesolithic settlement sites in the ancient deposits of Lake Pickering, in east Yorkshire.

No apology is offered for having delved so far back into the antecedents of the Star Carr project, since it would not otherwise have been possible to appreciate fully the strength of my drive to undertake and carry through the excavations or to account for the fact that Cambridge was so well prepared to seize the opportunity and make the most of it within the limits of prevailing concepts. The site at Star Carr in most respects matched the ideal I had set myself as a result both of experiencing the inadequacies of the existing British evidence on the nature of Mesolithic settlement and of being able to examine at first hand material obtained from the bog and mere sites of the West Baltic area. The main objectives were already clearly defined in my imagination years before the site of Star Carr, thanks to Mr Moore, was even discovered. In summary terms one needed:

(a) to establish the precise stratigraphic context of the material in order by pollen analysis and other means to learn something precise about the topographic and vegetational circumstances prevailing at the time;
(b) to uncover the whole extent of the site, determine the nature of the settlement, and establish the likely size of the social unit involved;
(c) to see whether there was any perceptible change in the artifacts recovered from different levels;
(d) to recover as complete a sample as possible, paying special attention to artifacts made from organic substances; and
(e) to discover precisely how the inhabitants utilized their environment, what they ate, and during what season or seasons they were present on the site.

Success depended on three main resources. The least important, though sometimes the most embarrassing, was lack of money. The difficulties facing anyone trying to raise funds for archaeological excavations with nothing more to commend them than the probability of increasing knowledge about an obscure period of the Stone Age were formidable in the England of the immediate post-war years. Sites threatened by destruction were the financial responsibility of the Ancient Monuments Branch. Research excavations were in a different position. Where a prominent monument was concerned, such as a hill fort, public appeals were often effective in providing funds, especially when the site was a feature of a well-loved tract of country. Little was available for investigating a site like Star Carr; and it need hardly be recalled that the British Academy was as yet so far from being able to offer discriminating aid to projects important to scholarship though deficient in popular appeal that its total government grant in 1949 amounted to only £2,500 (Wheeler, 1970, p. 23). The work at Star Carr had therefore to be carried out on a voluntary basis, that is, by institutions and individuals providing facilities and labour without payment. The total funds used amounted to no more than a few hundred pounds for the three seasons together. The money came from three sources: the General Board of the Faculties at Cambridge in return for the training function of the excavation in relation to undergraduate members of the University; a still anonymous donor; and, for the final season, the Prehistoric Society.[8]

Lack of money certainly inhibited the full success of the work. On a site where cuttings filled with water overnight, it was unfortunate that we had to rely on one small gasoline pump and a clumsy hand one; among other things, this prevented us from opening up extensive areas at the same time. It also meant that seasons had to be kept short, and it is very probable that given more leisure for experimentation we might have improved procedures for recovery. A slower tempo might have encouraged a greater use of water as an agent; water jets as these were later employed on the wooden ships investigated in a cofferdam in Roskilde Fjord (Crumlin-Pedersen and Petersen, 1959, 1968) might, for instance, have resulted in the recovery of such soft objects as wooden arrow-shafts.

On the other hand, the very shortage of funds enhanced the quality of co-operation and help afforded by participating institutions and individuals. At the all-important level of practical help the civic authorities at Scarborough gave huts and bedding for student labour and provided planking and other equipment for the excavations. The British Museum of Natural History gave sympathetic help in the identification and conservation of animal materials and, during the third season, provided an Experimental Officer (Mr P. E. Purves) and a vacuum tank for treating animal materials on the site.

Responsibility for the task of excavating and investigating the site rested with the Department of Archaeology and Anthropology and the Subdepartment of Quaternary Research at Cambridge. The active participation of Donald Walker and a number of young helpers ensured that the stratigraphic context of the occupation was correctly fixed and adequate samples were obtained for future analysis.

Hired labour was used only to remove over-burden and to refill. The task of excavating the cultural horizon, which one had to do to a large extent with the bare hands while supported on planks immediately above the occupation level, was carried out entirely by students. This had two advantages over the use of hired labour. It meant that the work was done entirely by intelligent, observant, and dedicated young men and women, nearly all of whom had been taught in the same department and who were fully seized of the unique importance of the site. The physical remoteness of the site and its extreme unattractiveness, compounded by mud, ooze, rising water, and all too attentive clegs (small horseflies), only served to enhance the morale of the party. Under such conditions concentration on the job was the only way out. The second advantage was educational in the true sense of bringing out personal qualities in the context of an exacting discipline. Everyone sharing an experience of this kind identifies to some degree with the total enterprise of archaeology and at the same time gains the kind of self-confidence required of anyone aspiring to an archaeological career.

Over the three-year period we had the help of 25 young archaeologists from the Cambridge department as well as one from London and one from Oxford, not to mention assistance from the Subdepartment. Not all those who came made their careers in archaeology, but it is significant that each of the six who came for all three seasons, as well as five others, in fact did so. Of those who came for three seasons two, John G. Hurst and Michael W. Thompson, joined the Inspectorate for Ancient Monuments for England, and both have continued to combine research and scholarship with their official duties: Hurst pioneered the systematic study of villages deserted during the medieval period, and Thompson, who with Hurst was one of the founders of the Society for Medieval Archaeology, has translated and edited some of the leading works by Soviet archaeologists besides excavating medieval sites on his own account. Two others, Ron M. Butler and Christopher H. Houlder, joined the staffs of the Royal Commissions on Historical Monuments for England and on Ancient Monuments for Wales respectively, and each has made significant contributions to knowledge on his own account, Butler to the study of Roman defensive works and Houlder to the prehistory of Wales and southwest England. Gale Sieveking, after a period of postgraduate work, served as Director of Museums in the Federation of Malaya and undertook important excavations while in that area before returning home to take up an appointment in the British Museum, where he has specialized in Paleolithic archaeology. The last of the six, Mrs Sylvia J. Hallam, after putting in an onerous period of research on the Romans in the fenland which has only recently come to fruition, accompanied her husband to Western Australia, where she has recently been able to resume archaeological activity on the Stone Age cultures of that region. On the others who entered archaeology professionally, John D. Evans turned as a young fellow of Pembroke College, Cambridge, to the prehistory first of the western and then of the central parts of the Mediterranean basin; and, since he succeeded Gordon Childe as Professor of European Archaeology at the London University Institute of Archaeology, he has concentrated on the eastern part of the basin. Another to enter university teaching was Peter Gelling, who joined the Department of Archaeology at Birmingham and whose personal researches have been mainly concerned with Dark Age archaeology. Jack Golson took his first post after graduating in the Department of Anthropology at the University of Auckland and, during his time in New Zealand, gave an immense stimulus to Maori archaeology besides concerning himself with the Pacific area as a whole. When he moved to Australian National University, where he was recently appointed Foundation Professor of Prehistory, the first in Australia and indeed in the Commonwealth, he focussed his interests mainly on the southwest Pacific and on the New Guinea highlands. During his work on the beginnings of horticulture in that region, where he has recovered cultivation plots and implements of tillage under peat, he has worked closely with Donald Walker, who led the Quaternary Research team at the Star Carr excavations. Walker first acquired a taste for work overseas while doing his National Service (after Star Carr) in an Army Operational Research Unit attached to the Geological Survey of the Federation of Malaya.

While in Malaya he contrived to study changes in land and sea levels during the Quaternary and to co-operate with Mrs Gale Sieveking, who as Ann Paull had worked as a first-year archaeologist in the final season at Star Carr, in investigating the Middle Pleistocene lithic industry at Kota Tampan. Finally, Thabit Hassan, who joined us from the London University Institute of Archaeology and entered fully into the excavations, later played a leading part in the archaeology of the Sudan.

One reason for discussing the excavating team in this way has been to emphasize its quality. The other is to point the educational moral that what matters about early field experience is its intensity rather than its specific nature. The sense of sharing in a defined objective in an atmosphere of Quaternary research was a valuable one, but as the record shows the young people who dug at Star Carr have made their careers in a wide range of archaeological specialties and in many different parts of the world.

PART TWO: REVISIONS AND DISCOVERIES SINCE 1953

After an excavation report is finally published, two things are likely to happen: on the one hand, there will be a need for minor revisions and additions; and on the other, confirmation and validation are likely to come from new discoveries which help to secure the ground already won. Since these are all matters of fact rather than of theory and have no significant bearing on the future course of research, they will be dealt with briefly and succinctly.

Canis sp.

The only serious revision on a matter of identification concerns the canid bones from the site, over which Drs Fraser and King had already expressed some degree of uncertainty in one of their interim reports (Clark, 1950, p. 128). These comprised a nearly complete skull of an older animal, whose identification as a wolf (*Canis lupus*) still stands, and parts of the cranium and upper jaw of a younger animal together with parts each of a tibia and femur both chewed by carnivores (Clark, 1950, pp. 71–3), all of which have been the subject of revision by Dr M. Degerbøl. Degerbøl's re-examination (1961), following on the doubts previously expressed by Fraser and King, convinced him that the cranium and jaw fragment belonged in reality to a fairly small domestic dog (*Canis familiaris*), which nevertheless had teeth larger than those of Neolithic dogs; whereas the long bones belonged to a larger variety of dog. As Degerbøl recalled, domestic dogs had long been known from Maglemosian sites in Denmark – among others Mullerup, Svaerdborg, Holmegaard, and Lundby – so that the Star Carr identification merely carried the story back a few hundred years in the context of northwestern Europe.

From a wider point of view, though, the interest of the Star Carr canid material was enhanced by the results of Degerbøl's review of the canid remains from a Natufian B context in the Mugharet el-Wad, Mount Carmel, previously accepted on the authority of Miss Bate as *Canis familiaris* (Garrod and Bate, 1937, pp. 175ff.): in Degerbøl's view it is 'highly uncertain whether the Palestine animal was domesticated. Probably a prehistoric large jackal is represented'. It appeared to Dr Degerbøl therefore that the Star Carr animals were the oldest so far identified as dogs. Further than this, he maintained that since 'the Star Carr dog is a true dog, and not a tamed wolf in the first generation of taming, the domestication must have started much earlier than the date of the site'. This suggested to Degerbøl that, if the appearance of the domestic dog in temperate Europe is to be regarded as in any sense 'a "loan" . . . from agricultural people', the occurrence of this animal in mid-eighth millennium B.C. Yorkshire must argue for an even earlier development of agriculture. On the other hand the Star Carr appearance is equally compatible with the notion that the dog may have been domesticated first in the north temperate zone of Europe or even, as might be thought at least as likely, that it was domesticated more than once over the broad area in which hunter-gatherers occupied the same territories as wolves. This last suggestion finds some confirmation in the occurrence of dogs at the mammoth-hunter station of Mezine in the Ukraine dating from the Late-glacial period (Pidoplichko, 1969, pp. 99 and 162, fig. 33).

Beaver (Castor fiber)

The point made by Fraser and King (Clark, 1950, p. 91) that the beaver remains probably came from a single family hardly suggests that the catching of this animal played more than an ancillary part in the economy of the occupants of Star Carr. The point might all the same have been made that in addition to their valuable pelts beavers are capable of providing useful meat and fat. It is significant that in describing the utilization of beaver by the Rupert House band of Algonkian Indians of Labrador, Rolf Knight (Leeds and Vayda, 1965, p. 35) emphasized that beaver meat might 'provide the main food of the winter camp'.

In view of Tove Hatting's observation (Hatting, 1969) that beaver jaws from Danish Maglemosian sites had in some cases been modified artificially to facilitate hafting so that the incisors could be used more effectively as tools, the beaver jaws from Star Carr were carefully re-examined. It was found that in most instances the lower jaws lacked their coronoid and condylar processes but that there was no sign of the edge trimming visible on Danish examples from Spjellerup and Lundby; nor, again, were the incisors found to show traces of wear. From this it is assumed that the Star Carr fractures were accidental.

New Maglemosian and pre-Maglemosian finds in England

Since the Star Carr excavations were published, three finds of outstanding interest have been made in England.

Thatcham, Berkshire (Wymer, 1962). Renewed and more extensive excavations by Mr John Wymer revealed that a series of sites, each defined by concentrations of worked flints, had existed on the edge of a low gravel terrace bordering a reed swamp at the junction of the Moor Brook and the Kennet River. The excavations confirmed the small size of bands occupying individual sites, and the radiocarbon dates from the heaths and the adjoining swamp, taken together, argued for visits over a period of some centuries. Excavations in the swamp brought to light an interesting though quantitatively inadequate body of faunal remains, and a disappointingly limited range of artifacts made from bone and antler. It is a fair comment that the radiocarbon determinations gave unexpectedly high dates that, where (as in the swamp) the deposits contained pollen, are not easy to reconcile with the zonation in terms of forest history.

Brandesburton and Hornsea, Holderness (Clark and Godwin, 1956). The recovery of six unilaterally barbed bone points and later of another two in the course of working gravel at Brandesburton confirmed the importance of Holderness as a focus of Maglemosian activity; and it is relevant that the find was made in a tunnel valley linking Hornsea with the Hull valley. Examination of the locality failed to produce a single flint flake, and it is likely that the objects were lost in the course of hunting or fishing activities. The technique by which the points were barbed is identical with that exhibited by the original Skipsea and Hornsea specimens, which also agree in being made of bone, probably of elk metapodial. All these specimens, it may be noted, occur within the radius of economic activity of a single site. Although borings were made in the alluvial deposits at Brandesburton and samples were subjected to pollen analysis, no trace was found of any settlement that might be related to the barbed points.

Opportunity was taken at the same time to report the discovery of a barbed point recovered from the foreshore at Hornsea in 1932. The object was found coated with seaweed, and this, as well as its location, is consistent with its having been eroded from a submarine deposit and cast up on shore. Both by being made from antler rather than bone and in the number and fineness of its barbs, the new Hornsea piece differs from the original finds and is closely comparable to the specimen dredged from between the Leman and Ower Banks off the Norfolk coast only a year previously.

Poulton-le-Fylde, near Blackpool, Lancashire (Barnes, Edwards, Hallam, and Stuart, 1971). The recent discovery of an almost complete skeleton of an elk will be discussed further in Part Three. Attention may be directed here to the foreparts of two barbed points found with it and likewise dated by pollen analysis to the Allerød horizon (Zone II). Their main interest in the present context is that they are rather similar to the five slender specimens with very short tangs from Star Carr, categorized as forming Group D. This may be a pointer to the indigenous origin of the tradition manifested in the Star Carr material. In this connection it is significant that the three specimens of Class D points levelled in at Star Carr all belong to the lower horizon; that is, they occurred within six inches (15.2 cm) of the base of the deposit.

Techniques of working antler and bone

The groove and splinter technique. One of the most interesting outcomes of the excavations was the recovery of unusually full information about the manner in which blanks suitable for shaping into barbed points were achieved. In the original monograph it was already recognized that the technique was widespread and of high antiquity among the antler-working hunters of the Late-glacial and early Postglacial periods in western Europe. Certainly the technique was employed among the reindeer hunters of North Germany and France dating from the Late-glacial period. Among red deer hunters its use went back to the Aurignacian in the Dordogne; in Spain it is found in a Magdalenian IV level at Parpalló in Valencia as well as in the Azilian of the Franco-Cantabric region (Clark and Thompson, 1953).

Fresh confirmation that the groove and splinter technique was an integral and continuing element in Upper Paleolithic industries has been provided by studies made by Soviet prehistorians on the fabrication of artifacts from mammoth ivory in south Russia and Siberia. Of special importance in this regard have been the studies made by M. M. Gerasimov and S. A. Semenov. The section entitled 'Longitudinal and Transverse Division of Bone with a Burin' in Semenov's book (Semenov, 1964, pp. 155–8) makes plain the prevalence of the technique in the Soviet Union. Evidently it extended over the whole territory from Spain to Siberia and was one of the major innovations made possible by the development of Mode 4 lithic industries (Clark, 1970, pp. 74–6).

Flaking of bone. Semenov also illustrated (Semenov, 1964, fig. 72) the manner in which the split long bone of a horse had been flaked by percussion by early man in south Russia. This had been done in precisely the same way split metapodial bones and portions of femur of aurochs (*Bos primigenius*) had been worked by the artificers of Star Carr.[9] Quite plainly the technique of flaking was transferred from lithic to bone technology, a transfer very easy to understand under conditions of undifferentiated handwork in which the same worker shaped different materials. Indeed the mere fact of transference of this kind could be used as evidence that this undifferentiated stage of hand labor prevailed at Star Carr.

Stag frontlet masks

One of the novel features of the Star Carr find was a series of stag frontlets with parts of the antlers still in place (fig.28.1). The antlers had been reduced in girth and hollowed with the apparent intention of reducing weight while retaining the profile. The interior of the frontal part of the skull had been shaped in such a way as to reduce the sharp features, and the parietal bones had been perforated. The objects were interpreted as masks and a guess was hazarded that they might equally have been used for stalking and attracting the attention of deer or for ceremonial activities such as dances connected with the increase or well-being of these animals.

The first parallel to appear from northern Europe was found already in 1953 in bridging the river Wuhle near Berlin-Biesdorf (Reinbacher, 1956). The find cannot be precisely dated, but since it occurred in calcareous mud at a depth of 5½ meters under peat, the presumption is that it probably dated from early in the Postglacial period. It consisted of a frontlet of a red deer stag with antlers extending as far as the trez-tines but reduced in girth and hollowed in precisely the same way as the Star Carr specimens. The burrs at

28.1 Star Carr, 1950. The author holding a stag frontlet. Professor V. Gordon Childe wearing his habitual black hat appears on the right. The student leaning forward on the left is John D. Evans, who later succeeded Childe as Professor of Archaeology at the Institute of Archaeology

the base of the antlers had been removed except in front, another characteristic of the Star Carr specimens. The only significant difference was that there were no perforations through the parietal bones, though the sharp features on the inner face of the cranium had been reduced.

A second parallel is provided by the frontlet excavated at the well-known Maglemosian site of Hohen Viecheln near Schwerin in 1961 (Schuldt, 1961, Taf. 56–7). In this case only the stumps of the antlers survived, but the burrs had been removed and it was possible to see that the beams had been reduced in girth and hollowed. The cranium itself was rather closer to the Star Carr than to the Berlin-Biesdorf find, for not only had the inner protuberances been reduced, but also the parietals had been perforated.

When the Star Carr frontlets were published certain parallels were quoted from the ethnographic literature. The present opportunity will be taken to note a particularly interesting one overlooked at the time. Writing of the California Indians, A. L. Kroeber wrote (Kroeber, 1925, p. 817, pl. 8): 'Deer were frequently approached by the hunter covering himself with a deer hide and putting on his own head a stuffed deer head.' But Kroeber made it clear in writing of the Karok and Yurok tribes on the Klamath river, peoples who depended for meat to an important extent on elk and deer, that they used the same gear for ceremonial purposes, more particularly in conjunction with dances held in the autumn to assist the renewal of the seasonal round. A vivid detail noted by Kroeber (1925, p. 103) is that 'When the hunter donned a deer hide and stuffed deer's head . . . he cushioned his hair over the nape and ran several skewers through it.'

Elk mattock-heads

In the original publication (Clark, 1954) a formal distinction was made between two types of mattock-head. In Type 1 the blade was made from the frontal bone of the elk, and in Type 2 the blade was formed of elk antler (Clark, 1954, pp. 157–8). Regarded in functional rather than morphological terms, these two types represent the optimum utilization respectively of elk antlers broken out of the skull of a slain animal and of shed antlers. In the former case it was possible, by cutting and rubbing away the burr at the base of the antler and the attached frontal bone, to obtain a tool with a more effective working edge of bone, whereas in the latter the working edge had to be made by bevelling the base of a shed antler. Elk antler was softer and less effective than bone, but for certain purposes it was presumably effective.

PART THREE: A BIOARCHAEOLOGICAL INTERPRETATION

Of much more general relevance than comparatively minor corrections or additional parallels to the data recovered from Star Carr has been the changing emphasis during the last twenty or thirty years in the way we regard archaeological data. Whereas for generations prehistorians were concerned with establishing the bare chronological and geographical framework of their subject – and plenty remains to be achieved at this level – in recent years there has been an increasing interest in interpreting the data so ordered in terms of human life. In proportion as the prehistory of any region emerges from its preliminary stage of groping, interest focusses on the attempt to extract some meaning from it about human societies.

This can hardly be achieved through the mindless accumulation of data, any more than by merely taking thought. What is required is that both the recovery and the analysis of data be informed and directed by coherent and explicit theory – explicit because it is only when theory is acknowledged that it is likely to be adequately tested. The theoretical objectives of the Star Carr excavations were from the outset recognized to be of two kinds. In current jargon, I had in mind two models, one basically paleontological, the other economic.

The first objective was to recover as complete a sample as possible of the archaeological and biological fossils of a particular phase of prehistoric settlement and at the same time to establish its chronological context in the unfolding history of the early Postglacial environment in northwestern Europe. The second was to discover as much as possible of the way of life of the people who occupied Star Carr at the period in question – in particular, to define the scale of the social unit involved and recover as much information as possible both about the basis of subsistence and about the technology of the inhabitants.

The first objective calls for little comment precisely because it was so adequately realized. One need only recall that the measure of success attained in the face of a chronic shortage of funds was due in the first place to the suitability of the site. This is hardly surprising in view of the fact that it was chosen for the exceptional prospects it offered for the survival of the organic evidence needed to answer the kind of questions we had in mind. Of no less importance were the human resources available in Cambridge at the time, including an excavating team of outstandingly able undergraduate members of the Department of Archaeology and Anthropology and the assistance of skilled scientists from the Subdepartment of Quaternary Research, not to mention generous aid from members of the staff of the British Museum of Natural History. The measure of success attained in meeting our first objective contributed ironically to a shortcoming in the second. So much novel material was brought to light and so many detailed observations were made that there was an overriding call for a prompt and basically descriptive monograph. As it turned out, *Excavations at Star Carr* was written and illustrated within a year and a half of the end of the excavation and published within three years. Quantitatively the accession of new data of a purely archaeological kind was formidable. To quote only one example, Star Carr yielded 193 barbed points made of antler and bone, whereas previously only six specimens were available in all, one each from as many sites. Even more important in many ways was the qualitative advance in our knowledge of the basic artifacts of this phase of settlement. Among entirely new categories were two forms of mattock-head made of elk antler, a remarkable series of frontlet and antler masks of red deer, a series of probable skin-working tools made from femurs and metapodials of aurochs, and a great wealth of debris resulting from the process of working red deer antler. To make all this available to learning involved concentration on the artifacts from a single site, not to mention their illustration often from more than one angle. Again, the faunal assemblage from Star Carr was far and away the largest of any yet obtained from a site of this period in England. And quite apart from its archaeological interest it represented, as F. C. Fraser and J. E. King explained, a substantial addition to the zoological records. For instance, the excavations added records of eleven elk to the eight previously listed from England; and the possibility of measuring a series of antlers and bones from a red deer population dating from the eighth millennium B.C. promised an insight into the size attained by these animals in Britain at that time. Last and far from least, the research carried out by Harry Godwin and Donald Walker on a series of samples from vertical series along traverses across the Vale of Pickering, as well as at Star Carr and neighbouring sites, merited detailed publication. The prime aim of *Excavations at Star Carr* was, with good reason, to record a wealth of new primary evidence about a little known phase of British prehistory.

Perhaps there is no need for me to emphasize that the economic objective was no less in mind, even if it was less completely met; proof of this can be seen in the primacy given in Chapter 1 to the economic implications of the site. If a brief autobiographical reference can be excused in this context, I had been engaged ever since being released from war service in researching the evidence bearing on economic life embedded so to speak adventitiously in the literature of European prehistory; and *Prehistoric Europe: the Economic Basis* (Clark, 1952), in which these researches were summarized and organized into a coherent theme, was in fact written between seasons of excavation at Star Carr. The drive to pursue this kind of research was a revulsion from the narrowly typological and stratigraphical studies in which I had been engaged up to the outbreak of war, a revulsion made easier by the enforced break in my archaeological career. The dichotomy, of which I was so keenly aware, between the ordering of material in typological, temporal, or cultural terms and its interpretation in terms of the lives of the communities responsible for it, is one that has run through prehistoric archaeology ever since Sven Nilsson wrote his *Skandinaviska Nordens Urinvånare* on the Swedish side of the Kattegat (Nilsson, 1838–43) and C. J. Thomsen compiled his epochal guidebook on the Danish (Thomsen, 1836). Yet such was the triumph of museum-oriented archaeology during the closing decades of the nineteenth and opening ones of the twentieth century that the dichotomy was for a time obscured. Its reappearance was due, among other things, to the foundation as recently as 1922 of the Biological-Archaeological Institute of the University of Groningen. Under its founder A. E. van Giffen and his successor H. T. Waterbolk the Institute has been dedicated to the study of human settlement as distinct from the archaeology of selected categories of human artifacts. It has been truly bioarchaeological. Both van Giffen and Waterbolk were biologists by training and initially by profession, but the first came to see that men were more interesting than their dogs, the second that human settlements were of more moment than the pollen grains that helped to throw light on their ecological setting and age. What ultimately fascinated these scientists was not the environment, but the use made of it by man. Van Giffen and Waterbolk were drawn into archaeology by the superior attraction of studying human society. The fact that they became archaeologists underscores the conclusion that bioarchaeology is not, in the final analysis, biological; it is archaeological because it is concerned with communities whose behavioural patterns were conditioned and mediated by and through culture – communities, moreover, whose members subscribed to socially transmitted and consciously held values. From this it follows that models appropriate to biology are insufficiently sophisticated to cope without qualification with all the complexities of human society. As I pointed out in 1939 (Clark, 1939, p. 52) and in more detail in 1953 (Clark, 1953, fig. 6) in proposing overall models (fig. 28.2) for the interpretation of archaeological data in terms of human society, the interrelations even of apparently remote aspects of life are liable to be complex and far-reaching in the case of human communities. This can only mean that elementary models based on only a few variables can hardly in themselves provide answers of more than provisional validity in respect of particular communities.

   Much of the interest of archaeology resides indeed in the appreciation of factors beyond the range of biological explanation. Even at the basic level of subsistence there is no reason to suppose that *Homo economicus*, a species known only to the writers of economics texts, ever huddled in the encampment at Star Carr. Yet if human behaviour, even the behaviour of people at the rather elementary level of technology with which we are here concerned, is to some degree specific to the particular historic communities in which men live, if the diversity of human societies at the same level of technology is the product of choices that may even run counter to the immediate logic of economics, it remains true that the behaviour of human as of other animal groups is subject to environmental constraints and takes advantage of environmental potentialities. These constraints and franchises are capable of definition and in many cases, when quantified, are capable of defining

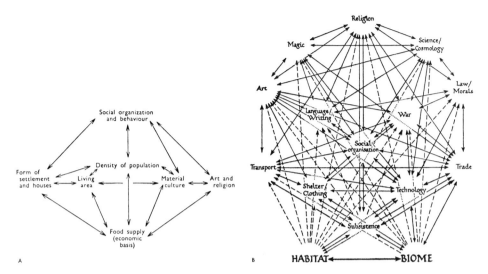

28.2 Models illustrating the interrelations among the economic, social and ideological aspects of human life and physical environment. Model A is taken from the author's *Archaeology and Society*, 1939 edition, and model B from the 1957 edition of the same work

regularities in archaeological phenomena that might otherwise remain undetected. Analysis of the manner in which the communities documented by archaeology appropriated and utilized the resources available to them, although it cannot explain the choices made, at least helps to define the options.

One way of assisting analysis of this kind is to think in terms of a simplified model tailored to the purpose in hand. Provided that the model's limitations are remembered, there can be no grounds for objecting to this procedure. As a tool for investigating Star Carr at its most elementary level as a base from which men obtained the raw materials they required for food, shelter, tools, and weapons, a convenient model may be reduced to three components:

Before such a model can be tested and used, it is first necessary to establish the relevant physical and social contexts.

28.3 Star Carr, 1950. Donald Walker, who later became Foundation Professor of Biogeography at the Australian National University, obtaining pollen samples. Between Walker's boots and the head of Thabit Hassan (later of the Sudan Antiquities Service) is the pointed stump of the felled birch tree lying recumbent in the background

Physical environment

Quite plainly, since any living community exists by manipulating its habitat and the various forms of life that this habitat is capable of supporting, the first task is to discover what these were like at the relevant period. The one certainty in dealing with an area strongly affected by the aftermath of glaciation is that even such controlling factors as sea level, climate, and vegetation will all have undergone more or less radical changes during the last 10,000 years. So far, then, as general environmental conditions are concerned, the first need is to establish the chronological context in the process of environmental change of whatever phase of settlement one is trying to study. This is one reason why one had to tackle Star Carr with a paleontological model in mind and proceed to deploy the resources of Quaternary research. As was emphasized in Part One, the whole enterprise of Star Carr stemmed to a significant degree from an involvement in Quaternary research that began at Cambridge in 1931–2.

The task of the Quaternary Research group at Star Carr was, first, to establish the date of the occupation and, next, to throw light on the

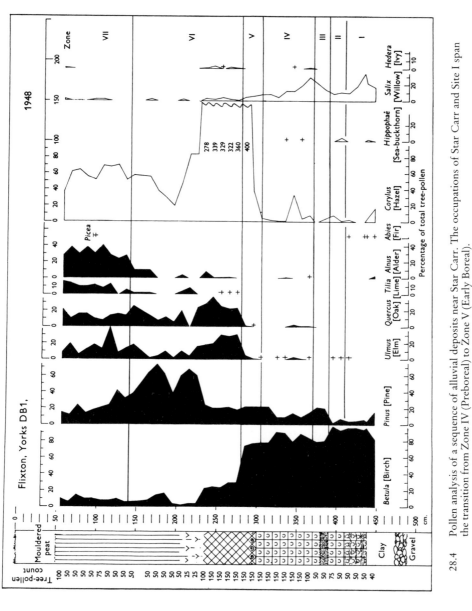

28.4   Pollen analysis of a sequence of alluvial deposits near Star Carr. The occupations of Star Carr and Site I span the transition from Zone IV (Preboreal) to Zone V (Early Boreal).

vegetation prevailing at the time, both on and immediately around the site and on the surrounding territory. Concerning the first part of the task, pollen analysis (fig. 28.3, fig. 28.4) showed that the occupation at Star Carr belonged to the closing phase of Zone IV in the forest history of Britain, equivalent to the late Preboreal climatic phase of the early Postglacial period in temperate Europe. Confirmation of this dating came with W. F. Libby's radiocarbon determination (7538 B.C.±350) based on an average of two samples from the cultural level. A point of further interest to which attention will be directed later is that Godwin and Walker referred the occupation of John Moore's site I, only a short distance away, to the transition from Zone IV to Zone V, that is, to the beginning of the Boreal climatic phase (Clark, 1954, p. 55). The dating of Star Carr in terms of forest history automatically made it possible to relate the site to changes of sea level, since 'moorlog' from about 20 fathoms (36.6 metres) under the North Sea between the Leman and Ower Banks had already been dated to Zone V (Godwin, 1933, pp. 42–3). At the time of Star Carr Britain would still have been joined to the continent (fig. 28.5), a fact which of itself makes it easier to understand the degree of cultural community that existed between sites as widely spaced as Star Carr, Klosterlund in Jutland (Mathiassen, 1937, pp. 132–51), and Henninge Boställe in Scania (Althin, 1954, pp. 143–4). And the greater extent of land especially west of the Pennines, whence it stretched unbroken to the Isle of Man (Movius, 1942, p. 88), is a factor that will need to be taken into account when assessing the territories open to human settlement during the early Postglacial period in northern England.[10]

The pollen dating also has implications for climate. Over northwestern Europe conditions were more continental, with seasons more sharply defined and winters colder, than they are today (Nordhagen, 1933, pp. 172–3). The nature of the vegetation was controlled in part by the climate, but in part also by local topography. Pollen analysis, reflecting as it does a broad zone, though weighted statistically in favour of territory closer at hand, revealed a vegetation dominated by forest trees. Birch was far and away the predominant tree, but pine, though represented macroscopically only by a single piece of bark, accounted for a sufficiently high proportion of the pollen rain to suggest that stands of this tree must have existed not very far away. Relatively high values for willow (up to 33 per cent in relation to the combined total of birch and pine) argue that this shrub flourished on the damp ground not far from the lake. The presence of macroscopic remains of open community plants like *Chenopodium*, *Polygonum*, and *Urtica* evidently reflected the existence of a clearing, hardly surprising in view of the fact that birch trees were felled to help form the platform on which the settlement rested.

Social context

To the pioneers of functional archaeology in Europe – and it was in Europe that the reaction against typological archaeology was most needed and sharpest when it came – to men like Gutmund Hatt,[11] Gerhard Bersu,[12] and P. P. Ephimenko[13] archaeology was basically the archaeology of human settlement, a point of view now more widely shared (for example, Chang, 1968). Settlements by their situation and form mirror the economy of the people who occupied them, in addition to being the primary sources of the biological materials relating to subsistence and of the artifactual traces of industrial activity. No less important, they are a main source of information about the social structure by means of which technology was organized to extract a living from the environment. The excavation of settlements is capable of giving the best insight into the scale of the social groups which form or ought to form the basic units of archaeological study, as well as into demography, hierarchy, and defence; but it is capable of doing these things only if extensive and, ideally, total areas are excavated or at least surveyed.

When excavating settlements of communities based on agriculture, the archaeologist seldom has any serious problem of definition, since he is likely to encounter more or less pronounced architectural features; and where these can be detected by geophysical means it is often possible to economize on actual excavation. As Ephimenko was perhaps the first to demonstrate, there is no need to despair of finding structural features when investigating sites occupied by hunter-fishers. Thanks to his initiative and that of other Soviet prehistorians our knowledge of the domestic structures of Upper and indeed of Middle Paleolithic men (Klein, 1969, fig. 2) is no longer confined to what can be revealed – when this is not destroyed by stratigraphy-oriented excavation – in the deposits accumulated in caves or rock shelters. Even where well-defined traces of structural features are not evident, it is often possible to recover significant indications by area excavation and the meticulous plotting of all introduced materials, whether timber, stone boulders, animal remains, or lithic artifacts and waste. In this respect the excavations at Star Carr set a pattern, even though the physical difficulties, in conjunction with insufficient funds, meant that in general the pinpointing of individual items had to yield to plotting in yard squares. Since Star Carr was published, area excavation has been carried out with particular success in sub-Saharan Africa, notably at Kalambo Falls (Desmond Clark, 1969) and Olduvai Gorge (Leakey, 1967), and information about the social life of man has been pushed far back into prehistory.

In excavating Star Carr the intention was to uncover the entire site. Apart from the northern margin, destroyed when the canalized version of the Hertford river was cut, the whole extent was investigated, although, because of the difficulty of coping with the water with minimal resources, the entire

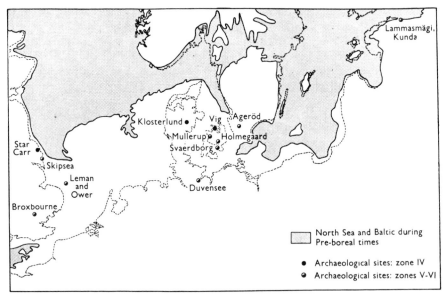

28.5 Britain in relation to the continent of Europe when sea level was 20 fathoms (36.6 m) lower than today. (The site of Hohen Vielchen near Schwerin is situated at the 'n' of Duvensee)

28.6 Star Carr, 1951. The southwest perimeter of the birch platform is visible. Glacial stones and stag antlers can be noted. The head is that of Richard West, later Director of the Subdepartment of Quaternary Research of Cambridge

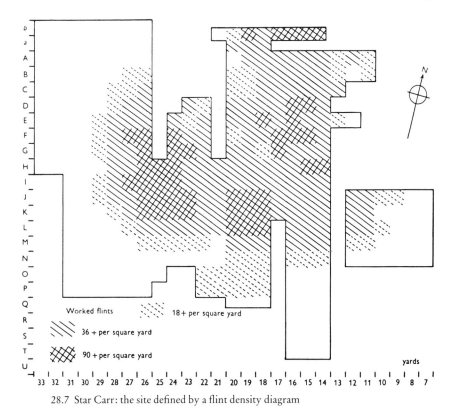

28.7 Star Carr: the site defined by a flint density diagram

occupation surface was never exposed at one time. On the southern water-logged half of the site the structure was well defined as a loose platform of birch brushwood incorporating glacial stones, wads of clay, animal antlers and bones, and flint implements and flaking debris (fig 28.6). On the landward half the brushwood and timber no longer survived, and antler and bone, when present at all, were in a badly decayed state. The only feature common to the occupation area as a whole was the relatively imperishable flint industry, and this was consequently used to establish the dimensions of the site. The wet and sludgy conditions made it impractical to pinpoint every flint, but the careful record of each square yard made it possible to produce an informative density diagram (fig. 28.7). Since the concentration of flint coincided on the southern half with the brushwood platform, the notion of treating it as a valid indicator for the whole site seems reasonable. As the diagram shows, the area of occupation so defined was such that hardly more than four family units can have camped on the site at one time. In other words, the group camping at Star Carr was of the same order of magnitude as the micro-bands encountered by anthropologists among recent hunter-gatherers. In addition, a size of three or four family units is what would be inferred on grounds of scale from rock shelters occupied during prehistoric times, for example, the Mugharet el-Wad, Mount Carmel (Garrod and Bate, 1937, chs. 2 and 3; Garrod, 1957), dating from about the same time as Star Carr.

Although the main point, that of scale, was established, no positive clues were obtained about the nature of the actual shelters that must surely have existed on the platform during the Preboreal winter. The disintegration of the platform in the course of excavation failed to reveal any trace of vertical or oblique posts, although these were specifically looked for. The only supposition one can make is that shelters were made either of skin tents or of bundles of reeds or other perishable vegetable material.

Although the social structure of the people inhabiting Star Carr must have been analogous in level of integration to that of cave and rock shelter dwellers, Star Carr, like other open sites, differs from caves or rock shelters in one important respect. Whereas a well-defined and readily available natural shelter was likely to be chosen as the home base of the same hunting band whenever it was exploiting the resources of that particular region, the selection of a location for camping on open sites was much less influenced by environmental features. Mr John Moore's discovery of a number of sites with an analogous flint industry in the immediate area of Star Carr suggests that there was a wide range of choice in the eastern end of the Vale of Pickering, though significantly, as it will appear, this was exercised only on the northern side that gave access to the North Yorkshire Moors. The fact that, as already pointed out, Site I, the only one other than Star Carr itself to be excavated (Moore, 1950), dated from Zone V in the local forest history reminds us that the territory was a place of resort over some period of time. The fact that Star Carr was only one of several locations used for camping does not mean that it was visited for only one season. It is only to be expected that, other things being equal, certain locations would prove more attractive than others and would thus be occupied on more than one occasion. An obvious method of discovering whether this had in fact happened at Star Carr was to test the stratigraphical context of artifacts peripheral to the platform and incorporated in rapidly formed alluvial deposits. Careful levelling revealed a slight but decisive gap between implements having finely barbed teeth, concentrated in the lower levels, and longer ones having larger, more widely spaced barbs, which occurred invariably at higher levels. This gap between the levels at which the different types of artifacts were located suggested that visits were made to the site on at least two occasions and that these may have been separated by some appreciable interval of time.

Seasonality

The next point to be determined is the time of the year at which the hunting band camped at Star Carr and alternative sites. This question was squarely faced at the time of the original investigation, since it was evident that we had to do with a community of people basically engaged in hunting and gathering. To judge from the ethnographic literature such a community was liable to be peripatetic even though its home base was commonly fixed during a certain season; in the course of the year the group would shift camp in exploiting the resources of what may best be termed its annual territory. Exceptions to this general rule can, of course, be quoted. When adequate and above all reliable sources of food were available all the year round, whether by continuing supply or by storage, it was possible at least for the women and children to occupy the same site the year round. A well-known example from the recent ethnographic past is that of the Indians of the northwest coast of North America (Forde, 1946, pp. 68–106; Drucker, 1965). By exploiting seasonal runs of salmon these people were able to accumulate sufficient food to maintain permanent villages, adorn large, solidly constructed houses with elaborate carvings, and support a colourful social life in which ceremonial destruction of wealth played a conspicuous part. From prehistoric times, an example recently documented by Japanese prehistorians in considerable detail is provided by the coastal settlements of the Jomon stage (Kidder, 1959, ch. 2). Families were able to live in these settlements all the year round thanks to a continuing supply of shellfish backed up by the proceeds of hunting and gathering in the interior, although study of fish bones shows that crews of able-bodied men must have been absent for lengthy periods catching fish on distant feeding grounds. As a general rule, people who depend on catching and gathering normally range over a considerable territory during the course of the year to hunt game, harvest wild plants, and secure other resources as these become available from season to season in different parts of their annual territory.

As Donald Thomson so well showed in respect of the Wik Monkan people of Cape York peninsula (Thomson, 1939), the seasonal movements of such people were far from random, being based on explicit knowledge of tribal lore concerning the breeding and ripening cycles of animals and plants. In order to maximize the intake of food from such resources, it was necessary to vary technology, move the home base, and sometimes even to vary the size of the band at different times of the year. Among the Wik Monkan it was the rainy season that witnessed the most prolonged period of settled life, and at this time of year the people occupied their most elaborate bark shelters. In the temperate zone of Europe one might on *a priori* grounds expect that the winter season would have been the one in which communities sheltered longest at one base; and this expectation would be all the stronger for a period when differences between summer and winter were more pronounced than they are today. Even in today's more equable climate red deer observe a seasonal rhythm at least in northern Britain, a rhythm which in territories with marked differences in level of the terrain takes the form of sheltering on low ground during the winter and moving up to higher ground in the spring to take advantage of vegetation that reaches maturity on higher ground during the summer.

It is one of the virtues of Star Carr that we do not have to rely on *a priori* notions, since water-logged deposits conserved the organic materials that alone permit direct inferences about seasonality. It is worth recalling in the first place that the botanists were impressed by the fact that the *Phragmites* reeds on which the settlement was based apparently survived human occupation; from this they concluded that the site can hardly have been occupied all the year round (Clark, 1954, p. 158). Much the most decisive and revealing evidence on seasonality, though, is that provided by faunal remains and above all by antlers of red deer, roe deer, and elk, discarded on the site, since these underwent in life processes of growth, shedding, and renewal

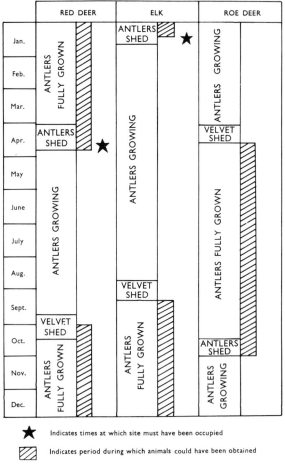

28.8   Indications of seasonality at Star Carr

which, though varying in date somewhat from year to year, were nevertheless keyed into an annual cycle. Fraser and King, who took great trouble with my query over seasonality (Clark, 1954, pp. 93–5), laid considerable emphasis on the fact that the great majority of red deer had been killed while still carrying their antlers, as indicated by the fact that 65 out of 106 antlers had been broken out of skulls and that, as opposed to 21 frontlets prepared as masks and still carrying the stumps of antlers, there were only three stag crania and two frontlets from which antlers had been shed. This fact argued that the main period of settlement coincided with the winter, during which the stags carried their antlers. On the other hand, the strikingly high proportion, two out of five, of shed to unshed antlers can be explained best by supposing that the site was occupied at least into early April, when antlers were normally discarded – the shed antlers were a valuable crop which unless collected fairly soon would be devoured by the stags themselves. Indeed, the presence even of a minority of skulls from which antlers had been shed might well imply that deer were hunted from the site until perhaps as late as the end of April. That the site was occupied during at least part of April is further suggested by the occurrence of substantial numbers of roe deer antlers, since roe deer do not discard their velvet until early in that month. As to when the occupation began there is greater room for speculation. An indication that the hunters were there before early January, when elk normally discard their antlers, is given by the circumstance that nearly half the antlers of this animal recovered from the site were broken out of the skull. A feature remarked by Fraser and King, and one that might at first sight be used to argue against occupation as early as October, since these animals discard their antlers at this time of year, is the total absence of shed roe deer antlers (Clark, 1954, p. 93). But such a conclusion would overlook the fact that the bones of game animals on the Star Carr site had all been brought there by man. The absence of shed roe deer antlers from the site would be significant in relation to seasonality only if it could be assumed that the hunters had some motive for collecting the shed antlers of this animal. In the case of red deer we know that they did have such a motive, since they relied heavily on the antlers of this animal for the material needed for their spearheads, and the utility of an antler for this purpose was not seriously affected by whether the antler was broken out of the skull of a slain animal or collected after shedding. By contrast there is not the slightest evidence that the Star Carr people made any use whatever of roe deer antler, despite the fact that this material is fully capable of serving for the manufacture of weapon heads, as is attested by the harpoon heads from the Kongemose stage in Denmark.[14] If the Star Carr community ignored roe deer antler as an industrial material, there would be no occasion to collect shed antlers of this animal. The absence of shed roe deer antlers, therefore, can hardly affect our diagnosis regarding seasonality.

Plants are another potential source of information on this topic. Yet, in contrast to animal bones, which often reveal traces of butchery, it is rarely possible to be sure that plant remains on archaeological sites, especially on open sites on which plants would have been growing in any case, were gathered for eating, a point which perhaps needs making at a time when notable advances have been made in the process of recovering plant remains from archaeological deposits. If one cannot be sure that plants were brought in or utilized by man, it is evident that these can hardly provide information about seasonality of settlement.

To sum up, analysis of antlers of red deer, elk, and roe deer suggests that Star Carr was occupied before the end of the year and into the following April (fig. 28.8). If, as is argued below, the period of occupation was related to the movement of red deer, it is likely that the site was occupied for around five months in the year.

Site territory

However different some aspects of the physical environment were in late Preboreal and early Boreal times, the topographic situation was the same then as now, with only two significant differences. On account of the lower sea level the coast was from 3.2 km (2 miles) to 6.4 km (4 miles) out from the existing line between Scarborough and Filey, and the territory available within a 10-km radius was commensurately greater. The other notable difference was the existence of the lake on whose northern shore, among other sites, the band camped at Star Carr. The precise extent of this lake as it existed at the time of the occupation has still to be plotted exactly, but on the basis of information obtained from a number of traverses Professor Walker[15] has suggested that it occupied approximately half the area shown as peat-covered in the Geological Survey of 1871, an estimate that would give it an area of approximately 7.25 sq. km (2.8 sq. miles). This lake must have been an attractive site for an encampment in part because of the extra food resources available on its perimeter both for game animals and for men, and in part for facilitating movement within the territory, a point reinforced by the recovery of a wooden paddle from Star Carr (Clark, 1954, p. 168).

It is a matter of some importance that traces of Mesolithic man are restricted to the north of the former lake,[16] since on this side there is a broad tract of territory warmed by the low winter sun and sloping gradually to the North Yorkshire Moors, whereas on the south there is only a narrow strip overshadowed by the steep escarpment of the chalk wolds (fig. 28.9). Again, whereas the chalk escarpment is relatively unbroken, the limestone to the north is penetrated by a series of rivers and streams running down from the Moors to the Vale of Pickering. Star Carr and Site I are situated only a little east of due south of one of the more obvious routes, that afforded by the Forge Valley which carries the Derwent River.

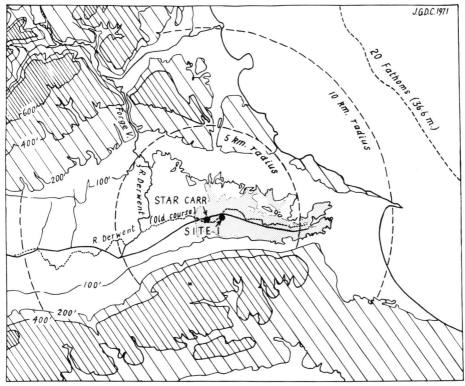

28.9 The situation of Star Carr in the Vale of Pickering between the North Yorkshire Moors and the Yorkshire Wolds. The circles enclose zones within one hour's and two hours' walk of the site; the likely site territory is contained within these circles. The area covered by peat in 1871 is indicated by light stipple. The lake might have occupied about half this area at the time of the occupation of Star Carr, which was situated on its northern margin

In determining the territory utilized from the Star Carr site, two guidelines suggest themselves. First, as has recently been emphasized (Vita-Finzi and Higgs, 1970), when men move on their own feet and have to carry food and other things on their own persons, a narrow limit is set to the radius over which it is practical to range from a fixed base. The second point to remember is that Star Carr was occupied during the winter, that is, at a time of year when herbivorous animals sought shelter on low-lying ground.

In seeking to define relevant parameters, therefore, account will have to be taken of a range for each of these variables. It will be assumed, on the one hand, that food was obtained within a radius of one or two hours' walk, that is, within 5 km (3.1 miles) or 10 km (6.2 miles), and that within these ranges the hunters are likely to have confined themselves to land under 30.5 metres (100 ft) of elevation or at most under 61 metres (200 ft). In calculating land areas further adjustments will be made to take account of topographical features. A deduction is required for the lake that filled part of the eastern end of the Vale of Pickering at the time of the settlement. The area of the lake is taken as 7.25 sq km (2.8 sq. miles). On the other hand, in the case of the broader (10 km) range a further adjustment is needed to account for the loss of land due to the rise of sea level in the North Sea some 20 fathoms (36.6 metres) since Early Boreal times. Allowing for the areas of high ground north and south of Cayton Bay and assuming that these were approximately symmetrical, we arrive at a loss of 23 sq. km below the present 61-metre (200-ft) contour but only 10 sq. km below the present 30.5-metre (100-ft) contour. After making these adjustments we are left with the site-catchment areas for each of the following constraints:

Range	Contour	Area
5 km (3.1 mi)	30.5 m (100 ft)	29 sq. km
5 km (3.1 mi)	61 m (200 ft)	44.8 sq. km
10 km (6.2 mi)	30.5 m (100 ft)	65.2 sq. km
10 km (6.2 mi)	61 m (200 ft)	107.5 sq. km

For what it is worth – and it is well known that hunter-fishers are capable of drawing raw materials of limited bulk from long distances through the network of social obligations linking different groups – almost all the raw materials known to have been used by the inhabitants of Star Carr could have been obtained within an hour's walk of their encampment. Antlers, bones, teeth, sinews, and hides were derived from the animals taken for food. The birch trees cleared to form the platform provided wood, bark, and the resin to be obtained from it, not to mention the tinder obtained by stripping the outer skin of the bracket fungus which adhered to the trunks. Hammerstones and rubbers were made from pebbles available in the local drift. Flint came in part from the same source, but in a tabular form was available in the chalk immediately south of the lake. The Lias pebbles used for beads were available in a local stream. Amber was presumably picked up on the shore, which even then lay only a short distance beyond the 10-km radius. The only substance for which a more distant source has been suggested is iron pyrites, which occurred in small lumps apparently showing signs of wear; presumably they were used for striking a light from flint. Although the Star Carr specimens were said to be available from the local drift, the late Dr Campbell Smith considered (Clark, 1954, p. 168) that they were closest in appearance to those from the Yorkshire Coal Measures, a suggestion that may prove significant.

Food supply

Plants. It is difficult to determine for certain to what extent the inhabitants of Star Carr availed themselves of plant food. On the face of it, it hardly seems likely that a landscape dominated by birch forest would have had much to offer in this respect, especially during the winter months. There is, for instance, no evidence for the local occurrence of hazel, the nuts of which were commonly eaten later in the Boreal period, and this shrub was only sparsely represented even in the pollen rain. What can be said is that several of the plants recovered from the mud containing the archaeological material would have been available at the time of year when the site was occupied in forms in which they are known to have been eaten in later times. These included two marsh community plants, *Phragmites communis* (reeds) and *Menyanthes trifoliata* (bog bean), the dried rhizomes of which are recorded as having been pounded into an edible meal by Swiss peasants as late as the nineteenth century (Brockmann-Jerosch, 1917); these plants could have been available in sufficient quantities to have served at the very least as a reserve of food. A number of open community plants were represented, but all of these were of types that would in any case be expected to have grown in the cleared area immediately around the site; and, as Godwin and Walker pointed out in the original monograph, three of them – *Urtica dioica*, *Stellaria media*, and *Chenopodium* spp. – were particularly fond of nitrogen such as would be generated from the refuse arising from human settlement.

Many of these open community species are known to have been eaten by European peasants (Clark, 1952, pp. 60–1) either in prehistoric or recent times, as is illustrated by table 28.1. Evidence that certain of these plants were being eaten down to modern times in Europe is well attested (Brockmann-Jerosch, 1917; Clark, 1952, pp. 60–1). The decisive evidence for prehistoric times comprises the comminuted residues washed out from the intestines of bog corpses from Tollund and Grauballe in Jutland, dating from the Roman Iron Age. Evidence that these plants were eaten in modern and recent prehistoric times does not, of course, prove that they were gathered for food by the inhabitants of Star Carr – unless there are indications of storage, it is difficult to see how this could be proved for a site without pottery or coprolites. What seems reasonably clear from the botanical evidence is that

Table 28.1.
Open community plants from Star Carr, with occurrences from peasant associations at Sipplingen (Bertsch, 1932), Osterbølle (Hatt, 1938), Tollund (Helbaek, 1950), and Grauballe (Helbaek, 1958)

Star Carr (Mesolithic)	Sipplingen (Late Bronze Age)	Osterbølle	Tollund (Roman Iron Age)	Grauballe	Recent peasant (19th–20th centuries)
Chenopodium album	X	X	X	X	X
Polygonum aviculare		X			X	X sp.
P. persicaria		X	X	X	
Rumex sp.		X	X	X	X
Galeopsis tetrahit	X	X	X	X	
Stellaria media		X	X	X	
Urtica dioica	X				X

the clearing was not extensive. The yield of open community plants can hardly have been appreciable. The only edible plants known to have been available in quantity were the marsh species – reeds and bog bean – mentioned above, a valuable resource if for any reason there was a shortage of meat.

Birds. Fowling can hardly have been more than a marginal activity at Star Carr. Although nine species of birds were represented among the faunal material, seven of them water birds, in no case was more than one individual involved.

Fish. The complete absence both of fish bones and of fish hooks was noted in the original monograph. The frequency with which certain bones and fish scales have been found in a reasonable state of preservation at bog sites elsewhere in northern Europe[17] argues that their absence from Star Carr is no accident, but an indication that fishing played little or no part in the food quest of the inhabitants of Star Carr.

Mammals. Beyond question the main source of food during the time of the Star Carr occupation was meat. Beavers were taken and presumably eaten, but the Star Carr hunters depended first and foremost on hoofed mammals (fig. 28.10). Red deer was by far the most important source of meat, but elk and aurochs contributed significantly to the food supply and roe deer and pig to a lesser degree. In estimating the amount of meat likely to have been available within daily reach of Star Carr it will be convenient to do so in terms of red deer, even if this accounted for only three-fifths of the total supply, since there is no reason to think that the conversion rate from foliage and pasture differed appreciably from one species to another. Many factors have to be taken into account. For example, there is a wide range of variation in the carrying capacity of different territories. In his study of red deer in the Scottish Highlands, Fraser Darling records (Darling, 1969) that some ground carried one deer to 40.5 hectares (100 acres), whereas only 12.1 to 16.2 hectares (30 to 40 acres) were needed to support a deer in other parts of the territory. Fraser Darling's lowest density of one deer per 40.5 hectares has been adopted for table 28.2 and fig. 28.11. In order to be on the conservative side, even though it could be argued that during the winter deer would be likely to crowd as closely for shelter as the exigencies of food would allow, other variables have been incorporated. Allowance has been made for four alternative site territories in terms both of distance from the encampment and of altitude. Again, calculations have been made on the basis of an annual culling rate both of 1/5 and of 1/6. In estimating yields of meat I have followed Dr Fraser's average of 190.5 kg (420 lb) deadweight for a stag, since his estimate was based firmly on metrical analysis of the material from the site (Clark, 1954, pp. 79–86). This suggested that feeding conditions must have been much more favourable than in the Scottish Highlands today. Measurement not merely of antler girths, but also of scapulae, humeri, radii,

Table 28.2.
Yields of meat from four alternative size territories centred on Star Carr at two rates of culling (the table has been prepared on the basis of a density of one red deer per 100 acres with meat at 60 percent of deadweight)

Site territory, sq. km	Population, numbers of deer	Cull, numbers of deer	Deadweight, kg	Meat, kg	Daily supply, kg
29	117.45	1/6: 19.56	3726	2236	6.1
		1/5: 23.49	4475	2685	7.4
44.8	181.44	1/6: 30.24	5761	3457	9.5
		1/5: 36.28	6911	4147	11.4
65.2	264.06	1/6: 44.0	8382	5029	13.8
		1/5: 52.8	10058	6035	16.5
107.5	435.37	1/6: 72.5	13811	8287	22.7
		1/5: 87.0	16574	9944	27.2

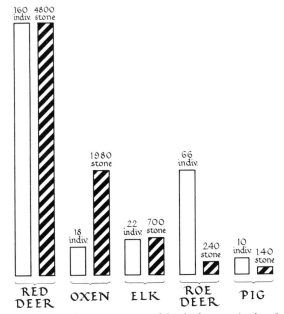

28.10 The relative importance of the chief game animals at Star Carr (1 stone = 14 lb)

metacarpals, metatarsals, and tibiae of mature stags from Star Carr showed that each one of them was larger and many of them were substantially larger than the largest comparable components of a recent British red deer represented in the collections of the British Museum of Natural History. Finally, the assumption is made that the yield of meat was approximately 60 per cent of the deadweight.

In constructing the diagram shown as fig. 28.12 it was assumed that on the average each family unit comprised two adults and three children; that the requirements of a man were 3,000, of a woman 2,400, and of each of three children 2,000 calories – that is, 22,800, 34,200, or 45,600 calories daily for a band of two, three, or four family units; and that these requirements could have been met respectively by 10.9, 16.3, and 21.7 kg of meat.[18] With these assumptions it can be seen that, on a basis of a one-in-five cull, sufficient meat could have been obtained to satisfy the caloric requirements of a band of up to but not more than four primary families by exploiting territory within a two hours' (10 km) radius up to the present 61-metre (200-ft) contour. Various gradations can be noted in the extent of the territory that would have had to be exploited to meet the needs of fewer than four family units. If the micro-band had consisted of two family units, its needs could have been met either by exploiting territory up to the 61-metre contour within one hour's walk (5 km) or, if hunting was confined to levels below 30.5 metres, by taking in a more extensive territory. Provision for a three-unit band could have been made by a modest extension of range provided that hunting was consistently carried out on higher ground up to 61 metres, by a wider extension of range at lower altitudes, or, alternatively and in practice more probably, by local variations of these options according to local conditions. At a culling rate of one in five it would still have been possible for a band of four families to obtain its requirements within a six-mile radius, though in this case most of the territory would have had to be exploited up to near the 61-metre contour.

On the more conservative assumption of a one-in-six cull, a more active exploitation of the site territory would have been necessary. Thus a two-family band would have had to range in places beyond the three-mile

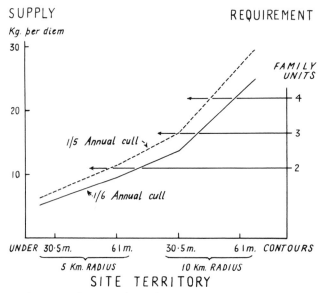

28.11 The potential supply of meat from low altitudes within the site territory of Star Carr in relation to the requirements of two, three, and four families

radius even if hunting up to the 61-metre contour, and a three-family band would have needed to push above the 30.5 metre contour even in the six-mile range. Yet, on the assumption that a certain modicum of food was obtained from plants, especially marsh plants, and from the occasional bird, even a four-family unit could just about have managed by exploiting the whole territory available within a two-hour walk and below the 61-metre contour.

Two broad conclusions seem to emerge from this model. Even on the more conservative assumptions both for the density and the culling rate of deer, there would have been sufficient meat alone for the caloric needs of a three-family unit and very nearly sufficient for a four-family unit. But secondly and no less emphatically, it would not have been possible for a band of more than four family units to have existed by hunting and by gathering a small amount of plant food within an economic range of the home base.

THE ECONOMIC INTERPRETATION OF STAR CARR

If we accept the conclusion that Star Carr was a winter settlement, we still must consider how it fitted into the annual cycle of activity and movement of the people who camped there. This question was not fully faced in the original monograph. It is time to face it now. If, as was shown, some three-fifths of the animal protein was obtained from red deer, we are entitled to look first at the annual movements and social groupings of this key animal. At a time when the northern temperate zone was affected by more pronounced seasonal variations than it is today, red deer and other animals directly dependent on vegetation must have responded to seasonal change by shifting their feeding grounds. In areas with any marked surface relief this would have taken the form of feeding on the highest ground during the summer and sheltering on low ground during the winter. Movement from the low-lying winter yards onto the moors must have been gradual since the vegetation on which the red deer and other mammals depended would have appeared in full abundance first on the lower slopes, reaching maturity on the higher slopes and crests only at the height of the summer. What brought the deer down to shelter was presumably snow or rather the anticipation of snow, at which red deer are particularly adept (Darling, 1969, p. 126). In choosing winter quarters deer have regard to shelter and sunlight. This makes it easy to understand why the Vale of Pickering and especially its northern side should have been chosen by deer coming down from the moors.

Another fact about red deer exceptionally relevant to Star Carr is that when they come down to their winter quarters or 'yards' they do so in segregated groups (Darling, 1969, p. 31), the adult stags separated from the hinds and immature animals. This is highly significant in view of the age and sex composition of the red deer assemblage at Star Carr. A point not emphasized in the original report is the great predominance of adult stags over hinds and young deer. This can only mean that the Star Carr hunters were culling stags during the winter months. This was a sensible thing to do. The long-term interest of the community – and after all it was only communities which served their long-term interest that survived to make archaeology – precluded the slaughter of hinds carrying their young. On the other hand, at this season the stags, concentrated in their 'yards' and for some part of the winter impeded by snowfall, were easier to take than when dispersed over their summer feeding grounds (Hickerson in Leeds and Vayda, 1965, p. 58).

The idea that in addition to hunting aurochs, elk, and roe deer, the inhabitants of Star Carr concentrated on culling red deer stags during the winter was derived from analysis of the animal material from the site. This idea is fully consistent with the evidence of the artifacts and indeed provides a convincing explanation for the pattern of material equipment. As was emphasized in the original monograph, 'Star Carr was a scene of intense activity in the fabrication of the tools and equipment needed in daily life' (Clark, 1954, p. 21). By far the most prominent activity was the preparation and utilization of red deer antler. The significance of this is, of course, that this animal is distinguished, for example, from reindeer, by the fact that only the stags carry antlers. The winter, when red deer stags were culled, would thus have been the season for replenishing stocks of the barbed points needed in hunting. The longish period of settlement on one site was another reason why industrial activities played so prominent a part in the activities of the winter months. This is indicated first and foremost by the utilization of red deer antler. It is worthy of note that an overwhelming proportion of the mature stag antlers, whether shed or broken out of the skull, showed signs of having been subjected to the process by which splinters, defined by deep grooves cut through the hard outer part of the antler, were obtained to form blanks for the spearheads (fig. 28.12). Thus 83 of the 102 stag antlers from the

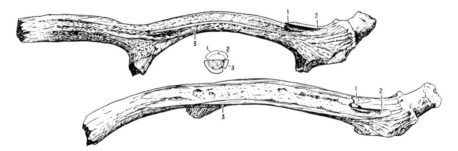

28.12 Antlers from slain red deer stag. The crown and tines have been removed and parallel grooves cut longitudinally through the hard outer wall of the antler beam. Two splinters have already been removed and a third has been partly defined by a groove

site had splinters removed, preparatory cuts had been made in 5 others, and 6 had been carried to the first stage of preparation, the removal of the crown. Conversely, 188 of the 191 barbed points from the site had been cut from stag antler splinters. Although we have no proof either that burins were the only tool employed in this work or that they were not also used for other purposes, there is evidently some degree of correlation between burins and the process of working antler and bone by the groove and splinter technique (Clark and Thompson, 1953). In this case it must be significant that burins

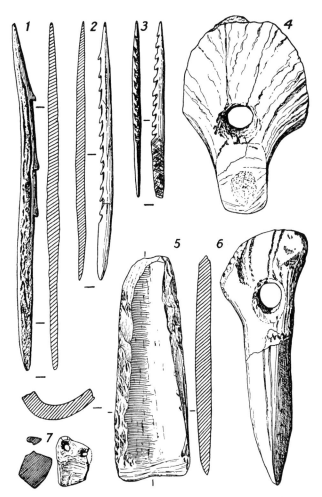

28.13 Antler and bone artifacts from Star Carr (two-thirds actual size): 1 barbed point from upper level; 2–3 barbed points from lower level; 4,6 perforated mattock-heads made respectively from a shed elk antler and from an antler with attached bone from a slain elk; 5 tool made from a portion of aurochs femur with flaked side and polished edge, used probably for leather-working; 7 perforated amber bead

were the single most common form of flint implement showing secondary working from Star Carr. There can be no question that the inhabitants of Star Carr took the opportunity of engaging in intensive industrial activity or that the leading single activity was the manufacture of barbed spearheads (fig. 28.13, 1–3) prepared from the antlers of their leading food animal.

Other indications of industrial activity to be briefly noted include finished forms and by-products of their manufacture made from the antlers and bones of the other two leading food animals, namely the elk and the aurochs. The labour involved in making mattock-heads from elk antlers taken from slain animals is particularly impressive (fig. 28.13, 6; fig. 28.14), but the systematic production of blanks for the manufacture of what were probably skin-working tools from the metapodial bones and humeri of *Bos primigenius* (fig.

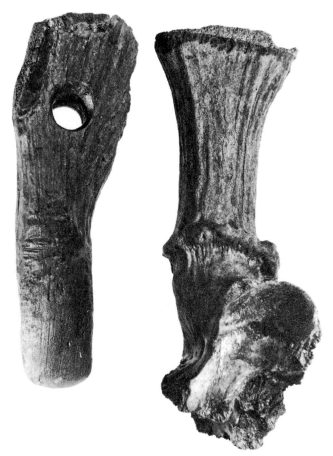

28.14 Illustration of the work involved in shaping a mattock-head from the antler and attached skull bone of a slain elk. The polished blade of the mattock-head is shown on the left. On the right it can be seen that the palmated part of the antler has been removed as an initial stage in the process

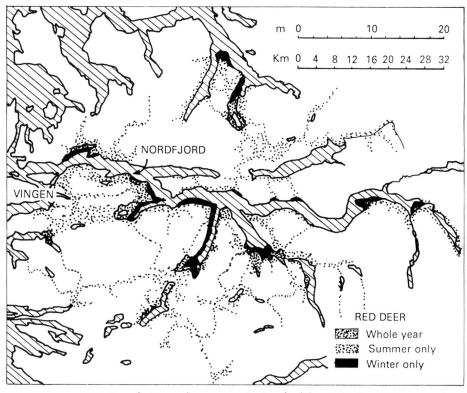

28.15 Map of winter and summer territories of red deer in the Nordfjord region of west Norway (After Ingebrigsten, 1924)

28.13, 5) is also worthy of note. Flint knapping was carried out actively on the site, and analysis of the industry in functional terms suggests that, apart from the adze blades used to clear the site, provide material for the platform, and fabricate wooden artifacts, the component types shaped by secondary flaking were predominantly concerned with hunting, the microliths being used to arm arrows, and with the utilization of animal products. Burins have already been mentioned in connection with the preparation of antler and, to a lesser degree at Star Carr, of bone. Convex scrapers made on flakes, which were hardly less numerous, are commonly accepted as well adapted, among other purposes, to preparing animal skins, along with the bone tools mentioned earlier in this paragraph. Although the biochemical conditions prevailing at Star Carr did not permit the survival of animal hide, there can hardly be any question of the value of clothing in a Preboreal winter, and it is difficult to see what alternative there can have been to animal skins in the cultural context of Star Carr.

Taken as a whole, the artifactual evidence from Star Carr is fully consistent with the conclusion drawn from the animal remains. The site was evidently occupied by a small hunting band which supported itself during the winter by the culling of red deer stags, supplemented by hunting elk, aurochs, and other game, and which took advantage of a period of settled existence to replenish the equipment needed during the course of the year.

Annual territory

What would the annual range of territory have been? One way of approaching this question is to consider the range of annual movement of red deer. Precision in this can hardly be expected, since the distances deer would have found it necessary to move in the course of the year would have been conditioned by several factors each of which was subject to variation in time and space; these factors include, among others, climate, vegetation, and topography. Ingebrigsten's study of the movements of red deer in the Nordfjord regions of southwest Norway is valuable because of its precision. (Ingebrigsten, 1924). It illustrates (fig. 28.15) very clearly the way in which the deer concentrated in low-lying sheltered territories for the winter and spread out over more extensive ones during the warmer seasons when suitable fodder was available on higher ground. However, Ingebrigsten's maps also point to a rather restricted range of movement, of the order of 12, 20, or 36 km in cases where territories are sufficiently distinct for measurement to be possible. In applying these results to Yorkshire it might be argued, on the one hand, that the rugged conditions of Norway necessitated more distant treks in search of food than would have been necessary in our case. On the other hand, it might be argued that the mere fact that the relief of the terrain was more gradual in Yorkshire would have increased the distances over which deer had to move in order to take advantage of the maximum range of altitude. Quite another approach to this problem of annual territory might be to extrapolate from the area of the site territory exploited during the winter – in round figures, 100 sq. km – on the assumption that the microband numbered 20 people. On the assumption that territory was used at the same rate for twelve months as it was for four, this would suggest an annual territory of about 300 sq. km. In terms of local topography and on the assumption that the Star Carr band exploited territory to the north of the Vale of Pickering, this requirement could have been met by taking in the area of limestone moors (part of the North Yorkshire Moors) east of the river Derwent. If, on the other hand, the deer were to take advantage of vegetation growing at the maximum range of altitude, this would have implied more extensive treks up to the Cleveland Hills, suggesting that one might have to think in terms of an annual territory of up to 600 sq. km. When it is recalled that deer occupy contracted territories during the winter, another feature brought out by Ingebrigsten's map, it seems reasonable to think that the wider range is more likely to be correct. On this assumption one might take the whole or greater part of the limestone moors as falling within the annual territory of the hunting band that camped in the eastern part of the Vale of Pickering during the late Preboreal and early Boreal periods. Alternatively, of course, the western and northern parts of the moors may have been exploited during the summer by groups having their winter base in the Vale of York or Teesmouth, where Maglemosian occupation is documented by a flint assemblage collected from the submerged forest at West Hartlepool (Trechmann, 1936).

It remains to ask whether the North Yorkshire Moors (fig. 28.17) have in fact yielded evidence for exploitation by Mesolithic man. Although the evidence leaves much to be desired, the answer must be an emphatic yes. There are no records of scientific excavations, and few of the large numbers of microliths collected from surface exposures can now be related to particular sites. All too many microliths have perished with their former owners, and few have received even the most cursory publication. Nevertheless certain points emerge from the information available. In the first place, the microlithic sites are commonly found on high ground, often on the highest available, such as the main mass of the moors west of the Derwent

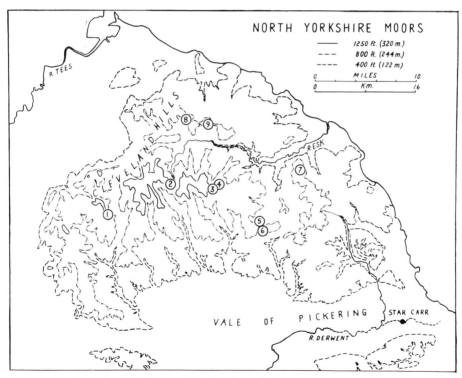

28.16 Contoured map of the North Yorkshire Moors showing microlithic sites: 1 Bilsdale; 2 White Gill, Stony Rigg; 3 Cock Heads; 4 Glaisdale; 5 Mauley Cross, Pickering Moor; 6 Trigger Castle; 7 Sil Howe Bog, Sleights Moor; 8 Brown Hill, Commondale; 9 Siss Cross, Danby Moor

and south of the Esk,[19] as well as the smaller areas to the east[20] and north[21] of these rivers respectively. It is true that upland sites, being more exposed and more subject to erosion, may have been more prone to discovery than the lower slopes, but the essential point remains that the highest parts of the moors must have been exploited by the people who made microliths. The other point is that most of the finds, at least of those known to me, belong to a microlithic industry marked by geometric triangles and rods, resembling the narrow-blade industry of the Pennines rather than the broad-bladed implements found at Star Carr. At the present time it can hardly be taken as established that the moors were exploited by the Star Carr band. On the other hand, if moors were included in the annual territory of one group of Mesolithic hunters, as we know they were in the Pennines, the presumption is that they would also have proved attractive to another.

The Pennines as a summer territory

In his basic study of the Pennine Mesolithic the late Francis Buckley recognized that, in addition to a narrow-blade microlithic industry character-ized by clear, brownish flint, small geometric forms, and narrow rods, there was another with broad blades and microliths of more elementary forms and often larger size, an industry distinguished from the former by the use of gray flint of supposed Lincolnshire or Yorkshire origin (Petch, 1924; Clark, 1932, pp. 21–8). No really convincing evidence was given for supposing the narrow-blade industry to be the earlier, and the indications now are that it was in fact relatively late – assemblages from Glaisdale[22] and from Stump Cross, Grassington (Walker, 1956), have each been referred on the basis of pollen analysis to the early Atlantic period, Zone VIIa. Interest really focuses on the broad-blade industry because, as Radley and Mellars were the first to point out (1964), this is comparable, with certain significant differences, to certain elements in the lithic component of industries of Maglemosian aspect dating from the late Preboreal and Boreal periods, industries of which Star Carr provides an early example. The significance of this fact is far more than merely typological. The occurrence of broad-blade industries at such sites as Warcock Hill (North) and Windy Hill, both at an elevation of about 380 metres (1,250 ft), and at Lominot at 426 metres (1,400 ft) on the very crest of the Pennines, and comprising no more than small round patches correspond-ing to tents or similar flimsy structures, can only suggest hunting activities at the peak of summer when game animals were cropping vegetation at the highest altitudes of their annual territory.

It is all the more interesting that Radley and Mellars should have discovered and excavated a closely similar flint industry at Deepcar with what appears to have been a hut emplacement at an intermediate altitude (152 metres or 500 ft) on a low spur overlooking the confluence of the Don and the Porter Rivers hardly more than 10 km from Sheffield. Having recovered a complete assemblage at Deepcar, Radley and Mellars were able to make a useful comparison with Star Carr (table 28.3). While noting, in support of their general argument, that axes and adzes and sharpening flakes from these occasionally occurred on the highland sites,[23] they nevertheless emphasized that such objects were relatively uncommon on these sites by comparison with lowland sites. Axes and adzes were a rare form at Star Carr, since they accounted for less than one per cent of the finished forms of flint implement. On the other hand, the number of sharpening flakes argues for intensive use of these tools. Evidently the need for forest clearance was greater on the lowland than it was on the highland summer territories. If we continue to interpret the two flint assemblages in functional terms, it is hardly surprising to find microliths strongly represented in both, since hunting was a common requirement at all seasons. Scraping tools on flakes are also well represented in both assemblages. The absence of core scrapers from Deepcar correlates with the comparative rarity of cores; and both are linked with the fact that the flint was obtained from a distance. On the other hand, there was a profound difference in the relative importance of burins. Whereas at Star Carr these are marginally the most numerous class of tool, at Deepcar they are relatively insignificant. This can be expressed in the form of ratios of burins to each of the other two categories. The ratio of burins to scrapers at Star Carr was 1:1.02; at Deepcar, 1:0.19. The ratio of burins to microliths at Star Carr was 1:1.35; at Deepcar, 1:0.10. So far as the Pennine assemblages from the Huddersfield region are concerned, no accurate idea of their composition can be made, but burins, though present, were certainly not important numerically. The significance of this pronounced difference is not cultural; it is economic. Burins played a key role in the technology of Star Carr because the inhabitants concentrated during the winter months on fabricating antler and bone equipment, including barbed bone points, and the

Table 28.3.
Comparison of proportions of different categories of flint artifact from Star Carr and Deepcar, Yorkshire

| | Star Carr | | Deepcar | |
	Percent	Number	Percent	Number
Burins	27.5	334	4.9	7
Scrapers (flake)	26.4	326	26.2	37
Microliths	20.4	248	48.2	68
Scrapers (core)	10.0	122	–	–
Awls on blades	8.8	107	–	–
Miscellaneous	5.8	71	19.8	28
Axes, adzes	0.6	7	0.7?	1?
Totals	100	1,215	100	141
Axe/adze sharpening flakes		26		0

most important material was the stag antler obtained by culling the stags of red deer at this time of year and gathering the crop of shed antlers in the early spring. By the same token, burins played a part of markedly less importance during the late spring, summer, and autumn, during which animals were hunted on higher ground and stags were culled only on a reduced scale and at a time of year when their antlers were only incipient or imperfectly formed. The relative infrequency of burins on upland sites by comparison with Star Carr can thus be explained in seasonal terms.

The fact that the Pennine sites are in a sense complementary to Star Carr does not mean that they were exploited by the same hunting band. The distance as the crow flies is of the order of 80 miles, and it has already been argued that the limestone moors would have afforded an ample annual territory for a group wintering in the Vale of Pickering. It is true that the late Dr Campbell Smith considered that pyrites lumps from Star Carr might have come from the West Riding coal measures, but this is not to imply that they were obtained directly from a distance of 50 miles, any more than the Beer Head flint from Dozmare Pool on Bodmin Moor (Wainwright, 1960, p. 197) was carried a similar distance by the makers of the flint industry concerned. More probably, to judge from present-day primitive people, materials travelled by way of a network of gift interchanges by means of which social obligations were maintained between different groups (Thomson, 1949; Clark, 1965); and in this connection it might seem important to determine objectively the source of the gray flint used at Deepcar and on the Pennine crests.

The location of Deepcar on an eastern spur of the Pennines argues that some at least of those who hunted the upper altitudes wintered somewhere between the Humber and the Trent. On the other hand, there is no reason why some of those who utilized territories reaching up to the crest of the Pennines should not have wintered west of the mountain chain (fig. 28.17). In this connection it has to be remembered that the Morecambe and Cheshire Plains, located west of the Pennines, are only vestiges of a much larger area of low-lying ground which in early Postglacial times extended to the Isle of Man and linked up with the river systems of the southern uplands of Lowland Scotland. Colour is lent to this fact by the recent discovery of an elk skeleton from Poulton-le-Fylde near Blackpool (Barnes, Edwards, Hallam, and Stuart, 1971), a find that links up with discoveries made earlier in the neighbourhood of Peel on the Isle of Man and in the Cree Valley of Wigtownshire (Reynolds, 1933). In 1934 when Reynolds wrote his mono-graph on the elk in Britain, it was still possible to say that, though present in the Cromer Forest Bed, this animal had never been recovered from glacial deposits in this country. However, the new find, like one previously made at Neasham near Darlington (Godwin, 1955, p. 18), shows that it made a tentative reappearance already during the Allerød phase of the Late-glacial

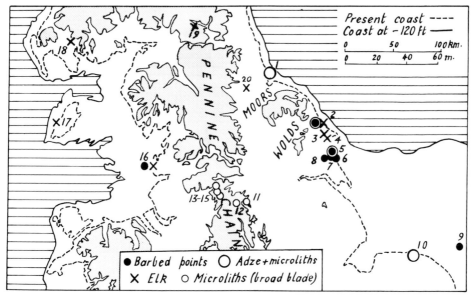

28.17 Map of Northern England and southern Scotland showing Early Mesolithic finds and discoveries of elk; 1 West Hartlepool; 2 Star Carr; 3 Thorpe Hall; 4 Carnaby; 5 Skipsea; 6 Hornsea (foreshore); 7 Hornsea (gasworks); 8 Brandesburton; 9 Leman and Ower Banks; 10 Kelling Heath; 11 Deepcar; 12 Pike Low; 13 Warcock Hill; 14 Lominot; 15 Windy Hill; 16 Poulton-le-Fylde; 17 Peel, Isle of Man; 18 River Cree, Wigtown; 19 Coldingham; 20 Neasham.

period. The distribution of elk finds in England (fig. 28.18), with concentrations in the Thames basin and East Yorkshire, agrees closely with that of early Postglacial settlement or, more accurately, with the low-lying winter sites of this phase of settlement, from which alone, unless in caves, animal material might be expected to survive. What makes the Poulton find unique, apart from its early age, is that the animal had evidently escaped the hunters while carrying in its body parts of two unilaterally barbed points resembling group D of those from Star Carr (Clark, 1954, fig. 54); moreover, examination of the skeleton revealed the existence of lesions resulting from an earlier attack. Although so far unique in this country, the Poulton find is comparable to the discovery of an elk at Taaderup in Denmark with which a unilaterally barbed point may likewise have been associated.[24] A detail of the highest interest is that the Poulton elk was in the process of shedding its antlers, a process that normally takes place early in January. From this it can be inferred that a winter settlement is likely to have existed within 5 or 10 km of the finding-place; there is an even chance that this may be under the Irish Sea, but an equally good one that a site awaits discovery on the Morecambe Plain.

Viewed in these terms the potentialities for research are immense. Wherever areas of high ground exist within range of a low-lying winter settlement,

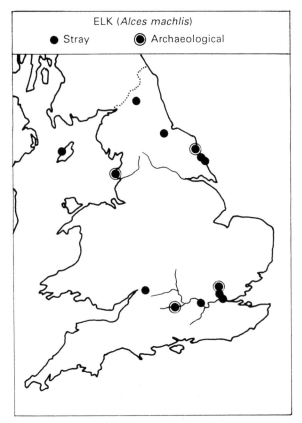

28.18 Finds of elk from Late-glacial and Early Postglacial England. Northern localities
are shown in fig. 28.17. Localities in and around the Thames basin include
Broxbourne, Ponder's End, Walthamstow, and Beckton Station in the Lea Valley;
Staines on the Thames; Thatcham on the Kennet; and Nailsworth in Glouces-
tershire

one may expect to find scattered traces of hunting dating from the warmer
time of the year. Conversely, the recovery of scattered microliths on high
ground should prompt a search for a winter base on low ground within the
annual range. To quote examples from the north of England, discoveries in
the forest bed at West Hartlepool (Trechmann, 1936) may well relate to a
winter site of a band whose annual territory included the eastern flank of the
North Pennines, and the numerous low-lying finds from Holderness (Clark
and Godwin, 1956) could have belonged to bands that hunted during the
summer on the Yorkshire Wolds. Again, in southern England, the bands
whose sites are found in the Colne (Layard, 1927; Clark, 1932, pp. 59–62),
Thames,[25] and Lea Valleys (Warren, Clark, et al., 1934) presumably
exploited the Chilterns[26] and the East Anglian Ridge during the summer; and
others centred on the Solent[27] may have ranged over Salisbury Plain (Higgs,
1959). Conversely, the flint industry studied by Geoffrey Wainwright at

Table 28.4.
The maximum potential population of England during the early Postglacial period according to various assumptions about the annual territory required by each group and the number of people in each group

Annual territories	Units	Total population	
		15 per unit	20 per unit
600 sq. km	220	3300	4400
500 sq. km	263	3945	5260
400 sq. km	329	4935	6560
300 sq. km	440	6600	8800

Dozmare Pool 900 ft above sea level on Bodmin Moor in Cornwall and correctly assigned to the Maglemosian tradition (Wainwright, 1960, pp. 197–9) must be presumed to represent the summer hunting of a band that wintered on the low ground to the north or south, now submerged by the sea.

In the light of what has been inferred about the likely extent of the annual territory of a hunting band on the scale of Star Carr during the early Postglacial period, it may be in order to speculate on the likely size of the population of England at the time. Nothing more can be done than to establish a series of parameters taking account of two main variables, namely the extent of the annual territory of each unit and the number of people in each (table 28.4). As a minimum, it is assumed that the annual territory might be three times the size of the winter territory in which game animals concentrated for shelter. Since animals might well have had to move over more extensive ranges to avail themselves of seasonal harvests of fodder, use has been made of a gradation of territories up to twice the suggested minimum. One way of testing these results is to compare them with population densities in Tasmania, another temperate island inhabited by people at a comparable level of technology. Accepting lower and upper estimates of 2,000 and 5,000 for Tasmania[28] and allowing for the difference in land area, the same density of population would yield from 4,133 to 10,455 inhabitants for England. Reference to table 28.4 and fig. 28.19 suggest that the match is reasonably good, especially for the lower end of the Tasmanian range.

This does not, of course, mean that the population of England at the time of Star Carr necessarily reached even the lower figure, though one might reasonably expect the Tasmanian estimates to provide a useful clue for the peak population of England immediately prior to the introduction of farming. The rapid spread of forest, which accompanied the onset of Postglacial climate, must indeed have been unfavourable to people who lived primarily by hunting hoofed game animals (Clark, 1968). Human settlement would have had to concentrate at this time, so far as lower ground was concerned, along watercourses and lake margins where breaks in the forest

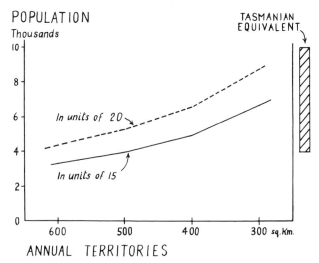

28.19 Diagram illustrating the maximum population in England during Mesolithic times. Among the various assumptions made are a number of estimates for the size of the annual territories

cover presented areas for the game animals to browse and where water plants and moisture-loving shrubs provided extra fodder. It was only as a result of inroads on the forest by felling and above all by fire in the course of driving game that potentialities for human settlement increased. In this connection it is relevant that the massive increase in hazel pollen, which British palynologists are inclined to attribute to the activities of Mesolithic man (Dimbleby, 1961; Smith, 1970), occurred in Zone V, that is, after the phase of settlement represented by Star Carr.

The archaeological evidence suggests that at the transition from Zone IV to Zone V the population of England was not merely very small, but was divided into two geographically distinct groups, one in the north in a region between the Humber and the Tees and extending to the Irish Sea, and the other in the south, concentrated in the Thames basin, a pattern which agrees in an interesting manner with that of finds of elk (fig. 28.19). The existence of these distinct provinces, separated by the Midlands and corresponding perhaps with endogamous groupings, helps to explain the independent courses of development followed during later Mesolithic times in the north and south of England.

Notes

1 The definitive publication covering the seasons 1949–51 appeared in book form (Clark, 1954; reprinted 1971). Interim reports appeared for each of the first two seasons (Clark, 1949, 1950). A brief paper emphasized the range of raw materials utilized (Clark, 1952–3).

2 This book was the outcome of doctoral research carried out under the supervision of Miles C. Burkitt, former pupil of the Abbé Henri Breuil and initiator of courses in prehistory at Cambridge University.

3 Named after the first site recognized in Denmark, Maglemose (*magle*, 'great'; *mose*, 'bog'), a locality at Mullerup, Zealand, excavated in 1900 (Sarauw, 1903).

4 The pronouncement was made when the spearheads were exhibited and described at the meeting of the British Association at Hull in 1922. The committee of experts appointed by the Royal Anthropological Institute based its opinion on the physical condition of the specimens and on detailed comparison with specimens from Kunda, Esthonia, at Cambridge. See *Man*, 1922, No. 75, and 1923, Nos. 31 and 83.

5 Each of these stemmed from fluctuations in the size of ice sheets. The weight of growing ice sheets depressed the earth's crust isostatically and recovery followed when the ice melted. Similarly, since ice sheets could grow only by incorporating water withdrawn from the oceans, periods of glaciation resulted in a eustatic lowering and periods of melting in a eustatic rise of sea levels. In estimating the effect of these processes account has to be taken of the fact that whereas eustatic effects were worldwide, the impact of isostatic change was more local, affecting only areas more or less immediately influenced by glaciation. Again, it is important to remember that, whereas the eustatic effect was immediate, the isostatic one was delayed in action so that, for instance, the land at the head of the Gulf of Bothnia is still gaining on the sea in response to the melting of the Scandinavian ice sheet. Another influence, especially important in territories where mountain building has occurred, is long-term tectonic adjustment that may greatly complicate the task of reconstructing geography from studies based on ancient strandlines.

6 German botanists, notably C. A. Weber and his school, made important contributions, but it was the Swedish state geologist Lennart von Post who first realized the full possibilities of the method and devised the basic diagram showing fluctuations in the proportions of pollen from different trees at successive levels in a vertical section. For a good account see Faegri and Iversen, 1950, pp. 12–14.

7 The true character of the 'roddons' first became fully apparent when modern drainage caused the upper peat to shrink and expose them as meandering banks of silt (Fowler, 1932, 1933, 1934a, 1934b).

8 The support of this society was appropriate since the Prehistoric Society of East Anglia, from which it sprang, had been responsible for publishing the first discoveries of Maglemosian material from England, including the flint site at Thatcham and the barbed points from Holderness and the North Sea.

9 A good parallel may be cited from the Predmost collection in the Moravian Museum at Brno, Czechoslovakia (Mus. No. 71844).

10 After citing submerged estuaries of the Ribble, Mersey, and Dee, as well as submerged forests off the coasts of Wirral and Formby, as evidence for a period of relatively low sea levels in the Irish Sea zone between the Late-glacial and Litorina transgressions, Movius concluded: 'Present evidence therefore makes it appear more than likely that the 20-fathom line represents a safe figure for indicating the amount of the uplift, although according to some authorities the estimate may be too high' (1942, p. 88).

11 While holding the chair of Geography at the University of Copenhagen, Gutmund Hatt carried out a remarkable programme of research on settlements, houses, and associated field systems, which had the effect of putting knowledge of the Danish Iron Age on a completely new footing (Hatt, 1937, 1938, 1949).

12 The excavations at Little Woodbury near Salisbury, England, were undertaken with the stated object of making a functional study of an archaeological site (Bersu, 1940). A large part of the interior of the enclosure revealed by aerial photography was stripped to disclose features of early settlement, notably postholes, pits, ditches, and hollows cut in the solid chalk. The excavator was able to show that the pits, so far from serving as dwellings, were in fact used for storage. The Iron Age farmers were shown to have lived in tall, round houses. Only one of these was occupied at a time, so that the site was a farmstead rather than a village; this made it possible to reinterpret sites previously excavated in their correct social terms (Hawkes, 1947, pp. 36ff.).

13 Although S. N. Zamiatnin was the first to excavate a convincing Paleolithic house, that at Gagarino in the Ukraine, as long ago as 1928, it was P. P. Ephimenko who made the largest contribution to this field of research, even if some of the social inferences he drew from his

plans were sometimes strained (Ephimenko, 1958). Analogous house plans have since been recovered from a number of sites in eastern and central Europe (Klima, 1963).

14 Examples may be quoted from the Kongemose level at Bloksbjerg (Westerby, 1927, fig. 33), from Langø (Broholm, 1928, fig. 19), from Horsens Fjord (Mathiassen, 1948, No. 164), and from a number of other sites.

15 In conversation, Cambridge, April 1971.

16 This information was obtained from Mr John Moore, who made the intensive surface study of the area that resulted in the discovery of Star Carr.

17 Many occurrences of pike (*Esox lucius*) are known (Clark, 1948, Appendix I). Pike are most commonly represented by jaws, vertebrae, or scales, the latter well seen at Holmegaard. Sheatfish (*Silurus glanis*) has been identified from Øgaarde, Holmegaard, and other Danish Maglemosian sites (Degerbøl and Iversen, 1942).

18 The information on which this paragraph is based was kindly supplied by Dr R. D. Keynes, F.R.S.

19 These include sites noted by Frank Elgee (1930, ch. 5), notably Cock Heads (elevation 394 metres, 1,300 ft) between Glaisdale and Rosedale, a site on the watershed between Farndale and Westerdale at over 305 metres (1,000 ft), and two sites between Hawnby and Chopgate, Bilsdale. I am indebted to Mr J. Rutter, Curator of Scarborough Museum, for information about the site at Mauley Cross on Pickering Moor noted by Mrs Gibbs-Smith; the whereabouts of the flints from this site is unknown. See also footnote 22.

20 For example, a site at Sil Howe Bog on Sleights Moor (Elgee, 1930, p. 30).

21 For example, sites at Siss Cross, Danby Moor (elevation 251 metres, 825 ft) and on Brown Hill, Commondale (274 metres, 900 ft).

22 At the instigation of Professor (later Sir) Harry Godwin, Dr David Churchill of the Sub-department of Quaternary Research at Cambridge examined a peat sample from a site on Glaisdale, investigated by Edward Wright and by John Bartlett, Director of the Kingston-upon-Hull Museums, which had yielded geometric microliths. Expressed as percentages of total tree pollen, his results were:

Forest trees		Other vegetation	
Betula	4	*Corylus*	53
Pinus	3	Grasses	9
Ulmus	18	Sedges	37
Quercus	31	Ericoid	1
Tilia	7	*Lonicera*	4
Alnus	37	*Umbelliferae*	3

These results are quoted from a letter from Godwin to me dated November 20, 1964.

23 For example, a complete axe with transversely sharpened edge was found on Ringstone Edge about 8 km (5 miles) northeast of the Windy Hill site on the Pennines west of Huddersfield (Davies and Rankine, 1960, fig. 1), and a sharpening flake was found at Pike Low (Radley and Mellars, 1964, p. 20).

24 Brøndsted, it is true, maintained (1957, pp. 78 and 372. s 81) that the finely barbed point was not certainly associated with the elk skeleton, but gives no reason other than a verbal communication from Dr Troels-Smith that the point was older. In the light of the new find one wonders whether the apparent association at Taaderup was not in fact a true one.

25 The Thames basin has yielded many finds, including stray barbed points from Battersea and Wandsworth (Clark, 1936, fig. 42, nos. 3 and 5), the key sites at Thatcham in the Kennet Valley (Clark, 1932, pp. 65–7; Wymer, 1962), and flint assemblages from Uxbridge in the Colne Valley (Clark, 1932, p. 67) and Broxbourne in the Lea Valley (Warren, Clark, et al., 1934).

26 Suggestive in this respect is the flint industry comprising transversely sharpened axes and adzes, obliquely blunted points, and other forms from Kimble, Buckinghamshire, at an elevation of about 183 metres (600 ft) on the Chilterns (Clark, 1932 pp. 67–8).

27 Among the numerous finds which suggest that important sites of the continental period

may be submerged under the Solent are the quartzite macehead with hourglass perforation, flint flakes, and pointed bone from dock excavations well below modern sea level at Southampton (Godwin, 1940, pp. 303–7; Rankine, 1949, pp. 70–1). It is further suggestive that Mesolithic flint industries, including axe or adze blades and microliths, have been found on the Isle of Wight (Poole, 1936).

28 *Chambers Encyclopaedia*, 1950 edition, vol. XIII, p. 473 b.

References

Althin, C. -A. (1954). *The Chronology of the Stone Age Settlement of Scania*, Vol. 1. Lund: Gleerup.

Armstrong, A. L. (1923). 'The Maglemose Remains of Holderness and their Baltic Counterparts', Proceedings of the Prehistoric Society of East Anglia, 4: 57–70.

Barnes, B., B. J. N. Edwards, J. S. Hallam, and A. J. Stuart (1971). 'The Skeleton of a Late Glacial Elk Associated with Barbed Points from Poulton-le-Fylde, Lancashire', *Nature*, 232: 488–9.

Bersu, G. (1940). 'Excavations at Little Woodbury, Wiltshire: Part I', *Proceedings of the Prehistoric Society*, 6: 30–111.

Bertsch, K. (1932). 'Die Pflanzenreste der Pfahlbauten von Sipplingen und Langenrain im Bodensee', *Bädische Fundberichte*, 2(9).

Brockmann-Jerosch, H. (1917). 'Die ältesten Nutz- und Kulturpflanzen', *Vierteljahrsschrift der Naturforschenden Gesellschaft in Zürich*, 62: 80–102.

Broholm, H. D. (1928). 'Langøfundet', *Aarboger*, 129ff.

Brøndsted, J. (1957). *Danmarks Oldtid*, vol. 1. Copenhagen: Gyldendal.

Chang, K. C., ed. (1968). *Settlement Archaeology*. Palo Alto, Calif: National Press.

Clark, J. Desmond (1969). *Kalambo Falls Prehistoric Site*, vol. 1. Cambridge: Cambridge University Press.

Clark, J. G.D. (1932). *The Mesolithic Age in Britain*. Cambridge: Cambridge University Press.

(1933). 'Report on an Early Bronze Age Site in the Southeastern Fens', *Antiquaries Journal*, 13: 266–96.

(1935). 'Report on Recent Excavations at Peacock's Farm, Shippea Hill, Cambridgeshire', *Antiquaries Journal*, 15: 284–319.

(1936). *The Mesolithic Settlement of Northern Europe*. Cambridge: Cambridge University Press.

(1939). *Archaeology and Society*, 1st ed. London: Methuen.

(1948). 'The Development of Fishing in Prehistoric Europe', *Antiquaries Journal*, 28: 45–85.

(1949). 'A Preliminary Report on Excavations at Star Carr, Seamer, Scarborough, Yorkshire', *Proceedings of the Prehistoric Society*, 15: 52–69.

(1950). 'Preliminary Report on Excavations at Star Carr, Seamer, Scarborough, Yorkshire (Second Season, 1950)', *Proceedings of the Prehistoric Society*, 16: 109–29.

(1952). *Prehistoric Europe: the Economic Basis*. London: Methuen.

1952–3. 'The Mesolithic Hunters of Star Carr', *Transactions of the Lancashire and Cheshire Antiquarian Society*, 63: 183–90.

(1953). 'The Economic Approach to Prehistory', *Proceedings of the British Academy*, 39: 215–38.

(1954). *Excavations at Star Carr, an Early Mesolithic Site at Seamer, near Scarborough, Yorkshire*. (Chapter II by D. Walker and H. Godwin; Chapter III by F. C. Fraser and J.E. King.) Cambridge: Cambridge University Press. Reprinted 1971.

(1965). 'Traffic in Stone Axe and Adze Blades', *Economic History Review*, 18: 1–28.

(1968). 'The Economic Impact of the Change from Late-Glacial to Post-Glacial Conditions in Northern Europe', *Compte rendu VIII, Congress of Anthropological and Ethnological Sciences*, Tokyo, pp. 241–4.

(1970). *Aspects of Prehistory*. Berkeley: University of California Press.

Clark, J. G. D., and H. Godwin (1956). 'A Maglemosian Site at Brandesburton, Holderness, Yorkshire', *Proceedings of the Prehistoric Society*, 22: 6–22.

Clark, J. G. D., and M. W. Thompson (1953). 'The Groove and Splinter Technique of Working Antler in Upper Palaeolithic and Mesolithic Europe', *Proceedings of the Prehistoric Society*, 19: 148–60.

Crumlin-Pedersen, O., and H. B. Petersen (1959). 'The Skuldelev Ships', *Acta Archaeologica*, 29: 161–74.

Darby, H. C. (1932). 'The Human Geography of the Fenland before the Drainage', *Geographical Journal*, 80: 1–16.

(1940). *The Draining of the Fens*. Cambridge: Cambridge University Press. Reprinted 1956.

(1952–67). *The Domesday Geography of England*. Cambridge: Cambridge University Press.

Darling, F. (1969). *A Herd of Red Deer*. Oxford: Oxford University Press.

Davies, J., and W. F. Rankine (1960). 'Mesolithic Flint Axes from the West Riding of Yorkshire', *Yorkshire Archaeological Journal*, 40: 209–14.

de Geer, Baron G. (1910). 'A Geochronology of the Last 12,000 Years', *Compte rendu XI, International Geological Congress*, Stockholm, vol. 1, pp. 241ff.

Degerbøl, M. (1961). 'On a Find of a Preboreal Domestic Dog (*Canis familiaris* L.) from Star Carr, Yorkshire, with Remarks on the Other Mesolithic Dogs', *Proceedings of the Prehistoric Society*, 27: 35–65.

Degerbøl, M., and J. Iversen (1942). 'On the Find of a Sheat-fish (*Silurus glanis*) from the Ancylus Period in Denmark', *Videnskabelige Meddelelser fra Dansk naturhistorisk Forening*, 105: 435–46.

Dimbleby, G. W. (1961). 'The Ancient Forest of Blackamore', *Antiquity*, 35: 123–8.

Drucker, P. (1965). *Cultures of the North Pacific Coast*. San Francisco: Chandler.

Elgee, F. (1930). *Early Man in North-east Yorkshire*. Gloucester: Bellows.

Ephimenko, P. P. (1958). *Kostienki I*. Moscow: Academy of Sciences.

Evans, H. M. (1932). 'Note on the Leman and Ower Harpoon', *Proceedings of the Prehistoric Society of East Anglia*, 7: 131–2.

Faegri, K., and J. Iversen (1950). *Text-book of Modern Pollen Analysis*. Copenhagen: Munksgaard.

Forde, D. (1946). *Habitat, Economy and Society*. London: Methuen.

Fowler, G. (1932). 'Old River-beds in the Fenlands', *Geographical Journal*, 70: 210–12.

(1933). 'Fenland Waterways, Past and Present. South Level District: Part I', *Cambridge Antiquarian Society's Communications*, 33: 108–28.

(1934a). 'Fenland Waterways, Past and Present. South Level District: Part II', *Cambridge Antiquarian Society's Communications*, 34: 17–32.

(1934b). 'The Extinct Waterways of the Fens', *Geographical Journal*, 83: 30–9.

Fox, C. (1923). *Archaeology of the Cambridge Region*. Cambridge: Cambridge University Press. Re-issued 1948.

Friis-Johansen, K. (1918–19). 'Une station du plus ancien âge de la pierre dans la tourbière de Svaerdborg', *Mémoires des Antiquaires du Nord*, pp. 241–359.

Garrod, D. A. E. (1957). 'The Natufian Culture: the Life and Economy of a Mesolithic People in the Near East', *Proceedings of the British Academy*, 43: 211ff.

Garrod, D. A. E., and D. M. A. Bate (1937). *The Stone Age of Mount Carmel*, vol. 1. Cambridge: Cambridge University Press.

Godwin, H. (1933). 'British Maglemose Harpoon Sites', *Antiquity*, 7: 36–48.

(1940). 'Pollen Analysis and Forest History of England and Wales', *The New Phytologist*, 39: 370–400.

(1943). 'Coastal Peat Beds of the British Isles and North Sea', *Journal of Ecology*, 31: 199–247.

(1945). 'Coastal Peat-Beds of the North Sea Region, as Indices of Land- and Sea-Level Changes', *The New Phytologist*, 44: 29–69.

(1955). *The History of the British Flora*. Cambridge: Cambridge University Press.

Hallam, S. J. (1964). 'Villages in Roman Britain: Some Evidence', *Antiquaries Journal*, 44: 19–32.

Hatt, G. (1937). *Landbrug i Danmarks Oldtid*. Copenhagen: Folkeoplysnings Fremme.

(1938). 'Jernalders Bopladser i Himmerland', *Aarbøger*, 119–266.

(1949). 'Oldtidsagre', Kongelige Danske Videnskabernes Selskabs Arkaeologisk-Kunsthistoriske Skrifter, 2(1).

Hatting, T. (1969). 'Er Baeverens Taender Benyttet som Redskabet in Stenalderen i Danmark?' *Aarbøger*, 116–26.

Hawkes, C. F. C. (1947). 'Britons, Romans and Saxons round Salisbury and in Cranbourne Chase', *Archaeological Journal*, 104: 27–81.

Helbaek, H. (1950). 'Tollundmandens Sidste Måltid', *Aarbøger*, 311–41.

(1958). 'Grauballemandens Sidste Måltid', *Kuml*, 83–116.

Higgs, E. (1959). 'Excavations at a Mesolithic Site at Downton, near Salisbury, Wiltshire', *Proceedings of the Prehistory Society*, 25: 209–32.

Ingebrigsten, O. (1924). *Hjortens Utbredelse i Norge*. Bergen: Naturvidenskabelige rekke No. 6. (First appeared in Bergens Museums Aarbok 1922–3.)

Kidder, E. J. (1959). *Japan*. London: Thames and Hudson. ('Ancient Peoples and Places' Series.)

Klein, R. (1969). 'The Mousterian of European Russia', *Proceedings of the Prehistoric Society*, 35: 77–111.

Klima, B. (1963). *Dolni Veštonice*. Prague: Czechoslovak Academy.

Kroeber, A. L. (1925). *Handbook of the Indians of California*. Washington, D.C.: Smithsonian Institution Bureau of Ethnology, Bulletin 78.

Layard, N. F. (1927). 'A Late Palaeolithic Settlement in the Colne Valley, Essex', *Antiquaries Journal*, 7: 500–14.

Leakey, M. D. (1967). 'Preliminary Consideration of the Cultural Material from Beds I and II, Olduvai Gorge, Tanzania', in W. W. Bishop and J. Desmond Clark, eds., *Background to Evolution in Africa*, Chicago: University of Chicago Press, pp. 417–46.

Leeds, A., and A. P. Vayda, eds. (1965). *Man, Culture, and Animals*. Washington, D.C.: American Association for the Advancement of Science.

Madsen, A. P., *et al.* (1900). *Affaldsdynger fra Stenalderen i Danmark*. Copenhagen: National Museum.

Mathiassen, T. (1937). 'Gudenaa-kulturen. En Mesolitisk Inlandsbebyggelse i Jylland', *Aarbøger*, 1–186.

(1948). *Danske Oldsager. I: Aeldre Stenalder*. Copenhagen: National Museum.

Moore, J. (1950). 'Mesolithic Sites in the Neighbourhood of Flixton, North-east Yorkshire', *Proceedings of the Prehistoric Society*, 16: 87–100.

Movius, H. J. (1942). *The Irish Stone Age: its Chronology, Development and Relationships*. Cambridge: Cambridge University Press.

Munthe, H. (1940). 'Om Nordens framst Baltikums, Senkvartära Utveckling och Stenaldersbebyggelse', *Kungliga Svenska Vetenskapsakademiens Handlingar*, 19 (Ser. III), No.1.

Nilsson, S. (1838–43). *Skandinaviska Nordens Urinvånare*. Lund: Gleerup.

Nordhagen, R. (1933). *De Senkvartaere Klimavekslinger i Nordeuropa og deres Betydning for Kulturforskningen*. Oslo: Aschehoug.

Peake, H. J. E., and O. G. S. Crawford (1922). 'A Flint Factory at Thatcham, Berks.', *Proceedings of the Prehistoric Society of East Anglia*, 3: 499–514.

Petch, J. A. (1924). *Early Man in the District of Huddersfield*. Huddersfield: Tolson Memorial Museum.

Phillips, C. W. (1951). 'The Fenland Research Committee, its Past Achievements and Future Prospects', in W. F. Grimes, ed., *Aspects of Archaeology in Britain and Beyond*, London: Edwards, pp. 258–73.

Pidoplichko, I. G. (1969). *Late Palaeolithic Dwellings of Mammoth Bones in the Ukraine*. Kiev: Institute of Zoology, Ukrainian Academy of Sciences.

Poole, H. F. (1936). 'An Outline of the Mesolithic Flint Cultures of the Isle of Wight', *Proceedings of the Isle of Wight Natural History and Archaeological Society*, pp. 551–81.

Radley, J., and P. Mellars (1964). 'A Mesolithic Structure at Deepcar, Yorkshire, England, and the Affinities of its Associated Flint Industries', *Proceedings of the Prehistoric Society*, 30: 1–24.

Rankine, W. F. (1949). 'Stone "Maceheads" with Mesolithic Associations from South-eastern England', *Proceedings of the Prehistoric Society*, 15: 70–6.

Reid, C. (1913). *Submerged Forests*. Cambridge: Cambridge University Press.

Reinbacher, E. (1956). 'Eine vorgeschichtliche Hirschmaske aus Berlin-Biesdorf', *Ausgrabungen und Funde (Berlin)*, 1: 147ff.

Reynolds, S. H. (1933). *A Monograph on the British Pleistocene Mammalia*. Alces (Supplement). London: Palaeontographical Society.

Sainty, J. E. (1924, 1925, 1927). 'A Flaking Site on Kelling Heath, Norfolk', *Proceedings of the Prehistoric Society of East Anglia*, 4: 165–75; 5: 56–61; 7: 283–7.

Salway, P., S. J. Hallam, and J. l'A. Bromwich (1970). *The Fenland in Roman Times*. London: Royal Geographical Society Research Series, No.5.

Sarauw, G. F. L.(1903). 'En Stenalders Boplads i Maglemose ved Mullerup, Sammenholdt med Beslaegtede Fund', *Aarbøger*, 148–315.

Schuldt, E. (1961). *Hohen Viecheln: ein mittelsteinzeitlicher Wohnplatz in Mecklenburg*. Berlin: Deutsche Akademie der Wissenschaft. Schriften der Section für Vor- und Frühgeschichte, 10.

Semenov, S. A. (1964). *Prehistoric Technology* (transl. M. W. Thompson). New York: Barnes and Noble.

Skertchley, S. B. J. (1977). *The Geology of the Fenland*. London: *Geological Memoir*.

Smith, A. G. (1970). 'The Influence of Mesolithic and Neolithic Man on British Vegetation: a Discussion', in D. Walker and R. G. West, eds., *Studies in the Vegetational History of the British Isles*, Cambridge: Cambridge University Press, pp. 81–96.

Smith, R.A. (1918). 'Our Neighbours in the Neolithic Period', *Proceedings of the Prehistoric Society of East Anglia*, 2: 479–507.

Steers, J.A., ed. (1934). *Scolt Head Island*. Cambridge: Heffer.

—— (1946). *The Coastline of England and Wales*. Cambridge: Cambridge University Press.

Thomsen, C.J. (1836). *Ledetraad til Nordisk Oldkyndighed*. Copenhagen: National Museum.

Thomson, D. (1939). 'The Seasonal Factor in Human Culture', *Proceedings of the Prehistoric Society*, 5: 209–21.

—— (1949). *Economic Structure and the Ceremonial Exchange Cycle in Arnhem Land*. Melbourne: Macmillan.

Trechmann, C. T. (1936). 'Mesolithic Flints from the Submerged Forest at West Hartlepool', *Proceedings of the Prehistoric Society*, 2: 161–8.

Vita-Finzi, C., and E. S. Higgs (1970). 'Prehistoric Economy in the Mount Carmel Area of Palestine: Site Catchment Analysis', *Proceedings of the Prehistoric Society*, 36: 1–37.

Wainwright, G. J. (1960). 'Three Microlithic Industries from South-west England and their Affinities', *Proceedings of the Prehistoric Society*, 26: 193–201.

Walker, D. (1956). 'A Site at Stump Cross, near Grassington, Yorkshire, and the Age of the Pennine Microlithic Industry', *Proceedings of the Prehistoric Society*, 22: 23–8.

Warren, S. H., J. G. D. Clark, *et al.* (1934). 'An Early Mesolithic Site at Broxbourne Sealed under Boreal Peat', *Journal of the Royal Anthropological Institute*, 64: 101–28.

Westerby, E. (1927). *Stenalderbopladser ved Klampenborg*. Copenhagen: Reitzels.

Westerby, E. (1931). 'Den Mesolitiske Tid i Norden', *Ymer*, 41–59.

Wheeler, R. E. M. (1970). *The British Academy 1949–68*. Oxford: Oxford University Press.

Wymer, J. (1962). 'Excavations at the Maglemosian Sites at Thatcham, Berkshire, England', *Proceedings of the Prehistoric Society*, 28: 329–61.

CHAPTER 29

PREHISTORIC EUROPE:
THE ECONOMIC BASIS

INTRODUCTION

In a field as inherently difficult as Prehistoric archaeology, in which we seek to recover the history of preliterate societies, a terrain with few signposts and almost limitless horizons, it is important at all times to know precisely where we stand and how we have come to be where we are. The history of research is a history of false trails as well as breakthroughs into new territory and it is important for the individual explorer not only to chart his own course but to be aware of the explorations of others. Only in this way is it possible to draw the maximum profit from the experiences, adverse or favourable, of the totality of competing, but also in a larger sense co-operating, individuals working in any particular field of archaeology. And it need hardly be added that experiences in one field may often be found to apply with varying degrees of qualification to cognate or even quite remote fields of archaeology. There is room, therefore, for a more technical kind of historical dialogue in the field of archaeological research than is commonly found in the literature. The history of archaeology in relation to other fields of inquiry and to the general movement of ideas need not be and indeed rarely is written by scholars dedicated to fundamental research in any particular branch. As the subject grows in maturity, on the other hand, a new need has become apparent, the need for a more technical assessment of the process of research in particular fields. Such treatment of particular aspects of archaeology, if successfully accomplished, ought to make us more effective because more consciously orientated towards purposeful goals.

The authors best qualified for the historical appraisal of particular fields are probably those who have held to a particular line and have made their position clear in a series of publications over a period sufficiently long to have witnessed basic changes in the course of archaeology. In my particular case I have been asked to explain why and how I came to write *Prehistoric Europe: the economic basis* and how the approach and concept embodied in it have contributed to and been modified by the onward progress of research. The first part of this assignment is the easier and the one the author is best qualified to discuss, and for that reason the one to which my attention will be directed.

A book is often said to be the child of its author. In reality the relationship is much closer. A parent contributes genes to his offspring, but the outcome is the product of a genetic mixture of overwhelming complexity extending backwards to countless generations. An author, on the other hand, at least has the illusion of being more in control of his product. Yet the words he inscribes on blank pages, though they are his and his alone, embody thoughts which, whatever the individual twist, derive to a greater extent than he can probably bring himself to admit from his social environment and his own historical context in the evolution of that environment. The fact remains that an author is an individual and a book the expression of an individual's point of view at a particular juncture of time under specific circumstances. It would be as false to pretend to a god-like independence of milieu as it would be to suggest that books emerge apart from their authors in response to influences or movements in the realm of ideas. A factual account of how I came to write my book is bound nevertheless to be autobiographical or a piece of pretentious humbug. Since authors stand in as much need of self-deception as the next man – and probably a good deal more so – it is well to recognize the dangers of reminiscence. The only objective manner of avoiding or at least of reducing the benefit of hindsight is to quote from books and articles written by myself and published at successive dates before 1952. By the same token, changes in my own way of looking at things at least can be documented from publications published since or in press.

The careers of most academics necessarily begin with a period of more or less intense specialization. The ever-increasing degree of specialization and the growing volume of publication necessitates choosing a restricted topic if worthwhile results are to be achieved within a prescribed period. In winning their doctorates, candidates are found to cut deep grooves as they penetrate the outer layers of academically approved doctrine and seek to explore some aspect of inner reality. The danger is that having succeeded, they fail to extract themselves from the grooves of their own creation. One reason for this is that they are too often unconscious of being walled in.

MESOLITHIC RESEARCH IN THE EAST ANGLIAN FENS

Before describing how I personally succeeded in discarding my Ph.D. shield, perhaps a word should be said about how I came to acquire it. The subject of my initial research – Mesolithic Britain – was suggested by my teacher Miles Burkitt in the Department of Archaeology and Anthropology at Cambridge. In those days at Cambridge, Miles was required to cover the whole field of prehistory up to the time when metallurgy was established. In attempting this he was made keenly aware of the fault or gap between the Old Stone Age

(Paleolithic) and the New (Neolithic), something thrown into strong relief by the different training and objectives of those primarily engaged in one or the other. Because he had to teach both he was all the keener to try to restore or discover the continuity of prehistory. To this end he undertook surveys of the data recovered since the beginning of the century on the European continent, which appeared to be of intermediate age and to date from the earlier part of Post-glacial times. One reason why he put me on to the task of investigating the evidence for a Mesolithic phase in Britain was that the most common clues would lie in the most durable residue, namely flint industries. As an undergraduate I had already been a passionate connoisseur for more than a decade, a result, perhaps, of having attended boarding schools from the age of seven, each of them situated on chalk downs (Sussex and Wiltshire), which were rich in flint industries.

My first task was a typological one. I had to comb through collections of flints, mostly collected by amateurs from the surface, to seek for parallels with Mesolithic material from Continental Europe. Other than this collection of Mesolithic material there were a small number of lithic assemblages obtained in the course of limited and not very sophisticated excavations and a few stray finds of antler and bone artifacts. It was on the slender basis of mere typological analogy, lacking stratigraphical or any other kind of dating that I presented the case for a Mesolithic phase of settlement in Britain (1933) and in particular for the presence in eastern England of flint industries and barbed antler and bone points resembling those excavated in Denmark and known as 'Maglemosian'. The comparative abundance of the material presented gave some ground for confidence but I was only too keenly aware of the need for an adequate chronological frame of reference.

The introduction of the technique of pollen analysis to Britain by Dr and Mrs Harry Godwin was to provide the best means for testing my hypothesis. By one of those contingencies which so often affect the course of research, a barbed point of 'Maglemosian' type was dredged from the bed of the North Sea between the Leman and Ower Banks by the trawler *Colinda* in September 1931. This discovery was just in time to be included in an appendix to my first book and, what is more important, occurred precisely at the moment when the Godwins were ready to apply their new technique. The new find, although differing in detail from those already known from Holderness, Yorkshire, and from the Thames Valley, strongly reinforced the notion that the Maglemosian culture extended across the North Sea at a time when the southern part of the sea was a vast freshwater fen. In their classic paper of 1933 (Godwin 1933:36–48), the Godwins were able to show that the North Sea specimen and that from Skipsea, Holderness, belonged to an early and late phase of the Boreal period, respectively; that is, that they were chronologically comparable with Maglemosian finds in Denmark. The analyses also gave some insight into the type of forest vegetation prevailing during the period when Britain formed an integral part of the North European Plain.

Godwin and I – he was already an established lecturer in the Department of Botany and I was still a research student in Archaeology and Anthropology – first came into contact through a common interest in the Fenland. This was the nearest point to Cambridge where a well-developed sequence of Post-glacial deposits of a kind likely to produce archaeological specimens in deposits containing identifiable pollen was known to exist. Cyril Fox (1923) had shown nearly ten years previously how Neolithic, and to a lesser extent Bronze Age finds, thickly clustered on the sandy Breckland, extended into the peat zone of the southeast Fenland. There seemed every hope that the area round Shippea Hill would provide opportunities for locating archaeological material from these periods in deposits capable of investigation by pollen analysis. Even more to the point, so far as I was concerned the Breckland contained in the Wangford-Lakenheath dune area a classic site for Mesolithic flints. There was a prospect that traces of this phase of settlement might also be located in the Fen sequence. A good deal was known about the Post-glacial stratigraphy of the Fenland thanks to the opportunities provided by the extensive cuts needed to maintain effective drainage. Skertchley's geological memoir showed that in the south eastern part of the basin including the Shippea Hill area, two major peat layers were commonly separated by a thick deposit of clay. The problem was how to establish the context of successive phases of human settlement to this well-defined stratigraphy. Since settlement in the Fenland has always been closely linked to waterways, an obvious lead was to follow the extinct course of the Little Ouse, which traversed the Shippea Hill Fens in the form of a low silt bank or 'rodden'. The decisive clue came with the discovery of a mixed assemblage of flints on the surface of sand ridges on either side of the former channel of the Little Ouse on Plantation and Peacock's Farms, Shippea Hill. The first find was made in 1931. The Fenland Research Committee was formed in 1932 under the Chairmanship of the distinguished paleo-botanist Sir Albert Seward, who then held the Chair of Botany at Cambridge, to insure that all the available skills of Quaternary Research were brought to bear on exploiting the potentials of the region (Phillips 1951: 158–273). Working as a team, Godwin and I succeeded before the end of 1934 in defining the ecological contexts of three phases of settlement – Late Mesolithic, Early Neolithic and Early Bronze Age – in the Shippea Hill Fens, by locating the peripheral scatter of waste from each phase of settlement, the first two at successive levels in the Lower Peat, the third in the base of the Upper Peat, and by seeing how these fitted into the sequence of vegetational history defined by pollen analysis (Clark 1935: 284–319). We had also by this time tied in an Early Mesolithic flint assemblage at Broxbourne in the Lea Valley between Cambridge and London. By the time this work had to come to an end in 1940 the sequence had been carried down to the Roman occupation of the Fenland. Although much of the basic work in the field and the laboratory fell to Godwin and myself, we received much help from working as members of a group. Much of the benefit accrued from the informal gatherings held each term to discuss research prior to publication and to enlist specialist aid in analyzing finds. Experience of this teamwork in Quaternary Research was an enduring influence.

Although drawn to Quaternary Research initially as a means of dating and validating traces of Mesolithic settlement, involvement soon made me aware of the importance of the environment in its own right as something to which man had necessarily to adapt. This made me impatient to see what had been achieved in the study of Mesolithic settlement in the countries which pioneered pollen analysis. In 1933 and 1934 opportunities were taken to visit excavations and museums in Denmark, Germany and Sweden. On my return I wrote a new book to show what had been achieved in these countries by viewing the archaeological data in its appropriate environmental setting (Clark 1936, 1969). The book's publication showed a fuller appreciation of the need to take account of the widest range of material equipment and in particular of objects made from antler, bone, bark, wood and other organic substances. Even more importantly, it revealed a real if still unsophisticated appreciation of the significance of physical environment: the change from Paleolithic to Mesolithic, for example, was viewed as in essence the outcome of adaptation to the new Post-glacial forested landscape. There was even a glimmer of an appreciation, evidenced, for example, by the fauna lists in Appendix One, that the people who practised industrial traditions in the context of Post-glacial environment actually lived by exploiting its resources.

ARCHAEOLOGY AND SOCIETY

Before this book appeared another decisive influence already had been at work and had made it possible to step out into a more spacious field. In 1935 I had been appointed to a lectureship at Cambridge. Experience of teaching soon awakened me to an awareness that archaeology was in effect a process of deploying techniques to increase knowledge of social life, something which in the ecstasy of classifying microliths in the cloistered world of a research student I had tended to overlook. The shock of having to teach novices after a spell of individual research is the greatest help in dispelling thesis neurosis. At such a juncture the effects of earlier training tend to assert themselves. Following the English tradition which still prevails in essentials, I specialized during my last year at school primarily on one subject, in my case history, and it was as a historian that I spent my first two years at Cambridge, since archaeology and anthropology in those days only rated half a course. It is so general in the United States for Prehistoric archaeology to be taught in the context of anthropology, that it may be worth emphasizing that Cambridge is one of the very few centres in Europe where this happens. I owe much to my training in history, which has always made me more interested in prehistory than merely in Prehistoric archaeology, but count myself doubly fortunate to have been brought up during the second half of my undergraduate training spent in the Department of Archaeology and Anthropology, on Radcliffe-Brown and Malinowski – and in due course on Evans-Pritchard and Thomson – as well as on Breuil and Childe. With such a training it was impossible to be content for long with ordering vestiges of material culture. When my time came to teach I was concerned to emphasize that archaeological fossils are social fossils and that what prehistorians were concerned with was in the final resort the process of social evolution. That is why I called the book I wrote for students at this time *Archaeology and Society* (1939), a book by the way, which after a third of a century remains obstinately alive. It seems hard to recall that the opening sentences of this book 'Archaeology is often defined as the study of antiquities. A better definition would be that it is the study of how men lived in the past . . .' should once have had an almost prophetic ring. What is certain is that Chapter Six headed 'Interpretation' contained in embryo the ideas developed in later writings down even to the diagrammatic model which in elaborated form illustrated and in a sense symbolized the theoretical position taken up in my Reckitt Lecture for 1953 (Clark 1953: 215–38).

PREHISTORIC EUROPE: THE ECONOMIC BASIS

If it had not been for the outbreak of war in the very year that *Archaeology and Society* appeared, *Prehistoric Europe: the economic basis* would probably have been written ten years earlier. Thus, when invited to contribute a book on *Prehistoric England* (1940) for a popular series – a task discharged while awaiting national service in 1940 – I found myself organizing the chapters not chronologically but functionally. Chapter by chapter the evidence was reviewed for the food quest, dwellings, handicrafts, mining and trade, communications, hill-forts (defence), burial and sacred sites. The basic ideas and an accumulation of notes were there. In the years of tedium and frustration that followed they no doubt simmered, but they could not be nourished by reading or research. An indication that this was so is given by the publication, while on war service, of the first two of a series of preparatory papers, one on bees (Clark 1942), the other on water (Clark 1944). In the first of these I made it plain that I intended to change the course of archaeological research by concentrating on social activities rather than upon objects. In the opening paragraph of the paper on bees I wrote:

As purveyors of honey and wax, substances rated high by early man, bees would seem to deserve more attention from archaeologists than they have in fact received.

In this respect they serve to point a moral. The tendency has all too frequently been to concentrate on those aspects of ancient cultures which lend themselves most easily to classification, to the neglect of those which promise the closest insight into the working of the societies under review, thus inverting the true outlook of the archaeologist and turning him away from the activities of human beings to a world of abstractions. The thesis we would like to urge is that the prime concern of archaeology is the study of how men lived in society, of how within the social framework they have striven to satisfy and multiply their wants. From such a standpoint the means adopted to gratify the taste for sweet things, a taste shared by man and beast and physiological in its basis, merits at least as much attention as current fashions in safety-pins and other topics beloved of 'museologists' (Clark 1942: 215).

I ended the paper by expressing the essence of an ecological viewpoint, linking honey with land-utilization and beeswax with bronze-casting. I noted how 'through the activities of bees, the pastoral background of Bronze Age Europe helped materially to fashion the most characteristic products of the period. Which tell us more, the bees or the bronzes? A question-begging question. In the study of any society, past or present, no aspect can safely be omitted, for all are interdependent.'

The article on 'Water in Antiquity' (Clark 1944) started off by recalling the basic importance of food and water 'and the all-pervading influence upon outlook and social structure exercised by the methods adopted to insure (their) adequate supply'. I acknowledged my debt to Social Anthropology implicitly by including myself among 'those who approach prehistory from a functionalist point of view' and explicitly by making footnote reference to books by Audrey Richards on diet and work in primitive society. On the other hand, the general organization of this article running through from the Old Stone Age to the modern hydro-electric era showed plainly enough a concern with history. Yet the essence of this paper is again ecological: the sources, methods of lifting and modes of utilization of water are considered as developing through time, but in step with basic subsistence and settlement patterns and subject to the natural possibilities of regions.

The fact that in these papers and those which followed immediately after the war I was consciously urging the need to break away from object-fetishism, does not mean that I was turning away from archaeological material. Quite the contrary, my idea was to use this as a means of documenting social life. In interpreting objects I sought to use every archaeological means, including the associations and contexts of data and iconography, but equally historical sources whether from classical or medieval antiquity or even from recent times. Again I did not hesitate to draw upon the extraordinary wealth of information assembled by anthropologists. In using this last source I was always aware of the need for sophistication. The principles I followed were described in an article written shortly after the war though it was not published until 1951 (Clark 1951). I began by emphasizing the falsity inherent in any attempt to apply the concept of unilinear evolution to human affairs. Cross-cultural comparison might indeed be suggestive: it could hardly in the nature of the case be definitive. More cogent results were likely when the comparisons were made within the same environment and when there was clear evidence of historical continuity between them. When seeking to interpret data about past behaviour and in particular about the way in which natural resources were utilized it was helpful to know how people occupying the same territory managed to provide for themselves before the rise of modern economies.

On resuming active scholarship after the war I lost no time in investigating the basic means of subsistence of prehistoric Europeans. The resulting papers fell into two groups: those concerned with hunting and catching activities and specifically with the exploitation of seals (Clark 1946) and whales (Clark 1947a) and with fowling (Clark 1948a) and fishing (Clark 1948b) and those connected with forest clearance (Clark 1945 a and b, 1947b), farming and stock-raising (Clark 1947c). Since the seal-hunting paper was the first of a series it may be taken as a type. Its purpose was made crystal-clear in the opening paragraph:

The research, on which the present paper is based, is part of a programme to further knowledge of prehistoric times by the study of social activities. Seal-hunting is here considered, not because it gave rise to objects which need classifying and dating, but simply because it was an activity of vital interest to certain coast-dwelling communities in northwestern Europe during the Stone Age (Clark 1946: 12).

I then proceeded to indicate the basic sources of my study. Since I went on to define my problem as 'basically biological' it is not surprising that I gave first place to zoology – to the identification of the seals from archaeological contexts and not least to the life habits of the various species which alone enables us 'to visualize the opportunities open to the old hunters'. Secondly, one depended on the findings of Quaternary Research both for dating stray finds and above all for information about contemporary coastlines. Thirdly, I drew upon ethnographic data bearing on the methods used to catch seals before the introduction of firearms: in this connection I made only circumspect use of data from Askimo territory, relying much more heavily on information about the way in which seals were hunted and exploited in northern Europe itself during historical times as recorded by historians and modern ethnographers. Finally, as was invariably and necessarily the case, I relied upon the archaeological data itself, the cultural and chronological contexts of seal bones and of the equipment used to catch them, information tabulated in a schedule and incorporated in a series of maps.

In discussing whales, fowls and fish, respectively, as factors in the subsistence and technology of the prehistoric inhabitants of Europe, I relied on the same kind of criteria as I had done in the case of seals and went out of my way to emphasize the degree of continuity in exploiting these particular resources. A point that may bear emphasis in connection with these papers on catching activities is that by stressing activities I was incidentally able to throw light on the way particular categories of artifact were used. The connection between form and function was frequently confirmed. For example, the formal distinction between stout harpoon heads with prominent barbs and some arrangement at the base for securing to a line emphasized the association with seal bones and isolated skeletons and the more slender finely barbed spearheads with tangs adopted for hafting to a wooden shaft emphasized the frequent association with remains of pike. Again, the association of stag antler mattock heads with the skeletons of stranded whales argued that one use of these artifacts was to detach blubber or meat from the carcass. Even more interesting, the sizes and shapes of fish-hooks could sometimes be linked with the classes of fish for which they were designed. The other, and by far the most significant consideration, is the stress laid on the behaviour and seasonality of the types of animal concerned, matters on which early man must have been well-informed as the price of survival and which provide us with a powerful key to the understanding of his way of life.

In considering the subsistence of people who practised mixed farming, much of the emphasis lay in vegetation and in particular on the way early man cleared the land, grew his crops and provided improved grazing for his livestock. In measuring the progress and nature of land clearance by far the most informative technique was that of pollen analysis. To appreciate the problem I was faced with, it is necessary to recall the orthodox position set out by Cyril Fox and which received general assent in British archaeological circles. In his work on *The Archaeology of the Cambridge Region* (1923), Fox observed that the earlier antiquities of the settled period were mainly concentrated on areas with light soils, mainly gravels, sands and chalk, which he termed a primary area of settlement. It was only later during the Roman period, but not seriously until Saxon times, that the heavier clay lands, commonly termed the secondary area of settlement, began to be taken up on any scale. In due course Fox generalized this observation and applied it to Britain as a whole (Fox 1932). The correlation was valid enough. Unfortunately, Fox went a step further and supposed that the primary zone was occupied first because it was free of forest or at least only lightly covered, whereas the secondary area was avoided by prehistoric man because it was forested. This supposition carried conviction because common observation showed that the present day woodlands were frequently (but of course by no means invariably) situated on clay lands whereas heaths and the chalk downland were commonly (though again by no means invariably) free of forest. From this it became common practice to 'restore' forests to distribution maps on the basis of geology and, conversely, to depict lighter formations as though these were free of forest. Thus, by a circular argument, when distributions of artifacts dating from the Neolithic to the Pre-Roman Iron Age were plotted they were almost invariably found to occur in 'open' country. The doctrine that forests were inimical to primitive farmers, one that could hardly have been entertained for a moment by anyone aware of the most elementary accounts of horticulturalists in the heavy forested areas of Africa, southeast Asia or South America, was also dominant on the European mainland during the early decades of the twentieth century. R. Gradmann and his followers, observing that traces of the earliest farmers were found on the loess and other formations presently supporting a mixed association of shrubs, grasses and bushes, supposed that farming spread on formations that carried relics of a *Steppenheide* vegetation (Gradmann 1906).

In order to understand the conditions under which farming economy was pioneered in temperate Europe it was necessary to understand what ecological conditions really were like during Neolithic times. There was one simple way to test the assumptions of Fox and the hypothesis of Gradmann and that was to discover by means of pollen analysis what kind of vegetation was in fact growing on the loess, light soils and calcareous formations at the time they were settled by Neolithic man. The result of systematic work carried out over a broad area of temperate Europe including Britain has been to show that at the peak of Post-glacial temperature when farming began in this part of the world the landscape was in fact dominated by forest which spread far and wide broken only by mountains, marshes, lakes, rivers and their flood plains and the sea coasts. Loess, chalk and breckland heath were alike forested. In so far as they are open today this is because they were among the first to be farmed. The first task of the Stone Age farmers was precisely to clear the forest, a long process in which several phases can be detected (Iversen 1941). In the same manner it was necessary for me to clear away misconceptions which stood in the way of understanding. So far from the forest being a barrier to farming, the earliest regime in temperate Europe was based on felling and burning, the regime of *brandwirtschaft*; and it was only when pressure of population caused the system to break down that permanent clearance and the creation of fixed fields and meadows began. It was into this picture that the cultivation of cereals and the maintenance of livestock (Clark 1947c), the twin pillars of mixed farming, had to fit.

The years 1945–8 which saw the publication of the papers on different aspects of subsistence were crowded ones. The war-time interruption had made men of my generation anxious to push ahead with their own work, but organized teaching had to be resumed and given an impetus and in my own case there was need to give a renewed impulse to *The Proceedings of the Prehistoric Society* which somehow had been brought limping through the war. Over and above this were the excavations which I regarded as part of my duty to carry on during the long vacation as a means of training students but which also could be used to demonstrate in practical terms the priorities in research that stemmed directly from the notions set out in my writings. It was no accident that the summers of 1949, 1950 and 1951, the years I was writing *Prehistoric Europe,* saw me at work in a waterlogged hole in the peat at Star Carr in East Yorkshire (Clark 1954, 1971). The same preoccupation that drove me to mine and quarry the literature and museum collections for information about how men exploited natural resources to maintain social life made me anxious to obtain the same kind of information for myself by means of excavation. Again, there was a certain justice in choosing a Mesolithic site for my demonstration. During my time as a research student twenty years previously I had been confined to the typological study of the most durable lithic residues and was helped out only by a few stray finds of antler and bone work. While teaching I had emphasized the need to remedy this situation by paying close attention to the conditions which determined the survival of a broader range of data and spelled out the potentialities in temperate Europe of sites where water-logging had inhibited or at least slowed down the process of bacteriological decay. It remained an objective to find such a site and when John Moore first showed me Star Carr in 1948 I realized that here was the chance I had been seeking. By systematically uncovering this site by the former Lake Pickering, one had the opportunity to recover at least some of the organisms on which Mesolithic man subsisted and at the same time of securing a far wider range of the equipment by which he adapted to and utilized the resources of his environment. The idea that most artifacts at least on Stone Age sites relate to the manipulation of environment is enough to indicate that research on a site like Star Carr needed to be carried out within the framework of interdisciplinary research. This was fortunately available. The work of the Fenland Research Committee was, as we have seen, essentially complete by 1940 and when Quaternary Research was revived at Cambridge after the war its horizons were altogether wider. The sub-Department of Quaternary Research was instituted at Cambridge in 1948. In 1949 and again in 1950 and 1951 members of its staff were on the site at Star Carr and in due course contributed significantly to the final publication.

When I came to write the preface to *Prehistoric Europe* I made it clear that I hoped to bring 'into focus two distinct lines of vision, those of the natural scientist and of the historian'. I was concerned to show not only how men sustained life but how over a period extending from the Late-glacial period to the foundation of cities in different parts of the Continent this life underwent progressive change. In defining the sources available for realizing this aim I distinguished the following main categories in my Introduction:
1 *Archaeological*
(a) Material equipment for which I emphasized the need to compensate for under-representation of the organic component and the importance of

studying materials and techniques of production as well as finished forms.

(b) Representations in the form of rock-art, models, engravings on metal-work or graffiti on pottery.

2 *Ethnographic and Ethnohistorical*

(a) Direct observation or records by trained ethnologists of the practices and equipment of indigenous peasant communities more especially in Scandinavia, the Alpine region and central and eastern Europe.

(b) Uncritical but still useful records by early writers, ranging from Strabo and Tacitus to King Alfred's edition of the history of Orosius or Olaus Magnus' *History of the Northern Peoples* published in the middle of the 16th century.

3 *Biological*

(a) Biological data on archaeological sites mainly in the form of food-refuse.

(b) Changes in vegetation revealed by pollen analysis and reflecting changes in land utilization.

The first chapter entitled 'Ecological Zones and Economic Stages' began by defining economy as 'an adjustment to specific physical and biological conditions of certain needs, capacities, aspirations and values'. This definition marked a considerable shift from the position taken up in *The Mesolithic Settlement of Northern Europe* in which changes in the cultural sphere were treated without comment as if they were straightforward adaptations to environmental change. Instead the relations between culture and the different aspects of the environment were now regarded as reciprocal. A direct appeal was made to the equilibrium model worked out by Evans-Pritchard in relation to the Nuer of the Sudan, the implication being that the status quo at any particular time or place could be expressed only in terms of interaction between cultural equipment and the main components of the natural ecosystem. But such a model was seen to be valid only for a very brief time. It was useful as a tool for investigating the workings of a functioning system and helped to explain why archaeological assemblages might retain their integrity long enough to form recognizable archaeological stages. To account for change, on the other hand, it was necessary to envisage forces that made for temporary disequilibrium. As soon as a long period of time was considered – and my book avowedly concerned itself with a period extending from the Late-glacial to the foundation of cities – stress had to be laid on the dynamic character of the adjustment between culture, habitat and biome. Changes in total ecosystems comprising human cultures in the context of their particular habitats and biomes, might be expected to proceed from any one of several directions. The equilibrium could be affected and even upset by changes in the environment, by what might be termed economic dynamism caused, for instance, by taking up all the available land, or by the effect of some labour-saving innovation, or again by the effect of contact between distinct cultures. Nevertheless, it was maintained that the climatic and vegetational zones into which Europe could be divided imposed certain limits to economic exploitation at any particular stage of technology. These zones, which shifted notably from the Late-glacial to the Post-glacial were defined as from north to south Circumpolar (fjäll-tundra and coniferous forest), Temperate and Mediterranean. Peasant societies based on mixed farming were seen as expanding to the northern frontiers of the Temperate zone and towns as emerging first in the Mediterranean zone, only developing as permanent institutions much later in the Temperate and Circumpolar zones.

The bulk of the book was given over to reviewing the evidence bearing on different aspects of economic life arranged in broadly chronological order in each chapter. The most complete treatment was accorded to the food quest, two chapters being devoted to catching activities (inland; coastal) and two to farming (clearance and cultivation; crops and livestock). Next followed, in logical order, shelter (houses and settlements); technology comprising the apparatus used to manipulate the environment (one chapter on artifacts of stone, bronze and iron; the other on other crafts, mainly those concerning working organic materials); and lastly, two chapters on distribution (trade; travel and transports). In presenting this material, particular care was taken to provide detailed documentation in the form of references to the extensive literature and a large number of illustrations.

This was necessary if the book were to succeed in its prime purpose, which was quite simply to convince professional archaeologists that their subject held more interesting possibilities than categorizing data in terms of cultural definition and periodization.

RETROSPECT

I responded eagerly to the pronouncement in 1935 of a revered senior, A. M. Tallgren, who stated 'Forms and types, that is products, have been regarded as more real and alive than the society which created them and whose needs determined these manifestations of life' (Tallgren 1937: 155).

From that time I began to accumulate notes bearing on the social function of archaeological data. As I've already mentioned, an invitation to write *Prehistoric England* for a popular series in 1939 gave me my first opportunity to try out a functional approach and the materials for papers written while on war service (Clark 1940) were drawn from notes accumulated during the immediate pre-war period. *Prehistoric Europe* was written with a considerable head of steam. How far it contributed to breaking the professional routine of the previous three generations it is not for me to say. Probably it would be best to regard the book as itself part of a reaction to what I have elsewhere termed 'Museological archaeology'. This reaction, so eloquently called for by Tallgren, was already beginning and was bound to come first in a territory like Europe in which the main spatial and temporal sorting of the primary data had already been accomplished.

The best form of attack depends very much on the intellectual and social context of the field of operations. My book was written in an English academic context. This is an unpromising field for dialectic. On the other hand, it does respond to facts, provided these are adequately validated. Translation of the book into eastern as well as western European languages shows that it must have met a need which was already being widely felt. Essentially the book represented a marshalling of facts which, in their totality, made it evident how much information could be gleaned about economic life even from material recovered with other ends in view, and specifically economic archaeology. By helping to channel the objectives of archaeological research also it has influenced, though to a lesser degree than one had hoped, the choice of sites for investigation and the methods used. The excavations at Star Carr which were not completed soon enough for more than a passing reference, are a case in point. Another is the continued investment of research time on the peat deposits of the Somerset Levels of southwest England, an investment which has already yielded important dividends of prehistoric causeways (Godwin 1960) and the practice of Neolithic archery (Clark 1963) and which promises even more valuable insights into the settlement and exploitation of the area by Neolithic and Bronze Age peoples. The systematic quest for sites offering the highest organic content is a logical and necessary counterpart of the kind of archaeology I was intent to foster. So long as archaeologists are absorbed in the preliminary task of establishing areas and distributions as they have to be in the initial stages of exploration in any area, there is a positive advantage in maintaining the ongoing ritual and getting on with the task of collecting stereotyped samples of a limited range of artifacts which because of their high survival value can be relied upon to recur. Once archaeology is regarded as a means of discovering how people lived, on the other hand, there is a powerful incentive to maximize the range of information by choosing the right kind of site and employing consistent and adequate sampling techniques. The choice of water-logged sites in the temperate zone is only one example of what I mean by choosing the right kind of site. Even more important is the need to concentrate on settlements and either excavate these completely or sample them in such a way as to make it possible to infer within a reasonable error of probability the scale and plan of structures. Again, in so far as economic archaeology is concerned with the way in which communities exploited natural resources, it follows that it ought to be pursued in the context of Quaternary Research. The Somerset tracks, for instance, only make sense in the context of ecological circumstances. They can only be recovered by means of pollen analysis and similar techniques; just as frequently they can only be dated by this method or directly by radiocarbon analysis.

The most trenchant criticism I received when the book first appeared came from Gordon Childe: 'Yes, Grahame, but what have you done about Society?' Childe was a good Marxist. He may well have had in mind a crucial passage from *Das Kapital* which presumably underlies the immense investment in Institutes of the History of Material Culture put forth by the Soviet Union and its satellites:

Relics of bygone instruments of labour possess the same importance for the investigation of extinct economic forms of society as do fossil bones for the determination of extinct species of animals. It is not the articles made, but how they are made, and by what instruments, that enables us to distinguish different economic epochs. Instruments of labour not only supply a standard of the degree of development to which human labour has attained, but they are also indicators of the social conditions under which that labour is carried on (Marx: 172).

A more wide-ranging criticism must be that the book was by its very nature too generalized, too divorced from actuality. Thus, in emphasizing the importance of studying archaeological and accompanying biological data in its ecological context, discussion was in practice limited to differences obtaining in the territories of four major macro-zones. Again, by abstracting the archaeological data from its social matrix and treating it as though it were the product merely of a generalized historical process, the social dimension of culture, the fact that archaeological, like anthropological data, in general, relates to specific communities was lost sight of. To conflate both the criticisms my treatment of the data inhibited consideration of it in terms of systems. With the benefit of hindsight it is easy to see this. Only two things need be said. These criticisms did not impair the immediate aim of the book, which was to make a very elementary, but in the context of the time, a very necessary point – namely, that even the data incidentally collected in the course of stratigraphic and culture-defining archaeology was capable of throwing light on the history of prehistoric economy. And, conversely, it implied that, if archaeologists were only to concentrate their attention on seeking answers to the right questions, there was every prospect of being able to throw far more light on the processes by which the prehistoric inhabitants of Europe exploited its resources in maintaining and improving their living standards. In other words, taking one elementary step did not preclude but made it easier to take further ones. In fact, certain steps have been and are currently being taken, in some instances, even by the present author.

STAR CARR

One way of making this last point is to compare the initial publication of the excavations at Star Carr (Clark 1954) with the treatment accorded after the lapse of nearly twenty years (Clark 1972). My prime objectives in excavating at Star Carr were to recover:

(a) an artifact assemblage of Early Mesolithic character combining equipment made from organic materials – antler, bone and hopefully wood – as well as from flint and stone, under conditions allowing dating in relation to phases in the history of Post-glacial vegetation in Britain;

(b) food-refuse, notably in respect of discarded meat bones, which might throw light on subsistence economy;

(c) information about the scale of social unit involved and if possible about the type of structures in which people lived.

The site on the northern edge of the lake which during Late-glacial and Early Post-glacial times filled the Vale of Pickering was chosen after prolonged search because it seemed to fulfill the main condition of success, namely an archaeological level in water-logged deposits. The success with which the first objective was realized can be seen from table I in Clark 1954, which brings out very clearly the way in which excavation of this single site enlarged our knowledge of Pre-Boreal and Boreal settlement in England. Not least of the finds was the quantity of waste resulting from the manufacture of artifacts of antler on the site. A disappointment was the rarity of wooden objects, which might conceivably have been mitigated if we had thought of using water jets as an excavating tool. A substantial body of food-refuse was obtained, principally animal bones, but including traces of edible plant foods, which may or may not have been gathered for food. The area of the site, indicated by plotting flints and noting the extent of a rough timber platform (only the lakeside half of which survived) made it plain that not more than a microband of three or four nuclear families can have occupied it at any one time. No information about actual shelters was obtained, except the negative one that we found no traces of vertical or oblique stakes in the underlying platform, which was composed entirely of birchwood, weighted with stones and wads of clay.

The main purpose of the publication was to make details of the find available with a minimum of delay to interested scholars. For this reason it carried many illustrations and was basically descriptive. An important feature of the book, as of the research on which it was based, was that it was interdisciplinary and included chapters on stratigraphy and vegetational history, and on the animal remains, as well as on the archaeology of the site. The presence in the field team of one or more qualified paleobotanists ensured that the stratigraphy was correctly established and samples taken from the positions best calculated to ensure that the occupation was fitted in correctly. This was invaluable not merely from a chronological but also from an ecological point of view: it allowed us to visualize fairly accurately the conditions under which the people responsible for the Star Carr assemblage were living while they occupied the site. Again, the identification of fruit and seeds gave us some idea of the plant food available at the time. The animal material was important because it marked an intermediate link in the food chain: on the one hand it gave us an idea of the kind of animals that fed on the vegetation revealed by pollen analysis and macroscopic identification – it was interesting to note for example the relatively high proportion of elk and aurochs and the low proportion of swine at a time preceding the formation of oak-mixed and older forests. On the other hand, it gave a direct insight into the range of animals exploited by the occupants of the sites as well as into their relative importance in the food quest. Yet very little was made of this in the original publication. As zoologists, Fraser and King were asked specifically whether they could pronounce on seasonality and whether they were able to show that the site was occupied during the winter and abandoned during the summer months. Important information was passed by, such as why this was the case, how it fitted in with the archaeological finds, where the hunters were during the rest of the year and in effect what the totality of information from animal bones and artifacts was able to tell us about the economic system. A certain amount of attention was paid to working out the calorific output of the animal material actually recovered from the site and this was shown to be enough, with certain corrections, to maintain a group of four nuclear families for over six years. This finding agreed well with the observed concentration of artifacts and the fact that stratigraphical evidence on the lakeward side was enough to indicate visits over a period of time. What was missing from the original publication on Star Carr agreed very well with what was lacking in *Prehistoric Europe*: in neither case was consideration paid to social groups in the round.

In the case of Star Carr an invitation to contribute to the McCaleb series of Modules in Anthropology (Clark 1972) gave me the opportunity to rethink the results free from the burden of presenting an adequate record of the primary data. In particular I had the chance to view what we had found in terms of the seasonal utilization of territory. In connection with his work on Paleolithic settlement at Epirus in northwest Greece, Eric Higgs had drawn special attention in association with C. Vita-Finzi to what he termed the catchment areas of sites (Vita-Finzi and E. S. Higgs 1970), that is, the area within an hour or two's walk of the actual home base which was fixed at a particular spot. Calculations made in relation to the north side of the former Lake Pickering showed that the carrying capacity of the low ground at the time of the year when red deer were present there would have been sufficient to maintain a group adequately so long as it did not exceed a microband of three or possibly four nuclear families. A close look at the red deer remains, which accounted for around two-thirds of the meat supply of the Star Carr encampment, brought out the important fact that those represented in the kill were predominantly adult stags. This fact went well with the circumstance attested by archaeology that a major industrial activity at the site was cutting strips from stag antler and fabricating these into barbed points for use as spearheads. This interpretation also agreed very well with the observation that during the winter when the herds come down to shelter on the lower ground adult red deer stags tended to occupy separate yards distinct from the hinds and young. Since at this time of the year most of the hinds were carrying young it was obviously consistent with good husbandry to concentrate on adult stags in winter, the time of the year incidentally when their antlers provided a valuable source of raw material. Where were the deer – and presumably their human predators – during the summer months? Or to put it the other way round, how far did the annual territory, that is, the territory exploited during the course of the year by the microband that wintered at Star Carr and doubtless other sites on the north shore of Lake Pickering, extend? To judge from available studies of red deer, notably those by Fraser Darling (1969) for Scotland and by Ingebrigsten (1924) for southwest Norway, the stags would have rejoined the herds and the animals would have moved up on to the lower slopes of the hills and progressively onto higher ground as vegetation ripened only to come down again at the approach of snow.

As is normally the case, once one has the key to the system – or better to begin with – once one has even formed a hypothesis to account for a limited range of facts – the chance comes to test it on its own terms. If in a territory of some marked surface relief, as we find in Yorkshire, we suppose that herds and their predators were exploiting high ground, does archaeology support this? In the case of Yorkshire the answer is surely, 'Yes'. On the very crests of the North Yorkshire moors or of the Pennines, lithic industries of Mesolithic aspect had long been known in localities which by common consent were too exposed to have been occupied by man during the winter months. Such industries were indeed among the first of their kind to be known in England. Because they differed in certain formal respects from those on lower ground they were generally attributed to distinct cultures: thus we had Tardenoisian industries on the high Pennines and Maglemosian ones on the low ground of East Yorkshire to go no further afield. Viewed bioarchaeologically (or by the archaeology of how individual communities in fact lived in their environments), it begins to look as if at least some of the Pennine industries relate to the summer hunting grounds of people who camped on lower ground during the winter. The microlithic and scraper component of the 'broad-blade' group of Pennine industries could be lost in the lithic assemblage at Star Carr and such differences as we can see can be explained in ecological/seasonal terms. For instance, the absence of axes and adzes from the high Pennine sites above the tree-line is hardly surprising; nor is the much lower proportion of flint burins, which at Star Carr were linked with intense activity in working stag antler by the groove and splinter technique, since during the summer antlers were still in the process of growth. One of the morals of the rethink of Star Carr is the need to correct generalized concepts like 'culture' (e.g., Early Maglemosian) and environmental zones (e.g.,

Birch-pine forest) by getting down to basic bioarchaeology – the study of how communities lived – by exploiting the resources of specific territories. In the case of people who depended on animals that shifted their territories seasonally this implied moves of the home-base and its attendant resource territory over a more extensive annual territory.

A model for this kind explains something, but it is nevertheless inadequate for the basic reason that human societies, even at a comparatively elementary technical level, differ profoundly from the animal aggregations which serve them as prey. The predator in chief moves in an extra dimension, the dimension of social territory. Aggregations of mammals achieve human status to the extent that their behaviour conforms to or reacts against social patterns, that is, patterns transmitted and added to by virtue of belonging to historically constituted societies. The integrity and cohesion of these societies both determines and is reinforced by a certain patterning of behaviour in the same way that individuals signal their identity by conforming to (or of course dissenting from) social norms. Since human societies occupy and defend territory it is useful to speak of social territory as a third and peculiarly human level in the territorial hierarchy. At an economic level, one may define social territory as the territory drawn upon for resources by any community by virtue of belonging to larger social groupings. If in *Prehistoric Europe* I ignored these groupings, which define themselves in the archaeological record in a variety of ways but notably by virtue of sharing idiosyncratic features of style which suffice to reinforce a sense of social identity, I did so intentionally. My aim in writing the book was quite simply to wake archaeologists from a situation in which, to repeat Tallgren's words, 'forms and types . . . [were] regarded as more real and alive than the society which created them'. If it helped in any way to promote economic prehistory or bioarchaeology it did what I set out to do. Now a generation later one can afford to admit: yes, communities had to exist by utilizing natural resources and by deploying the appropriate techniques and artifacts, *but* they did so as communities, that is, as human, culturally defined, historically-based com-munities. From this it follows that form and style analysis, so long as it is pursued with the object of defining social territories and, as societies advanced in complexity, of defining classes, and not as an end in itself, retains a highly significant place in scientific archaeology.

It is possible and, as I tried to point out in *Prehistoric Europe: the economic basis*, highly desirable when one encounters artifacts to ask the question that a paleontologist asks of a fossil, 'What was this *for*?' meaning something more than that this artifact or this fossil helps me to systematize or order my data as archaeologist or as paleontologist. An archaeologist, like a paleontol-ogist, values the object he handles, not only as a means of controlling his material, but as a means of gaining insight into the lives of the organisms to which they relate – how they were structured, how they ate, what territories they occupied, how they adapted to environment and how they moved about it. But people are more complex beings than fossil mammals and archaeology is that much more difficult. It is concerned with a new dimension, a new territory. When we speak of use we must in the case of artifacts think not merely of material use, but of social, symbolic use. The fact that the vast majority of the finest artifacts were never intended to be used at a banal, material level does not mean that their makers were wasting their time or merely shaping prize museum specimens. These things had their uses but they were social uses. By isolating the socio-cultural from the economic factor I did what I intended to do, but in doing so did violence to the total reality. For instance, I devoted a chapter to what, drawing on the vocabulary of our own quite different type of society I termed 'trade', without so much as recognizing that redistribution is not only a basic characteristic and mark of human society, but patterns of redistribution satisfied social as well as merely economic purposes. I first woke up to the meaning of the patterns of redistribution to which archaeologists have been paying increasing attention as a result of spending a term in the Department of Anthropology at Otago working in a country with a strong ethnohistorical tradition. The paper I wrote on the so-called stone axe 'trade' (Clark 1965) is one sign of awakening. At the present moment, half-way through my book on *The Older Age Settlement in Scandinavia*, I am beginning to appreciate more fully what Childe meant in 1952, when he commented, 'Yes, Grahame, but what have you done about Society?'

References

CLARK, GRAHAME
1933 *The Mesolithic Age in Britain*. Cambridge, Cambridge University Press.
1935 Report on Recent Excavations at Peacock's Farm, Shippea Hill, Cambridgeshire. *Antiquaries Journal* 15: 284–319.
1936, 1969 *The Mesolithic Settlement of Northern Europe*. Cambridge, Cambridge University Press. New York, Greenwood Press.
1939, 1947 *Archaeology and Society*. London, Methuen. 1960, 1965 New York, Barnes and Noble.
1940 *Prehistoric England*. London, Batsford.
1942 Bees in Antiquity. *Antiquity* 16: 208–15.
1944 Water in Antiquity. *Antiquity* 18: 1–5.
1945a Farmers and Forests in Neolithic Europe. *Antiquity* 19: 57–71.
1945b *Man and Nature in Prehistory, with special reference to Neolithic Settlement in Northern Europe*. University of London Institute of Archaeology, Occasional Paper 6: 20–8.
1946 Seal-hunting in the Stone Age of North-Western Europe, a study in Economic Prehistory. *Proceedings of the Prehistoric Society* 12: 12–48.
1947a Whales as an Economic Factor in Prehistoric Europe. *Antiquity* 21: 84–104.
1947b Forest Clearance and Prehistoric Farming. *The Economic History Review* 17: 45–51.
1947c Sheep and Swine in the Husbandry of Prehistoric Europe. *Antiquity* 21: 122–36.
1948a Fowling in Prehistoric Europe. *Antiquity* 22: 116–30.
1948b The development of Fishing in Prehistoric Europe. *Antiquaries Journal* 28: 45–85.

1951 Folk Culture and the Study of European Prehistory, in *Aspects of Archaeology in Britain and Beyond. Essays presented to O. G. S. Crawford*, W. F. Grimes, ed. London, Edwards.

1952, 1965 *Prehistoric Europe: the economic basis*. London, Methuen. 1966, Stanford, Stanford University Press.

1953 The Economic Approach to Prehistory. *Proceedings of the British Academy* 39: 215–38.

1954, 1971 *Excavations at Star Carr, an Early Mesolithic Site at Seamer, near Scarborough, Yorkshire* (with chapters by D. Walker, and H. Godwin and F. C. Fraser and J. E. King). Cambridge, Cambridge University Press.

1963 Neolithic Bows from Somerset, England and the Prehistory of Archery in north-west Europe. *Proceedings of the Prehistoric Society* 29: 50 ff.

1965 Traffic in Stone Axe and Adze Blades. *The Economic History Review* 18: 1–28.

1972 *Star Carr: A Case Study in Bioarchaeology*. Reading, Mass., Addison-Wesley Modular Publications: McCaleb Module 10.

COLES, J. M.; HIBBERT, F. A. AND CLEMENTS, C. F.

1970 Prehistoric Roads and Tracks in Somerset, England: 2. Neolithic. *Proceedings of the Prehistoric Society* 36: 125 ff.

DARLING, FRANK FRASER

1969 *A Herd of Red Deer*, Oxford, Oxford University Press.

FOX, CYRIL

1923, 1948 *Archaeology of the Cambridge Region*. Cambridge, Cambridge University Press, Maps I, II.

1932 *The Personality of Britain*. Cardiff.

GODWIN, H.

1933 British Maglemose Harpoon Sites. *Antiquity* 7: 36–48.

1960 Prehistoric Wooden Trackways of the Somerset Levels: their construction, age and relation to climatic cleavage. *Proceedings of the Prehistoric Society* 26: 1 ff.

GRADMANN, R.

1906 Beziehung zwischen Pflanzengeographie und Siedlungsgeschichte. *Geogr. Z.* 12: 305–25.

HIGGS, E. S.

1971 Further information concerning the environment of Palaeolithic man in Epirus. *Proceedings of the Prehistoric Society* 37: 367–80.

1972 *Papers in Economic Prehistory*. Cambridge, Cambridge University Press.

Note: the fact that the British Academy should have chosen to adopt an investigation into the Early History of Agriculture as its first Major Research Project is an interesting portent.

INGEBRIGSTEN, O.

1924 *Hjortens Utbredelse i Norge*. Bergen.

IVERSEN, J.

1941 *Land Occupation in Denmark's Stone Age*. Danmarks Geologiske Undersøgelse. IIR, 66. Copenhagen.

MARX, KARL

Das Kapital. Everyman Edition, vol. 1. New York, E. P. Dutton.

PHILLIPS, C. W.

1951 The Fenland Research Committee, Its Past Achievements and Future Prospects, in *Aspects of Archaeology in Britain and Beyond*. W. F. Grimes, ed. London, Edwards.

TALLGREN, A. M.

1937 The Method of Prehistoric Archaeology, *Antiquity*: 152–61. See page 155. This was translated from the original written in French and published in *Eurasia Septentrionalis Antiqua* x (1935).

VITA-FINZI and HIGGS, E. S.

1970 Prehistoric Economy in the Mount Carmel Area of Palestine: Site Catchment Analysis. *Proceedings of the Prehistoric Society* 36: 1–37.

CHAPTER 30

PREHISTORY SINCE CHILDE[*]

THE MAN AND HIS CAREER

In initiating what will hopefully prove to be a fruitful series dedicated to the memory of Professor V. Gordon Childe, the first full-time Director of this Institute, it seems appropriate to begin by saying something about the man and his career. Let me admit that the first part of this undertaking is difficult. Childe was personally reticent and had few close friends. To a quite unusual degree the man was his work. If he had been a more rounded person he might have been with us still. On the other hand he might not have achieved what he did if he had conformed more exactly to the psychiatrists' stereotype. Even his 'Valediction', received at this Institute by surface mail a few days after his death in the Blue Mountains of New South Wales on 19 October 1957, maintained that reticence about himself which makes his prefaces so unrewarding to anyone concerned with the man.

The bare facts of his life can be simply told. He was born in 1892, the son of the Rector of St Thomas's Church in North Sydney. He never married. He attended the Church of England Grammar School at Sydney and Sydney University. In 1914 he took up a graduate scholarship in Classics at Queen's College, Oxford. The only record of formal instruction in archaeology I have (and I owe this information to Mr John Boardman, F.B.A.) is that he embarked on the course for the Diploma in Classical Archaeology under J. D. (later Sir John) Beazley and Marcus Todd. Unlike his fellow candidate Joan (later Dame) Evans he did not complete the course. Instead he took a B.Litt. for a study on an Indo-European topic.

He returned to Australia in the middle of the First World War to join the Australian Union of Democratic Control and campaign against conscription. By 1919 he was private secretary to the leader of this movement, John Storey. His efficiency and zeal is indicated by the fact that he retained this position when Storey became state premier in 1920. Looking back at the end of his life Childe referred to this period as 'a sentimental excursion into Australian politics'. Yet if Storey had not died suddenly in 1921, this lecture might not have been written. Childe found himself out of a job and his attempt to

560

obtain a university post failed owing no doubt to his political activities.[1] His immediate needs were met by the then Labour premier of Queensland who found him a clerical job in the State Public Service. According to Smith, Childe 'endured this position for about six months and then sailed for Europe'. Perhaps he stuck it out to save his fare. What is sure is that Childe was by now thoroughly disillusioned with his native land. This was not only on account of his own personal ill-treatment. Still more influential was his disgust with the avarice and apathy of the Australian workers and the corruption of the Australian Labour leaders. If anyone has any doubts about this let him read the embittered pages of *How Labour Governs*. Did he sail for England by repulsion to get away from a scene of failure and disillusion? Or did the archaeology of the Aryan speakers exert a positive pull? Or did he turn to European prehistory to resolve doctrinal Marxist issues?

A point to remember is that by 1922 Childe was already 30, an age at which most men are already well forward in their careers. Moreover the career of prehistorian did not yet exist. All was uncertainty, the potentially creative uncertainty deplored by planners. One of the few things we know about this period (1922–5) is that in March 1924 he was confident enough to lecture to the Society of Antiquaries on the context of British beakers in European chronology. In 1925 he published his first archaeological book, *The Dawn of European Civilization*, which Crawford (1926:89) hailed as 'the most important of its kind that has hitherto been published', and landed his first job in England, the librarianship of the Royal Anthropological Institute. From this vantage he proceeded to write in rapid succession *The Aryans, The Most Ancient East* and *The Danube in Prehistory*.[2] In those days it was perhaps not so surprising that he should have been invited to fill as foundation professor the new Abercromby Chair of Prehistoric Archaeology at Edinburgh.

The main facts about Childe's professional career may be found in Professor Piggott's Academy obituary (Piggott, 1958:305 – which is the key source for Childe's career in Britain). Although he was conscientious in offering courses for the ordinary degree Childe had only one honours candidate in archaeology during his 20 years at Edinburgh. According to Piggott he had no 'natural aptitude or liking for teaching'. In one's own experience he was a poor lecturer, though no worse than some scholars of at least equal eminence. Excavation was also a chore and here again Piggott was frank: 'he was a poor excavator'. During his decade as Professor in this Institute his pupils remained small in number – the primary degree course is after all only a recent innovation – but in some at least he inspired devotion. Whatever his deficiencies as a lecturer – and they were as nothing one gathers to his defects as an administrator – he was transparently honest, cared for his subject and treated his pupils with respect. Throughout his professional career he gave his time mainly to research and writing. He brought out new editions of his scholarly works – those of *The Dawn* were numerous – wrote textbooks for students (Childe, 1930, 1935, 1940, 1946a, 1950) and the series of paperbacks for the public which brought him world fame.

Let me return to Childe briefly as a person. In his obituary Piggott sought to account for his reticence in the lapidary phrase 'He was very ugly and he was an Australian.' But did Childe realise he was very ugly? If he did he had come to terms with it by the time I knew him. He was at least as willing as the next man to be photographed, he was able to make himself agreeable to the ladies at a social level and his habit of stroking his moustaches while lecturing always seemed to me to suggest some measure of self-satisfaction. Yet at a deeper level it may well be true that it affected his subconscious attitudes, fanning the fierceness of his revolt against his upbringing and leading him to protect himself by reticence. Jack Lindsay gives more than a hint of this in his description of Childe during the Brisbane days of 1921 (1958:136). 'His odd though likeable face, I felt certain, contributed to his refusal to come too far out of his inner refuge'. His Australianness was also important, not perhaps in making him retiring or causing him to become absorbed in his work – neither characteristic after all of the Australian character – but in a more positive sense. It meant that he came to the subject of prehistoric Europe freshly and even sentimentally with a determination to seek out its essence. When all is said, the fact is that Childe returned to England a wounded, disillusioned man. To quote Lindsay again (1958:135), at this time Childe's 'strong socialist convictions were being outraged by the insights he was gaining into the realities behind the facade in the political world'.

This is not the place to discuss Childe's attitude to Marxism in any detail. The topic has recently been dealt with by Peter Gathercole (1971:225) and my topic is not Childe so much as Prehistory since Childe. A few words must however be said.

From an external behaviourist point of view I think his friends would agree he was the most bourgeois person in the world. When he ostentatiously came into a summer conference of the Prehistoric Society with *The Daily Worker* under his arm, you can be sure he had spent the night in the best hotel. His favourite haunt in London was The Athenaeum, where the waiters handed him his 'usual' (about the nature of which there are varying accounts) without the formality of being asked. His entry in *Who's Who* admitted to nothing more revolutionary than bridge, walking and motoring. He complained from Australia on his final trip at the absence of his Athenaeum comforts and my impression is that he included in these the deference he considered his due.

Intellectually and emotionally on the other hand there is no doubt in my mind that, having once propelled him into archaeology on the rebound so to say, Marxism exerted a seriously inhibiting effect on his middle years. It helps to explain why after 1930 or so Childe's creative period was essentially over and why at the end of his life he realised that his prophet had played him false. Whereas in 1946 he could still argue (1946b:251) that there was a 'prospect of reaching general laws indicative of the direction of historic progress', in his 'Valediction' he had to admit that while Marxism had once seemed to make intelligible the development of each culture it 'completely failed to explain the differences between one culture and another and indeed obliterated or dismissed the differences observed' (1958:6).

I have said something – very little in effect – about Childe as a person. What about the first and second words of my title? Childe was a prehistorian and I have chosen to speak about prehistory, not about archaeology as such. Yet no one realised more keenly than Childe himself that archaeology was his main tool in trying to reconstruct what happened in prehistory and in particular how European civilisation achieved its unique character. His attitude was stated very explicitly on the opening page of *Scotland before the Scots* in which he declared his aim to 'extort from the archaeological data a story of development, of a process in time . . .' Note the word 'extort'. One can hardly dissociate the writing of prehistory – for prehistory is paradoxically something which only exists when it is written down – from the process of extortion from archaeological data. What we know – what we can know about prehistory – is conditioned by the methods we use to extract information from the debris just as these in turn are conditioned by what we seek to learn about prehistory. There is a feed-back between the aims of the prehistorian and the procedures of the prehistoric archaeologist just as vital as there is between the various aspects of the life of the communities which existed in prehistoric times.

It is important I think to realise that, like some of the seniors still with us, Childe was virtually self-taught as an archaeologist. He came to Oxford as a classicist and received very little formal training in archaeology. What he did get was an insight into the formal analysis of pottery from Beazley, something which stood him in good stead for the rest of his life and, even more important perhaps, an impression from the example of Arthur Evans of what could be done in the way of distilling history from artifacts. It can hardly be a coincidence that he should have begun his first lecture to the Society of Antiquaries (1925b:159) as follows:

The publication of the first volume of Sir Arthur Evans' *Palace of Minos* (1921) marks the beginning of a new era in the prehistory, not only of the Aegean, but of Europe as a whole.

He ended his lecture with a table synchronising the prehistoric successions in Britain, the Nordic province, Silesia and the South Danube between *c.* 2500–1500 BC with Evans' periods EM II–LM Ia. During the discussion Mr Reginald Smith is recorded as having confessed to feeling much refreshed by the infusion of so much material from the continent in the discussion of a problem in British prehistory. This was high praise from Mr Smith.

By whatever means, Childe became convinced that it was possible to extract from raw archaeological data the kind of information needed to understand the genesis of 'European civilization as a peculiar and individual manifestation of the human spirit' which he proclaimed as his aim in the opening paragraph of *The Dawn*. Since he had not been trained as a prehistoric archaeologist he had in that supremely creative period in the wilderness between 1922 and 1925 to think out for himself how he was going to achieve this. The drawback was that having once made this effort Childe made no further contribution of importance to the discipline of prehistoric archaeology as such. He had achieved what he was going to achieve in this genre essentially by 1930. In so far as I speak of Prehistoric Archaeology since Childe I will in effect be speaking of what happened since then. As a prehistorian on the other hand Childe is in a real sense still with us. We are working in a world which was to a significant extent of his making.

THE CLASSIFICATION OF ARCHAEOLOGICAL DATA: PERIODS AND CULTURES

Before turning to this larger prospect I must dwell for a moment on his own contribution as a prehistoric archaeologist. It is originality that gives impact to a book. For most of you it must take some effort of the historical imagination to appreciate the impact of the original *Dawn*. I am in an easier position because I was still an undergraduate when the 2nd edition – in effect a reprint with a single page addendum – appeared in 1928. In thinking about this lecture I turned up my copy with its undergraduate scorings. To myself and the very small handful of contemporaries reading archaeology as an undergraduate course *The Dawn* had something of the character of a sacred text. How did it appear to my seniors? We know Crawford's reaction. He had all the flair of a born journalist for new ideas. He realised at once that Childe had produced a truly original book. It was original not merely for presenting to insular readers an enlarged perspective to European prehistory, something I shall return to, but also in the way Childe used the raw data. He supplemented an exclusively chronological by a cultural approach. By this I do not mean that he rejected the need for periodisation. Far from it. Periodisation formed the basic framework of *The Danube in Prehistory*. No one realised more clearly that in dealing with traces of prehistoric societies, which by definition left no written records, it was all the more necessary to find objective means of plotting the flow of time. But for Childe the temporal sequence was only the beginning, not the end of archaeology. The end was to define and understand the prehistoric communities to which the archaeology related.

Childe appeared at the right moment. In the more advanced archaeological countries of Europe the gross outlines of periodisation were already defined by the end of the 19th century and by the First World War much of the detail had been filled in. During the 1920s most of the professionals were still trapped in their museums but it must have been evident to someone coming fresh to the scene as Childe did from Australia that the returns to be gained from chronological system-building were rapidly diminishing over much of Europe. It must have been equally apparent that without some understanding of the nature and spatial reference of the data there was little to be learned even from its detailed periodisation. Above all Childe realised that the kind of abstract treatment accorded to geological formations was totally inadequate for dealing with traces of human societies. What was needed was a method of distinguishing between the different societies represented by archaeological data. How Childe set about this is formulated most explicitly in the Preface to *The Danube in Prehistory* (v/vi). When 'certain types of remains – pots, implements, ornaments, burial rites, house forms constantly recur(ring) together', he wrote, we term 'such a complex of regularly associated traits . . . a "cultural group" or just a "culture".' Such 'cultures' were conceived of as occupying space as well as time. This was formalised in *The Dawn* by the provision of maps showing the extent of different cultures at four periods of time spanning the Neolithic and the earlier half of the Bronze Age, as well as by chronological tables relating to a number of defined geographical zones and recording the extent in time of cultures. Childe conceived archaeological data as existing in two dimensions, in space as well as time. This was his essential contribution to prehistoric archaeology.

When Childe came to archaeology it is not surprising in view of the state of the subject that he should have regarded a more adequate system of classification as a first priority. Such training as he had in Classical Archaeology gave him a keen appreciation of form analysis. Throughout his life he had an amazing visual memory understandable in a pupil of Beazley but all the more remarkable in that he found it difficult to represent objects graphically. His concept of the archaeological culture was a decisive contribution which served his purpose, but it was one which trapped him in the sense that he never took the next step. We must remember that he was already 33 when *The Dawn* appeared. Thereafter his new thinking was devoted to prehistory rather than to prehistoric archaeology as such. Over 20 years on, in what must have been one of his first publications, if not the first, since his appointment to the Directorship of the Institute, we find him still hammering away at the notion that both are 'classificatory sciences' (1946b:243). It is revealing also that he should have been so preoccupied with the ancient issue of diffusion *v.* evolution that he was inclined to dismiss the functionalism expounded by Malinowski and Radcliffe Brown as 'not a little affected by the reaction against this windy controversy'. There is no sign that Childe was to the slightest degree influenced in his approach to archaeological material by the seminal writings of these men whose *Argonauts of the Pacific* and *Andaman Islanders* appeared in 1922, the year he returned to England. When years later he showed signs of being aware of what they were getting at, it was rather as a bystander. In his 'Valediction' he admitted (p. 2) that

A deeper analysis and ecological description of recognised cultures directed towards disclosing the functional integration of their surviving constituents and reconstructing the economic and sociological linkages between the latter are suitable themes for doctoral theses . . .

This was hardly the language of immediacy or personal involvement and the passage came from a paper written 36 years after the publication of the decisive books. The ecological approach to archaeological data ventilated nearly 20 years before the 'Valediction' was nevertheless 'since Childe'. Before I turn to this it will be convenient to say a little more about Childe and anthropology. Although he failed to profit from the most significant development of his day in this field, he was paradoxically strongly influenced by the writings of such ancients as Tylor and Morgan. On the other hand he was sufficiently aware of the fallacy inherent in Fraser's method to avoid the error into which it has become fashionable to fall to-day, more especially one might add in the media and what might charitably be termed post-T.V. books. No one realised more keenly the folly of picking and choosing scraps of evidence from different cultures and applying them out of context. By doing so the same archaeological phenomena could of course be 'explained' in a multitude of different ways. To quote again from his 'Valediction', Childe wrote:

. . . it is fun to find the same pattern on an Arunta churinga and an Irish grave slab. Let us not waste our time in deciphering such sepulchral carvings by reference to the recorded meaning of similar patterns in aboriginal Australia. The value of such ethnographic comparisons is just to show the funny kinds of meanings and purposes that may be attached to the queerer kind of archaeological data.

THE ECOLOGICAL APPROACH: SYNCHRONIC

Since Childe developed the notion of the archaeological culture, the logical next step was to seek to reconstitute the lives of the communities implied by these assemblages. It was necessary to introduce a third dimension – to add life to time and space. Before discussing the ecological approach – has one got to say model? – I think it important not to overlook the fact that new ways of looking at archaeological data seldom invalidate older ones, though they sometimes help them to be followed in a more sophisticated manner. Just as Childe realised that there was a continuing need to devise and refine archaeological chronology, more especially in new or less well explored territories, so we may recognise the continuing need to distinguish the communities which existed in prehistoric times. Indeed the application of more refined quantitative methods should make it possible to establish these with greater certainty and precision than the impressionistic methods used in the past. Yet just as chronological systems can be devised more intelligently when account is taken of the spatial extent of particular artefact assemblages, so the validity of archaeological cultures can often be tested when the data is viewed in ecological terms. The very notion of a third dimension implies after all the existence and equal importance of the other two.

Historically the source of three-dimensional archaeology was derived in part from the kind of functional anthropology initiated by Malinowski and Radcliffe-Brown and in part from the development of animal and plant ecology. Both these were mainly British. Anyone reading both Archaeology and Anthropology at Cambridge before the war was indeed privileged. I can still hear Col. Hudson telling us that the essence of Anthropology was food and sex, keeping alive and perpetuating, not forgetting the social arrangements evolved by different communities to ensure these things. Radcliffe-Brown was compulsory as well as compulsive reading. And, as I've told elsewhere, the 1930s were the years in which pollen-analysis, a principal tool of environmental archaeology, was not merely being developed in the Botany Department but being applied to the prehistory of human settlement in the Cambridgeshire Fens (Clark, J. G. D., 1974:35; see also Phillips, 1951:258). Living systems and the interactions between their components were so to speak in the air. One grew up with a view of archaeology which some seem only to have rediscovered lately and by way of transatlantic proponents of the so-called New Archaeology.

The concept of human societies operating as systems, in which every component contributed to the functioning of the whole, was set out as a basis for the interpretation of the archaeological traces of former states of society in a widely used and several times translated text written just before the war and published in 1940 (Clark, J. G. D., 1940:152) as well as in a slightly more elaborate form, in the Reckitt Archaeological Lecture for 1952 (1952:215; 1957:175). I would ask you to observe two things about these diagrams. First, the arrows linking different dimensions are double ended. This was intended to denote that inter-relationships were dynamic and reciprocal. In more modern jargon they demonstrate the importance of feed-back within the system. Diagrams of this sort are necessarily flat. A better impression might have been given by building the kind of model with coloured symbols threaded onto wire used by molecular biologists to demonstrate the complexity of the genetic code. The other thing I would like you to note is that in the 1952 diagram human social systems are specifically integrated with the biological and physical aspects of total ecosystems. This stemmed in part from involvement in Quaternary Research, first in the work of the Fenland

Research Committee (1932–40) and later in connection with Star Carr (1949–52) (Clark, J. G. D., 1972a). No less influential was the overtly ecological interpretation of two of the most original successors of Malinowski and Radcliffe-Brown, namely Donald Thomson whose study of the seasonal aspects of Wik Monkan culture was published in 1939 and E. Evans-Pritchard whose *Nuer* appeared in the following year. It is important to note here that the ecological approach was not only free from, but was a denial of the dreary determinism of some of the earlier geographical approaches to archaeology. The relationships between the several dimensions of human life and different facets of the natural environment were seen not as one-way but as two-way. Each of the manifold relationships was held to be reciprocal. If the environment set constraints on economy, forms of economic life affected the environment. Similarly if economic factors influenced social organisation and ideology and value-systems, the converse is equally true. No wonder that Childe in the end had to abandon Marxism as an adequate tool for explaining prehistory.

You will have noticed that studying archaeological data in terms of ecosystems by no means implies any neglect of geographical references: on the contrary ecosystems are based on and indeed incorporate territories. It is merely that archaeological cultures in the sense distinguished by Childe are

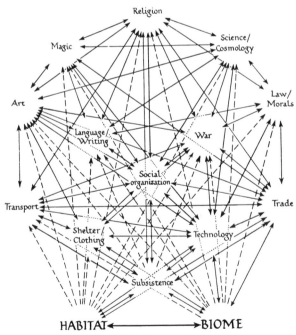

30.1 Simplified diagram illustrating some of the synchronic interrelations of aspects of human ecosystems

considered as relics of once living systems instead of merely or mainly as aggregations of traits useful for the purpose of territorial classification. The same methodological problem arises, that of definition. Individual eco-systems, like archaeological cultures, only exist as isolates for convenience of study. Although in general I intend to leave questions of methodology on one side, I must say just a word about the problem how we are to define phenomena which are only isolates for the purposes of study. It is perhaps significant that Malinowski and Radcliffe-Brown both chose small islands for their pioneer studies. In this way the unit of study was neatly and impartially defined by geography. Even so one cannot forebear to mention that not even islands in the midst of the Bay of Bengal or the Pacific Ocean can always remain in isolation. Had this been the case they could hardly have been populated by man. On the other hand archaeologists and anthropologists as well are for most of the time confronted by more extensive territories, whether continents or large islands, likely to have been shared by communi-ties united by different values, having distinct social systems, equipped by distinctive technologies and utilising their environments in different ways or at different levels of intensity. In short the problem remains of defining the areas occupied by communities united by distinctive cultural traditions or by different ecosystems or social territories, however one prefers to term them. Childe himself was well aware of the value of distribution maps in this regard. Those in *The Dawn* were abstract in the sense that they embodied his own considered views without indicating their material basis. In *The Danube in Prehistory* he had more scope to be concrete. It is evident that he relied primarily on pottery. He did so for the familiar reasons. In early times it was primarily a local product, it was made in abundance, it survived relatively well and although representing only a single craft, which may in some cases have played a relatively unimportant role, the product was complex and involved a number of variables, including composition, building, firing and shape as well as the technique, form and disposition of ornamentation. But Childe was also prepared to take account of any cultural preference consistently reflected in the archaeological data. The difficulty was that his criteria were eclectic, even impressionistic. He would throw in barrow forms, metal types, ornamental motifs, religious practices, anything in fact that helped to fill out distributional patterns and define territories. Some of his contemporaries were less catholic. Indeed, in extreme instances they went to the length of defining cultural territories and even of inferring series of invasions on the basis of variations in single traits, as with Harold Peake's bronze sword hilts and on this precarious basis seeking to explain the course of prehistory. It is interesting that, although Childe entitled his Oslo lectures of 1949 *Prehistoric Migrations in Europe*, we find him in the first one quoting with approval the long held Russian view that one should always seek explanations in terms of local developmental processes before having recourse to external causes and stating in so many words that he himself proposed to 'make a minimal use of migrationist hypotheses'. To-day the task of defining socio-cultural territories is recognised as a problem calling for a more methodical approach. Specifically it is one of the many problems in archaeological method from which we may expect increasingly valuable results from the application of mathematical procedures. As was so well illustrated at the recent Anglo-Romanian Conference dedicated to this theme, mathematics can provide tools, which so long as they remain tools, are capable of extorting history from an increasingly broad range of material phenomena (Hodson *et al.*, eds., 1971; Doran and Hodson, 1975).

Let me now consider some of the implications of adding a third dimension to archaeology. First, I think, it transforms our attitude to the raw data. One has only to glance through the pages of *The Dawn* to see how vestigial is the evidence used to define the dimensions of time and space, by comparison with that needed to reconstruct living systems. At the primary, elementary level of excavation, the enlarged objective requires a changed order of priority in the selection of sites and in the methods used to recover data. That is why, in a simple text entitled advisedly *Archaeology and Society* written in the middle of Childe's tenure of the Abercromby chair, I laid so much stress (ch. III) on the factors controlling the survival of different kinds of archaeological data. Star Carr was not dug to find yet more microliths nor would I have supported the researches in the Somerset Levels being carried on by Dr John Coles and his team so consistently out of an anxiety for the recovery of yet more polished axes or Neolithic pots. Projects of this kind have been selected explicitly in order to widen the range of data. Let me make the point appropriately by reference to arrowheads. When I was a boy they were one of my chief prizes as a flint collector. In the pre-Childe literature leaf arrows, like long heads and long barrows were classified as Neolithic and barbed-and-tanged arrowheads along with short heads and round barrows as Bronze Age. Childe assigned leaf-shaped arrowheads to the Windmill Hill and barbed-and-tanged to the Beaker culture. Both were very approximately correct. But it is also right to see these pieces of flint as the armatures of arrows that were propelled by pulling bows. It was indeed the recovery by peat diggers of the Neolithic bows from Ashcott and Meare (Clark, 1963:50) that still further enhanced interest in the Somerset levels already famous for the state of preservation of the Glastonbury and Meare Lake Villages, for the Quaternary Research work of Sir Harry Godwin (1960:1) and his associates and not least for their timber trackways (Coles *et al.*, 1968, 1970, 1973a, 1975). Study of bows, like any other category of archaeological find in functional terms opens up manifold fields of research. Details from a broad range of archaeological sources previously studied in isolation take on new meanings when focused on activities rather than on categories of objects. Conversely the desire to investigate activities defines areas of ignorance, the essential prerequisite for creative research as distinct from the mere salvage of material objects or structures. In particular it points to the need to obtain adequate samples of materials hitherto neglected because irrelevant to the needs of conventional temporal or cultural classification. Here again we have a feedback from research needs to techniques. The development of the froth flotation apparatus by the British Academy Early History of Agriculture Project at Cambridge (Jarman *et al.*, 1972:39) is only one of a multitude of instances.

The three-dimensional approach has another advantage. Since reciprocal relations exist between different spheres both of the natural environment and also of social life, it follows that each can be manipulated to probe others not always at first sight connected. In the case of arrows the relevance to subsistence and so to settlement is of course evident. It can among other things serve as a useful check on the nature of man–animal relations at particular sites. If all was love and understanding between men and reindeer at Stellmoor (Rust, 1943:85) or between men and red deer at Star Carr[3] one might well ask why arrows were so prominent at both and why the skeletal remains of both species should show evident signs of their use. Again, where archery is established in the archaeological record it can sometimes be used to account for enigmatic representations in art. Thus the clear representation of a bow and its attendant quiver helps to confirm that the engraving on the inner face of one of the slabs in the burial chamber of Göhlitsch in fact depicts the inner wall of a gabled timber house (Clark, 1963: pl. ix lower). Conversely and more frequently the iconography of rock-art for example may complete information about archer's equipment and still more usefully tell us about the bow's tactical use in hunting: rock-paintings in Eastern Spain for instance show ibex encircled by and red deer driven into bowmen. The various elements in the make-up of ecosystems embracing human societies compare with the strands in a prehistoric textile: Professor Vogt (1937) found that the best way to unravel the sometimes complex weave of Cortaillod samples was gently to tug individual strands and see how they related to others.

The fact that much can be learned by studying different aspects of social life, as represented by archaeological fossils, in conjunction is hardly contradicted by the fact that at an advanced level the pursuit of three-dimensional archaeology has increasingly to be carried on by specialists. Here I am not thinking so much of regional or temporal specialisation as of preoccupation with different aspects of the subject, whether environmental, economic, demographic, technological, social, political, conceptual or aesthetic, or again as Dr David Clarke (1968) has so amply demonstrated with the different techniques brought to bear on the analysis of archaeological data. Indeed the more we think in terms of three-dimensional archaeology the more necessary it becomes to draw on the maximum range of expert knowledge in respect both of the activities, organisation and conceptual life of communities of men and of the techniques and procedures available for analysing the material detritus of these. Anglers, toxologists, musicians, wood-turners, boat-builders, sailors – these and many more such – have special kinds of knowledge only available by accident to the professional archaeologist. This is an area, I believe, where the amateur can do most for archaeology, not by doing in his spare time what the professional is better equipped to effect, but contributing his special knowledge of how things work to the interpretation of archaeological data. I repeat what I have often said before that there is no kind of knowledge, no kind of experience, which cannot be of value to the elucidation of the past once this and not the manipulation of the data is regarded as the main object of the prehistorian or for that matter the historian. Professor Evans (1975:8) expressed it perfectly in his recent inaugural lecture as Director when he remarked that 'one of the beauties of archaeology is that almost any talent may turn out to be relevant'.

The most impressive outcome of the new approach is surely the emergence and growth to maturity of science-based archaeology.[4] Here one can see very clearly the extent of the feed-back between aims and methods. To take only one instance, so long as the chief and indeed in some cases only aim was classification, then adequate dating and the analysis of form and style of artefacts were sufficient. In so far as the role of artefacts in social life comes into question as a principal aim on the other hand it becomes important to define the precise source of materials, the processes by which they were manufactured into useful objects and the exact manner in which they were used. This leads directly to the appropriate branches of natural science and technology. Conversely it is known to have provided important stimuli to research in these fields. Again, as new apparatus or procedures, developed it may be in industry or in medical or military science, become available, historians and prehistorians may be encouraged to ask new and more searching questions. Such a process of continuous feed-back between the arts and sciences is one reason why archaeology has such a high potential as a subject of general education. The converse is no less true that the best prehistorians are likely to be those most aware of the possibilities in both camps. In the study of prehistory there is a constant interaction between aims and methods. Investigation of social structure for example has been immensely facilitated by computer technology and conversely the availability of this technology has led prehistorians to tackle problems previously considered beyond their reach (Leone, 1972, gives an instructive review of the field). The systematic coding and programming of graves, skeletons and grave-goods, to quote only one example, offers new insights into demography and social organisation. Similar insights can be won from the disposition of finds on settlements and within dwellings. In each case the basic requirement is pre-excavation survey and total excavation, each of which has been facilitated by a variety of chemical and geophysical techniques, air photography and mechanised precision excavators. The needs and requirements of three-dimensional archaeology are indeed formidable, but the returns in new knowledge are immeasurably greater than the mere salvage of repetitious data that too often passes for archaeology.

An aspect of antiquity traditionally emphasised by archaeologists, even if some of them have long ceased to merit the jibe that they were more interested in *Homo faber* than in *Homo sapiens*, is of course technology, though even here, as I've already pointed out, there has been a welcome extension of range from that needed for mere classification. During the generation just past on the other hand two additional fields have claimed attention, notably Environmental Archaeology in which this Institute has long played a leading role and Economic Prehistory. A particular aspect of this latter, The Early History of Agriculture, was adopted by the British Academy in 1966 as its first Major Research Project. Among the many publications issuing from this may be cited the three volumes edited by Mr E. S. Higgs (1972, 1975 and forthcoming), director of the Project during its decade of operation. Latterly we have seen and welcomed developments in other fields. The claims of Social Archaeology, grotesquely overlooked in the past, have received a welcome advertisement in Professor Colin Renfrew's recent Inaugural Lecture at Southampton University (Renfrew, 1973).[5] The archaeology of man's conceptual life has also recently been claiming increasing notice: I need only mention Alexander Marshack's (1972) illuminating study of notational markings on Palaeolithic art objects or the many fields of research considered in the course of the symposium held by the Royal Society and the British Academy on early astronomy (Kendall *et al.*, 1974, particularly A. Thom's paper on the astronomical significance of prehistoric monuments in Western Europe).

At an operational level mention should be made of Experimental Archaeology recently surveyed by Dr John Coles (1973b: a much fuller bibliography of various aspects of the field is given in Hester and Heizer, 1973). Plainly the more emphasis laid on the archaeology of once living systems, the greater the importance of devising experimental tests. For instance I've spoken of prehistoric bows. By constructing accurate models in the same kinds of wood and testing them in practice something measurable can be learned of their range and accuracy. Again it is valuable to test the functional labels of such flint forms as burins by using replicas and then comparing traces of wear on these with that observable on prehistoric specimens. Dr Coles' experiments on shields and musical instruments are other cases in point. And we should not forget the experiments in early farming methods carried out by the National Museum of Denmark, experiments ranging from clearance of forest by axe and fire to the sowing, reaping and grinding of cereals.

THE ECOLOGICAL APPROACH: DIACHRONIC

The data we study relate not merely to abstract time, to space and to real societies that existed in time and space, but to societies that changed their configurations in the course of time. Ecosystems have historical as well as existential dimensions. We can only hope to understand the course of change if we first understand function. The antithesis between Social Anthropology as a subject concerned with the synchronic study of society and Archaeology as one dealing with diachronic phenomena is no longer drawn so sharply as it once was. Social Anthropologists now feel sufficiently sure of themselves to admit that history is an undeniable dimension of any human society and archaeologists, as I have tried to indicate, are showing more interest in the way societies operate. Yet it is still true that Social Anthropology's main contribution to intellectual life rests on its ability to gain insights into the way societies operate in the short term, whereas the unique property of Pre-historic Archaeology is the ability to discern and explain changes in human affairs over the enormously long periods of time at its disposal. By facilitating the task of reconstructing the socio-cultural systems functioning in particular spatial and temporal contexts, the ecological approach has made it possible to attempt the even more formidable task of seeking to unfold the process of change through time, which in effect constitutes prehistory. In more concrete archaeological terms it is capable both of offering a more adequate interpret-ation of the data from single periods of occupation than a merely formal analysis of artefacts can do and of accounting for the differences existing between material from successive occupations.

When prehistoric archaeologists confront material from long sequences they consistently find evidence for what appear to have been relatively long periods of stability separated by phases of rather drastic change.[6] Yet quantitative analysis shows that behind a succession of distinct cultural configurations there is often evidence for continuous but gradual change in respect of individual components. To be acceptable a theory of cultural change needs to take account of both phenomena. This is what the ecological approach allows. We can accept as a working premise that the total environments in which any ecosystems operate are subject to change. For systems to operate effectively – and if they are not effective they will not long survive by any archaeological reckoning – it is necessary for at least some components to undergo a process of adaptation. Yet systems only survive in so far as they retain their coherence and integrity. Up to a point this can be achieved by adjusting to such adaptations on the part of certain components. Beyond this on the other hand the cost of maintaining the *status quo* may become so excessive that it is less demanding and therefore adaptively advantageous to effect a radical change and achieve a new configuration, a new kind of pattern to which members of society conform and which appears in the stratigraphic record as a new culture or at least as a new phase of cultural development. This would be no less true because certain components persist, though often modified in form or relative importance, through successive configurations.

It happens that in my own areas of specialisation I have focused more particularly on changes in habitat and biome, notably the contraction of ice-sheets, changes in land and sea levels and their effect on topography and the availability of resources, climate, vegetation and animal life. Childe significantly referred these to what he termed the 'external' environment. From an ecological standpoint on the other hand habitat and biomes are themselves integral parts of systems comprehending human societies. Moreover there is commonly a significant feed-back relationship, so much so that one often expects to gain information about basic economic activities like farming through the study of vegetational change. On the other hand there can be no question of changes in habitat or biome determining the course of prehistory. They were merely some among a number of changes to which human societies adapted through their cultural apparatus and in some cases let us not forget they were themselves the outcome of changes in the socio-cultural sphere.

In so far as Childe and his contemporaries sought to explain why one culture gave place to another, they did so in a perfunctory manner. There was a limited number of stock explanations. Cultural changes were accounted for by and large in terms of biological, climatic or geographical changes and/or in terms of the socio-cultural environment, notably 'influences' from other systems or more specifically trade or conquest and ethnic replacement. The author plumped for one or a combination and left it at that. There was little attempt at explanation or testing. More satisfying conclusions can be reached, I suggest, in terms of ecological theory. A point of departure is that ecosystems only exist in isolation for the convenience of analysis. In reality they intermesh with others, even ones remote in space. If this is true for instance of plant communities, which may be influenced by the movement of fruits, pollen or spores from far away, it applies with even more force to systems comprehending human societies. This is so because these are positively constituted by sharing, by the redistribution of goods and skills and above all perhaps of ideas, something made possible by the incomparable range and efficiency of communications within and between human societies.

Now just as the unique configurations embodied in archaeological cultures are the product of interaction between the individual communities occupying social territories (Clark, 1975:14), so it must be supposed were the larger societies themselves subject to influences not merely between neighbours through conflict or interchange, but also from afar through the movements of individuals and above all of objects and ideas. It is true enough that the very nature of societies, constituted by sharing territories and a whole configuration of ideas, techniques and values, not forgetting a common social structure, made them to a large extent proof against this bombardment so long as they were functioning effectively. The fact remains that ideas are potent and never more so than when systems are under strain. Whether in any situation we can hope to identify the final straw that tipped the balance is perhaps less important than seeking to estimate the pressures which over lengthy periods of time threaten the integrity of any system and can only be accommodated by adopting a new one with a different configuration. One indication of the importance of external influences in promoting cultural change, which I only have time to mention, is of course the relationship between centrality and progress and between isolation and stagnation. Another topic about which I must be brief is invasion or wholesale immigration, the most violent and, if substantiated, sweeping kind of external influence. If I have deplored the use of invasion as a *deus ex machina* (Clark, 1966:172) it is for the good methodological reason that it has tended in the past to inhibit research into alternative causes for the changes in our rough island history. It is often argued that the fact that ethnic movements can be documented from history implies that they operated in prehistory. I would prefer to put it the other way round and suggest that prehistorians, by treating invasions as hypotheses and testing them against the evidence as adequate explanations for cultural change, could well put in question not merely the implications but sometimes even the validity of such historical sources. In any case arguing backwards in time is an outrage in historio-graphic terms, since it is of the essence of history to weigh evidence in its contemporary context. What applies in one cannot be assumed to apply in another. Another point to remember is that not even the resources of the most modern military science have succeeded in obliterating peoples. As for cultures conquest has rarely been as effective as an agent of change as peaceful processes operating through time.

Another and in the long term more significant factor making for change was what I have elsewhere referred to (1975:27) as the inherent dynamism of human societies. I refer to the built-in trend towards a more effective and intensive utilisation of natural resources, making possible a greater density and concentration of population, a greater sub-division of functions and in consequence more effective and explicit political institutions. I have used the word built-in advisedly, since as I argued in *Aspects of Prehistory* (1970, ch. 2) the more effective use of resources and all that follows was an adaptive advantage so potent that it was a main factor in social selection. And let us not forget, failed societies leave no archaeology or at least none worth looking at. At this point I ought I suppose to refer to Childe's Neolithic and Urban Revolutions which exist in our thoughts whether or not they did in prehistory. I would only comment that the new methods of approaching prehistory, while they have not destroyed the familiar trilogy of Savagery, Barbarism and Civilisation as a parable, have disposed of its claim to offer what can be accepted as in any sense an explanation of prehistory. What prehistorians now visualise is the operation of inexorable processes, inexorable because, except in the refuge areas beloved of the classic Social Anthropologists, conformity to them was the price of survival. All prehistorians can hope for is to define the thresholds from one form of social life to another. Whether particular thresholds were revolutionary in the sense of being abrupt or whether they were smooth and gradual can only be assessed in terms of local research. There is nothing in ecological theory which rules out the possibility of comparatively rapid changes. On the other hand, as more than one speaker during the recent symposium on the Early History of Agriculture argued, the more closely the process of domestication, the basis of the first of Childe's 'Revolutions', is studied, the more gradual it is seen to be.[7] Paradoxically, although in the abstract everyone admits the reality of different states of society, these can often only be defined in the archaeological record by statistical means.

THE SCOPE OF PREHISTORY

In the course of this lecture I have intentionally kept to the higher ground, if not as some of you may think even to the world of clouds and theory. If I had done otherwise I could not possibly have covered more than a fraction of the territory. To conclude, let me touch briefly on the more banal matter of the temporal and spatial scope of prehistory. Although Childe wrote occasionally on the Palaeolithic he did so without much conviction. His real concern began with the Mesolithic contrivers of his Neolithic Revolution. Yet, since Childe, concern with the definition and meaning of man has again focused attention on the earliest periods of prehistory. Of recent years this quest has centred on Africa and more especially in East Africa. It is interesting to observe that even for the remoter periods of prehistory there has been a distinct shift from exclusive concern with stratigraphy and cultural classification to attempts to recover the forms of dwellings and analyse in detail the activity patterns to be inferred from the precise plotting of artefacts and palaeontological material. This in turn has involved, as was outstandingly the case at Kalambo Falls, Zambia (Clark, J. Desmond, 1969), and the much older beds in the Olduvai Gorge, Tanzania (Leakey, 1967:471; *cf.* Isaac, 1969), the application of stripping and plotting techniques of the kind originally worked out in connection with the settlement archaeology of later prehistoric Europe. If one of the main contributions Prehistory can make is to man's understanding of his place in the world, it is understandable that one of the main areas of research in a temporal sense must lie far back in the Early Pleistocene and perhaps even earlier when he was in the very process of emerging from his hominid antecedents.

In his first Inaugural Lecture Professor Evans claimed as one of Childe's basic tenets 'the necessity of mastering and using in our studies the widest possible range of comparative material' (Evans, 1958:49). It is true enough that Childe himself wrought a revolution in this regard. When he came to England again in 1922 he found British Archaeology divided into two camps working 'very nearly in watertight compartments' (Childe, 1929a:v). British insular archaeologists organised on a quasi feudal basis conducted their local and even national researches with only the barest if any reference to the European continent. On the other side were those concerned with the archaeology of the classical and bible lands whose activities focused on the Mediterranean and the Middle East. In between there was a virtual blank. It was a major contribution of *The Dawn* to set later prehistoric Britain in the context of temperate Europe, temperate Europe in that of central Europe and the Aegean and that of the Aegean in that of *The Most Ancient East*. Yet Childe remained a prisoner of Europe and the territories which influenced it in prehistory. If he looked to China it was not on account of Far Eastern civilisation but to pursue the origins of socketed bronze spearheads. He showed no interest in the New World, Sub-Saharan Africa, the Pacific or even his native Australia.

The half century since Childe came to prehistory has witnessed a world-wide expansion of archaeological research which is now pursued as extensively as botany or geology. What is at least as important is that since 1949 the technique of radiocarbon analysis has made available that form of 'trustworthy chronology, independent of archaeology and of any historical assumption' to which Childe was still looking forward in his 'Valediction'. Without a world-wide system of dating there was no possibility of extorting a world prehistory from the mere multiplication of local archaeological sequences. It is a matter of record that if the basic research leading to the development of radiocarbon analysis was carried out in the Institute of Nuclear Physics at Chicago, much of the impetus and direction came from the human sciences. The preface to the first edition of *Radiocarbon Dating* acknowledged the financial support of the Wenner-Gren Foundation for Anthropological Research during the crucial years 1948–50, as well as the help in selecting samples offered by the Committee on Carbon 14 of the American Anthropological Association and the Geological Society of America under the chairmanship of Fred Johnson (Libby, 1949; also 1970).[8] In this field anthropology was the patron, natural science the creative agent. The feedback or pay-off was tremendous. The foundations for a truly world-wide prehistory were being laid during the years preceding Childe's 'Valediction' and the structure, however incomplete in detail, has long since been taken for granted. Within the last 50,000 years or so of its effective range radiocarbon analysis has contributed more than any other single technique to making this possible, complemented for the remoter periods by such other chronometric methods as potassium/argon and uranium fission track.

The enlarged scope of prehistory allows us to view Childe's objective in a new light. European civilisation can now be seen more clearly to have been only one of a number of unique manifestations of the human spirit. Indeed from an ecological point of view, making all allowances for contacts, it would be inconceivable to view any culture otherwise than as constituting an essentially unique system. It is ironical that if Childe had taken a more ecumenical view he might have freed himself much earlier from the anti-quated folk-lore of Karl Marx. It is pathetic to find him admitting in his 'Valediction' that

Universal laws of social development are fewer and far less reliable than Marxists before 1950 thought.

It was as a great prehistorian, a man dedicated to his subject, to an unusual degree unconcerned for himself, that we salute the memory of Gordon Childe. His integrity shines through in his published works. In these he drew a clear distinction. He never tried to score debating points off colleagues by appealing to a lay public. In his professional writing he was scrupulous in documenting his facts and in keeping his works up to date. In addressing the general public, which perhaps wisely he did through the printed word, his tone was never condescending or dogmatic. He sought merely to engage interest. If he took the trouble to write a series of books for the general reader from *Man makes Himself* (1936) to the posthumous *The Prehistory of Human Society* (1958), this was because he thought his subject was one of broad human concern.

If like the rest of us Childe was in a measure a prisoner of his own past, I need quote only one sentence from his 'Valediction' to show that by the end of his life he saw well enough the way things were moving in the study of Prehistory.

The economic, sociological and ultimately historical interpretation of archaeological data has, I believe, now become a main task.

Notes

*The first Gordon Childe Memorial Lecture given at the Institute on 29 April 1975.

1 According to F. P. Smith in his foreword (pp. v–x) to the 2nd edition of Childe's first book *How Labour Governs* (1923), Childe obtained, but only briefly retained, a post in the Department of Tutorial Classes at the University of Queensland. In fact it has since appeared that it was the Senate of the University of Sydney which failed to ratify his appointment to a tutorship in ancient history: see J. Allen (1962), a reference for which I am indebted to Professor J. V. S. Megaw. It is nevertheless clear from Jack Lindsay's book (1958:135–7) that Childe did spend a period in the Brisbane area, presumably when he was holding the clerical job he took up following the debacle: a reference I owe to Mr Peter Gathercole.

2 According to the Preface (xii) 'The text was completed in September 1927, but owing to various difficulties final publication had to be postponed until 1929.'

3 Re-examination of the red deer bones from Star Carr by Dr Nanna Nøe-Nygaard of the Institute of Historical Geology and Palaeontology of the University of Copenhagen has revealed traces of the use of weapons on Mesolithic herbivores from Denmark (1974).

4 A useful survey of the field is given in Brothwell and Higgs 1969. The importance of this topic has recently been acknowledged in joint discussions between the British Academy and the Royal Society on the funding of research in this field.

5 For a pioneer survey, see Gutorm Gjessing's essay 'Socioarchaeology': one of those offered to Kaj Birkett Smith on his 70th birthday (Gjessing, 1963). See also J. G. D. Clark (1972b, esp. 10 ff.)

6 Thus in the long sequence at the Haua Fteah in Cyrenaica Dr Charles McBurney discerned 'two major change-overs from one basic pattern of composition to another' in addition to 'lesser changes, implying no more than adjustment of the material culture within the framework of an unbroken tradition'. McBurney was only following convention in equating the former with 'actual ethnic movement involving clear-cut cultural replacement' (McBurney, 1967:135).

7 Nowhere better seen than in the history of the exploitation of plant food in the Valley of Mexico revealed by R. S. MacNeish's excavations (McNeish, 1972).

8 Willard F. Libby (1949 and 1970) recalls that the father of Dr J. Arnold, his colleague along with Dr Anderson in the early stages of the research, 'was an enthusiastic amateur archaeologist'. Dr Libby himself had a keen interest in the antiquity of man in the New World.

References

ALLEN, J. 1962 Aspects of V. Gordon Childe, *Labour History*: 52 f.

BROTHWELL, D. and HIGGS, E. 1969 *Science in Archaeology. A Survey of Progress and Research*, revised ed., London: Thames and Hudson.

CHILDE, V. G. 1923 *How Labour Governs* (second edition 1964), Melbourne University Press.

1925a *The Dawn of European Civilization*, London: Kegan Paul, Trench & Trubner.

1925b When did the Beaker-Folk arrive? *Archaeologia*: 159.

1926 *TheAryans*, London: Kegan Paul, Trench and Trubner.

1929a *The Danube in Prehistory*, Oxford: The University Press.

1929b *The Most Ancient East*, London: Kegan Paul, Trench and Trubner.

1930 *The Bronze Age*, Cambridge: The University Press.

1935 *The Prehistory ofScotland*, London: Kegan Paul.

1940 *Prehistoric Communities of the British Isles*, London: Chambers.

1946a *Scotland before the Scots*, London: Methuen.

1946b Archaeology and Anthropology, *Southwestern Journal of Anthropology* 2, 3: 243–51.

1950 *Prehistoric Migrations in Europe*, Oslo.

1958 Valediction, *Bull. Inst. Arch. London* I, 1–8.

CLARK, J. DESMOND 1969 *Kalambo Falls Prehistoric Site I*, Cambridge: The University Press.

CLARK, J. G. D. 1940 *Archaeology and Society*, London: Methuen (3rd edn 1957).

1952 Economic Approach to Prehistory, *Proc, Brit. Acad.* 39, 215–38.

1963 Neolithic bows from Somerset, England, and the Prehistory of Archery in North-western Europe, *P.P.S.* 26 1–36.

1966 The Invasion Hypothesis in British Archaeology, *Antiquity* 40: 172–89.

1970 *Aspects of Prehistory*, University of California Press.

1972a *Star Carr: a case study in Bioarchaeology*, Reading, Mass.: Addison-Wesley.

1972b The Archaeology of Stone Age Settlement, *Ulster J. of Archaeology* 35:3–16.

1974 Prehistoric Europe: The Economic Basis, *Archaeological Researches in Retrospect* (Ed. Gordon R. Willey), Cambridge: Winthrop.

1975 *The Earlier Stone Age Settlement of Scandinavia*, Cambridge: The University Press.

CLARKE, D. L. 1968 *Analytical Archaeology*, London: Methuen.

COLES, J. M. *et al.* 1968 Prehistoric Road and Tracks in Somerset, England, *P.P.S.* 34: 238–58.
1970 Prehistoric Road and Tracks in Somerset, England: 2, *P.P.S.* 26:125–51.
1973a Prehistoric Road and Tracks in Somerset, England: 3 The Sweet Track, *P.P.S.* 39: 256–93.

COLES, J. M. 1973b *Archaeology and Experiment*, London: Hutchinson.

COLES, J. M. *et al.* 1975 *Somerset Level Papers I*, Hertford: Somerset Levels Project.

CRAWFORD, O. G. S. 1926 *Antiquaries Journal* 6:89–90.

DORAN, J. E. and HODSON, F. R. 1975 *Mathematics and Computers in Archaeology*, Edinburgh: The University Press.

EVANS, J. D. 1958 Two Phases of Prehistoric Settlement in the Western Mediterranean, *13th Ann. Rep. and Bull. Inst. of Arch.* London: 49–70.
1975 Archaeology as Education and Profession, *Bull. Inst. Arch. London* 12: 1–12.

EVANS-PRITCHARD, E. 1940 *The Nuer*, Oxford: The University Press.

GATHERCOLE, P. 1971 Patterns in prehistory: an examination of the later thinking of V. Gordon Childe, *World Archaeology* 3, 2: 225–32.

GJESSING, G. 1963 Socioarchaeology, *Foll 5*: 103–11.

GODWIN, H. 1960 Wooden Trackways of the Somerset Levels: their construction, age and relation to climatic change, *P.P.S.* 26: 1–36.

HESTER, T. R. and HEIZER, R. F. 1973 *Bibliography of Archaeology I: Experiments, Lithic Technology and Petrography*, Reading, Mass.: Addison-Wesley Modules in Anthropology 29.

HIGGS, E. S. (ed.) 1972 *Papers in Economic Prehistory*, Cambridge: The University Press.
1975 *Palaeoeconomy*, Cambridge: The University Press.

HODSON, F. R. *et al.* (eds) 1971 *Mathematics in the Archaeological and Historical Sciences*, Edinburgh: The University Press.

ISAAC, GLYNN LI. 1969 Studies of early culture in East Africa, *World Archaeology I*, 1–28.

JARMAN, H. N. *et al.* 1972 Retrieval of plant remains from archaeological sites by froth flotation, *Papers in Economic Prehistory* (Ed. E. S. Higgs) Cambridge: The University Press: 39–48.

KENDALL, D. G. *et al.* (eds) 1974 *The Place of Astronomy in the Ancient World*, London: The British Academy.

LEAKEY, M. D. 1967 Preliminary Survey of the cultural material from Beds I and II, Olduvai Gorge, Tanzania, in *Background to Evolution in Africa* (eds W. W. Bishop and J. Desmond Clark), Chicago: 417–46.

LEONE, M. P. (ed.) 1972 *Contemporary Archaeology: A Guide to Theory and Contributions*, Southern Illinois University Press.

LIBBY, W. F. 1949 *Radiocarbon Dating*, Chicago: The University Press.
1970 Radiocarbon Dating in *The Impact of the Natural Sciences on Archaeology* (ed. T. L. Allibone), The British Academy: 1–10.

LINDSAY, J. 1958 *Life rarely tells: an autobiographical account ending in the year 1921 and situated mainly in Brisbane, Queensland*, London: The Bodley Head.

McBURNEY, C. B. M. 1967 *The Haua Fteah (Cyrenaica) and the Stone Age of the South-east Mediterranean*, Cambridge: The University Press.

MACNEISH, R. S. 1967 A Summary of Subsistence, *The Prehistory of the Tehuacan Valley I* (ed. D. S. Byers), University of Texas Press: 290–310.

MARSHACK, A. 1972 *The Roots of Civilization. The cognitive beginnings of man's first art, symbol and notation*, New York.

NØE-NYGAARD, N. 1974 Mesolithic hunting in Denmark illustrated by bone injuries caused by human weapons, *J. of Arch. Sci.* 1: 217–48.

PHILLIPS, C. W. 1951 The Fenland Research Committee in *Aspects of Archaeology in Britain and Beyond* (ed. W. F. Grimes), London: Edwards, 258–71.

PIGGOTT, S. 1958 Obituary in *Proc. Br. Acad*: 305–12.

RENFREW, A. C. 1973 *Social Archaeology*, Southampton: University Press.

RUST, A. 1943 *Die Alt-Und Mittelsteinzeitlichen funde von Stellmoor*, Neumünster: 85–7.

THOMSON, D. 1939 The Season Factor in Human Culture, *P.P.S.* 5, 209–21.

VOGT, E. 1937 *Geflechte und Gewebe der Steinzeit 3*, Basel.

CHAPTER 31

ARCHAEOLOGY IN INDIA SINCE WHEELER

INTRODUCTORY

I ended my first lecture by summarizing very briefly what I believe to be Sir Mortimer Wheeler's essential legacy to India. I intend to devote the greater part of this one to considering what use India has in fact made of it during the last thirty years. As every teacher knows, the real measure of his success is the speed and extent to which his pupils outgrow his own achievement. It is his main task, not to imprint the younger generation, but to give its members confidence to make their own adaptations to changing circumstances, not least to new states of knowledge, new climates of opinion and new sets of problems. I emphasize this in case anyone should interpret anything said in this lecture as criticism of Sir Mortimer Wheeler in whose honour you have invited me to lecture.

THE CONTINUING NEED FOR AND THE LIMITATIONS OF STRATIGRAPHIC EXCAVATION

So far as an observer from outside can judge, the basic principles set out by Sir Mortimer Wheeler have continued to inform the practice of archaeology in India since he left its shores. This can be illustrated for example by the precise manner in which B. K. Thapar, a former member of the Taxila School, and now himself the Director General of the Survey, cut his sections at Maski[1] in south Deccan or again his cellular grid at Purana Qila.[2] Indeed I would go further and suggest that the progress made by Indian archaeologists since Independence stems in large measure from their observance. On the other hand the dynamic quality of Wheeler's leadership has ensured continuous progress in the elaboration of procedures, the development and adoption of novel techniques and above all in the constant definition of new objectives. Again, India like the rest of the world has fallen more and more under the influence of contemporary science and its accompanying modes of thought. Without in any way abrogating its place among the humanities, as Wheeler himself visualised it, archaeology has found it easy to gain from the advance of natural science since its very method reflects an experimental rather than traditional approach to a study of the past. It is a paradox to which I shall return at the end of this lecture that India has stepped onto the

582

31.1 Section through the Chalcolithic site of Maski, south Deccan, 1954, prepared for record by B. K. Thapar

31.2 Grid of cellular layout of excavations, carried out by B. K. Thapar at Purana Qila, Delhi, 1969-70

stage of history as an independent nation state at a time when cultural diversity and the sense of identity that this is capable of conferring is threatened as never before by the homogenizing pressures of a world-wide technology and the universalizing and generalizing categories of scientific thought.[3]

The remoter phases of prehistory, of which Mortimer Wheeler appreciated the significance without himself embarking on them, exemplify how early it was that Indian archaeology began to be enmeshed with modern science. As Professor H. D. Sankalia wrily commented almost in the same tenor in his recent book 'whatever interest we behold today (in this subject) is solely due to the impact of western thought and science'.[4] The foundations of our knowledge of the Palaeolithic phase of Indian prehistory were in fact laid by the English geologist Bruce Foote,[5] who arrived at the outset of his long career in 1862 within three years of the publication of Darwin's *Origin of Species* and the validation by Evans, Lyell and Prestwich of Boucher de Perthe's discovery of Palaeolithic implements in association with remains of extinct animals in the valley of the Somme, France. Western contributions have continued to make themselves felt in this area of Indian prehistory down to the present day, though latterly supplemented and, in due course, greatly outweighed by the work of Indian prehistorians. In this connexion I could mention my own teacher M. C. Burkitt whose study[6] of the collections formed by the British-Indian civilians Cammiade and Richards was particularly important for making the Indian Stone Age more widely known. Of greater moment for the future was the Yale-Cambridge expedition which operated under de Terra and Paterson[7] in Kashmir, the Punjab, the Narmada Valley and Madras, and for the first time linked Stone Age industries with the major climatic divisions of the Quaternary period.

Further contributions to the implanting of Quaternary research as a way of dating and interpreting the prehistoric sequence in India were made by Professor F. E. Zeuner,[8] whose chair was based on the London University Institute of Archaeology, founded by Mortimer Wheeler, and more recently by Andrew Goudie, Bridget Allchin, and K. T. M. Hegde's investigation of fossil dunes in Gujarat.[9] Perhaps the best indication that Quaternary research is well and truly established and practised by Indians on their own soil is afforded by the foundation of the periodical *Man and Environment*, the first issue of which appeared only last year (1977).[10] In this new periodical we can see one of the many realizations of the hopes expressed by Mortimer Wheeler in his presidential address to the Indian Science Congress of 1946.[11] The need for a forum for prehistoric archaeologists, geologists, hydrologists, geomorphologists, palaeobotanists, palaeontologists, soil scientists and others working in the field of Quaternary studies is manifest not merely for refining chronology, but even more for pursuing archaeology in depth. Whether one's concern is primarily ecological or economic it is obvious to us today that we need to study not merely artefacts but all the components of the systems in which human societies necessarily exist and these not in isolation but in interaction. If this interplay is to be free and so yield the greatest returns, archaeologists, while keeping their historic aims in view, must step down from the commanding height that Sir Mortimer found it so natural to assume[12] and stand on the same ground as their colleagues. The chronological ordering of the Indian Stone Age summarized in Sankalia's book complemented Mortimer Wheeler's concern for the chronology of the later prehistoric and protohistoric phases of the Indian sequence.

The main steps can be summarized very briefly. As recently as 1954–5, Professor Sankalia established the stratigraphic succession at Nevasa on the Pravara river, that has since been validated over a large part of India, south of the Ganges basin, of a Lower Palaeolithic (Series I) with handaxes and cleavers overlaid by a Middle Palaeolithic (Series II), comprising scrapers, points and blade-like tools.[13] More recently, the stratigraphic position of an Upper Palaeolithic (Series III) assemblage, marked by massive flakes, blades, burins and scrapers, has been established by Goudie, Allchin and Hegde in the upper levels of the Gujarat dunes.[14] To complete the sequence the same workers recovered a microlithic assemblage (Series IV), comparable to that occurring over extensive areas of the Old World during early neothermal times from deposits overlying the dunes and so post-dating the Late Pleistocene arid phase. Recent intensive work on analogous assemblages has lent precision to their dating, notably through radiocarbon analysis of samples from Sarai Nahar Rai[15] and Bagor,[16] as well as beginning to open up new dimensions in this phase of Indian prehistory. For the first time other prospects indicate that the mere temporal ordering of stone assemblages in the context of Quaternary geology may not be sufficient. The horizontal, diachronic study of cemeteries and settlements and the systematic analysis of organic residues are already beginning to give an insight into the social grouping, forms of settlement, economies and burial rituals prevailing during this phase of Indian prehistory. Thus, a crucial link is being forged between the still shadowy if long-enduring Stone Age and the protohistoric period that saw the birth of Indian civilization. The people who made the microlithic industries were after all the indigenous population of India.

It remains to see what Quaternary research can reveal about the transition from a hunter-forager to a farming economy in different parts of the Indian sub-continent. Clearly, advances can only be made and consolidated as the result of carefully planned and long sustained programmes, but promising beginnings have already been made. One avenue of research, the application of pollen-analysis to early neothermal deposits, was initially explored by Gurdip Singh and his collaborators,[17] who sought to interpret fluctuations in plant cover in terms of changes in land use in the style pioneered by Johs. Iversen in Denmark.[18] Both in Kashmir and Rajasthan changes in vegetation,

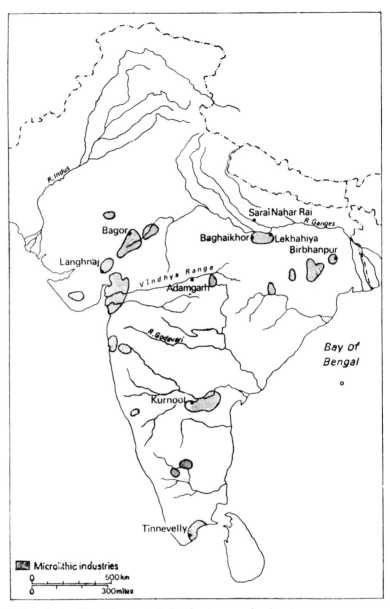

31.3 Map of microlithic industries in India, showing some key locations.

interpreted in terms of clearance by man, were held to imply the practice of agriculture possibly as far back as *c.* 6000 BC. More recently, a more critical attitude has been taken to the palynological evidence. Vishnu-Mittre in particular has pointed to the fact that analogous vegetational fluctuations have been noted well back in the Pleistocene not only at Hoxne in eastern England but notably at Kakathope, Madras.[19] As we know from observation of the practices of Australian aborigines,[20] hunter-foragers are capable of making a profound impact on vegetation, which can on occasion resemble closely that made by primitive agriculture. The conclusion seems inescapable that although pollen-analysis can provide invaluable clues, the actual practice of agriculture can only be proved by evidence from archaeological sites themselves. Much remains to be done in India, as elsewhere, in improving the standard of recovery of plant residues and even in adopting well tried methods and apparatus.[21] Even the incomplete and defective data presently available shows that agriculture has certainly been practised in India for over four millennia.[22] Further, there are signs that cultivation may have begun some time before it has been documented by archaeology. The range of weeds from Neolithic sites like Burzahom, in Kashmir, or Chirand, in Bihar, not to mention occurrences on Harappan and other chalcolithic settlements, argues that foraging continued alongside farming and points to what might be learnt by recovering plant residues from earlier neothermal sites. Again, the fact that the earliest Indian crop plants so far recovered were fully developed suggests, more particularly in the case of a local domesticate like Indian dwarf wheat (*Triticum sphaerococcum*), a longish antecedent stage in the progressively more effective utilization of plant resources.

In his Preface to the volume of studies presented to Sir Mortimer Wheeler to mark his eightieth birthday the Director of the Royal Asiatic Society recalled the recipient as 'already a "complete" archaeologist of international character' before India first claimed[23] him. Certainly, the new Director

31.4 Plan of a chalcolithic house, revealed by horizontal stripping at Inamgaon, District Pune, by the Deccan College Team

General was a professional archaeologist at the height of his powers and, certainly also, he already enjoyed an international reputation before he came to you. On the other hand, like many Englishmen, dating from the last generation of the imperial age, he was intensely British, not to say insular. The European continent was of little interest to him apart from the light it could throw on British phenomena. When as a very young man he visited the Rhineland[24] it was to check the date of Romano-Rhenish pottery, important to him at that time because of its occurrence in Britain. Similarly, when in 1936 he undertook a brief tour of the Near East it was to prepare for taking up the direction of the new London Institute of Archaeology. Again, the forays he made with flying squads of excavators into Brittany and Normandy in 1938–39 were aimed at tracking down the sources of exotic features of the Pre-Roman Iron Age in southern England.[25] When in later years he looked back on these excursions he did so with some complacency. As he recalled in respect to western Asia:

From the Sinai border to . . . northern Syria, I encountered such technical standards as had not been tolerated in Great Britain for a quarter of a century . . . The scientific analysis of *stratification*, upon which modern excavation is largely based, was almost non-existent. And the work was being carried out upon a lavish and proportionately destructive scale.[26]

Again, when his excavations in Brittany were officially inspected by the French authorities:

We were able to display . . . an orderly British excavation in full blast, the first of its kind, I suppose, in the annals of Breton archaeology.[27]

It was true enough that Wheeler's sections were a marvel by comparison with anything to be seen in France or the Near East at the time. On the other hand, if he had made an archaeological tour of Germany or Denmark during the interwar years he would have found something very different. There, the archaeologists of the *Siedlungsarchäologie* school had advanced to another stage of research: having established their sequences they were seeking to recover the way of life of the communities that had left their successive traces in the soil. A decisive advance was made both in Germany and Denmark during the decade preceding Wheeler's excavations at Maiden Castle. As early as 1927, Gerhard Bersu had revealed the plans of five phases of prehistoric settlement on the Goldberg,[28] a defended site near Nördlingen in south Germany, by stripping successive levels and revealing extensive areas in plan. Even more extensive operations were carried on by Buttler and Haberey between 1930 and 1934 at Köln-Lindenthal in the Rhineland[29] where the stripping of *c.* 35,000 sq. m of Neolithic surface revolutionized ideas about this phase of European prehistory. By uncovering the total plan of a settlement comprising long rectangular houses, granaries and drying racks they succeeded in illuminating not merely the economy but also the demography and social structure of the peasant communities established on the loess of West Germany at a period we now know to have been around six thousand years ago. Meanwhile, during the nineteen-thirties Gudmund Hatt[30] had been at work applying horizontal excavation to settlements of the Pre-Roman and Roman Iron Age in north Jutland and amplifying his studies by extensive surveys of adjacent field systems and careful analysis of food residues. In a word, both in Denmark and Germany archaeological sites were being planned and excavated with the prime object not of refining sequences of artefacts or determining their affiliations at home and overseas, but rather of reconstructing as far as possible the way of life of the communities that made and used them.

In British archaeological circles, receptive to what was going forward in the archaeologically more advanced parts of Europe, these developments were followed with intense interest. When Gerhard Bersu, rightly apprehensive of trends in Hitler's Germany, came to Britain he was invited to apply his methods to Little Woodbury,[31] a site discovered by air-photography on the chalk near Salisbury and hardly more than 60 km from Maiden Castle. Complete excavation was prevented by the war, but about 7 out of 15,000 sq. m of its total extent were cleared down to the chalk surface. Area excavation revealed a farmstead, comprising at any one time a single house with associated structures, notably granaries, drying racks, storage-pits and corn drying kilns. After the war, examination of Pitt-Rivers's excavation report on an analogous site at Woodcuts showed that in the light of Bersu's work the General had himself been digging a farmstead and not a village as, following tradition, he had assumed.[32] Already before the war the virtual monopoly of the Maiden Castle style of excavation, directed primarily to the refinement of chronology, and directed, therefore, to parts of the site most susceptible to change, notably the entrances to the defended area, was under challenge, not merely on the continent but on the very chalk of southern England on which Maiden Castle and the Pitt-Rivers estate were situated. This implies no criticism of Mortimer Wheeler, rather the contrary. In any endeavour, whether in natural science, archaeology or any other field, it necessarily happens that the more decisively one set of questions is answered, the more surely new ones will obtrude themselves, questions that as a rule will require new procedures for their resolution. It is a measure of Mortimer Wheeler's success in establishing a chronological framework for the Pre-Roman Iron Age in southern Britain that new methods should have pressed so rapidly and so insistently on those he had himself perfected.

It was much the same story in India. The stratigraphical ordering, both of the Stone Age and of the succeeding protohistoric period, along the lines demonstrated by Wheeler, would of itself have been enough to shift the emphasis of Indian archaeology away from exclusive preoccupation with chronology and external relations. No one could have put this more succinctly than Sir Mortimer Wheeler himself in his foreword to the first edition (1956) of the still regretted Bendapudi Subbarao's *The Personality of India*. Sir Mortimer joined with Subbarao and his colleagues in looking forward:

to the time when the necessary initial vertical digging – the search for a cultural time-table – can be supplemented increasingly by horizontal digging – by the systematic revelation of the ancient towns and villages of India and a clear demonstration of the sort of life that was lived in them.[33]

INTERDISCIPLINARY RESEARCH

This tendency has been accelerated and intensified by the systematic deployment during the last two decades of the technique of radiocarbon dating, a happy consequence of the high standard attained by the physical sciences in India. The establishment of a C 14 Laboratory in the Tata Institute of Fundamental Research, Bombay (now shifted to the Physical Research Laboratory, Ahmadabad), dedicated to the exploitation and refinement of Willard Libby's new method of dating,[34] greatly facilitated the cooperation between physicist and archaeologist on which success in this field so largely depends. The extent of the Indian sub-continent and the wide range of cultural attainment prevailing in different parts of it at any one time made it a peculiarly favourable theatre for the deployment of the new method. In the upshot, India has proved to be an outstanding exemplar of what radiocarbon dating is capable of achieving in opening up archaeology.[35] Inevitably, its success meant increased speed of the run-down of the initial phase of research in Indian archaeology to which Wheeler had applied his energy and sense of direction with such conspicuous success. Stratigraphic excavation will always be needed, and wherever it is carried on in India in the future, one may hope that it will continue to be executed in true Wheelerian style. On the other hand, the focus of interest has now shifted away from the primary task of establishing sequence and datable contacts to investigate structures in relation to the social life of the people who occupied them. Here again we have a parallel with Britain. In each country the superlative elan imparted by Wheeler and the admirable methods of excavation he imparted hastened the time when the main concentration would focus on what he himself had always held to be the ultimate aim of archaeology, the more perfect understanding and appreciation of man's past, whether or not this had been recorded in documentary researches.

The investigation of a settlement mound at Inamgaon on the right bank of the river Ghod in the neighbourhood of Pune by a research team from Deccan College[36] illustrates conveniently what I mean by speaking of a Post-Wheeler stage in Indian archaeology. The zeal and disciplined attention to detail in respect of excavation, record and retention of data are fully maintained, but a notable change of objective is reflected in excavation procedure. A feature which merits particular mention is that the project was a collective one in which objectives were clarified in discussion before the work began and a plan of operations agreed upon to ensure that aims were at least pursued if not in the event always fully realized. This in itself betrays a recognition that every excavation is at once a dialogue and an experiment and tacitly rejects the idea firmly fixed in the mind of Gen. Pitt-Rivers and not a few of his successors that one had only to dig and record to reveal objective truth. It was decided early on to abstain from cutting 'one long trench across the mount, in Wheelerian fashion' on the ground that since it was already known that the site was inhabited between *c.* 1600–700 BC during Malwa, Early Jorwe and Late Jorwe times (Periods I–III) there was no point in doing so. It was accepted that since a prime aim was to investigate the lifeways and settlement patterns of the inhabitants through the life-time of the occupation, a first necessity was to clear a sufficient area off the settlement to reveal its overall plan at each level as well as details of individual structures. Again, following in this case a favourite maxim of General Pitt-Rivers, it was agreed not merely to recover enough artefacts to date the various occupations, but instead to retain 'all the objects – useful or otherwise' and to observe and record not merely their stratigraphic context as with Pitt-Rivers but also their position in relation to individual structures. Particular stress was laid on the need to record the nature and position of refuse in relation to dwellings: instead, for instance, of merely keeping the pottery from different levels distinct, it was decided to relate pots and sherds to individual houses in the hope of recovering information about the social dimension.

Another aspect of team-work was the inclusion of experts not merely as authors of specialist reports on which the director could draw when writing his final report, but as fully fledged members of a seminar. Instead of the head archaeologist selecting items to buttress his hypothesis and in this way too often conducting a circular argument, questions were to be debated from different angles by independent minds equipped with their own expertise. Even from a summary account one is beginning to see the advantages of this kind of approach. In respect of subsistence the point of departure must always be the ecological setting. S. N. Rajagurus's conclusion from his examination of the Inamgaon territory is that it was 'characterised by high variability of rainfall and consequent threat of drought'. M. D. Kajale's identification of two cereals (barley and wheat) and of four pulses (beans, horse-gram, lentils and peas) led him to suggest on his own account that the chalcolithic farmers must have 'made use of available water resources very intelligently'. How intelligently, was verified by the discovery, through extensive excavation, of an embankment of rubble and mortar, built during period I, and plausibly interpreted as designed to pond back flood-water which in case of need could be used for irrigation. As to the composition of diet much remains to be learnt. G. L. Badam found that the inhabitants were probably roasting and certainly eating a variety of domesticated animals, among which humped oxen predominated, as well as several kinds taken in the chase. On the other hand, he also noted that the deplorable dental pathology of a man of thirty-five or so suggests stress due to 'a diet composed primarily of grains'. By this stage of course it cannot be assumed that diet was by any means uniform throughout the population, and one of the main objects of extensive excavation is precisely to uncover information on social structure. The Inamgaon site has indeed produced evidence in the shape of a large, multi-room house, contrasting with the normal run of small single-room dwellings, for at least a certain degree of social hierarchy. Again, detailed recording of small finds and waste in relation to structures has shown that craftsmen in potting, gold-smithing and ivory carving were concentrated on the western margin of the settlement. It is particularly significant that this should have been so throughout the Inamgaon occupation and above all that it should still apply to the villages of Maharashtra down to the present day.

THE ECOLOGICAL APPROACH IN INDIAN ARCHAEOLOGY

Since Indian archaeologists have been free to concern themselves with something beyond establishing bare sequences they have addressed themselves to many problems and followed many roads. It would be tedious and otiose to enumerate these for an Indian audience. I will only touch on some which have struck me as of particular interest. One of the outstanding features of India and its archaeology is the immense diversity and range which it displays. One of the leading questions to obtrude itself must surely be how it has been that during the last four millennia down to the present day so wide a range of cultural attainment is displayed by different parts of the subcontinent at one and the same time? In his *The Personality of India*,[37] the title of which must surely have been inspired by Sir Cyril Fox's *The Personality of Britain*, Bendapudi Subbarao sought the key in geography. Two factors were of predominant importance, first that during protohistoric times at least overland cultural intrusions came from the north and predominantly, though not exclusively, from the north-west, and second that they found their way south along paths to a large extent laid down by geographical circumstances. In particular, Subbarao followed Professor O. H. K. Spate's lead[38] in distinguishing relatively accessible nuclear zones and areas of relative isolation. Whereas exotic impulses penetrated the former relatively easily, the latter were so much more resistant that in some cases they have continued to shelter tribal communities of simple culture down to our own times. Subbarao went further than emphasizing the difference between territories that attracted and those that sheltered from new impulses.

He went a certain way to adopting an ecological concept of culture whereby 'there is always at any time, an essential equilibrium between the various factors like the physical environment, and human communities in relation to their material culture and technological achievement'.[39] Further, he appreciated that this equilibrium was notional and in fact liable at any time to be upset 'when any one of these factors changes'. The degree to which human communities adapted to such upsets determined whether they progressed or stagnated. It was communities unable to effect the necessary adjustments that contracted out by withdrawing to areas of relative isolation. Thus geographic factors exerted a selective role in the process of cultural evolution and contributed to the diversity of culture in the subcontinent.

If Subbarao had lived we can well believe that he would himself have applied ecological notions to the further elucidation of archaeology, as the present writer had been doing in relation to European prehistory since 1952.[40] It was left to D. P. Agrawal to expound in a truly brilliant chapter some of the possibilities stemming from an application of such notions to the protohistory of India.[41] Agrawal has not fallen into the determinist trap that caught so many geographers who thought it fun to explain cultural and historical change in terms of climatic or some other environmental fluctuation. In framing an ecological hypothesis to account for the diversity of cultural patterns and the limited scale of individual settlements in a territory like Baluchistan for instance, he began by rejecting as unproven Aurel Stein's theory of desiccation. Instead he points to two aspects of the habitat still characteristic of the region, namely low rainfall and a topography marked by narrow basins separated by mountain barriers. And these he sees as factors constraining greater homogeneity and larger scale settlements rather than as compelling the pattern reflected in the archaeological record. When he does acknowledge the impact of changes in habitat or biome he commonly attributes these in themselves to the impact of demographic or directly cultural forces. Thus, while assuming that the climate of the Sind-Punjab region had remained within certain limits stable during recent millennia, he notes that the agricultural wealth on which the Harappan civilization ultimately rested itself depended on the silt deposited by annual melt-waters. This in turn was conditioned by the degree to which the flow was retarded by vegetation. Thus the breakdown of the Harappan civilization was built into the system. The more effective the technology, the more marked the increase of population, the greater the impact on vegetation. And the regenerative forces began to decline, degradation set in, vegetation became less effective in slowing down the flood waters and the amount of silt deposited and by consequence the prosperity of the Harappan civilization declined. Often then interaction between the natural and socio-cultural components in ecosystems were highly complex and on occasion the leading role might be played by a more or less drastic change in the habitat. In the case of Rajasthan the determining factor seems to have been a change in the course of the Sutlej which by drastically impairing conditions for farming, led a population adjusted to more favourable circumstances to weigh too heavily on vegetation and convert the territory into a marginal desert even less favourable to human settlement. As a last example I would touch upon one of the most striking regional contrasts in all of Indian protohistory, that between the fate of the Indus and Ganga basins as foci of human settlement. The question why the Harappan did not spread into the adjacent basin is all the more insistent that the empires of historic times were commonly based upon it. I for one have found the ecological explanation furnished by Agrawal all the more satisfying at least as a working hypothesis that it takes full account of the essential dimension of time. The contrast between the fertile silt of Sind and Punjab and the hard calcareous silt of the Doab only weighed in favour of the Indus, so long as the Harappans had not pushed their 'success' to the point at which it fatally impaired the ability of the vegetation to promote the deposition of silt; and conversely the hard soils and heavy forest of the Ganga basin ceased to be serious obstacles to farming once an effective iron technology had been established during the period of the Painted Grey Ware during the first millennium BC.

If the many stimulating hypotheses put out by Agrawal and others about the way in which the different environmental systems of the subcontinent were exploited at different periods of prehistory and protohistory are ever to be conclusively tested, it is evident that substantially greater resources will need to be invested in Quaternary research.

This includes geomorphological studies of the kind recently reviewed at the Physical Research Laboratory, Ahmadabad,[42] as well as the palaeobotanical ones already touched upon (above, p. 587) and the mineralogical, petrological, chemical and technical studies needed to investigate sources of raw materials and the techniques used to shape them into increasingly specialized artefacts. Inter-disciplinary studies of this kind, involving archaeologists and natural scientists are capable of bringing profit to both, provided only that the integrity of the various disciplines is scrupulously observed.

This in turn has a powerful bearing on an issue of great practical importance, namely how to finance fundamental research on the scale needed if worthwhile results are to be gained from fundamental research on such topics as the refinement of dating techniques, the exploitation and shaping of the environment and the sources and techniques of working the raw materials used in making the material equipment of the cultural apparatus. The cost of such research extended over periods of years is far beyond the range of funding open to the humanities. Experience in Britain suggests that one way of closing the gap is to convince natural scientists of the benefits that can flow back to science from participation in joint research. Substantial progress has been made on a public level through the joint symposia held of recent years between the Royal Society and the British Academy,[43] but the influence of cooperation at a less formal level between natural scientists and archaeologists, engaged on joint projects, has probably in the aggregate been even more significant. At least we can point to one practical outcome in the very recent formation by the Science Research Council, which broadly controls the disbursement of government funds for research in the natural sciences in Britain, of a special Science-based Archaeology Committee with powers to make grants within a prescribed national budget for the furtherance of research specifically on the interface between Archaeology and the Natural Sciences.

THE ANTHROPOLOGICAL APPROACH TO ARCHAEOLOGY IN INDIA

Another topic on which I would like to touch concerns the approach of professional archaeologists to their own cultural data. This is largely determined or at least powerfully influenced by the nature of their training. Here, one may note a broad contrast between the Old World where archaeologists tend to emerge from a background in the history of their own historical tradition and Australasia and the New World where they came mainly from schools in which archaeology or at least prehistoric archaeology was studied in the context of anthropology. Many British archaeologists, including Sir John Marshall and Sir Mortimer Wheeler, were trained in the Greek and Roman classics. One of the great benefits of such an education, well displayed in Wheeler's own life, was the emphasis it placed on humanity, on real people and communities, rather than on abstractions. On the other hand, there is irony in the designation common in Scottish universities of Professors of Classics as Professors of Humanity, when in reality these scholars are endowed to profess the values of a very particular, and from a global point of view, a very restricted segment of humanity. As always, there are exceptions, of whom Sir James Fraser is perhaps the most eminent, but the conventional classicist tends not merely to be culture-bound but, what is worse, blissfully unaware of his condition. When Mortimer Wheeler came to India he identified first, as we have seen, with the Greeks in the north-west and next with the Romans in the south. If there was a sound methodological reason for this in the need to calibrate Indian stratigraphy with a known system of historical dates, it is hard not to believe that he was drawn by deeper and probably unconscious tides. It was not merely that he took the classical peoples as a basis for exploring the archaeology of India, as he previously had done in England and Wales. One must remember that the Greeks and Romans regarded the peoples with whom they came into contact as barbarians and by implication as inferiors. Similarly archaeologists coming from a classical or indeed historical tradition sometimes fall into the trap of grading cultural manifestations in terms of the degree to which they approximate to their own and at the same time of employing a terminology appropriate to their own society for others of quite different traditions, and at quite different stages in social evolution. Semantic confusions and unacknowledged value judgement have only added to the already formidable difficulties of deciphering the unwritten past. None of us can claim immunity for these faults. They are an inherent part of our being as men, that is primates conditioned by inherent and, therefore, by particular cultures. It is the inevitability of prejudice that emphasizes the need to be aware of it, while at the same time endowing us with our humanity. From personal experience I believe the best preparation is to be educated both in the history of one's own tradition and in the broader perspectives of anthropology. If it is not asking too much in an age of specialization, an awareness at least of the ways in which the natural sciences work and enough facility in mathematics to manipulate and quantify archaeological data are hardly less to be desired. Is it any wonder that educationalists as such should find archaeology an ideal meeting ground of specialists, an area of mutual understanding and shared insights?

A broadly anthropological approach on the part both of overseas and indigenous scholars to the phenomena encountered in archaeological excavations is already yielding fruit. The interpretation of the Deccan ash-mounds is a case in point. Since these were first noted by a British surveyor at the beginning of the nineteenth century they have been the subject of much idle speculation. Some people held them to be the outcome of natural processes, including volcanic activity, whereas others were nearer the mark in ascribing them to human activity generally of an industrial nature, including brick-making, potting, class-manufacture and iron smelting, but also extending to mass *sati*. When Bruce Foote, the real pioneer of Stone Age studies in India, addressed himself to the problem in 1886, it was natural for him at a time before prehistoric archaeology had diverged from the general body of cultural anthropology to recall the explorer Stanley's description in his book *In Darkest Africa* of the accumulations of cow-dung outside the *zariba* or thorn-fence of the East African village.[44] It was this recollection that gave him the clue to his theory that the ash-mounds were nothing more than accumulations of cow-dung. Despite the fact that Foote's hypothesis was confirmed by chemical analysis of the ash at Presidency College, Bombay, it passed into limbo during the silly season that ensued when archaeologists became too absorbed in organizing their data to mediate seriously on what it meant. When, following Sir Mortimer's stratigraphic demonstration of the age of the Neolithic in south India, Raymond Allchin returned to the problem of the ash-mounds as monuments to the actual life of the people of the Deccan during the second millennium BC, he returned to Bruce Foote and at Utnur in particular tested, and as it turned out, vindicated his hypothesis by excavation. Sufficient of the old ground surface was stripped to reveal traces of the actual wooden pens, as well as cattle bones and even hoof-imprints,[45] and F. E. Zeuner's test of the overlying ash confirmed that it was in fact burnt cow-dung. The only difference concerned the circumstance under which the mounds of dung were fired. This is not the moment to discuss whether Allchin was right to reject Foote's idea that the firing was accidental in favour of the notion that it was carried out intentionally as a part of a magico-religious rite concerned with warding off disease and promoting fertility. The only point I would make is that Allchin was guided by his knowledge of rites still practised in rural India.[46] Ethnographic comparisons, if they cannot of themselves offer decisive proof, at least offer hypotheses grounded in reality rather than mere fancy, but they still need to be tested and if they are not amenable to testing are barely worth making.

One thing the Utnur excavation proved for certain is that cattle were of key importance in the Deccan already by the beginning of the second millennium BC. And the multitude of representations of humped cattle painted on and pecked into rock-surfaces around the Piklihal ash-mount[47] further suggests that cattle were already of more than merely economic importance. One impression made on Allchin by his work in the Deccan was his sense of cultural continuity: '. . . many of the basic elements of life in the Karnataka region then established have continued down to the present day'.[48] Put the other way round one could comment that India had achieved

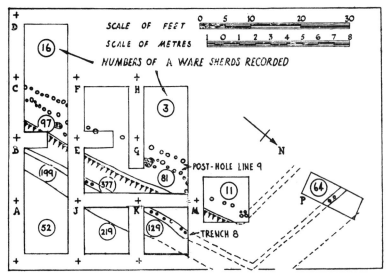

31.5 Utnur ash-mound, Deccan: F. R. Allchin's plan, showing one corner of cattle-pen, dating from Period I

its identity a very long time ago. As Allchin commented in his Utnur Report 'The keeping of cattle is, in India, as old as civilization'.[49] The humped cattle painted on the Togau and Zhob wares of Baluchistan and further afield on the Iranian plateau recall those engraved on the seals and modelled in clay at Harappan sites. It is hardly surprising, in view of the continuity of settlement displayed by the chalcolithic sites of the Malwa and Jorwe phases, dating from the run down of the Harappan civilization to *c.* 700 BC,[50] that so many of the basic activities of economic life noted at the Indus cities still operate in modern India. To judge from marks in the sub-soil, the Harappan settlement at Kalibangan was found to be built over an earlier period ploughed field, cultivated at the present day by traction ploughs.[51] Cotton was already among the crops raised alongside cereals. Again, the humped oxen depicted on seals and still familiar today were presumably used to draw not only the ploughs but also the solid-wheeled wagons represented in baked clay toys from Harappan levels and reproducing precisely those still in use.

In looking to the future it is of vital importance to touch upon a more fundamental way in which anthropological insights ought increasingly to be brought to bear on archaeological research in India. The instances so far mentioned relate after all to a relatively simplistic phase in the history of

31.6 Kalibangan: Pre-Harappan ploughed field with furrow-marks showing traces of cultivation of modern type exposed by B. K. Thapar under the settlement mound.

archaeological research. Mortimer Wheeler and, it must be confessed, nearly all his successors in Indian archaeology, have acted on the assumption that their main task was to recover data in a disciplined manner. The emphasis lay on the material evidence and on the means used to secure it. This was understandable enough when the objective was still the elementary one of building temporal sequences. On the other hand, in proportion as this

31.7 Clay model of Harappan bullock cart

31.8 Modern bullock cart

objective is realized, archaeology, if it is to be more than a hobby and a destructive one at that when excavation is involved, needs to be pursued at a more sophisticated level. It is no longer enough to accumulate data, however, meticulously, and then ask what it means. Thought and notably the formulating of problems and questions need to precede action, if action is to yield understanding rather than result in the destruction of potential evidence. Above all, since archaeology is concerned with such lengthy vistas of time, we need to discover not merely how socio-cultural systems operated at particular periods, but how and by what processes they underwent the changes documented in the archaeological record while at the same time maintaining the underlying continuity that issued ultimately in each of the diverse historic civilizations of mankind. In this context I would strongly recommend S. C. Malik's book published already ten years ago.[52] I would only add that in the context of India and more particularly in relation to the protohistoric period, historical and literary scholarship have at least as much to contribute by way of posing significant questions as anthropology.

THE DIVERSITY OF CULTURE

I would like to end this lecture on a more general note and one of which I believe Sir Mortimer Wheeler would have approved. If we accept that, however scrupulous we ought to be to pursue archaeology in the controlled and disciplined manner proper to any scientifically conducted pursuit and, however assiduous we should be enlisting natural scientists to extract the most from archaeological data, our aim is all the same humanistic, then we ought not to be afraid to regard archaeology as something capable of enhancing our lives. One way in which we can do so is to deepen our sense of corporate identity at the same time as it enriches our awareness and enjoyment of culture. It is widely and, in my view, rightly accepted that prehistoric archaeology is valuable for reminding us of our common identity as men, distinct from other primates, by virtue of sharing a common inheritance of culture. It is true enough that for by far the greater part of prehistory the cultural stock was by and large common to all men in every part of the then inhabited world. The flint and stone industries of Lower, Middle and early Upper Pleistocene Age, were notably homogeneous over those parts of Africa, adjacent parts of Europe and Asia as far east as China, to which settlement was then confined. It was when settlement first expanded into a greater range of environments later on in the Upper Pleistocene that we begin to observe perceptible regional diversification and some notable increase in complexity, but it was not until the adoption of a more sedentary form of life, based on domestication of the animals and plants, occupying many different habitats, that there was any pronounced acceleration. Above all, it was during the protohistoric phase in India as elsewhere that the

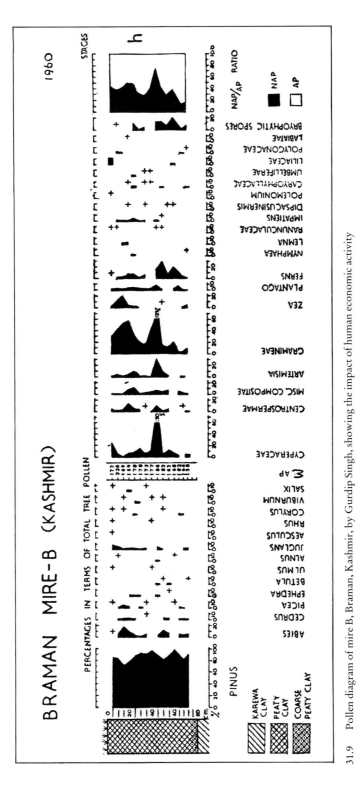

31.9   Pollen diagram of mire B, Braman, Kashmir, by Gurdip Singh, showing the impact of human economic activity

CARBON-14 DATINGS OF PROTOHISTORIC CULTURES OF INDO-PAKISTAN SUBCONTINENT

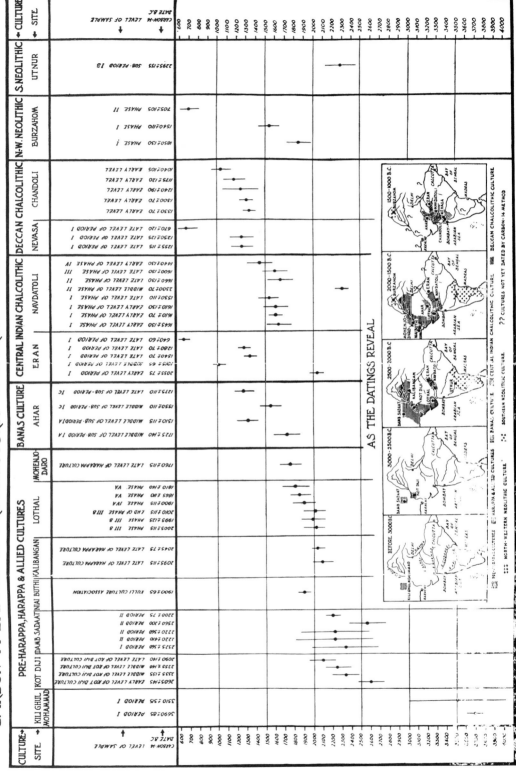

31.10 Diagram illustrating the use of radiocarbon dating in Indian archaeology

distinctive civilizations we know today began to emerge. It is I suggest precisely in the achievement of diversity that human communities attained their fullest humanity.

This diversity is not only infinitely precious. It is also increasingly under threat from the dominant forces in modern society. We are told it is unscientific to be Indian or English or even European. Natural science is not interested in diversity but in generality. So is modern business. And so are many modern politicians. The most efficient manufacture depends on standard machines and operatives trained to man them. Similarly, the most effective market is the widest and most standardized, and consumption, to be maximized, requires the flattening of social hierarchy, the elimination of cultural preferences and the most speedy and uniform communication systems, whether for the movement of goods, people or ideas. If maximizing the production and consumption of goods is the be all and end all of human life, then we can view the dissolution of culture with equanimity as the removal of an impediment to the unrestricted forward movement of progress. If on the contrary we accept the verdict of archaeology that men have achieved their humanity precisely by developing the culture and maximized their humanity by intensifying, localizing and diversifying their heritae, then I suggest we should not only deplore the homogenizing tendencies of our age, but proclaim the positive value to us as human beings of our particular traditions.

The dilemma we face is that whereas throughout the greater part of history and the whole of protohistory and prehistory social selection made for a progressive intensification and diversification of culture, the influence of industrial production and natural science has been driving us all into even greater cultural impoverishment. The progressive dehumanization of man is not inevitable, though it is already far advanced. As archaeologists surveying the total range of man's history, we are uniquely placed to proclaim the values we stand in danger of losing. Unless the danger of losing these values is proclaimed they will not merely be betrayed, but betrayed in the names of profit, progress and science.

Notes

1 B. K. Thapar, 'Maski, 1954: A Chalcolithic Site of the Southern Deccan', *Ancient India*, 13 (New Delhi, 1957), pp. 4–142.

2 B. K. Thapar, 'The Buried Past of Delhi'. *Expedition*. 14, no. 2 (Winter 1972), pp. 21–6.

3 Grahame Clark, 'Archaeology and Human Diversity', *Annual Review of Anthropology*, Palo Alto (California, 1979).

4 H. D. Sankalia, *The Prehistory and Protohistory of India and Pakistan*, new edition (Poona, 1974), p. 13.

5 For a brief history of his activities in India see Notes in *Ancient India*, 18–19 (1963), pp. 1–3.

6 L. A. Cammiade and M. C. Burkitt, 'Fresh Light on the Stone Ages of South-east India', *Antiquity*, 4 (1930), pp. 327–39.

7 H. de Terra and T. T. Paterson, *Studies on the Ice Age in India and Associated Human Cultures*. Carnegie Institute Publication, no. 449 (Washington, 1939).

8 F. E. Zeuner, *The Stone Age and Pleistocene Chronology in Gujarat*. Deccan College Monograph Series: 6 (Poona 1950).

9 A. S. Goudie, B. Allchin and K. T. M. Hegde, 'The former extension of the Great Indian Sand Desert, *Geographical Journal*, 139, pt 2 (London, 1973). pp. 243–57.

10 Edited by V. N. Misra, Deccan College, Poona, for the Indian Society for Prehistoric and Quaternary Studies. Physical Research Laboratory, Ahmadabad.

11 Wheeler's Presidential Address reprinted in *Ancient India*, 2 (1946), pp. 125–33.

12 As when he asked (*ibid.*, 127) 'how are we in India to harness the natural sciences in the service of the study of man'.

13 H. D. Sankalia, 'Animal-fossil and Palaeolithic Industries from the Pravara Basin at Nevasa, District Ahmadnagar'. *Ancient India*, no. 12 (New Delhi, 1956), pp. 35–52; also 'Middle Stone Age Culture in India and Pakistan', *Science* 1964, vol. 146, no. 3642 (Washington, 1964), pp. 365–75.

14 A. S. Goudie *et al.*, *op. cit.* (1973), pp. 243–57.

15 G. R. Sharma, 'Mesolithic lake cultures in the Ganga Valley, India', *Proceedings of the Prehistoric Society*, new series, 39 (1973), pp. 327–39.

16 V. N. Misra. 'Bagor – a late mesolithic settlement in north-west India', *World Archaeology*, 5 (1973), pp. 92–110.

17 G. Singh, R. D. Joshi, S. K. Chopra and A. B. Singh, 'Late Quaternary history of vegetation and climate of the Rajasthan Desert, India'. *Philosophical Transactions of the Royal Society of London*, 267, no. 889 (1974), pp. 467–501; G. Singh, 'A preliminary Survey of the Post-glacial Vegetational History of the Kashmir Valley', *The Palaeobotanist*, 12, no. 1 (Lucknow, 1963), pp. 73–108.

18 *Landnam i Denmarks Stenalder* (Land Occupation in Denmark's Stone Age), Danmarks Geol. Unders. IIR, no. 66 (Copenhagen, 1941).

19 Vishnu-Mittre, 'Palaeobotanical evidence in India', *Evolutionary Studies in World Crops*, ed. J. Hutchinson (Cambridge, 1974), pp. 3–30.

20 S. J. Hallam, *Fire and Hearth*, Australian Institute of Aboriginal Studies (Canberra, 1975).

21 A notable example is the froth flotation apparatus developed by the Cambridge unit of the British Academy Major Research Project in the Early History of Agriculture. For specification see, H. N. Jarman, A. J. Legge and J. A. Charles, 'Retrieval of plant remains from archaeological sites by froth flotation', *Papers in Economic Prehistory*, ed. E. S. Higgs (Cambridge, 1972).

22 Vishnu-Mittre, 'Palaeobotanical evidence in India', pp. 3–30.

23 John Burton-Page in *J. Roy. Asiatic Soc.* (Cambridge, 1970).

24 Sir Mortimer Wheeler, *Still Digging* (London, 1955).

25 Wheeler, *op. cit.* (1955), ch. 8.

26 *Ibid.*, p. 112.

27 *Ibid.*, p. 118.

28 G. Bersu, 'Vorgeschichtliche Siedlungen auf dem Goldberg bei Nördlingan', *Deutschtum and Ausland*, hft 23/4 (1930), pp. 130–43.

29 W. Buttler and W. Haberey, *Die Bandkeramische Ansiedlung bei Köln-Lindenthal* (Berlin and Leipzig, 1936).

30 The most useful single reference is G. Hatt, 'Jernalders Bapladser i Himmerland', *Aabger* (1938), pp. 119–266.

31 G. Bersu, 'Excavations at Little Woodbury, Wiltshire', *Proceedings of the Prehistoric Society*, 6 (1940), pp. 30–111.

32 C. F. C. Hawkes and S. Piggott, 'Britons, Romans and Saxons round Salisbury and in Cranborne Chase: reviewing the excavations of General Pitt-Rivers, 1881–1889', *The Archaeological Journal*, 104 (1947), pp. 27–81.

33 B. Subbarao, *The Personality of India. A Study in the Development of Material Culture of India and Pakistan* (Baroda, 1956), p. vi. As Subbarao himself put it (*op. cit.*, 1): 'The emphasis on vertical sequence is justified in the initial stages over a vast unexplored country. But once a rough outline has emerged . . . we will be able to revert to large-scale

horizontal excavations to fill in the details and to reconstruct the physical and cultural environment of the Prehistoric and Historic civilizations of India.'

34 Willard F. Libby, *Radio-carbon Dating* (Chicago, 1955). See also contributions by Lilly and others to *The Impact of the Natural Sciences on Archaeology*, British Academy, ed. T. E. Allibone *et al.*, 1970, pp. 1–75.

35 D. P. Agrawal and A. Ghosh (eds.) *Radio-carbon and Indian Archaeology*, Tata Institute of Fundamental Research (Bombay, 1973); D. P. Agrawal., *The Copper Bronze Age of India* (New Delhi, 1971).

36 H. D. Sankalia, M. K. Dhavalikar and others, 'Inamgaon Seminar', *Man and Environment*, 1 (Ahmadabad, 1977), pp. 40–60.

37 B. Subbarao, *The Personality of India*, M. S. University Archaeology Series, no. 3 (Baroda, 1956).

38 O. H. K. Spate, *India & Pakistan – A Regional and General Geography* (London, 1954).

39 Subbarao, *op. cit.* (1956), p. 64.

40 The notion of studying socio-cultural systems alongside habitat and biome as aspects of ecosystems was first developed by social anthropologists, notably by E. Evans-Pritchard in respect of the Sudan (*The Nuer*, Oxford, 1940). The present author applied the concept to archaeological data in 1952 (*Prehistoric Europe: the economic Basis* (London), ch. 1, and in more detailed fashion in his Albert Reckitt Archaeological Lecture of the following year (*Proceedings of British Academy*, 39, pp. 215–38).

41 Agrawal, *op. cit.* (1971), ch. 7.

42 *Ecology and Archaeology of Western India*, eds. D. P. Agrawal and B. M. Pande (Delhi, 1977).

43 The following volumes of papers delivered at symposia organized jointly for the Royal Society and the British Academy have so far been published by the Oxford University Press: T. E. Allibone, Sir Mortimer Wheeler, I. E. S. Edwards, E. T. Hall and A. E. A. Werner, *The Impact of the Natural Sciences on Archaeology*, 1970; D. G. Kendall, S. Piggott, D. G. King-Hele and I. E. S. Edwards, *The Place of Astronomy in the World*, 1974: and Sir Joseph Hutchinson, Grahame Clark, E. M. Jope and A. Riley, *The Early History of Agriculture*, 1977.

44 R. B. Foote 'Notes on some recent Neolithic and Paleolithic finds in South India', *Journal of Asiatic Society of Bengal*, 56 pt 2 (1887), pp. 259–82.

45 F. R. Allchin, *Neolithic Cattle-keepers of South India: a Study of the Deccan Ashmounds* (Cambridge, 1963), p. 65, figs. 3 and 17.

46 F. R. Allchin noted significantly: 'Indeed it is probable that if we could record more complete accounts of the whole complex of related cattle rites throughout India, we should be able to find evidence of survivals of the ashfire cult'. Allchin, *op. cit.* (1963), p. 175.

47 F.R. Allchin. *Piklihal Excavations* (Hyderabad, 1960), pp. 11–17.

48 Allchin, *op. cit.* (1960), p. 134.

49 Allchin, *op. cit.* (1963), p. 100.

50 H. D. Sankalia, B. Subbarao and S. B. Deo, *The Excavation at Maheshwar and Navdatoli 1952–53* (Poona, 1968); H. D. Sankalia, S. B. Deo, Z. D. Ansari and S. Ehrhardt, *From History to Pre-history at Nevasa 1954–56* (Poona, 1960); and H. D. Sankalia *et al.* in 'Inamgaon Seminar', *Man and Environment*, vol. 1 (1977), pp. 44–6.

51 B. K. Thapar, Kalibangan: 'A Harappan Metropolis beyond the Indus Valley', *Expedition*, 17, no. 2, pp. 19–32.

52 S. C. Malik, *Indian Civilization, the Formative Period*, Indian Institute of Advanced Study (Simla, 1968).

CHAPTER 3 2

THE PREHISTORIC SOCIETY: FROM
EAST ANGLIA TO THE WORLD*

THE BEGINNINGS

It is doubly appropriate that the Prehistoric Society should celebrate its jubilee in Norwich. The Society was born in the Castle on 23 February 1935 of a parent conceived improbably enough in the Public Library at a meeting held on 26 October 1908 to inaugurate an East Anglian Society 'for the study of all matters appertaining to prehistoric man'. The question I want you to consider in this address is how the Prehistoric Society of East Anglia developed so rapidly to the point at which it achieved national status as The Prehistoric Society. Let me begin by removing one misapprehension. My hands are not dripping with East Anglian blood nor have I just wiped them clean. The Prehistoric Society was not the outcome of a revolutionary putsch. It stemmed from nothing more dramatic than a recognition that the Prehistoric Society had long ceased to be East Anglian. When we met at Norwich Castle for our Annual General Meeting in 1935 and passed the resolution which eliminated the words 'of East Anglia' from our title we were merely recognizing a fact, that we had long ceased to be East Anglian in anything but name. There were no dissentient votes.

The two men who between them set the Prehistoric Society on its feet came from different but complementary backgrounds. W. G. Clarke was Norfolk born and bred and earned his living as a working journalist in Norwich, while cultivating a wide-ranging interest in natural history and prehistoric archaeology. Dr W. G. Sturge came of a well-known Quaker family and spent his retirement, from a lucrative medical practice in Nice, in Suffolk carrying on his specialized hobby of collecting flints. He settled in Icklingham Hall partly in order to have room for his prestigious collection of worked flints and partly to give himself the opportunity of adding to it. Clarke was the prime mover and effective founder of the Society and, although a busy man, served as Secretary for the first twelve years. Sturge acted as President and to some extent as patron. Between them they ensured that Norfolk and Suffolk were joint partners in the new society.

According to the rules of 1909 the purpose of the society included:
1 the 'promotion of friendly intercourse between prehistorians'
2 'the study of all matters connected with prehistoric man in East Anglia'

3 the dissemination of 'knowledge of prehistory by means of papers and exhibitions of implements'.

The Society was very much a grass-roots affair. Three quarters of the 107 members listed in 1910 lived in Norfolk or Suffolk. Apart from museum curators, all were amateurs of prehistory and few, if any, were graduates (aside from medical practitioners and parsons). What they did share was a passion for flints, an interest in Quaternary geology and a readiness to further the aims of the society by personal effort. Their faith is well displayed by their decision to publish *Proceedings* in 1911. The Society had no endowment and a minuscule income from subscriptions. At the previous AGM the treasurer had only been able to report a small balance on an income of £6 14s. The subscription had been raised in 1909 from 1s 6d. (7½p) to 2s 6d. (12½p) and was only raised to 5s (25p) in 1918 to take account of wartime inflation. The decision to print 500 copies, nearly five times the membership, was courageous, even allowing for the fact that non-members had to pay as much as 3s 6d (17½p) a copy, and was only possible through Dr Sturge's generosity. It should be remembered that the society received no public funding of any description. Our forebears paid their way and laid the foundations of our society in the currency of private effort sustained by a faith in the value of prehistory.

How was it that such a small group of amateurs without formal qualifications, only the slenderest finances and positively no public support managed in a single generation – one interrupted by the First World War at that – to create the prototype of the Prehistoric Society? Superficially the members were animated by a shared passion for flint implements. To give this an outlet W. G. Clarke began by organizing excursions to the Breckland, in those days an open waste given over to rabbits and littered with flints. The members would be lectured in gravel-pits, let loose to collect surface flints and guided to Icklingham Hall, there to gloat over the largest private collection of flints in the country and refresh themselves with Mrs Sturge's tea. The formal meetings at Ipswich and Norwich were largely given over to displaying, comparing and talking about flints. The excitement was so great that it was sometimes impossible to transact even vital formal business. Clarke decided to try to harness the ruling passion by organizing an excavation. The project of excavating at Grimes Graves was sanctioned in October 1913, funds were collected and two pits explored in May 1914. The Report, a volume of 245 pages, 30 plates and 86 figures, appeared in 1915. The total cost of fencing, excavating, preparing for publication and producing an edition of 500 copies came to £247 19s 3½d., well within the estimate of £250. All services were of course rendered free, including that of auditing the accounts carried out by a Norwich firm. The Grimes Graves venture was creditable for its day on the part of a regional society, but could hardly be seen as pointing the way to a rapid advance to national status.

JAMES REID MOIR

This could only be done by reference to an idea of broad concern. The idea that flints were clues to the antiquity of man and the evolution of human society was one capable of exerting an appeal transcending any province or country and extending potentially over the world as a whole. The East Anglian who most effectively identified the society with this appeal and in this way converted a provincial association of flint hunters into the prototype of our present society was James Reid Moir (Keith 1944). How was it that a man of such limited education and devoid of formal qualifications managed to impose himself and his ideas on the scientific establishment of his time?

According to Prof. P. G. H. Boswell (1945), who had been given school prizes by the father and as a professional geologist had followed his son's researches in the field, the explanation lies in a conflict between father and son. Lewis Moir was a strong-willed Scot who had set up as a tailor and outfitter in Ipswich, where he became something of a public figure, a town councillor, a JP, vice-chairman of the Ipswich School board and an elder of the Presbyterian Church. Moir senior had no doubts about his only son's future. The boy was sent to a commercial school and before he reached the age of sixteen was apprenticed to his father. Although Reid Moir had no positive idea as yet of what he wanted to do with his life, he was sure of one thing: he had no intention of settling down for longer than he could help as a tailor and outfitter. In the meantime he took refuge in books and for a time became obsessed with Tibet. He found his way following his other hobby, golf. Approaching the final green on Rushmere golf course his partner bent down and picked up a barbed and tanged flint arrowhead. In Moir's own words, 'The sight of it thrilled me, and from that moment archaeology claimed me. This may sound dramatic, but it is literally true'. Reid Moir had been born again.

As a convert he began by acquiring the sacred book, Evans's *Ancient Flint Implements*, a work that had captivated our founder as a boy as it later did myself. He next sought out fellow members of the cult. He first met Lt Col Underwood who, as it happened, was to succeed Dr Sturge as president of the Prehistoric Society of East Anglia. Through him he met W. G. Clarke and so obtained access to the Sturge collection. It was from Underwood, also, that Moir acquired his concern for the earliest flint industries. To find them he spent his spare time searching exposures of Tertiary and Early Pleistocene deposits in commercial workings. Something of the flavour of those early days is captured in his recollection that 'it was sometimes necessary to go out digging on Sunday afternoons with the spade, for decency's sake, concealed in a specially made canvas case'.

Moir made his break through on 3 October 1909, in Boulton and Laughlin's brickfield, Ipswich. There he recovered flints apparently flaked by man in a deposit containing shells, bones and teeth derived from the Red

Crag. Moir conveyed his exciting news to the East Anglians at a meeting held at Ipswich in March 1910. Boswell did his best to restrain him from seeking wider publicity until the geological age of the flints could be established. Moir on the other hand saw his chance and took it. In a letter to *The Times* which appeared on 17 October 1910 he claimed to have found evidence for a drastic extension in the history of man. The controversy this provoked was the final straw for Lewis Moir. He had long seen his son's hobby as a distraction from business. He now discerned a threat to religion. He promptly sacked the young man. Reid Moir experienced happiness he had never previously imagined. He had not only found an object in life. He was now free to pursue it, whatever the financial hardship.

In establishing himself as a prehistorian Moir employed a two-pronged tactic. He cultivated his home base, the Prehistoric Society of East Anglia, to provide himself with a platform and hopefully an avenue for publication. At the same time he sought to establish contact with men possessed of the qualifications he knew himself to lack and able by their influence to advance the standing of the Society. In pursuit of his first objective Moir followed his *Times* letter by delivering a revised version of his Ipswich lecture at Norwich on 12 December 1910 under the title 'The Flint Implements of Sub-Crag Man' (Moir 1910). He used this occasion to bring the society to the point of decision. Beginning by reading a list of thirteen persons headed by Sir Ray Lankester as accepting that his flints had been worked by man, he went on to observe that Mr S. Hazzledine Warren and Professor Boyd Dawkins held the contrary view, that the Sub-Crag flints were 'undoubtedly the result of natural forces and nothing else'. This opened the way for the Society to appoint a Special Committee to reach a decision. It can hardly be said that those appointed were impartial: four were among those already on record as accepting the humanity of some of the flaking on Moir's flints and the fifth, W. G. Clarke, had already anticipated Moir in finding humanly flaked flints of Sub-Crag age in Norfolk. Hardly surprisingly the Committee, meeting at Icklingham Hall, declared 'not the slightest hesitation' in accepting that some at least of the flints submitted by Moir had been shaped by man. In the meantime their geological age had been referred to two Fellows of the Royal Society, Dr J. Marr of Cambridge and Mr Whittaker of the Geological Survey. In the light of their report the Special Committee (1910) felt confident in assigning some at least of the flints to 'the Pleistocene and possibly, in the case of some, to a "pre-Pliocene" age'.

In the meantime, between the Ipswich and Norwich lectures Moir took his first and, as it turned out, his most decisive step in winning support from established figures by inviting Sir Ray Lankester to inspect his flints and visit the scene of their discovery (Moir 1910). Sir Ray, a former Linacre Professor of Comparative Anatomy at Oxford and latterly Director of the British Museum of Natural History, was serving as President of the Ipswich

Museum in his retirement. It is possible that Moir was encouraged to approach him because, apart from his local standing as President of Ipswich Museum and the reputation he enjoyed from his earlier work on the fossils of the Red Crag, he had retained the interest in prehistory which had led him as a young man to make a pilgrimage to Boucher de Perthes. To occupy his time in retirement Ray Lankester (1907) had written a popular book on the subject and in an article in the *Daily Telegraph* had written of eoliths that they had been made 'at least as far back beyond the Palaeoliths as these were from the present day'. It is perhaps not surprising that he responded to Moir's invitation. In the event he was deeply impressed and was convinced that there was substance in Moir's claims. Indeed the more he thought about it the more it seemed to him that Moir's discoveries merited wider attention than they would be likely to receive if left solely in the hands of the Prehistoric Society of East Anglia. He therefore determined to lay the evidence before the Royal Society in a formal lecture. In preparation he brought his formidable powers as a morphologist to bear on the lithic material from Moir's Ipswich sites, including also material from Norfolk recovered by W. G. Clarke. One outcome was the original definition of the rostro-carinate, a beak-like form which later played a key role in controversies surrounding Pliocene man. The title he gave his Royal Society Lecture (Lankester 1912), 'On the Discovery of a Novel Type of Flint Implements below the base of the Red Crag in Suffolk, proving the existence of Skilled Workers of Flint in the Pliocene Age', must have been music to Reid Moir's ears. In concluding his lecture Ray Lankester expressed the hope that no one would waste the society's time by suggesting that the Sub-Crag flints had been flaked by natural agencies. The President, Sir Archibald Geikie, advised those present to ignore this and feel free to express their own opinions. Only one dared to do so. In reply the lecturer said he had listened with amazement at remarks of a kind he might have expected to hear from a member of an uncivilized race. Perhaps it is not surprising that, as Sir Arthur Keith recalled (1944, 737), Sir Ray Lankester's address was 'received by the Royal Society with an extreme degree of scepticism'. But Sir Ray was a formidable man. His lecture was printed in full with many illustrations in the *Philosophical Transactions of the Royal Society* for 1912.

Ray Lankester afforded the moral support Moir badly needed at this stage in his career (Moir 1929). He confirmed his sense of destiny as a man engaged on nothing less than a massive extension of the kingdom of man. Just as Boucher de Perthes, with whom he liked to compare himself, had earlier won acceptance for Quaternary man, so he, Reid Moir, felt he was going to achieve the same for Tertiary man. In his Royal Society paper Ray Lankester had provided him with a formidable weapon. As we know from Reid Moir himself (1935, 45) he also taught him how to use it. Moir would read drafts of his papers to his mentor and receive detailed advice on tactics and wording. Sir Ray Lankester even went so far as to communicate Moir's 'Transitional forms connecting the rostro-carinate flint implements with the tongue-shaped implements of river terrace gravels' to the Royal Society in 1917 (Moir 1935, 78). When invited to address the meeting at the end he glanced round in a threatening manner, saying: 'If there are any present who do not accept these conclusions, Mr Moir and I will no doubt be able to deal with them'. This time there were no volunteers.

His success with Ray Lankester encouraged Moir to forge links with other FRS's. The discovery by labourers of a human skeleton apparently sealed by boulder clay in the Ipswich area (Moir 1912; 1927, 133; Keith 1912) gave him a pretext to make contact with Sir Arthur Keith. He boldly despatched the bones, still encased in clay and sand, to the Royal College of Surgeons. The skeleton proved to belong to a man of modern type. Keith was delighted, because it appeared to confirm the antiquity of the famous Galley Hill find of a skeleton of similar type made in 1888 ostensibly in the Middle Pleistocene Gravels of the 100 ft terrace of the Thames. It no longer signifies that both skeletons are now recognized to have been intrusive. Moir had attracted the foremost human palaeontologist in the country. Sir Arthur Keith not merely joined the society and remained a member for life. He also served as a Vice-President and arranged for the society to hold some of its earliest London meetings in the Royal College of Surgeons.

Moir had already taken steps to secure his western flank by inviting Dr Marr of the Geology Department at Cambridge to pronounce on the age of his flints for the Special Committee appointed by the Prehistoric Society at its Norwich meeting. He followed this up by sending assemblages of flints to the Sedgewick Museum. It was in discussing these with one of his pupils, Miles Burkitt, that Marr unwittingly secured as one of Moir's earliest disciples the man who was to initiate the formal teaching of prehistory at Cambridge (Burkitt 1925, xi). It is significant that rostro-carinates featured both in Burkitt's text-book *The Old Stone Age* (1933) and in the first edition of Louis Leakey's rival *Adam's Ancestors* (1934).

Oxford was another target, and here also Moir aimed at Geology in the person of Professor W. J. Sollas, FRS, to whom he sent a particularly seductive flint. Sollas was so taken that he decided to describe it to the Geological Society. Unlike Ray Lankester or Moir himself, Sollas made the fatal mistake of temporizing. The geologists turned down his paper. Moir bided his time. Two years later Sollas was invited to lecture to the Prehistoric Society. By this time he had overcome his doubts and offered his congratulations to Moir on 'his well-deserved triumph'. His paper was accepted for publication (Sollas 1920). Sollas attributed his change of view to the weight of distinguished authority: if Ray Lankester, Marr, Miles Burkitt and 'so I am informed, that most distinguished authority, the Abbé Breuil' accepted Moir's flints, who was he to disagree? Sollas was not the last man to succumb to the domino effect.

Moir found the French harder going. They had been rejecting similar claims since 1867 and they were insulated from the domino effect by the Channel. Still, the high priests of prehistory had to take note of heresy when given currency in the *Philosophical Transactions of the Royal Society*. Marcellin Boule, Director of the Institute of Human Palaeontology at Paris, hurried over to Ipswich with the Abbé Breuil in his train. The verdict was delayed until 1915 when Boule pronounced in *L'Anthropologie* his virtual certainty that the rostro-carinates of Suffolk were the products of purely physical causes (Boule 1915). Moir for his part stigmatized Boule's report as 'the most biassed statement it has ever been my misfortune to read'. Breuil's attitude is reflected in a letter he addressed to F. N. Haward, one of Moir's stoutest opponents:

As with all their eolith-loving confreres it is difficult to discuss with these gentlemen. They affirm their opinions with too much enthusiastic conviction which prevents them from appreciating the right of others to doubt.

Miles Burkitt did not give up hope. In 1921 he persuaded Breuil to revisit Ipswich to inspect the Foxhall flints. At a congress held later that year at Liège which Burkitt attended, the Abbé admitted that some of the Foxall flints had probably been flaked by man. Burkitt (1921) in announcing the Abbé's conversion reported it as another triumph for Reid Moir.

There are no signs that Moir was more than irritated by what he regarded as Gallic obtuseness. The British bandwaggon was gathering pace. One of its most prominent passengers was Mr Reginald A. Smith of the British Museum. Reginald Smith was certainly not recruited by Reid Moir. His eyes had been fixed from the outset on Dr Sturge's collection of flint implements and when this came to the museum on the owner's death in 1919 the preparation of the book on *The Sturge Collection*, published in 1931 'as a tribute to the testator's memory', was among his fondest concerns. Smith refrained from joining the society until he was made an Honorary Member in 1915. As President in 1918 he did much to wean it from its exclusive preoccupation with East Anglia. For one thing, by refusing to lecture away from London, he encouraged it to meet more often in London, where the society had first met in 1913 in the rooms of the Royal Anthropological Institute. In 1914 and again in 1920 meetings were held at the Royal College of Surgeons. In 1923–24 the society met in the rooms of the Geological Society and in 1924–29 at the Royal Anthropological Institute. In 1930, following Reginald Smith's appointment as Director of the Society of Antiquaries of London, the society began its present practice of meeting in the rooms of that body. Reginald Smith (1918) also sought to persuade the

East Anglians to take more account of the European context of their finds. In the world of flints he was at that time an almost god-like figure and his views were all the more influential in that as yet he had no effective competition from universities. It was fortunate for Reid Moir and for that matter for the Prehistoric Society of East Anglia that he accepted the Sub-Crag flints as having been shaped by man. Indeed, it was Reginald Smith who set the official seal of approval on Moir. The table printed at the beginning of the British Museum guide to *Stone Age Antiquities* published in 1921 was acknowledged to be 'based for the most part on Mr Reid Moir's discoveries of human work in East Anglia at geological horizons which till recently were regarded as long anterior to the human period'. It is significant that in the index to the guide Moir rated eight references against his nearest rivals, the Abbé Breuil, Flinders Petrie and others with no more than five.

If acceptance from such a quarter must have gratified Reid Moir, coming as it did within little more than a decade of his famous letter to *The Times*, it did not silence his critics in the Prehistoric Society. As Sir Arthur Keith (1944, 741–42) was later to observe (in a not wholly felicitous phrase), Sir Ray Lankester may have 'slaughtered the opponents of Moir's thesis, but he failed to silence them'. Unhappily the conflict between those who accepted the Sub-Crag flints as having been shaped by man and those who held them to be purely natural could not be resolved by rational argument. Moir's new life was founded on his original claim. He had no choice but to defend it by evasion, parrying, intimidation and above all by reiteration. If in hindsight the society may seem to have expended an undue proportion of its effort during its opening decades arguing a problem incapable of resolution in terms of the data available in East Anglia, the tension which it generated did much to consolidate the membership.

SUB-CRAG FLINTS: NATURAL PRODUCTS OR THE WORK OF PLIOCENE MAN?

The conflict opened in 1911 when Moir replied to a paper by the Abbé Breuil (1910) describing flints from Eocene deposits at Belle Assize in France, which although exhibiting flaking of human appearance had demonstrably been flaked by the pressure of geological deposits. In his reply Moir (1911) described practical experiments made by shaking flints in sacks to test percussion and subjecting them to pressure in an old letter-press, experiments which he claimed allowed him to distinguish by objective means between the work of man and nature in respect of flint flaking. Even so he was careful to make it plain that he was directing his experiments to testing Harrisonian eoliths, not his own Sub-Crag flints which were excluded since 'their form and flaking is so obviously human'. Moir's lecture was followed at the same meeting by one from F. W. Haward (1911), a professional engineer, who argued that insufficient attention had been paid to the impact of natural forces. Haward suggested that the only artificial component in eoliths was their selection by collectors from quantities of evident rubbish. When he returned to the attack in 1919 Haward brushed aside Moir's evasion by directing attention specifically to 'The Origin of the Rostro-carinate implements and other chipped flints from the basement beds of East Anglia' (Haward 1919). Moir replied two months later to this direct attack and resorted to mild intimidation by inviting his audience to take their choice between Mr Haward and Sir Ray Lankester (Moir 1919, 158). Two years later he adopted a subtler and probably more effective method by acknowledging the help he had received from a distinguished body of men, including six Fellows of the Royal Society, headed by Sir Ray Lankester, and Mr Reginald Smith, when introducing his paper on investigations at Foxhall and other sites near Ipswich (Moir 1921).

Haward's frontal onslaught gave Moir food for thought. In 1924 he returned to the question of Harrisonian eoliths. Since these first appeared in detritus beds underlying the Suffolk Red Crag they must certainly have been older in origin than his own Sub-Crag assemblages. Assuming, as he did, that Harrisonian eoliths had been shaped by man, his own pre-palaeolithic assemblages could no longer be regarded as marking the most primitive phase of flint-working (Moir 1924). In the same paper Moir noted that implements of eolithic form appeared in much later assemblages, Acheulian or even Late Mousterian in character, and stated his conviction that 'these primitive forms, are, without question, of the same age as the well-made hand-axes with which they were found associated'. If the thought ever obtruded that the most economical explanation for the occurrence of eoliths over so vast a span of cultural history was that they were products of natural agencies, this was effectively censored by his overriding commitment to Tertiary man. The same inhibition operated when he was confronted by 'Gigantoliths' on the foreshore at Sheringham (Moir 1934). These objects resembled hand-axes but were so heavy, weighing up to a stone or more, that he was moved to exclaim 'we simply do not know why these specimens were made or to what use they were put'. Once again the explanation that they were natural was not one he could entertain.

One of the greatest handicaps imposed on upholders of any dogma is the way it impairs their ability to assess evidence in an objective manner. This certainly applied to the East Anglian believers. Whenever they were confronted by new claims or discoveries there was a strong temptation to overlook them if they opposed but to view them with indulgence if they appeared to confirm or strengthen the central dogma.

An obvious weakness in Moir's thesis, which his critics did not fail to emphasize, was the absence of physical remains of Tertiary man. This made him highly susceptible when he encountered an illustration of the jaw exhibited by an American, R. H. Collyer MD, to the Ethnological Society of London in 1863, and described by him as 'the oldest relic of the human animal in existence'. What excited him in particular was that the specimen was described as having come from Foxhall, Ipswich, a site with exposures of Sub-Crag deposits (Moir 1921, 392–98). He was sufficiently excited to undertake one of his major investigations in the Foxhall Hall pit in the hope of recovering fossils of Tertiary man. He did so in the face of objections which would have discouraged less powerfully motivated investigators. For one thing the jaw bone had no adequate provenance. All we know is that it had been given to Dr Collyer by an Ipswich druggist who had bought it for half a crown (12½p) from the finder. It is also recorded that it was examined by T. H. Huxley at a crucial period in human palaeontology and that this leading authority found no reason to ascribe it 'to an extinct or aberrant race of mankind'. Last, but not least, the illustration depicts a palpably modern jaw. The Foxhall investigations yielded plenty more eoliths, but no fossils of Tertiary Man. It is perhaps fortunate that the jaw was lost to science when its owner returned to the United States.

Another impediment to a more widespread acceptance of Tertiary man was his lack of cultural attributes more appealing than rostro-carinates and associated flints. It was doubtless anxiety to display his humanity in a more convincing and sympathetic light that led the East Anglians to take so seriously the Red Crag Shell Portrait exhibited to the Society in 1913 by Dr Marie Stopes (1921). So seriously was this taken that a special committee was appointed, comprising Sturge, Moir, Burrell and W. G. Clarke, to report on its credentials. The sheer banality of the design ought to have put the Society on its guard, not to mention its lack of scientific provenance. The story unfolded by Dr Stopes was bizarre. The shell was said to have been found at Colchester by a young clerk described as a 'red-hot atheist' who 'rejoiced at what appeared to him to be a crushing blow to Scripture'. The young man's joy was replaced by embarrassment when shortly after he experienced conversion at a local Revival Meeting. Displaying the shell to Dr Stopes's father he suggested that it ought to be destroyed. This touched a raw nerve in Mr Stopes who promptly put it in his pocket and declared that he would be no party to the destruction of scientific evidence. As he was the stronger man, the shell survived and was duly cherished by his famous daughter. Indeed Dr Stopes joined the Society expressly to put on record the precious evidence salvaged by her father. One wonders whether she was surprised at the warmth with which her communication was received. The Committee appointed to sit in judgement must have been sorely tempted. Its members felt that 'the weight of evidence was in favour of the Pliocene age of the human work on the shell'. However discretion (provided one suspects by W. G. Clarke) prevailed and their report ended by stating that 'they considered that it was impossible to speak with absolute certainty on the point'.

Moir would have been well advised to confine himself to his home territory. When he exposed himself to an unfamiliar environment and audience, his lack of self-criticism and elementary caution was made even more painfully evident. He was first attracted to the Irish Stone Age in 1929, by which time he had become accustomed to reiterating dogmatic pronouncements to largely captive audiences. Moir visited Rosse's Point, Co. Sligo, at the invitation of his friend J. P. T. Burchell who had found an assemblage of what he claimed to be palaeolithic artefacts. The fact that some dismissed these as products of 'the collision of limestone boulders set in motion by the violent action of Atlantic storm' only strengthened Moir's determination to subject them to the same tests as he had applied to his own Sub-Crag flints. Having done so he was convinced that 'the Rosse's Point specimens (were), without question, the result of a purposeful and highly skilful flaking process'. Indeed Moir went so far as to express his 'admiration of the ancient artificers of Sligo'. As if this was not enough he concluded in words of almost paranoid certitude: 'I entertain no more doubt that the specimens collected by Burchell are of human origin than I do that the pen with which I am writing this article was made by man' (*The Irish Times*, 5 March 1929).

Moir's bond with the Irish Stone Age persisted. At the Annual General Meeting at Norwich in 1932, at which he presided for the first time during his second tenure of the chair, he gave strong support to Burchell's claim to have found lower palaeolithic flints in Ulster (Burchell and Moir 1932). Indeed, he felt sure enough of their age by analogy with East Anglian flints to end his report on a note he must surely have learned from his old master, Sir Ray Lankester: 'It remains for those who think otherwise to put forward acceptable evidence that the above conclusions are erroneous'. No one attending that Annual General Meeting in Norwich Castle ventured to think, or at least to express himself, otherwise. Nor did Adolf Mahr (1937) when five years later he delivered his Presidential Address on Irish Prehistory which in its printed form was by far the longest paper ever published by the Prehistoric Society. Silence is often more eloquent than words.

Moir devoted his second Presidential Address (1932) to the topic to which he owed his career, 'The Culture of Pliocene Man'. Since he had been hammering away on this theme for a generation the President assumed that his audience accepted Tertiary Man as a verity, and decided to enlarge on the idea that the Sub-Crag men were relatively advanced by comparison with the makers of Harrisonian eoliths. If the truth be told he was not able to muster a very impressive body of evidence. It amounted to a couple of would-be burins, an enigmatic egg-shaped stone, identified some years previously by the Abbé Breuil as a sling-stone, and a considerable quantity of bone fragments eroded to the point at which any traces of human work they may once have exhibited had long since been worn away (Burkitt 1955, III). He therefore ended his address by looking to the future, claiming that

Prehistoric archaeology is entering upon a new and revolutionary era. The old view that the first human being appeared in the earlier part of the comparatively recent Pleistocene period, is being recognized as erroneous, and the trail of ancient man is leading investigators into a region, archaic and unexplored, and, in all probability, rich in material of profound interest and importance to science. (Moir 1932, 14)

Prehistoric archaeology, and not least its earliest phases, was indeed on the verge of profound changes, but one effect of these was to consign Moir's most prized discoveries to the dust-bin. The new advances bearing on the remotest periods of prehistory were to occur, not in East Anglia but in East Africa, and to date not from the Pliocene but from a greatly extended Lower Pleistocene. As Leakey (1953, 66–69) was the first to recognize, the discoveries first made effectively in East Africa exposed the Sub-Crag flints of East Anglia as irrelevant.

The quest for Tertiary Man in East Anglia, however delusory it ultimately proved to be, had put the Society on the scientific map, drawn into its ranks men of influence in many fields relevant to prehistoric studies and through the tensions generated by controversy helped to bind the society together. Yet it would be wrong to leave the impression that under the lead of Reid Moir with Sir Ray Lankester behind him the Society was dedicated solely to rostro-carinates and kindred matters. For one thing it was responsible for effecting a revolution in Pleistocene stratigraphy. As Professor Marr (1920) pointed out in his Presidential Address for 1920, the acceptance of Tertiary man implied a great expansion of prehistory. This in turn high-lighted the need to establish the stratigraphy of the Pleistocene by promoting co-operation between Quaternary geologists and prehistoric archaeologists. Moir was encouraged to embark on a systematic attempt to establish the context of successive assemblages of flint artefacts in the Pleistocene strati-graphy of East Anglia as a whole. In this he received much help from archaeological colleagues, among whom J. E. Sainty[1] was prominent, as well as many geologists, notably Boswell, Dewey and Marr, mindful of Sturge's dictum that 'flint implements were the true fossils of the gravels'. The East Anglians investigated a sequence of deposits ranging from the Cromer Forest Bed to the Brown Boulder Clay of Hunstanton, as well as investigating a number of important palaeolithic sites, including High Lodge, Hoxne and Whitlingham. It is some measure of their success that the Abbé Breuil began his address as the last President of the Prehistoric Society of East Anglia in 1934 by admitting his indebtedness to them in reforming French prehistory (Breuil 1934, 289).

THE TRANSFORMATION OF THE PREHISTORIC SOCIETY

Although on the surface the Prehistoric Society came into being when a motion was passed abbreviating the title of the parent society at the annual general meeting for 1935, the formal act was only the culmination of a series of changes which had already set in before the outbreak of the First World War. These related both to its membership and to its intellectual concerns. As to membership, the main changes occurred in geographical composition and in professional affiliation (fig. 32.1). At the outset just on three-quarters (74%) of the members were domiciled in Norfolk and Suffolk, slightly more than a tenth (11%) in the capital and the remainder elsewhere in the United Kingdom and Ireland. The rapid growth in membership which accompanied publication of the *Proceedings* led to a progressive reduction in the predominance of East Anglians. Although the number of members from Norfolk and Suffolk continued to increase up till the outbreak of the First World War, the accession of new members from elsewhere was so much more rapid that already by 1914 the proportion of East Anglians had fallen to under a half of the total. The more successful the society and the wider the appeal of its *Proceedings*, the more pronounced this demographic shift became. By 1921 the East Anglians had sunk to under a third, by 1924 to under a quarter and by 1934 to only 15% of the total membership of the Prehistoric Society of East Anglia. By 1969 East Anglians accounted for less than 2%. On the other hand the proportion of members with London addresses was no greater in 1969 than it had been in 1914. The British membership remained provincial, though now much more widely distributed. A notable development occurred in respect of overseas members. Whereas there were none to begin with, they already amounted to 3% by 1914 and by 1934 to 11%. By 1969 the proportion had almost doubled to 21% and this included 140 institutions from thirty-four countries, a significant indication of wide international acceptance.

A change of even greater importance was the accession of members professionally qualified in areas germane to prehistoric studies. By 1914 the society had been strengthened by Professors Ridgeway, Seligman and Arthur Keith in the fields of archaeology, anthropology and human palaeontology, by the geologist Dr J. E. Marr and by the youthful Miles Burkitt. During and immediately after the First World War the society was joined by ethnologists Henry Balfour and A. C. Haddon and geologists P. G. H. Boswell and K. S. Sandford. The society secured its first prehistoric archaeologist as yet holding an official post when it elected Reginald Smith an Honorary Member in 1915. The representation of prehistoric archaeology was improved by the adhesion of O. G. S. Crawford and Dorothy Garrod in 1922 and of Cyril Fox in 1923, but it was the accession of Stuart Piggott and myself in 1929 and of Gordon Childe, Leslie Grinsell and Charles Phillips in 1930 that marked the beginning of the great influx of prehistorians responsible for shaping the Prehistoric Society in its modern form. It is a striking fact that ten of the first eleven presidents and 71% of all the officers of the Prehistoric Society during its first quarter century were former members of the Prehistoric Society of East Anglia.

The most direct insights into the intellectual concerns of the Society are to be found in the papers published in its *Proceedings*. One of the most striking features about the Prehistoric Society of East Anglia was its preoccupation with the Stone Age which accounted for nine out of ten of the papers published up till 1928. Furthermore, within the Stone Age members were mainly interested in its earlier stages. Even in the final volume of the *Proceedings of the Prehistoric Society of East Anglia* these accounted for more than half the articles. One of the most powerful thrusts behind the formation of the Prehistoric Society in its present form was the strong influx of new members in the final years of the East Anglian society whose interests focused on the Neolithic and later periods of prehistory. The watershed is neatly fixed by the publication of *The Axe Age* (Kendrick 1925). In this book T. D. Kendrick contrasted what he termed 'the intimate acquaintance with the remarkable series of civilizations' of the palaeolithic with the 'unfortunate neolithic' which remained 'in very much the same state in which it was first arranged in the fifties of the last century' (Kendrick 1925, 2–5). Seldom can such a true assessment have been so rapidly overtaken by events. That very year Alexander Keiller began the systematic excavations at Windmill Hill, Avebury (Smith 1965), which led to the rapid advance in our knowledge of Neolithic Britain incorporated in Stuart Piggott's classification of British Neolithic pottery in 1931 (Piggott 1931; 1954). Even more significant in some

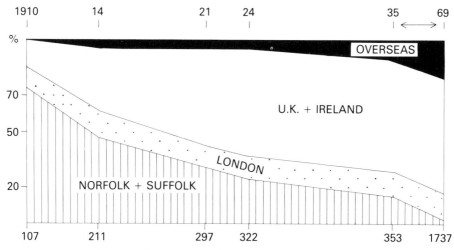

32.1 Changes in the proportion of members of the Prehistoric Society with addresses in East Anglia, London, other parts of the United Kingdom and overseas

respects was the appearance, while *The Axe Age* was still in proof (Kendrick 1925, 62), of V. Gordon Childe's *The Dawn of European Civilization* (1925). At one stroke Thurnam's long-headed builders of long barrows with their polished flint and stone axes and their leaf-shaped arrowheads, were seen to inhabit a small corner of the European continent, the home of a variety of distinct neolithic communities. Further, Childe (1928) went on to claim in *The Most Ancient East: The Oriental Prelude to European Prehistory* that the neolithic peoples of Europe needed to be studied in the context of more advanced societies in Egypt and South-west Asia. The influx of members whose interests focused on settled communities is reflected in the more balanced temporal coverage of the *Proceedings of the Prehistoric Society* by contrast with its prototype. During the first twenty-five years up to two or even three fifths of articles dealt with Bronze or Early Iron Age topics. In summary, whereas the East Anglians concentrated on *la préhistoire*, the Prehistoric Society has taken fuller account of the phases of prehistory assigned by Déchelette to *la protohistoire*.

The geographical coverage of articles published in the *Proceedings* since 1911 reflects an overall shift from East Anglia to national and increasingly to

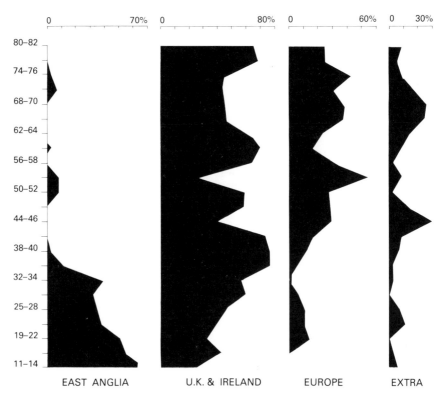

32.2 Changes in the geographical composition of articles in the Proceedings (*Proc. Prehist. Soc. East Anglia* 1911–34, *Proc. Prehist. Soc.* 1935–82)

international spheres of interest (fig. 32.2). As one might expect, articles dealing with Norfolk and Suffolk remained important throughout the life of the parent society, even though falling from *c.*70 to 40% between 1911–14 and 1932–4. On the other hand a rapid decline set in during the final years of the East Anglian society and in early volumes of the *Proceedings of the Prehistoric Society* articles dealing with East Anglia declined to vanishing point, only to reappear spasmodically in later issues. To a substantial extent the decline in East Anglian articles was compensated by a rise in the proportion of ones dealing with other parts of Great Britain and Ireland. Between 1911–14 and 1929–31 these rose from 26 to 60% and in early issues of the *Proceedings of the Prehistoric Society* attained a peak of 77%. Articles covering territories overseas, although never more than a minor component of the East Anglian publication, were never wholly absent. East Anglians keen on flints and stones liked to pursue their hobby wherever they might find themselves and made a practice of reporting back to home base. The very first volume of the *Proceedings of the Prehistoric Society of East Anglia* contained articles by Seton-Karr (1914) on palaeoliths from the Madras Presidency of South India and by R. S. Newall (1913), later of Stonehenge fame, on a microlithic industry collected from a prehistoric hut site while he was engaged in sheep-mustering in West Australia. Again, when Capt. Francis Buckley found himself involved in countering the German offensive of 1918 in northern France, he took the opportunity of collecting Mousterian flints from the parapets of trenches dug to defend Coigneux (Buckley 1921). His only complaint was that he could have found more if only he could have excavated the parapets at suitable points. Collections of flint and stone implements made by East Anglians and other Britons in different parts of the old empire frequently ended up in the great museums which combined archaeological with ethnographic material, notably the British Museum, the Pitt-Rivers Museum at Oxford and the University Museum of Archaeology and Ethnology at Cambridge. When the Curator of the Pitt-Rivers, Henry Balfour, addressed the Prehistoric Society of East Anglia as president for 1924, he broke new ground by choosing a topic which in his own words had 'no direct bearing upon East Anglia, nor, indeed, upon Great Britain in general', namely the lithic industries of the Tasmanians (Balfour 1925).

Henry Balfour was not the first Oxford man to show an interest in the Tasmanian lithic industries and his attitude marked an important advance over that of his predecessor. Prof. W. J. Sollas thought of the Tasmanians as if they represented peoples whose industries were stratified in the palaeolithic cave deposits of Europe and assigned them variously to the Aurignacian and Mousterian stages in different editions of *Ancient Hunters and their Modern Representatives*. Balfour, as a professional ethnologist, was more inclined to treat the Tasmanian industries on their own terms and emphasized that they showed more differences than similarities by comparison with European analogues. It was left to Dorothy Garrod (1928), a woman of Ipswich stock, who had graduated at Cambridge in history, taken a diploma in anthropology at Oxford and received her training as a prehistorian at Paris at the hands of the Abbé Breuil, to make clear in her presidential address for 1928 the essential need to treat archaeological data in terms of cultural rather than of natural history. Miss Garrod began her address, which in this respect notably anticipated Gordon Childe's plea made in the course of the inaugural presidential address to the Prehistoric Society in 1935 (Childe 1935), by reminding her audience that de Mortillet's classification of the palaeolithic applied only to Europe and predominantly to western Europe. If one wished to recover the prehistory of other regions, this could only be done by conducting excavations 'in the great regions outside Europe whose prehistory is still unknown'. Archaeological sequences could not be extrapolated from Europe. They could only be established by the spade. This had drastic implications for prehistoric studies. The more archaeological sequences were treated as the outcome of cultural rather than of natural history, the more essential it was seen to be to extend prehistoric research over the world as a whole. Miss Garrod put her words into practice by her systematic excavations in Kurdistan and Palestine and by contributing her classic paper 'The Upper Palaeolithic in the light of Recent Discovery' to the *Proceedings* (Garrod 1938). Furthermore her election to the Disney Chair of Archaeology at Cambridge in 1938 earned by these achievements put her in a position to increase the flow of young professionals needed, if the vision of cultural diversity adumbrated by herself for the palaeolithic and by Gordon Childe for the settled communities, which gave rise to the various and contrasting civilizations of mankind, was to be realized at an acceptable speed.

When Professor Garrod took office in 1938 prehistoric archaeology was already well established at Cambridge at the level of undergraduate teaching and post-graduate research. Formal lectures in the subject by Miles Burkitt had first been given in 1916 and prehistoric archaeology took its place in the syllabus of the then one-part Archaeological and Anthropological Tripos in 1927 when E. H. (later Sir Ellis) Minns became the first full-time Disney Professor and Miles Burkitt his University Lecturer. The fact that prehistory at Cambridge was taught from the beginning in conjunction with social and physical anthropology in a Museum of Archaeology and Ethnology disposed its graduates to view their subject in a world-wide context. Louis Leakey, encouraged by A. C. Haddon, had embarked in 1926 as a future Fellow of St John's on what proved to be his epoch-making programme of research in Kenya and, in conjunction with Burkitt's interest in the prehistory of South Africa, this must have helped to influence the choice of Africa as a destination for some of the first graduates of the Cambridge school. Desmond Clarke headed for Northern Rhodesia (Zambia), Thurstan Shaw for the Gold Coast (Ghana), Bernard Fagg for Nigeria and T. P. O'Brien for Uganda, the first three of whom went on to contribute reports on their discoveries to our *Proceedings*.

The full impact of Professor Garrod's regime was delayed until academic life was resumed in 1945/46. Before retiring in 1952 she had the satisfaction of leaving behind a syllabus which continued to require a grounding in Anthropology as well as Archaeology, but in its second phase provided for specialization in a number of archaeological options, teaching for which was provided by a number of cognate faculties. Meanwhile greater provision for post-graduate research had made it possible for increasing numbers to engage in advanced studies. This in turn qualified them for posts in the archaeology departments opened up in an increasing number of universities both in Britain and in the English-speaking world overseas, as well as in museums, the public services concerned with the conservation and recording of ancient monuments, and in British institutes and schools in the Mediterranean, the Near East and East Africa.

The Prehistoric Society was able to derive maximum profit from, as well as assist in promoting, this world-wide activity by reason of the fact that its *Proceedings* were edited for some four and a half decades in Cambridge. This put us in the position to publish some of the most original work of generations of young prehistorians including not merely our pupils, but their pupils in an increasing number of universities and not least those who came to Cambridge from overseas to seek qualifications or undertake research. The benefits conferred on the Prehistoric Society can be judged from its *Proceedings*. The index for volumes I–XXX shows entries from at least forty-five and for volumes XXXI–XL from forty different states. In return the Prehistoric Society was able to promote the exchange of ideas and information which made possible the advance of a true world prehistory, that is a prehistory based on original field-work and reflecting the diversity of human achievement during prehistoric times.

This is a theme which could well form the subject of an instructive volume. Here I will allude to only one example to illustrate the value of reciprocal contacts mediated by our *Proceedings* between universities as widely separated from Cambridge as Melbourne, Australia. When Donald Thomson came to Cambridge on the eve of the Second World War to recharge his batteries, as he put it, from A. C. Haddon, long-term member of the Prehistoric Society and veteran of the Torres Straits expedition of 1898, he wrote one of the most influential papers ever published in our *Proceedings*. 'The Seasonal Factor in Human Culture' (Thomson 1939) read in typescript by Haddon was based on original field-work carried out on the Wik-Monkan tribe of Cape North. This influenced me strongly when thirty years later I was engaged in rethinking Star Carr (Clark 1972) and it was ever present in the minds of those who still later worked on the British Academy's Early History of Agriculture Project at Cambridge under the leadership of E. S.

Higgs (Hutchinson *et al.* 1977; Jarman *et al.* 1982). The reception given to his first article for the *Proceedings* encouraged Donald Thomson to let us have another, this time on the technology of the Bindibu tribe of west-central Australia (Thomson 1964), an article which specialists in lithic typology might well take to heart more than they have yet done. When D. J. Mulvaney followed in his footsteps some years later as a lecturer in history at Melbourne, he elected to take the Cambridge tripos and gained experience in cave stratigraphy with Charles McBurney at the Haua Fteah in Cyrenaica. Returning home, Mulvaney undertook the critical review of the problems confronting Australian prehistory summarized in his masterly article 'The Stone Age of Australia' published in our *Proceedings* (Mulvaney 1961). The carefully planned and vigorously pursued campaigns which followed (Mulvaney and Joyce 1965) made it possible for Mulvaney as early as 1969 to publish *The Prehistory of Australia*, a book which at one stroke added a new continent to world prehistory. Much more could be said of the part played by the Cambridge school, mediated through our *Proceedings*, in advancing the prehistory of Australia, New Guinea and New Zealand, as indeed of many territories geographically less remote. The pioneers who laid the foundations of the Prehistoric Society may have begun by concentrating for the most part on the old stone age in East Anglia, but in pursuing early man they had willy nilly entered on a quest that could only be satisfied by exploring his traces the world over. T. H. Huxley, whose protégé Ray Lankester did so much to float the prototype of our society, would surely have rejoiced to see the outcome of our East Anglian forebears making up for their lack of means and formal qualifications by their zeal for prehistory. The Prehistoric Society as it celebrates its jubilee can take pride that the part it has played in promoting the study of prehistoric man has attracted leading exponents from as far afield as Australia, China and the New World.

Notes

*   This paper was read to the Society at its 50th Anniversary Conference, held in Norwich, on 29 March 1985.

1   J. E. Sainty, B.Sc., joined the Society in 1914 and lived in Norwich while teaching at the City of Norwich School. His most important contribution was his work on 'An Acheulian Palaeolithic workshop site at Whitlingham near Norwich' (*Proc. Prehist. Soc. East Anglia* 5, 1927, 176–213). He served as President in 1929, when he addressed the Society on 'Problems of the Crag' (*Proc. Prehist. Soc. East Anglia* 6, 1929, 57–78). In retirement he lived at West Runcton and for the next twenty-five years kept a close watch on the cliff exposures of the north Norfolk coast.

Bibliography

BALFOUR, H., 1925. 'The status of the Tasmanians among the Stone Age people', *Proc. Prehist. Soc. East Anglia* 5, 1–15.

BOSWELL, P. G. H., 1945. 'James Reid Moir, F.R.S. (1879–1944)', *Proc. Prehist. Soc.* 11, 66–88.

BREUIL, H., 1910. 'Sur la présence d'éolithes à la base de l'Eocene parisien', *L'Anthropologie* 21, 385–408.

— 1934. 'Presidential Address for 1934', *Proc. Prehist. Soc. East Anglia* 7, 289–322.

BUCKLEY, F., 1921. 'Finds of flint implements in the Red Lines trenches at Coigneux, 1918', *Proc. Prehist. Soc. East Anglia* 3, 380–8.

BURCHELL, J. P. T. and MOIR, J. R., 1932. 'The evolution and distribution of the hand-axe in N.E. Ireland', *Proc. Prehist. Soc. East Anglia* 7, 18–34.

BURKITT, C. 1921. 'Congress at Liège', *Proc. Prehist. Soc. East Anglia* 3, 453–7.

— 1925. *Prehistory*, 2nd ed. Cambridge University Press.

— 1933. *The Old Stone Age*, 1st ed. Cambridge University Press.

— 1955. *The Old Stone Age*, 3rd ed. Bowes and Bowes, Cambridge.

CHILDE, V. G., 1925. *The Dawn of European Civilization*, 1st ed. Kegan Paul, Trench, Trubner and Co., London.

— 1928. *The Most Ancient East: The Oriental Prelude to European Prehistory*. Kegan Paul, Trench, Trubner and Co., London.

— 1935. 'Changing methods and aims in prehistory', *Proc. Prehist. Soc.* 1, 1–15.

CLARK, J. G. D., 1972. *Star Carr: a case study in bioarchaeology*. Addision-Wesley, Reading, Mass.

GARROD, D. A. E., 1928. 'Nova et Vetera: a plea for a new method in Palaeolithic archaeology', *Proc. Prehist. Soc. East Anglia* 5, 260–67.

— 1938. 'The Upper Palaeolithic in the light of recent discovery', *Proc. Prehist. Soc.* 4, 1–26.

HAWARD, F. W., 1911. 'The chipping of flints by natural agencies', *Proc. Prehist. Soc. East Anglia* 1, 185–93.

— 1919. 'The origin of the rostro-carinate implements and other chipped flints from the basement beds of East Anglia', *Proc. Prehist. Soc. East Anglia* 3, 118–46.

HUTCHINSON, SIR J., CLARK, J. G. D., JOPE, E. M. and RILEY, R. (eds), 1977. *The Early History of Agriculture*. Oxford University Press for the British Academy.

JARMAN, M. R., BAILEY, G. N. and JARMAN, H. N. (eds), 1982. *Early European agriculture, its foundations and development*. Cambridge University Press.

KEITH, SIR A., 1912. 'Description of the Ipswich skeleton', *Proc. Prehist. Soc. East Anglia* 1, 203–9.

— 1944. 'James Reid Moir', *Obituary Notices of Fellows of the Royal Society* 4, 733–45.

KENDRICK, T. D., 1925. *The Axe Age*. Methuen, London.

LANKESTER, SIR E. R., 1907. *The Kingdom of Man*. Constable, London.

— 1912. 'On the discovery of a novel type of flint implements below the base of the Red Crag in Suffolk, proving the existence of skilled workers of flint in the Pliocene age', *Phil. Trans. Roy. Soc.* Ser. B 202, 283–336.

LEAKEY, L. S. B., 1934. *Adam's Ancestors*, 1st ed. Methuen, London.

— 1953. *Adam's Ancestors*, 4th ed. Methuen, London.

MAHR, A., 1937. 'New aspects and problems in Irish prehistory', *Proc. Prehist. Soc.* 3, 262–436.

MARR, J. E., 1920. 'Man and the Ice Age', *Proc. Prehist. Soc. East Anglia* 3, 177–92.

MOIR, J. R., 1910. 'The flint implements of sub-crag man', *Proc. Prehist. Soc. East Anglia* 1, 17–43.

— 1911. 'The natural fracture of flint and its bearing upon rudimentary flint implements', *Proc. Prehist. Soc. East Anglia* 1, 171–84.

— 1912. 'The occurrence of a human skeleton in a glacial deposit at Ipswich', *Proc. Prehist. Soc. East Anglia* 1, 194–202.

— 1919. 'A few notes on the sub-crag flint implements', *Proc. Prehist. Soc. East Anglia* 3, 158–61.

1921. 'Further discoveries of humanly-fashioned flints in and beneath the red crag of Suffolk', *Proc. Prehist. Soc. East Anglia* 3, 389–430.

1924. 'Some archaeological problems', *Proc. Prehist. Soc. East Anglia* 4, 234–40.

1927. *The Antiquity of Man in East Anglia.* Cambridge University Press.

1929. 'Obituary. Sir Edwin Ray Lankester, K.C.B., F.R.C., L.l.D. 1847–1929', *Proc. Prehist. Soc. East Anglia* 6, 140–42.

1932. 'The culture of Pliocene man', *Proc. Prehist. Soc. East Anglia* 7, 1–17.

1934. 'A giant hand-axe from Sheringham, Norfolk', *Proc. Prehist. Soc. East Anglia* 7, 327–32.

1935. *Prehistoric Archaeology and Sir Ray Lankester.* Norman Adlard, Ipswich.

MULVANEY, D. J., 1961. 'The Stone Age of Australia', *Proc. Prehist. Soc.* 27, 56–107.

1969. *The Prehistory of Australia.* Thames and Hudson, London.

MULVANEY, D. J. and JOYCE, E. B., 1965. 'Archaeological and geomorphological investigations at M. Moffat Station, Queensland, Australia', *Proc. Prehist. Soc.* 31, 147–212.

NEWALL, R. S., 1913. 'Stone implements from Millstream Station, W. Australia', *Proc. Prehist. Soc. East Anglia* 1, 303–19.

PIGGOTT, S., 1931. 'The Neolithic pottery of the British Isles', *Archaeol. J.* 88, 67–158.

1954. *Neolithic Cultures of the British Isles.* Cambridge University Press.

SETON-JARR, H. W., 1914. 'A recent expedition after Indian palaeos', *Proc. Prehist. Soc. East Anglia* 1, 440–42.

SMITH, I. F., 1965. *Windmill Hill and Avebury. Excavations by Alexander Keiller 1925–39.* Clarendon Press, Oxford.

SMITH, R. A., 1918. 'Our neighbours in the Neolithic period', *Proc. Prehist. Soc. East Anglia* 2, 479–507.

SOLLAS, W. J., 1911. *Ancient Hunters and their Modern Representatives.* 2nd ed., 1915; 3rd ed., 1924. Macmillan, London.

1920. 'A flaked flint from the Red Crag', *Proc. Prehist. Soc. East Anglia* 3, 261–67.

Special Committee, 1910. 'The report of the Special Committee', *Proc. Prehist. Soc. East Anglia* 1, 24–43.

STOPES, M. C., 1921. 'The Red Crag shell portrait', *Proc. Prehist. Soc. East Anglia* 3, 323–32.

THOMSON, D. F., 1939. 'The seasonal factor in human culture illustrated from the life of a contemporary nomadic group', *Proc. Prehist. Soc.* 5, 209–21.

1964. 'Some wood and stone implements from the Bindibu tribe of central Western Australia', *Proc. Prehist. Soc.* 30, 400–22.

INDEX

Page numbers in *italics* refer to illustrations